Women Transforming Politics

Women Transforming Politics

AN ALTERNATIVE READER

EDITED BY

Cathy J. Cohen,
Kathleen B. Jones,
and Joan C. Tronto

NEW YORK UNIVERSITY PRESS
New York and London

NEW YORK UNIVERSITY PRESS
New York and London

Library of Congress Cataloging-in-Publication Data
Women transforming politics : an alternative reader / edited by Cathy
J. Cohen, Kathleen B. Jones, and Joan C. Tronto.
p.   cm.
Includes bibliographical references (p.   ) and index.
ISBN 0-8147-1557-5 (clothbound : acid-free paper).—ISBN
0-8147-1558-3 (paperbound : acid-free paper)
1. Women in politics—United States.   2. Women political
activists—United States.   3. Feminism—United States.   I. Cohen,
Cathy J., 1961–   . II. Jones, Kathleen B., 1949–   . III. Tronto,
Joan C., 1952–   .
HQ1236.5.U6W668   1997
306.2'082—dc21   97-19645
                   CIP

New York University Press books are printed on acid-free
paper, and their binding materials are chosen for strength
and durability.

Manufactured in the United States of America
10 9 8 7 6 5 4 3 2 1

CONTENTS

ACKNOWLEDGMENTS

There are many words to describe what we have endured together in the last three years. This process has been long, hard, challenging, but most importantly, fun. In the course of the three years that we have been working on this book, many people have been influential in its development and completion. Cecelia Cancellaro cajoled us to pursue this project despite our concerns that each of us had other (less) important things to do.

Toward the completion of the project, Eric Zinner assumed editorial responsibility at NYU Press. We are grateful for his guidance and support. Despina Papazoglou Gimbel has been an extraordinary managing editor; she and her staff have been invaluable, carefully reading and rereading every page of this manuscript.

Throughout the history of this book, a number of supporters, most of them wearing multiple hats at the same time (feminist political scientists, grass roots activists, students), have contributed their insights and provided their encouragement. From lunches at APSA meetings to suggestions for authors and articles to occasional queries such as "which year will the book be available for my classes?" we have gained much from all of these colleagues.

The authors in the book are really special. Many have not been either traditionally or formally associated with the field of women and politics. This unfamiliarity highlights the gaps in the field that we describe in the introduction. The good news is that these authors, and many more like them, will now become familiar to a new generation of feminist scholars and political activists. We believe that the continuing work of these authors will reshape not only the field of women and politics, but also how we conceptualize politics and political life in general. Our profoundest thanks go to each of these authors (even though some were punctual and some were not).

Cathy Cohen wishes to thank many of the graduate students in political science and African and African American studies at Yale University. Their expertise and assistance range from contributing essays to looking up citations. She wishes to thank her family back in Toledo and her political family in New York for all of their support and care.

Kathy Jones wishes to thank her students in Women and Politics at San Diego State University and the University of California at San Diego, who were among the first to respond to the book's organizing framework and who made important suggestions and criticisms that helped to fine-tune it. She also wants to thank several students at San Diego State University who helped with bibliographic questions, and the support staff of the Department of Women's Studies and the College of Arts and Letters' Dean's Office. Finally, she thanks her family — her partner Amy, her sons Ari and Jed — for being so patient with the many phone calls, trips, and sacrifices that surrounded this book.

Joan Tronto wishes to thank her students at Hunter College of the City University of New York, who provide constant challenge and inspiration. She also thanks the staff of the Hunter College Library, who aided with bibliographic questions. Some of this work was done while she was supported by the Institute for Human Sciences in Vienna, Austria, and she is most grateful for this support.

The importance of the friendship that has developed among us extends beyond the pages of this book (which, given its length, may seem hard to believe). Even had this book never been completed, our friendship made the past three years rewarding in themselves. Luckily, for each of us, and hopefully for the reader, we finished these three years with a book and a friendship. We end this very long project with a promise/warning: stay tuned for the second edition!

One last wish: best of health to Cathy's father!

New York City
February 1997

Introduction: Women Transforming U.S. Politics: Sites of Power/Resistance

CATHY J. COHEN,
KATHLEEN B. JONES,
AND JOAN C. TRONTO

More than once within the last decade political pundits have announced the "Year of the Woman." Expecting that differences in the voting patterns of men and women would have a major impact on the division of political power between the two parties in Congress, or would decide the outcome of the presidential election, voters and media alike had been primed to study women and politics.[1] However, once the so-called gender gap proved not to be as wide as it had been predicted to be, analysts lost interest in women and politics, and politics as usual — dominated by men and their interests — returned to center stage. Yet even without the predicted impact of a gender gap on electoral outcomes, women's involvement in politics has persisted in being more complex, unusual, and unprecedented than most media reports have captured. By continuing to define politics as what happens exclusively within the institutional arena of the governmental process, or by allowing traditional practices of political interest brokering to limit the scope of our understanding of the political process, political analysts have missed the ways women's actions have transformed politics even though women do not hold the majority of seats in the legislature or have access to most of the economic power. To appreciate the transformative impact of women's actions on politics, we have to understand the contradictory effects of two decades of change in women's lives. In the last two decades more women have been elected to public office in the United States than ever before, yet the number of women of color and working-class women who are among their ranks remains insignificant.

During this same period, feminists have exploited the gender gap to wrest some important national concessions from political parties and officeholders, while the conditions confronting most women in terms of job and career options, economic stability, and sheer survival continue to deteriorate. In the area of public policy, women have experienced an improvement of their legal status. Federal laws have been passed that guarantee equal credit for women regardless of marital status and equal pay for equal work. Title VII and Title IX of the Civil Rights Act of 1964 extended civil rights in employment and education to women. Despite the fact that programs such as affirmative action have increased educational and employment opportunities for some women, the net impact of these programs had barely been felt before a declining economy brought increasing poverty rates for female-headed households to postwar record highs. Nearly 50 percent of all female-headed households with children under eighteen, and between 60 and 70 percent of such households headed by women of color, live in poverty. At the same time, the Supreme Court's ruling in *Roe v. Wade*, which had secured the legal right to reproductive choice for women, began to be challenged. First, a court ruling (*Harris v. McRae*) prohibited the use of federal Medicaid funds for abortions. This decision effectively shifted onto the states, and onto women themselves, the burden of securing economic assistance if poor women were to exercise their reproductive rights. Then increasing numbers of states enacted laws restricting women's reproductive choice to such an extent that, today, women in 85 percent of counties in the United States lack abortion services.

Although record numbers of women were employed outside the home, complaints that women and children were draining the nation's productivity by swelling the ranks of the welfare rolls were heard increasingly during the 1980s and 1990s. The fact that the overwhelming majority of women on welfare sought public assistance as a temporary safety net between jobs, and that a large number of women on public assistance were employed at low-paying, part-time jobs that offered no health care benefits carried little or no political weight. Opponents of federal income assistance programs instead sustained public hostility to the poor, especially targeting poor women of color. The Reagan administration made the first series of massive cuts in federal social spending, shifted fiscal responsibility for subsidized health care onto the states, and approved a tax cut and subsequent tax reforms that increased the proportion of federal taxes paid by the middle class. Under the Bush administration and, later, near the close of Clinton's first term in office, attacks on welfare heightened. In 1996, with the Republicans in control of Congress, and with Clinton concerned about his reelection, a "welfare reform" bill was passed and signed into law imposing strict limits on eligibility for public assistance. These limits included the elimination of noncitizen legal residents from eligibility and capped public assistance to any family at five years over their lifetime. The bill ended more than sixty years of federal support for families with dependent children. Yet despite cries of the financial burden and immorality of welfare, from 1984 to 1994, the gap between the rich and the poor widened; the top 1 percent of the population of the United States now owns 48 percent of the nation's financial wealth, while the bottom 80 percent owns only 6 percent.

How do we explain the fact that many women's lives have significantly improved in the United States during the last two decades, and that all women have seen their legal status enhanced, while for many women daily life has become more tenuous and threatening? What kinds of political responses to these paradoxical effects of improved legal status and declining quality of life have different women undertaken? The authors in this volume believe that it is in the contradictory experience of progress and oppression that the transformative power of women's political work is located. *Women Transforming Politics* explores these paradoxes and argues that despite great gains in many arenas, women's continuing marginalization in politics is not the problem of women. Instead, the problem rests in the ways we conceptualize and practice politics in the United States.

Any theory of women's political behavior must account for the particular tension between the "ascribed role of woman and the achieved role of politician."[2] The tension between "being a woman" and "being a politician" is not experienced uniformly; it varies among women of diverse racial and class backgrounds. The reason is that despite an evidently shared biology, all women are not the same. Their life experiences and social affinities mark them off from one another in such radically distinct ways that even sisters who are presumed to share a cultural heritage do not necessarily share a political outlook. At the same time, what counts as politics to any one individual or to a particular class, sexual, or racial group may be at odds with mainstream definitions of the political, and is affected by histories and geographies that bind different groups to a political system in different ways. An obvious example is that what counts as political action is different for those members of the political community whose ancestors have survived and resisted the political experience of slavery or conquest than it is for those whose ancestors have shared a history of relative freedom and privilege.

Women Transforming Politics begins from the critical stance that systemic forms of domination operate to shape the lives of women and men in our society and to create sites of power/resistance. We start from the premise that racism, sexism, class exploitation, homophobia, and other institutions of control are interrelated sites of domination and struggle that have left a long legacy in U.S. politics and continue to shape the life choices of all those who find themselves in North America. These systems of power create political divisions such as race, gender, economic and social class, sexual orientation, ability, ethnicity, religion, age, region, and language by making these categories formative of our sense of who we are and where we stand. Furthermore, these categories constitute identities whose complexity we cannot grasp when we isolate discourses of race, class, gender, or sexuality from one another. Yet the persistence of thinking and living in terms of these divisions — as when pollsters divide public opinion into gendered or racialized categories — constructs our sense that these categories of identity are "normal" or "natural." In fact, power is most effective when it makes the results of any system of political differences appear to be the primary, "taken-for-granted" given or premise of reality.

The coupling of racism and sexism in the lives of most women demands a more integrated approach to studying women and U.S. politics.[3] Despite the insights that have been gained over the last quarter century of research, we have yet to incorporate fully and systematically the implications of this intersection in our research. Understanding this process means recognizing that power relations do not produce the same effects on all persons, not even on all those who appear to share similar traits or social locations, such as gender, race, sexuality, class, citizenship, or social status. If, for example, gender is understood as a system of power in which some persons (usually men) are positioned to exercise power over others (usually women), not all persons (usually women) who would likely be controlled by others (usually men) are constrained by this system in the same way or to the same extent. In other words, women become "Real Women" in any culture or time not only by becoming different from (some) men, but by becoming different from one another.

We consider it essential to our struggles against dominant power to decenter the experiences, values, and perspectives of dominant groups. In the field of women and politics, this means decentering the focus on elite women, especially elite white women, which has continued to dominate research. Only by including those women whose lives do not fit neatly into the categories of what has been regarded tradition-ally as politics—women whose realities have been constructed by attempts to obscure political accountability, but who have struggled to resist these impositions—can we perceive the limits and the profoundly deep problems, as well as the opportunities, in American political life. In this collection we have foregrounded the experiences of women of color, working-class women, lesbians, and others who have been perceived, or have perceived themselves, to be marginal in American politics. In doing so, we intend to portray the complexity of domination and resis-tance and to examine the obscurity, yet penetrability, of political accountability that makes this inclusion necessary to any adequate political science.

Although the last two decades have seen the greatest interest in research on women and politics in the United States since the 1920s, and despite the prolifera-tion of political analyses featuring gender as a central variable, we still have not exhausted a radically deep feminist critique of politics suggested by pioneering researchers more than twenty years ago. *Women Transforming Politics* responds to the long unheralded plea to alter research paradigms in order to account for the diversity and range of women's involvement in and contributions to politics, and constitutes a conceptual shift in our understanding of politics. This shift enables us to explore how being on, or in, the margins has an impact on women's social location, identity, and consciousness, while not preventing them from transforming the shape and quality of public life. Our authors attest to the richness of women's political life in the multiple sites of power/resistance that produce contemporary politics in the United States.

Women have always been politically active. Historians have documented the extensive and varied ways women have shaped the public realm. Although few women have occupied key governmental positions, the daily activities of women as daughters, mothers, wives, lovers, sisters, nurses, teachers, workers, friends, and confidants have been critical to the system's running in predictable ways. Without the woman on the assembly line of a factory in a free trade zone, fearful of unionization, forced to "willingly accept" lower pay because she fears that she might lose her job to workers out of the country, the engines of modern capitalism would come to a halt and the government's trade deficit would increase exponentially. Without the resistant woman who lobbies, without benefit of a large budget or staff, against the location of a toxic dump site in her neighborhood, the exploitation of poorer communities would continue unchecked. Without the women mobilizing to increase public attention to women's health care needs around the issues of breast cancer or domestic violence, the inadequate investment of research money into issues disproportionately affecting women would go unnoticed.

Yet students of politics remain largely ignorant of the enormity of women's historical and contemporary contributions to the meaning and quality of public life. What has made women marginal has been the way politics has been defined in mainstream political analysis. Key among the factors that have left women out of the political picture has been the excessive reliance on dominant institutions to mark the space of politics, which marginalizes women's ways of looking at and being involved with politics.[4] Another factor has been that material on different women's political action has been organized in texts in a way that treats women of color or working-class women as deviating from a political norm established by elite white women.

Over the last twenty-five years, women's studies scholars, political scientists, historians, and others interested in women's political participation have been producing an impressive body of work that challenges conventional approaches to the study of politics.[5] Rather than treat the scope of politics as a given, researchers who have made gender central to their analysis have problematized the basic category of "politics," thus altering both the methods and the conceptual frameworks of the field of contemporary political science. Minimally, these new studies of women and politics have established that gender structures the arena of politics itself and shapes our understanding of it. That is, they have shown how the particular boundaries that any culture constructs to mark off behavioral norms of "masculinity" from behavioral norms of "femininity" are related to the boundaries constructed between "public life" and "private life."

Women Transforming Politics builds on the insights of these prior works, yet pushes beyond them to address more fully the criticisms of a number of scholars who have contended that existing research still tends to treat elite women's political experiences as constitutive of the parameters of political research itself. We have chosen to broaden the scope of political analysis as well as expand the subjects of study. Traditional studies of women and politics, like much of political science, focus either on the functioning of governmental institutions or on the behavior of individuals isolated from those social contexts of power that both constrain action and create opportunities for resistance. Studies of women and politics in this volume, however, explore connections between the actions of "citizens" and "leaders" in the public, official arena of politics and the different structures of opportunity in the so-called private sphere, or the realm of "civil society." Thus, interdisciplinary studies that elaborate on the connections between structures of power in the private realm and the constellation of power relations in the public realm have a radical impact on the field of political science research.

To remove the traditional boundary markers that circumscribe the field of politics is to change the methods and conceptual framework of political science. As a result, new sets of issues and needs emerge on the political landscape, and new actors and

social movements demand recognition as already politically engaged, primary play-
ers in the expanded political arena. Challenging the public/private boundary broad-
ens our understanding of how we all are "politicized" differently or produced as
specific sorts of political actors even when we seem to share certain social locations.
In this way, the politically constructed categories of race, gender, class, sexuality,
nation, and culture can be brought into sharper, more central focus.

This broadened understanding of politics also foregrounds the cumulative impact
of differentially distributed "resources," such as language, literacy, wealth, marital
status, permissible sexuality, and nationality, on the process of politicization and the
dynamics, modes, and means of political action. Through this wider lens, we can
perceive the myriad ways politics is produced and resisted through the "activities
that are carried on in the daily lives of ordinary people and are enmeshed in the
social institutions and political-economic process of . . . society."[6] It allows us to
explore how citizens have been created by, and have in turn influenced and
transformed, the contours of political life.

Women Transforming Politics argues that all women's full integration into politics
presents a radical challenge to the nature of any political system and necessitates
systemic changes. Women constitute the majority of the population; we would
expect their incorporation to alter existing political relations and processes drastically.[7] Women are not simply another interest group once excluded from public life
and now more fully present. Instead, women are a diverse group whose varied needs
and interests are not easily fit into the traditional structures of politics, nor easily
accommodated through the traditional mechanisms of policy making, nor appropriately understood as homogeneous and necessarily compatible with one another. Any
analysis of politics should include awareness of the "political nature of existing social
arrangements."[8] Seeing the "political nature of existing social arrangements" means
seeing institutions of work, family, sexuality, ethnicity, and so forth as contingent
rather than inevitable, and thus capable of being changed.[9]

In *Women Transforming Politics*, we make research that furthers the process and
possibility of social change central to our study of women and politics. In addition
to making our text multicultural in its foundation and broadening those actions
defined as political, we have chosen to organize our material around the perspective
of political change. Our assumption is that the study of women and politics is the
study of changing politics and the politics of change. We adopt the point of view
that radical change, which we take to occur on the "left" as well as on the "right," is
a function of collective action. Yet we understand "collective action" to occur not
only through the organizing efforts of self-conscious movements for change, but also
through the cumulative effects of individual acts of resistance in multiple political
arenas.

The authors in this volume describe the systematic forms of domination that
permeate American culture, society, and politics in order to enable us to ask, What
can be done? How can these circumstances be changed? To make change happen,
people have to become aware of the need to act, and they must be willing to act.
But as several of the essays in this collection demonstrate, the irony is that political
action is never so neat and rational as it appears to be after the fact. In other words,

people become more fully aware and clear about the goals and direction of their actions only in the middle of political action itself.

The effectiveness of both collective action and acts of individual resistance depends on how accurately we identify the multiple sources of oppression and marginality. As surely as domination and resistance along the axes of gender, race, ethnicity, language, sexuality, and so forth provide power to some and not others, so, too, these structures of domination and resistance often obscure some lines of accountability in favor of others. For example, as long as political authorities can claim that they are not responsible for the economic hardships of groups such as the women workers in Tennessee (discussed in Eve S. Weinbaum's chapter), that economic dislocation is the function of the automatic working of market forces, then they cannot be held to account. Engaging in a politics of change means, in part, seeing the connections — the lines of accountability and the failures of responsibility — that have created the situations in which we find ourselves marginalized.

Working toward accountability means acknowledging how dividing lines between modes of power relations have been constructed artificially. These dividing lines make no sense from the perspective of those whose lives are situated outside the current, dominant "centers" of power. For example, the division between "culture" and "politics" may seem real to elites whose political power is intact and whose cultural identities are fairly well reflected in the media. Yet that same division appears to be something artificial and arbitrary to Marisela Norte, a Latina spoken prose artist.

As Michelle Habell-Pallán explains in her essay in this volume, Norte's cultural works are political because through them Norte forges a resistant identity that refuses to be limited to the narrow spaces constructed and imposed on her by stereotypical images of Latinas in both the mainstream culture and her "own" community of color. This essay, along with others in this volume, attempts to provide a richer understanding of the complex contexts of political engagement — family and intimate relationships, friendships, neighborhood, community, work environment, structural limits of language, race, religious, and other cultural groupings — that structure perceptions of opportunities for political participation.

The thematic approach that we have developed in this anthology reflects the ways research in the fields of women's studies, African American studies, Chicana/o and Latina/o studies, Asian American studies, American Indian studies, and gay and lesbian studies has transformed the conceptual framework of political science. In other words, the book's scope, contents, and organization represent the conceptual and methodological changes that this new research has wrought. Not only are new examples of traditional topics examined, but also the range, intensity, modes, arenas, and purposes of political action are redefined. Consequently, readers will be encouraged to think critically about the diverse ways that "bringing women in" to the space of politics and public life has generated a radical change in our understanding of what politics is and how we study it.

In order to highlight the intersections of discourses and structures of race, class, ethnicity, sexuality, nationality, and ability on women's political roles, we have made the strategic decision not to isolate the experiences of women of color and/or working-class women in separate sections. Rather, we include a diversity of materials in every thematic section of *Women Transforming Politics*. Any essay can be considered a case study of the section's major theme, but each changes the angle of vision used to examine that theme. We expect readers to think through the consequences of using different women's experiences to tell the section's story and to consider critically the social context of all knowledge claims.

Many of the topics that teachers of women and politics frequently investigate — voters and elections, interest groups and lobbies, the institutions and mechanisms of official lawmaking and policy making — are analyzed in new ways in *Women Transforming Politics*. Authors such as Elsa Barkley Brown, Jane Junn, and Paule Cruz Takash examine electoral politics not only by documenting the political attitudes and rates, directions, and modes of political participation among different groups of women, but also by analyzing different leadership and participation strategies of women of diverse cultural backgrounds and political experience. Other infrequently studied topics are explored extensively herein: the history of social movements in the United States; the development and emergence of feminist consciousness in groups and among individuals; women's everyday, grassroots political actions; cultural modes of political engagement, such as arts, literature, and music; and the politics of personal life, sexuality, and intimate relations.

Our intention is to encourage readers to investigate the varied — sometimes conflicting — ways that different women's social location and cultural heritage have changed the contours of public life and structured women's consciousness of themselves and their worlds. As argued above, making gender central to the study of politics requires situating gender in a particular cultural context and political history. We therefore stress the importance of developing a historical framework for understanding the concept of gender and women's changing relationship to politics. Without a historical perspective on and inclusion of the diversity of the political experiences of women in different social locations, we cannot adequately comprehend why women's struggle for equality and women's demands for the right to participate fully in public life and be recognized as political actors on their own terms have different meanings to different groups. For instance, Hazel V. Carby explores how concerns of both African American and white elites about the impact of the early twentieth-century migration of many single African American women to Northern cities could be read as anxieties about class expressed in terms of anxieties about sexuality.

Carby notes that efforts on the part of middle-class Blacks to suppress the cultural expressions of working-class Black women, such as jazz, reflected the not-unfounded fear that middle-class power and status would be threatened by changing behavioral norms. Taking a more contemporary example, Alice Echols considers the ways the different experiences of white women and African American women in the civil rights movements and in the anti–Vietnam War movement had a critical impact on their consciousness. Differences in lived experience and consciousness manifested themselves in differences in emphasis on which issues should be central to the struggle for women's equality.

The essays in this collection aim to convince readers of the need to redefine politics by being more inclusive of the range of actions that count as political and the actors who participate in politics. The most fundamental insight these essays share is that the places or sites of power in U.S. politics always are also sites of resistance. In other words, we do not locate power in one place and resistance in another. Rather, we seek to demonstrate that even in those institutions of power that are thought to be "dominant," critical actions can subvert the traditional mode of power, challenging its direction and purpose. For example, Frances K. Pohl examines how activists concerned with sexual harassment in the military used the documents and artifacts collected in the official investigation of Tailhook '91 to raise questions about the way the military sexualizes women's and men's roles so as to define the characteristics of "fighter pilot" and "military hero."

Women Transforming Politics redefines concepts and develops new conceptual frameworks for political science. Many of the essays deal with traditional concepts in political science; yet few leave these concepts intact. Jane Junn's survey of women of color's participation, for example, shows that the usual associations between increasing income and increasing participation do not apply among African American and Asian American women. R. Darcy, Charles D. Hadley, and Jason F. Kirksey look at the effects of electoral systems on African American women and discover that for this group the impact of certain electoral systems, such as district elections in municipal politics, may not be as predicted. Yvette Alex-Assensoh and Karin Stanford present data that belie the image of the weakened, socially isolated, female-headed households in Black urban centers. Paule Cruz Takash challenges the usual dividing line between grassroots politics and electoral politics by examining the complex political lives of Latina and Chicana elected officeholders in California. Carol Hardy-Fanta's description of adult socialization challenges models of childhood socialization. Rina Benmayor and Rosa M. Torruellas's concept of "cultural citizenship" stands in counterpoint to many usual understandings of American citizenship.

Perhaps one of the most contested ideas in these essays is the notion that there are simple, easily identifiable, and a priori known interests that grow out of an individual's experience, and that provide the only basis for political activity. Although the model of interest-motivated politics may describe well the activities of mainstream, relatively affluent political actors, this account of "interest politics" does not describe most of the actors in these essays. In many cases, individuals do not see their interests as outside or opposed to communal or collective interests. Rather, ideas about what interests should be pursued emerge through the process of political activism itself, rather than being clear and fully articulated from the outset. In few of these cases considered in this collection can any simple form of "identity politics" serve as the beginning and end point for analysis.

New concepts or arenas of concern are also introduced into political science by other essays in this volume. Several authors emphasize the importance of "the body" as a category of political discussion. Sarah Banet-Weiser, for example, explores how cultural ideals of beauty in the United States reflect and reinforce certain norms of appearance and practices of sexuality that depend on the representation of Blacks as threatening to these norms and practices. Others investigate cultural ideals as they are represented in different contexts of power and privilege. In her contribution, Frances K. Pohl raises the constructions of masculinity and femininity to the level of political, and not simply cultural, phenomena. Moreover, some of the essays explore how modes of political action vary in accordance with different political goals. Debra C. Minkoff suggests that for women of color, organizational mobilization takes a different form because the women in the organizations want to put the institutions to different uses.

A number of the essays challenge distinctions among realms of "the state," "the economy," "society," or "culture." For instance, Jacqueline Stevens shows how our ideas about marriage as a "natural" institution depend on certain norms and behaviors being legitimated by the state and do not derive automatically from anything in either human biology or sexual desire. Doreen J. Mattingly explains how power relationships between female domestic workers from Mexico and their female employers are affected by patterns of immigration that are, in turn, altered by shifting U.S. policy and broad economic trends. In each case, understanding the intersections of state action with culture or with the economy is as important as studying what has traditionally been defined as the "political" part of the topic under discussion, whether that topic is marriage, beauty pageants, or union organizing.

Finally, each of these essays represents an invitation to readers to become more politically engaged in a self-conscious way. By calling attention to new ways to understand how to act politically, we provide vehicles through which we can shape contemporary U.S. politics. By exploring the complexity of public policy issues, such as just policies for immigrants and undocumented workers in the United States or fair criminal sentencing policies, we expose the sexism and racism constructing the current political system. And by thinking about politics in a global perspective, that is, beyond the boundaries of the group with which we most immediately identify, we confront the inevitable interconnectedness of all of our actions.

In sum, *Women Transforming Politics* constitutes a conceptual shift in political analysis in three ways. First, we refuse to define political activity in traditional ways, thus broadening the scope of politics. By rejecting traditional delineations between "public" and "private" spheres of action, we expose the simultaneity with which we are produced as isolated "citizens" with equal standing before the law while we struggle to exist in the context of different communities and social groups as "women" and/or "men," and/or "Latina," and/or "lesbian," and/or "working-class." Second, by highlighting the experiences of women of color and their communities, we challenge hierarchical social systems that distribute privileges around a normative white, male, middle-class, heterosexual, able-bodied model of the individual. By decentering the focus on both elite political action and dominant groups' grassroots claims, we displace those who have traditionally occupied center stage, including the white, upper- and middle-class, privileged women who have dominated most feminist works on women and politics. Third, by redefining basic political concepts, such as "citizenship," "leadership," and "representation," we provide new frameworks for a political science of the twenty-first century that is self-critically descriptive, self-consciously engaged and committed to social change, and self-reflectively inclusive.

Women Transforming Politics introduces the student of politics to new ways of thinking about the field of political science and suggests ways to further transform political research. The "successful" transformation of politics and the discipline of political science in order to accommodate the complexity of women's political needs and demands depends on what criteria we use to measure success in the first place. These criteria, like the concept of politics itself, are contested. In the final analysis, then, we want to foster debate about the success of women's movements for change in the United States. Is movement success best measured by the degree to which more women are integrated into the elite of a political system? Or is the integration of individual women ultimately less significant than the degree to which the structure of the system itself has changed? *Women Transforming Politics* makes a persuasive case for defining success as systematic change. Only from such a perspective will the study of women in politics be changed from a "portrait of marginality" to a vision of political transformation.

NOTES

1. See Carol M. Mueller, *The Politics of the Gender Gap: The Social Construction of Political Influence* (Sage, 1988).

2. Marianne Githens and Jewel Prestage, introduction to *A Portrait of Marginality: The Political Behavior of the American Woman*, ed. Githens and Prestage (David McKay, 1977), 6.

3. Ibid., 9.

4. Inez Smith Reid, "Traditional Political Animals? A Loud No," in *Portrait of Marginality*, ed. Githens and Prestage, 366–78. For an analysis of marginality that recognizes how the marginalized can manipulate their political locations to forge resistant identities and ideologies, see Cathy Cohen, "Contested Membership: Black Gay Identity and the Politics of Aids," in *Queer Theory/Sociology*, ed. Steve Siedman (Blackwell, 1996), x–xx; and the chapter by Andrea Densham in this collection.

5. Sandra Baxter and Marjorie Lansing, *Women and Politics: The Visible Majority*, rev. ed. (University of Michigan, 1983); Sandra Bookman and Ann Morgan, eds., *Women and the Politics of Empowerment* (Temple University Press, 1988); Susan Carroll, *Women as Candidates in American Politics* (Indiana University Press, 1985); Susan Carroll and Wendy Strimling, *Women's Routes to Elective Office: A Comparison with Men's* (Rutgers University, Center for the American Woman and Politics, 1983); R. Darcy, Susan Welch, and Janet Clark, *Women, Elections, and Representation*, 2d ed. (University of Nebraska Press, 1994); Irene Diamond, *Sex Roles in the State House* (Yale University Press, 1977); Linda Lovelace Duke, *Women in Politics: Insiders or Outsiders?* 2d ed. (Prentice Hall, 1996); Janet Flammang, *Political Woman: Current Roles in State and Local Government* (Sage Press, 1984); Patricia Gurin and Louise A. Tilly, eds., *Women, Politics, and Change* (Russell Sage Foundation Press, 1990); Jane Jaquette, *Women in Politics* (Wiley and Sons, 1974); Rita Mae Kelly and Mary Boutelier, *The Making of Political Women* (Nelson Hall, 1978); Jeanne Kirkpatrick, *Political Woman* (Basic Books, 1974); Ruth Mandel and Debra Dodson, "Do Women Office Holders Make a Difference?" in *The American Woman*, ed. Sara E. Rix (Norton, 1992); Virginia Sapiro, *The Political Integration of Women* (University of Illinois Press, 1984).

6. Sandra Bookman and Ann Morgan, "Rethinking Women and Politics: An Introductory Essay," in *Women and the Politics of Empowerment*, ed. Bookman and Morgan, 4.

7. Kathleen B. Jones, "Citizenship in a Woman-Friendly Polity," *Signs* 15, no. 4 (1990); and idem, "Identity, Action, and Locale: Thinking about Citizenship, Civic Action, and Feminist Politics," *Social Politics* 1, no. 3 (1994).

8. Kay Boals, "Review Essay: Political Science," *Signs* 1 (1974): 161.

9. Jane Jaquette, "Review Essay: Political Science," *Signs* 2 (1975): 147.

PART ONE

Politics, Economics, and Culture
How Women Live

ONE

Women of Color in the Eighties
A Profile Based on Census Data

TAMARA JONES AND ALETHIA JONES

The common understanding of what it means to be a woman of color in the United States continues, by and large, to be more informed by social myth than empirical evidence. Images of the sexually promiscuous Latina, the passive Asian geisha girl, and the Black welfare queen, to name just a few examples, act as a sort of social dictionary for those who have been unable or unwilling to discern the complexities of the lives of women of color. These images have played a significant and insidious role in the social, political, economic, and institutional histories of the United States. As a result, the historical debate on what it means to be a woman has often been racialized. For example, the Victorian ideal of femininity characterized (White) women as delicate, passive, chaste, and the apotheosis of morality. In contrast, Black women were portrayed as physically strong, aggressive, sexually promiscuous, and lacking in moral worth. The Victorian ideal of femininity collided sharply with stereotypes of Black women, for whom this ideal was never intended and rarely applied.[1] Sojourner Truth's challenge — "And ain't I a woman?" — speaks just as much today as it did in 1851 about the important ways race and gender combine to produce unique experiences among different groups of women.[2]

The racializing of gender is also complemented by traditions within communities of color in which gender has been used in particular ways to understand and articulate racial and ethnic identities. Consider the Million Man March on Washington in October 1995. Black men gathered from across the country to reflect on their identities and roles as male members of their communities. Not only did this exclude Black women, but the march in its very formulation made certain assumptions about what the role of Black women should be. Black women had a narrowly defined place in the necessary dialogue about the role of Black men, about what ails the Black community, and about what needs to be done to rebuild the community. Such thinking reduces Black women to helpmates and assumes them to have very little of importance to contribute to this work. Further, it delegitimizes Black women's leadership within Black communities. The march thus demonstrated some of the ways particular social and political agendas in communities of color are premised on the silence and relative invisibility of women of color.

We must consider the impact of any social, political, or economic belief or strategy on the lives of women of color. Women of color constitute the majority of the global population and a significant percentage of the population of the United States. A society in which women of color are valued and fully empowered will have made significant gains in the ongoing struggle against oppression and all forms of social inequality.

This essay presents data to address some of the assumptions about the lives of women of color in the United States. We hope this information can also guide those who organize for social change. We ask, What have been the actual experiences of women of color in the United States during the 1980s? In so doing, we extend work presented by Vilma Ortiz in her 1994 essay on women of color.[3] Using Ortiz's 1980 data as a baseline and the now available 1990 census data, we focus on the rates of change during the last decade along dimensions discussed by Ortiz.

The national census allows us to make reliable statistical comparisons among women of different racial and ethnic groups. But it is important to acknowledge the types of information the census does not provide. The macroscopic view that this type of data supplies is simply incapable of answering detailed questions about women's experiences. For that, we must turn to descriptive and personal accounts of women's lives. However, we must consider both quantitative analyses and a multiplicity of descriptive stories to reach a fuller understanding of the lives of women of color. Former president Ronald Reagan's use of the image of the "welfare queen" as the archetype of welfare recipients is a good example of how reliance on a single source (albeit a contested one) can lead to erroneous conclusions. His depiction of women receiving public assistance lacked the empirical evidence necessary for such a sweeping assertion, but succeeded nonetheless in promulgating the public image of Black women as unconscionable cheats. Those who would move closer to the truth must consider the ways statistical and qualitative data combine to portray a more complete picture. Census data provide a small but necessary piece of the puzzle. Studies of national phenomena are almost by definition crude measures, and often fail as complete explanatory models. The national census is no exception to this general rule.

This is a comparative study. We present data for five broad racial categories and try to show differences within racial groups as well by highlighting some ethnic communities. We have been necessarily constrained by the categories and definitions used by the Census Bureau, and thus the reader will discover that the designations Black and Native American do not account for the ethnic, cultural, and tribal differences that define the women in these groups. Additionally, the census includes more ethnic groups under some of the broader racial categories than are presented in this essay. For example, the broader categories "Asian" and "Latina" each comprise several ethnic groups. Individually, these ethnic groups in turn can, and often do, present a picture that differs significantly from that of the racial group taken as a whole. The reader is directed to the appendix for a complete description of the groups included in this study, as well as some important notes on census terminology and data collection.

The census data cannot speak to all differences within the subgroups themselves (for example, the impact of sexual orientation on women's lives) and inevitably obscure the human stories behind the numbers. The reader should consider these data a map of highways; with such a model, one needs to gather additional information to travel local roadways and to gain a fuller picture of the terrain in which women live.

Although we acknowledge the invidious effects of patriarchy, we offer no comparisons to men in this study. We believe that the experiences of women can and, at times, should be evaluated on their own terms. Further, comparisons among women of color can clarify how statistical data can be used to render some women of color groups invisible. The experiences of non-Black and non-White women have much to contribute to our common understanding of what it means to be a woman in modern America. Data on White women are included not as a normative standard, but rather as a backdrop against which we can more fully appreciate the effects of race in a system that is both patriarchal and racist. The main body of the essay presents the quantitative data on women's experiences. The conclusion discusses some of the political implications of the data and identifies possible areas of further research.

It is important to draw the reader's attention to data presented on rates of percent change versus actual percentages. Actual percentages represent the simple proportion of women with the discussed characteristic. Percent change represents the proportional change among women. It more accurately represents the degree of shift. Thus, if a percentage dropped from 30 percent to 15 percent, this is a percent change, or decrease, of − 50 percent.

Population

All the groups of women included in this essay experienced population growth during the eighties, although the growth rates varied from a low of 5 percent for White women to a high of 138 percent for Vietnamese women (see table 1.1). Interestingly, almost all the groups experienced a decline in their fertility rates (see figs. 1.5, 1.6, and 1.7), while the proportion of foreign-born simultaneously increased (see table 1.2). Obviously, most of the increase in population size is attributable to immigration.

Asian communities increased significantly between 1980 and 1990. As an aggregate group, the Asian female population almost doubled its size, but there were significant differences among the particular Asian ethnic groups. Japanese women had the lowest rate of growth among Asian women, at 21 percent. However, the Chinese, Korean, and Vietnamese female populations grew by over 100 percent each, and Asian Indian and Filipino women by over 85 percent each. In all these

TABLE 1.1.

U.S. Population Size, 1980 and 1990, Ranked by 1990 Data

(in Thousands)

	Female			Total population		
	1980	1990	% Change	1980	1990	% Change
WHITE	96,985 (1)	102,306 (1)	5	189,035 (1)	199,827 (1)	6
BLACK	13,973 (2)	15,818 (2)	13	26,482 (2)	29,931 (2)	13
LATINO	7,329 (3)	10,771 (3)	47	14,604 (3)	21,900 (3)	50
Mexican	4,268 (4)	6,444 (4)	51	8,679 (4)	13,393 (4)	54
ASIAN	1,926 (5)	3,701 (5)	92	3,726 (5)	7,227 (5)	94
Puerto Rican	1,028 (6)	1,353 (6)	32	2,005 (6)	2,652 (6)	32
NATIVE AMERICAN	777 (7)	1,017 (7)	31	1,535 (7)	2,015 (7)	31
Cuban	421 (8)	535 (8)	27	806 (9)	1,053 (10)	31
Filipino	405 (9)	763 (9)	88	782 (10)	1,420 (9)	82
Chinese	401 (10)	827 (10)	106	812 (8)	1,649 (8)	103
Japanese	388 (11)	469 (11)	21	716 (11)	866 (11)	21
Korean	207 (12)	448 (12)	116	357 (13)	797 (12)	123
Asian Indian	194 (13)	363 (13)	87	387 (12)	787 (13)	103
Vietnamese	118 (14)	281 (14)	138	245 (14)	593 (14)	142
Total Women of Color	23,791	30,915	30			
Total People of Color				45,943	60,285	31
Total Women	116,499	127,538	9			
Total People				226,546	248,710	10

SOURCES: 1980 data from U.S. Bureau of the Census, *1980 Census of Population: General Social and Economic Characteristics* (PC80-1-C1, 1983) (hereafter cited as *General Social and Economic Characteristics*), tables 74 and 75. 1990 data derived from U.S. Bureau of the Census, *1990 Census of Population: Social and Economic Characteristics, United States* (CP-2-1, 1993) (hereafter cited as *Social and Economic Characteristics*), tables 4 and 40.

NOTE: Figures in parentheses indicate rank in 1980 and 1990 respectively. Capitalized categories represent totals for all subgroups, including those not listed. The Latino figure includes two groups of Latinos, those who clearly indicate a racial origin group (White, Black, Asian, Native American) and those who do not answer the question or give multiple racial origins (Other Race Latinos). Other Race Latinos are approximately 50 percent of the Latino population. Latinos who clearly identify a racial group category are double counted. A black Latino, for example, is included in the category Black and again in the category Latino. But Latinos in the Other Race category appear only once, in the Latino numbers. Calculations of totals in this table (the last four rows) eliminate this double count when it occurs. The general category of Other Race includes non-Latinos. Non-Latinos are 3 to 5 percent of that category and are also taken into account. See appendix for explanation of census terminology and methods.

cases, the rate of increase of the female population roughly matches the rate of increase of the total population of the group. Yet despite these increases, Asian ethnic groups continue to rank among the least populous groups in the United States.

Much of the increase in population size in Asian communities is attributable to the large number of immigrants. Amazingly, over 65 percent of the general Asian population in 1990 were born outside the United States. Of this number, 57.5 percent entered the United States for the first time between 1980 and 1990. During the decade, the percentage of immigrants increased in all Asian ethnic communities except among the Vietnamese. Vietnamese communities continued to have the highest percentage of recent immigrants among all the categories included in this study, despite a drop in the proportion of foreign-born Vietnamese who were recent immigrants, from 77.5 percent in 1980 to 61.8 percent in 1990.

Other women of color groups experienced more modest rates of increase in their populations during the eighties. Overall, the Latina population grew by 47 percent.

Mexicans constituted the largest group and also had the largest rates of increase. The rate of growth of the female population matched that of the total population for both Native Americans and Blacks, at 31 percent and 13 percent respectively.

The percent of foreign-born remained relatively unchanged among White women (increasing slightly from 4.9 percent in 1980 to 5 percent in 1990) and Latinos (increasing from 35.2 percent to 35.8 percent). Mexicans were the fastest growing immigrant community among Latinos — in 1990, slightly over 50 percent of the Mexican foreign-born population were recent immigrants, compared to 28.5 percent in 1980. The population of foreign-born in Black communities increased from 3.1 percent to 4.9 percent.

In general, we can observe that during the eighties, the immigration population increased in every group except among Vietnamese and Koreans. It declined among the Vietnamese because they have experienced a simultaneous drop in their foreign-born and recent immigrant populations. The Korean immigrant population re-

TABLE 1.2.
Percentage of Population Foreign-Born, 1980 and 1990,
by Racial/Ethnic group

	Foreign-born		Recent immigrant[a]	
	1980	1990	1980	1990
WHITE	4.9	5.0	—	—
BLACK	3.1	4.9	—	—
LATINO	35.2	35.8	25.0	50.7
Mexican	26.0	33.3	28.5	50.4
Puerto Rican[b]	51.0	46.2	20.0	—
Cuban	77.9	71.7	7.2	25.8
ASIAN	58.6	65.6	44.7	57.5
Chinese	63.3	69.3	35.1	56.8
Japanese	28.4	32.4	35.9	54.4
Filipino	64.7	64.4	34.8	49.0
Korean	81.9	72.6	50.1	56.5
Asian Indian	70.4	75.3	43.9	58.3
Vietnamese	90.5	79.9	77.5	61.8
NATIVE AMERICAN	2.5	0.0	—	—

SOURCES: 1980 data taken from Vilma Ortiz, "Women of Color: A Demographic Overview," in *Women of Color in U.S. Society*, eds. Maxine Baca Zinn and Bonnie Thornton Dill (1994) (hereafter cited as Ortiz, "Women of Color"). 1990 data from *1990 Census of Population: Asians and Pacific Islanders in the United States* (CP-3-5, 1993) (hereafter cited as *Asians in the U.S.*), table 1; *1990 Census of Population: Persons of Hispanic Origin in the United States* (CP-3-3, 1993) (hereafter cited as *Persons of Hispanic Origin*), table 1; and *Social and Economic Characteristics*, tables 6, 7, 116.

[a]Calculated among the foreign-born only. Recent immigrants are those who entered the United States during the previous decade (e.g., 1970–80). Foreign-born are all those who are not U.S. natives, that is, born in the United States, its territories (Guam, Puerto Rico, U.S. Virgin Islands, and Northern Mariana Islands), or born abroad with at least one American parent. Both recent immigrants and the foreign-born respondents can be naturalized citizens.

[b]Puerto Ricans are technically not immigrants. However, given their distinctive Latino culture and adjustment experiences on the mainland, they are more like immigrants. For the purposes of this discussion, those born in Puerto Rico are considered part of the foreign-born population.

NOTE: A dash means that no census figures have been published, except in the case of Puerto Ricans, for whom comparable data to 1980, given our unique calculation of foreign-born, could not be derived. For this table and those that follow, the number for total Asians does not include Pacific Islanders who constitute .05 percent of the Asian population.

mained constant as a percentage of the total Korean population; the drop in the percentage of Korean foreign-born was offset by an increase in the percentage of recent immigrants.

Our study confirms data presented elsewhere documenting the changing racial demographics of the United States. In 1980, the ratio of the total White population to the total population of people of color and the ratio of White women to women of color were roughly four to one. In 1990, the ratios had decreased to roughly three to one. In short, people of color accounted for a larger percentage of the total U.S. population by the end of the decade.

Education

While increased schooling guarantees neither a well-paying job nor job security, it has proven to be an important factor for those seeking to improve their economic status and social standing.

The percentage of women completing high school and college[4] has increased for all groups except Vietnamese women, who experienced a slight drop in their number of high school graduates (see figs. 1.1 and 1.2). In 1990, the average graduation rate for all women was 66.1 percent for high school and 16 percent for college. This represented an increase since 1980, when 57.6 percent of all women graduated from high school and 12.2 percent from college.

Some of the most impressive educational gains have been made by Latinas. Although as of 1990 they still trailed all other racial groups in both high school and college graduation rates, 16.9 percent more Latinas graduated from high school, and 38.3 percent more graduated from college compared to 1980. Puerto Rican women achieved the greatest gains among Latinas, enjoying a 36.8 percent and a 95.8 percent increase in completion of high school and college respectively. However, these remarkable percentage increases must be understood in the context of the low numbers of Puerto Rican female graduates at the start of the decade. In 1980, 39.1 percent of all Puerto Rican women finished high school and only 4.8 percent completed college. But despite their gains, only slightly more than half (53.5 percent) of Puerto Rican women have a high school diploma and only about one in ten (9.4 percent) earned an associate or bachelor's degree in 1990. Cuban women continue to enjoy a tradition (since at least 1970) of the highest graduation rates among Latinas. The number of Cuban women earning high school diplomas was 53.3 percent in 1980 and 55.8 percent in 1990; 13.2 percent of Cuban women graduated from college in 1980, and 14.9 percent in 1990. Mexican women also increased their graduation rates, but still, less than half (44.5 percent) finished high school and only 5.6 percent completed college in 1990.

Black and Native American women have also made consistent gains in their education: 63.8 percent of Black women received their high school diplomas in 1990, compared with 51.5 percent in 1980; 11.7 percent of Black women graduated from college in 1990, against 8.3 percent in 1980. In 1990, 65.4 percent of Native American women earned a high school degree, versus 54.3 percent in 1980; 8.7 percent received a college degree in 1990, versus 6.4 percent in 1980.

FIG. 1.1.

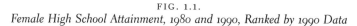

FIG. 1.1.
Female High School Attainment, 1980 and 1990, Ranked by 1990 Data

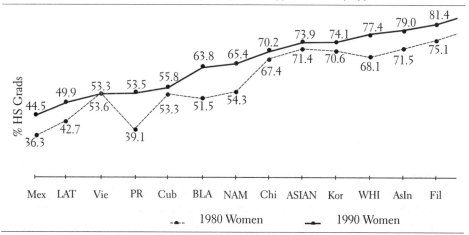

SOURCES: For 1980 data, see Ortiz, "Women of Color." 1990 data derived from *Social and Economic Characteristics*, tables 42, 106, 115.

NOTE: Based on females 25 years and over.

KEY: ASIAN: All Asians; AsIn: Asian Indian; BLA: All Blacks; Chi: Chinese; Cub: Cuban; Fil: Filipino; Ja: Japanese; Kor: Korean; LAT: All Latinas; Mex: Mexican; NAM: All Native Americans; PR: Puerto Rican; Vie: Vietnamese; WHI: All Whites

FIG. 1.2.
Female College Attainment, 1980 and 1990, Ranked by 1990 Data

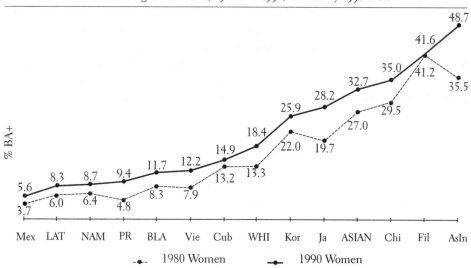

SOURCES: For 1980 data, see Ortiz, "Women of Color." 1990 data derived from *Social and Economic Characteristics*, tables 42, 106, 115.

NOTE: Based on females 25 years and over.

KEY: ASIAN: All Asians; AsIn: Asian Indian; BLA: All Blacks; Chi: Chinese; Cub: Cuban; Fil: Filipino; Ja: Japanese; Kor: Korean; LAT: All Latinas; Mex: Mexican; NAM: All Native Americans; PR: Puerto Rican; Vie: Vietnamese; WHI: All Whites

The data for White women show a steady increase in educational attainment: 13.7 percent more White women completed high school between 1980 and 1990. The number of White women completing college also increased by 38.3 percent. At the end of the decade, White women ranked first and second for high school and college graduation rates respectively when comparisons were made among general racial categories of women (i.e., against Black, Latina, Asian, and Native American women). However, they rank fourth and seventh when these categories are broken into ethnic subgroups.

As a racial group, Asian women continue to attain higher educational levels than other categories of women of color. Taken as a whole, 71.4 percent completed high school and 27 percent finished college in 1980. In 1990, the rates had increased to 73.9 percent and 32.7 percent, respectively. Japanese women had the highest rank for high school graduation rates in both 1980 (79.5 percent) and 1990 (85.6 percent). Asian Indian women led in college graduation rates in 1990 (48.7 percent), up from 35.5 percent a decade earlier. Vietnamese women had the lowest graduation rates among Asian women in both 1980 and 1990. Indeed, they were the only category of women to experience a decline ($-.6$ percent) in high school educational attainment.

Although we have utilized a rank order among the categories of women to facilitate our discussion, it is important to note that despite their educational gains, less than half of the women in any of the racial or ethnic groups managed to attain a college degree. The implications of this are sobering in a world economy that increasingly demands higher skill levels and educational preparedness of its workers. The disparity in graduation rates among women is also quite startling. Almost nine times as many Asian Indian women as Mexican women graduate from some type of college. Almost twice as many Japanese women as Mexican women graduate high school. More research needs to be done before we can more fully understand the factors responsible for these observed differences among women.

Labor Force Participation

Many of the current political debates concerning communities of color center on economic issues, particularly employment rates and the availability of jobs. Thus we ask, How have women of color fared on the job market? What kinds of jobs do they typically hold? How has their earning power changed, if at all? Did the level of poverty among them vary significantly during the 1980s?

Census data are based on self-reporting along very broad and unrefined dimensions. Thus, for example, the data on labor force participation do not incorporate activities within the hidden economy.[5] Nor does the census count those who have withdrawn from the labor market, discouraged by their repeated failure to find jobs. As we shall see, these are important distinctions if one wishes to fully map the contours of the experiences of women of color in this area.

Overall, women accounted for 60 percent of the total labor force growth between 1982 and 1992.[6] They experienced their highest rate of participation in the labor

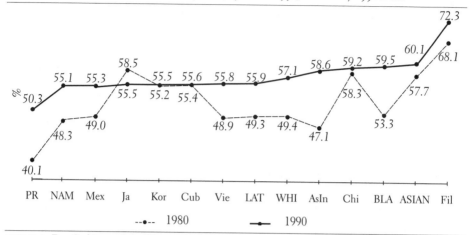

FIG. 1.3.
Female Labor Force Participation, 1980 and 1990, Ranked by 1990 Data

SOURCES: For 1980 data, see Ortiz, "Women of Color." 1990 data derived from *Social and Economic Characteristics*, tables 44, 108, 117.
NOTE: Based on female population 16 years and over.
KEY: ASIAN: All Asians; AsIn: Asian Indian; BLA: All Blacks; Chi: Chinese; Cub: Cuban; Fil: Filipino; Ja: Japanese; Kor: Korean; LAT: All Latinas; Mex: Mexican; NAM: All Native Americans; PR: Puerto Rican; Vie: Vietnamese; WHI: All Whites

market in 1992 at 58 percent. By 1990, all groups of women had over 50 percent of their members represented in the labor force.

Women of color had an average participation rate of 52.2 percent in 1980 and 57.7 percent in 1990. White women had an average participation rate of 49.4 percent in 1980 and 57.1 percent in 1990 (see fig. 1.3). Thus, while historically a higher percentage of women of color have worked, between 1980 and 1990 the gap between women of color and White women's participation rates in the labor market narrowed from five to less than one percentage point. White women may have entered the formal labor market in significant numbers at a later historical date, but during the past decade they made gains at a much faster rate than did women of color.

The labor force participation rate increased for all groups of women between 1980 and 1990, with the exception of Japanese women, whose participation in the formal labor force declined from 58.5 percent to 55.5 percent. As a racial group, Asian women entered the decade with the highest rate of participation. However, we again note disparity in rates among various Asian ethnic groups. Filipino women continued to have the highest rate of participation: almost three out of four Filipino women were accounted for in the labor market by the end of the decade (68.1 percent in 1980 and 72.3 percent in 1990). In 1980, Asian Indian women had the fewest percentage of women engaged in the visible economy (47.1 percent). By 1990, Japanese and Korean women had the lowest rates of participation among Asian women (55.5 percent each). Both Chinese and Korean women remained relatively stable in their labor force rates, each with increases of less than 2 percent. Asian Indian women, on the other hand, experienced an increase of 24.4 percent, jumping from 47.1 percent in 1980 to 58.6 percent in 1990.

Between 1980 and 1990, 1.5 million additional Black women found work in the formal economy, bringing their total labor force rate to 59.5 percent. This made Black women the group with the third largest rate of labor force participation — an increase from 1980, when they ranked seventh among all groups of women. Although unemployment rates for Black women dropped from 14 percent to 11 percent between 1980 and 1990, the eighties were very uneven for this group — unemployment reached a high of 19 percent for Black women in 1983.[7]

In 1980, 48.3 percent of Native American women participated in the labor force; in 1990, this figure had jumped to 55.1 percent. Despite this, Native American women continued to rank twelfth in the 1990 distribution of all women's labor force participation rates. Puerto Rican women had the lowest labor force participation rate in both 1980 and 1990, at 40.1 percent and 50.3 percent, respectively. More Mexican women worked in the formal economy, while Cuban women's participation rate remained more or less unchanged.[8]

Even a cursory glance at figure 1.3 reveals a remarkable flattening out of differences in labor force participation rates among all categories of women in 1990. With the exception of Filipino women, all the categories fall between 50 percent and 60 percent. Does the fact that all groups of women moved closer to being employed in the formal economy at the same rates during the 1980s also mean that they had increasingly similar job experiences? Were they more likely to hold the same types of jobs? Did they all share similar rates of growth in their income levels? Have the poverty levels among these women dropped to reflect the fact that more of them are employed than ten years previously? It is to these questions that we now turn our attention.

Full-Time Year-Round Employment Experiences

1989 data directly comparable with 1979 figures on full-time year-round female employment were not published by the Census Bureau. Consequently, it is not possible to determine how the rate of full-time year-round female employment changed between the beginning and the end of the decade. Table 1.3 can, however, provide a snapshot of women's employment experience during that time.[9]

Of the women who worked in 1989, 46.4 percent held full-time year-round jobs. There was little difference between the percentages of White women and those of women of color in these types of jobs: 46.2 percent of working White women and 46.6 percent of working women of color. Cuban, Filipino, and Japanese women were the only groups in which over 50 percent of working women did so on a full-time basis throughout the year. Mexican and Native American women had the lowest proportion of women in such jobs, at 40.3 and 40.7 percent respectively.

We should remember that trends in labor force participation and full-time employment can really be informative only when we consider the types of jobs women hold. The following data tell an uneven story in this regard. Almost all groups of women increased their numbers in managerial and professional jobs;[10] the number of self-employed has also increased in each group.[11] However, there is considerable variation in women's experiences in service jobs and in technical, sales, and administrative occupations.

TABLE 1.3.
Women Employed Full-Time Year-Round, 1989

	% Worked full-time year-round	Total women working full-time year-round (in thousands)	Total women working in 1989 (in thousands)
Cuban	52.9 (1)	138	261
Filipino	52.3 (2)	234	447
Japanese	51.4 (3)	126	245
BLACK	48.9 (4)	3,490	7,137
ASIAN	48.5 (5)	828	1,708
Vietnamese	47.8 (6)	54	113
Chinese	47.2 (7)	199	422
Puerto Rican	46.5 (8)	226	486
WHITE	46.2 (9)	23,460	50,748
Asian Indian	44.4 (10)	72	162
Korean	43.7 (11)	86	197
LATINA	42.6 (12)	1,833	4,304
NATIVE AMERICAN	40.7 (13)	170	418
Mexican	40.3 (14)	980	2,433
Total Women of Color	46.6	6,321	13,567
Total Women	46.4	28,715	61,905
Total People	55.5	74,660	134,529

SOURCE: *Social and Economic Characteristics*, tables 47, 109, 118.

NOTE: Ranked by column 1. Capitalized categories represent totals for all subgroups, including those not listed. Figures based on women 16 years and over who worked in 1989. Total women of color category calculated as a mean average of corresponding capitalized categories. Total women category calculated as the mean average of all capitalized categories. For this table and those that follow, Latinos are double counted in calculations of totals. This is an unavoidable artifact of published census data.

On average, 21.5 percent of all women held managerial and professional jobs in 1979; this number increased to 27.8 percent in 1989 (see table 1.4). In 1979, 22.4 percent of White women were employed in managerial and professional occupations, versus 17.6 percent of all women of color. In 1989, the figures were 29.3 percent for White women and 21.3 percent for women of color. Thus, White women increased their standing in management and professional jobs by 31 percent, while women of color in similar jobs increased by only 21 percent.

The distribution of both percentage change and actual percentages of women in management and professional positions varied greatly among women of color. Latinas had the greatest percentage increase among all women; 36 percent more Latinas held these white-collar jobs by the end of the decade. Puerto Rican and Cuban women saw the largest increases of all groups, with 57 percent and 54 percent more women in these jobs respectively. Despite this, fewer than one in four Puerto Rican or Cuban women worked in managerial or professional jobs in 1989. Mexican women increased their representation by 41 percent, Black women by 29 percent, and Native American women by 23 percent. Yet these groups also remain significantly underrepresented in managerial and professional jobs. Again, the initial low percentages of female managers and professionals at the start of the decade explain how substantial proportional changes occurred and yet still resulted in persistently low percentages of women in these jobs.

The gains of Asian women in professional jobs might appear small in contrast to the gains experienced by other groups of women (only a 6 percent increase for Asian

TABLE 1.4.

Percentage of Women in Managerial and Professional Occupations, 1979 and 1989, Ranked by 1989 Data

	1979	1989	% Change
WHITE	22.4 (6)	29.3 (1)	31
Japanese	23.1 (5)	28.8 (2)	25
Filipino	27.4 (2)	27.7 (3)	1
Chinese	24.9 (3)	27.7 (3)	11
Asian Indian	33.4 (1)	27.4 (4)	−18
ASIAN	23.8 (4)	25.2 (5)	6
Cuban	15.7 (10)	24.1 (6)	54
NATIVE AMERICAN	17.7 (7)	21.7 (7)	23
Korean	17.4 (8)	21.3 (8)	23
BLACK	16.5 (9)	21.3 (8)	29
Puerto Rican	13.4 (11)	21.1 (9)	57
LATINA	12.5 (12)	17.0 (10)	36
Mexican	10.8 (14)	15.2 (11)	41
Vietnamese	11.3 (13)	14.8 (12)	31
Total Women of Color	17.6	21.3	21
Total Women	21.5	27.8	30
Total People	22.7	26.4	16

SOURCES: 1979 data derived from *General Social and Economic Characteristics*, tables 89, 163, 169. 1989 data derived from *Social and Economic Characteristics*, tables 45, 110, 119.

NOTE: Figures in parentheses indicate rank in 1979 and 1989 respectively. Capitalized categories represent totals for all subgroups, including those not listed. Percentages based on total employed women 16 years and over. Total women of color category calculated as a mean average of corresponding capitalized categories. Total women category calculated as the mean average of all capitalized categories.

women in general). However, most Asian women began the eighties with higher percentages of women represented in these jobs (an average of 23.8 percent). Further, there was a wide variation within this group (from a decrease of 18 percent to an increase of 31 percent). Both of these factors contributed to a lower overall rate of increase. In 1989, Japanese women had the highest percentage among all women of color, with 28.8 percent in professional positions, compared to 23.1 percent in 1979. The proportion of Filipino women in these jobs was virtually unchanged over the decade, moving from 27.4 percent to 27.7 percent. Chinese women increased their showing from 24.9 percent in 1979 to 27.7 percent in 1989. Asian Indian women were the only group to experience a decline in the number of women in managerial and professional jobs. They dropped from 33.4 percent to 27.4 percent. Among Asian women, Korean and Vietnamese women had the lowest percentages of women working professionally: 21.3 percent of Korean women worked in such jobs in 1989, against 17.4 percent in 1979. Vietnamese women also had the lowest rates among all groups of women: 14.8 percent in 1989, versus 11.3 percent in 1979.

Self-Employed Women

More women went into business for themselves during the 1980s (see table 1.5). The total number of self-employed women increased from 3.7 percent to 5.1 percent. In 1979, 4 percent of White women were self-employed, versus 2.6 percent of all women of color; in 1989, 5.6 percent of White women were self-employed, versus 4.1 percent of women of color.

Korean women had the largest percentage of self-employed women throughout the decade: 7.8 percent in 1979 and 13.7 percent in 1989. Vietnamese women were especially active in this regard: 134 percent more Vietnamese women started their own businesses, which made them the group with the second largest percentage (6.1) of self-employed women in 1989. Chinese and Japanese women each had 5.5 percent self-employed in 1989, up from 5 percent and 4.5 percent respectively. Asian Indian women had 5 percent self-employed in 1989, versus 4 percent in 1979. Filipino women continued to trail among self-employed Asian women, increasing to 2.7 percent from 1.9 percent.

The number of self-employed Latinas almost doubled, from 2.1 percent to 3.9 percent. Cuban and Mexican women did well in this group. Self-employed Cuban women increased from 2.6 percent to 3.8 percent. The number of Mexican women in business for themselves grew from 2 percent to 3.7 percent. Puerto Rican women did less well among Latinas in this category: 1.2 percent were self-employed in 1979, up to 2.2 percent in 1989.

Fifty-seven percent more Native American women also became self-employed during this time. Measured in absolute terms, a smaller percentage of Black women were self-employed in the eighties than any other group of women: 2.1 percent in 1989, compared to 1.2 percent in 1979. However, for thirteen of the groups in our list

TABLE 1.5.
Percentage of Women Who are Self-Employed, 1979 and 1989,
Ranked by 1989 Data

	1979	1989	% Change
Korean	7.8　(1)	13.7　(1)	76
Vietnamese	2.6　(6)	6.1　(2)	134
ASIAN	4.0　(4)	5.6　(3)	40
WHITE	4.0　(4)	5.6　(3)	39
Chinese	5.0　(2)	5.5　(4)	10
Japanese	4.5　(3)	5.5　(4)	22
Asian Indian	4.0　(4)	5.0　(5)	25
NATIVE AMERICAN	3.0　(5)	4.7　(6)	57
LATINA	2.1　(7)	3.9　(7)	86
Cuban	2.6　(6)	3.8　(8)	45
Mexican	2.0　(8)	3.7　(9)	86
Filipino	1.9　(9)	2.7 (10)	44
Puerto Rican	1.2 (10)	2.2 (11)	82
BLACK	1.2 (10)	2.1 (12)	73
Total Women of Color	2.6	4.1	58
Total Women	3.7	5.1	37
Total People	6.8	6.9	1

SOURCES: 1979 data from *General Social and Economic Characteristics*, table 168; Ortiz, "Women of Color." 1989 data derived from *Asians in the U.S.*, table 4; *Persons of Hispanic Origin*, table 4; *Social and Economic Characteristics*, table 47.

NOTE: Figures in parentheses indicate rank in 1979 and 1989 respectively. Capitalized categories represent totals for all subgroups, including those not listed. Percentages based on total employed women 16 years and over. Total women of color category calculated as a mean average of corresponding capitalized categories. Total women category calculated as the mean average of all capitalized categories.

TABLE 1.6.

*Percentage of Women in Technical, Sales, and Administrative Support
Occupations, 1979 and 1989, Ranked by 1989 Data*

	1979	1989	% Change
Cuban	42.8 (3)	45.5 (1)	6
Puerto Rican	42.0 (4)	44.9 (2)	7
WHITE	47.3 (1)	44.7 (3)	−6
ASIAN	40.1 (7)	39.7 (4)	−1
LATINA	38.9 (8)	39.1 (5)	0
BLACK	35.2 (11)	38.7 (6)	10
Mexican	37.5 (10)	38.7 (6)	3
Filipino	40.9 (5)	38.6 (7)	−6
NATIVE AMERICAN	38.5 (9)	38.2 (8)	−1
Japanese	46.0 (2)	37.8 (9)	−18
Korean	29.8 (13)	34.7 (10)	16
Chinese	40.2 (6)	33.2 (11)	−17
Asian Indian	40.2 (6)	32.9 (12)	−18
Vietnamese	32.3 (12)	32.4 (13)	0
Total Women of Color	38.2	38.9	2
Total Women	45.6	43.6	−4
Total People	30.3	31.7	5

SOURCES: 1979 data derived from *General Social and Economic Characteristics*, tables 89, 163, 169. 1989 data derived from *Social and Economic Characteristics*, tables 45, 110, 119.

NOTE: Figures in parentheses indicate rank in 1979 and 1989 respectively. Capitalized categories represent totals for all subgroups, including those not listed. Percentages based on total employed women 16 years and over. Total women of color category calculated as a mean average of corresponding capitalized categories. Total women category calculated as the mean average of all capitalized categories.

of fourteen, fewer than six out of every one hundred individuals became self-employed.

The experiences of women in technical, sales, and administrative jobs have been more varied (see table 1.6).[12] Overall, the percentage of White women in these jobs dropped from 47.3 percent in 1979 to 44.7 percent in 1989, while women of color, as an aggregate group, remained at roughly the same rate (38.2 percent in 1979 and 38.9 percent in 1989). However, there are considerable differences among women of color.

The number of Black women in these jobs increased from 35.2 percent to 38.7 percent. This represented the second largest increase (10 percent) among all groups of women in such jobs. The percentage of Native American women in these jobs remained relatively stable over the decade, dropping slightly from 38.5 percent to 38.2 percent. Latinas also remained constant as a racial group: roughly 39 percent worked in technical, sales, or administrative jobs. Puerto Rican women had the largest percent increase among Latinas and the third largest increase among all groups of women, growing from 42 percent to 44.9 percent. Cuban women had the largest percentage of women employed in these blue-collar jobs among all groups of women in 1989 (45.5 percent). Mexican women saw a more modest increase, from 37.5 percent to 38.7 percent.

Among Asian women, only Korean women had an increase in their rate of employment in these types of jobs. Korean women filled technical, sales, and administrative jobs at a faster rate than any other group of women. Between 1979 and 1989, the number of Korean women working in these occupations increased from 29.8 percent to 34.7 percent. The employment rates of Vietnamese women in this area remained constant at approximately 32 percent. Japanese, Chinese, and Asian Indian women each had a lower percentage of women working in these jobs: 18 percent fewer Japanese and Asian Indian, and 17 percent fewer Chinese women than in 1979. Representation of Filipino women also declined, from 40.9 percent to 38.6 percent. In short, more Korean, Black, and Latina women worked as technicians, salespersons, and administrative support personnel, even as the percentage of other groups of women in these areas dropped.

Latinas emerged as the fastest growing group in the service occupations (see table 1.7).[13] More Latinas worked as maids, security guards, police officers, and the like during the eighties. Among all groups, Mexican women had the second highest percentage of women working as service providers in 1989: 23.6 percent, up from 22.8 percent in 1979. Puerto Rican and Cuban women had the highest rates of increase. The percentage of Puerto Rican women in these jobs grew from 15.2 percent in 1979 to 17.6 percent in 1989, and for Cuban women, from 12.4 percent to 13.7 percent.

All other groups of women underwent a decline in the percentage working in service occupations. Black women dropped from 29.3 percent to 25.1 percent, and Native American women from 25.2 percent to 22.7 percent. The percentage of White women service providers also declined, from 16.3 percent to 15.4 percent. Asian Indian and Japanese women shared the largest rate of decline (− 31 percent): Asian

TABLE 1.7.
Percentage of Women in Service Occupations, 1979 and 1989,
Ranked by 1989 Data

	1979	1989	% Change
BLACK	29.3 (1)	25.1 (1)	− 14
Mexican	22.8 (4)	23.6 (2)	4
LATINA	20.8 (5)	23.5 (3)	13
NATIVE AMERICAN	25.2 (2)	22.7 (4)	− 10
Korean	22.9 (3)	18.0 (5)	− 22
Vietnamese	17.9 (6)	17.7 (6)	− 1
Puerto Rican	15.2 (10)	17.6 (7)	16
Filipino	16.7 (8)	16.2 (8)	− 3
ASIAN	17.2 (7)	16.1 (9)	− 6
WHITE	16.3 (9)	15.4 (10)	− 5
Cuban	12.4 (13)	13.7 (11)	10
Japanese	17.2 (7)	11.9 (12)	− 31
Chinese	13.8 (11)	11.9 (12)	− 14
Asian Indian	13.0 (12)	9.0 (13)	− 31
Total Women of Color	23.1	21.8	− 5
Total Women	17.9	16.9	− 6
Total People	12.9	13.2	2

SOURCES: 1979 data derived from *General Social and Economic Characteristics*, tables 89, 163, 169. 1989 data derived from *Social and Economic Characteristics*, tables 45, 110, 119.

NOTE: Figures in parentheses indicate rank in 1979 and 1989 respectively. Capitalized categories represent totals for all subgroups, including those not listed. Percentages based on total employed women 16 years and over. Total women of color category calculated as a mean average of corresponding capitalized categories. Total women category calculated as the mean average of all capitalized categories.

Indian women in the service industry decreased from 13 percent to 9 percent, and Japanese women from 17.2 percent to 11.9 percent. Korean women also saw a significant drop, from 22.9 percent to 18 percent.

Women's Personal Income

Table 1.8 shows median income levels for individual women workers.[14] Most Asian women continued to have higher earnings than any other racial category. Japanese, Chinese, Filipino, and Asian Indian women were the top four income earners in both 1979 and 1989. Vietnamese and Korean women did less well among Asian women in both years. In general, Asian women's salaries increased by 9 percent during the eighties.

Among Latinas, we note the continuation of a trend documented by Ortiz: Puerto Rican women outearn Mexican (and now Cuban) women and are more likely among Latinas to have full-time year-round jobs, despite the fact that Puerto Rican women have the lowest labor force participation rate (see table 1.3 and fig. 1.3).[15] Ortiz offers a feasible explanation, that this is the result of the concentration of Puerto Rican women in the Northeast, where there are higher-salaried jobs that demand greater skills. Consequently, while fewer Puerto Ricans are able to find work, those who do work enjoy higher material returns. Mexican, Native American, and Black women had the lowest income levels among all women.

TABLE 1.8.
Median Income for Female Full-Time Year-Round Workers, 1979 and 1989,
Ranked by 1989 Data

	1979	1989	% Change
Japanese	$20,257 (2)	$24,133 (1)	19
Chinese	20,215 (3)	23,277 (2)	15
Filipino	20,412 (1)	21,690 (3)	6
Asian Indian	20,058 (4)	21,590 (4)	8
ASIAN	19,553 (5)	21,335 (5)	9
WHITE	17,870 (6)	19,916 (6)	11
Vietnamese	15,744 (11)	18,771 (7)	19
Korean	17,447 (7)	18,760 (8)	8
Puerto Rican	15,963 (9)	18,717 (9)	17
Cuban	15,269 (12)	18,283 (10)	20
BLACK	16,291 (8)	18,005 (11)	11
NATIVE AMERICAN	15,786 (10)	16,613 (12)	5
LATINA	15,169 (13)	16,307 (13)	8
Mexican	14,647 (14)	15,478 (14)	6
Total Women of Color	16,700	18,065	8
Total Women	17,646	19,570	11

SOURCES: 1979 data from *General Social and Economic Characteristics*, table 170; Ortiz, "Women of Color." 1989 data derived from *Social and Economic Characteristics*, tables 48, 111, 120; *Characteristics of American Indians*, table 6.

NOTE: Figures in parentheses indicate rank in 1979 and 1989 respectively. Capitalized categories represent totals for all subgroups, including those not listed. Figures based on all women 15 years and over with income in 1979 and 1989. Total women of color category calculated as a mean average of corresponding capitalized categories. Total women category calculated as the mean average of all capitalized categories.

The gap between the highest- and lowest-earning groups of women grew during the decade, even when the figures are adjusted to constant dollars.

Family Income and Poverty

Family income levels convey how much demand is being placed on every dollar earned better than individual earnings do.[16] The distinction can be conceived as the difference between an income of $20,000 supporting a family of four versus a single individual. Thus, we consider income and poverty levels among families in general, and among female-headed families in particular.

Table 1.9 shows the median income for all families, that is, families headed by a single male, a single female, or a couple. For ease of comparison, we have adjusted 1979 income dollars to 1989 dollar value. In 1979, the median family income was $35,420 for Whites and $27,073 for communities of color. By 1989, the median family income for Whites had increased by 5 percent to $37,152, and by only 2 percent to $27,673 for families from communities of color. In 1979, the average family in communities of color made 76.4 percent of what White families earned. By 1989, families in communities of color earned 74.5 percent of White families' income. The gap in income levels between White families and families in communities of color widened during the eighties.

The top four median incomes among all groups of women were held by Asian families, and Japanese families had the largest median income ($46,502 in 1979 and $51,550 in 1989). In 1989, Vietnamese families had the lowest income level among Asian families but still outearned all other non-Asian families of color, with the exception of Cuban families. In fact, Vietnamese families experienced the greatest gains in their income levels — an astounding 40 percent. This can be compared with Black families, who had roughly the same income level as Vietnamese families in 1979, but who witnessed only a 5 percent gain by the end of the eighties. Puerto Rican families had the highest rate of increase among Latinos, but continued to have lower income levels and higher poverty levels than both Mexican and Cuban families. Mexican, Native American, and Korean families actually saw a decline in their incomes. Puerto Rican, Black, and Native American families had the lowest median incomes in 1989.

The difference between the top and bottom income-earning families was quite dramatic: in both 1979 and 1989, the Japanese median family income was around twice that of the lowest income-earning families.

The poverty levels for most families remained unchanged during the eighties (see fig. 1.4). Fewer Puerto Rican families were at or below the poverty level during the eighties, but Puerto Ricans remain the poorest community in the United States. Vietnamese families saw the largest decline (-32 percent) in their poverty rates, and yet almost one in four Vietnamese families lived below the poverty line between 1979 and 1989. Japanese and Filipino families saw not only some of the biggest decreases but also some of the lowest poverty rates among all the groups.

Native American, Mexican, and Korean families had the largest increases in their

TABLE 1.9.
Median Family Income, 1979 and 1989, Ranked by 1989 Data
(in 1989 Dollars)

	1979	1989	% Change
Japanese	$46,502 (1)	$51,550 (1)	11
Asian Indian	42,488 (2)	49,309 (2)	16
Filipino	40,268 (3)	46,698 (3)	16
ASIAN	38,612 (4)	41,583 (4)	8
Chinese	38,350 (5)	41,316 (5)	8
WHITE	35,420 (6)	37,152 (6)	5
Korean	34,780 (7)	33,909 (7)	− 3
Cuban	31,017 (8)	32,417 (8)	5
Vietnamese	21,828 (12)	30,550 (9)	40
LATINO	25,010 (10)	25,064 (10)	0
Mexican	25,101 (9)	24,119 (11)	− 4
BLACK	21,417 (13)	22,429 (12)	5
Puerto Rican	18,248 (14)	21,941 (13)	20
NATIVE AMERICAN	23,253 (11)	21,619 (14)	− 7
Total People of Color Families	27,073	27,673	2
Total Families	33,859	35,225	4

SOURCES: 1979 data from *General and Social Economic Characteristics*, table 170; Ortiz, "Women of Color." 1989 data derived from *Social and Economic Characteristics*, tables 48, 111, 120.

NOTE: Figures in parentheses indicate rank in 1979 and 1989 respectively. Capitalized categories represent totals for all subgroups, including those not listed. Figures based on all families with income in 1979 and 1989. Total people of color families calculated as a mean average of corresponding capitalized categories.

FIG. 1.4.
Percentage of Families at or Below Poverty, 1979 and 1989, Ranked by 1989 Data

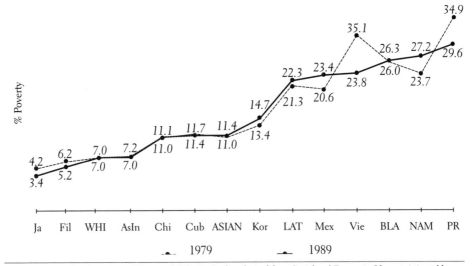

SOURCES: 1979 data from Ortiz, "Women of Color." 1989 data derived from *Social and Economic Characteristics*, tables 49, 112, 121.

NOTE: The average poverty threshold was $7,412 in 1979 (or $12,600 in 1989 dollars) and $12,674 in 1989.

KEY: ASIAN: All Asians; AsIn: Asian Indian; BLA: All Blacks; Chi: Chinese; Cub: Cuban; Fil: Filipino; Ja: Japanese; Kor: Korean; LAT: All Latinas; Mex: Mexican; NAM: All Native Americans; PR: Puerto Rican; Vie: Vietnamese; WHI: All Whites

poverty rates, at 15, 14, and 10 percent respectively, while the poverty rate for Blacks increased by only 1 percent.

Income Levels and Poverty among Female-Headed Families

In 1989, Blacks had the largest percentage of families headed by women (43 percent), followed by Native Americans (26 percent) and Latinas (22 percent). Twelve percent of White and Asian families were headed by women.[17]

A comparison of median family income (table 1.9) with median income for female-headed families (table 1.10) shows that female-headed families continue to be poorer than other families, partly because they have only one wage earner. In 1979, the average median income for female-headed families was less than half that of families in general ($16,932 for female-headed families, versus $33,859 for all families). By 1989, the gap had narrowed somewhat to roughly one half ($17,414 versus $35,225).

In 1979, White women who headed families had a median family income of $15,535, compared to $12,054 for families headed by women of color. By 1989, their respective incomes were $20,340 and $14,812. Families headed by women of color earned about 78 percent of what their White counterparts made in 1979, and only 73 percent by 1989. Families headed by women of color became poorer during the eighties compared to families headed by White women.

As a racial group, Asian female-headed families had the largest change in family income, undergoing a 49 percent increase in ten years. In general, Asian female-headed families outearned Latina, Black, White, and Native American female-headed families in both 1979 and 1989. White, Latina, and Black female-headed families all had higher incomes in 1989. Native American female-headed families were the only group to see a decline — their income levels dropped from $11,213 to $10,635.

Families headed by Japanese women had the largest increase of any group: their income rose from $19,038 to $32,675 — an increase of 72 percent! Asian Indian, Chinese, and Filipino female-headed families also had high incomes, in relation to other groups of women. Vietnamese female-headed families earned less pay than other families headed by Asian women: their income increased by only 2 percent during the eighties, resulting in a median income of $11,926 in 1989. Puerto Rican female-headed families remained the poorest of all female-headed families: the median income for Puerto Rican female-headed families was $7,808 in 1979 and only $8,912 in 1989.

In 1989, many more families headed by women of color lived in poverty (41.5 percent) than did White female-headed families (23.2 percent) (see table 1.11). However, it should be noted that White female-headed families were also among the five groups of women whose poverty rates *increased* over the decade. White female-headed families underwent a 4 percent increase in poverty, along with families headed by Mexican women (2 percent increase), Vietnamese women (3 percent increase), Native American women (9 percent increase), and Asian Indian women (31 percent increase). All other groups experienced a decline in poverty

TABLE 1.10.
Median Income for Female-Headed Families, 1979 and 1989, Ranked by 1989 Data
(in 1989 Dollars)

	1979	1989	% Change
Japanese	$19,038 (1)	32,675 (1)	72
Filipino	18,263 (3)	30,950 (2)	69
Chinese	18,297 (2)	26,928 (3)	47
ASIAN	15,929 (5)	23,686 (4)	49
Asian Indian	17,554 (4)	22,245 (5)	27
WHITE	15,535 (6)	20,340 (6)	31
Cuban	13,629 (8)	19,511 (7)	43
Korean	13,881 (7)	19,127 (8)	38
Mexican	11,266 (10)	12,714 (9)	13
BLACK	10,962 (12)	12,522 (10)	14
LATINA	10,112 (13)	12,406 (11)	23
Vietnamese	11,647 (9)	11,926 (12)	2
NATIVE AMERICAN	11,213 (11)	10,635 (13)	−5
Puerto Rican	7,808 (14)	8,912 (14)	14
Total Women of Color Families	12,054	14,812	23
Total Female-Headed Families	16,932	17,414	3

SOURCES: 1979 data from *General and Social Economic Characteristics*, table 170; Ortiz, "Women of Color." 1989 data derived from *Social and Economic Characteristics*, tables 48, 111, 120.

NOTE: Figures in parentheses indicate rank in 1979 and 1989 respectively. Capitalized categories represent totals for all subgroups, including those not listed. Figures based on all female-headed families with income in 1979 and 1989. Total women of color families calculated as a mean average of corresponding capitalized categories.

TABLE 1.11.
Poverty Level among Female-Headed Families, 1979 and 1989, Ranked by 1989 Data

	1979	1989	% Change
Puerto Rican	66.8 (1)	57.3 (1)	−14
NATIVE AMERICAN	46.5 (4)	50.8 (2)	9
Vietnamese	47.8 (3)	49.0 (3)	3
LATINA	48.2 (2)	45.7 (4)	−5
Mexican	44.3 (6)	45.4 (5)	2
BLACK	46.3 (5)	44.5 (6)	−4
Asian Indian	21.0 (11)	27.4 (7)	31
Korean	32.1 (7)	25.9 (8)	−19
Cuban	27.2 (8)	25.3 (9)	−7
ASIAN	25.7 (9)	24.9 (10)	−3
WHITE	22.3 (10)	23.2 (11)	4
Chinese	22.3 (10)	19.9 (12)	−11
Filipino	20.4 (12)	14.2 (13)	−30
Japanese	14.5 (13)	9.6 (14)	−34
Total Women of Color Families	41.7	41.5	0
Total Female-Headed Families	30.3	31.6	4
Total All Families	9.6	10.0	4

SOURCES: 1979 data from *General Social and Economic Characteristics*, table 171; Ortiz, "Women of Color." 1989 data derived from *Social and Economic Characteristics*, tables 49, 112, 121.

NOTE: Figures in parentheses indicate rank in 1979 and 1989 respectively. Capitalized categories represent totals for all subgroups, including those not listed. The average poverty threshold was $7,412 in 1979 (or $12,600 in 1989 dollars) and $12,674 in 1989. Total women of color calculated as a mean average of corresponding capitalized categories. Percentages based on all female-headed families with income and those below poverty in 1979 and 1989.

ranging from −4 percent for Black families to −34 percent for Japanese. Families headed by Puerto Rican women remained the poorest of all female-headed families, although the proportion of Puerto Rican families living in poverty declined from 66.8 percent in 1979 to 57.3 percent in 1989.

Fertility

Fertility rates measure the number of live births per thousand women, regardless of marital status. Figures 1.5, 1.6, and 1.7 present data on three age groups. But first a word of caution. The reader might be tempted to read the chart on the fertility rates of fifteen- to twenty-four-year-olds as a precise barometer of teen pregnancies. This would be a mistake. These data do not speak to the distribution of births within an age group; we do not know whether more of the babies are being born to fifteen- and sixteen-year-olds or to women in their early to mid-twenties.

Young Puerto Rican, Mexican, Black, and Native American women have higher birth rates than young women in other ethnic groups. However, contrary to popular perceptions, young Puerto Rican and Black women recorded a decline in their rates by the end of the decade. Births among young Puerto Rican women dropped from 548 births per thousand women (bpt) to 524 bpt, and among young Black women from 537 bpt to 516 bpt. The fertility rates of young Native American women, however, increased from 530 bpt to 533 bpt. Young Cuban women were another exception to the trend of decreasing rates, with a 16 percent increase in births, from 192 to 222 bpt.

FIG. 1.5.
Fertility Rate for Women Aged 15 to 24, 1980 and 1990, Ranked by 1990 Data

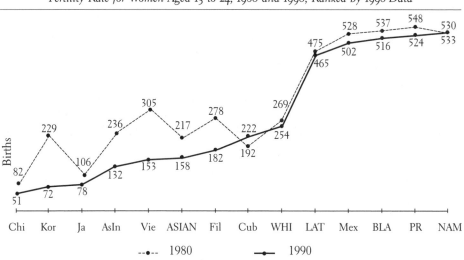

SOURCES: 1980 data from Ortiz, "Women of Color." 1990 data derived from *Asians in the U.S.*, table 1; *Persons of Hispanic Origin*, table 1; *Social and Economic Characteristics*, table 41.
NOTE: Births = live births per thousand women.
KEY: ASIAN: All Asians; AsIn: Asian Indian; BLA: All Blacks; Chi: Chinese; Cub: Cuban; Fil: Filipino; Ja: Japanese; Kor: Korean; LAT: All Latinas; Mex: Mexican; NAM: All Native Americans; PR: Puerto Rican; Vie: Vietnamese; WHI: All Whites

FIG. 1.6.
Fertility Rate for Women Aged 25 to 34, 1980 and 1990, Ranked by 1990 Data

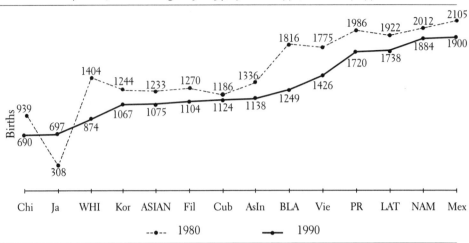

SOURCES: 1980 data from Ortiz, "Women of Color." 1990 data derived from *Asians in the U.S.*, table 1; *Persons of Hispanic Origin*, table 1; *Social and Economic Characteristics*, table 41.
   NOTE: Births = live births per thousand women.
   KEY: ASIAN: All Asians; AsIn: Asian Indian; BLA: All Blacks; Chi: Chinese; Cub: Cuban; Fil: Filipino; Ja: Japanese; Kor: Korean; LAT: All Latinas; Mex: Mexican; NAM: All Native Americans; PR: Puerto Rican; Vie: Vietnamese; WHI: All Whites

FIG. 1.7.
Fertility Rate for Women Aged 35 to 44, 1980 and 1990, Ranked by 1990 Data

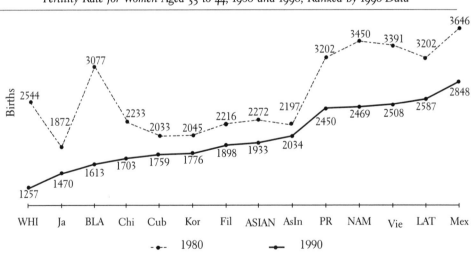

SOURCES: 1980 data from Ortiz, "Women of Color." 1990 data derived from *Asians in the U.S.*, table 1; *Persons of Hispanic Origin*, table 1; *Social and Economic Characteristics*, table 41.
   NOTE: Births = live births per thousand women.
   KEY: ASIAN: All Asians; AsIn: Asian Indian; BLA: All Blacks; Chi: Chinese; Cub: Cuban; Fil: Filipino; Ja: Japanese; Kor: Korean; LAT: All Latinas; Mex: Mexican; NAM: All Native Americans; PR: Puerto Rican; Vie: Vietnamese; WHI: All Whites

At the start of the 1980s, the birth rates varied widely among young Asian women. Young Asian women had significant drops in their fertility rates. Young Korean women had the largest decline in fertility rates (− 69 percent), from 229 bpt in 1980 to 72 bpt in 1990. Young Chinese women consistently had the lowest fertility rate of all groups: 82 bpt in 1980 and 51 bpt in 1990. Younger White women's fertility rates also decreased, by roughly 6 percent.

The story of declining rates persists among older women as well (figs. 1.6 and 1.7). The only exceptions were Japanese women between the ages of twenty-five and thirty-four. The number of births in this group increased by 126 percent, from 308 bpt to 697 bpt. Even so, Japanese women had the second lowest number of births in 1990. Additionally significant were the declining rates for both White and Black women among both twenty-five- to thirty-four-year-olds and thirty-five- to forty-four-year-olds. White women's fertility rates in the former age group decreased by 38 percent, from 1,404 bpt in 1980 to 874 bpt in 1990. (Rates in excess of 1,000 can be explained by the fact that a single woman can have multiple births while she is a member of a single age category. For example, a woman may have two children while she is between the ages of 25 and 34.) Black women's rates dropped by 31 percent, from 1,816 bpt to 1,249. In this age bracket, Chinese women had the lowest fertility rates in 1990 (690 bpt), while Mexican women had the highest rates (1,900 bpt).

Among thirty-five- to forty-four-year-olds, all the groups had lower numbers of births by the end of the decade. White and Black women had the largest decreases, with declines of 51 percent and 48 percent respectively. In 1990, White women also had the lowest fertility rate (1,257 bpt), while Mexican women had the highest (2,848 bpt). For all the ethnic and racial groups, women between the ages of thirty-five and forty-four had higher fertility rates than women younger than thirty-five in the same group.

Marital Status

The proportion of women who were ever married changed little during the eighties, although quite significant shifts are discernible for some groups among the proportion of single women and those whose marriages have been disrupted (see tables 1.12, 1.13, and 1.14). With the exception of Chinese and Black women, the percentage of women who were ever married declined among all groups. Chinese women's marriage rates increased by 1 percent over the decade, from 59.3 percent to 60 percent, and the percentage of Black women in marriages increased by only one tenth of a percentage point, from 35 percent to 35.1 percent. Black and Puerto Rican women are the least likely to be married among all women, having the lowest rates of marriage and among the highest rates of single women. However, once married, Black women were 20 percent *less* likely to see their marriages disrupted, while the proportion of Puerto Rican marriages ending in divorce, separation, or widowhood remained unchanged.

Asian women had the highest rates of marriage, with the exception of Vietnamese women. Asian women were also the least likely among all women to see their marriages disrupted, although Filipino and Japanese women witnessed an increase in the number of disrupted marriages. Native American women had lower percentages of single and married women. However, they experienced a 12 percent increase in disrupted marriages.

TABLE 1.12.

Percentage of Women Ever Married, 1980 and 1990, Ranked by 1990 Data

	1980	1990	% Change
Asian Indian	71.5 (1)	70.0 (1)	−2
Korean	68.2 (2)	62.1 (2)	−9
ASIAN	61.7 (4)	60.1 (3)	−3
Chinese	59.3 (6)	60.0 (4)	1
Japanese	60.9 (5)	59.8 (5)	−2
Filipino	62.4 (3)	59.1 (6)	−5
WHITE	57.5 (7)	55.5 (7)	−3
Cuban	54.5 (10)	53.5 (8)	−2
Mexican	55.6 (9)	53.2 (9)	−4
Vietnamese	56.7 (8)	52.6 (10)	−7
LATINA	52.8 (11)	50.4 (11)	−5
NATIVE AMERICAN	48.0 (12)	46.1 (12)	−4
Puerto Rican	43.0 (13)	40.1 (13)	−7
BLACK	35.0 (14)	35.1 (14)	0
Total Women of Color	49.4	47.9	−3
Total Women	51.0	49.4	−3

SOURCES: 1980 data from Ortiz, "Women of Color." 1990 data from *Asians in the U.S.*, table 1; *Characteristics of American Indians*, table 3; *1990 Census of Population: General Population Characteristics, United States* (CP–1–1, 1992) (hereafter cited as *General Population Characteristics*), table 40; *Persons of Hispanic Origin*, table 1.

NOTE: Figures in parentheses indicate rank in 1980 and 1990 respectively. Capitalized categories represent totals for all subgroups, including those not listed. Percentages based on women 15 years and older. Total women of color category calculated as a mean average of corresponding capitalized categories. Total women category calculated as the mean average of all capitalized categories.

TABLE 1.13.

Percentage of Women Never Married, 1980 and 1990,
Ranked by 1990 Data

	1980	1990	% Change
BLACK	34.4 (1)	40.2 (1)	17
Vietnamese	31.7 (2)	35.1 (2)	11
Puerto Rican	31.1 (3)	34.1 (3)	10
LATINA	27.5 (6)	29.3 (4)	7
Mexican	27.3 (7)	29.3 (4)	7
NATIVE AMERICAN	28.6 (4)	28.2 (5)	−1
Chinese	28.4 (5)	28.0 (6)	−1
Filipino	26.0 (8)	27.0 (7)	4
ASIAN	25.0 (9)	26.6 (8)	6
Korean	18.6 (13)	23.8 (9)	28
Japanese	24.3 (10)	23.6 (10)	−3
Asian Indian	15.1 (14)	22.0 (11)	46
WHITE	21.2 (12)	20.7 (12)	−2
Cuban	22.3 (11)	19.1 (13)	−14
Total Women of Color	28.9	31.1	8
Total Women	27.3	29.0	6

SOURCES: 1980 data from Ortiz, "Women of Color." 1990 data from *Asians in the U.S.*, table 1; *Characteristics of American Indians*, table 3; *General Population Characteristics*, table 40; *Persons of Hispanic Origin*, table 1.

NOTE: Figures in parentheses indicate rank in 1980 and 1990 respectively. Capitalized categories represent totals for all subgroups, including those not listed. Percentages based on women 15 years and older. Total women of color category calculated as a mean average of corresponding capitalized categories. Total women category calculated as the mean average of all capitalized categories.

TABLE 1.14.
*Percentage of Women Maritally Disrupted, 1980 and 1990,
Ranked by 1990 Data*

	1980	1990	% Change
Cuban	23.2 (4)	27.5 (1)	19
NATIVE AMERICAN	23.3 (3)	26.1 (2)	12
Puerto Rican	25.9 (2)	26.0 (3)	0
BLACK	30.6 (1)	24.6 (4)	−20
WHITE	21.4 (5)	23.7 (5)	11
LATINA	19.7 (6)	20.2 (6)	3
Mexican	17.1 (7)	17.5 (7)	2
Japanese	14.7 (8)	16.5 (8)	12
Filipino	11.7 (13)	14.3 (9)	22
Korean	13.2 (11)	14.1 (10)	7
ASIAN	13.3 (10)	13.3 (11)	0
Vietnamese	11.6 (14)	12.4 (12)	7
Chinese	12.2 (12)	12.1 (13)	−1
Asian Indian	13.4 (9)	8.1 (14)	−40
Total Women of Color	21.7	21.1	−3
Total Women	21.7	21.6	−0

SOURCES: 1980 data from Ortiz, "Women of Color." 1990 data from *Asians in the U.S.*, table 1; *Characteristics of American Indians*, table 3; *General Population Characteristics*, table 40; *Persons of Hispanic Origin*, table 1.

NOTE: Figures in parentheses indicate rank in 1980 and 1990 respectively. Capitalized categories represent totals for all subgroups, including those not listed. Percentages based on women 15 years and older. The category "maritally disrupted" combines those who are separated, widowed, and divorced. Total women of color category calculated as a mean average of corresponding capitalized categories. Total women category calculated as the mean average of all capitalized categories.

Taken singly, each of these variables seems to tell a different and, at times, contrasting story. Broadly speaking, the lives of women of color seem to have improved during the eighties. More graduated from high school and college. More held managerial and professional jobs. In addition, women of color are increasingly self-employed, a fact that might testify to their increasing economic independence. In general, more women of color participated in the labor force during the 1980s. Some groups of women experienced increases in their income levels of up to 22 percent. Despite this, half the groups of women in this study saw almost no change in their poverty level (experiencing shifts of less than 1 percent); two-thirds of the remaining half experienced increases in their poverty rates. Of the women who had jobs, fewer of them had the security of full-time annual employment.

Taken together, what does it all mean? One way of negotiating this puzzle is to compare the expectations inherent in one set of the data with the actual experiences indicated by another set. For example, if we think that increased schooling increases employability and earning potential, then we might expect that increased graduation rates would correspond to increased income levels. And this does indeed seem to be the case for some groups. However, it does not explain the declining income levels and increasing poverty among Mexican women. These women had the third largest increase in women graduating high school and the third largest increase in women receiving college degrees, but their median income experienced the second lowest rate of increase, only 6 percent.

A second strategy is to ask about the women who are not accounted for in these tables. For example, only 23 percent of Black women are accounted for in the 1989 list of women in managerial/professional occupations and who are self-employed (see tables 1.4 and 1.5). It is reasonable to ask what kinds of jobs the other 77 percent of employed Black women have. One published report by the Department of Labor notes that while Black women have "increased their employment in a wide variety of professions," their number has declined in some well-paying jobs. Indeed, during the past decade, jobs as retail sales clerks, nursing aides, secretaries, cashiers, cooks, elementary school teachers, and janitors and cleaners (of private households and buildings) have accounted for most of the employment of Black women — as much as 33 percent of total Black female employment in 1990.[18] The report goes on to note that these jobs "offer low pay, require little training and few skills, demand little work experience, and offer very limited chances for advancement." Additionally, many of these are part-time positions, which the Department of Labor characterizes as "among the fastest growing in the near future." Clearly, the declining number of Black women in full-time annual employment is not explained by Black women choosing to work fewer hours for comparable pay.

There is stark evidence of the continued development of a two-tiered, racially polarized society among women, in which some Asians and Whites experience economic prosperity and some Latinas, Blacks, and Native Americans disproportionately fill dead-end, low-skill jobs. Yet a third strategy for understanding these data is to question the root causes of the racial and ethnic differences in the achievements of women of color, and the institutions or practices that perpetuate this pattern. For example, we could ask, Why do some Asian groups have a higher percentage of women who have graduated from high school and college, and who have achieved a higher level of financial success? To point to the supposed stronger work ethic of Asians is to ignore the high rates of poverty and low graduation rates among some Asian groups, like the Vietnamese. To suggest a specific cultural factor is to homogenize culturally complex communities and to overlook significant intracommunity differences. Rather, it may be more productive for us to consider the ways prior education and financial prosperity of immigrant groups prepare them to succeed in the United States; or the ways schools in the United States, drawing on prevailing racial stereotypes, track Asian students into science and math fields. There are many other possible factors, of course. Our point is simply that the explanations for the wide variations among women of color are not always self-evident. The statistical data presented in this essay indicate outcomes, not causes; thus, additional quantitative evidence and more refined analytical work are needed before we can fully understand the observed variations among women of color.

The number of those living in poverty will continue to increase as a result of the growing capitalist predisposition to equate business efficiency and profits with a "streamlined" workforce. The new world economic order is one in which the exploitation of cheap and unskilled workers in lesser developed countries directly contributes to increased unemployment and poverty in more industrialized states. In addition, technology is increasingly viewed as a substitute for, rather than an aid to, human labor. The combined effect is increased layoffs — already the hallmark of business in the 1990s — and a growing population of the poor. More women and men of all races and ethnicities will continue to fall into poverty. While the percentage of those living in poverty remained relatively unchanged for most groups in the 1980s, the increased size of those communities means that the same percentage now represents larger actual numbers of those who are poor.

However, racial discrimination and changing family structures guarantee that women of color will continue to be disproportionately poor. The lower earning power of women of color, the decreasing likelihood of finding full-time jobs with decent benefits, and the high numbers of women who are single parents all suggest that women of color will continue to be among the poorest of people in the United States. Against the backdrop of these economic realities, the accounts that blame individual women for their lack of success and for the deteriorating social fabric are revealed to have a misplaced focus. Such ideologies fail to consider the ways larger economic and social structures shape the life choices of individuals.

Consider the poverty rate among women of color. Capitalist economies require a pool of underemployed and unemployed labor; competition for jobs keeps wages (particularly for unskilled labor) low. This feature of capitalism has meant that workers have always been especially vulnerable to exploitation. There has always been a direct relationship between the difficulty of finding work and the willingness to accept degrading conditions of work. Poor and working-class women (and men and children) in this country work fourteen-hour shifts in sweatshops to produce the jeans that hang in local department stores, are sprayed with pesticides as they pick produce to stock grocers' shelves, and are burned to death because their supervisors have locked them in to ensure that they work. These are not idle imaginings; they are actual accounts reported in U.S. newspapers over the last decade.[19] It is easy to dismiss these stories as aberrations in a system that generally treats its workers well. But there is mounting evidence that conditions of workers in the United States are worsening and are increasingly tenuous.[20]

Further, transnational corporations are characterized by their ability to transfer their capital to wherever costs are lowest and profit margins highest. There is little incentive for U.S. corporations to employ domestic labor. U.S. companies, in industries as varied as clothing, computers, automobiles, and carbonated beverages, to name just a few, routinely manufacture their products in other countries. Even products that are labeled "Made in America" are often only assembled in the United States. Such products are often manufactured in countries where workers (typically women of color) are forbidden by law to form unions, are paid at the discretion of companies that are not constrained by minimum wage requirements, are offered no benefits, are laid off if they get sick, and are subject to unsafe and unhealthy work environments. It is no wonder that immigration rates continue to rise even as more U.S. jobs move to other countries.

Immigrant women of color suffer many of the same hardships as those who are born in the United States. They are among the most marginal members of society and become the scapegoats for social ills. The woman of color who is a single mother, particularly if she is poor, comes to symbolize the failure of the individual worker and the disintegration of the nuclear family structure. Further, poor and working-class women of color are often portrayed as noncitizens who stand outside the social contract. As such, they are not believed to be subject to the rules that structure relationships between citizens and the state. Women of color thus become the target of a myriad of regulative policies, from enforced sterilizations to mandated workfare and dead-end jobs.

Any political action whose goal is the improvement of the lives of women of color in the United States must, first, recognize the international dimensions of systems of oppression that are structural in nature and, second, acknowledge how those systems create hierarchical differences among women of color. Further, activists must question the degree to which beliefs are informed by the empirical evidence of the lives of women of color. Finally, we must work to fully empower women of color and make their concerns central to national debates.

APPENDIX

- Most 1980 data are taken from Vilma Ortiz's article. We indicate when 1980 data are used directly from the census. All 1990 data are based on the 1990 *Census of Population* (see bibliography for full list of references). The Current Population Survey, which updates data between the decennial censuses, was not available for all groups when research was conducted for this chapter.
- Some words on language. We have replaced the government's label of "Hispanic Origin" with the term "Latina" because it recognizes the African, Spanish, and Indigenous bases of Latino culture; "Hispanic Origin" highlights only the Spanish contribution to this complex and diverse culture. We substitute "Native American" for "American Indian" because the latter reference perpetuates Columbus's erroneous belief that he had reached India. This reference does not include Eskimos and Aleuts, whose legacy is distinct from that of the numerous tribal nations.
- Importantly, Latinas, who may be of any race, are counted twice: once as Latinas and again as members of other racial groups. Thus, a woman who identified herself as both Black and Latina would be included in both categories. Census data distinguish between Latinas and non-Latinas in summary statistics for racial groups (Whites, Blacks, Asians) but not when they provide detailed information on ethnic subgroups (such as Japanese, Korean, Asian Indian). The general trends for a population are not altered by their inclusion, however. Latinos represent 5 percent of all Whites, 2 percent of all Blacks, 7 percent of all Native Americans, and 4 percent of Asians/Pacific Islanders. Their inclusion in both categories also allows us to maintain consistency with calculations performed using 1980 data.
- This essay does not discuss all the Asian and Latino subgroups described in the census. Rather, we have followed Ortiz's scheme in order to facilitate comparisons with her 1980 data. While the census reports twelve Asian subgroups, the six Asian subgroups included in our discussion represent 89 percent of all (i.e., both men and women) Asians. Similarly, the three Latino subgroups included

here represent 78 percent of the total population of Latinos to be found in the thirteen ethnic subgroups. In the charts and tables, the general categories of "Asian" and "Latina" include all subgroups, even those not listed. The unlisted groups are, for Asians, Cambodians, Hmongs, Laotians, Thais, Indonesians, Pakistanis; for Latinos, Dominicans (from the Dominican Republic, not Dominica), Costa Ricans, Guatemalans, Hondurans, Nicaraguans, Panamanians, Salvadorians, Argentinians, Chileans, Colombians, Ecuadorians, Peruvians, Venezuelans. However, please note that in this essay, the general category Asian excludes Pacific Islanders (Hawaiian, Samoan, Tongan, Guamanian, and Melanesian) and the Native American category excludes Eskimos and Aleuts. The Chinese category includes the Taiwanese.

- With the addition of the "Other Asian/Pacific Islander" category in 1990, the census improved its measurement of the Asian population by capturing groups who were once assigned to the "Other" category. This change contributes to the increased counts of Asians, as well as high rates of immigration during the 1980s. There were no substantive measurement changes between 1980 and 1990, so the data for the two censuses are directly comparable.

- The inflation rate for 1979 dollars is based on the implicit price deflators in the *Economic Report of the President*, February 1994.

NOTES

The authors wish to acknowledge and thank Lynne Huffer for her careful readings and precise suggestions, the staff of the Government Documents Center at Yale University, and the editors of this volume. Their efforts contributed to the strengths of this essay. That which is found wanting remains the sole responsibility of the authors.

1. Class status also played an important role in this nineteenth-century Victorian image of women. Poor and working-class White women were certainly not regarded as the embodiment of womanly virtues. According to this way of thinking, their poverty and lack of formal education precluded the expression of their womanly "natures." However, poor White women, along with non-White women, could be (re)educated and reformed to more closely resemble the womanly ideal.

2. Remarks by Sojourner Truth at the 1851 woman's rights convention in Akron, Ohio, in *Black Women in Nineteenth-Century American Life: Their Words, Their Thoughts, Their Feelings*, ed. Bert James Loewenberg and Ruth Bogin (University Park: Pennsylvania State University Press, 1976).

3. Vilma Ortiz, "Women of Color: A Demographic Overview," in *Women of Color in U.S. Society*, ed. Maxine Baca Zinn and Bonnie Thornton Dill (Philadelphia: Temple University Press, 1994).

4. College graduation rates include both two-year associate degree and four-year bachelor degree programs.

5. It is not possible to provide a distinct definition of the phenomenon that is variously termed the hidden, informal, or underground economy. The economic activities that qualify as such occur in a wide variety of contexts and in many forms: from the "salesgirl" who is paid cash "off the books" to the woman who "does hair" in her apartment. Generally,

however, the term applies to economic activities that escape government scrutiny and legal regulations.

6. "20 Facts on Women Workers," *Facts on Working Women* (U.S. Department of Labor Women's Bureau), no. 93–2 (June 1993). Data available only on Black, Chinese, Filipino, Japanese, Mexican, Native American, Puerto Rican, and White women.

7. "Black Women in the Labor Force," *Facts on Working Women*, no. 90–4 (June 1991).

8. However, the fact that Latinas are "one of the fastest growing groups in the Nation" leads the Bureau of Labor Statistics to project that the number of Latinas in the labor force will increase by over 70 percent by the year 2005. This would be the "second largest [increase] among all other groups of women or men, regardless of race. Their labor force participation is expected to reach 58 percent." The report forecasts that Asian and Pacific Islander women will see the largest increase of women in the labor force during this period (86 percent). The same document notes that as of 1993, the rate of participation for Cuban women had dropped to 47.9 percent, "the lowest figure in the past decade" for that group, and that Mexican women had the highest rate of participation among all Hispanic women that year. "Women of Hispanic Origin in the Labor Force," *Facts on Working Women*, no. 94–2 (December 1994).

9. The census questionnaire asks women to describe the type of jobs they held in the week preceding their completion of the census form. This sample is then used to determine women's employment experience for 1989 and for the immediate past decade.

10. The categories of management and professional occupations represented a broad array of middle-class jobs and stable working-class jobs. Managerial and professional occupations include executive, administrative, and managerial jobs, and professional specialty occupations such as engineering, health diagnosis, health assessment and treatment, as well as teaching, library work, and counseling.

11. In the self-employed category there may be some underreporting by those working in the hidden economy who might fear discovery and punishment by the federal government.

12. Technical, sales, and administrative support occupations include health and non-health technicians and technologists, sales personnel, and administrative support staff (including clerical workers, computer equipment operators, secretaries, typists, financial record processors, mail and distribution workers).

13. The service occupations include maids, police and firefighters, security guards, food service workers, and cleaning and building personnel.

14. The *median* level should not be confused with the *mean* level of income. The mean average would be the sum of all the individual incomes earned by women divided by the total number of women (or what is commonly referred to as simply the average). The median average is the particular income level at which 50 percent of the women earn below that figure and 50 percent earn above it.

15. Ortiz, 31.

16. The formula used by the Census Bureau (and employed in this essay) to calculate poverty in families takes into account the varying sizes of families. Additionally, the census defines "family" to include groups of related individuals, in contrast with the category "household," which includes unrelated individuals.

17. U.S. Bureau of the Census, 1990 *Census of Population: Social and Economic Characteristics, United States*, CP-2-1, 1993.

18. "Black Women in the Labor Force," 4.

19. "Made in the USA Lobby Running after Nike," *Business Times*, November 5, 1992, 17; Frank Swoboda, "Sears Agrees to Police Its Suppliers: Retailer Addresses Issue of Forced

Labor," *Washington Post*, March 31, 1992, C1; "Statement by Jay Mazu, President International Ladies' Garment Workers' Union on Model Agreement between San Francisco Manufacturers and Contractors," *Business Wire*, January 6, 1994; Maria Echaveste and Karen Nussbaum, "The Sweatshop Is Reborn," *New York Times*, March 6, 1994, 13 (Maria Echaveste is the administrator of the Wage and Hour Division of the Labor Department; Karen Nussbaum is the director of the department's Women's Bureau); Ketty Mobed, Ellen B. Gold, and Marc B. Schenker, "Occupational Health Problems among Migrant and Seasonal Farm Workers: Cross-Cultural Medicine: A Decade Later," *Western Journal of Medicine* 157, no. 3 (September 1992): 367; Tony Horwitz, "Modern-Day Sweatshops," *Arizona Republic*, February 5, 1995, D1; Scott Bronstein " 'They Treated Us Like Dogs,' Say Workers at Plant Where 25 Died: Bitter Employees Say Conditions at Poultry Facility Were Unsafe," *Atlanta Journal and Constitution*, September 5, 1991, A6.

20. Sean Reilly, "The Case for Unions: Labor Movement Reform," *Washington Monthly* 27, nos. 7–8 (July–August 1995): 26.

BIBLIOGRAPHY

Aguilar-San Juan, Karin, ed. *The State of Asian America: Activism and Resistance in the 1990s.* Boston: South End Press, 1994.

Bronstein, Scott. " 'They Treated Us Like Dogs,' Say Workers at Plant Where 25 Died: Bitter Employees Say Conditions at Poultry Facility Were Unsafe." *Atlanta Journal and Constitution*, September 5, 1991, A6.

Council of Economic Advisers. *Economic Report of the President.* Washington, DC: U.S. GPO, 1994.

Echaveste, Maria, and Karen Nussbaum. "The Sweatshop Is Reborn." *New York Times*, March 6, 1994, F13.

Horwitz, Tony. "Modern-Day Sweatshops." *Arizona Republic*, February 5, 1995, D1.

Loewenberg, Bert James, and Ruth Bogin, eds. *Black Women in Nineteenth-Century American Life: Their Words, Their Thoughts, Their Feelings.* University Park: Pennsylvania State University Press, 1976.

"Made in the USA Lobby Running after Nike." *Business Times*, November 5, 1992, 17.

Mobed, Ketty, Ellen B. Gold, and Marc B. Schenker. "Occupational Health Problems among Migrant and Seasonal Farm Workers: Cross-Cultural Medicine: A Decade Later." *Western Journal of Medicine* 157, no. 3 (September 1992): 367.

Omolade, Barbara. *The Rising Song of African American Women.* New York: Routledge, 1994.

Ortiz, Vilma. "Women of Color: A Demographic Overview." In *Women of Color in U.S. Society*, ed. Maxine Baca Zinn and Bonnie Thornton Dill. Philadelphia: Temple University Press, 1994.

Paik, Sook Ja. "Korean-American Women's Underemployment and Dual Labor Burden." In *The Korean-American Community: Present and Future*, ed. Tae-Hwan Kwak and Seong Hyong Lee. Seoul: Kyungnam University Press, 1991.

Reilly, Sean. "The Case for Unions: Labor Movement Reform." *Washington Monthly* 27, nos. 7–8 (July–August 1995): 26.

Rodriguez, Clara E. "Beyond the Census Data: A Portrait of the Community." In *Puerto Ricans: Born in the U.S.A.* Boston: Unwin Hyman, 1989.

Sassen, Saskia. "The Informal Economy: Between New Deal Developments and Old Regulations." *Yale Law Journal* 103, no. 8 (June 1994): 2289–2304.

"Statement by Jay Mazu, President International Ladies' Garment Workers' Union on Model Agreement between San Francisco Manufacturers and Contractors." *Business Wire*, January 6, 1994.

Swoboda, Frank. "Sears Agrees to Police Its Suppliers: Retailer Addresses Issue of Forced Labor." *Washington Post*, March 31, 1992, C1.

Takaki, Ronald. *Strangers from a Different Shore*. Boston: Little, Brown, 1989.

U.S. Bureau of the Census. *Characteristics of American Indians by Tribe and Language*. Section 1 of 2. CP–3–7, 1994.

———. *Characteristics of the Black Population*. CP–3–6, 1994.

———. *How We're Changing: Demographic State of the Nation, 1994*. Current Population Reports. Series P–23, no. 187 (January 1994).

———. *How We're Changing: Demographic State of the Nation, 1995*. Current Population Reports. Series P–23, no. 188 (December 1994).

———. *1980 Census of Population: Characteristics of the Population*. Vol. 1. *General Social and Economic Characteristics*, chap. C, pt. 1. PC80–1–C1, 1983.

———. *1990 Census of Population: Asians and Pacific Islanders in the United States*. CP–3–5, 1993.

———. *1990 Census of Population: General Population Characteristics, United States*. Washington, DC: U.S. Department of Commerce, CP–1–1, 1992.

———. *1990 Census of 1990 Census of Population: Persons of Hispanic Origin in the United States*. CP–3–3, 1993.

———. *1990 Census of Population: Social and Economic Characteristics, United States*. CP–2–1, 1993.

U.S. Department of Labor Women's Bureau. "American Indian/Alaska Native Women Business Owners." *Facts on Working Women*, no. 89–9 (December 1989).

———. "Asian American Women Business Owners." *Facts on Working Women*, no. 89–8 (December 1989).

———. "Black Women Business Owners." *Facts on Working Women*, no. 89–7 (September 1989).

———. "Black Women in the Labor Force." *Facts on Working Women*, no. 90–4 (June 1991).

———. "20 Facts on Women Workers." *Facts on Working Women*, no. 93–2 (June 1993).

———. "Women in Management." *Facts on Working Women*, no. 89–4 (December 1989).

———. "Women of Hispanic Origin in the Labor Force." *Facts on Working Women*, no. 94–2 (December 1994).

———. "Women Who Maintain Families." *Facts on Working Women*, no. 93–3 (June 1993).

———. "Women Workers: Outlook to 2005." *Facts on Working Women*, no. 92–1 (January 1992).

———. "Working Mothers and Their Children." *Facts on Working Women*, no. 89–3 (August 1989).

Waldman, Elizabeth. "Profile of the Chicana: A Statistical Fact Sheet." In *Mexican Women in the United States: Struggles Past and Present*, ed. Magdelana Mora and Adelaida R. Del Castillo. Los Angeles: Chicano Studies Research Center, University of California, 1980.

Wilson, William Julius. *The Truly Disadvantaged*. Chicago: University of Chicago Press, 1987.

TWO

"Working Men" and "Dependent Wives": Gender, "Race," and the Regulation of Migration from Mexico

DOREEN J. MATTINGLY

In January 1993, the search for a U.S. attorney general brought national media attention to the generally invisible practice of employing undocumented immigrant women as paid household workers. Zoe Baird's disclosure that she had employed two undocumented Peruvian immigrants, one as a child care provider and one as a driver, cost her a position in Clinton's cabinet and led to the deportation of her employees. Baird was guilty of breaking two laws: first, she did not pay Social Security taxes for her employees, and second, she violated immigration law by employing immigrants who did not have "lawful permanent resident status," or who were, in everyday language, "illegal aliens."

As "Nannygate" unfolded, it became evident that Baird was not the only one illegally employing household help. In its coverage of the Baird story, the *San Diego Union-Tribune* baldly claimed that "The hiring of undocumented migrants for domestic help is as much a part of California culture as surfing" (Jones and Spivak 1993). Employing undocumented immigrants has been illegal since 1986, when the practice was banned by the Immigration Reform and Control Act (IRCA). Yet IRCA has not eliminated the employment of undocumented immigrants; it has merely driven it underground. In fact, as undocumented immigrants have found it increasingly difficult to find jobs in companies, more have turned to employment in private homes. So perhaps not so ironically, a law originally intended to limit illegal migration has instead increased the availability of affordable child care, cleaning services, and gardening for many middle-class American households.

In this chapter I take a closer look at the connections between the employment of immigrant domestic workers and the 1986 Immigration Reform and Control Act. My analysis draws on in-depth interviews with immigrant domestic workers in San

Diego, California. My intent is to make evident the role of gender and racial ideologies in IRCA and to suggest the impact of such ideologies on the lives of immigrant men and women. I begin the essay with a discussion of the recent expansion of women's undocumented migration from Mexico, illustrating the role of domestic service employment in that migration. I then shift my focus to U.S. immigration policy, arguing that the past regulation of Mexican migration has been shaped by racialized and gendered ideals that I call "working men" and "dependent wives." I then turn to a detailed discussion of the role of gender and racial ideology in IRCA, showing how gendered stereotypes are embedded in the law's provisions. In the conclusion I briefly discuss the impact of the same stereotypes on California's Proposition 187, a referendum prohibiting the use of some public services by undocumented immigrants.

Before proceeding, I want to make clear my use of the terms "gender" and "race." Gender refers to the socially constructed ideologies of difference between men and women, not to biological difference. Gender is an important dimension of all social life, and shapes the lives of both men and women. Immigration law, like other aspects of life, is gendered, in that "it is shaped by social and cultural ideals, practices, and displays of masculinity and femininity" (Hondagneu-Sotelo 1994, 2). In this essay I am using the term "race" to also refer to an aspect of identity that is socially — not merely biologically — constructed. Omi and Winant (1994) define "race" as a "concept which signifies and symbolizes social conflicts and interests by referring to different types of human bodies" (55). Throughout the essay, I have placed the term "race" in quotation marks, to remind readers that I am speaking of a dimension of social life that makes reference to biological difference, but is in fact constantly being challenged, manipulated, and redefined. The "racial" categorization of Mexican immigrants and Chicanos (American citizens of Mexican descent) — or of any people of color — is an aspect of social life that is embedded in political and economic processes. The two aspects of social identity cannot be separated; gender differences and hierarchies are fundamentally linked to "racial" differences and hierarchies (Mohanty 1991; Glenn 1992; Sacks 1989; hooks 1984). The experience and meaning of being a man or a woman — and this is true for people of all "races" — is shaped by the experience and meaning of being black, or white, or Latino. Looking at the gender dimensions of Mexican immigration means always keeping in mind both how experiences of Mexican immigrant men and women are shaped by the "racialization" of Mexicans in the United States, and how the construction of Mexican immigrant identity has been gendered (see also Hondagneu-Sotelo 1994).

Domestic Service and Women's Migration from Mexico

To better understand the connections between gender ideology, domestic service, and immigration law, I interviewed thirty-two immigrant Mexicana domestic workers in San Diego.[1] The interviews took place between January and May 1994, and were conducted with the aid of Bertha Palenzuela Jottar, a bilingual interviewer. Domestic workers were recruited for the study in several ways. Some were referred by contacts in the immigrant community, while others were contacted through a church with a large immigrant congregation. We also distributed flyers and recruited workers at bus stops, clinics, and city parks where we knew domestic workers frequented.[2] Each interview lasted between one and two hours, and included questions on a wide variety of topics, including the impact of IRCA on the lives and work of the women.

The domestic workers interviewed were a diverse group of women, ranging in age from eighteen to seventy-two. Among the workers interviewed, eleven (34 percent) were live-in workers whose responsibilities included child care, and twenty-one (66 percent) were live-out housekeepers who worked for several different employers. The women varied dramatically in their English language ability. Roughly a fifth were fluent enough to communicate easily in English, while close to another fifth spoke only a few words. The educational background of respondents varied as well; 23.3 percent have less than a primary school education, while 36.7 percent have some education beyond high school (called *secundaria* in Mexico). Fifteen (47 percent) of the domestic workers were resident aliens at the time of the interview, although all had been undocumented when they first migrated to the United States.

Paid household work includes work by live-in child care workers (nannies) and housekeepers.[3] Some housekeepers live in the homes of the employers, but most clean the homes of several different employers on a weekly or bimonthly basis. Although official statistics report that household employment in the United States has been declining steadily for several decades, numerous observers agree that the occupation is flourishing in areas with large immigrant populations (Hondagneu-Sotelo 1994; Cornelius 1992; Rieff 1991; Colen 1990). Domestic service is an important occupation for immigrant women from the West Indies, the Philippines, Central America, and Mexico (Repak 1994; Colen 1990; Enloe 1989). Large surveys of undocumented immigrant women in San Diego (Solórzano-Torres 1991), Houston (Cárdenas et al. 1982), and the San Francisco Bay area (Hogeland and Rosen 1990) have found domestic service to account for one-third to one-half of the jobs held by employed immigrant Mexicanas.

Domestic work is, in some ways, an obvious choice for immigrant women. Although the work is hard, it provides women who do not speak English, have no marketable skills, or who are in the country illegally with an opportunity to earn relatively high wages. Among the immigrant women I interviewed, the average hourly wage was $8.00 for live-out housekeepers and $2.70 for live-in child care workers. Many of the women I interviewed, particularly those who had migrated recently, knew before they came that domestic work would be the only job available to them in the United States. Imelda Nieto, a former teacher in Mexico, has been living and working illegally in the United States since 1989.[4] Despite her education, Imelda feels there are no other jobs for her until she becomes a resident alien: "When you first arrive in the U.S. this [cleaning houses] is the first job you look for. When you go to the houses, many people don't mind if you have no papers. Some do, but if they had to hire another white woman they would have to pay more than $40."

Growing numbers of women, like Imelda, have been leaving their homes in

Mexico and illegally coming to the United States. Evidence from a variety of sources shows that since the mid-1980s the illegal immigration of women and children has *increased*, both in absolute numbers and relative to male migration (Cornelius 1992; Solórzano-Torres 1991; Bean et al. 1990; Bustamante 1990; Woodrow and Passel 1990). Although women have been migrating from Mexico since Southwestern states first became U.S. territory, recent increases in women's migration are part of a larger transition in Mexico-U.S. migration patterns. Until the late 1970s, a large percentage of migrants were young men who lived and worked in the United States for part of their lives while their families remained in Mexico. Since that time, the permanent settlement of families (men, women, and children) has increasingly replaced temporary male labor migration. Researchers studying Mexico-U.S. migration have found that in the last decade there is more migration by whole family units (moving together), more family-reunification migration (women and children joining family heads already in the United States), and more migration by single women (Hondagneu-Sotelo 1994; Cornelius 1992; Bean et al. 1990).

There are three important reasons for the increases in women's migration. First, Mexico's deepening economic crisis has prompted the exodus of many people, including working- and middle-class women from parts of Mexico that have not traditionally sent migrants to the United States (Cornelius 1992). Limited employment opportunities for women in Mexico often contribute to women's decisions to migrate to the United States. Second, the persistent demand for low-wage workers in the United States, particularly in urban service sector jobs like domestic service, has continued to draw immigrants (Sassen and Smith 1992). For some Mexican women, migrating to the United States can be the only way to meet their financial obligations. Francesca supports her mother and seven-year-old daughter in Mexico City with her earnings as a live-out housekeeper in San Diego. Francesca finished a year of college in Mexico and has worked as a receptionist and office manager there. Still she could not earn enough without migrating. Francesca summed up the sentiments of most of the women interviewed: "In our country we earn too little. We have nothing because in our country we couldn't earn anything with the low salaries. So we come with that idea, that here we will make more money, maybe someday build a house. I think that this is the reason a lot of us work like this."

In addition to these economic push and pull factors, women's migration is often made easier by the presence of friends and family already living in the United States. While both male and female migrants often follow others from their community, migration networks are particularly important for women. Single women are often restrained from migrating alone by restrictive gender norms and family responsibilities. The presence of female family members in the United States is a particularly important factor in the migration of single women. In my research I found that many immigrant women followed, and were aided in their migration by, other immigrant women already employed in domestic service in San Diego. As the number of settled immigrants in the United States has grown, it has become ever easier for immigrant women to make homes in the United States (Hondagneu-Sotelo 1994; Massey et al. 1987).

Although economic forces and social networks are the most important factors affecting international migration flows, their impact is mediated by immigration laws and policies. At present, the Immigration Reform and Control Act plays an important role in the migration and employment patterns of men and women. As was also the case with earlier immigration laws, IRCA is not neutral when it comes to gender and "race." Rather, the intent and enforcement of the law have been informed by powerful stereotypes about the identity of immigrants. Before discussing in detail the impacts of IRCA, I will explain how ideologies about the gender and "race" of Mexican immigrants have historically been embedded in U.S. immigration law.

U.S. Immigration Law and Mexican Migration

Migration from Mexico — both legal and undocumented — is substantial and increasing. From 1980 to 1993, over four million immigrants from Mexico were legally admitted to the United States, accounting for 28.8 percent of all legal migrants admitted during the period (U.S. Immigration and Naturalization Service 1993). In addition to legal immigrants, an unknown number of undocumented immigrants from Mexico also live in the United States. Woodrow and Passel (1990) estimated that close to two million undocumented immigrants resided in the United States in 1988, roughly 60 percent of whom were from Mexico.

In the United States, immigration from Mexico is unique not only in its magnitude. The proximity of Mexico, the historical conquest of Mexican territory by the United States, and the long presence of Mexican immigrants and their descendants have all made immigration from Mexico a special case in U.S. immigration law. In what Cockroft (1986) has called a "revolving door" policy, U.S. immigration law has at times recruited Mexican immigrants and at other times singled them out for exclusion. For example, during World War II, the Bracero Program recruited Mexican male laborers to fill wartime labor shortages. At other times, U.S. immigration policies have tried to stop or forcibly reverse the flow of migrants from Mexico. This was the case in 1954, when the Bracero Program was replaced with "Operation Wetback," and an estimated one million migrants were deported to Mexico (García 1980). Such conflicting treatment of Mexican immigration has been informed by numerous factors, including cycles of economic growth and recession and fluctuating racial tensions in the United States. Through alternating labor recruitment and deportation programs, immigration law has set the terms for the treatment of immigrants from Mexico: they have been welcomed as workers but discouraged from settling and having families in the United States.

Underlying and influencing the regulation of Mexican immigration have been persistent and powerful gender and "racial" ideologies about Mexican immigrants. "Racial" ideologies and politics have always influenced policies determining who could migrate to the United States and under what terms. In the late nineteenth and early twentieth centuries, immigration laws limited the migration of Asians, and for much of the twentieth century immigration quotas have intentionally favored people emigrating from countries in Northern and Western Europe (Cose 1992; Takaki 1993). Ideologies of difference are particularly important to immigration policy, since immigration is one of the key mechanisms through which citizenship is shaped and regulated. As markers of difference, "race" and ethnicity are crucial to most definitions of citizenship, dividing "insiders" from "outsiders." As Judith Shklar (1991) points out, even the founding fathers defined American citizenship in exclusionary terms, "by distinguishing themselves from their inferiors, especially from slaves but also from women" (15).

Mexican immigrants have been "racialized" by policies that treat them as laborers rather than as full citizens. In the Southwestern United States, the lives of Mexican immigrants and Mexican Americans have been shaped by pervasive occupational segregation, which has limited their employment to agricultural and other manual labor (for men) and service work (for women). Although many have claimed that the limited job options of new immigrants are due to their lack of skills or inability to speak English, the enduring similarity of the experiences of Chicanos and Mexican immigrants reflected a discrimination based on physical "racial" markers (Romero 1992). The combination of "looking Mexican" and working in low-wage jobs has played a central role in the social construction of the "racial identity" of Mexican immigrants and Chicanos.

The "racialization" of Mexican immigrants, as well as their citizenship, also has an important gender dimension. Feminist scholars have shown that one of the ways gender shapes citizenship in liberal welfare states (such as the United States) is through the distinction between "public man" and "private woman" (Elshtain 1981). Feminists have emphasized the conceptual division of the world into the public (masculine) sphere of employment and politics and the private (feminine) sphere of the family and interpersonal relations (Rosaldo and Lamphere 1974). Because of the ideology of separate spheres, men's relations to the state are largely shaped by their paid work, while women's relations are based on their familial or marital roles (Orloff 1993; Gordon 1990). For the most part, citizenship in the United States has been defined in terms of participation in the public sphere, and therefore equated with male forms of employment and political participation (Jones 1990; Lloyd 1986). As a result, the ideal citizen has been understood to be an employed man with a dependent spouse and children.

These insights from feminist theory are useful in understanding the role of gender ideology in the regulation of Mexican immigration. Specifically, the treatment of Mexicans under immigration law has been gendered through the prevalent notions of "working man" and "dependent wife." Mexican immigrant men have historically been valued for their role in paid production, especially in farming, manufacturing, and mining. But while immigrant men have at times been recruited to fill the demand for cheap labor, immigration law has historically treated women immigrants from Mexico as dependents, either as wives or as wards of the state. Unlike their male relatives, Mexican women were never directly recruited for their labor power; rather, they were encouraged to remain in Mexico so that male workers would return when they were no longer needed. Thus Mexican men have been granted partial citizenship rights: as workers but not as fathers. Mexican women, on the other hand, have not even been valued as workers, and their immigration has never been encouraged by immigration policy.

By discouraging the permanent settlement of immigrant families and periodically deporting Mexican immigrants, the U.S. government has geographically shifted the costs of social reproduction of Mexican workers back to the Mexican government and the unpaid work of Mexican women. The term "social reproduction" refers to "the array of activities and relationships involved in maintaining people both on a daily and intergenerational basis" (Glenn 1992, 1). Male immigrant workers have been "cheap labor" not only in terms of wages; they are also cheap in terms of social costs, since they were raised, educated, and cared for in illness and old age in Mexico. Of course, Mexican women have been migrating to the United States since the Mexican-American War, many have been employed in the United States, many are U.S. citizens, and many have made use of government-funded schools, medical care, and other social services. It is interesting to note, however, that Chicanas and Mexicanas have consistently been concentrated in domestic work in private homes as well as in institutional service work, such as cleaning in motels, rest homes, and hospitals (Glenn 1992; Romero 1992). Thus Mexicana immigrants have been discouraged from raising their own families in the United States by immigration law, but they have been employed in jobs that contribute to the reproduction of middle-class Anglo families.

In the past, when Mexican migration was dominated by single men, the U.S. economy and government benefited from the unpaid reproductive work of women residing in Mexico. Recent increases in women's migration and the permanent settlement of more Mexican immigrant families in the United States have obviously modified the gender dynamics of Mexican immigration. "Working men" no longer make up the vast majority of Mexican immigrants, and the United States is increasingly bearing the costs of supporting the social reproduction of immigrant families. Nevertheless, the ideals of "working men" and "dependent wives" remain embedded in contemporary policies regulating Mexican immigration, including IRCA.

The Immigration Reform and Control Act

The Immigration Reform and Control Act was passed in 1986, partly in response to the perception of U.S. citizens that undocumented immigration was growing too rapidly and was contributing to the unemployment of citizens. IRCA used a "carrot and stick" approach to stop undocumented immigration. On the "stick" side, the law increased the border patrol and made it illegal to employ undocumented immigrants.[5] On the "carrot" side, IRCA granted amnesty to a limited number of qualified illegal immigrants.[6] Over three million illegal immigrants, 70 percent of whom were from Mexico, registered for legalization under the program (U.S. Immigration and Naturalization Service 1989). Despite the law's intent, there is substantial evidence that illegal immigration from Mexico has not declined since IRCA's passage.[7] Instead, IRCA has driven the employment of undocumented immigrants underground, often worsening working conditions and lowering wages (Sassen and Smith 1992).

Like earlier immigration policies, IRCA was based on the assumption that most undocumented Mexican immigrants were "working men." As a result, both the policies granting amnesty to illegal immigrants and the policies seeking to stop the employment of illegal aliens were shaped by gender stereotypes. In the amnesty component of IRCA, both the "working man" and "dependent wife" stereotypes of Mexican immigrants served to make it more difficult for women than for men to qualify for amnesty. In the words of Maria Blanco, an immigration lawyer in San Francisco, IRCA's programs "were implemented in ways that excluded thousands of women from the amnesty program by ignoring the work and home realities of immigrant women" (1991, 6–7). To receive amnesty under IRCA, immigrants had to prove continuous residence in the United States between 1982 and 1986. Yet the rules for proving continuous residence were modeled after men's experiences. Because women's names were less likely to appear on household records, such as utility bills and rent receipts, it was harder for them to prove residency than it was for men. Proof of continuous employment was also accepted by the Immigration and Naturalization Service (INS), but again, women had a more difficult time providing the necessary papers. Domestic workers in particular rarely had paycheck stubs or tax forms to prove that they had been employed. Among agricultural workers, where the family labor system predominates, male heads of households tend to be credited with and paid for the labor of the entire family, limiting women's ability to prove that they had worked in the fields. In addition, women who took breaks from employment for childbearing had a harder time proving continuous residence (Blanco 1991; Hogeland and Rosen 1990; Fuentes 1987).

IRCA's amnesty programs were also shaped by the negative stereotype of immigrant Mexicanas as "dependent wives." In particular, the law sought to prohibit immigrant women from becoming public dependents (Chang 1994). Like most immigration laws, IRCA sought to prohibit the migration of persons "likely to become a public charge." Unlike earlier immigration laws, however, IRCA expanded the definition of "public charge" to include persons who had received public benefits in the past (Chang 1994; Wheeler and Zacovic 1987). As a result, many undocumented women who had previously received AFDC for their U.S.-born children were ineligible for legalization (Chang 1994).[8] Because of these biases, women were less likely to have been legalized under the program. According to one estimate, 300,000 eligible immigrant women did not apply for legalization (U.S. Immigration and Naturalization Service 1989).

The ideologies of "working man" and "dependent wife" also had a profound effect on rules prohibiting the employment of undocumented immigrants, particularly with respect to domestic workers. Under the law, individuals are required to verify that their employees are citizens or resident aliens, and employers are fined if they knowingly employ workers who are in the country illegally. People are not, however, responsible for knowing the legal status of independent contractors, defined by IRCA as those workers "hired to do a piece of work according to his or her means and methods and subject to control only as to results" (CIRRS 1988, 9). Gardeners, roofers, carpenters, and garbage haulers are all considered independent contractors because they provide their own tools. In the regulations, domestic workers are explicitly categorized as employees rather than as independent contractors, since domestic workers do not provide their own tools (CIRRS 1988, 13). So if a household employs a housekeeper and a gardener, both of whom are in the country illegally, the household is violating federal law when it hires the housekeeper, but not when it hires the gardener.

Despite the clear illegality of employing undocumented immigrants as domestic workers, the law has not stopped the practice, as Nannygate made eminently clear. In fact, IRCA appears to be having the opposite effect, pushing even more undocumented immigrants into informal employment: working in sweatshops, landscaping, and domestic service. One explanation for this contradictory outcome lies in the uneven enforcement of employer sanctions. When compared to other employers of undocumented workers, those who pay their workers "under the table" (as do most employers of domestic workers) are much less likely to be prosecuted. Since the intent of IRCA was to keep undocumented immigrants from taking away jobs from American workers, it is not surprising that the enforcement of the law has focused its limited resources on large firms with relatively high-paying and often male-dominated jobs (see, for example, Mines and Avina 1992). Jobs in domestic service are an especially low priority for the enforcement of employer sanctions (Ruiz 1991). The Immigration and Naturalization Service conducted over thirty thousand investigations of nonagricultural employers between 1987 and 1990. Only forty-three of these were of private households (U.S. Department of Labor 1991, 29). In her study of maids in El Paso, Vicki Ruiz (1991) found that although INS officials would take domestic workers into custody if caught at the border, they would not search private residences. As one INS official told her, "it doesn't make sense looking for one illegal maid . . . when we could be removing an alien from a good paying job" (72).

By making it more difficult (although by no means impossible) for undocumented immigrants to find work in factories, nurseries, hotels, and restaurants, IRCA has actually compelled more women to look for work in private homes. My interviews with domestic workers provide extensive evidence that since the passage of IRCA, domestic service has become a more important source of employment for immigrant women. Twenty (62.5 percent) of the domestic workers interviewed said that since IRCA, jobs open to undocumented women were basically limited to domestic work. This opinion was particularly strong among domestic workers who were undocumented and those who had recently arrived in the United States. All the women who migrated after 1986 said that they thought the women were pushed into domestic service because it was the only job they could get without papers, and 82.4 percent of all undocumented women said this. In the words of Maria Velasco, an undocumented immigrant who arrived in 1988,

> It is more difficult in general, because in many jobs they ask for papers. But I have noticed in this kind of job they don't ask much about papers. . . . In a company they know what a real green card looks like or if it's a fake one, so it is more difficult to find a job in those places than in a particular home. If [people hiring domestics] ask for papers, they don't recognize if they are fake or not.

In addition to pushing more women into domestic work, IRCA has also had indirect effects on women's work in domestic service because it has made it more difficult for men to find work. As one live-in worker put it, "Since IRCA it is difficult because people lost their jobs, and for men it is more difficult to find jobs than for women, because women can live in houses." The experiences of Lydia and Jorge Cortez drive the point home. Jorge lost his factory job in 1992, when his social security number was discovered to be false. Since that time he has only been able to find sporadic work with Lydia's brother, a gardener. Lydia is eight months pregnant with her second child, and although she has made plans for her sister-in-law to clean her houses when she delivers, for now she is still working three days a week: "Even with my jobs we barely make it. He pays the rent but I have to pay for the lights and sometimes the water, and we always need more food." Like many domestic workers interviewed, Lydia now earns more money than her husband does. Half of the live-out workers earned at least half of their household income, and when married workers were asked whether their families could survive without their income, only one-third said they could; another third said they probably would survive, but it would be difficult, while a final third said that their families could not survive. Women's income is even more crucial for undocumented immigrants: two-thirds of the undocumented married women said their families could not survive without the money they earn cleaning houses.

The importance of domestic workers' income illustrates one of the ironies of IRCA. Although informed by the gendered and "raced" stereotypes of "working man" and "dependent wife," the law has contributed to a breakdown of those roles in real life. The ability of immigrant women to earn wages equivalent to, or at times higher than, those earned by their male partners increases the authority and autonomy of immigrant women within their families and communities (see also Hondagneu-Sotelo 1994). As Hondagneu-Sotelo points out, employed immigrant women "simultaneously expand their spatial mobility in the public sphere and exercise greater status in the family" (146).

Yet while IRCA may have increased the relative earning potential of immigrant domestic workers, it has also worsened their working conditions. There is increasing evidence that since IRCA employment discrimination against all Mexican-origin workers has increased, regardless of the workers' legal status (U.S. General Accounting Office 1990). The brunt of the law, however, has been borne by undocumented workers. Among the domestic workers interviewed, twenty-nine (90.6 percent) felt that IRCA had reduced the wages and working conditions of undocumented immigrants. Many of the undocumented women told stories of employers who had implicitly or explicitly used the workers' legal status to control them. One recalled an employer who threatened to call the INS when the worker refused to add ironing to her regular tasks; another told of an employer who threatened to "call her lawyer" when the worker pressed for a raise. Imelda Nieto summed up the opinions of most of the undocumented domestic workers: "[Americans] like it that we [immigrants] do this work, I think they prefer us. . . . When you don't have papers they think you are secure, that you won't leave the job. At a certain level they exploit us. They know that for little money they can demand a lot of work because the people need the jobs."

More of the Same?

In both its legalization policies and enforcement practices, IRCA has been shaped by gendered and "racialized" conceptions of "working men" and "dependent wives." Like earlier laws restricting immigration, IRCA focused on undocumented male workers and treated women as economic dependents. As a result, it was more difficult for undocumented immigrant women to receive amnesty. Under IRCA, employer sanctions have not been enforced as tightly against women's employment, particularly in domestic service. So because of its gendered assumptions that immigrant women are not workers, IRCA has had the ironic effect of increasing immigrant women's employment in paid household work. Further, by restricting employment opportunities for men, IRCA has also made women's earnings from domestic work more important to immigrant families, potentially changing gender relations in those families.

Although the traditional division of labor in immigrant households appears to be eroding — in part because of IRCA — the ideologies of "working men" and "dependent wives" continue to inform immigration policies and politics. In particular, immigrant Mexicans remained negatively stereotyped as "dependent." As the community of undocumented workers in the United States has become more diverse, more immigrant families have looked for health care, education, and other reproductive support in the United States rather than in Mexico. Although immigrants have been found to use social services at much lower rates than citizens (Hayes-Bautista 1993), many U.S. citizens have become enraged that American society is responsible for supporting some of the reproductive needs of workers who are not citizens. Immigrant use of social services became the touchstone issue for the most recent attempt to control immigration. In November 1994, California voters passed Proposition 187, a controversial and potentially unconstitutional voter referendum prohibiting undocumented immigrants from receiving many state-funded services, including public education and nonemergency medical care. The proposition reiterated a theme central to U.S. regulation of Mexican immigration: you are welcome as a productive worker but you are not entitled to government support for your reproduction.

Like earlier immigration laws, Proposition 187 is also gendered, in that it seeks to limit the immigration of women because they are economic dependents. The position of immigrant domestic workers, who are both paid service workers in other people's homes and unpaid workers in their own homes, makes clear the gender and "racial"-ethnic bias of Proposition 187. Immigrant women have become political targets for using collective resources to conduct their own family and community reproductive work in the United States. Yet at the same time, the employment of undocumented immigrant women as domestic workers in private homes is tolerated, and even encouraged, since it contributes to the reproduction of middle-class American households. Thus, in immigration law, immigrant Mexican women and men have generally been perceived in terms of particular gender and "racial"-ethnic stereotypes. By creating policies informed by these stereotypes, the U.S. government has contributed to the further construction of such stereotypes, gendering and "racializing" Mexican immigrant women and men.

The experiences and options of women and men who migrate to the United States from Mexico are influenced by many factors: their family roles and responsibilities, the skills and attitudes they bring with them, the availability of employment and housing in the United States, and government policies that regulate their immigration and employment. Gender and "race" also play a role in their lives as migrants, not as factors distinct from other factors, but as dimensions of all of them. In focusing on immigration law, I do not mean to argue that it is the most important factor shaping the experiences and options of immigrants, nor to suggest that laws are the only aspect of social life shaped by ideologies of gender and "race." Rather, I have tried to show the impact of ideologies of identity on a single aspect of immigrant life. My goal in doing so has been to make visible the complex ways that power, politics, and privilege shape the gender and "race" of all people.

NOTES

This research was partially supported by a grant from the National Science Foundation (SES 9304771). For their comments on earlier drafts of this paper, I thank Kirstin Dow, Kathy Jones, Joan Tronto, and Cathy Cohen. Bertha Palenzuela Jottar provided invaluable research assistance.

1. The terms "paid household work" and "domestic service" are used interchangeably in this essay.

2. Respondents were paid ten dollars for their participation in the project.

3. Some people who do housekeeping work are employed by cleaning companies, rather than by households. This group of domestic workers is not discussed in this essay.

4. All the names used are pseudonyms.

5. Under IRCA, employers who knowingly hire undocumented workers are subject to fines ranging from $250 to $2,000 for each employee, with the possibility of up to six months imprisonment for a repeated "pattern and practice" of such violations (CIRRS 1988, 8).

6. IRCA contains two legalization programs, a regular legalization program (LAW) offering legal status to immigrants who could prove continuous residence in the United States between 1982 and 1986 (1.77 million applicants, 70 percent of whom are from Mexico, and roughly 11 percent from Central America), and a legalization program for special agricultural workers (SAW) who had worked at least ninety days in U.S. agriculture the previous year (1.3 million applicants) (U.S. Immigration and Naturalization Service 1989).

7. Studies using data from daily border counts, sending communities in Mexico, and immigrant communities in the United States have all found that IRCA has not deterred immigration (Donato et al. 1992; Bustamante 1990; Chavez et al. 1990; Cornelius 1989a, 1989b).

8. The constitutionality of the "special rule" excluding past aid recipients is presently being challenged in court. For a full discussion, see Chang 1994.

REFERENCES

Bean, Frank D., Barry Edmonston, and Jeffrey S. Passel, eds. 1990. *Undocumented Migration to the United States: IRCA and the Experience of the 1980s.* Washington, DC: Urban Institute Press.

Blanco, Maria. 1991. Senate testimony in support of SB 1734 to repeal employer sanctions. Mimeo available from Equal Rights Associates, San Francisco.

Bustamante, Jorge A. 1990. Undocumented migration from Mexico to the United States: Preliminary findings of the Zapata Canyon Project. In *Undocumented Migration to the United States: IRCA and the Experience of the 1980s,* ed. Frank D. Bean, Barry Edmonston, and Jeffrey S. Passel, 211–26. Washington, DC: Urban Institute Press.

Cárdenas, Gilbert, Beth Anne Shelton, and Devon Peña. 1982. Undocumented immigrant women in the Houston labor force. *California Sociologist* 5 (2): 98–118.

Chang, Grace. 1994. Undocumented Latinas: The new "employable mothers." In *Mothering: Ideology, Experience, and Agency,* ed. Evelyn Nakano Glenn, Grace Chang, and Linda Rennie Forcey, 259–85. New York: Routledge.

Chavez, Leo R., Estevan T. Flores, and Marta López-Garza. 1990. Here today, gone tomorrow? Undocumented settlers and immigration reform. *Human Organization* 49:193–205.

CIRRS. 1988. Alternative employment strategies for immigrants and refugees. San Francisco: Coalition for Immigrant and Refugee Rights and Services.

Cockroft, James D. 1986. *Outlaws in the Promised Land.* New York: Grove.

Colen, Shellee. 1990. "Housekeeping" for the green card: West Indian household workers, the state, and stratified reproduction in New York. In *At Work in Homes: Household Workers in World Perspective,* ed. Roger Sanjek and Shellee Colen, 89–118. Washington, DC: American Anthropological Association.

Cornelius, Wayne. 1989a. Impacts of the 1986 Immigration Law on emigration from rural Mexican sending communities. *Population and Development Review* 15:687–705.

———. 1989b. The United States' demand for Mexican labor. In *Mexican Migration to the United States,* ed. Wayne A. Cornelius and Jorge A. Bustamante, 25–47. La Jolla, CA: Center for U.S.-Mexican Studies, University of California at San Diego.

———. 1992. From sojourners to settlers: The changing profile of Mexican migration to the United States. In *U.S.-Mexico Relations: Labor Market Interdependence,* ed. Jorge A. Bustamante, Clark W. Reynolds, and Rául A. Hinojosa Ojeda, 155–95. Stanford: Stanford University Press.

Cose, Ellis. 1992. *A Nation of Strangers: Prejudice, Politics, and the Populating of America.* New York: William Morrow.

Donato, Katharine M., Jorge Durand, and Douglas S. Massey. 1992. Stemming the tide? Assessing the deterrent effects of the Immigration Reform and Control Act. *Demography* 29 (2): 139–57.

Elshtain, Jean Bethke. 1981. *Public Man, Private Woman.* Princeton: Princeton University Press.

Enloe, Cynthia. 1989. *Bananas, Beaches, and Bases: Making Feminist Sense of International Politics.* Berkeley: University of California Press.

Fuentes, Anette. 1987. Immigration reform: Heaviest burden falls on women. In *Listen Real Loud.* Philadelphia: American Friends Service Committee.

García, Juan Ramon. 1980. *Operation Wetback: The Mass Deportation of Mexican Undocumented Workers in 1954.* Westport, CT: Greenwood.

Glenn, Evelyn Nakano. 1992. From servitude to service work: Historical continuities in the racial division of paid reproductive labor. *Signs* 18 (1): 1–43.

Gordon, Linda, ed. 1990. *Women, the State, and Welfare.* Madison: University of Wisconsin Press.

Hayes-Bautista, David E. 1993. Mexicans in Southern California: Societal enrichment or wasted opportunity? In *The California-Mexico Connection,* ed. Abraham F. Lowenthal and Katrina Burgess, 131–46. Stanford: Stanford University Press.

Hoffman, Abraham. 1974. *Unwanted Mexican Americans in the Great Depression: Repatriation Pressures, 1929–1939.* Tucson: University of Arizona Press.

Hogeland, Chris, and Karen Rosen. 1990. *Dreams Lost, Dreams Found: Undocumented Women in the Land of Opportunity.* San Francisco: Coalition for Immigrant and Refugee Rights and Services, Immigrant Women's Task Force.

Hondagneu-Sotelo, Pierrette. 1994. *Gendered Transitions: Mexican Experiences of Immigration.* Berkeley: University of California Press.

hooks, bell. 1984. *Feminist Theory from Margin to Center.* Boston: South End.

Jones, Kathleen B. 1990. Citizenship in a woman-friendly polity. *Signs* 15, no. 4.

Jones, Sharon L., and Sharon Spivak. 1993. National furor over Nannygate hits close to home. *San Diego Union-Tribune,* February 12.

Lloyd, Genevive. 1986. Selfhood, war, and masculinity. In *Feminist Challenges: Social and Political Theory,* ed. Carole Pateman and Elizabeth Gross, 63–76. Boston: Northeastern University Press.

Massey, D. S., R. Alarcón, J. Durand, and H. Gonzalez. 1987. *Return to Aztlan: The Social Process of International Migration from Western Mexico.* Berkeley: University of California Press.

Mines, R., and J. Avina. 1992. Immigrants and labor standards: The case of the California janitors. In *U.S.-Mexico Relations: Labor Market Interdependence,* ed. Jorge A. Bustamante, Clark W. Reynolds, and Raúl A. Hinojosa Ojeda, 397–428. Stanford: Stanford University Press.

Mohanty, Chandra Talpede. 1991. Cartographies of struggle: Third world women and the politics of feminism. In *Third World Women and the Politics of Feminism,* ed. Chandra Talpede Mohanty, Ann Russo, and Lourdes Torres, 1–50. Bloomington: Indiana University Press.

Omi, Michael, and Howard Winant. 1994. *Racial Formation in the United States: From the 1960s to the 1990s.* 2d ed. New York: Routledge.

Orloff, Ann Shola. 1993. Gender and the social rights of citizenship: The comparative analysis of gender relations and welfare states. *American Sociological Review* 58:303–28.

Repak, Terry. 1994. Labor market incorporation of Central American migrants in Washington, D.C. *Social Problems* 41 (4): 114–28.

Rieff, David. 1991. *Los Angeles: Capital of the Third World.* New York: Simon and Schuster.

Romero, Mary. 1992. *Maid in America.* New York: Routledge.

Rosaldo, Michelle Zimbalist, and Louise Lamphere. 1974. *Women, Culture, and Society.* Stanford: Stanford University Press.

Ruiz, Vicki L. 1991. By the day or the week: Mexicana domestic workers in El Paso. In *Women on the U.S.-Mexico Border: Responses to Change,* ed. Vicki L. Ruiz and Susan Tianopp, 61–76. Boulder: Westview.

Sacks, Karen Brodkin. 1989. Toward a unified theory of class, race, and gender. *American Ethnologist* 16 (3): 534–50.

Sassen, Saskia, and Robert C. Smith. 1992. Post-industrial growth and economic reorganization: Their impact on immigrant employment. In *U.S.-Mexico Relations: Labor Market Interdependence,* ed. Jorge A. Bustamante, Clark W. Reynolds, and Raúl A. Hinojosa Ojeda, 372–96. Stanford: Stanford University Press.

Shklar, Judith. 1991. *American Citizenship: The Quest for Inclusion.* Cambridge: Harvard University Press.

Solórzano-Torres, Rosalía. 1991. Female Mexican immigrants in San Diego County. In *Women on the U.S.-Mexico Border: Responses to Change,* ed. Vicki L. Ruiz and Susan Tiano, 41–60. Boulder: Westview.

Takaki, Ronald. 1993. A *Different Mirror: A History of Multicultural America.* Boston: Little, Brown.

U.S. Department of Labor. 1991. *Employer Sanctions and U.S. Labor Markets: Second Report.* Washington, DC: U.S. Department of Labor, Bureau of International Labor Affairs, Immigration Policy and Research, Report 3.

U.S. General Accounting Office. 1990. *Immigration Reform: Employer Sanctions and the Question of Discrimination.* Report to the Congress. March.

U.S. Immigration and Naturalization Service. 1989. *Statistical Yearbook of the Immigration and Naturalization Service.* Washington, DC: U.S. GPO.

———. 1993. *Statistical Yearbook of the Immigration and Naturalization Service.* Washington, DC: U.S. GPO.

Wheeler, Charles, and Beth Zacovic. 1987. The public charge ground of exclusion for legalization applicants. *Interpreter Releases* 64 (35).

Woodrow, Karen A. and Jeffrey S. Passel. 1990. Post-IRCA undocumented immigration to the United States: An assessment based on the June 1988 CPS. In *Undocumented Migration to the United States: IRCA and the Experience of the 1980s,* ed. Frank D. Bean, Barry Edmonston, and Jeffrey S. Passel, 33–76. Washington DC: Urban Institute.

THREE

On the Marriage Question

JACQUELINE STEVENS

In 1843 Karl Marx wrote "On the Jewish Question," an essay that established the grounds for subsequent claims that economic or other social relations may not be constrained, or even all that deeply affected, by legal ones.[1] Some feminist theorists have used this essay to show that the elimination of legally codified inequalities does not overthrow a social order in which men dominate women. Elaborating Michel Foucault's insights on power reproduced at the margins rather than descending from a sovereign, still other feminists heuristically enhance women's perspective and agency by focusing on these ostensibly nonstatist experiences.[2] State interventions of marriage law, however, remain important for the reproduction of gender roles and the state itself. The meanings of the most apparently "cultural" or "natural" roles of mother and father are constituted by and through the state.

I borrow from anthropological theory to define the state as a political organization that creates intergenerational identities through kinship rules that distinguish between sacred and profane forms of sexuality and reproduction. Whereas liberal social contract theorists grapple with the modern state as a membership organization constituted by individual consent and Marxist theory views the state as an egalitarian facade for exploitative market relations, this essay conceptualizes the state as using invocations of birth and marriage to maintain the allegiance of its members, through the constitution of a legal family form that provides rules for inclusions and exclusions of citizens.[3]

While others have shown the inconsistency of marriage and liberal theory[4] or the illogical requirement of a hierarchical private sphere for women in the construction of an egalitarian public sphere for men,[5] this essay shows the ways that marriage genders the fully developed political state and its citizens, even when it appears that the state does not have sex-specific requirements for the duties of "husband" and "wife."[6] While gender distinctions are effaced in many other parts of the law,[7] and while there are far fewer explicitly discriminatory laws that regulate marriage than when the state was more explicitly patriarchal, marriage still creates political status roles.

The state actively participates in establishing the distinction between what is *profane* (instrumental, everyday life) and what is *sacred* (ritualistic expressions of group particularity).[8] Marriage in the modern state names the relations between parents and children, such that the mother's relation is putatively profane or natural but the father's is not. With the appellation "husband," fathers have the prerogatives of paternity that they would lack were the sacred/profane distinctions of marriage not in place. By legally privileging what is "political" (fathers) over what is "natural" (mothers) through marriage, the state engenders parenting roles in a hierarchical fashion.

Marx incorrectly defines the fully developed liberal state as one that has eliminated all political status relations.[9] The modern state has eliminated the "aristocrat," the "knight," the "lord," the "serf," and the "peon," but one juridical status relation still remains: that of "husband" and "wife."[10] A large number of social and economic benefits go to people who fit the legal definition of the married couple, many of which flow from the state itself using this definition in contexts ranging from tax returns to social security benefits to citizenship criteria. The state clearly favors the married couple over any other dyad or individual.

In the United States, family law is far more egalitarian than it was as recently as thirty years ago. Indeed, it is the egalitarian quality of much of the marriage relation that renders the exceptions all the more telling. Specifically, court opinions in the United States continue to insist that a husband must be a "man" and a wife a "woman," in the name of nature, the Bible, or a particular kinship pattern in which women's bodies reproduce children for state-licensed husbands to control. In relation to the profane/sacred character of marriage's sexual roles — denoting legitimate and illegitimate partners and children — marriage also contributes to the constitution of national and racial identities. Marriage provides one criterion for citizenship, and through miscegenation laws it also has played a role in the construction and perpetuation of racial identity in the United States.

I focus on court decisions for the analysis of marriage because law constitutes marriage. It does not passively reflect or regulate preexisting marriage norms. Unlike most other laws, marriage law is what language philosopher J. L. Austin calls "performative." Austin writes that when one's utterance is performative one is "*doing* something rather than merely *saying* something." Austin's first example of this is a marriage ceremony: "Suppose, for example, that in the course of a marriage ceremony I say, as people will, 'I do' — (sc. take this woman to be my lawful wedded wife)."[11] Performatives may "misfire" if the context is inappropriate, for instance, according to Austin, if one attempts to divorce one's wife by "standing her squarely in the room and saying, in a voice loud enough for all to hear, 'I divorce you.' Now this procedure is not accepted . . . at least not in this country and others like it."[12] Of all his examples it is only marriage that requires a specifically legal context for the statement to be felicitous.

Law is not definitive in the same way for most other activities that it regulates. Whereas it is possible but illegal to drive ninety miles an hour or to enable a nine-year-old to drink beer, it is not possible to be married in any way other than that which one's state legislature recognizes. One does not look to law for what counts as "ninety miles an hour" or "nine years old." Although in any particular case facts may be subject to dispute, I know of no case in which a speeding law was challenged because if one followed another calendar, say, based on a "twelve-hour-day," then one was really going only forty-five miles an hour. Nor am I familiar with a person pleading "not guilty" to selling to a minor because in base 3 the child was twenty-two. No one experiences the state arbitrarily constituting the terms of these regulated activities. I use court decisions and statutes as the evidence for what counts as marriage in this country. Not only is marriage formally constituted through the state, but the judiciary recognizes its own interventions as artifice and accords itself, as the guardian of the state, the epistemological position of being able to make these determinations.[13]

I focus on the United States because it is the country Marx, with good reason, held up as exemplary of the most "completely developed political state," that is, the one with the fewest status requirements for political membership and participation.[14] That Marx's focus was on religion in particular, and that marriage is closely tied to religious discourse, also renders a return to his analysis of the United States especially relevant.

"On the Jewish Question"

Marx argues in his essay that law may provide conditions for equality that are not actually realized in daily life. He describes two spheres that exist in relation to each other: *political society* (relations constituted by the state and its laws) and *civil society* (all other relations). Political society and civil society do not exist autonomously, according to Marx; civil society is not the equivalent of a Lockean "state of nature." Rather, political society and civil society require each other. All social relations defined as "nonpolitical" are created by the state, by the rules and laws of political society. For instance, the "right" to practice one's religion is constituted by a legal document (the Constitution, in the United States) that is interpreted by state agents (the Supreme Court). The relation of husband to wife, constituted by the state through marriage laws, is another example of the state's creation, through law, of a sphere of "private" relations ostensibly outside the "public" realm.

Feminist Theory and "On the Jewish Question"

The modern liberal state and its laws, for the most part, seem gender-neutral; legislation does not specify who must do the housework any more than it specifies who may accumulate capital. Nonetheless, men have more power and authority than women in our society. How is this so? Wendy Brown, in her essay on abortion rights, uses Marx to explain this: "The *political* emancipation of women (suffrage, equal rights, etc.) leaves intact the fact of sexism with regard to reproductive relations just as 'political emancipation from religion leaves religion in existence.' "[15] Similarly, Catharine MacKinnon writes that the apparent gender-neutrality of the liberal state serves the hierarchies of civil society: "civil society, the domain in which women are distinctively subordinated and deprived of power, has been placed beyond reach of legal guarantees. Women are oppressed socially, prior to law, without state acts, often in intimate contexts."[16] Brown's and MacKinnon's observations seem to make sense, at least at first glance, since women in the United States have the same individual political rights as men — rights that some in the 1920s thought would be the first step to the alleviation of gender inequalities — and yet women continue to suffer from various forms of violence, exploitation, and discrimination, especially in the "private" realms of family and market.

It is important to bear in mind that there is no private sphere present from when proto–*Homo sapiens* rose from the muck, a point obscured in the writings of some feminists, such as MacKinnon and Brown. Rather than leave women alone, in some pre-legal limbo, juridical discourse itself makes certain activities "private." That is, through law the state creates the "private" realm where sexual and other violence is permitted. When men in the past have gotten away with beating their wives, this is because the state positively excuses certain forms of violence. Marriage law makes this especially clear: the Anglo common law did not ignore wife beating, it articulated its "reasonable bounds";[17] marital rape exemptions did not ignore rape within marriage, they explicitly required the state to protect this form of violence. Sir Matthew Hale wrote, "the husband can not be guilty of a rape committed by himself upon his lawful wife, for by their mutual matrimonial consent and contract the wife hath given herself in this kind unto her husband and which she can not retract."[18]

The marriage relation also creates public, that is, politically relevant identities. Of this historian Nancy Cott writes, "Marriage is commonly thought to lie in the realm of private decision making, but . . . the institution of marriage is and has been a public institution and a building block of public policy."[19] She goes on to detail nineteenth-century law and court decisions in the United States that show marriage as crucial to the regulation of race relations and religious affiliation, and as constitutive of the modern state; she concludes that "heterosexual marriage" is the "most direct link of public authority to gender formation."[20]

Marriage and the State

Today gender-neutrality in law seems to be becoming the norm, as many of the more obvious inequalities associated with the status roles of "husband" and "wife" no longer exist. For instance, most states lack any gender-specific language in matters of property ownership, divorce, alimony, and adultery. Marital rape exemptions have been abolished in at least nineteen states.[21] Feminist legal theorist Martha Fineman writes,

> during the 1970s there were successful attempts in most states to make laws gender neutral. Such campaigns were particularly significant in the family law area, where gendered rules had been the norm. Feminists concerned with law reform considered the push for degendered rules a symbolic imperative, even when they recognized that such rules might actually result in removing an arguable advantage for women, as in the case of maternal preference rules for deciding custody cases.[22]

These trends might suggest that the state may be in the process of withdrawing from the regulation of marriage, at a rate faster when it comes to gender roles than to gender status. That public authority contributes to gender by controlling marriage, then, appears to be a matter of merely heuristic — not political — interest, if that distinction implies no power dynamics between husband and wife.

Cott, however, contends that the state cannot simply leave marriage alone:

> One might go so far as to say that the institution of marriage and the modern state have been mutually constitutive. As much as (legal) marriage does not exist without being authorized by the state, one of the principal means that the state can use to prove its existence — to announce its sovereignty and its hold on the populace — is its authority over marriage.[23]

The regulation of marriage remains of paramount concern to the state because marriage plays a role in the creation of the state's citizens. Marriage functions in this fashion in three ways. First, in some cases it names the *terms of legitimacy* that render some children citizens and others aliens. Second, it announces a *form* of kinship relations. Third, it marks people as *full citizens*. The juridical privileging of a certain kinship structure marked by marriage — in tax law, welfare policy, educational policy, and immigration law — continues to render the married couple the ultimate unit worthy of full political rights.

Citizenship

There are three routes to citizenship by birth in the United States. Though not all of these depend on marriage per se, they all presume a certain kinship form of state membership, one that is intimately associated with marriage. To be a citizen in the United States, (1) one is born in the sovereign territory of the United States; (2) one's mother is a U.S. citizen; or (3) one's father is a U.S. citizen and married to one's mother.[24] Resident alien status procedures are similar. In the last case a marriage certificate, and not only the citizenship of a biological parent, determines whether certain children are eligible to be U.S. citizens. Citizenship by marriage occurs when an alien is married to a citizen in a ceremony deemed consistent with U.S. marriage laws. Hence, if a male U.S. citizen marries three wives in Iran, those marriages will not be recognized in the United States and the wives will not receive citizenship. Similarly, if a same-sex couple are wed in Denmark, the fact that one partner is a U.S. citizen will not render his or her non-American spouse a citizen, because that marriage practice is not recognized in any of the fifty states of the United States. So it is not "marriage" but a specifically "American" form of marriage that constitutes U.S. citizens. Marriage has also meant the loss of citizenship for women.[25]

Racial Identities

Marriage plays a key role in the construction of racial identity as well, in the United States and elsewhere.[26] Here the courts have construed the correct and hence legal marriage form as simultaneously "Christian" and "European." This collapsed racial/religious rubric articulates the American marital relation. One of the most famous marriage cases, *Reynolds v. United States* (1878), upholds penalties for polygamous marriage against Mormon assertions of the First Amendment's free exercise clause, on the grounds that "Polygamy has always been odious among the northern and western nations of Europe, and, until the establishment of the Mormon Church, was almost exclusively a feature of the life of Asiatic and of African people."[27] In this opinion, Europe is conflated with northern and western Europe, as a racialized experience in contrast with those of "Asiatic and of African people." Obviously the category is confused. Of interest here is not the content or logic of the classification, but the formal articulation of a specifically national marriage structure within a framework of a phenomenologically racialized religion. What counts as marriage is what forms the proper racial/religious contour for an "American."

The twentieth-century anxiety over illegitimacy, a product of marriage law, also has racial overtones. Patriarchal monogamy is perceived as European, while anything else is regarded by the state as Asian or African. What's it to the state whether a father is married to the mother of his child, or whether, relatedly, kinship is matrilocal or even matriarchal? At least Daniel Patrick Moynihan was honest enough to admit the cultural specificity of the preference for a patriarchal, married family in his still influential *Report on the Negro Family*:

> There is, presumably, no special reason why a society in which males are dominant in family relationships is to be preferred to a matriarchal arrangement. *However, it is clearly a disadvantage for a minority group to be operating on one principle, while the great majority of the population, and the one with the most advantages to begin with, is operating on another.* This is the present situation of the Negro. Ours [i.e., White society] is a society which presumes male leadership in private and public affairs.[28]

That is, most people in this country are White; Whites have power over Blacks; Whites have patriarchal values; therefore, African Americans should be more patriarchal as well.[29]

Former vice president Dan Quayle, responding to the 1992 riots in Los Angeles prompted by the initial verdict on the police beating of Rodney King, blamed the riots on the "breakdown of the family structure." His speech begins with a discussion of the "legacy of racism that has been overcome," moves to a Moynihanesque discussion of poverty statistics and an example of the "single mother raising her children in the ghetto," and concludes with the worry that "our cultural leaders in Hollywood" establish bad role models: "It doesn't help when prime time TV has Murphy Brown — a character who supposedly epitomizes today's intelligent, highly paid, professional woman — mocking the importance of fathers by bearing a child alone and calling it just another 'life style choice.' "[30] Perhaps Quayle's real worry runs the other way around: perhaps the anxiety is that White men are not at the center of "their" White households, the way that White conservatives imagine men not at the head of the African American household. In any case, the family form, legally and more broadly, is perceived as one indicative of a racial status: patriarchal monogamy is European, White, Christian, and preferable; anything else is African or Asian.[31]

Not only is the form of marriage specifically racialized, its rules have also relied on the state to reproduce racial identities. "Antimiscegenation" laws prohibited so-called interracial marriage in this country until 1967.[32] Since the purpose of these laws was to regulate the "Whiteness" of the country — marriage regulation being used as a proxy for physical restraints against interracial heterosexual intercourse — relatively few children were officially reported as being the offspring of interracial couples, even where the actual identities of the parents were known. With "miscegenation" and "fornication" both against the law, interracial children were either legal nonentities or evidence of a crime.

In an early decision allowing a railroad to have "separate but equal" seating, the Court relied on "the Creator's" thoughts on marriage:

> Conceding equality, with natures as perfect and rights as sacred, yet God has made them dissimilar, with those natural instincts and feelings which He always imparts to His creatures when He intends that they shall not overstep the natural boundaries He has assigned to them. The natural law which forbids their intermarriage and that social amalgamation which leads to a corruption of races, is as clearly divine as that which imparted to them different natures.... From social amalgamation [sitting next to someone of a different race on a train] it is but a step to illicit intercourse, and but another to intermarriage.[33]

Of special interest is that *intermarriage*, not illicit sex, is the furthest one might stray from a Christian God's intention. As late as 1967 it was illegal for Blacks and Whites to marry in many states, so that the children of interracial marriages were classified as having a father of the same race as the mother.[34] Insofar as birth certificates (by stating one's parents' race) continue to name one's race (as do driver's licenses in some states), in the fully developed nation-state drinking fountains may lack any distinguishing signs, but the state labels its citizens "Black" and "White."[35]

This political status upholds racist forms of discrimination in two ways. The first is through law, in political society: whether through slavery or Jim Crow, racial classifications were the first step to state-sponsored racism. These forms of discrimination no longer exist; however, the state-constituted grid of racial identity perpetuates the form of race difference that manifests exploitative consequences in other practices. Racism is deeply enmeshed in psychological, sociological, and cultural paradigms of inequality. Although these discourses do not necessarily emanate from the state, the racial subject positions that circulate through them certainly do. In brief, the scaffold of racism is the concept of race, a concept that has been structured by and through the state and its documents, including those of marriage.

Marriage and Gender

To connect the relation of marriage to nationality and to race does not take feminists away from gender, but rather leads them right back to it, since it is the marriage form of husband and wife that constitutes our kinship structures. Social identity is constituted and maintained through the regulation of sex and sexuality.

Yet the gender dynamic that Cott associates with the state — although harmful for those who desire other forms of marriage, for those women who are not White (and hence unable to benefit from White privilege reproduced through marriage law), and for those who are uninterested in a partnership with a man — does not seem especially harmful to women as a class. Not only women are hurt by the constructions of marriage as strictly a relation between husbands-as-men and wives-as-women. Thus some might argue that the exclusion of homosexual marriage from kinship possibilities renders marriage an institution that reproduces "heterosexuality" but not necessarily "gender," since the state does not determine the content of the female "wife" 's and male "husband" 's roles.

Perhaps Cott would be more correct in saying that heterosexual marriage is the "most direct link of public authority" to *sexuality* formation, but not to "*gender* formation," which is her claim.[36] If all that is required for marriage is a "man" and a "woman," with no other gendered attributes required of these partners — as opposed to the past, when to be the "man" was to own all the property, for instance — then the state seems not to be filling in the blank of what it means to be a (male) husband and a (female) wife. Any sex-specific roles would seemingly emerge from extrajuridical contexts.

Yet the apparent equality of the political statuses "husband" and "wife" actually obscures an underlying dynamic that continues to render marriage a site of gendered political inequality. Marriage statutes, as interpreted by the courts, position women as part of nature and men as part of political society. Marriage constitutes men's control over women's labor when it gives "husbands" custody rights "fathers" lack.[37] The state, then, awards men control over the labor of women's bodies (children) by virtue of the political conventions of marriage. When married to a woman, a man is always the legal father not only of children he begets with her, but also of any child she bears. Hence women are to nature as men are to politics, since her relation to the child is by birth (natural), while his is by marriage (political).[38]

It is true that the politics/nature distinction has sometimes been gendered in an apparently opposite fashion as well. Rousseau's work is an example of this, as was the temperance movement in the late nineteenth and early twentieth centuries in the United States, when women's and Christian organizations figured the state as an institution that would domesticate the savage sexuality of its male citizens. Law as a feminine, maternal force underscores the compensatory character of the state's masculinity, in a manner similar to that of the Catholic Church (among others) — which is at once patriarchal and feminine. This conjunction suggests that when men appropriate birth, qua "fathers," their control of birth (which remains the central function of religious and national institutions) remains an ultimately feminine, that is, maternal, activity.[39]

The state as a site of compensatory masculinity is at once fatherly (political) and maternal (tied to birth). In its insistence on controlling marriage, the state positions itself as constitutive of intergenerational identities — and here I follow Durkheim —

by arrogating to itself the authority to distinguish (and hence to constitute) what is profane (sex as "fornication," children as "illegitimate") and what is sacred (sex within marriage, legitimate children).[40]

The modern state's constitution of kinship relations is masculine in two ways. First, the privileged, sacred status always devolves to men; their sacred marital status of husband-father trumps a natural father's claim to his children, and it also trumps a mother's "natural" status — as the laws on surrogacy make clear. A woman's right to make decisions about her children is substantially undermined if she is married. Not biological paternity, but marriage creates these subject positions. Second, and relatedly, the state's rules are oriented toward controlling and displacing the "natural." Insofar as the courts associate women with nature, the state's articulations of the maternal relationship suggest the appropriation and displacement of this feminine status.[41]

Recent Court Cases

The court decisions most constitutive as well as illustrative of the above points offer opinions on child (really infant) custody in cases where the biological parents are not married.[42] These include surrogacy cases, adoption cases, and cases of artificial insemination. According to most statutes and court decisions, when parents are unmarried and when the father has demonstrated no interest in either the mother or the pregnancy, the mother has the prerogative to make the determination of whether to allow the child to be adopted, without the permission of the father. Apparent exceptions to this are emerging, although all are cases in which the father has shown an interest in the pregnancy and in the child. In these exceptional cases the courts have named an equivalence between the mother bearing a child and the father establishing a trust fund in the child's name; on this basis, biological fathers have custody rights similar to those of married fathers. In all these cases the state holds the prerogative not simply to enforce "the law" or use the law to enforce contracts and status relations decided in civil society, but also to assign status itself. "Wife," "husband," "father," and "mother" are all state creations. As Judge Montgomery said, "We know what a child is. But what is a father, mother, or parent? It is time to redefine such once simple words from a perspective of the law. . . . [W]hat exactly *is* a daddy? Is it a noun or a verb?"[43] In addressing similar questions the courts have established the system of custody rights illustrated in table 3.1.[44] Of interest here is the language the courts use to establish equivalences among different status relations. In *Caban v. Mohammed* (1979), a frequently cited decision, a Supreme Court majority ruled that paternity per se does not entail custody rights: "The mother carries and bears the child, and in this sense her parental relation is clear. The validity of the father's claim must be gauged by other measures. By tradition, the primary measure has been the legitimate familial relationship he creates with the child by marriage with the mother."[45] In *Lehr v. Robertson* (1982), the Court ruled that the "mere existence of a biological link" does not merit protection of paternal rights, so that an unwed mother may allow her child to be

TABLE 3.1.
Biological Fathers' Rights to Custody

	Father has custody rights	Father lacks custody rights
Biological parents unmarried and father does not contribute financially or show legal interest in pregnancy[a]		X
Biological parents unmarried and father contributes financially and shows interest during pregnancy[b] or later[c]	X	
Biological parents unmarried and father shows financial and emotional commitment to child, but mother's husband wants custody[d]		X
Biological parents married and father shows no commitment to child and provides no financial support[e]	X	

[a]*Lehr v. Robertson*, 463 U.S. 248 (1982); *Caban v. Mohammed*, 441 U.S. 380 (1979); *re Adoption of Reams*, 557 N.E.2d 159 (1989).

[b]*Abernathy v. Baby Boy*, 437 S.E.2d 25 (1993); Michael Azzariti, "Domestic Law," *South Carolina Law Review* 46 (1994): 48–54; Norman Allen, "*Adoption of Kelsey S.*: When Does an Unwed Father Know Best?" *Pacific Law Journal* 24 (1993): 1633–80.

[c]*Petition of Kirchner*, 649 N.E.2d 328, 333 (1995).

[d]*Michael H. v. Gerald D.*, 491 U.S. 110 (1989).

[e]This is the presumption that inheres in the "best interest" standard; see Lenore Weitzman, *The Marriage Contract: Spouses, Lovers, and the Law* (New York: Free Press, 1981); see also *Matter of Baby M.*, 537 A2d 1227 (1988).

adopted without the father's consent.[46] Only her consent and that of her husband are required.

The mother's biological link to the child is assumed to be of a different character than that of an unwed father, and hence the Court did not recognize an equal protection claim. The defense of this position is that the mother has a "continuous custodial responsibility,"[47] not the father. However, in this case and in others, the reason the mother has this responsibility is that she did not allow the father to visit or to assume any responsibility. According to the facts recounted in the dissenting opinion, Lehr visited the hospital when his daughter Jessica was born and tried to maintain contact. However, after the mother was released from the hospital, she "threatened Lehr with arrest unless he stayed away and refused to permit him to see Jessica."[48] The majority discounted Lehr's interest because it did not take the proper, that is, legal, form, which required him to follow New York guidelines for signing up on the "putative father registry."[49] The dissent emphasizes the importance of the biological tie and the actual interest shown,[50] while the majority emphasizes the importance of sticking to the rules — essentially holding that the state, not biology, constitutes the family.

The importance of the marriage tie is announced in *Reams* and other surrogacy situations that require the consent of the surrogate mother's *husband* before the child may be declared that of the biological father.[51] As the court stated in *Reams*, "legal parentage, not to be confused with biological parentage, must be established before the issuance of custody can properly be decided."[52] The husband of the mother is, in all but one or two states, presumptively the father.[53] This has been held when either the father/sperm donor wants custody[54] or the mother wants to arrange adoption without paternal consent.[55] The apparent state interest here is in the protection of the husband's custody of his wife's children against that of a biological father.

In the case of *Reams* — pertaining to a woman who was artificially inseminated with sperm belonging to neither the prospective adoptive father nor her own husband — her husband's consent was necessary for the adoption to proceed: "even though Norma Stotski [biological mother] and Leslie Miner [biological father] executed consent forms which they thought to be valid, neither could relinquish legal custody of Tessa to Mr. Reams through the adoption process" because "Mr. Stotski, by virtue of the fact that he is married to Norma Lee Stotski, *shall be treated in law and regarded as the natural parent* of Tessa Reams. Thus, it is Mr. Stotski's consent, in addition to Mrs. Stotski's consent, that is required to effectuate an adoption of Tessa Reams."[56] The actual natural father's consent is irrelevant.[57] By self-consciously dubbing political men ("husbands") "natural fathers" when recognizing someone else as the biological father, the state commits a telling semantic mistake. On the one hand, the courts maintain that a political relation is always, in marriage law, privileged over a natural one. On the other hand, the courts regard this legal status as "natural." The courts constitute this privileged relation by naming those who are husbands (fathers by law) "natural," providing legal "husband-fathers" with the recognition that natural "natural-fathers" lack.

In *Michael H. v. Gerald D.* (1989), Michael and Carol signed a statement stipulating that "Michael was Victoria's natural father," although after she reconciled with her husband, Gerald, Carol "instructed her attorneys not to file the stipulation."[58] Michael, supported by a court-appointed advocate for Victoria, sought visitation rights and was granted them, until Gerald intervened on the grounds that he was the "presumptive father," so that Michael had no grounds on which to file for visitation rights.[59] The decision begins, "California law, like nature itself, makes no provision for dual fatherhood."[60] This being the case, the Court must decide who the father will be. This is purely a status decision, one in which individual rights cannot be pressed until one subject position achieves a legal, not natural, recognition.

The question before the Court, then, is who is the father? The husband or the father? The answer: the husband. This is because, according to Scalia, for centuries our laws have protected the custody claims and responsibilities of husbands, and ignored those of biological fathers.[61]

The majority argument advances in three steps. First, Scalia asserts that a child may have only one father — the genetic one or the legal one, by marriage. Second, Scalia assesses the different rights at issue for the genetic father as opposed to those of the husband: "Here, to *provide* protection to an adulterous natural father is to *deny* protection to a marital father, and vice-versa. If Michael has a 'freedom not to conform' (whatever that means), Gerald must equivalently have a 'freedom to conform.'"[62] Third, a legal choice must be made, even when it is conceded that "multiple fatherhood" would be most beneficial to the child: "[W]hatever the merits of the guardian's ad litem's belief that such an arrangement can be of great psychological benefit to a child, the claim that a State must recognize multiple fatherhood has no support in the history or traditions of this country."[63]

The child advocate's point, that such a ruling would deny Victoria a relationship with her genetic father that "legitimate" children enjoyed — and thus deny her equal protection — was rebutted by Scalia on the grounds that "Illegitimacy is a legal construct, not a natural trait," and that under California law, Victoria is "legitimate" (the daughter of her mother's husband). In other words, the "natural" relation of paternity can be overridden by a legal definition. In essence, the Court develops a self-consuming argument in which genetics qua nature is the model of "single fatherhood," determining the limits of a single legal father; once in place, based on a view of nature, the natural father model is trumped by the legal father model.[64]

In apparent contradiction with the above cases, readers might recall two high-profile custody disputes in the early 1990s. Both involved mothers who had allowed their newborn children to be adopted without obtaining the fathers' consent. In the cases that were referred to in the media as those of Baby Jessica and Baby Richard, the biological mothers subsequently married the biological fathers and then pursued custody through the courts. In both cases the biological parents ultimately prevailed.

The principles invoked to decide these cases reflect the reasoning of others discussed in this essay, insofar as they rely on a very particular definition of a parent. The Michigan legal code defines "parents" as "natural parents" "if married prior or subsequent to the minor's birth."[65] Since both biological couples are also married couples, the courts can say that *Michael H.* and the others are about "denying the unwed father's rights" and do not establish precedent for "establishing that non-parent custodians" have rights by virtue of having custody.[66] "Natural," that is, married, parents lose their custody rights only if they are shown to be unfit.[67]

The Group, the State, and Kinship

To understand the underlying logic of what Cott regards as the state's use of marriage to control its own existence — manifest above in its paternity decisions — I turn to Durkheim, who shows that the regulation of kinship roles is the way groups maintain the continuity of the group in the face of the natality and mortality of its individuals. The practices that express this are what Durkheim calls "religious," although the term has wide applications:

> [N]early all the great social institutions have been born in religion. Now in order that these principal aspects of the collective life may have commenced by being only varied aspects of the religious life, it is obviously necessary that the religious life be the eminent form and, as it were, the concentrated expression of the whole collective life. *If religion has given birth to all that is essential in society, it is because the idea of society is the soul of religion.*[68]

It is not specific rules per se, Durkheim suggests, but the possibility of their being institutionalized in an ongoing fashion characteristic of a particular group that is the hallmark of "religion." Durkheim describes the nation-state as an organization that follows this pattern: "What essential difference is there between an assembly of Christians celebrating the principal dates of the life of Christ, or of Jews remembering the exodus from Egypt or the promulgation of a new moral or legal system of some great event in the national life?"[69] The specific practices to which Durkheim points as bringing about community, however, are not grand ceremonies, but the sacred/profane distinctions of kinship systems.

Durkheim locates communities achieving this continuity in events surrounding marriage, birth, and death. The totem of a clan, which distinguishes it from other clans, belongs only to members of that clan: "[I]ts name is also the name of a determined species of material things with which it believes it has very particular relations," and these are "especially relations of kinship."[70] One's totem is not elective (just as citizenship is not), but determined by the kinship rules of the group: "It is a part of the civil status of each individual; it is generally hereditary; in any case, it is birth which designates it, and the wish of men counts for nothing."[71] The same holds for citizenship status in a nation-state. One is a citizen by virtue of birth in a particular nation-state, or of parents who are citizens in a particular nation-state.[72]

Durkheim explores the sacred/profane distinctions associated with invocations of birth. Relatedly, group membership by *kinship* depends on the specific "incarnation" of this figure, not a diffuse association of an individual with a mythical god or hero. This occurs at birth and related rituals.[73] The passing on of a totem of the father uses not a biological account, but a religious one (group-constructed). For instance, Durkheim refers to a study of the Aranta in which the authors write that "commerce of the sexes is in no way the determining condition of generation, which is considered the result of mystic operations."[74] The transmission hangs on marriage, not sex. In some tribes, it is the husband's totem in the form of a spirit, not his sperm, that is responsible for conception,[75] while for others, the matrimonial clan provides the totem.[76] The sacred part of the child, the identity as part of the clan in distinction from the generic features held as a profane body, are determined, Durkheim explains, through a society's kinship rules.

These rules can be characterized as masculine, or paternal. By focusing on birth as the site of membership, kinship rules name women's activity as that which is essential and subject to appropriation, by souls in trees, the husband's totem, or the state's customs. Birth need not be regarded as an inherently feminine power for one to note the ways that societies represent reproduction as a female activity that ulterior rules also appropriate, as when rituals perform group initiation, by men, in relation to invocations of birth.[77] Again, "real men," like Rousseau, may recognize this appropriation for what it is and think it unmanly for a community to worry so much about birth. Whether the "cause" of this paternity structure is the sometimes anonymity of paternity, a psychologically rooted compensatory urge to control birth when one does not give birth, or something else is beyond the scope and method of this essay.

In this country the state's interest in regulating birth through marriage appears to require rules that denigrate women's control and that discriminate against same-sex couples. Only heterosexual marriage guarantees paternal rights. The very representation of a mother's "natural" relation with the infant requires a legal system that performs a comparable relation for the husband, if paternity is to be institutionalized as sacred. The singularity of the totem — of the nation-state and the paternal name — is what requires exclusions. If women could marry women and men marry men, or if a plurality of forms of parenting were recognized, this compensatory paternal rule would have no privileged place in law, and hence no privileged place in our kinship system.

The history of patrilineality suggests that fatherhood in an ongoing family line is extremely important in this society. Preventing same-sex couples from marrying affirms the sex-specificity in the husband and wife relation and hence the sacred character of the husband-father's relation to the child. If roles were not sex-specific, the kinship system as a whole could be sacred, but the sex-specificity of "paternity" would not be. Another way to think about this is that "paternity" requires exclusions, as do all identities. The "father" requires the "not-father." If this father is to be sacred for males, associated with masculinity per se, then husbands — the sacral fathers — must be men. Were women eligible to become husbands, the determinacy of the gender/sex mapping fades. Again, there is no biological basis for this rule of exclusion; it is part of the same system that places paternity rights of husbands over those of fathers.

I would like to close with some reflections on the Hawaii Supreme Court and First Circuit Court decisions that have called sex-specific marriage roles into question.[78] Hawaii has a fairly recent experience with non-Christian marriage roles and practices. Although the Christian missionaries have left their mark and many in Hawaii oppose same-sex marriage, representatives of the Sovereign People's movement and other non-European organizations in Hawaii have endorsed the possibility of same-sex marriages on the grounds that this was "traditional" to the precolonial peoples of those islands.[79]

In *Baehr v. Lewin* and in *Baehr v. Mike*, the Court held that same-sex couples should be allowed to apply for marriage licenses, that "husband" and "wife" need not be sex-specific roles — unless the state could prove that the "sex-based classification is justified by compelling state interests and the statute is narrowly drawn to avoid unnecessary abridgements of the applicant couples' constitutional rights."[80] The state supreme court and the First Circuit Court drew on the state's Equal Rights Amendment, holding that if a man could be a husband, then it might well be unconstitutional discrimination to prevent women from applying to be husbands as well, and vice versa. The state attorney general is appealing these rulings, attempting to show that Hawaii has a "compelling interest" in maintaining its current marriage practices, so same-sex marriages are still prohibited, but the responses to the possibility are instructive.

As of September 1996, sixteen states have passed laws banning the recognition of same-sex marriages. And Congress passed the Defense of Marriage Act, which holds that at the federal level "the word 'marriage' means only a legal union between one man and one woman as husband and wife, and the word 'spouse' refers only to a person of the opposite sex who is a husband or a wife." The bill also holds that no state shall be required to legally acknowledge a "relationship between persons of the same sex that is treated as a marriage under the laws" of another state.[81] In the event that Hawaii (or another state) recognizes same-sex marriages, these laws will invite constitutional scrutiny, since the Commerce Clause in the U.S. Constitution has been interpreted to require states to recognize marriages performed in other states. This has prompted the Reverend Lou Sheldon of the Traditional Values Coalition to call for amending the Constitution: "if you destroy the heterosexual ethic, then you are destroying a major pillar of Western civilization," a move that may prompt conservatives to attempt to "strike down the 'full faith and credit' provision of the U.S. Constitution."[82]

In sum, the status relations of marriage contribute to the reproduction of a particular political society — even if it is a procedurally liberal one — and as long as marriage is legally codified, gendered depictions of birth will be as well. It is the liberal state's assertion of its power to define parental roles, *not* the roles some imagine as handed us by nature, that assures the continuity of this sex/gender system. This is revealed in the state's constitution of the sacred/profane distinctions that guarantee the immortality of its identity by the appropriation of the birth practices that yield national and racial identities for its citizens.

NOTES

This paper has benefited tremendously from the comments on an earlier draft provided by Julia Adams, Don Herzog, Kathleen Jones, Hanna Pitkin, Sonya Rose, Margaret Somers, Ann Stoler, Joan Tronto, and Elizabeth Wingrove. Thanks to Paula Ettelbrick for sharing her insights on some of the controversies in the same-sex marriage challenges. This essay is part of a booklength manuscript, *Reproducing the State.*

1. Karl Marx, "On the Jewish Question" [1843], in *The Marx-Engels Reader,* ed. Robert Tucker (New York: Norton, 1978), 26–52.

2. The literature I have in mind includes feminist standpoint epistemologies as well as Foucauldian influenced work.

3. The primary theoretical sources for this argument are Emile Durkheim, *The Elementary Forms of Religious Life,* trans. Joseph Swain (1912; New York: Free Press, 1965); and Claude Levi-Strauss, *The Elementary Structures of Kinship,* trans. James Bell, John von Sturmer, and Rodney Needham (1949; Boston: Beacon Press, 1969). These choices indicate my attempt to highlight the chasm between the paradigms of political *membership by choice* (debated in the social contract — and post–social contract — literatures of liberals, Marxists, and feminists) and the political fact that citizenship in all modern states is constituted by *references to birth,* either by "blood" or by land. Concepts of birth are imbricated in kinship structures, and hence this essay explores the gendered character of the "mother" and "father" simultaneously produced by and constitutive of the state.

4. Sara Ketchum, "Liberalism and Marriage Law," in *Feminism and Philosophy,* ed. Mary Vetterling-Brogin, Frederick Elliston, and Jane English (New York: Rowman and Littlefield, 1977), 264–76; J. S. Mill, *The Subjection of Women* (1869; Rutland, VT: Everyman's Library, 1985), esp. chap. 2; Susan Okin, *Justice, Gender, and the Family* (New York: Basic Books, 1989); Carole Pateman, *The Sexual Contract* (Stanford: Stanford University Press, 1988), esp.

chap. 6, "Feminism and the Marriage Contract,"; Mary Shanley, "Marital Slavery and Friendship: J. S. Mill's *The Subjection of Women*," in *Feminist Interpretations and Political Theory*, ed. Carole Pateman and Mary Shanley (Cambridge: Polity Press, 1991); Mary Wollstonecraft, *A Vindication of the Rights of Woman* (1792; Rutland, VT: Everyman's Library, 1985).

5. Marx, "On the Jewish Question"; Catharine MacKinnon, *Toward a Feminist Theory of the State* (Cambridge: Harvard University Press, 1991), esp. chap. 8; Katherine O'Donovan, *Sexual Divisions in the Law* (London: Weidenfield and Nicolson, 1985).

6. Older accounts of the gender-specific, exploitative aspects of marriage are still relevant, especially in states with marital rape exemption laws, discussed below. On the history of marriage as an inegalitarian institution, see Frederick Engels, *The Origin of the Family, Private Property, and the State* (1884; New York: Pathfinder Press, 1972); Gerda Lerner, *The Creation of Patriarchy* (New York: Oxford University Press, 1986); Mary Shanley, *Feminism, Marriage, and the Law in Victorian England, 1850–1895* (Princeton: Princeton University Press, 1984); Carol Smart, *The Ties That Bind: Law, Marriage and the Reproduction of Patriarchal Relations* (London: Routledge & Kegan Paul, 1984).

7. By "law" I mean simply interpretations of the written documents that outline the scope of state action and restrictions. Law is what announces what the state can do, as opposed to what "the people" or individuals cannot do. I put it this way to emphasize the constitutive aspects of law sometimes lost in analyses of liberal states, on the part of pluralists as well as Foucauldians; see Alan Hunt, *Explorations in Law and Society: Toward a Constitutive Theory of Law* (New York: Routledge, 1993), esp. "Foucault's Expulsion of Law: Toward a Retrieval" and "Law as a Constitutive Mode of Regulation."

8. I follow Durkheim's use of this dichotomy, described by him as central to the reproduction of group identity, *Elementary Forms of Religious Life*, 431 and elsewhere. Critics of what has been called "heteronormativity," or what Michael Warner has called "repro culture," have noted the persistence of state interventions in the construction of sexuality. See Richard Collier, *Masculinity, the Law, and the Family* (London: Routledge, 1995); Lisa Duggan, "Queering the State," *Social Text* 39 (summer 1994): 1–14; David Evans, *Sexual Citizenship: The Material Construction of Sexualities* (London: Routledge, 1993); Janet Halley, "The Construction of Heterosexuality," in *Fear of a Queer Planet*, ed. Michael Warner (Minneapolis: University of Minnesota Press, 1994); Gayle Rubin, "Thinking Sex: Notes for a Radical Theory of the Politics of Sexuality," in *Pleasure/Danger: Exploring Female Sexuality*, ed. Carole Vance (Boston: Routledge & Kegan Paul, 1984); Jacqueline Stevens, "Leviticus in America: On the Politics of Sex Crimes," *Journal of Political Philosophy* 1 (2) (June 1993), 105–36.

9. Marx, "On the Jewish Question," 33.

10. The state interest in marriage is stated in a late nineteenth-century case, *Maynard v. Hill* 125 U.S. 190 (1888). A frequently quoted passage maintains that marriage is an "institution, in the maintenance of which in its purity the public is deeply interested, for it is the foundation of the family and of society, without which there would be neither civilization nor progress" (211). Marriage, according to this decision, "is not so much the result of private agreement, as of public ordination" (quoting from *Noel v. Ewing*, 9 Indiana 37 [1857], 4–50). While other contracts are passively enforced by the state, the state itself actively creates the status of husband and wife in its "public ordination" of marriage. More recent constitutional law treats marriage as a "right" as well as a status; see *Loving v. Virginia*, 338 U.S. 1 (1967); *Zablocki v. Redhail*, 434 U.S. 374 (1977).

11. J. L. Austin, "Performative Utterances," in *Philosophical Papers* (Oxford: Clarendon, 1961).

12. Ibid., 225.

13. On the relevance of the epistemology of law to certain practices, see Hunt, *Explorations in Law.*

14. Marx, "On the Jewish Question," 30. Of course Marx could not have been thinking about sex roles when he wrote this, since at that time only a very small proportion of women could vote or run for office, a fact that would require a major qualification of the United States as "completely developed."

15. Wendy Brown, "Reproductive Freedom and the Right of Privacy," in *Families, Politics, and Public Policy: A Dialogue on Women and the State,* ed. Irene Diamond (New York: Longman, 1983), 327, quoting from Marx, "On the Jewish Question," 31.

16. MacKinnon, *Toward a Feminist Theory of the State,* 165.

17. William Blackstone, *Commentaries on the Laws of England,* 8th ed. (Oxford, 1775), 444–45, quoted in Henry Kelly, "*Rule of Thumb* and the Folklore of the Husband's Stick," *Journal of Legal Education* 44 (September 1994): 351–52. See also Ann Jones, *Next Time She'll Be Dead* (Boston: Beacon, 1994); and Susan Schechter, *Women and Male Violence* (Boston: South End, 1982).

18. M. Hale, *Historia Placitorum Coronas* 628, 629, quoted in Sandra Ryder and Sheryl Kuzmenka, "Legal Rape: The Marital Rape Exemption," *John Marshall Law Review* 24 (winter 1991), 394–95; see also O'Donovan, *Sexual Divisions,* 119–45; and Robin West, "Equality Theory, Marital Rape, and the Promise of the Fourteenth Amendment," *Florida Law Review* 42 (1990): 45–79. On the engagement of the law in this area, Aryeh Neier writes that the "law cannot be neutral on this issue. It either protects the victims of rape or it protects the rapist. If the law exempts husbands from rape charges, the implication is that it condones husbands raping wives." Quoted in Ryder and Kuzmenka, "Legal Rape," 419.

19. Nancy Cott, "Giving Character to Our Whole Civil Polity: Marriage and the Public Order in the Late Nineteenth Century," in *United States History as Women's History: New Feminist Essays,* ed. Linda Kerber, Alice Kessler-Harris, Kathryn Sklar (Chapel Hill: North Carolina University Press, 1995), 107.

20. Ibid., 121.

21. Ryder and Kuzmenka, "Legal Rape," 417.

22. Martha Fineman, *The Illusion of Equality* (Chicago: University of Chicago Press, 1991), 80. In her more recent work, Fineman recognizes the "sacred" character of marriage, but sees this as an extension of — not in tension with — the view of the nuclear family as "natural." Fineman thus understands the challenge to the "natural" family as emanating strictly from feminists, and not the courts and the state, as this essay proposes. Fineman proposes two policy reforms. The first is to "abolish marriage as a legal category"; the second is to privilege the "Mother/Child dyad" as a "caregiving family ... entitled to special, preferred treatment by the state." She adds the caveat that "men could and should be Mothers" and that the Child "stands for all forms of inevitable dependency." *The Neutered Mother, the Sexual Family, and Other Twentieth Century Tragedies* (New York: Routledge, 1995), 146–47, 155, 172–73 n. 36, 228, 230–31; 234–35.

23. Cott, "Giving Character," 109.

24. *Fiallo v. Bell,* 430 U.S. 787 (1977). A June 1995 report from a governmental commission on immigration policy recommends reducing the number of spaces available for immigration based on work skills and extended family relations and suggests that the state "emphasize the importance of the nuclear family as the basic unit of immigration" on grounds that it is "not in the national interest" for nuclear families to be apart. Robert Pear, "Change in Policy for Immigration Is Urged by Panel," *New York Times,* June 5, 1995, A1, A7.

25. In 1907 Congress passed a law "merging . . . the nationality of an American woman in that of her alien husband," thereby revoking her U.S. citizenship. This law consolidated previous court rulings that adopted similar positions, and was amended in 1922 to restore citizenship to these women. For a wonderful survey of seventy-two countries' rules on marriage and nationality through 1928, see House Committee on Immigration and Naturalization, *Hearings before the Committee on Immigration and Naturalization*, 70th Cong., 1st sess., *Effect of Marriage Upon Nationality*, statement by Emma Wold, May 19, 1928 (Washington, DC: GPO, 1928). See also E. P. Hutchison, *Legislative History of American Immigration Policy, 1798–1965* (Philadelphia: University of Pennsylvania Press, 1985).

26. Cott, "Giving Character," 118–19; David Fowler, *Northern Attitudes towards Interracial Marriage: Legislation and Public Opinion in the Middle Atlantic States and the Old Northwest, 1780–1930* (New York: Garland Press, 1987); Michael Grossberg, *Governing the Hearth: Law and the Family in Nineteenth Century America* (Chapel Hill: University of North Carolina Press, 1985), 126–39; Ann Stoler, *Children of the Imperial Divide* (Ann Arbor: University of Michigan Press, 1992); idem, *Sexual Affronts and Racial Frontiers* (Ann Arbor: University of Michigan Press, 1991); Carol Weisbrod and Pamela Sheingorn, "*Reynolds v. U.S.*: Nineteenth Century Forms of Marriage and the Status of Women," in *Domestic Relations and the Law*, ed. Nancy Cott (London: K. G. Saur, 1992), 345–75.

27. *Reynolds v. United States*, 98 U.S. 145, 165 (1878).

28. Daniel Patrick Moynihan, "The Negro Family: The Case for National Action," in *The Moynihan Report and the Politics of Controversy*, ed. Lee Rainwater and William Yancey (Cambridge: MIT Press, 1967), 75, emphasis added.

29. For an affirmative statement about this difference, see Karen Sacks, *Sisters and Wives* (Westport: Greenwood, 1977).

30. Dan Quayle, speech made to the Commonwealth Club of California, May 19, 1992, transcribed by News Transcripts, Inc., in "Excerpts from Vice President's Speech on Cities and Poverty," *New York Times*, May 20, 1992, A20.

31. Current court opinions continue to support a particular form of marriage in the name of "enlightened nations" and "our traditions," so that the cultural specificity of this marriage form is recognized and privileged, but the courts do not name the specific other compared to which "ours" is enlightened. See, for example, *Singer v. Hara*, 522 P.2d 1197 (1974); the current marriage form is justified due to the "prevailing mores and moral concepts of this age," which the court finds rooted in "scriptural, canonical, and civil law," *Adams v. Howerton*, 486 F. Supp. 1119, 1123 (1980); polygamy is a "blot on our civilization" and "contrary to the spirit of Christianity and of the civilization which Christianity has produced in the Western world," *Mormon Church v. U.S.*, 136 U.S. 49 (1889); *Moore v. East Cleveland*, 431 U.S. 495, 503 (1976); *Caban v. Mohammed*, 441 U.S. 397 (1979). On the constitutional status of the specifically Christian form of marriage in this country, see Carol Weisbrod, "Family, Church, and State: An Essay on Constitutionalism and Religious Authority," *Journal of Family Law* 26 (1987–88): 741–70; she writes that "co-option of the state by the church must now be justified by the state in entirely secular terms" (765). The Supreme Court does not follow this practice consistently, as in the references to Leviticus in *Bowers v. Hardwick*, 478 U.S. 186 (1986); and a still influential federal court decision against same-sex marriage held that different-sex marriages are as "old as the book of Genesis." *Baker v. Nelson*, 191 N.W. 2d 185 (1971).

32. In another telling portrait of the multiple layers of marriage politics, colonial law in Virginia prohibited "fornication" between "Negroes" and "Christians," suggesting that the religion, race, gender, nationality, and sexuality are always politically intertwined. Cott, "Giving Character," 388 n. 45.

33. *West Chester and Philadelphia Railroad Co. v. Miles*, Pennsylvania Supreme Court at 211 (1867).

34. Paul Lombardo writes, "Administrative enforcement by minor state bureaucracies also perpetuated the accepted mythologies, especially those involving the miscegenation taboo." He describes a twenty-year racist correspondence between Virginia's head of the Registrar of Vital Statistics and John Powell, founder of the Anglo-Saxon Clubs of America (ASCA), which begins in the early 1920s. "Miscegenation, Eugenics, and Racism: Footnotes to *Loving v. Virginia*," *University of California Davis Law Review* 21 (winter 1988): 427. See also R. Sickels, *Race, Marriage, and the Law* (Albuquerque: University of New Mexico Press, 1972); and Raymond Diamond and Robert Cottrol, "Codifying Caste: Los Angeles' Racial Classification Scheme and the Fourteenth Amendment," *Loyola Law Review* 29 (spring 1983): 255–85.

35. The statute challenged in *Loving v. Virginia* reads, "It shall hereafter be unlawful for any white person in this state to marry any save a white person; or a person with no other admixture of blood than white and American Indian. For purposes of this chapter, the term 'white person' shall apply only to such person as has no trace whatever of any blood other than Caucasian," quoted in *Loving* at 5 n. 4. Since this "drop" is assigned by who one's parents are, and who one's parents are is determined by marriage, the restrictions on marriage restrict racial identities. See also *Doe v. State*, 479 So. 2d 369 (1985). Alexis de Tocqueville recognized the insidious consequences of this kind of policy, and believed that the only way the United States could overcome racial divisiveness would be through the children of mixed marriages: "I have said before that the real link between the European and the Indian was the half-breed; in the same way, it is the mulatto who forms the bridge between black and white; everywhere where there are a great number of mulattoes, the fusion of the two races is not impossible." *Democracy in America* (1835; New York: Anchor Books, 1969), 356.

For an excellent history of *Loving*, see Walter Wadlington, "The *Loving* Case: Virginia's Anti-Miscegenation Statute in Historical Perspective," *Virginia Law Review* 52 (1966). On current racial classification policies of the federal government, see Lawrence Wright, "One Drop of Blood," *New Yorker*, July 1994, 46–55.

36. Cott, "Giving Character," 121.

37. By positioning children as the objects of women's labor, the state defines children as property, and though this contributes to an alienated relation to one's personality (as children "belong to" their parents, not themselves), this dynamic is not the focus of this essay. Rather, I focus on the ways that marriage decisions constitute women's bodies as natural, thereby derogating to law, to the state, the function of the supranatural authority that can decide paternity and custody.

38. Sherry Ortner, "Is Female to Male as Nature Is to Culture?" in *Women, Culture, and Society*, ed. Michelle Rosaldo and Louise Lamphere (Stanford: Stanford University Press, 1974). As examples of the devaluation of females, Ortner writes, "female exclusion from a most sacred rite or the highest political council is sufficient evidence." The fact that the state constitutes the sacred quality of marriage, one that excludes women from the sacred position of "husband," similarly situates women in the realm of nature and men in the realm of politics. Ortner writes, "[M]y thesis is that woman is being identified with — or, if you will, seems to be a symbol of — something that every culture defines as being of a lower order of existence than itself." This realm, according to Ortner, is nature, or the profane. But whereas Ortner develops an essentialist argument about women's "natural procreation functions" as the root of this identification, mine is a phenomenological argument about the ways this culture figures itself politically vis-à-vis reproduction.

39. Norman O. Brown makes a similar point in *Love's Body* (New York: Random House, 1966).

40. See also Fineman, *Neutered Mother*, 146–47.

41. Susan Griffin has shown the ways European philosophers, scientists, politicians, and novelists — virtually all men — developed and sustained a long history of associating women with nature and then asserting the superiority of masculinity by noting the triumph of men over both women and nature. This argument has been misread by many, who believe Griffin describes an essential identity of woman with nature. *Women and Nature* (New York: Harper and Colophon, 1978). Like Griffin's work, this essay maps the ways the courts assign women a particular status and then use and build the state's authority by manipulating that realm named "feminine" and "natural."

42. See *Child Custody and the Politics of Gender*, ed. Carol Smart and Selma Sevenhuij-sen (London: Routledge, 1989). Smart points out that the rhetoric on the child's need for the father aligns the father and child against the mother: "The more men's interests and children's interests are seen to coincide, the more mothers are disempowered." Ibid., 10. Nancy Erikson, "The Feminist Dilemma over Unwed Parents' Custody Rights," *Law and Inequality* 2 (1984): 447–72; Kathryn Katz, "Ghost Mothers: Human Egg Donation and the Legacy of the Past," *Albany Law Review* 57 (1994): 733–80.

43. Judge Montgomery, "Child Abuse and Changing Definitions," address at the annual meeting of the Child Abuse and Neglect Committee, published in *Texas Bar Journal* 57 (September 1994): 886.

44. A few words on the meaning of these decisions are in order. First, marriage statutes are written by state legislatures, which means they vary. Among the variations is the person authorized to signify that a wedding has been performed. Most states require a religious official or state magistrate; but some states exclude certain minister-by-mail "denominations," while a few allow anyone to sign the form. Second, some of what follows is taken from state supreme court opinions, and these also reveal discrepancies. I have provided information, when relevant, on the frequency of certain policies, such as surrogacy laws. Finally, these decisions are on cases the courts themselves deem "unique," "exceptional," or "unusual," and so one might wonder whether they help us understand the daily practices of most citizens. However, it is law that renders these situations marginal, not the parental disputes per se; without marriage law there is no "unique" marriage arrangement. In prompting a careful consideration of the "logic" of marriage rules, these cases provide insights that otherwise normalized understandings of marriage preclude.

45. *Caban*, 441 U.S. at 397, cited in *Lehr v. Robertson*, 463 U.S. 248, 260 (1982).

46. *Lehr*. States vary in requirements of paternal consent. In New York consent is not required, a law that Lehr said deprived him of a fundamental right. The court disagreed.

47. Ibid. at 267–68.

48. Ibid. at 269.

49. Ibid. at 248.

50. Ibid. at 268–76.

51. As of 1992, eighteen states had some regulations of surrogacy practices. Of these, eleven explicitly voided surrogacy contracts; four allowed surrogacy contracts, but held the surrogate's husband as the putative father, so that his consent for adoption was necessary; one made the father the legal parent (Arkansas); and one simply said that surrogacy contracts should not be considered "child selling" (West Virginia). I have relied for these numbers on the information provided in the appendix of Alice Hofheimer, "Gestational Surrogacy: Unsettling State Parentage Law and Surrogacy Policy," *New York University Review of Law*

and Social Change 19 (1992): 613–16. The states voiding the contracts have the same implications as those requiring the husband's consent for adoption, since if the contract is not recognized, the husband will be considered the legal father.

52. See *re Adoption of Reams*, 557 N.E.2d 159, 162 (1989).

53. Arkansas is clear on this, but the statute in New Hampshire is not so clear. On the one hand, it says that the husband is the putative father, but on the other hand, it says that "the paternity presumption is rebuttable." Ibid., 615. This seems to suggest an easy case for a biological father with a paternity test, but as we will see below, marriage may trump the "rebuttable presumption."

54. *Matter of Baby M.*, 537 A.2d 1227 (1988), and at 1253, 1254.

55. See *Lehr* and others.

56. *Reams* at 165, 164, emphasis added.

57. The Uniform Parentage Act, adopted by eighteen states as of 1993, says, "If, under the supervision of a licensed physician and with the consent of her husband, a wife is inseminated with semen donated by a man not her husband, the husband is treated in law as if he were the natural father of a child thereby conceived." Quoted in Hollace Stevenson, "Donor Anonymity in Artificial Insemination: Is It Still Necessary?" *Columbia Journal of Law and Social Problems* 27 (fall 1993): 162.

58. *Michael* at 2338.

59. The California statute reads, "the issue of a wife cohabiting with her husband, who is not impotent or sterile, is conclusively presumed to be a child of the marriage." Cal. Evid. Code Ann. Para. 621a. Michael's case was dismissed when Gerald was ruled the father, on the grounds that to do otherwise would "impugn the integrity of the family unit." Supp. App. to Juris. Statement, A-91, quoted in *Michael H. v. Gerald D.*, 491 U.S. 110 (1989). Michael appealed on the grounds that this decision violated his procedural and substantive due process rights, and was supported by Victoria's advocate, *Michael* at 2338, 2339.

60. *Michael* at 2339.

61. Ibid. at 2342 n. 3.

62. Ibid. at 2346.

63. Ibid.

64. The reasoning here resembles that of the decision in *Karin T. v. Michael T.*, 484 N.Y.S.2d 780 (1985), in which Michael T. was born "Marlene T." and held by the court as "indeed a female" (at 782). Nonetheless, the court held Michael T. responsible for child support payments, even though the marriage was "fraudulent" (784) and New York's Domestic Relations Law recognized parents only in "biological terms." The Court holds that since the legal form of Michael's commitment mirrored the legal form of a biological parent's commitment, Michael should be held responsible: "The actions of this respondent in executing the Agreement above referred to certainly brought forth these offspring as if done biologically. . . . This Court finds that under the unique facts of this case, respondent is indeed a 'parent' to whom such responsibility attaches" (784). When Michael took on the legal responsibility of a parent by agreeing to raise the children as Karin's husband — a legal status the state would not recognize — Michael effectively took on a biological status that the court would recognize, that of a "parent."

65. MSA 25.244 (1)b, cited in *Re: Baby Girl Clausen*, 1993 (No. 96366, Nos. 96441, 96531, 96532). Text from LEXIS on-line database.

66. Ibid.

67. Ibid., n. 45.

68. Durkheim, *Elementary Forms of Religious Life*, 466, emphasis added.

69. Ibid., 475.

70. Ibid., 123. Durkheim adds, "[T]he primitive family organization cannot be understood before the primitive religious beliefs are known; for the latter serve as the basis of the former. This is why it is necessary to study totemism as a religion before studying the totemic clan as a family group" (126 n. 24).

71. Ibid., 188.

72. The apparent exception of "naturalization" does not undermine kinship terms for membership, but is a copy that affirms the logic of the original. The words "nation" and "naturalization" share the same Latin root, *nasci*, which means birth.

73. Durkheim, *Elementary Forms of Religious Life*, 197.

74. Ibid., 284, paraphrasing Baldwin Spencer and F. J. Gillen, *The Native Tribes of Central Australia* (London, 1899); and *Northern Tribes of Central Australia* (London, 1904), cited in Durkheim, 110.

75. Ibid., 281 n. 49.

76. Ibid., 285.

77. Alice Adams, *Reproducing the Womb: Images of Childbirth in Science, Feminist Theory, and Literature* (Ithaca: Cornell University Press, 1994).

78. *Baehr v. Lewin*, 852 P.2d 44 (1993).

79. The organizations supporting same-sex marriage in Hawaii include the Japanese-American Citizens League, the Native Hawaiian Legal Corporation, and the National Asian Pacific American Bar Association. My source for this information is the Hawaii Equal Rights Marriage Project, http://www.xq.com/hermp/faq.html.

80. *Baehr* at 59–60. See also Noel Myricks and Roger Rubin, "Legalizing Gay and Lesbian Marriages: Trends and Policy Implications," *American Journal of Family Law* 9 (spring 1995): 35–44.

81. HR 3396, S 1740, 104th Congress, 2d Session, 1996.

82. Quoted in Elaine Herscher, "When Marriage Is a Tough Proposal," *San Francisco Chronicle*, May 15, 1995, A1, A10. Another anecdotal example associating the reproductive culture of heterosexuality with the well-being of the nation-state is Zimbabwe's president Robert Mugabe, who refused to allow a lesbian/gay booth to display texts at an international book fair in his country, saying that the exhibit would promote sodomy, which in turn would promote the view that men should give birth, which in turn would ruin the country. *New York Times*, August 2, 1995, A1, A10.

FOUR

American Sweatshops 1980s Style Chinese Women Garment Workers

PETER KWONG

The suffering of Chinese women in garment sweatshops is not a new story; they are only the latest group of immigrant women trapped in this industry, where in this age of computers they are still slaving away for subsistence wages, on century-old machines, at piece rate, under a primitive labor management setup. Today, with the available third world labor, garment manufacturers have shifted their production overseas seeking higher profits, throwing the whole industry into turmoil. Chinese factory owners in this country have lowered the workers' wages even further. The paternalistic labor union, overwhelmed by these developments, is more concerned for its own survival. Ultimately, the Chinese garment workers at the bottom bear the brunt of all these transgressions.

The conventional understanding is that Chinese immigrant women are docile and willing to withstand such treatment. Yet they are militant. Their consciousness is developing. One does not hear about them because as housewives, as employees, and as rank-and-file union members, isolated in ethnic communities, they are systematically deprived of their own voices and their right to make decisions affecting them. What they are experiencing is the oppression of sex, race, and class at its worst.

The Rise of the Chinese Garment Industry

Old Chinese communities in America had few women. The 1965 new immigration law made it possible for families to immigrate here as a unit. The number of Chinese women increased dramatically. The majority of them are able-bodied housewives of childbearing age between twenty and forty (Sung 1978; Sassen-Koob 1982).

Generally, Chinese with poor English and no marketable skills tend to live and look for jobs in Chinese communities. The men work in restaurants, where hours are long and wages low and there is no health insurance or job security. To supplement and safeguard the family finances, most wives find work in garment factories (Wu 1980). In the unionized factories, the women are able to get the critically needed health insurance for their families. With this pool of "willing" labor, factories in New York's Chinatown mushroomed; at present, there are 450 Chinese garment factories hiring 20,000 Chinese women workers (Kwong 1987, 30).

The Garment Industry and Its Structures

The garment industry's production and management structure is the most backward of all the industries in this country. On the top are the manufacturers, who determine what and how much to produce, and take charge of designing and pattern making, supply the fabric, and provide shipping and cutting facilities. The actual production is given to contractors, the factory owners, who hire workers to sew the garments. Once the garments are completed, the manufacturers merchandise them to retailers. So there are three levels: the manufacturers, the contractors, and the workers. Manufacturers require large capital to start, and since they initiate and receive the sales value of the products, they have decisive advantages over the contractors, who are small, require limited financing, and have many competitors. When the former offer lower prices to the contractors, they take the bid in order to beat out competitors and compensate the loss by squeezing the workers.

In this setup of unequal power, the manufacturers always try to maneuver themselves by shifting all the disadvantages downward. The garment industry is by nature seasonal and unstable, subject to changes in fashion, taste, and the health of the economy. In adverse circumstances, manufacturers simply stop ordering. The management of workers is left to the contractors. When workers demand higher wages, it is the contractors they confront, although the manufacturers are more responsible for the lower wages offered. Furthermore, the contractors are just labor managers with machines in a rented space. They have no incentive to invest in improving the technical and production processes and no incentive to improve the conditions of the workplace. This explains the barbaric, unhealthy, unsafe conditions the workers have to endure.

Today, manufacturers are investing in third world countries where the wages are one-tenth of those paid here. The number of jobs in the industry decreased dramatically. Between 1969 and 1980 in New York City alone, garment jobs fell by 40 percent. This was so in every part of New York except Chinatown, where jobs expanded from 8,000 to 20,000 during this same period. This is surprising, but it also defines the very conditions of work in Chinatown.

Garment work is harsh. Contractors always try to press wages down to the subsistence level. The work is at piece rate. The contractors treat the workers like slaves and the workers are their own slave drivers. To make more pieces and therefore more money, they do not stop to take breaks or lunches; they work as many hours as possible, which may mean from early morning to seven or eight o'clock at night, six days a week. The intensity of this labor is possible for the young and strong — after a few years most will not be able to keep up, and some develop painful backache or muscular disease. Those reaching their mid-thirties quit or take on less strenuous jobs such as cutting threads at even lower wages.

American-born workers, even those who are unemployed, would not stand for these conditions. The use of American-born workers in the past has proved to be unreliable, with high turnover and absentee rates. Historically, therefore, garment factories employ the weakest and most vulnerable in this society, that is, immigrant women.

The threat of imports puts pressure on many immigrant women of different ethnic backgrounds, but for many reasons many of them did not want to work in the garment industry (Petras 1980). The fact that these jobs are expanding in Chinatown shows that the structure of control in the Chinese community provides the additional elements needed to extract that extra surplus from the women workers.

Chinese Contractors

Chinese contractors are generally family businesses run by a male head of the household. They work extra hard, contending with a small margin of profits. They expect their workers to work hard as well. In their process of primitive accumulation, contractors squeeze surplus from every conceivable circumstance. They underpay the workers by cheating on the piece rates, do not pay overtime, ignore minimum wage and overtime rules, ignore safety and health regulations, underreport, and use double accounting or cash transactions to evade taxes. They make no apology to their workers, for they believe these new immigrant women are lucky to get jobs from them to begin with. And most contractors are from Hong Kong and Taiwan, where there is little tradition of fair labor practices.

But the productiveness of the Chinese garment industry has to be understood from the social and political environment of Chinatown. Historically, the community has been controlled by feudal village and clan associations and tongs with a rigid male hierarchical structure. These associations are the speakers for the community and are controlled by landlords, factory owners, and successful businessmen. Their leaders take the position that the prosperity of the garment industry is in the interest of the whole community and that the workers should "appreciate" the difficulties of the contractors and unite with them.

At the same time, contractors use all possible means to divert the class division within the community into racial issues against the outside. They claim to be victims of racial discrimination from "American manufacturers, white government inspectors, and Jewish union officials," all of whom, these contractors imply, have taken advantage of them because they are Chinese. These are powerful arguments at this time of heightened "racial" consciousness, even for liberal social workers and local Chinese media. At the least, they would all like to see problems between labor and management resolved within the community. Leaders of associations (all of whom are men), social welfare agencies, and Chinese newspapers all appeal to the "racial pride" and "common community interests" of the women workers and speak out, in their name, without their interests in mind.

In this pro-contractor environment, workers are constrained and unable to voice their grievances. And since most Chinese women have no other job options, they are discreet and not likely to take actions that would jeopardize their livelihood. One finds a job in a garment factory through word of mouth and through personal contact. Undisciplined or activist workers are easily screened out. "Troublemakers" on the job are fired and blacklisted. Two years ago a worker complained to the union about her employer. She was fired and the next day her picture appeared in several Chinatown papers with an "appeal" to have some kindhearted employer take her, since she is a good worker, but is not happy working at Factory X. Other workers who had challenged the bosses are known to receive threatening phone calls and find broken machines on their jobs.

These control systems make Chinese women workers "quiet" and "reliable." At the same time, Chinese contractors operating on the basis of the community "senti-ment" are able to extract high productivity from their workers. That is why the factories in the community are "doing well."

The Union and Chinese Women Workers

Considering their conditions, it is surprising that all Chinatown garment workers were organized by Local 23-25 of the International Ladies' Garment Workers' Union as early as 1974. Some union officials argue that the lack of improvement of these bad conditions is due to the fact that Chinese workers do not speak out and willingly cooperate with their Chinese employers. This is unfair. As a matter of fact, the ILGWU has one of the worst reputations among unions for its inability to organize the rank and file.

This reputation is not without justification, because from the start the union has never seen itself as primarily organizing the workers. The ILGWU believes that struggle solely against the contractors would not go very far, because they are, after all, marginal businesses. Meaningful union negotiations have to include manufac-turers, who ultimately have the money that affects the wage scale. The union tries to appeal to manufacturers' desire for "stable" production conditions by committing them to award jobs only to those contractors that hire union workers. So the ILGWU normally begins by organizing the manufacturers and not the workers first. Once the union comes to an agreement with large manufacturers, it then goes to the contractors. The contractors usually agree, because the union has control over the supply of work from manufacturers. Finally, through the contractors, the union unionizes the workers. This organizing method is from the top down rather than the other way around.

In this configuration, the union has divided loyalties. As a union, it represents the workers, but it also has to be sensitive to the problems of the manufacturers and contractors, otherwise they move away, or threaten to do so. Therefore, during contract negotiations the union "moderates" its demands to both, allowing them to make "'some money" and to "stay in business," and retaining for itself the right to organize the workers. It acts like a mediator among the three parties. For this reason, the union is sensitive to spontaneous rank-and-file movements that might throw off this delicate balance. No wonder the ILGWU over the years has earned the reputation of being a paternalistic union.

The Chinatown garment industry was organized the same way. When the American manufacturers recognized the "productive environment" of the Chinese community, they willingly signed an agreement with the union in the early 1970s to stabilize the labor situation in Chinatown. This was a very important breakthrough for the ILGWU, which was experiencing a rapid decline in membership everywhere else. It got the most out of this opportunity by signing up all the Chinatown contractors. It was a success; 95 percent of all Chinatown shops were organized and the union increased Local 23-25's Chinese membership to 20,000.

Chinatown was organized through the contractors; this was the easiest, quickest, and cheapest way for the union. However, Chinese women became members of the union without the experience of struggle. Once they joined, the ILGWU provided normal services, but made little effort to organize them. It had not established its own apparatus within the rank and file. This is a real problem. Most Chinese women have no union experience. Since they work in such an isolated ethnic setup, the power of the management remains dominant. In many factories shop stewards were chosen by management. In other cases ILGWU business agents, who represent the union in overseeing individual shops, are reported to get along better with and side regularly with the management. They look the other way when violations exist. There were even charges of agents taking bribes. Some observers suggest that this is inevitable, for if the union were to enforce all the rules in the contract, most of the Chinese contractors would be out of business.

When asked, union officials generally agree that there may be a few instances of this type, but insist that the union would prosecute "vigorously" if the workers filed complaints. In Chinatown few ever did. Furthermore, the union claims that Chinese workers cooperate with management by knowingly working off the books, not reporting management's cheating on piece rates, secretly working on jobs gotten from nonunionized manufacturers, or even taking jobs to do them at home. This type of behavior makes the union's enforcement impossible.

In any event, the union, at least before 1982, seemed to take the position that Chinese women are difficult to organize because they are too passive and too tied down by the Chinatown political and social structure. Nor did the union see the potential of these women to play a significant role in the labor movement or in the Chinese community. Chinese members, on the other hand, did not expect the union to do much either. They saw it as but another bureaucratic authority: they paid dues to it and got health benefits in return.

Activism of Chinese Women

Then, in the summer of 1982, during the negotiation of a new contract, the image of passive Chinese women was shattered. It was a regular three-year contract renewal, with standard increases. The manufacturers signed, and the union and the negotiating unit for the contractors (i.e., the Greater Blouse, Skirts, and Undergarment Association [GBSUA]; this is translated as "Foreigners' Garment Merchants' Association" in Chinese) also agreed with the terms. Unexpectedly, the Chinese contractors as a group balked and claimed that the GBSUA did not represent them, because it did not consult them throughout the negotiation. They were angry, for even though 85 percent of the firms were Chinese, no Chinese were on the negotiating team. Furthermore, Chinatown shops were the only group that was doing well, and thus were the backbone of New York's garment industry. As the vital segment of Chinatown's economy, they expected the Chinese community to rally behind them, particularly in this clear instance of "racial discrimination." This was the time, thought the Chinese contractors, to exert their influence by pushing back the power of the union.

The union had not expected this and wanted to head off this challenge by a show of force. Demonstrations to defend the contract were called. According to some accounts, the union leaders had no idea how the Chinese women would react. The staff who worked with the Chinese were not close enough to the members to be able to predict. Some people doubted that the Chinese women would turn out on a class issue, in order to confront their own people in Chinatown.

Once the call went out, the reaction was overwhelming. Hundreds of women volunteered: some operated the phone bank to contact individual members, others made bilingual leaflets, banners, and propaganda material. Different shops were mobilized by militant leaders who came out from the rank and file. On the day of the first demonstration, 20,000 workers showed up. This was a historic event. Never before had the Chinese turned out on this scale for a labor issue, much less the Chinese women. The contractors backed off right away and the workers won a new contract.

This event showed that Chinese women were conscious, but could not act on isolated individual factory floors. They were silenced by the community's conservative establishment, which represents owners and landlords. If this tight grip was to be broken, intervention had to come from outside. The ILGWU's call for mass mobilization was what the Chinese women needed to rally around and act together. The critical point was that the union had showed its support for the workers, who realized that they did not have to cooperate with the management and in fact repudiated those who did.

The 1982 event also showed that mobilized Chinese women are a powerful force to be reckoned with. As a group, they can challenge reactionary forces and shift the balance of the community to their advantage. However, the ILGWU as an institution has never been comfortable with "activated" rank and file, for they threaten the maneuverability of union leadership in bargain negotiations, and the power of control over membership by the union officials.

Over the years, the ILGWU has developed different techniques to keep control. The most controversial one is restricting leadership to white men (Liebman 1979) even though membership of the International Ladies' Garment Workers' Union has always been overwhelmingly female, and the ethnic composition has changed over the years from Jewish to Italian, to Black, to Puerto Rican, and is now mainly Chinese and Hispanic (Laurentz 1980). At present 85 percent of Local 23-25 members are Chinese. Only in the past few years has the union replaced more and more of its staff with Chinese; none, however, are in the top ranks. And the general understanding is that only the non-Chinese union officials make important decisions. Recently, reporters from a number of Chinese newspapers organized a series of forums inviting different concerned parties to exchange ideas on the upcoming union negotiation. The highest ranking Chinese on the union staff was asked and agreed to come, but at the last minute those higher up told him not to. Representatives from the contractors' side came, and the papers reported only their side of the story.

Another method of control is to recruit activists and politically conscious elements onto the union staff and direct their energy into "acceptable" projects. Local 23-25 has recruited several of the most militant workers of the 1982 strike onto the union staff. The purpose was to get them involved in Chinatown affairs to make the union's presence in the community felt. In this way, progressive and labor forces in the community can count on the union to form a united front, thereby improving the position of all the Chinatown working people. These are honorable objectives, and the Chinese staff members are energetic and committed, but they are involved with so many high-profile issues that one begins to wonder whether this is simply the union's public relations stance. At one time, several ILGWU staff members' pictures were shown in Chinese papers in a demonstration at the South African consulate against apartheid. This is a worthy cause; however, most members were more upset with the union's cutback on health benefits, and more concerned about the uncertainty of the upcoming contract negotiations. No wonder a commentator once observed that the ILGWU has a complete foreign policy but not a position on its workers.

Present Problems and the New Contract Negotiations

The garment industry in America is confronting a devastating crisis. In the last twenty years, imports have jumped from 11 percent to 54 percent of the U.S. market. This means that manufacturers are leaving, including those who originally signed contracts with the union. Today, the unionized manufacturers that remain can provide jobs for only one-third of the Chinatown factories. Some shops only get sporadic orders, thus laying off workers for weeks at a time. And since the health insurance, which is managed by the union, is mainly funded by manufacturers' contributions, their withdrawal has brought the whole system to the verge of bankruptcy. The union is forced to increase membership contributions and to make more stringent rules, excluding those who make less than $4,100 a year. Women working in factories that do not get sufficient job orders do not make enough to qualify for benefits. This is particularly bad for cutters and the unskilled newcomers, who don't make much more than ten dollars a day. The union's new health benefits rule, therefore, caused panic in the community, for most Chinese women are dependent on the union health benefits to protect their families.

In the meantime, the Chinese contractors have solicited jobs from nonunion manufacturers to fill the void, but refuse to report this to the union to avoid having to pay contributions to the union membership funds. This is a clear contract violation, but cheating on this level is so widespread that the union is not able to control it. In fact, some factory managers simply give the material to the workers and ask them to do the work at home.

The industry's prospect is so bleak that the union is unable to unionize new manufacturers to replace those that left. The workers are caught in a bind: in order to have jobs to live on, they are forced to cooperate with the management. Again, the contractors try to use this opportunity to isolate the union by appealing to workers' ethnic solidarity. They claim that the union, an outside force, is not sensitive to the problems of the Chinese and that its unreasonable demands will kill the "community industry." Some even go so far as to suggest that the workers should leave the union, promising that they would provide a much better health benefit plan for the workers.

Up to this point, the union has explained little to the workers about the strategy to protect the workers in this new contract negotiation, insisting that bargaining positions are not to be discussed in public. In the meantime, it blames all the problems on imports. In fact, the union sponsored a citywide demonstration against imports. One can imagine the difficulties for the Chinese women to march in such a demonstration, which is aimed mainly at imports made by Chinese in Hong Kong, Taiwan, and the Chinese People's Republic.

The Workers' Struggle for Women's Rights

At the bottom of all these contradictions is the issue of sexism. The dominance of men in this general environment is so absolute that women's rights as an issue have not even surfaced. At the first meeting of the 1985 contract talks, all the representatives of the manufacturers and contractors were men, on the union side they were also all men, and the reporters from local Chinese newspapers covering the event were all men. Each side had a chance to voice its own version of the difficulties it faced, but the female workers did not have this chance, even though they are the foundation on which the whole industry rests. Their interests are represented by male union officials, who were not even sensitive enough to know of their own sexism. These are the oppressive conditions that Chinese women are under; they are exploited by the Chinese owners, silenced by the community feudal institutions, and disenfranchised of their rights of representation by the union.

Yet Chinese women have not been passive. The mobilization of 1982 has stirred up Chinese women's interests in union affairs, and caused them to expect more and be more critical of the union. The women realized that the union's commitment to them was limited. Changes could come about only by their own conscious and organized efforts to push the union forward. A group of activists gathered. At first, they met as members of a Chinese choral group, to avoid hostile union attention. After a few meetings together, one urgent issue stared them in the face: the need for day care. Among the 20,000 members, there are parents of an estimated 1,000 preschool children. Since working mothers labor long hours and cannot leave their children at home, they bring them to work. But the unhealthy and unsafe factory conditions are hazardous. Several children were injured when they fell into elevator pits. Members of this original group appealed to the union for action. The president of the union local at the time was outraged at such suggestions, claiming that this was not a union concern, much less the concern of the rank and file. Furthermore, if the union set up a day care center for the Chinese, all other ethnic groups in the union would want it too. Lastly, the union had no money. The official was suspicious of such spontaneous demands made by members. Only when he was sure the workers had no ulterior motives, and also realized the explosive nature of such a popular demand, did he acquiesce. The union raised enough funds and took the credit for establishing a day care center presently accommodating seventy-five children.

Many more women became involved over the day care issue. They requested the formation of a Chinese chapter of the Committee of Labor Union Women (CLUW) within the local. The objectives of this nationwide organization are stated vaguely: to promote women's rights and fight for the unionization of unorganized women. The union gave consent, after making sure the top leaders of this chapter were from the union staff. The need to form a women's chapter to promote the women's cause inside this supposedly women's union is most ironic. But for the women, CLUW offered them a separate base with a degree of autonomy to organize among the Chinese women workers.

At their first fund-raising banquet, the organization's potential was apparent. Chinese women from the factories came out in full strength to support this event. Within one week, six hundred dinner reservations and thousands of raffle tickets were sold. This was done mainly through the women's informal but extensive social networks. For the first time, it seemed that the women felt that they had their own organization to work for. They were full of energy, optimism, and a sense of solidarity.

The effectiveness of this group in influencing the union is yet to be seen. But it's clear that Chinese women workers are not docile, for they want a better life for themselves and their families. That is why they are straining to find ways to pull themselves out of these isolated ghetto exploitations. It is in this spirit that they had supported the union, and will continue to do so even though the union has not fully protected and supported them as it should. In time they will develop unity and strength; their progress cannot be stopped, with or without the help of the union.

REFERENCES

Kwong, Peter. 1987. *The New Chinatown.* New York: Hill and Wang.
———. 1996. *The New Chinatown.* Rev. ed. New York: Hill and Wang.
Laurentz, Robert. 1980. "Racial/Ethnic Conflict in the New York City Garment Industry, 1933–1980." Ph.D. diss., SUNY Binghamton.
Liebman, Arthur. 1979. *Jews and the Left.* New York: Wiley.

Local 23-25 International Ladies' Garment Workers' Union and New York Shirt and Sportswear Association. 1983. *The Chinatown Garment Industry Study.* By Abeles, Schwartz, Haeckel, and Silverblatt. June.

Petras, Elizabeth McLean. 1980. "Toward a Theory of International Migration: The New Division of Labor." In *Source Book on the New Immigration*, ed. Roy Simon Bryce-Laporte. New Brunswick, NJ: Transaction.

Sassen-Koob, Saskia. 1982. "Recomposition and Peripheralization at the Core." In *The New Nomads*, ed. Marlene Dixon and Susanne Jonas. San Francisco: Synthesis.

Sung, Betty Lee. 1978. *Chinese Population of Lower Manhattan, 1978.* U.S. Department of Labor, Employment and Training Administration.

Wu, Yuan-Li, ed. 1980. *The Economic Condition of Chinese Americans.* Monograph 3. Chicago: Pacific/Asian American Mental Health Research Center.

FIVE

Women, Work, and the Politics of Fetal Rights

RACHEL ROTH

In 1979, women chemical workers at the American Cyanamid plant in Willow Island, West Virginia, were told that their work was dangerous for fetuses, and that they could not keep their jobs if they were even capable of getting pregnant. This effectively forced them to choose between being sterilized or unemployed. In a cruel twist of irony, the women who got tubal ligations were all laid off the following year anyway, when their department in the plant was closed (Petchesky 1984, 350; Bertin 1989, 278).

"Fetal protection" policies like American Cyanamid's are not isolated practices, but part of a broader political trend to reinforce women's subordination. Over the past twenty years, the assertion of fetal rights has been used to regulate women's most fundamental decisions in every state in the United States, diminishing women's power to live independent, purposeful lives. Women have been subject to a range of intrusions that men have not, ranging from unsolicited advice from waiters when they order drinks to invasive medical procedures without their consent and criminal prosecution for failing to follow their doctor's orders during pregnancy (see Kantrowitz 1991; Kolder et al. 1987; Warren 1987).

Because rights claims resonate so deeply with American political and cultural values, fetal rights claims have been taken seriously in the political arena, and courts and legislatures have granted rights to fetuses. The logic of fetal rights depends on certain rhetorical constructions. Proponents of fetal rights oppose them rhetorically to women's rights, constructing a contest of equal antagonists with only one possible winner (see Condit 1995). Another frequent formulation opposes fetal rights to women's responsibilities. These formulations have become so pervasive that supposedly neutral figures like news reporters use them without thinking about their implications. But what both of these constructions do is obscure the way fetal rights function to distribute costs. When a court or other institution decides to award rights, it has to assign the costs of those rights to some individual or collectivity. Fetal rights impose tangible costs on women. These costs can't be measured solely in terms of money, although that is certainly at stake. Women also experience costs to their freedom, physical and mental security, identity, and privacy when they are subjected to court-ordered cesarean operations against their will and when they incur added civil and criminal penalties for using drugs or alcohol during pregnancy (Roth 1993). When women are assigned responsibility for taking care of fetuses, without being given the resources they need to do this, they can lose their confidence in the fairness of social institutions, and that in turn creates costs for all of society.

What is so problematic about fetal rights is that *women* are made to bear almost all the costs, rather than the costs being distributed more evenly across society. Consider, for instance, how the demands of disabled people to participate fully in American life have led to newly articulated rights of access to education, transportation, and work. In this case, when government actors and institutions decided that those rights claims had merit, they distributed the attendant costs broadly to taxpayers, employers, and consumers (see, e.g., the Americans with Disabilities Act). In the case of workplace fetal protection policies, the opposite is true: only women are made to pay, and the very high price exacted is to protect *potential* fetuses that may never even be conceived. Had either the courts or American Cyanamid taken women's rights, workers' rights, or even fetal rights seriously, the company would have been compelled to clean up the workplace instead of discriminating against women.

Fetal protection policies starkly dramatize the socially ascribed tension between women's economic and reproductive activity. This essay will describe the struggle over fetal protection policies in the courts, paying special attention to this tension. Court decisions matter because of the significant impact they have on people's lives. Court decisions are also interesting and important for a second reason. Courts don't simply announce decisions; they have to explain them in written opinions, and those opinions offer rich texts that allow us to analyze what is at stake in the negotiation of social conflicts. After a brief historical overview of how the Supreme Court has understood pregnancy and motherhood among women workers, this essay will examine the case of *United Auto Workers v. Johnson Controls, Inc.* in depth, showing how the social construction of gender in judicial discourse influences rulings. The final section compares the *Johnson Controls* case to other fetal rights struggles over pregnant women's medical care and drug use. The politics of fetal rights in the workplace hinges on gender and economics; in many other arenas, race also plays a significant role in shaping the terrain of fetal rights politics.

Women Workers and the Next Generation

Discrimination against women in employment on the basis of reproduction is not new (Baer 1978). Historically, such discrimination has been justified not because it benefits women but because it benefits the next generation. In its 1905 decision

Lochner v. New York, the U.S. Supreme Court struck down a maximum hours law as unconstitutional interference with a worker's right to contract. Then three years later it upheld an Oregon law specifically prohibiting *women* from working more than ten hours per day, because their role as mothers allegedly rendered them weak, dependent, and inferior. The Court reasoned in *Muller v. Oregon* (1908) as follows:

> That woman's physical structure and the performance of maternal functions place her at a disadvantage in the struggle for subsistence is obvious. This is especially true when the burdens of motherhood are upon her. . . . [A]s healthy mothers are essential to vigorous offspring, the physical well-being of woman becomes an object of public interest and care in order to preserve the strength and vigor of the race. . . .
> . . . [T]here is that in her disposition and habits of life which will operate against a full assertion of [her] rights. . . . [S]he is so constituted that . . . her physical structure and a proper discharge of her maternal functions — having in view not merely her own health, but the well-being of the race — justify legislation to protect her. . . . The limitations which this statute places upon her contractual powers . . . are not imposed solely for her benefit, but also largely for the benefit of all. (208 U.S. 412, 416–17, 421, 422)

Interestingly, the ideology of protection did not always hold when it came to other kinds of employment regulation, like setting minimum wages. The Supreme Court ruled in *Adkins v. Children's Hospital* (1923) that the District of Columbia's establishment of a minimum wage for women workers unduly interfered with their freedom of contract. The Court claimed that the matter of wages could be distinguished from the matter of hours, which had to do with women's unique physical limitations. In addition, the Court specifically argued that the Nineteenth Amendment, granting women the vote, forbade singling women out for such special protection.

In his dissenting opinion, Justice Taft criticized the Court's reliance on the myth of freedom of contract. Taft wrote that legislatures adopting minimum wages "proceed on the assumption that employees in the class receiving least pay *are not upon a full level of equality of choice* with their employer," and therefore need government protection from exploitation (my emphasis; 261 U.S. 525, at 562).

Whatever interest the Court had previously displayed in the well-being of women workers' children seems to disappear here, for surely the amount of money a woman could earn would have an impact on the "strength and vigor" of her children, and hence "the race." Although the Court did not use the language of fetal rights, its reasoning is familiar today: society protects "children" while they are in the womb. Once they are born and therefore actually *become* children, their "rights" cease to exist.

During the 1960s Congress passed comprehensive civil rights legislation. Martha Gilbert and other female employees of G.E. used Title VII of the 1964 Civil Rights Act (prohibiting discrimination in employment on the basis of race, color, national origin, religion, or sex) to launch a class action suit against the company's disability benefits policy, which did not cover routine pregnancy care. Gilbert argued that the exclusion of pregnancy from coverage discriminated against her and other women workers because of sex (*General Electric v. Martha Gilbert et al.* (1976), 97 S.Ct. 401). The lower court ruled for Gilbert, but the Supreme Court did not. Quoting from an earlier decision, the Court asserted that "while it is true that only women can become pregnant, it does not follow that every legislative classification concerning pregnancy is a sex-based classification" (97 S.Ct. 401, at 407).[1] Rather, it found that "an exclusion of pregnancy from a disability benefits plan providing general coverage is not a gender-based discrimination at all," because "for all that appears, pregnancy-related disabilities constitute an *additional* risk, unique to women" (emphasis in original; 97 S.Ct. 401, at 408 and 410). This logic exposes the androcentric bias in law: women are being measured against a male standard, and any way that women deviate from men is considered extraordinary, or at the very least "extra."[2] Biased benefits packages like G.E.'s reflect the continuing assumption that men are primary breadwinners and women merely supplemental workers.

After the *Gilbert* decision, a coalition of feminist and labor groups lobbied Congress to make it clear that treating women workers differently on the basis of pregnancy *does* mean treating them differently on the basis of sex, and in 1978 Congress added the Pregnancy Discrimination Act to Title VII. Specifically, the act prohibits discrimination against workers on the basis of "pregnancy, childbirth, or related medical conditions," and requires that pregnant or potentially pregnant workers similar to other employees in their "ability or inability to work" must be "treated the same" for all employment-related purposes (42 U.S.C.A. 2000e(k)). As we shall see, discrimination on this basis can be upheld only under very restricted circumstances.

From Limits to Exclusion

The most significant "fetal protection" case is *United Auto Workers v. Johnson Controls, Inc.* (1991), in which a group of unions and workers challenged Johnson Controls' sweeping exclusion of all fertile women from jobs working with lead *and* jobs from which they could be promoted to positions working with lead. This is the first and only of several cases challenging fetal protection policies brought during the 1970s and 1980s to reach the Supreme Court. The case exemplifies how sexist ideology embedded in culture and law shapes judicial outcomes. The reasoning of the lower court opinion epitomizes this kind of biased jurisprudence, and for that reason is very important, even though it was ultimately overruled (see Kenney 1992 for a comprehensive review of litigation).

Based in Milwaukee, Johnson Controls is the nation's biggest manufacturer of automobile batteries. Lead is an essential ingredient in batteries, and one that can adversely affect neurological development in fetuses or young children and increase the risk of strokes and heart attacks in adults. In 1977, Johnson Controls started a program to warn employees of the reproductive risks associated with exposure to lead, and required women to sign a form indicating that they had been informed. Five years later, the company switched from a policy of informing women to a policy of shutting them out.

The policy excluded all women up to age seventy who could not prove they were sterile, regardless of their intentions to become parents or to have more children. The workers who sued the company included a woman who had been sterilized in order to keep her job, a man who was refused a temporary transfer in order to reduce the level of lead in his blood so that he and his wife could plan a pregnancy, and a woman who had been transferred out of her production job to one washing other workers' protective equipment. Most of the female plaintiffs were over fifty years old. Johnson Controls justified its policy by noting that during a five-year period (1979–83), a total of eight employees became pregnant while their blood lead levels exceeded the threshold recommended by the Occupational Safety and Health Administration for *male and female* workers planning children. There was no proof of birth defects or other abnormalities among the children. The company successfully defended its policy in the district court, and the union appealed.

The Seventh Circuit Court of Appeals saw this case as a question of disparate impact rather than disparate treatment. Under Title VII of the Civil Rights Act, workers can challenge a discriminatory policy in two ways. They can claim to suffer from disparate *impact* when a neutral-sounding policy has a discriminatory effect on an identifiable group, or they can claim disparate *treatment* when a policy explicitly treats one group differently from another. In cases of disparate treatment, employers must prove that the trait by which they discriminate is a BFOQ, a "bona fide occupational qualification reasonably necessary to the normal operation of that particular business or enterprise" (42 U.S.C.A. 2000e-2(e)). In contrast, employers can justify neutral policies that have a disparate impact on one sex with a more lenient defense known as "business necessity," which can be met if the practice serves legitimate employment goals (*UAW v. Johnson Controls, Inc.*, 866 F.2d 871, at 887). Although these standards may sound vague and similar to each other, courts have interpreted them differently. The term "reasonably necessary" has been interpreted quite narrowly, so that an employer must prove that the discrimination is very important to the proper functioning of the business and that less restrictive alternatives have been exhausted. The business necessity defense is less stringent and also shifts the burden of proof from the employer to the plaintiff, who must establish that she suffered discrimination (see Becker 1994 for an overview of Title VII doctrine). The Seventh Circuit Court upheld Johnson Controls' policy in a seven to four decision by interpreting it as a facially neutral policy, arguing that even though it applied only to women, it "effectively and equally" protected the offspring of male and female employees, and was therefore not illegal sex discrimination (866 F.2d 871, at 885).

In its opinion, the court transforms the potential fetuses that fertile women working at the factory might someday conceive into "unborn children." It then attributes compelling interests to these unborn children, on which they cannot act in their own behalf. These interests must be balanced against the employer's and employees', but ultimately everyone's interests are fulfilled except women's. The employer continues operating the business without fear of tort liability; the fetus can be conceived in a body free from lead contamination; and the woman loses her well-paid union job. Johnson Controls assumes, and the court allows, that female employees have only maternal interests, and that these are equivalent to their born or unborn children's. But the court goes even further, approving of "Johnson's interest in protecting the health of the unborn *through* the female employee" (my emphasis; 866 F.2d 871, at 899). Here, the court allows the company to turn women into vehicles for the interests of others, even the interests of nonexistent beings.

All the justices seem to assume that women who become pregnant always carry their pregnancies to term. But women's reproductive experiences are not dichotomous — either sterility or mandatory childbearing. Women can and do control their fertility through birth control and abortion, a fact that neither the majority nor the dissenting opinion mentions. Women who want to work in battery production and postpone childbearing can exercise their legal right to have an abortion if they get pregnant while working in a high-lead environment. The omission of this possibility is consistent with the majority's implicit view that women are incapable of deciding for themselves what job they want, what level of risk is acceptable, and what childbearing plans to make.

Because the court defined Johnson Controls' policy as gender-neutral, it evaluated it under the disparate impact/business necessity model. The business necessity defense can include such considerations as how hiring certain workers will affect costs and safety to customers or other third parties. However, it is not so broad as to include general ethical or moral concerns. When courts violate this standard and accept general societal interests in the health of future unborn children as a legitimate "business necessity" defense for restricting women, they hold women exclusively responsible for producing healthy children who will not be economic burdens on society. Here, where pregnancy is grounds for constraining a woman, pregnancy is considered of general social interest. More often, when pregnancy might be grounds for providing aid to women, as in the case of poverty, pregnancy is considered a woman's "private" affair, carrying no social entitlement to adequate wages or health care. If companies that manufacture hazardous products really cared about the health of future generations, not to mention the health of its workforce, they would take steps to make the workplace as safe as possible. One of the dissenting opinions noted cynically that the majority had to analyze the case as disparate impact, because the company couldn't win otherwise (866 F.2d 871, at 910). *Johnson Controls* recalls *Muller v. Oregon*, portraying women as having one primary role in life — reproduction.

Rejecting the lower court's reasoning, the Supreme Court unanimously struck down Johnson Controls' fetal protection policy in the spring of 1991. Although all nine justices concurred in the judgment, they filed three separate opinions disputing the scope of the precedent they wanted to set.[3] The majority held that a fetal protection policy excluding women cannot be upheld, because it singles out some workers on the basis of their ability to become pregnant, and that clearly violates the Pregnancy Discrimination Act.

The Supreme Court correctly saw the case as a question of disparate treatment. As discussed earlier, when employers like Johnson Controls discriminate overtly, they can justify their policies only by satisfying the BFOQ defense. In other words, to justify requiring sterility of women, an employer must prove that pregnancy or the potential to become pregnant interferes materially with a woman's ability to do her job. In this case, the court rejected the claim that childbearing capacity impairs women's ability to make batteries. The majority considers its ruling neither remarkable nor unprecedented; it does "no more than hold that the Pregnancy Discrimination Act means what it says" (111 S.Ct. 1196, 1210).

The decision in a 1990 California case about the same policy further exposes the way paternalistic biases swayed the ruling of the Seventh Circuit Court of Appeals. The California case arose when a woman at Globe Battery, a Johnson Controls subsidiary, was denied a production job exposing her to lead. She challenged the policy under state law instead of under Title VII, and a court of appeals agreed that excluding fertile women violated California's fair employment laws and regulations. The court summarized,

> The Company's policy is predicated upon the presumption that the employer is better situated to safeguard the interests of a woman's future offspring, should there be an unexpected pregnancy, than is the woman herself — i.e. that society's interest in fetal safety is best served, not by fully informing women of the risks involved and allowing them to make informed choices, not by fixing the workplace, but rather by removing from women the opportunity to make any choices in the matter at all. (*Johnson Controls, Inc. v. California Fair Employment and Housing Commission*, 90 Daily Journal D.A.R. 2410)

This critique captures an attitude that is widely shared by employers and judges, who frequently treat women as incapable of making important decisions. In fact, women have to make important decisions all the time under real material constraints, such as job availability and income. Women took jobs at American Cyanamid because they offered the only living wage in the area (Faludi 1991, 441). At fifteen to twenty dollar per hour, Johnson Controls' battery production jobs are among the highest paying in Bennington, Vermont (Kilborn 1991). Queen Foster sued Globe Battery in Fullerton, California, because she wanted to double her income by becoming a machine operator instead of a clerical worker (Glanton 1988). These factories are often the biggest employer in town, and exist alongside primarily low-paying service sector jobs that do not provide health benefits or opportunity for advancement. The "choice" women are supposed to make is untenable when they have families they must support or when they need money now but may want children later. The rhetoric of free choice simply doesn't measure up to economic reality.

In its 1977 warning policy, Johnson Controls recognized that trying to assume prospective parents' responsibility to protect future children would infringe on their employees' rights "as persons." But fear of having to pay damages to their employees' children made them change their moral stance. Dropping its concern for women as persons, the company shifted its concern to children only, announcing, "To knowingly poison unborn children is morally reprehensible. Johnson Controls will do everything in its power to avoid having that happen at our manufacturing plants" (cited in Daniels 1993, 64).

Why, then, did Johnson Controls refuse to allow male workers concerned about harming their future children to transfer temporarily out of production jobs involving lead? This refusal belies any full commitment to fetal welfare, or to cost control, since the children of male workers might sue the company. Instead, it reveals a false construction of the problem of workplace safety as one resting entirely with women, which led to a "solution" of discrimination instead of other possible arrangements the company could have made.

Compared with men, women have borne the full moral costs, the blame, for imperfect children. Both scientific research and employment restrictions have singled them out.[4] No one talked about excluding men from the workplace, because no one took seriously the possibility that they could harm their children prior to conception. As Johnson Controls' expert witness put it, "If you don't look for a problem, you don't find it" (*Johnson Controls, Inc. v. California Fair Employment and Housing Commission*, 2414). After all, if companies excluded both fertile men and women from their factories, they would have to close down.

Future litigation on more narrowly tailored fetal protection policies will have to determine the ultimate scope of women's right to work. As things now stand, the Supreme Court will not permit employers to allay their concerns about fetal vulnerability by externalizing all the costs of fetal protection onto women. Because of this decision, women should not be closed out of some twenty million jobs involving exposure to toxins (Greenhouse 1991). However, sharp disagreements divide the Court. For instance, White, Rehnquist, and Kennedy believe that a policy excluding only pregnant women could meet the BFOQ defense. The changing composition of the Court, along with changes in technology, politics, and culture, leaves open the question of women's equality in employment.[5]

The Politics of Fetal Rights

Not only is *Johnson Controls* the most significant case about a fetal protection policy, it also represents the most significant victory for women over the politics of fetal rights. Women have been less successful in challenging other kinds of restrictions where the logic of fetal rights continues to prevail.

Three key ideological components at work in the decision of the Seventh Circuit upholding Johnson Controls' policy appear in other fetal rights struggles, especially those over pregnant women's medical care and drug use: that women have only maternal interests; that women are vehicles for the interests of others; and that women are incapable of making decisions. It is beyond the scope of this essay to investigate whether these ideologies are constituted by categories in addition to gender; however, their translation into practice has very much to do with race and poverty.

Since the 1970s, pregnant women's control over their own medical care has been seriously eroded. Pregnant women are treated differently from all other patients in 71 percent (thirty-five) of the states that allow people to specify in living wills how doctors should treat them if they become injured or terminally ill and can no longer communicate their wishes. In fully 42 percent (twenty) of these states, a pregnant woman's living will is categorically invalidated, regardless of the stage of gestation; only three states explicitly permit women to give instructions regarding pregnancy (Roth 1995). Pregnant women have been ordered by judges to submit to cesarean deliveries and other invasive medical procedures against their will, compromising the commitments to informed consent and bodily integrity that law and medicine supposedly embrace. Procedures are most likely to be forced on women who are socially marginal in some way: poor women, members of a minority religious group that proscribes medical intervention, or members of a racial or ethnic minority, including immigrant communities that do not speak English as a primary language (see Kolder et al. 1987). Currently, policy makers are calling for mandatory testing and treatment of pregnant women in response to the results of a study suggesting that giving AZT to HIV-positive women during pregnancy and delivery can reduce the incidence of HIV among their newborns. Many doctors feel encouraged to adopt this protocol, regardless of whether AZT is indicated for the pregnant woman *herself* (Farber 1995; Kolata 1994). This change in protocol will have a significant impact on the treatment of Latina and Black women, who are disproportionately infected with HIV ("Update" 1995).

During the past decade, a second trend of singling out pregnant women for different treatment has emerged: the prosecution of pregnant women who take drugs or drink alcohol. Women have been charged with everything from prenatal child abuse and assault with a deadly weapon to distributing drugs to a minor through the umbilical cord (Paltrow 1992). These charges are usually the work of a creative district attorney who relies on laws written for other purposes, since no legislature has yet passed a law treating drug use during pregnancy differently from any other drug crime. While the charges are ad hoc, the pattern of prosecution is not. Only 30 percent of the women prosecuted have been white, even though white women use illegal drugs and alcohol during pregnancy at rates comparable to those of women of other races (Paltrow 1992; see also Roberts 1991). This criminalization of pregnancy has taken place in a national context of grossly inadequate drug and alcohol treatment services for pregnant women (Chavkin 1990).

The idea that women have only maternal interests is especially resonant in all three of the medical care examples: women should put the interests of their fetus's health ahead of their own. This point is closely related to the second, that women are merely vehicles for the interests of others. While few people see women in the drug prosecution scenario as having maternal interests, the same ideology is still at work setting the standards by which these women are judged. People frequently assume that pregnant women who use drugs — out of addiction or for recreation — have no maternal interests at all, but rather are some kind of monstrous anti-mothers (Tsing 1990). Because they are seen as monsters, it is even easier to treat them as means rather than ends, to focus on punishing women for harming the fetus rather than on rehabilitating them, and to take their children away after birth. Pregnant women with HIV, many of whom have drug addictions, are similarly seen as pariahs.

Finally, the idea that women cannot make decisions and should defer to the expert judgments of others bolsters the political viability of all these practices. Women's decisions to give birth vaginally are overruled when doctors think that it will be dangerous, although in hindsight doctors have often been proved wrong. Women's deliberations about their desires for life-sustaining treatment are completely nullified in the presence of an embryo or fetus, regardless of their own views about being kept alive as a human incubator in an unconscious state. For the sake of their fetus, all pregnant women with HIV are now expected to take AZT, a drug well known for its toxic properties, regardless of what stage their infection has reached and whether the drug would be prescribed for them were they not pregnant.[6] In all these instances, pregnant women are held to standards of behavior that would not be enforceable against any other member of the community. The fetus's "rights" are held to trump any interest women have in determining their own care during pregnancy, regardless of the harm women incur in the process.

Women with substance abuse problems are held responsible for their initial decisions to take drugs, but are not given much assistance or compassion when drug dependence does compromise their ability to make decisions. The prosecution of women for conduct during pregnancy probably represents the most vicious complex of ideological forces — the promotion of fetal rights at women's expense combines with racism, abandonment of the inner city, and the "war on drugs" to leave poor Black, Latina, and Native American women with a precarious hold on their civil rights and their health.

Although there are many ideological similarities among medical, prosecution, and workplace fetal rights practices, there are important structural differences that help account for the different political outcomes. As Cynthia Daniels explains, *Johnson Controls* was an excellent test case because the policy was so extremely broad and because lead is perhaps the best understood workplace toxin (Daniels 1993, 91, 65). The Pregnancy Discrimination Act provided an effective means to challenge the policy and an effective forum as well — the federal courts and ultimately the Supreme Court, whose decisions have national jurisdiction. Because the stakes were so high, resources could be marshalled from a wide array of feminist, civil liberties, labor, and public health groups to press the case.

Most other fetal rights battles are being fought at the state and local levels, which means that even important victories are geographically circumscribed, and change is more incremental. It is harder to rally assistance for an ongoing series of individual cases than for a single high-profile case. In the absence of explicit state legislation on things like forced medical treatment or the application of drug trafficking laws to pregnant women, women have successfully argued that the laws and reasoning applied to their cases were being used in a way that the legislature did not intend. The case of Jennifer Johnson in Florida is probably the most celebrated: the state supreme court overturned her conviction for delivering drugs to a minor through her umbilical cord on these grounds (*Johnson v. State of Florida*, 602 So.2d 1288 (1992); see also Paltrow 1992; and *In re A.C.*, 573 A.2d 1235 (D.C. App. 1990)). Hence, it is the due process guarantees in law, and not any explicit recognition of gender discrimination, that has proved women's most powerful tool.

These cases and practices show that reproduction is socially organized in ways that disadvantage women. Social norms and institutions that adopt fetal rights define women solely in reproductive terms, denying women their full humanity and severely compromising their pursuit of economic security and equality. Fetal rights politics is an acute expression of how women's disproportionate responsibility for reproduction perpetuates their subordination: it punishes women without treating their addictions, forces needless medical interventions on women, and "protects" women out of jobs.

It is significant that fetal protection policies have been implemented only in male-dominated industries where women are considered marginal workers. Both nursing and elementary school teaching, almost exclusively female occupations, are surprisingly hazardous, exposing workers on a daily basis to chemicals and infections known to cause reproductive damage, and yet no one suggests closing those jobs to women (Scott 1984). Seen in this fuller context, fetal protection policies do not look like sound policies to protect fetuses, safeguard women's health, or enhance work-place safety. The failure to accommodate men's concerns about their future children reveals fetal protection policies for what they are: protection of corporate profits and the gender status quo. These policies reassert traditional social arrangements by limiting women to a reproductive role and denying men any such role at all. The vindictive quality of many fetal rights practices reinforces the conclusion that what fetal rights do best is undermine women's autonomy.

Some feminists have warned against celebrating *Johnson Controls*, arguing that it legitimates the false choices women are supposed to make between parenthood and work, and between health and work (see, e.g., Rosen 1991). While I still consider the decision an important victory, these critics are right to reject simple arguments about individual choice as sufficient to describe or ensure women's autonomy. As Rosalind Petchesky observes, the critical issue in reproductive politics "is not so much the content of women's choices, or even the 'right to choose,' as it is the social and material conditions under which choices are made" (Petchesky 1984, 11). In the United States today, the social and material conditions shaping women's lives include widening inequalities of wealth, polarizing race relations, and rampant antifeminism. A political movement to create genuine choice and autonomy for women must continue striving to transform these conditions. Specifically, it must fight against the dangerous practices described in this essay, and take on the difficult task of redistributing the costs of reproduction in an increasingly stratified society. Women's self-determination requires freedom from the excessive and oppressive burdens of fetal rights.

NOTES

For their helpful engagement with this essay, I would like to thank Barbara Blodgett, Ann Ferguson, Alexa Freeman, Jennifer Manion, Corey Robin, Rogers Smith, Eve Weinbaum, and the editors of this volume. I am also grateful to the Five College Women's Studies Research Center at Mount Holyoke College, the Woodrow Wilson Foundation Women's Studies Dissertation Grant Program, and the American Association of University Women for their institutional and material support.

1. The earlier case was *Geduldig v. Aiello*, 417 U.S. 484 (1974), in which women employees posed an unsuccessful challenge to a similar benefits policy under the Fourteenth Amendment to the U.S. Constitution.

2. For discussions of the male standard in law, see MacKinnon 1987 and Kenney 1992, chap. 2.

3. Justice Blackmun, joined by Marshall, O'Connor, Souter, and Stevens, wrote the majority opinion. Justice White, joined by Kennedy and Rehnquist, and Justice Scalia wrote concurring opinions.

4. Because of the cultural predisposition to view reproduction as a female matter, the vast majority of reproductive health research has been conducted on women. According to the Office of Technology Assessment, "most suspected hazards have not been thoroughly researched for their reproductive effects in both males and females," and companies have singled out women for exclusion on the basis of research that "generally fails to confirm or disconfirm a need for differential exposure standards for men and women" (OTA 1985, 26). What epidemiological research has been done on men indicates that exposure to a wide range of occupational and environmental substances, including lead, nuclear radiation, herbicides and pesticides, paints, and solvents, may damage men's sperm, leading to their own sterility, their partners' miscarriages, or leukemia, kidney tumors, heart abnormalities, mental retardation, and learning disabilities in their children (Blakeslee 1991).

At least one known hazard to men's reproductive health, the pesticide DBCP, was banned; the alternative would have been to force men to choose between their jobs and their fertility (Bertin 1989, 280).

5. See Kenney (1992, chap. 7) for an analysis of the failure of American occupational health and safety law to provide a remedy for exclusionary policies. Although many advocates prefer to cast fetal protection policies as health problems for all workers, the current status of the law makes it difficult to sustain a challenge outside the sex discrimination paradigm. The union representing workers at American Cyanamid lost their health and safety case in court. Several women filed a discrimination lawsuit under Title VII, obtaining some relief through a pretrial settlement with the company. This fact of American law "is what creates the false impression that, in bringing cases on exclusionary policies, women seek the right to poison themselves and their children" (Kenney 1992, 211).

6. Moreover, the regime is still controversial even as far as fetuses are concerned, because AZT's long-term effects on the developing nervous system are not known, and so the approximately 75 percent of children who would have been born without HIV in any case are subjected to a potentially dangerous drug for no reason.

REFERENCES

Adkins v. Children's Hospital. 1923. 261 U.S. 525.

Baer, Judith. 1978. *The Chains of Protection: The Judicial Response to Women's Labor Legislation.* Westport, CT: Greenwood.

Becker, Mary. 1994. "Reproductive Hazards after *Johnson Controls,*" *Houston Law Review* 31 (1): 43–97.

Bertin, Joan. 1989. "Reproductive Hazards in the Workplace." In *Reproductive Laws for the 1990s,* ed. Sherrill Cohen and Nadine Taub, 277–305. Clifton, NJ: Humana Press.

Blakeslee, Sandra. 1991. "Research on Birth Defects Turns to Flaws in Sperm." *New York Times,* January 1.

Chavkin, Wendy. 1990. "Drug Addiction and Pregnancy: Policy Crossroads." *American Journal of Public Health* 80 (4) (April): 483–87.

Condit, Deirdre. 1995. "Fetal Personhood: Political Identity under Construction." In *Expecting Trouble: Surrogacy, Fetal Abuse, and New Reproductive Technologies,* ed. Patricia Boling. Boulder: Westview.

Daniels, Cynthia. 1993. *At Women's Expense: State Power and the Politics of Fetal Rights*. Cambridge: Harvard University Press.

Faludi, Susan. 1991. *Backlash: The Undeclared War against American Women*. New York: Crown.

Farber, Celia. 1995. "AIDS Words from the Front." *Spin*, April (Internet).

General Electric v. Martha Gilbert et al. 1976. 97 S.Ct. 401.

Glanton, A. Dahleen. 1988. "Job Bias Plea Clashes with Firm's Fetus Safety Rules." *Los Angeles Times*, May 15, 15.

Greenhouse, Linda. 1991. "Court Voids Limits to Women in Jobs on Basis of Fetus." *New York Times*, March 21.

Johnson Controls, Inc. v. California Fair Employment and Housing Commission. 1990. 90 Daily Journal D.A.R. 2410.

Kantrowitz, Barbara. 1991. "The Pregnancy Police." *Newsweek*, April 29.

Kenney, Sally. 1992. *For Whose Protection? Reproductive Hazards and Exclusionary Policies in the United States and Britain*. Ann Arbor: University of Michigan Press.

Kilborn, Peter T. 1991. "Employers Left with Many Decisions." *New York Times*, March 21.

Kolata, Gina. 1994. "Discovery That AIDS Can Be Prevented in Babies Raises Debate on Mandatory Testing." *New York Times*, November 3.

Kolder, Veronika, Janet Gallagher, and Michael Parsons. 1987. "Court-Ordered Obstetrical Interventions." *New England Journal of Medicine* 316 (19): 1192–96.

Lochner v. New York. 1905. 198 U.S. 45.

MacKinnon, Catharine. 1987. "Difference and Dominance." In *Feminism Unmodified: Discourses on Life and Law*. Cambridge: Harvard University Press.

Muller v. Oregon. 1908. 208 U.S 412.

Office of Technology Assessment (OTA). 1985. *Reproductive Hazards in the Workplace*. Washington, DC: U.S. GPO.

Paltrow, Lynn. 1992. *Criminal Prosecutions against Pregnant Women: National Update and Overview*. New York: Reproductive Freedom Project, American Civil Liberties Union.

Petchesky, Rosalind. 1984. *Abortion and Woman's Choice: The State, Sexuality, and Reproductive Freedom*. Boston: Northeastern University Press.

Roberts, Dorothy. 1991. "Punishing Drug Addicts Who Have Babies: Women of Color, Equality, and the Right of Privacy." *Harvard Law Review* 104 (7) (May): 1419–82.

Rosen, Ruth. 1991. "What Feminist Victory in the Court?" *New York Times*, April 1.

Roth, Rachel. 1993. "At Women's Expense: The Costs of Fetal Rights." *Women & Politics* 13 (3–4): 117–35.

————. 1995. "Forced Medical Intervention on Pregnant Women." Unpublished manuscript.

Scott, Judith. 1984. "Keeping Women in Their Place: Exclusionary Policies and Reproduction." In *Double Exposure: Women's Health Hazards on the Job and at Home*, ed. Wendy Chavkin. New York: Monthly Review Press.

Tsing, Anna. 1990. "Monster Stories: Women Charged with Perinatal Endangerment." In *Uncertain Terms: Negotiating Gender in American Culture*, ed. Faye Ginsburg and Anna Tsing. Boston: Beacon.

United Auto Workers v. Johnson Controls, Inc. 1989. 866 F.2d 871.

————. 1991. 111 S.Ct. 1196.

"Update: AIDS among Women — United States, 1994." 1995. *JAMA: Journal of the American Medical Association*. 273 (10) (March 8): 767–68.

Warren, Jennifer. 1987. "Case against Woman in Baby Death Thrown Out." *New York Times*, February 27.

SIX

The Wage Effects of Sexual Orientation Discrimination

M. V. LEE BADGETT

Over the past three decades, legislators at the federal, state, and municipal levels have moved toward a general public policy stating that employers should employ and pay people based on what they can produce on the job, not who they are. The Civil Rights Act of 1964 prohibits employment discrimination because of an individual's race, color, religion, sex, or national origin. Other laws forbid employment discrimination based on individuals' age or physical or mental disability. Other salient aspects of human identity remain outside this form of legal protection, however. Most notably, employment discrimination against individuals who are or are perceived to be lesbian, gay, or bisexual remains legal in most workplaces in the United States. This essay is the first econometric study of the possible wage effects of such discrimination.

Much of the debate about adding sexual orientation to civil rights laws has centered on the need for such legislation. Proponents of civil rights protections for lesbian, gay, and bisexual people argue that these people experience employment discrimination and that it causes them economic and psychological harm. Opponents of civil rights protections argue that such laws are unnecessary and would grant gay people "special privileges" (Carroll 1992). Citing survey data purportedly showing that lesbian and gay people have higher than average incomes (see, for example, "Clinton Administration Backs Bill" 1994), they assert that lesbians and gay men are an affluent group without need of further protection, and call into question the very existence of discrimination against them.

Existing economic studies of lesbian and gay people, however, are based on biased samples and inappropriate statistical comparisons. In this essay I apply econometric tools developed in the study of race and gender discrimination to the newer question of employment discrimination based on sexual orientation. Data pooled from the 1989–91 versions of the General Social Survey, a national random sample, allow econometric testing for the effects of sexual orientation discrimination on earnings. In its use of a random sample and multivariate analysis, this study constitutes a significant methodological advance over other quantitative studies of such discrimination and past efforts to compare earnings by sexual orientation.

Conceptual Framework

Before we evaluate labor market outcomes for evidence of employment discrimination against a group, it is reasonable to ask whether there is some reason to expect differential treatment of that group. Historical, sociological, and psychological research demonstrates the existence of homophobia (the fear of homosexuals and homosexuality) and heterosexism (the belief that heterosexuality is superior to homosexuality and should be an enforceable social norm) and the effects that such attitudes have in the everyday experience of lesbians and gay men: the lack of social or legal recognition of family structures, the persistence of threatened and actual violence, and the perpetuation of false stereotypes (see, in general, Gonsiorek and Weinrich 1991). Individuals with a bisexual orientation may also encounter such attitudes, although at other times those individuals may be perceived as being (or at least behaving as) heterosexual (see Garnets and Kimmel 1991, 149).

If employers or coworkers have a distaste for gay identity, behavior, or "lifestyle," employers may develop a taste for discrimination (following Becker 1971). This taste for discrimination is necessary but not sufficient for the occurrence of discrimination against gay employees, however. Unlike race or gender, for instance, sexual orientation is not generally an observable characteristic. (In this respect, sexual orientation is more like religion or national origin.) For the social stigma attached to homosexuality and bisexuality to result in direct employment discrimination, *disclosure* of a gay employee's sexual orientation is necessary.

Lesbians and gay men who voluntarily disclose their sexual orientation to employers or coworkers may trade off the risk of diminished career advancement or income loss for some future return (for anecdotal examples, see Woods 1993, 216–22). The future return may be psychological (enhanced self-esteem), political (a more supportive and accepting workplace), or economic (extension of benefits to domestic partners or spousal equivalents). Given these potential trade-offs, disclosure is likely to be endogenous, that is, at least partly determined by workplace factors.

An important workplace factor, of course, is income, but the direction of influence is difficult to determine a priori. First, compared to lower-income workers, higher-income workers may occupy jobs that allow them to manage the harmful effects of social stigma more comfortably, increasing their probability of disclosure. Second, higher levels of income could cushion the financial burden of some adverse workplace reactions, such as a loss of promotion, again leading to more disclosure by high-income people. In the other direction, however, people earning high incomes would lose more if fired, for instance, particularly if they feared that information about their sexual orientation would hinder their job search.[1] Schneider (1986, 479) found that lesbians with higher incomes were less likely than those with lower incomes to disclose their sexual orientation; that study, however, used a nonrandom sample.

Disclosure of sexual orientation may also be involuntary, although the extent of this kind of disclosure is unknown. Inferences of a lesbian or gay identity can be made by employers or coworkers from numerous sources of information: military discharge records, arrests or convictions, marital status, residential neighborhood, silences in conversations, and so on. In some cases, these inferences may even be incorrect, and a heterosexual employee may be wrongly perceived as being gay. Furthermore, voluntary disclosures to coworkers increase the likelihood of involuntary disclosure, whether accidental or deliberate.

Disclosure, whether voluntary or involuntary, may result in sanctions by coworkers, supervisors, or employers. Negative reactions will vary across workplaces. Coworkers might harass a gay or lesbian coworker, with adverse effects on the worker's productivity, income, and advancement. Supervisors or employers may harass, fire, or refuse to promote lesbian, gay, or bisexual employees.[2] This form of *direct discrimination* results in equally productive individuals being compensated differently.

Although disclosure is necessary for direct discrimination to occur, even successfully passing as heterosexual might not preclude negative economic effects. Evidence suggests that nondisclosure (or "passing" as heterosexual) is a common strategy for avoiding discrimination (Badgett, Donnelly, and Kibbe 1992). As Escoffier (1975) pointed out, passing may require a conscious effort to avoid potentially awkward social interactions that contribute to job satisfaction or advancement for other workers. The isolation involved in many passing strategies could lead to higher absenteeism and job turnover, and the energy devoted to passing might reduce productivity. In this case, the behavior is not an intrinsic characteristic of the worker but an effect of *indirect discrimination* within a workplace perceived as threatening. Two individuals with equal productive abilities would have differential productivity and, therefore, differential wages because of the work environment's effect on the gay individual's productivity. A different passing strategy could lead to a positive effect on productivity if gay workers, "driven by a half-conscious belief that if they just show themselves productive enough, worthy enough, good enough, they will overcome the invisible stigma," become workaholics (Mohr 1988, 149).

Overall, the likely wage effect of successfully passing as heterosexual in the workplace is ambiguous. In theory, one could distinguish the effects of direct discrimination in wages from the indirect effects by controlling for individuals' productivity differences. In practice, however, this distinction will be difficult to make, as will be discussed below.

Evidence on the Economic Status of Lesbians and Gay Men

Legal cases provide well-documented evidence of particular instances of employment discrimination against lesbians and gay men. Further evidence of employers' attitudes comes from a 1987–88 survey of employers in Anchorage, Alaska. Of the 191 employers surveyed, 18 percent said they would fire homosexuals, 27 percent said they would not hire them, and 26 percent said they would not promote them (Brause 1989). Some evidence that attitudes do translate into discrimination comes from nonrandom surveys of self-identified lesbian, gay, and bisexual people. A recent review of twenty-one surveys found that between 16 percent and 46 percent of survey respondents reported having experienced some form of discrimination in employment (in hiring, promotion, firing, or harassment) (Badgett, Donnelly, and Kibbe 1992).[3]

If discrimination does commonly occur and results in similarly qualified and productive people being treated differently only because of their sexual orientation, an economist might expect to observe differences in wages. The paucity of available data for large numbers of lesbians and gay men has made comparisons of income by sexual orientation difficult. Table 6.1 presents data from three relatively recent national surveys of lesbians and gay men. None of these surveys included heterosexual people, so the comparison group in the last column of table 6.1 is the national median income for full-time male or female workers, most of whom will be heterosexual.

The first survey, conducted in 1988 and reported in *Out/Look* magazine, asked respondents to indicate in which $5,000 range their income fell. The median range reported for gay men, $25,000 to $29,999, overlapped the national male median, but the median range for lesbians was higher than the median for women nationally. This same pattern showed up in the 1989 Teichner survey for the *San Francisco Examiner*, which found no clear difference between gay men's incomes and the national male median but higher median incomes for lesbians than for women nationwide. The 1988 Simmons Market Research Bureau survey appears second in the table and shows the most dramatic differences between gay and national incomes, with gay individuals (86 percent of whom were men) earning 35 percent more than the median male.

These comparisons are questionable for several reasons. In the two nonrandom surveys (*Out/Look* and Simmons), lesbian and gay respondents tended to be disproportionately white, urban, and well educated, all of which are factors associated with higher average incomes. (The difficulties in collecting data on a representative sample of a stigmatized population are discussed in the next section.) The extraordinarily high incomes found in the Simmons study most likely reflect sample selection bias. Surveys were inserted into eight gay/lesbian newspapers, and responses were mailed in.[4] This sampling technique guaranteed a highly educated sample (59.6 percent of respondents were college graduates, 16.8 percent had a master's degree, and 6.8 percent had a Ph.D.) and, therefore, higher than average incomes.

But even the survey with the least biased sampling technique (Teichner used random digit dialing and interviewed self-identified lesbian/gay/bisexual people) found that lesbians' median income was well above the median female income. Although the willingness of respondents to identify themselves as gay or lesbian to an unknown interviewer may vary along income lines within gender groups, which could be a source of observed differences, some further explanation is necessary. Furthermore, if experience and education are not controlled for, comparisons of the median or average income for the gay sample with the national medians may be

TABLE 6.1.
Survey Data on Income of Lesbian, Gay, and Bisexual People

Survey	Year	Instrument	N	Gender	L/G/B income	National income[a]
Out/Look	1988	Magazine survey, mail-in	510	Men	25K–29K[b]	27,342
				Women	20K–24K[b]	18,823
Simmons Mkt. Research Bureau	1988	Gay newspaper inserts			36,900[c]	(see above)
Teichner/*San Francisco Examiner*	1989	Phone survey, random digit dialing	400	Men	29,129[b]	28,605
				Women	26,331[b]	19,643

SOURCES: "Work and Career" 1988; Gravois 1991; Teichner 1989. National medians from *Economic Report of the President,* Feb. 1990 and Feb. 1991.

[a] "National income" is median income for full-time, full-year workers.
[b] Median income for sample.
[c] Average income for sample.

misleading. As in the standard economic approach to race and gender discrimination, we need a multivariate analysis of a random sample to properly compare the earnings of lesbian, gay, or bisexual workers to the earnings of heterosexual workers.

Data

As mentioned above, one reason we know little about the economic effects of sexual orientation is that reliable and representative data matching sexual orientation to economic outcomes are extremely rare. One important nationally representative survey, the General Social Survey (GSS) conducted by the National Opinion Research Center, has collected information on labor market variables (employment status, income, and occupation) and, beginning in 1989, on sexual behavior with partners of either sex (Davis and Smith 1991).[5] While the GSS does not specifically ask about sexual orientation or identity, same-sex sexual experiences are likely to be highly correlated with a self-identified gay or bisexual orientation (see Lever et al. 1992).

Because of the design of the GSS, not all respondents were asked all questions in each survey. Following elimination of those without information on sex partners[6] or income[7] (and a few with missing data on other variables), the sample pooled from the 4,426 respondents in the 1989–91 surveys contains 1,680 people who were employed full-time when surveyed.[8] Of this subsample, 4.8 percent reported having had at least one same-sex sexual partner since the age of eighteen, a proportion that falls well within the range found by studies of sexual orientation (Gonsiorek and Weinrich 1991). For purposes of this essay, those respondents are classified as *behaviorally* lesbian, gay, or bisexual.

The lack of data on self-identified sexual orientation is disappointing, but using behavior to infer identity may not be inappropriate. First, society may not make such fine distinctions.[9] Both behavior and identity are stigmatized and are sufficient to trigger legal sanctions in the United States. For instance, the *act* of sodomy is still prohibited in about half of the states (*Harvard Law Review* editors 1991, 9), as is the solicitation of "noncommercial, consensual same-sex sexual activity" in many places (27). In some cases, these laws (and the presumption that lesbians and gay men violate the sodomy laws) have been used to justify employment discrimination (see the discussion of *Childers v. Dallas Police Department* in Rubenstein 1993, 334).

Second, although respondents are not asked when their sexual activity took place, both absolute and relative numbers of same-sex sexual partners are likely to indicate whether this behavior was temporary or experimental or whether the behavior reflects the individual's underlying sexual identity and orientation. Therefore, this study uses four measures of gay sexual behavior: (1) having had *one or more* same-sex sexual partners (the most general definition, identifying 4.8 percent of the sample); (2) having had *more than one* same-sex sexual partner (3.0 percent); (3) having had *at least as many* same-sex sexual partners as opposite-sex sexual partners (3.0 percent); and (4) having had either more than one same-sex sexual partner or at least as many same-sex sexual partners as opposite-sex sexual partners (that is, either (2) or (3), a definition that takes in 3.8 percent of the sample).

An issue related to the use of this data is their reliability. The questions on sexual behavior in the GSS were self-administered and were accompanied by assurances of confidentiality and by the explanation that "frank and honest" responses were important for understanding how to deal with the AIDS epidemic.

One final drawback of the GSS data set is that respondents were asked to select one of twenty categories to indicate their pretax employment earnings from the previous year, rather than to name exact figures. The income ranges for each category increase with income, but the analysis uses natural logarithms, which evens the ranges out. Medians were calculated for the GSS ranges using Current Population Survey data on full-time workers.[10] All medians were converted to 1988 dollars for the purposes of calculations in this essay.

Methodology

The most common econometric approach for capturing the effects of discrimination is to see whether people who are similar in all observable and economically relevant ways have similar labor market outcomes. This essay uses a basic OLS model of wage determination with the log of income as the dependent variable. Separate equations for men and women will take into account any differences in men's and women's labor market decisions and experiences. Independent variables include individual characteristics related to productivity (such as education, occupation, marital status, and experience)[11] and other labor market influences (region, SMSA residence, and race). The main effect of discrimination, if any, will be captured by the coefficient on a dummy variable for being behaviorally lesbian, gay, or bisexual. A statistically significant negative coefficient would imply discrimination in the form of lower wages. Discrimination may also exist in the process of allocating individuals among occupations.

A variable measuring the extent of workplace disclosure of gay behavior or identity would be more appropriate to include in the wage equation, since disclosure is necessary for direct discrimination to occur. Unfortunately, this information is not available. As a result, the hypothesized discrimination characteristic is measured with error, violating one of the usual OLS assumptions. With no information on disclosure, statistical correction is not feasible, but the interpretation of the results can be adjusted.

Overall, this selection bias problem is likely to reduce any measured effect of discrimination, biasing the procedure against the discrimination hypothesis. Consider figure 6.1, a matrix of disclosure decisions for behaviorally lesbian, gay, or bisexual people. The framework described above suggests that gay employees disclosing their sexual orientation, the people in groups A and C, are vulnerable to direct workplace discrimination. The variable created from the General Social Survey combines people in groups A and B but does not (and cannot) distinguish people in those two groups, although we would expect only those in group A to face direct discrimination. Lesbian, gay, and bisexual individuals in group B, who have not disclosed their sexual orientation at work, might still face indirect discrimination if expectations of discrimination reduce productivity. Given the imperfect proxies for productivity and the inability to measure disclosure, then, the GSS sexual orientation variable will pick up the effect of both direct and indirect discrimination against groups A and B. If indirect discrimination lowers earnings less than direct discrimination, or if the net effect of nondisclosure is to induce gay employees to work harder and to *increase* productivity, then the sexual orientation coefficient will *underestimate* the negative effect of direct discrimination on earnings.

The impact of imperfectly measuring the sexual orientation variable can be analyzed similarly. Individuals in group D are not coded by the GSS variable as being gay. As with group B, they are unlikely to face direct discrimination but might have lower incomes from indirect discrimination. Workers in group C are likely to face discrimination but cannot be identified with the GSS data. Overall, though, the effect of misclassifying group C and D workers is likely to be negligible. First, if, as seems reasonable, the economic and social risk from disclosing sexual behavior to a survey interviewer is less than the risk from workplace disclosure, the combination of survey nondisclosure and workplace disclosure will be rare and the size of group C will be small. Second, unless the overall group of lesbian, gay, and bisexual adults is quite large, the addition of the potentially lower-income group C and D workers to the heterosexual total will have a relatively small effect on the average income against which behaviorally gay respondents' income is measured. And even a large combined group of C and D workers facing both indirect and direct discrimination would pull the average down, *reducing* the observed income difference between gay and heterosexual workers. Thus the errors both in measuring behavior and in using behavior as a proxy for disclosure result in a bias *against* finding discrimination.

As discussed above, workplace disclosure may be systematically related to income, and Schneider (1986) found that disclosure is less likely as income increases, resulting in another form of selection bias. This pattern is consistent with the hypothesis that gay workers make cost-benefit calculations before disclosing their sexual orientation, and that disclosure is less likely among high-income workers because they have more to lose. The earnings loss for lower-income workers who disclose their sexual orientation and face direct discrimination will not, therefore, be representative of the loss faced by the average worker. But in that case the average worker has a *higher* expected loss of income, which is why he or she does not disclose,

FIGURE 6.1.
Voluntary Disclosure Decisions of Lesbian, Gay, and Bisexual Workers

	Disclosure in workplace	No disclosure in workplace
Disclosure in survey	A	B
No disclosure in survey	C	D

suggesting that, again, this source of selection bias will result in underestimates of the average effect of disclosure and discrimination.

Aside from the effect of indirect discrimination on the productivity of gay workers who do not disclose their sexual orientation, other sources of ability or productivity differences that are unobservable to the researcher might be related to sexual orientation. For instance, some economists measuring racial earnings differentials have hypothesized racial differences in unobserved quality (usually differences in schooling quality) that, if properly accounted for, would reduce the difference in earnings attributed purely to racial discrimination (for example, Smith and Welch 1989; Juhn, Murphy, and Pierce 1991). This is less likely to be an issue in the case of sexual orientation, however, since observed levels of education are quite similar across heterosexual and homosexual groups and there is no reason to expect systematic differences in the quality of schools attended by lesbian, gay, or bisexual people. Furthermore, much of the gay and lesbian identity development process occurs in the late teens and early twenties, suggesting that sexual orientation is unlikely to influence educational decisions (Garnets and Kimmel 1991).[12]

Other components of unobserved ability — work experience and labor force attachment — also cause concern when OLS models are used to measure discrimination against women (Bloom and Killingsworth 1982), and these factors, unlike the school quality component, may be correlated with sexual orientation. Lesbians and bisexual women may have stronger labor force attachment and more work experience than heterosexual women, since they usually have weaker economic incentives to specialize in home production: their partners (or spousal equivalents) are women who face the same potentially discriminatory labor market. Furthermore, the legal benefits of partnership are fewer, and the economic penalties for not working are greater even for lesbians who share economic resources and expenses with a partner, since few employers who provide health care benefits for employees' legal spouses do so for employees' same-sex domestic partners (Bowman and Cornish 1992). As a result, lesbians' labor force experience might not be interrupted as often as heterosexual women's, which would make the potential experience variable available from the GSS a closer proxy for lesbians' actual experience (see note 11).

If these unobserved components of wage determination are correlated with sexual orientation, then OLS coefficients are biased *against* finding discrimination, since the unobserved components mean that lesbian and bisexual women are more productive than heterosexual women who are identical in their observed characteristics. This problem can be at least partly corrected with information gained from modeling the female worker's decision to work full-time. To the extent that the unobservable component involved in the full-time work decision is correlated with the unobservable determinants of wages (for instance, actual experience and labor force attachment), adding a Heckman correction term — the inverse Mills ratio representing the probability of being a full-time worker — to the OLS model will reduce the bias (Bloom and Killingsworth 1982). In addition, the possibility that the potential experience variable more closely proxies lesbians' actual experience than heterosexual women's actual experience will be accounted for by interacting experience and sexual orientation.

Results

Table 6.2 presents the means for the variables used in both procedures. Unlike the data derived from the surveys described in table 6.1, the behaviorally lesbian/bisexual women earn approximately 18 percent less, on average, than do behaviorally heterosexual women in the GSS, and gay/bisexual men earn 7 percent less than heterosexual men. Two likely sources of the differences between the survey results in tables 6.1 and 6.2 are differences in sampling techniques (the GSS is a probability sample, the other surveys are not) and in sexual orientation definitions (the GSS definition is based on behavior, the others on self-identity). Within the GSS, some of the unadjusted difference between lesbian/bisexual women and heterosexual women could come from the fact that the gay sample is slightly younger and less likely to be white, factors that would tend to reduce average incomes. For men, there are no obvious factors pulling down gay/bisexual men's earnings. The major difference seems to be in the occupational distribution, but this difference would not necessarily mean lower incomes: the gay male respondents are less likely to be in managerial and bluecollar occupations but are more likely to be in professional/technical and service occupations.

Table 6.3 presents the OLS coefficient estimates from regressions on the subsample of the 1,680 respondents who had full-time jobs when the survey was taken.[13] Columns 1–3 and 4–5 present the results for women and men, respectively. Columns 2, 3, and 5 supplement the basic specification in 1 and 4 with dummies for broad occupational category. (The small size of the gay sample prevented more detailed categories.) Table 6.3 reports the OLS results using only the most stringent definition of lesbian/gay/bisexual (having had at least as many same-sex as opposite-sex sexual partners). Using the three alternative definitions changes the L/G/B coefficient (as noted below), but the other coefficients vary only slightly. In all specifications, for both men and women, the education, occupation, marriage, race, sex, and experience coefficients have the usual signs, and most of them are significant at the 5 percent level.

When controls are included for the other factors influencing income, being behaviorally lesbian, gay, or bisexual reduces income, but the difference is statistically significant only for men. For women (column 1), the dummy variable for lesbian, gay, or bisexual is -0.35 using this L/G/B definition, and the coefficient ranges from -0.29 to -0.36 using the other three definitions (not reported in table 6.1). The t-statistics are small, however, in each case. The null hypothesis that the coefficient is zero can be rejected in a one-tailed test at the 10 percent level for two

TABLE 6.2.
Variable Means for Full-Time Workers, Pooled 1989–91 Data
(Standard Deviations in Parentheses)

Variable	Lesbian/ bisexual women	Heterosexual women	Gay/ bisexual men	Heterosexual men
Annual earnings (in 1988–90)	15056	18341	26321	28312
	(8284)	(11334)	(16937)	(16842)
% 0 to 9,999	29.4	21.2	10.6	8.8
% 10 to 19,999	35.3	36.2	29.8	22.5
% 20 to 29,999	29.4	25.8	21.3	26.2
% 30 to 39,999	5.9	12.0	17.0	19.4
% 40,000 and up	0.0	4.7	21.3	23.1
Education (in years)	13.6	13.6	13.6	13.6
	(3.0)	(2.5)	(4.0)	(2.9)
Age	34.0	39.4	41.3	39.1
	(10.3)	(11.1)	(12.2)	(11.8)
Potential experience[a]	15.4	20.8	22.6	20.4
	(10.8)	(11.6)	(13.2)	(12.1)
% White	79.4	85.2	89.4	90.7
% Married	23.5	51.0	40.4	67.7
% In large SMSA	55.9	51.9	55.3	45.8
Region (%):				
Northeast	17.6	20.2	25.5	18.4
Midwest	23.5	26.9	29.8	26.6
West	17.6	19.3	12.8	19.6
South	41.2	33.5	31.9	35.3
Occup. (%):				
Manager	8.8	14.8	12.8	17.9
Prof./Tech.	26.5	25.4	31.9	20.0
Clerical/Sales	14.7	35.7	17.0	12.9
Craft/Operative	23.5	12.3	27.7	40.6
Service	26.5	11.9	10.6	8.7
N	34	698	47	901

SOURCE: Author's calculations from General Social Survey (Davis and Smith 1991).
    NOTE: The lesbian/gay/bisexual sample is made up of those with one or more same-sex sexual partners.
[a] Potential experience = age − years of education − 5.

of the four definitions, which define as lesbian or bisexual both those with more than one same-sex sexual partner and those with either more than one or at least as many same-sex as opposite-sex sexual partners (definitions 2 and 4 above).[14]

For men (column 4), the sexual orientation effect is stronger than for women: the coefficient is −0.28 and is significantly different from zero at the 1 percent level in a one-tailed test. This finding suggests that the income penalty for gay or bisexual men could be as much as 24.4 percent.[15] The coefficient using the other three definitions ranges from −0.12 to −0.24 in the specifications without occupation dummies. Two of those coefficients are significantly different from zero at the 5 percent level in a one-tailed test, and the third (having one or more same-sex sexual partners, the most general one) is significant at the 11 percent level in a one-tailed test. In general, as the definitions become more stringent, the income effect becomes more negative, suggesting that having more than one same-sex sexual partner or mostly same-sex sexual partners may identify those gay/bisexual men who are more likely to disclose their sexual orientation at work.

Escoffier (1975) suggested that some gay people might choose occupations in which workplace disclosure of sexual orientation is least damaging. In this case, disclosure is a compensating differential for the gay worker. An alternative explanation that would account for the same observations is that gay workers are segregated or crowded into more tolerant occupations that have lower wages. To see whether occupational choice or crowding can explain lower gay incomes, I added four occupational dummy variables to each specification (the dummy variable for service occupations was excluded). The effect seen in columns 2 and 5 was similar for all L/G/B definitions.

Adding occupation dummies has a very different effect on men and women. For women, both the coefficients and t-statistics for the sexual orientation variable drop considerably, and the occupation dummies have large, significant effects on income. In other words, accounting for the differences in occupational distribution explains some of the sexual orientation income difference (which also becomes statistically

TABLE 6.3.
Determinants of Annual Income in General Social Survey: Income in 1988–90
(Regression Coefficients; Absolute Value of t-Statistics in Parentheses)

Variable	(1) Women	(2) Women	(3) Women	(4) Men	(5) Men
Constant	7.17**	7.12**	5.5**	7.84**	7.96**
	(37.1)	(34.6)	(4.1)	(60.0)	(51.6)
L/G/B[a]	−0.35	−0.32	−0.12	−0.28**	−0.31**
	(1.1)	(1.1)	(0.3)	(2.3)	(2.6)
Education	0.13**	0.10**	0.13**	0.09**	0.07**
	(11.1)	(7.6)	(4.1)	(12.5)	(8.5)
Currently married	−0.08	−0.08	−0.26	0.27**	0.26**
	(1.4)	(1.5)	(1.6)	(5.8)	(5.6)
White	0.11	0.10	0.25	0.09	0.06
	(1.4)	(1.3)	(1.5)	(1.2)	(0.9)
Potential experience	0.04**	0.04**	0.10**	0.04**	0.04**
	(5.1)	(5.1)	(2.1)	(6.2)	(6.1)
(Exper)^2	−0.00**	−0.00**	−0.00*	−0.00**	−0.00**
	(3.9)	(4.0)	(1.8)	(4.3)	(4.3)
Exp*L/G/B	0.01	0.02	0.01		
	(0.8)	(1.0)	(0.3)		
Big SMSA	0.26**	0.28**	0.35**	0.19**	0.17**
	(4.5)	(5.0)	(3.5)	(4.4)	(4.1)
Northeast	0.07	0.06	−0.08	0.17**	0.18**
	(0.9)	(0.8)	(0.5)	(2.9)	(3.6)
Midwest	−0.02	−0.01	−0.12	0.20**	0.19**
	(0.2)	(0.1)	(0.9)	(3.8)	(3.6)
West	−0.05	−0.05	−0.17	0.09	0.08
	(0.6)	(0.6)	(1.1)	(1.6)	(1.4)
Manager		0.58**	0.57**		0.35**
		(5.6)	(5.6)		(4.1)
Prof/Tech		0.58**	0.57**		0.31**
		(5.8)	(5.8)		(3.5)
Clerical/Sales		0.46**	0.46**		0.13
		(5.3)	(5.4)		(1.5)
Craft/Operative		0.36**	0.35**		0.11
		(3.4)	(3.4)		(1.4)
Lambda			0.90		
			(1.2)		
Adj. R^2	0.21	0.25	0.25	0.28	0.29
N	732	732	732	948	948

NOTE: Dummy variables for service occupation and South are excluded.
  [a] Definition of L/G/B: Number of same-sex sexual partners ≥ number of opposite-sex sexual partners.
  * Statistically significant at the 10% level; ** at the 5% level (two-tailed tests).

insignificant in all the specifications, including occupation). Lesbian/bisexual women tend to be in lower-paying occupations, as the means in table 6.2 suggest: half of the lesbian/bisexual women work in the lowest-paying occupations for women in this study (craft/operative and service). After the selection bias correction in column 3, both the coefficient and the t-statistic are insignificantly different from zero.[16] In a similar specification without occupation controls, the L/G/B/ coefficient was −0.11 with a t-statistic of 0.2. (In the selection-corrected specifications using the other definitions, the coefficient on L/G/B was sometimes positive and sometimes negative but never significantly different from zero.)

For men, adding the occupation variables *increases* the negative effect, revealing as much as a 26.7 percent income disadvantage (from column 5). Although occupational sorting might be observed at a finer level of detail not possible in this study, these results suggest that gay/bisexual men are in higher-paying occupations but earn less than heterosexual men within these broad categories.

Why does the effect of sexual orientation vary between men and women? The results for women from the selection-corrected specifications are sensitive to the sexual orientation definition used. With actual measures of these unobserved characteristics, the sexual orientation income gap might widen for women. Also, behavior may not be a good proxy for identity as lesbians; the expected income difference would be reduced if identity is more stigmatizing than behavior, as seems likely. The variable means in table 6.2 demonstrate that lesbian/bisexual women are not better off economically than gay/bisexual men, suggesting that gender is more important than sexual orientation in determining income for lesbian and bisexual women. On average, lesbian/bisexual women earn 57.2 percent of a gay/bisexual man's income; the female-to-male ratio among heterosexuals is 64.8 percent.

Another possible explanation is that gay/bisexual men face greater discrimination than lesbian/bisexual women for other reasons. Bloom and Glied (1989) suggested that employers might use perceived sexual orientation as a proxy for susceptibility to HIV and AIDS, since the Americans with Disabilities Act prohibits employment discrimination because of HIV status. This might account for some of the difference, since HIV is much rarer among lesbians.

Finally, the form of discrimination against lesbians may differ from that against gay and bisexual men. The results in table 6.3 suggest that at least some of lesbian/bisexual women's earnings disadvantage comes from being in lower-paying occupations, perhaps as a result of discrimination. Indirect discrimination might affect women differently from men, since women already face the potential for sex discrimination and might not fear sexual orientation discrimination as much as gay men do. Or double jeopardy might encourage lesbians to work harder to avoid discrimination. In other words, the coefficients in table 6.3 will then *underestimate* the impact of direct discrimination on earnings.

Conclusion

The findings of this study provide evidence that economic differences exist between people with differing sexual orientations (as defined by their behavior). Behaviorally gay/bisexual men earn from 11 percent to 27 percent less than behaviorally heterosexual men. Because this economic disadvantage holds after education and occupation are controlled for, it appears that equally productive gay people are being treated differently, that is, they are being discriminated against. Although the findings for lesbians are not consistently statistically significant, the behaviorally lesbian/bisexual women in this sample earn less than similar behaviorally heterosexual women. The difference for lesbians ranges from 12 percent to 30 percent, dropping greatly in size and significance when occupation and a selection bias correction are taken into account. The lack of statistical significance could reflect the small size of the sample of lesbians or could result because the model does not adequately control for unobservable differences between lesbians and heterosexual women in labor force experience and work attachment.

Might this discrimination wither away on its own, as suggested by a taste discrimination model? An employer with a less intense taste for discrimination ought to be able to hire productive gay employees for a smaller outlay than other employers must pay for equally productive heterosexual workers, eventually bidding up the wage of gay employees. Many firms have added sexual orientation to their nondiscrimination policies, as the model predicts.

At least two factors suggest, however, that firms with nondiscrimination policies have not been responding simply to competitive pressures. First, anecdotal evidence suggests that some of these firms changed their official policies in response to state or local antidiscrimination ordinances (Badgett 1990, 207). Others changed their policies at least partly in response to pressure and actions by individual gay employees and company groups ("Building Community" 1992), and groups of customers and investors have also attempted to influence corporate policies. Second, in some cases, labor costs might actually be higher for those companies than for more intense discriminators if antidiscrimination policies lead to changes in the company's benefits programs, such as the introduction of benefits for the domestic partners of gay employees. Therefore, it is hard to see this trend as resulting from the process generated within the Becker discrimination model.

If, as policy decisions over the past three decades suggest, the United States is moving toward a general policy of prohibiting employment discrimination on the basis of nonproductive characteristics, then this essay's finding that sexual orientation discrimination exists in the workforce identifies another policy need: adding sexual orientation to antidiscrimination laws.

NOTES

1. Such a firing occurred in the case of Jeffrey Collins, a former Shell Oil employee. A California court found that Shell had fired Collins for being homosexual, violating the implicit employment agreement between Shell and Collins. Furthermore, Shell informed corporate headhunters of the reason for Collins's dismissal ("Right to Privacy" 1991).

2. Schneider (1986) showed that negative reactions reduce the probability that a lesbian will repeat the disclosure of her sexual orientation in the future.

3. These perceptions of discrimination are similar in magnitude to those of African American workers, 36 percent of whom reported experiences of racial discrimination in a 1990 survey (Turner, Fix, and Struyk 1991, 7).

4. Michael Gravois of the Rivendell Marketing Company provided me with information on the survey in a phone conversation on November 7, 1991. Some results appeared in an article in the *Wall Street Journal* (Rigdon 1991).

5. More specifically, respondents were asked two questions: "Now thinking about the time since your eighteenth birthday (including the past twelve months), how many male [female, in the second question] partners have you had sex with?"

6. The procedures described below were repeated on the sample of all full-time workers, including those without data on sexual partners, who were identified by a dummy variable. This procedure resulted in coefficients virtually identical to those produced by the procedures described in the next section.

7. Respondents were asked about income earned in the previous year from their current occupation. Thus nonrespondents to the income question are those who earned no income last year from their current occupation, suggesting that those reporting incomes ar strongly attached to the labor force.

8. Individuals were included if employed full-time when surveyed or if they normally worked full-time but were not at work because of a temporary illness, a vacation, or a strike.

9. The distinction between behavior and identity is important in some cultures, however, including cultures that are represented in large ethnic groups in the United States, such as Latino cultures (Alonso and Koreck 1989).

10. The CPS medians were calculated for all workers, with no differentiation by race or gender. This procedure would tend to narrow the race and gender differences in median earnings in the GSS, since the distribution of earnings *within* a particular range is likely to vary by race and gender. Since this study disaggregates the GSS analysis by gender, observed racial earnings differences in the GSS are likely to be more affected. This probably explains the relatively small OLS coefficients and low t-statistics on the dummy variable for being white seen in table 6.3.

11. Since actual work experience is not available, potential experience is calculated as (age $-$ years of education $-$ 5).

12. Although adolescents in the early stages of gay identity development might have painful high school experiences, the effect of this internal conflict on educational attainment is not clear (Gonsiorek 1988, 474–77).

13. All calculations in this essay were derived using LIMDEP.

14. Also, the degree of statistical significance achieved depends on the specification of the model. Although the interaction of sexual orientation and experience is included for economic reasons, it should be noted that without that variable, the L/G/B coefficient is half as large and is statistically insignificant for all four definitions.

15. The percentage decline is calculated using $\delta = \ln (1 + d)$, where δ is the coefficient on L/G/B and d is the percent difference in mean incomes between the gay and heterosexual groups.

16. The selection correction involved first modeling the probability of women holding full-time jobs. The independent variables in this probit model included all the variables in table 6.3 except for occupation. The coefficient on L/G/B was always positive, regardless of the definition, but never statistically significant.

REFERENCES

Alonso, Ana Maria, and Maria Teresa Koreck. 1989. "Silences: 'Hispanics,' AIDS, and Sexual Practices." *Differences* 1, no. 1 (winter): 101–24.

Badgett, M. V. Lee. 1990. "Racial Differences in Unemployment Rates and Employment Opportunities." Diss., University of California, Berkeley.

Badgett, Lee, Colleen Donnelly, and Jennifer Kibbe. 1992. "Pervasive Patterns of Discrimination against Lesbians and Gay Men: Evidence from Surveys across the United States." National Gay and Lesbian Task Force Policy Institute.

Becker, Gary S. 1971. *The Economics of Discrimination.* 2d ed. Chicago: University of Chicago Press.

Bloom, David E., and Sherry Glied. 1989. "The Evolution of AIDS Economic Research." *Health Policy* 11, no. 2 (April): 187–96.

Bloom, David E., and Mark R. Killingsworth. 1982. "Pay Discrimination Research and Litigation: The Use of Regression." *Industrial Relations* 21, no. 3 (fall): 318–39.

Bowman, Craig A., and Blake M. Cornish. 1992. "A More Perfect Union: A Legal and Social Analysis of Domestic Partnership Ordinances." *Columbia Law Review* 92, no. 5 (June): 1164–1211.

Brause, Jay. 1989. "Closed Doors: Sexual Orientation Bias in the Anchorage Housing and Employment Markets." In *Identity Reports: Sexual Orientation Bias in Alaska.* Anchorage: Identity Inc.

"Building Community at PG&E." 1992. *Gay/Lesbian/Bisexual Corporate Letter* 1, no. 2 (November–December): 3–6.

Carroll, Vincent. 1992. "Coloradans on the Gay Amendment." *Wall Street Journal,* December 15.

"Clinton Administration Backs Bill to Ban Job Bias against Gays." 1994. *Daily Labor Report,* August 1, D16.

Davis, James Allan, and Tom W. Smith. 1991. *General Social Surveys, 1972–1991.* Machine-readable data file and codebook. Principal investigator, James A. Davis; director and co-principal investigator, Tom W. Smith. National Opinion Research Center, Chicago (producer); Roper Center for Public Opinion Research, University of Connecticut, Storrs (distributor).

Economic Report of the President. 1990, 1991. Washington, DC: GPO.

Escoffier, Jeffrey. 1975. "Stigmas, Work Environment, and Economic Discrimination against Homosexuals." *Homosexual Counseling Journal* 2, no. 1 (January): 8–17.

Garnets, Linda, and Douglas Kimmel. 1991. "Lesbian and Gay Male Dimensions in the Psychological Study of Human Diversity." In Jacqueline D. Goodchilds, ed., *Psychological Perspectives on Human Diversity in America.* Washington, DC: American Psychological Association, 137–92.

Gonsiorek, John C. 1988. "Mental Health Issues of Gay and Lesbian Adolescents." *Journal of Adolescent Health Care* 9. Reprinted in Linda D. Garnets and Douglas C. Kimmel, eds., *Psychological Perspectives on Lesbian and Gay Male Experiences.* New York: Columbia University Press, 1993, 469–85.

Gonsiorek, John C., and James D. Weinrich. 1991. "The Definition and Scope of Sexual Orientation." In John C. Gonsiorek and James D. Weinrich, eds., *Homosexuality: Research Implications for Public Policy.* Newbury Park, CA: Sage, 1–12.

Gravois, Michael. 1991. President, Rivendell Marketing Company. Telephone conversation with author, November 7.

Harvard Law Review editors. 1991. "Sexual Orientation and the Law." Cambridge: Harvard University Press.

Juhn, Chinhui, Kevin M. Murphy, and Brooks Pierce. 1991. "Accounting for the Slowdown in Black-White Wage Convergence." In Marvin H. Kosters, ed., *Workers and Their Wages: Changing Patterns in the United States.* Washington, DC: American Enterprise Institute Press, 107–43.

Lever, Janet, David E. Kanouse, William H. Rogers, Sally Carson, and Rosanna Hertz. 1992. "Behavior Patterns and Sexual Identity of Bisexual Males." *Journal of Sex Research* 29, no. 2 (May): 141–67.

Mohr, Richard. 1988. *Gays/Justice: A Study of Ethics, Society, and Law.* New York: Columbia University Press.

Rigdon, Joan E. 1991. "Overcoming a Deep-Rooted Reluctance, More Firms Advertise to Gay Community." *Wall Street Journal,* July 18, B1.

"The Right to Privacy: A $5.3 Million Lesson for Shell?" 1991. *Business Week,* August 26.

Rubenstein, William B., ed. 1993. *Lesbians, Gay Men, and the Law.* New York: New Press.

Schneider, Beth E. 1986. "Coming Out at Work: Bridging the Private/Public Gap." *Work and Occupations* 13, no. 4 (November): 463–87.

Smith, James P., and Finis R. Welch. 1989. "Black Economic Progress after Myrdal." *Journal of Economic Literature* 27, no. 2 (June): 519–64.

Teichner, Steve. 1989. "Results of Poll." *San Francisco Examiner,* June 6, A19.

Turner, Margery Austin, Michael Fix, and Raymond J. Struyk. 1991. *Opportunities Denied, Opportunities Diminished: Racial Discrimination in Hiring.* Urban Institute Report 91-9. Washington, DC: Urban Institute Press.

Woods, James D. 1993. *The Corporate Closet: The Professional Lives of Gay Men in America.* New York: Free Press.

"Work and Career: Survey Results." 1988. *Out/Look* 1, no. 3 (fall): 94.

SEVEN

Fighting the Violence against Our Sisters: Prosecution of Pregnant Women and the Coercive Use of Norplant

SUZANNE SHENDE

The latest assault on low-income women of color, which in this year's incarnation is the virtual gutting of "welfare," should be no surprise. The relentless repression, exploitation, and scapegoating of poor women of color has a long, consistent history in this country, and the failure of our various movements to adequately address the systematic problems at each juncture ensure that this tactical assault shall continue. The factors of race, gender, and class make individuals and groups vulnerable to systemic oppression, whether it be in the sphere of government benefits cuts, reproductive health constraints, immigration restrictions, affirmative action rollbacks, or initiatives against lesbians and gay men.

Although the most marginalized women have always resisted and struggled, they have been met with an equally prevalent obstacle: the tendency for privileged members of their own community, the elite "leaders," to allow or participate in the oppression of their "sisters." Women of color and their issues are often relegated to second-class status even in the feminist, nationalist, reformist, or revolutionary movements where they struggle.

The struggle of women of color and low-income women to make the battle for reproductive freedom relevant and liberatory has a long history.[1] The birth control movement, begun in the 1800s and held dear by white feminists, flourished with underlying beliefs in "more children from the fit, less from the unfit."[2] Birth control was intended, through the 1900s, as population control for communities of color and poor people in general. This premise of domination and control over poor women and communities of color continues, as 81 percent of the women forced by court order to have cesarean sections against their will have been women of color.[3] Recently, a Black woman with a low income who was HIV-positive was forced to have an abortion because doctors decided she was not fit: neither to be a parent nor to make an informed decision of her own.[4]

The modern mainstream women's movement has not recognized these realities and has reflected white, middle-class concerns: for example, it has concentrated on the *legality* of abortion without demanding that *affordability* be as crucial an element. In 1980 the Supreme Court upheld the denial of funding for abortion, yet women's organizations respond to recent threats to *Roe* as if they are only *now* losing something meaningful, rarely acknowledging that choice was lost for poor women over a decade ago.[5]

In the same way that birth control has been used as a strategy of domination of communities of color, so has forced sterilization. In the early 1970s, poor twelve- and fourteen-year-old Black girls were sterilized in Alabama; this was sanctioned and financed by Medicaid.[6] Women are sometimes not told of the operation at all, believing they are having only an abortion or delivery performed; sometimes they are not informed of the irreversibility of the operation; they are sometimes forced to sign forms they cannot read, either because they are illiterate or because the forms are not in their native language.[7] Sterilization is still funded largely by the government,[8] while the government increasingly will not fund abortions, quality family planning services and obstetric care. In some areas of the United States over 50 percent of the Latina women have been sterilized, as have 42 percent of Native American women nationally.[9] Women in prison and mentally ill women continue to be subjected to punitive sterilization. And when abortion funding was banned in 1988 in Michigan, women were forced to resort to sterilization; the number of sterilizations jumped, with a projected increase of 1,500 over two years.[10] While some women's groups have paid lip service to opposing forced sterilization, sterilization cannot be correctly regarded as solely a "women's issue": in Puerto Rico, where over a third of the female population has been sterilized, it was blatantly used to tailor the labor force to the needs of U.S. corporations, which by 1930, thirty-two years after U.S. troops invaded the island, owned over half the land there.[11] Not only were women used as cheap labor in factories, which had sterilization clinics on the very premises, but they were used as guinea pigs for contraceptive pills twenty times stronger than those now marketed.[12] The threat has not lifted: a bill only recently defeated in Ohio proposed punishing female drug offenders with forced sterilization.[13]

Meanwhile, a mostly white, middle-class women's movement and the forces fighting racism and imperialism in communities of color have failed to address the oppression faced by women of color and poor women, or to include them meaningfully. The reality is that poor women of color face not just vicious sexism, or isolated racism, but unemployment or dead-end jobs, homelessness, chemical addiction, racist and sexual violence, lack of access to housing, health care, and education, and imprisonment for supposed economic and moral crimes like sex work, welfare fraud, and shoplifting. The state controls women of color and their reproductive functions, but has no concern for their quality of life and their opportunities. Nine million women have no health insurance, and 52 percent of Black female-headed families live in poverty.[14] Black infant mortality is almost twice that of white, and one main cause, low birthweight, is totally preventable if women have access to care. However, 25 percent to 30 percent of inner-city Black women receive little or no prenatal care, and the number is rising.[15] Currently, only sixteen states fund abortions for poor women, and only 18 percent of counties have even one abortion provider.[16] In 1970, 80 percent of the deaths in New York City from botched illegal abortions were of Black and Latina women; the death rate nationally for women of color from illegal abortions was twelve times that of white women.[17]

This reality demands a new, comprehensive vision of antiracist, feminist, leftist politics speaking to the lives of women of color and poor women. Reproductive freedom is clearly more than mere freedom from government interference: it means the right to bear children; to have access to safe, affordable health care, preventive care, hospitals, and pre- and postnatal care; to obtain culturally relevant information and education about sexuality, reproduction, contraception; and to make informed, uncoerced choices, whether the potential coercion be physical or financial. It means addressing the problems that exist in our communities, and not just in our wombs.

Given this background on the restriction of reproductive freedom for women of color and low-income women, it is not surprising that the symbiotic relationship of race, class, and gender is highlighted in this most recent crisis. Women have been prosecuted for drug addiction during pregnancy, for supposed "delivery of drugs to minors" or "child abuse," with the words "child" and "minors" actually referring to the fetus. The number of cases has exploded, from two to over sixty in two years.[18] By mid-1992, over 160 women in twenty-four states had been arrested and criminally charged for drug or alcohol use during pregnancy; innumerable others continue to face deprivation of custody through civil court procedures.[19]

Although substance use is equally prevalent across socioeconomic and racial lines, almost all the women arrested have been poor, and over 80 percent have been women of color, primarily Black, Latina, and Native American.[20] Public hospitals often systematically test and report their patients, who are often on Medicaid, while private doctors with insured patients and a profit incentive do not.[21] A study in Florida showed that about 15 percent of Black and a slightly *greater* percentage of white women used substances during pregnancy, but Black women were *ten* times more likely to be reported; 60 percent of those women reported had incomes of less than $12,000 a year.[22]

The criteria that determine who will be tested target poor women and women of color. For example, one criterion is absent or late prenatal care, and in South Carolina, one of the primary prosecuting states, Medicaid does not cover prenatal care until the nineteenth week of pregnancy; a second criterion is relatively small fetal size, which is likewise linked to access to care and proper nutrition.

While the entire program is racially discriminatory, it is also punitive and counter-productive. On one hand, there is *not* adequate, affordable drug treatment for chemically addicted women who are pregnant: over half the drug treatment programs in New York City exclude pregnant women, and two-thirds refuse women whose costs are paid by Medicaid.[23] In some states, Medicaid will not cover crack addiction treatment costs. The beds of those few that are left are often full, or don't have any child care — so women risk losing custody of their children to take care of themselves. Nationally, there are over 67,000 people on waiting lists for drug treatment.[24] Two-thirds of the hospitals report having nowhere to refer pregnant, drug-using women.[25]

Drug treatment programs that do exist are primarily designed for white males and are unresponsive to the needs of these women, including their psychological, social, and economic conditions.[26] It is estimated that up to 90 percent of women addicts are survivors of rape or incest, many grew up in a home with chemically addicted people, and many are currently in battering relationships.[27] Drug use then must be seen and responded to as a way of alleviating such pain, and treatment must address these related problems.

Groups that are as far from radical as the American Medical Association,[28] the the American College of Obstetricians and Gynecologists,[29] and American Academy of Pediatrics[30] have publicly opposed the prosecutions as counterproductive, because mandatory reporting and the threat of prosecution deter women from obtaining prenatal care. Prenatal care can be medically more determinative of the health of the fetus than occasional drug use. Studies have shown that it is "safer" for a fetus to be born to a woman who is a drug user, anemic, or diabetic with prenatal care than to be born to a medically "normal" woman without prenatal care.[31] Some reports link nicotine and alcohol use more directly to fetal difficulties than illicit substance use,[32] but the "War on Drugs" fuels counterproductive, ignorant hysteria that demonizes addicts of crack cocaine.

The actual effects of crack use may be overstated, or at least prematurely presumed to be documented and understood. As stated in a *Journal of the American Medical Association* commentary, "predictions of an adverse developmental outcome of these children are being made despite lack of support of scientific evidence."[33] Where deleterious effects are seen in infants that have been exposed to crack, preliminary studies have shown that only a quarter of the harm may be attributable to crack: a full three-fourths may be attributable to the effects of poverty, malnutrition, stress, and lack of prenatal care.[34] Additionally, unsupervised withdrawal from drug use, even if possible, can actually damage the fetus,[35] again showing the importance of getting women into care, not driving them away. By the prosecutions, women are deterred from seeking the care they need, as acknowledged by even the U.S. General Accounting Office,[36] and they are dissuaded from disclosing negative health information fully to health care workers, knowing that doctor-patient confidentiality will be violated.

What these prosecutions have done, other than discourage women from seeking care, and harm women and infants, is to make pregnancy a crime for women, especially poor women of color, who suffer from the disease of chemical addiction. Criminally, laws meant to apply to sellers of drugs are being warped to apply to these situations, and elevate drug use to a *felony* for pregnant women. In the extreme case, one woman was charged with assault with a deadly weapon.[37] In legal terms, we argue that this violates constitutional guarantees of due process, the right to freedom from cruel and unusual punishment, and notice as to what behavior is criminal.

These laws also unconstitutionally infringe on a woman's fundamental right to make decisions about procreation, her right to privacy, her right to freedom from unreasonable search and seizure, her right to bodily autonomy, and her right to freedom from discrimination on the basis of gender and race.[38]

Underlying the prosecutions is an approach that again dictates to an "unfit woman" her lack of options, plays on racist, sexist stereotypes, and treats her as incapable of responsible decision: a child, a savage, an entity less important than the fetus, a mere factory for the production of people. It pretends to protect a fetus while in actuality it endangers both fetus and woman, and cares nothing for the lives of the infant once born and the poor individuals and communities of color at large. It holds women to a standard it does not hold men: men's drinking has been linked to fetal abnormalities, but they are not held accountable for that, nor for the fact that one in twelve women is battered by a partner during pregnancy. And finally, it holds individual women blameworthy but exculpates a system that cut federal drug and alcohol funding by 40 percent in 1981.

Illustrating how the issue is about the control of women is a case in which a woman was actually charged with failing to follow doctor's instructions to stay off her feet and to refrain from sexual intercourse.[39] Another woman, when she went to the hospital emergency room fearing that the beating her husband had inflicted on her may have affected the fetus, was arrested for having had a drink.[40] A third is forbidden to use alcohol, go to bars, or associate with people who use alcohol, for fifteen years. Thus, police and prosecutors become "trustees" of the fetus, tyrannically controlling the lives of women. In South Carolina, the *parents* of a pregnant woman are charged with neglect of their daughter and their apparent "grand fetus"; another woman was sentenced to ten years, which is a sentence unheard of for simple drug use. Yet another was guarded by officers during labor, prohibited from seeing her newborn — who was hidden in the nursery under a pseudonym — and taken to jail, literally still bleeding from delivery.[41]

While appellate level courts in Florida, Kentucky, Michigan, Ohio, and California have ruled that it is improper to apply the drug delivery or child endangerment statutes to prenatal conduct,[42] states continue to deprive women of custody because of drug use during pregnancy.[43] Perhaps more important, most women may not have the luxury of challenging their loss of custody, arrest, or conviction, or of rejecting a plea to the charged crime, which may get them probation.

Sixteen percent of U.S. children are mentally and neurologically damaged, according to the *New England Journal of Medicine* — from lead exposure, mostly paint peeling in substandard housing.[44] Women of color are forced to live in neighborhoods bounded by toxic waste dumps, work under inhumane and dangerous conditions, suffer battering, rape, poverty, and lack of health care — and then are prosecuted for conduct that is deemed hazardous to the health of the fetus.

Any feminist cry about freedom of *choice* rings hollow to these women in economic and racial subjugation. And a Black, Latino, Native, or other agenda for liberation that does not acknowledge these particular repressive acts toward women is incomplete. Chemically addicted women, without access to drug treatment or a change in the circumstances that have led to drug use, do not make a "choice" to continue drug use during pregnancy. And where abortion and family planning are unavailable to women without resources, some women do not make a "choice" to become and remain pregnant, but instead are forced to carry to term.

The prosecutions of pregnant women for drug use during pregnancy have diverted attention from governmental indifference to 67,000 people on waiting lists for drug treatment nationwide. The issue has been transformed into one of individual blame and "deviant subcultures." Through the prosecutions, the state has provided vindication for police brutality, license for greater arbitrary and discriminatory civil intrusions, and justification for its ongoing systemic assaults on communities of color and low-income communities, while simultaneously dismantling those communities' scant social services and developmental resources. With this form of state-sanctioned violence against women, the government has designed strategies to overlook substance abuse by whites and middle and upper classes while punishing, stigmatizing, and scapegoating the poor, Blacks, and Latinas/os. It has laid the groundwork for the retraction of fundamental civil liberties guaranteed in the Bill of Rights. It has implanted in people's minds the image of women addicted to crack as the greatest threat to the health of newborns, even though poverty has been found to have an effect three times that of crack on infant health. It has absolved itself from any responsibility for an infant mortality rate higher than that in eighteen other countries, and its position as one of only two industrialized countries that fail to provide universal health coverage, child care, and parental leave. It has created an ahistorical, decontextualized explanation of drug use, and appeared engaged in anti-drug activity without actually threatening the profitable drug trade. It has obscured the real issues of lack of access to health care and treatment (making recovery from addiction impossible), unemployment, and inadequate education (rendering recovery pointless). It has failed to reduce chemical addiction, to actually take responsibility for addressing the complex societal problems at hand; its supposed "War on Drugs" has been counterproductive, irresponsible, and a predictable, miserable failure. Without recognizing that all these issues are interrelated, feminists risk missing the point altogether, and losing the battle as well as the war.

While women are imprisoned, homeless families starve on the streets, and the government provides billions for food and shelter only when it sustains soldiers in its imperialist wars — where is the outcry? It seems to be business as usual — with a bit of depressing new business on the reproductive front: one of the first publicized uses of a new birth control method, Norplant, was an attempt by a California judge to sentence a woman to forced surgical implantation of the device as a condition of her probation upon conviction of child abuse.[45]

Norplant, like all forms of birth control, has its strengths and weaknesses.[46] It was finally approved by the FDA in December 1990. It would have been encouraging if we could have seen this new device, the first major new form of birth control in over twenty years, as a much needed option for women, a technological advancement that could offer a little more choice to women. Then we could have entered the fray trying to be sure that it was available to poor women, that women were fully informed about it before they made their decision, that it was used safely. Instead of that expansion of choice, we see this new product immediately being used coercively, used to limit the options of women, and used to punish the women who most need access to health care and control of their lives: poor women and women of color.

Norplant use involves six three-centimeter silicone rubber capsules filled with a steroid that must be surgically implanted and removed with the use of a local anesthesia by a person trained in counseling, insertion, and removal.[47] There are a variety of possible adverse effects of Norplant,[48] and the implantation of Norplant may be contraindicated for women with certain health conditions.[49] In fact, the woman sentenced to Norplant in California, Ms. Johnson, was a low-income Black woman who suffered from three such contraindications: high blood pressure, diabetes, and a slight heart murmur.

The decision to choose to use Norplant, a prescription drug, should be a medical and a personal decision. It requires not only the full consent of the woman patient, who must be fully informed about the risks, but also the advice and counsel of a health care worker who is knowledgeable about Norplant and the patient's medical history.[50] The judge taking on an unlicensed practice of medicine in the Johnson case, Judge Broadman, is rumored to have tried to put a woman on Norplant before it was even approved by the FDA. It is not, however, an individual bad judge per se that is the problem. The sentence, although ultimately not carried out, reflects the ongoing bias against women of color.

The judge sentenced Johnson to one year in prison and three years probation, and added as a condition of probation that she have Norplant surgically implanted. To have it removed, she would have to get permission from the court and go back to a doctor. While the judge claimed that she agreed to this, he never explained that it was to be surgically implanted, and even admitted in the hearing, "you probably haven't heard of it," and later, "you're probably losing what I am saying right now."[51] As soon as she realized what the judge was imposing on her, Johnson refused, and her attorney filed an appeal.

The originator of Norplant immediately responded to the sentence as well, saying that he was "totally and unalterably opposed to the use of Norplant for any coercive or involuntary purpose. It was invented to improve reproductive freedom, not restrict it."[52] Medical and legal professionals alike have insisted that the kind of informed consent required for medical procedures is not possible in this kind of criminal justice setting.

In the inadequate legal terms (stemming from the fact that law itself is structurally a system of repression in this society), we talk about this type of sentence violating a woman's rights to liberty, privacy, and bodily integrity and the right to freedom from cruel and unusual punishment under the state and federal constitutions. It also violated California law requiring probation conditions to be reasonable: that they be related to past and future criminality and illegal conduct.[53] No court has upheld a condition that requires sterilization, contraception, castration, marriage before conception, or celibacy as a condition of probation.[54]

In the law, there is the requirement that probation include the restoration of self-esteem, integration into a working environment, and the inculcation of social responsibility.[55] Forced contraception surely fails to improve a woman's self-esteem or teach her to be "responsibly free." Coerced contraception does nothing to address the underlying conditions that led to child abuse or teach coping skills, nor will it enable a woman to be a better parent or prevent future abuse. Any program that would be narrowly tailored, as is required when fundamental rights such as procreation are infringed, to rehabilitate an abuser and address child abuse would look very different from one mandating such surgery: counseling, parenting classes, prenatal care, job assistance, and child care are all more relevant. Like an Orwellian nightmare, it seems society can only use drugs and punishment to express its vengeance, rather than having offered adequate social services, information, education, opportunities, access to birth control, and relevant counseling.

While it is clear that this is a punishment that falls only on women, in the case of Johnson, the judge revealed other race and class biases that underlie such actions, commenting on Johnson's status as a single mother and as a recipient of public assistance.[56] While child abuse crosses racial and socioeconomic lines, the people under the scrutiny of the government, who face biased intervenors from the state, are people receiving public assistance, and in this country the poor are disproportionately people of color. It has also been documented that child abuse procedures have historically been imbued with cultural and racial ethnocentrism and class bias.[57]

The judge also came forth as self-appointed guardian of her fetus by ordering Johnson not to smoke cigarettes in jail or drink beer or wine,[58] activities both legal and totally unrelated to her conviction. He commented in the press on her past record — which is not one of child abuse, but forged checks and petty theft. These crimes may speak more to her economic need and desperation to provide for a family in the face of governmental indifference than any sort of "criminality," and his comments may illuminate his racist assumptions about Black criminality.

As egregious as Judge Broadman's actions were, they are unfortunately indicative of the sentiments of more than a few of the people in power. A Kansas legislator proposed to pay women with children who receive public assistance $500 to have Norplant implanted in order to prevent populating this nation with what he seemingly thinks are undesirables.[59] Although the government generally is unconcerned about basic health maintenance or preventive health measures, for this procedure the state would pay for annual checkups, and would pay fifty dollars each year the device stayed implanted. These draconian measures are often proposed by individuals with strong antichoice views, revealing the hypocrisy of the fallaciously named "pro-life" lobby. While the Kansas legislator felt "something must be done to reduce the number of unwanted pregnancies," an antichoice administration denies funding to even educate about birth control.[60]

How have we gotten to a stage where a woman can be jailed for being a pregnant addict, where poor women and women of color can be openly bribed or ordered to not have children? For one, while these and the attacks on welfare emerge as new crises, what they reflect are just new manifestations of unaddressed chronic deprivation: poverty, racism, and lack of health care, opportunities, and control over our own lives.

Second, these crises reflect the success of government repression of any resistance that began to effectively respond to the material realities of the race and class dimension of people's lives in an empowering, self-determining way, whether it's the government's murderous COINTELPRO against the Black Panthers or current repression against Native American activists, Puerto Rican independentistas,[61] or AIDS demonstrators.[62]

And finally, it reflects a failure of a white, middle-class-dominated feminist movement, a failure of communities of color to get beyond narrow capitalist nationalism, middle-class integrationism, and/or male-defined agendas. There has been a failure to make movements truly inclusive; issues of the disenfranchised, the poor, women, lesbians and gay men, drug users, and others have been marginalized. Movements have replicated hierarchy and stratification, as have institutions within communities that were designed to provide support.

A solution to these crises involves the need for political organizing to obtain concrete improvements — drug treatment, health services, day care, job leave, prenatal care and education — while also addressing the underlying causes of race, class, and gender inequality, using a revolutionary analysis. This is where the work of leftists, activists, and feminists should be focused, work that must be inclusive and complete, work that is centered around input from, impact on, and empowerment of the most marginalized in our communities. Liberatory politics must provide more than mere antiracist slogans, tokenism, and noblesse oblige; feminist leftist politics must give up privileges, share power, expand leadership and agendas, and provide a real vehicle to challenge those structures of domination. We must overcome a myopic vision and travel far beyond literary criticism, rhetoric, and commodification of culture and identity to engage in day-to-day diligent community work, coalition building, and revolutionary resistant action.

NOTES

1. On the legacy of government control over Black women, from enslavement to its present forms, see Berrien, "Pregnancy and Drug Use: The Dangerous and Unequal Use of Punitive Measures," 2, no. 2, *Yale Journal of Law and Feminism* 239 (1990); and Davis, *Women, Race and Class* 202–21 (1983).

2. See, e.g., Davis, *Women, Race and Class* at 208–14.

3. See Paltrow, Goetz, and Shende, "Overview of ACLU National Survey of Criminal Prosecutions Brought against Pregnant Women," *ACLU Reproductive Freedom Project Memorandum*, October 3, 1990, at 2 n.2; Kolder, Gallagher, and Parsons, "Court-Ordered Obstetrical Interventions," 316 *New England Journal of Medicine* 1192–96 (May 7, 1987); and National Health Law Program, *Court-Ordered Caesareans: A Growing Concern for Indigent Women* 1064 (Feb. 1988). See *In re A.C.*, 573 A.2d 1235 (D.C. App. 1990).

4. See, e.g., *Doe v. Jamaica Hospital*, No. 31248/89 (N.Y. Sup. Ct. Kings Cty. filed 1989), where abortion was not a choice but was imposed on a woman: she was not allowed to consider the prospect of herself or her family raising the child; her informed consent was never obtained; and it was never explained to her that approximately 50 percent to 80 percent of infants sero-convert (become HIV-negative) within a few months of birth; see Amaro, "Women's Reproductive Rights in the Age of AIDS: New Threats to Informed Choice," in Fried, *From Abortion to Reproductive Freedom: Transforming a Movement* 252–53 (1990).

5. *Harris v. McRae*, 448 U.S. 297 (1980) (permitting the government to exclude abortion from the services funded by Medicaid).

6. Davis, *Women, Race and Class* at 215–16.

7. Davis, "Racism and Reproductive Rights," in Fried, *From Abortion to Reproductive Freedom* at 22–23; Flores, Davison, Mercedes Rey, Rivera, and Serrano, "La Mujer Puertorriqueña, Su Cuerpo, y Su Lucha por la Vida: Experiences with Empowerment in Hartford, Connecticut," in Fried at 224–25.

8. Fried, "Abortion and Sterilization in the Third World," in Fried, *From Abortion to Reproductive Freedom* at 63.

9. Flores et al. at 224–25; Davis, "Racism" at 23; Dixon, Ross, Avery, and Jenkins, "The Reproductive Health of Black Women and Other Women of Color," in Fried, *From Abortion to Reproductive Freedom* at 159.

10. Chargot, "Abortion and the Poor," *Detroit Free Press*, August 5, 1990.

11. *La Operación*, film produced and directed by Ana Maria Garcia (1982); and Mujeres en Acción Pro Salud Reproductiva: Northeast Project on Latina Women and Reproductive Health, *Puertorriqueñas: Sociodemographics, Health, and Reproductive Issues among Puerto Rican Women in the U.S.* 5 (released by the Hispanic Health Council, Hartford, CT).

12. *La Operacion*; see also Beneria and Sen, "Accumulation, Reproduction, and Women's Role in Economic Development: Boserup Revisited," *Signs* 279 (winter 1981); note the history of genocidal government experimentation on people of color, such as the Tuskegee experiment, Jones, *Bad Blood: The Tuskegee Syphilis Experiment — A Tragedy of Race and Medicine* (1981).

13. S. 324, 118th General Assembly, Regular Session 1989–90 (introduced by Senator Cooper Snyder). See also Berrien at 240–41.

14. Roberts, "The Future of Reproductive Choice for Poor Women and Women of Color," 12 *Women's Rights Law Reporter* 59, 64 (1990) (also presenting thorough, well-contextualized overview); see also Dixon et al. at 157–59.

15. Children's Defense Fund, *The Health of America's Children: Maternal and Child Health Data Book* (1989); Wilkerson and Mitchell, "Staying Alive! The Challenge of Improving Black America's Health," *Emerge Magazine*, September 1991, at 24; see McNulty, "Pregnancy Police: The Health Policy and Legal Implications of Punishing Pregnant Women for Harm to Their Fetuses," 16 *New York University Review of Law and Social Change* 277, 293–99 (1987–88); Berrien at 248.

16. Pollitt, "A New Assault on Feminism," *Nation*, March 26, 1990, at 409, 414.

17. Davis, *Women, Race and Class* at 204.

18. See Paltrow and Shende, "State by State Case Summary of Criminal Prosecutions against Pregnant Women," *ACLU Reproductive Freedom Project Memorandum*, April 2, 1991.

19. Center for Reproductive Law and Policy, "Punishing Women for Their Behavior during Pregnancy: A Public Health Disaster," *Reproductive Freedom in Focus*, Center for Reproductive Law and Policy, February 14, 1996.

20. *Id.*; see also Paltrow, Goetz, and Shende at 1–2; Kolata, "Racial Bias Seen on Pregnant Addicts, *New York Times*, July 20, 1990, at A13. Racism in the supposed fight against drug use is nothing new; see Aldrich, "Who Was Using It? Racism in the Formation of U.S. Drug Policy," a slide talk presented at the International Conference on Drug Policy Reform, Washington, DC (October 31–November 4, 1990).

21. Chasnoff, Landress, and Barrett, "The Prevalence of Illicit Drug or Alcohol Use during Pregnancies and Discrepancies in Mandatory Reporting in Pinellas County, Florida," 322 *New England Journal of Medicine* 1202 (April 26, 1990).

22. *Id.*; see also Winslow, "Black Pregnant Women Far More Likely to Be Reported for Drug Use," *Wall Street Journal*, April 27, 1990.

23. Chavkin, "Help, Don't Jail Addicted Mothers," *New York Times*, July 13, 1989.

24. Survey done by the National Association of State Alcohol and Drug Abuse Directors in 1989.

25. *Testimony before House Select Committee on Children, Youth and Families*, 101st Cong., 1st sess. (April 27, 1989) (opening statement by Rep. and Chair George Miller).

26. Reed, "Developing Women-Sensitive Drug-Dependence Treatment Services: Why So Difficult?" 19 *Journal of Psychoactive Drugs* 151 (1987); Finkelstein, "Treatment Issues: Women and Substance Abuse," prepared for the National Coalition on Alcohol and Drug Dependent Women and Their Children (September 1990).

27. Walker, "Abused Mothers, Infants, and Substance Abuse: Psychological Consequences of Failure to Protect," prepared for the American Psychological Association Division on Clinical Psychology and Georgetown University Child Development Mid-Winter Conference on Mothers, Infants and Substance Abuse, Scottsdale, AZ (January 19–20, 1990); Kilpatrick, "Violence as a Precursor to Women's Substance Abuse: The Rest of the Drug-Violence Story," presented at the Topical Mini-Convention on Substance Abuse and Violence, American Psychological Convention, Boston (August 1990); Finkelstein, Duncan, Derman, and Smeltz, *Getting Sober, Getting Well: A Treatment Guide for Caregivers Who Work with Women* 244 (1990); Leff, "Treating Drug Addiction with the Woman in Mind," *Washington Post*, March 5, 1990, at E4; Malaspina, "Clean Living," *Boston Globe Magazine*, November 5, 1989, at 20; Randall, "Domestic Violence Begets Other Problems of Which Physicians Must Be Aware to Be Effective," 264 *Medical News and Perspectives* 940 (1990); Amaro, Fried, Cabral, and Zuckerman, "Violence during Pregnancy and Substance Abuse," 80 *American Journal of Public Health* 575 (1990).

28. "Legal Interventions during Pregnancy" 262 *Journal of the American Medical Association* 2663 (November 28, 1990).

29. A.C.O.G. Committee on Ethics, *Committee Opinion — Patient Choice: Maternal Fetal Conflict*, no. 55 (October 1987).

30. American Academy of Pediatrics, Committee on Substance Abuse, "Drug Exposed Infants," 86 *Pediatrics* 639–42 (1990).

31. "Taxpayers Pay for Lack of Prenatal Treatment," *St. Petersburg Times*, November 3, 1986, at 7B.

32. Mofensen and Caraccio, "Cocaine," 16 *Pediatric Annals* 864, 872 (1987); Krieger, "Study Finds Babies Born as Addicts Can Lead Normal Lives," *San Francisco Examiner*, February 6, 1990, at A10.

33. Mayes, Granger, Bornstein, and Zuckerman, "The Problem of Prenatal Cocaine Exposure: A Rush to Judgment," 267 *Journal of the American Medical Association* 406 (January 15, 1992). See also Karel, " 'Crack' Babies: Earlier Reports Drew Premature Conclusions," *Psychiatric News*, March 19, 1993, at 9; and Fackelmann, "The Crack Baby Myth," *Washington City Paper*, December 11, 1991, at 25.

34. Murphy and Rosenbaum, "Blame Poverty for their Learning Disabilities," *New York Times*, February 27, 1991, at A27.

35. Finnegan, "Management of Drug Dependent Women," 562 *Annals of New York Academy of Sciences* 135 (1988).

36. U.S. General Accounting Office Report to the Chairman [*sic*], Committee on Finance, U.S. Senate, "Drug Exposed Infants: A Generation at Risk," GAO/HRD-90-138 (June 1990).

37. *North Carolina v. Inzar*, No. 90CRS6960, 90CRS6961 slip op. (N.C. Super. Ct. April 9, 1991) appeal dismissed, No. 9116SC778 (N.C. App. August 30, 1991).

38. See infra n. 42; *State of South Dakota v. Christensen*, No. CR 90–377 (S.D. Cir. Ct. 2d Div., Cty. of Minnehaha Filed 1990); also McNulty; Berrien; and Gallagher, "Prenatal Invasions and Interventions: What's Wrong with Fetal Rights," 10 *Harvard Women's Law Journal* 9 (1987).

39. See *State of California v. Stewart*, No. M508197 (Cal. Muni. Ct. Cty. February 26, 1987) (reporter's transcript) (charges were dismissed following public outrage and protest).

40. *State of Wyoming v. Pfannenstiel*, No. 1–90–8CR (Wyo. Cty. Ct. filed January 5, 1990).

41. Goetz and Fox, *ACLU Reproductive Freedom Project Initial Report: Poor and Pregnant? Don't Go to South Carolina* (February 1, 1990); Paltrow, Goetz, and Shende; and Paltrow and Shende.

42. *People v. Hardy*, 469 N.W.2d 50 (Mich. Ct. App. 1991); *State v. Gray*, 584 N.E.2d 710 (Ohio 1992); *Reyes v. Superior Court*, 75 Cal. App. 3d 214 (1977); *Johnson v. State*, 602 So.2d 1288 (Fla. 1992); *Welch v. Commonwealth*, No. 92–SC-490–DG, slip op. (Ky. September 30, 1993); *People v. Morabito*, 580 N.Y.S.2d 843 (Geneva City Ct. 1992) aff'd, slip op. (Ontario Cty. September 24, 1992); *State v. Luster*, 419 S.E.2d 32 (Ga. App. 1992); *State v. Gethers*, 585 So.2d 1140 (Fla. App. 1991); *State v. Carter*, 602 So.2d 995 (Fla. App. 1992). See also, e.g., trial-level victories: *People v. Stewart*, No. M508197 (Cal. Muni. Ct. February 26, 1987); *State v. Andrews*, No. JU 68459 (Ohio C.P. June 19, 1989); *Commonwealth v. Pelligrini*, No. 87970, slip op. (Mass. Super. Ct. October 15, 1990); *State v. Bremer*, No. 90–32227–FH slip op. (Mich. Cir. Ct. January 31, 1991); *North Carolina v. Inzar, supra* at n. 37.

43. See, e.g., *In re Monique T.*, 4 Cal. Rptr. 2d 198 (Ct. App. 1992); *In re Dustin T.*, No. 1949 (Md. Ct. Spec. App. 1992); *In re Theresa J.*, 551 N.Y.S.2d 219 (App. Div. 1990); *In the Matter of Nash*, 419 N.W.2d 1 (Mich. Ct. App. 1987); *In re Ruiz*, 27 Ohio Misc.2d 31 (Wood Cty. C.P. 1986). Some courts have rejected these arguments, e.g., *In re Valerie D.*, 223 Conn. 492 (1992); *State ex rel. Juvenile Dept. of Marion Cty. v. Randall*, 773 P.2d 1348 (Or. Ct. App. 1989); *Cox v. Ct. of Common Pleas*, 537 N.E.2d 721 (Ohio Ct. App. 1988); *In re Solomon L.*, 236 Cal. Rptr. 2 (Ct. App. 1987); and *In re Dittrick Infant*, 263 N.W.2d 37 (Mich. Ct. App.).

44. Pollitt at 409.

45. *State of California v. Johnson*, No. F015316 (Cal. 5th App. Dist. filed April 24, 1991). Johnson was convicted of child abuse: this was her first offense. She pleaded guilty to hitting two of her children with a belt and an electrical cord when she found them smoking cigarettes and playing with wire in an outlet.

46. The medical and scientific information on Norplant is from Hatcher, Stewart, Trussell, Kowal, Guest, Stewart, and Cates, "Implants, Injections, and Other Progestin-Only Contraceptives," in *Contraceptive Technology, 1990–1992,* 301–14 (1990); Bardin, "Norplant Contraceptive Implants," 2:1 *Obstetrics and Gynecology Report* 96–102 (winter 1990); and the Population Council, *Norplant: A Summary of Scientific Data* (1990).

47. For five years, the pregnancy rate of users was about 1 percent to 3 percent. Its effects are reported to be completely reversible soon after removal. It works by suppressing ovulation, impairing sperm penetration by thickening cervical mucus, and other mechanisms.

48. These include the possibility of infection at the site of insertion, headache, depression, nervousness, fatigue, dizziness, nausea, an increased risk of ectopic pregnancy, dermatitis, weight gain, breast tenderness, hair loss, anemia, ovarian cysts, an increase in cholesterol level, altered glucose tolerance, and multiple menstrual problems.

49. Such conditions include high blood pressure, diabetes, jaundice, unexplained vaginal

bleeding, a history of blood clots, heart attacks, chest pain, epilepsy, fibrocystic disease of the breast, migraines, mental depression, and gall bladder, heart, kidney, or liver disease.

50. In tests, 20 percent of the women terminated their use of Norplant in the first year. Thus, despite its long-term advantages, it is not ideal for every woman, even a woman who initially thinks it might be suitable.

51. *State of California v. Johnson*, Transcript at 6–9.

52. *New York Times*, January 6, 1991, editorial page.

53. See brief filed for the ACLU Reproductive Freedom Project and the ACLU of Northern California in *State v. Johnson* (No. F015316) (Cal. 5th App. Dist. filed April 24, 1991).

54. Green, "Depo Provera, Castration, and the Probation of Rape Offenders: Statutory and Constitutional Issues," 12 *University of Dayton Law Review* 1 (fall 1986); *People v. Pointer*, 15 Cal. App. 3d 1128 (1984); *In re Dominguez*, 256 Cal. App. 623 (1967); *State v. Mosburg*, 768 P.2d 313 (Kan. App. 1989); *Thomas v. State*, 519 S.2d 1119 (Fla. App. 1 Dist. 1986); *State v. Norman*, 484 S.2d (La. App. 1 Cir. 1986); *Smith v. Superior Court*, 726 P.2d 1101 (Sup. Ct of Ariz. 1986); *People v. Gauntlett*, 352 N.W.2d 310 (Mich. App. 1984); *Howland v. State*, 420 S.2d 919 (Fla. App. 1 Dist. 1982); *Wiggins v. Florida*, 386 S.2d 46 (Fla. App. 4 Dist. 1980); *Rodriguez v. State*, 378 S.2d 7 (Fla. App. 2 Dist. 1979); and *State v. Livingston*, 372 N.E.2d 1335 (Ohio App. 1977); see also *Skinner v. Oklahoma*, 316 U.S. 535 (1942).

55. See, e.g., *People v. Richards*, 17 Cal. 3d 614 (1976); *In re Martinez*, 86 Cal. App. 3d 577 (1988); and *People v. Keller*, 76 Cal. App. 3d 827 (1988).

56. Transcript at 6. Despite the fact that there are no allegations or evidence regarding the use of any illegal substance, he says he is "concerned about drug use," Transcript at 2.

57. This is not to say that abuse is not a real problem, but to warn of the dangers in such punitive measures, discriminatorily applied.

58. Transcript at 4, 9.

59. Kansas House Bill 2089, proposed by Representative Patrick, January 31, 1991. A *Philadelphia Inquirer* editorial, which was so soundly denounced as racist by staff and readers that the paper was forced to print an apology, proposed the same scheme.

60. Note the recent conservative success in prohibiting women from receiving accurate and thorough pregnancy-related information — the *Rust v. Sullivan* decision, which forbids federally funded facilities from providing basic information about the existence of abortion.

61. See, e.g., Churchill and Vander Wall, *Agents of Repression* (1988).

62. Dunlap, "FBI Kept Watch on AIDS Groups during Protest Years," *New York Times*, May 16, 1995.

EIGHT

Cultural Survival and Contemporary American Indian Women in the City

JENNIE R. JOE AND
DOROTHY LONEWOLF MILLER

Prior to their conquest and subsequent colonization, Indian women in most tribes held important positions as healers, teachers, and leaders. Moreover, because of their resourcefulness and ability to gather and store seeds, roots, and berries, and to hunt small game, they were able to feed their families when big game was scarce and hunting was poor. In some tribes, the women were the agriculturists and thereby provided the major food source for their families. The European conquest, however, greatly altered the world of most Native Americans.

The erosion of the role and position of Indian women began with missionization and education. Indian girls were forced to go to school to learn to be homemakers or handmaidens for non-Indian families. Others who dared to return to the reservations found themselves alienated until they either had to relearn traditional skills for survival and/or return to the non-Indian world to find work. This loss of values among Indian peoples was accelerated as more and more tribes were forced into a paternalistic or wardship position with the federal government. The fabric of many tribal cultures, however, survived because in many instances women of the tribe used whatever means were available to protect their children and their men. Unfortunately, they were no match for the powerful arm of the federal government, an institution that was bent on "civilizing" the Indians. Tribes may have been able to save some elements of their language or their cultural traditions, but these efforts did not stem the tide of other changes, which have resulted in poverty and the loss of psychological well-being.

Various forms of oppression and poverty continue today for many Indian women and their families. Forced by public outcry to improve the lot of American Indians, the federal government over the years has periodically initiated programs to deal with some of these problems. One economic alternative was the relocation of young Indian women and men to urban areas where the federal government had arranged contracts with trade schools and employment agencies for job placement. Jobs were primarily unskilled or semiskilled, and resettlement was in urban ghettos. Thus, other than when World War II manpower shortages permitted Indian women to be recruited to work in war plants (the first large-scale out-migration), the federal relocation program of the 1950s and 1960s was the first major out-migration of Indian women from the reservations. The relocation program, however, favored single young adults, which meant that many of the young women had to leave their children behind with grandparents or other extended family members. Once settled, they could arrange child care and other services; then women brought their children to the city and/or started their family in the city.

The government-sponsored relocation program uprooted many single young Indian women as well as young married women. Although the relocation was necessary for the economic survival of many women and their families, that policy, along with the push toward wage labor, began to erode the traditional extended family units that had acted as a buffer against many of the daily stresses of poverty and other hardships. Since the move to the city left them lacking the psychological support of kin and friends, many young women and their children were forced either to seek out other Native Americans in the city or to save enough money to finance frequent trips home. Frustrations and stresses in the city were compounded by problems of discrimination and loneliness. In addition, poverty and unemployment continued to plague many of the families — a situation that continually undermined the economic roles of men and, in some instances, shifted the burden of family support to the women. Because they were far from the reservation, many Indian women who had children had to assume sole responsibility for maintaining cultural continuity and tribal identity for their children.

Today, the future of Indian culture continues to be threatened by the increased migration to the cities. For example, the move to the city often breaks down the geographical boundaries of a reservation that help maintain tribalism and/or continuity of culture. This is not to say that reservation life remains unaffected by modernization and culture change. The erosion of cultural values and beliefs has been and continues to be widespread, so that the geographic boundaries are not enough. With time, the pressures toward assimilation have bred a number of "marginal" individuals, those who have no firm footing in either the Indian or the non-Indian world. The marginal existence has wrought devastation intergenerationally, and the scars from this experience continue to surface in various self-destructive behaviors: alcoholism, suicide, homicide, and/or permanent disability associated with other forms of "careless" behavior. Given these past experiences and their devastating consequences for many Indian families, the cultural strengths that kept tribal identity and families together have centered on the role of women in most tribes. For example, one Navajo woman leader (Wauneka 1987, 2) posits that "When Indian women move to the city or marry a non-Indian, the continuity of the tribal culture is threatened. . . . most of us learn about our 'Indianness' from our mothers."

Thus, continuity of culture and tribal identity is of paramount concern for most

Native American communities. For example, many legal and policy debates today focus on such issues as tribal membership and degree of Indian blood of the membership. As a result of this interest, there is an increased concern about whom an Indian woman marries and whether her children will be eligible for tribal membership. Urbanization, because it often results in marrying out and detribalization, is seen as a real threat to tribal and cultural continuity. In this chapter we explore how the responsibility for cultural continuity is accentuated for women in the city; we will examine the lives and experiences of a small sample of American Indian women in Tucson, Arizona, who have found ways to promote or construct cultural and tribal linkages for their children in the urban world.

Urbanization

Today, over half of the 1.9 million American Indians and Alaska Natives live in off-reservation communities, especially cities such as Los Angeles, Denver, San Francisco, and Chicago (U.S. Department of Commerce 1991).[1] As stated before, relocation to urban centers is viewed by many tribal leaders as one of the major threats to cultural continuity. Their fears are not unfounded. For example, these leaders point to the increasing number of intertribal and interracial marriages among the Indian population residing in the cities, and the increasing number of Indian children born and reared in the cities who have little or no knowledge of their tribal traditions or languages. One American Indian demographer has confirmed the tribal leaders' prediction; he estimates that by the year 2080, the percentage of urbanized American Indians with one-half or more Indian blood will decrease from the present (1980 census) 87 percent to 8 percent (Thornton 1987, 237).

In 1970 only one-third of all American Indians were married to non-Indians, but by 1980 this percentage increased to 50 percent (Thornton 1987, 236). As a result of intertribal and interracial marriages, the tribal identification among urbanized Indians appears to have become more generic over time. For example, Indians living in the cities are more likely than those living on the reservation to identify themselves generically as American Indians rather than as members of a specific tribe. It also is not uncommon to find an Indian child claiming lineage from more than one tribe because his or her parents also claim lineage from more than one tribe. In addition, because these Indian children are reared in ethnically diverse urban neighborhoods, they may not speak their tribal language and are less likely to hear their tribal language spoken.

Although there is no information yet available from the 1990 census as to how many urbanized Indians speak their tribal language, in 1970, 26 percent of urbanized Indians and 32 percent of Indians on the reservation indicated a tribal language as the first language learned (Thornton 1987, 238). In Los Angeles, where there is a sizable Indian population, 23 percent of the 54,569 American Indians interviewed in 1979 reported English as their second language (UCLA 1987). Matthew Snipp and Gary Sandefur (1988) found that 18 percent of the urban-dwelling Indians and 41 percent of the reservation Indians use their native language in their homes.

American Indian Women in Tucson

The Indian women who are subjects of this study either were born in the city of Tucson or have lived in Tucson for a number of years. Unlike the Indian women in Los Angeles, whose family history may include involuntary relocation, most of these women have always lived in Tucson or voluntarily moved there from nearby reservation communities. Yet despite voluntary relocation and prolonged urbanization, most of these women have acculturated but not assimilated. They are bicultural and bilingual. It could be said that for most of these women and their families, the walls of their houses, apartments, or mobile homes serve as psychological boundaries that help them maintain their cultural and tribal identity. These psychological boundaries therefore serve to encapsulate against assimilation.

Tucson, the second largest urban center in Arizona, is home to 6,868 American Indians, mostly Tohono O'odham, Pima, and Yaqui tribal members (Tucson Planning Department 1985). These three tribal groups constitute 89 percent of all Indians living in the city (Evaneshko 1988). The city sprawl is adjacent to the vast desert homelands of the Tohono O'odham (formerly Papago). One Tohono O'odham community and the two Yaqui villages (one on a new reservation) are within Tucson city limits. The Indian families in the city therefore live close to relatives and friends, and thus most familial and other social ties are maintained.

The urban experiences of these Indian women in Tucson afford an opportunity to examine some of the explanations regarding the forces present in their lives that help them maintain or foster cultural traditions and tribal identity for their children and themselves. This study therefore examines data from two tribal groups of women who were selected from a sample of clients — twenty-three Tohono O'odham and ten Yaqui women — who utilize the urban Indian health clinic in Tucson. These women were part of a larger study that began with a sample of one hundred Indian clients utilizing the Tucson urban Indian clinic.[2]

Tohono O'odham

The Tohono O'odham were residing in southern Arizona when the Spanish explorers first entered the region, and the O'odham view the valley of Tucson as part of their ancestral homeland. Their reservation is vast, covering a large part of southwestern Arizona, and a few tribal members live below the Mexican border in the state of Sonora. There exists a considerable ethnographic literature of the O'odham people (Densmore 1929; Underhill 1939; Spicer 1949, 1962; Shaw 1968; Bahr 1969).

The O'odham have undergone three major waves of invasion and conquest, by Spain, Mexico, and the United States. The Spanish and Mexican regimes introduced Catholicism into tribal life, beginning with construction of missions and winning of souls for the church. As a result, for a number of decades Tohono O'odham children were largely educated in Catholic schools that dotted the reservation. Yet, as is true throughout the Southwest, Catholicism was modified by the O'odham to mesh with their traditional religious beliefs. The cycles of conquest resulted in loss of vast lands, the depletion of water resources, and the influx of a large non-Indian population that grew into the city of Tucson. Under Anglo colonization, Tohono O'odham children were sent to government schools both on and off the reservation while their parents were forced into wage labor. With few or no job skills, most began to follow seasonal work, picking cotton or fruit in nearby areas. Other adults, because of poor health, age, or lack of job skills, became increasingly dependent on public welfare programs.

Yaquis

Unlike the Tohono O'odham, the Yaquis are newcomers to Tucson. They fled from northern Mexico in the late nineteenth and early twentieth centuries, and settled in a number of small villages and enclaves between Tucson and Phoenix. Historically and culturally, the Yaquis have remained distinct from their neighbors of northern Mexico and their new neighbors, the Tohono O'odham (Chaudhuri 1974). After years of work and countless efforts, the Yaquis were officially granted federal recognition in 1978 as an American Indian tribe (Locust 1987, 4). Although not all Yaquis are enrolled as members of this newly recognized tribe, today there is nevertheless a strong sense of tribal identity, and the new reservation of New Pascua serves as headquarters for the Yaqui tribal government.

Like the Tohono O'odham, the Yaquis have experienced diverse conditions since the 1890s. The Mexican Revolution and its aftermath divided the Yaqui communities in Mexico. Some Yaquis were captured and sent to Yucatan, others served in the Mexican Revolutionary armies, and still others fled to southern Arizona. Since the Spanish conquest of Mexico, Catholicism has been deeply embedded among the Yaquis. Despite their conflicts with the Mexican government, they became heavily Mexicanized, adopting many Mexican customs of food, dress, and social activities during their two centuries under Mexican government (Spicer 1949; Kelley 1978). Despite their Mexicanization, many Yaquis claim loyalty to the Yaqui culture. Yaqui women, for example, are especially sensitive to the accusation that they may "become Mexican." For example, one Yaqui woman, referring to her former daughter-in-law who was now married to a Mexican, observed, "She is not a Yaqui anymore — she became Mexican." Older Yaqui women are very deeply religious, as is shown by their collections of *santos* (religious statues) and religious pictures.

The Subjects: A Statistical Portrait

The statistical profile of the Indian women in this study indicates that Tohono O'odham women were younger, had a few more years of education, and had slightly more children than the Yaqui women. Table 8.1 summarizes the average ages, education, and family size.

Thirty percent of these women from both tribes were head of their household, a somewhat higher number in comparison to the 23 percent found among the Indian households in Los Angeles County (UCLA 1987). In addition, all ten Yaqui women

TABLE 8.1.
Average Age, Education, and Number of Children of
Tohono O'odham and Yaqui Mothers
(N = 33)

Tribe	Age	Education (years)	Number of children
Tohono O'odham	34.7	9.6	2.7
Yaqui	45.4	6.9	2.3

in the sample were born and reared in the city of Tucson, compared to 30 percent of the Tohono O'odham women.

Although a majority of both groups were members of the Catholic Church and said that marriage in the church was desirable, about 30 percent indicated that they had been married more than once, often outside the church. Over 44 percent declared themselves single on public documents, but some were living with a mate who may or may not be the father of their children. Only 18 percent of these Indian mothers were married to a man from their tribe, 40 percent were single parents, and others had companions who were from other tribes or who were Mexicans. Only one reported that an Anglo man resided with her. Perhaps as a result of the Catholic religion, there are not many divorces. Some of the fathers of their children had either deserted the family or had never legitimized the children by marriage. Thus some of these women were financially dependent on Aid to Families with Dependent Children (AFDC) and whatever cash they could obtain from domestic or other part-time work.

Nearly half of these mothers were born on their reservation or in their village. Tohono O'odham women were more likely to be born in their reservation communities than were Yaqui women (52 percent versus 30 percent). One-third of these Indian mothers speak their native language (many are trilingual: English, Spanish, and their native language). Fifteen percent of their children speak their native language. In addition, 82 percent of all the children are enrolled in their mother's tribe, a crucial element in maintaining tribal ties and continuity of Indian identity. Tribal enrollment becomes very crucial in obtaining health and education benefits as well as providing a structural basis for deeper psychological definitions of the self.

An examination of the cultural identities of the sample population is presented in table 8.2. The women from the Tohono O'odham and Yaqui communities, for the most part, identify themselves as either O'odham or Yaqui. Children likewise speak of themselves as O'odham or as Yaqui, although in school, their non-Indian teachers and schoolmates frequently refer to them as "Indians." At home, specific tribal identity is more common. For example, when asked about cultural values and identity, some of the responses were "To be O'odham is to be good. To be special. To do things in a certain way." To be Yaqui is to "live the Yaqui way." In many instances, for the women as well as for their children, language and skin color provide two dimensions of the variations of their view of the non-O'odham or non-Yaqui world. Although language and skin color may be most visible, proximity to the reservation and age are also factors. Younger women place less emphasis on tribal

TABLE 8.2.
Indicators of Tribal Identity of Urban O'odham and Yaqui Mothers

	Yaqui (N = 10) N (%)	O'odham (N = 23) N (%)	Total (N = 33) N (%)
Mother born on reservation	3 (30)	12 (52)	15 (47)
Mother speaks native language	3 (30)	8 (35)	11 (33)
Child speaks native language	3 (30)	2 (9)	5 (15)
Child enrolled in tribe	8 (80)	19 (83)	27 (82)
Married, same tribe	3 (30)	3 (13)	6 (18)
Use medicine people	4 (40)	9 (39)	13 (39)
Use Indian remedies	6 (60)	7 (30)	13 (39)

identity than do older women. This observation parallels that of Jane Kelley (1978), who posits that Tohono O'odham can be expected to adhere less precisely to indigenous beliefs when they are away from members of their social group or away from their family life. On the other hand, Kelley also notes that there comes a time in life (middle age) when old beliefs reappear and are reinforced by that social group.

In addition, the cultural ties to traditional medicine and Indian lifestyles of these women are indicated by the fact that nearly 40 percent used medicine people and Indian remedies during times of illness. Thus the blending of secular and sacred medicine for illnesses is common among both groups.

The Tohono O'odham and Yaqui women share many characteristics that are relevant to their adaptation to urban life. First, these women tend to be welfare mothers, often separated from stable incomes or enduring relationships with an employed man; second, the core of their cultural life is the blend of Catholicism and the native belief system that they practice in their daily lives; and third, they live separate from the mainstream of Tucson urban life — they reside in segregated residential areas, they know Tucson Anglos "look down" on Indians, and they avoid confrontation or do not expect equal employment or economic opportunities. Thus, these women are forced to maintain their native identities as best they can (often without viable structural tribal support).

Public welfare and Anglo racism, on the one hand, and tribal identity and relationships, on the other, keep these Yaqui and O'odham women bound to the rapidly changing cultural remnants of their indigenous lifestyles. However, using Catholicism, tribal religious activities, and extended family networks, these women manage to socialize their children to be bicultural and to have a tribal identity.

The tribal identification of these women is important and is underscored by the actions of each tribe. For example, in their battle to obtain federal recognition as an Indian tribe, the Yaquis kept reemphasizing that despite the overshadowing Mexican influence, they were nevertheless Yaqui, an Indian tribe. Similarly, the Tohono O'odham fought to have their tribal name changed from Papago, a Spanish word with a derogatory connotation, to Tohono O'odham, which means the Desert People, the name by which they have historically called themselves. Table 8.3 lists how these women described the cultural orientation of their families.

Because they have had prolonged exposure to the Mexican culture, the Yaquis, more so than the O'odham, have often been described as tricultural, and many still continue to blend the three cultures. And because the Spanish language is more functional in dealing with the outside world, many of the children of these women learned Spanish instead of Yaqui (Chilcott et al. 1979). Since the mid-1980s, however, the Yaqui community has aggressively supported a Yaqui-English bilingual education program for their children.

The Tohono O'odham children in the city are predominantly taught their native language by their mothers and grandmothers. Sometimes the children are placed in boarding schools on the reservation so that they may be with other O'odham children, in order to retain or learn the O'odham language. In the Tucson public schools, Indian bilingual teachers are employed to work with the Indian children. The Indian committees that oversee these programs are usually made up of women — mothers of some of the children enrolled in these schools.

Although not all the Yaquis are enrolled as members of their tribe, most of the mothers carefully guard birth certificates and other records so that their children will not be counted as non-Indian by the schools. Most of the Tohono O'odham mothers also said that their children are enrolled in the tribe, and enrollment information is kept in a safe place.

These women said they pass on their "Indianness" or tribalism by giving their children Indian names, allowing their children to live with their grandmothers or other relatives on the reservation, taking their children to native healers, teaching their children some of the stories and customs of the tribe, and teaching them to appreciate "Indian food" and "Indian music." Some of the mothers who work hired other Indian women to care for their young children so that their children would be with Indian people.

In the larger urban arena, these women participate in activities that are Indian-oriented. The Indian Center in Tucson is directed by a woman, as is the urban Indian health program. A majority of the women employed in these facilities are Indian. They also advise and serve on cultural enrichment programs such as the Johnson-O'Malley and Title IV Indian Education Programs.[3] They usually help hire Indian tutors and assist with other cultural programs in the Tucson community.

Similarly, in Los Angeles, the major urban Indian health program is directed by an Indian woman, and, as in Tucson, a majority of the human service workers in this agency are women. They help organize the powwows, arrange special outings for the elders and the youth, and serve on committees advising various agencies on how best to serve the Indians in the city. They also help support the popularity of Indian arts and crafts by buying from Indian craftspeople.

TABLE 8.3.
Cultural Orientation of Subjects

Cultural orientation	Tohono O'odham (%)	Yaqui (%)
Mostly Indian	40	30
Bicultural	43	40
Mostly non-Indian	17	30

This description of Indian women residing in the city represents those who are most often married to Indians and who continue consciously and unconsciously to be the culture bearers. Indian women who are married to non-Indians, on the other hand, are less likely to be actively involved in types of activities that are designed for the Indian clients, although they may support the cultural survival activities in other ways. They may, for example, attend fund-raising functions. Because they often keep themselves marginal to the world of other Indian women, most remain invisible to the Indian network unless their children, upon finding that they have Indian heritage, begin to frequent the Indian center or participate in some of the programs.

Life in the city is complicated by a variety of problems. Table 8.4 summarizes some of these problems, as reported by the women in the study. As indicated, poverty is an important factor in the daily life of Indian women and their families; two-thirds of them were receiving public assistance as their primary source of financial support. Although public welfare funds provide a safety net against economic collapse, the level of support guarantees a life trapped in a culture of poverty. That, combined with a mother-headed household (58 percent) and the impact of alcohol and drugs on the family (24 percent), undoubtedly contributes to the high dropout and school problem rate (33 percent) of the children of these women. The combination of being Indian, being poor, and living in the segregated neighborhood pockets of Tucson presents Indian mothers with many structural barriers to survival or to rising in the mobile Anglo world, but their tribally oriented, encapsulated world helps them survive psychologically and culturally. But these women's survival in the city is not without psychological cost, as the levels of stress in table 8.5 show.

These subjects took the Health Opinion Survey (HOS), a self-reporting mental health scale that has been used with other tribes. HOS helped gauge the degree of stress among these Indian mothers. As shown in table 8.5, 70 percent scored in the moderate-high range of stress; 70 percent stated they often "get discouraged" and are in "poor spirits." One-third reported they frequently have "bad dreams." These psychological symptoms are serious for women who are less acculturated and who hold to forces of positive power, avoiding states of discouragement and being in poor spirits. "Bad dreams" are often perceived as serious warnings of forthcoming disaster that require the services of medicine people to lift the negative forces at work in one's life.

Other data indicate how these Indian mothers deal with these serious social and psychological pressures. They turn to medicine people (30 percent); they turn to families and relatives on the reservation (27 percent); they turn to family and friends in the city for help (39 percent). All these help-seeking patterns provide coping strategies as well as messages and behaviors that strengthen the women's sense of identity.

The cultural endurance and encapsulation of Indian women and their families in the city are the consequences of poverty and racism, two negative structural properties of American life. On one hand, Indian women bring to the city a strong sense of identity with their tribal life and land base, and on the other hand, they are assigned to a separate status as a lower caste and class group, living in segregated

TABLE 8.4.
Urban Yaqui and O'odham Mothers: Social Problems

Social problem	Yaqui N (%)	O'odham N (%)	Total N (%)
On public assistance	5 (50)	17 (74)	22 (67)
Single parent	4 (40)	15 (65)	19 (58)
Child school problem, dropout	4 (40)	7 (30)	11 (33)
Alcohol, drug problem in family	3 (30)	5 (22)	8 (24)

TABLE 8.5.
Psychological Effects of Urban Living on Yaqui and O'odham Mothers

Psychological effects	Yaqui N (%)	O'odham N (%)	Total N (%)
Moderate-high stress score	8 (80)	15 (65)	23 (70)
Bad dreams	3 (30)	8 (35)	11 (33)
Gets discouraged	8 (80)	15 (65)	23 (70)
In poor spirits	8 (80)	15 (65)	23 (70)

communities, largely dependent on some form of welfare. Thus both poverty and racism work to keep American Indians from melting into American urban life.

By maintaining cultural boundaries, some women seek ways to avoid racial assignment within the urban culture. Thus they remain predominantly tribally oriented rather than take on the more generic identification of "Indian," as they are commonly referred to by their non-Indian neighbors. By encapsulating themselves within their tribal identity, these women may become culturally pluralistic but rarely are assimilated. There are several explanations offered as to why American Indians have not become totally assimilated over hundreds of years of conquest and governmental pressures. Among these are four major explanations.

1. Indians have been isolated geographically and have not been given the necessary opportunity for education and resources that would enable them to integrate fully into the American mainstream. This is the "taken-for-granted" view held widely by the public and by social and political planners.

2. Forced acculturation has resulted in high degrees of resistance to change in Indian cultural patterns (Dozier 1955). This resistance has been aided by the "draining off" of the most acculturated segment of the reservation population, leaving a residue of those Indians who hold more firmly to their culture and increase their resistance to "forced change" (Vogt 1957). Edward Spicer spoke of the acculturation admixture as follows: "Political domination stimulated the Indians in a variety of ways to resist submergence in the conquering societies. Moreover, in the dominant nation, the tendency was ultimately reinforced by the recognition of the Indian entities and even encouraged their continued existence as distinct ethnic groups" (1962, 157).

3. It is the nature of culture that while material aspects of a culture change, family and kinship institutions are more persistent, so those aspects of a way of life, the implicit values of the core culture, and the cultural orientations and

personality types are even more persistent (Linton 1936; Vogt 1957; Spicer 1962; Hallowell 1945; Bruner 1956).

4. The organized communal structure, such as that found on many reservations, preserves Indian cultural beliefs and functions in the urban environment (Wolf 1955).

This study of Tucson Indian women revealed an acculturative strategy of encapsulation. Four adaptive strategies utilized by these women are especially evident: (1) strong tribal identity, (2) cultural beliefs, (3) American racism, and (4) welfare lifestyle, that is, institutionalized poverty. All four of these factors operate to prevent total assimilation of these Tohono O'odham and Yaqui mothers residing in Tucson, Arizona. These "push" and "pull" forces stalemate the assimilative process and serve as counterweights to aid the women in their tribally oriented life way.

As mothers, most of these women translate their cultural heritage within the framework of their everyday life, particularly as they socialize their children into the values and behaviors of their tribal culture. As mothers they also see to it that their tribal affiliations are kept intact by making certain that their children are registered with their tribe and that the tribal identity is maintained from one generation to the next. In contrast, the man's role, under conquest, has deteriorated and has become devalued in contemporary urban society. Although forced cultural change has meant that their men are often unable to be fathers, these women as mothers maintain their role as caretakers of the children.

As mothers, these women face the racism of segregated housing and must struggle to keep their family ties intact (Blumer 1958). They comfort their children when other children ridicule them as "Injuns" or "savages," or beat them up at school. As mothers, they protest and defend their Indian children against racism and, indirectly, against assimilation into the broader non-Indian world.

Some of these women are welfare mothers. Public assistance programs such as AFDC have always relied on mothers to hold their families together, albeit at a level of financial assistance that assured they would live in a culture of poverty. Thus, despite a history of government programs aimed at assimilating them into the mainstream, these women have clung to their cultural identities as tribal members. The reasons for the failure of the rapid assimilation are complex, and include the struggles of these women to maintain their cultural continuity and tribal identity for themselves and their children, despite the powerful forces of racism and poverty.

Sometimes, these women worry more about losing their men and their children to the ravages of alcoholism and drugs than to losing their offspring to mainstream society. As long as they themselves identify with their tribal heritage, they find ways to manipulate the home and social environment as much as possible to ensure that their children do not forget "who they are." They may not speak the language or share all the beliefs and teachings of the tribe, but these women do instill in their children information and identification about their tribal roots.

In the field of women's studies, we need to note the contributions of Indian women not only in terms of the strategies they use to foster tribalism and "Indianness" but also in terms of the way they define these important concepts within their contemporary worldview and self-identity.

NOTES

This study was supported by a grant from the National Institute on Disability and Rehabilitation Research (NIDRR), U.S. Department of Education (#G0083C0094). We would also like to thank our colleague, Robert Young, for his valuable suggestions, and Trudie Narum, who helped with this study.

1. It should be noted that although the relocation was often viewed as a major urbanization experience for Indian people, migration to the cities was not a new phenomenon for some, especially those who were among the first to be dispossessed from their land and those whose homelands were near the urban growth centers. In fact, social and other problems of Indians in the city were mentioned in the 1928 Meriam report (Meriam 1928).

2. The study was intended to be an assessment of the health needs and problems of the clients utilizing the urban clinic (Joe et al. 1988).

3. The Johnson-O'Malley Act, enacted in 1934, permitted the federal government to contract with public schools to educate Indian children. Title IV of the Indian Education Act (P.L. 92-318).

REFERENCES

Agar, Lynn P. 1980. "The Economic Role of Women in Alaskan Society." In E. Bourguigan, ed., *A World of Women*, 305–18. New York: Praeger.

Albers, Patricia C. 1983. "Introduction: New Perspective on Plains Indian Women." In Patricia Albers and Beatrice Medicine, eds., *The Hidden Half: Studies of Plains Women*, 1–26. Lanham Park, MD: University Press of America.

———. 1985. "Autonomy and Dependency in the Lives of Dakota Women: A Study in Historical Change." *Review of Radical Political Economics* 17: 109–34.

———. 1989. "From Illusion to Illumination: Anthropological Studies of American Indian Women." In Sandra Morgen, ed., *Gender and Anthropology*, 132–70. Washington, DC: American Anthropological Association.

Albers, Patricia C., and Beatrice Medicine. 1983. "The Role of Sioux Women in the Production of Ceremonial Objects: The Case of the Star Quilt." In Patricia Albers and Beatrice Medicine, eds., *The Hidden Half: Studies of Plains Indian Women*, 123–42. Lanham Park, MD: University Press of America.

Allen, Paula Gunn. 1986. *The Sacred Hoop: Recovering the Feminine in American Indian Traditions*. Boston: Beacon.

Bahr, Donald. 1969. "Pima Shamanism: The Sickness." Ph.D. diss., Harvard University.

Bataille, Gretchen, and Kathleen M. Sands. 1984. *American Indian Women Telling Their Lives*. Lincoln: University of Nebraska Press.

Black, Mary. 1984. "Maidens and Mothers: An Analysis of Hopi Corn Metaphors." *Ethnology* 23: 279–88.

Blackwood, Evelyn. 1984. "Sexuality and Gender in Certain Native American Tribes: The Case of Cross-Gender Females." *Signs: Journal of Women in Society and Culture* 10: 27–42.

Blumer, Hubert. 1958. "Race Prejudices as a Sense of Group Position." *Pacific Sociology Review* 1: 3–7.

Bruner, Edward M. 1956. "Cultural Transmission and Cultural Change." *Southwest Journal of Anthropology* 10: 191–99.

Buckley, Thomas. 1982. "Menstruation and the Power of Yurok Women: Methods in Cultural Reconstruction." *American Ethnologist* 32: 37–56.

Bysiewicz, Shirley, and Ruth Van de Mark. 1977. "The Legal Status of Dakota Women." *American Indian Law Review* 3: 255–312.

Chaudhuri, Joystpul. 1974. *Urban Indians of Arizona: Phoenix, Tucson, and Flagstaff.* Tucson: University of Arizona, Institute of Government Studies.

Chilcott, John, Barbara Buchanan, Felipe Molina, and James Jones. 1979. *An Education-Related Ethnographic Study of a Yaqui Community.* Tucson: University of Arizona Press.

Conte, Christine. 1982. "Ladies, Livestock, Land and Lucre: Women's Network and Social Status on the Western Navajo Reservation." *American Indian Quarterly* 6: 105–24.

Cruikshank, Julie. 1975. "Becoming a Woman in Athapaskan Society: Changing Traditions in the Upper Yukon River." *Western Canadian Journal of Anthropology* 5: 1–14.

Densmore, Frances. 1929. *Papago Music.* Bureau of American Ethnology, Bulletin 90. Washington, DC: U.S. GPO.

Downs, James. 1972. "The Cowboy and the Lady: Models as Determinant of the Rate of Acculturation among the Pinon Navajos." In Howard M. Bahr, Bruce A. Chadwick, and Robert E. Day, eds., *Native Americans Today,* 275–90. New York: Harper and Row.

Dozier, Edward. 1955. "Forced and Permissive Acculturation." *American Indian* 7:38–41.

Evaneshko, Veronica. 1988. *Demographics of Native Americans in the Traditional Indian Alliance Catchment Area.* Tucson: University of Arizona, College of Nursing.

Green, Rayna. 1980. "Native American Women." *Signs: Journal of Women in Society and Culture* 7: 248–67.

———. 1983. *Native American Women: A Contextual Bibliography.* Bloomington: Indiana University Press.

Hallowell, A. I. 1945. "Socio-psychological Aspects of Acculturation." In Ralph Linton, ed., *The Science of Man in the World Crisis,* 171–200. New York: Columbia University Press.

Joe, Jennie R. 1982. "Cultural Influences on Navajo Mothers with Disabled Children." *American Indian Quarterly* 6: 170–90.

Joe, Jennie R., Dorothy Lonewolf Miller, and Trudie Narum. 1988. *Traditional Indian Alliance: Delivery of Health Care Services to Arizona Indians.* Tucson: University of Arizona, Native American Research and Training Center, Monograph Series, no. 4.

Kehoe, Alice. 1976. "Old Woman Had Great Power." *Western Canadian Journal of Anthropology* 6: 68–76.

———. 1983. "The Shackles of Traditions." In Patricia Albers and Beatrice Medicine, eds., *The Hidden Half: Studies of Plains Indian Women,* 53–76. Lanham Park, MD: University Press of America.

Kelley, Jane H. 1978. *Yaqui Women: Contemporary Life Histories.* Lincoln: University of Nebraska Press.

Keohane, Nannerl, Michelle Zimbalist Rosaldo, and Barbara Gelpi, eds. 1982. *Feminist Theory: A Critique of Ideology.* Chicago: University of Chicago Press.

Kidwell, Clara Sue. 1979. "The Power of Women in Three American Indian Societies." *Journal of Ethnic Studies* 6: 113–21.

Klein, Alan. 1983. "The Plains Truth: The Impact of Colonization on Indian Women." *Dialectical Anthropology* 7: 299–313.

Knack, Martha. 1980. *Life Is with People: Household Organization of the Contemporary Southern Paiute Indians.* Anthropological Papers 19. Socorro, NM: Ballena Press.

Lamphere, Louise. 1977. *To Run after Them.* Tucson: University of Arizona Press.

Landes, Ruth. 1971. *The Ojibwa Woman.* New York: Norton.

Lincoln, Kenneth. 1983. *Native American Renaissance.* Berkeley: University of California Press.

Linton, Ralph. 1936. *The Study of Man.* New York: Appleton-Century.

Locust, Carol. 1987. *Yaqui Indian Beliefs about Health and Handicap.* Tucson: University of Arizona, Native American Research and Training Center, Monograph Series.

Lurie, Nancy. 1961. *Mountain Wolf Woman: Sister of Crashing Thunder, a Winnebego Indian.* Ann Arbor: University of Michigan Press.

Lynch, Robert. 1986. "Women in Northern Paiute Politics." *Signs: Journal of Women in Society and Culture* 11: 253–66.

Medicine, Beatrice. 1978. *The Native American Woman: A Perspective.* Austin, TX: National Educational Laboratory Publications.

———. 1987. "Indian Women and the Renaissance of Traditional Religion." In Raymond J. DeMallie and Douglas R. Parks, eds., *Sioux Indian Religion: Tradition and Innovation,* 159–71. Norman: University of Oklahoma Press.

Meriam, Lewis. 1928. *The Problem of Indian Administration.* Baltimore: Johns Hopkins University Press.

Metcalf, Ann. 1979. "Reservation Born — City Bred: Native American Women and Children in the City." In Ann McElroy and Carolyn Matthiasson, eds., *Sex Roles in Changing Cultures: Occasional Papers in Anthropology,* 21–34. Buffalo: State University of New York Press.

Schlegel, Alice. 1973. "The Adolescent Socialization of the Hopi Girl." *Ethnology* 12: 449–62.

Shaw, Daniel R. 1968. "Health Concepts and Attitudes of the Papago Indians." Master's thesis, University of Arizona.

Snipp, C. Matthew, and Gary D. Sandefur. 1988. "Earnings of American Indians and Alaska Natives: The Effects of Residence and Migration." *Social Forces* 66: 994–1008.

Spicer, Edward H. 1949. *Pascua, a Yaqui Village of Arizona.* Chicago: University of Chicago Press.

———. 1962. *Cycles of Conquest.* Tucson: University of Arizona Press.

Thornton, Russell. 1987. *American Indian Holocaust and Survival: A Population History Since 1492.* Norman: University of Oklahoma Press.

Tucson Planning Department. 1985. "1985 Computer Printout of Tucson Census Data." Tucson: Tucson City Government.

UCLA Ethnic Studies Center. 1987. *Ethnic Groups in Los Angeles: Quality of Life Indicators.* Los Angeles: UCLA, Ethnic Studies Center.

Underhill, Ruth. 1939. *Social Organization of the Papago Indians.* New York: Columbia University Press.

U.S. Department of Commerce. 1991. *1990 Census: National and State Population Counts for American Indians, Eskimos, and Aleuts.* Washington, DC: Bureau of the Census.

Vogt, Evon Z. 1957. "The Acculturation of American Indians." *Annals of the American Academy of Political and Social Science* 311: 137–46.

Wauneka, Annie D. 1987. "Navajo Women." Keynote presentation at the Navajo Nation Conference on Women, Tsaile, Arizona.

Weaver, Sally. 1972. *Medicine and Politics among the Grand River Iroquois.* Ottawa: National Museum of Man.

Williams, Walter. 1986. *The Spirit and the Flesh: Sexual Diversity in American Indian Cultures.* Boston: Beacon.

Wolf, Eric R. 1955. "Types of Latin-American Peasantry: A Preliminary Discussion." *American Anthropologist* 57: 456–57.

NINE

Policing the Black Woman's Body in an Urban Context

HAZEL V. CARBY

> The problem of the unemployed negro woman in New York city is proba-
> bly more serious than that of any other class of worker. She is unquestion-
> ably shut out from many lines of occupation, and through her increasing
> inefficiency and desire to avoid hard work, the best households and hotels
> and restaurants are gradually supplanting her with whites. This means in
> many instances that she must rely upon odd jobs and employment in the
> questionable house. . . .
>
> Negro women who are led into immoral habits, vice and laziness, have
> in too many instances received their initiative from questionable employ-
> ment agencies. . . . Some preventive measure must be taken for the col-
> ored girl going to work for the first time, and for the green helpless negro
> woman brought up here from the South — on promises of "easy work, lots
> of money and good times."
>
>   — Frances A. Kellor, "Southern Colored Girls in the North"

The migration of black people to cities outside the Secessionist
states of the South in the first half of the twentieth century transformed America
socially, politically, and culturally. Of course, the migration of black people is not a
twentieth-century phenomenon. In the antebellum period the underground railroad
was the primary conduit out of the slaveholding states; in the late 1870s there was
significant black migration to Kansas and in the 1880s to Oklahoma. Before 1910
there were major changes in the distribution of the black population between rural
and urban areas within the South. The proportion of black people in southern cities
more than doubled between 1870 and 1910 and, consequently, the proportion of the
black population that continued to live in rural areas decreased significantly from 81

to 70 percent.[1] Historians and demographers seem to agree that what is now called the Great Migration needs to be viewed in the context of these earlier migratory patterns and in light of the fact that black people were becoming increasingly urbanized before they left for northern cities.

When we consider the complex cultural transformations that not only accompany but are an integral part of these demographic shifts, it is important to challenge simplistic mythologies of how a rural black folk without the necessary industrial skills, untutored in the ways of the city, "green" and ignorant, in Frances Kellor's opinion, were exploitable fodder for the streets of New York, Chicago, Detroit, Cleveland, Philadelphia, and Pittsburgh.[2] Certainly, male and female black migrants suffered economic and political exploitation, but it is important to separate the structural forces of exploitation, but it is important to separate the structural forces of exploitation from the ways black migrants came to be regarded as easily victimized subjects who quickly succumbed to the forces of vice and degradation.

I am going to argue that the complex processes of urbanization had gender-specific and class-specific consequences for the production of African American culture in general, and for the cultural representation of black women in particular. The movement of black women between rural and urban areas and between southern and northern cities generated a series of moral panics. One serious consequence was that the behavior of black female migrants was characterized as sexually degenerate and, therefore, socially dangerous. By using the phrase "moral panic" I am attempting to describe and to connect a series of responses, from institutions and from individuals, that identified the behavior of these migrating women as a social and political problem, a problem that had to be rectified in order to restore a moral social order.[3] These responses were an active part of a 1920s bourgeois ideology that not only identified this moral crisis but also produced a language that provided a framework of interpretation and referentiality that appeared to be able to explain for all time the behavior of black women in an urban environment. Kellor's indictment of the sexual behavior of black migrant women registers the emergence of what would rapidly become a widely shared discourse of what was wrong with black urban life.

Frances Kellor was the general director of the Inter-Municipal Committee on Household Research in New York City, and her "Southern Colored Girls in the North" appeared in Charities, "A Review of Local and General Philanthropy." Her article provides important evidence that as early as 1905 the major discursive elements were already in place that would define black female urban behavior throughout the teens and twenties as pathological.[4] The subjects of Kellor's article are migrating black women who are looking for work, and she implicitly assumes that these women are alone, either single or, at least, without men. Therefore, according to Kellor, they need "protection." On the surface, it looks as if Kellor is inciting moral alarm in defense of the rather abstract quality of female virtue, but it is quickly evident that she does not believe that black women have any moral fiber or will of their own that can be mobilized in the defense of their own interests. On the contrary, she believes that they become prostitutes because they are unable to protect themselves. Kellor's report makes a strong case for the creation of an alternative set of institutions to police the actual bodies of migrating black women. While Kellor is apparently condemning the existence of employment agencies that create a situation of economic dependency and exploitation in order to channel black women into houses of prostitution, she is actually identifying the "increasing inefficiency and desire [of black women] to avoid hard work" as the primary cause of the "problem."

Kellor has three major recommendations to make in addition to the establishment of more respectable and law-abiding agencies. First, she suggests the use of "practical and sympathetic women," like those on Ellis Island "who guide and direct the immigrant women," to "befriend" and act as "missionaries" toward black women when they arrive from the South. Second, she advocates the institution of a controlled system of lodging houses where black women can be sent at night and kept from going off on their own into the streets. Finally, she argues for the creation of training schools to make black women "more efficient."[5] This discourse, however, establishes a direct relationship between the social supervision of black women migrants and the control of their moral and sexual behavior, between the morally unacceptable economics of sex for sale and a morally acceptable policing of black female sexuality. In other words, Kellor characterizes the situation not as the lack of job possibilities for black women with the consequent conclusion that the employment market should be rigorously controlled, but, on the contrary, as a problem located in black women themselves, who, given the limited employment available to them and their "desire to avoid hard work," will sell their bodies.[6] Therefore, the logic of her argument dictates that bodies, not economic markets, need stringent surveillance.

The need to police and discipline the behavior of black women in cities, however, was not only a premise of white agencies and institutions but also a perception of black institutions and organizations and the black middle class. The moral panic about the urban presence of apparently uncontrolled black women was symptomatic of and referenced aspects of the more general crises of social displacement and dislocation that were caused by migration. White and black intellectuals used and elaborated this discourse so that when they referred to the association between black women and vice, or immoral behavior, their references carried connotations of other crises of the black urban environment. Thus the migrating black woman could be variously situated as a threat to the progress of the race; a threat to the establishment of a respectable urban black middle class; a threat to congenial black and white middle-class relations; and a threat to the formation of black masculinity in an urban environment.

Jane Edna Hunter, who was born in 1882 on the Woodburn plantation in South Carolina and trained as a nurse in Charleston and then at the Hampton Institute, arrived in Cleveland in May 1905 with little money. In an attempt to find accommodations, she mistakenly arrived at a brothel, and her search for a place to live, she says, gave her an insight into the conditions that a black girl, "friendless and alone," had to face.[7] Hunter reflects that at home on the plantation she was well aware that some girls had been seduced, but she was totally unaware of what she calls a "wholesale organized traffic in black flesh" (*NP*, 68). When she goes to a dance she is shocked to see that the saloon on the first floor of Woodluff Hall is "the resort of bad women," and that the Hamilton Avenue area is the home of "vice." Hunter's discovery of what she identifies and criticizes as organized vice is interspersed with a description of her own difficult search for legitimate employment. Although highly trained, she cannot find a doctor who wants to employ a black nurse, and she depends on a cousin to find cleaning jobs for her.[8] Eventually Hunter alternates work as a domestic with temporary nursing assignments until she finds a permanent position in the office of a group of doctors.

In her autobiography, A *Nickel and a Prayer*, Hunter states that her experiences led her to conclude that "a girl alone in a large city must needs know the dangers and pitfalls awaiting her" (*NP*, 77). While Hunter never situates herself as a helpless victim, she carefully creates a narrative that identifies and appears to account for the helplessness of other black migrating women, and as she does so she incorporates Kellor's analysis, strategies, and conclusions. Hunter turned the death of her mother, from whom she had become estranged, into a catalyst to devote her life to political and social activity on behalf of the black women she designated as helpless. As a young woman Hunter was forbidden to see the man she loved, and she blamed her mother for forcing her into marriage with a man forty years older than herself. However, she walked out of the marriage fifteen months later and went to Charleston to find work, declaring that "a great weight rolled from my mind as I left him, determined to find and keep the freedom which I so ardently desired" (*NP*, 50). Hunter's mother died in 1911, after Hunter had lived in Cleveland for four years, and the realization that reconciliation was now impossible occasioned deep despair. In the midst of contemplating suicide, Hunter found herself asking the question, "how could I best give to the world what I had failed to give her?" (*NP*, 81). Hunter's self-interrogation resulted in her making her mother, rather than herself, a symbol for the helplessness of all migrant women. Hunter characterized her mother as both "immature and impulsive" and imagined that her mother would have been totally helpless if she had been a migrant. What Hunter cannot explicitly acknowledge is that a figure of such helplessness stands in direct contrast to the way she writes with confidence and self-determination about her own need to gain and retain her freedom through urban migration. But the designation of her mother as helpless enables Hunter to occupy the absent maternal space. The daughter becomes mother as Hunter listens to the strains of a spiritual and is moved by the words, "ah feels like a motherless child." At this moment she decided on her "supreme work," dedicating her life to helping "the young Negro girl pushed from the nest by economic pressure, alone and friendless in a northern city; reduced to squalor, starvation; helpless against temptation and degradation" (*NP*, 83).

The fruit of Hunter's labors and the institutionalization of her maternal role into that of a matriarch is the formation of the Working Girls' Home Association, which later became the Phillis Wheatley Association, with Hunter as president. The Phillis Wheatley Association was the equivalent of the "controlled system of lodging houses" that Kellor recommended in her report, but under black, not white, control. In cooperation with the National Association of Colored Women, other similar institutions were established in cities across the country; Hunter served as chair of the Phillis Wheatley department of the NACW. The board that was established in 1913 to oversee the home included white as well as black patrons, and Hunter argued that the Phillis Wheatley Association was "one of the strongest ties between the Negro and white races in America" (*NP*, 165). It was not only at the level of management, however, that Hunter was proud of the association as a model of interracial cooperation. The home was a training ground to prepare young black women for domestic service, and one of Hunter's aims was to improve relations between white mistress and maid by producing a happy and efficient servant. As Hunter states,

> The most important factor in successful domestic service is a happy and human relation between the lady of the house and the maid — on the part of the maid, respect and affectionate regard for her employer; on the part of the employer, sympathy and imagination. Perhaps it is not going too far to say that the lady of the house should stand in the relation of a foster mother to the young woman who assists her in the household tasks. . . .
>
> The girl who is fairly well-trained and well-disposed will become interested in the life of the family that she serves, and will be devoted to its happiness. (*NP*, 161–62)

Hunter asserted that the Phillis Wheatley Association was "an instrument for [the] social and moral redemption" of young black women (*NP*, 157). A prerequisite for this redemption, Hunter maintained, was surveillance over all aspects of the lives of the girls in the home:

> In fact it was necessary at all times to guard our girls from evil surroundings. I kept a vigilant ear at the switchboard in my office to catch conversations of a doubtful character, and to intercept assignations. No effort we made to restrict tenancy to girls of good character could exclude the ignorant, the foolish, and the weak, for these had to be protected as well. In the company of a policeman whom I could trust, I would sometimes follow couples to places of assignation, rescue the girl, and assist in the arrest of her would-be seducer. (*NP*, 128–29)

There are extraordinary contradictions present in this narrative reconstructing the life of a woman who when young had declared her independence from both the patriarchal power of her husband and the maternal power of her mother by walking away from both of them to "find and keep the freedom [she] so ardently desired," only to find herself in her mature years thwarting the desires of other young women by lurking in hallways to eavesdrop on their telephone calls and marching off into the night accompanied by the police to have their lovers arrested. And yet, Hunter clearly tries to establish a maternal framework to disguise and legitimate what are actually exploitative relations of power. Exploitation becomes nurturance when Hunter describes the white mistress acting as a "foster mother" to a young black domestic worker and when she herself dominates the lives of her charges in the Phyllis Wheatley Association. Hunter, remembering her own mother as weak and helpless, created the association as a matriarchy that allowed her to institutionalize and occupy a space of overwhelming matriarchal power over younger black women.

Although Hunter is uncritical of and, indeed, manipulates and abuses the possibilities of matriarchal power, she is explicit in her criticism of the ways an abusive patriarchal power becomes embedded in the corrupt legal and political machinery of city governance. Hunter is trenchant in her analysis of the mutually beneficial relations between "unscrupulous politicians," the "rapacity of realtors," the creation of the segregated ghetto, and organized vice in Cleveland. But urban blacks are situated as merely the victims of the forces of corruption: the politicians, Hunter felt, played "upon the ignorance of the Negro voter to entrench themselves in office, and then deliver[ed] the Negro over to every force of greed and vice which stalked around him" (*NP*, 121).

Hunter utilizes the forces of matriarchal power to declare war on what she feels to be her most formidable enemy, "commercialized vice." She describes her battle in the most epic of biblical language, a battle in which she fights a "dreadful monster . . . spawned by greed and ignorance . . . hideous to behold. 'Out of its belly came fire and smoke, and its mouth was as the mouth of a lion . . . and its wages were death' " (*NP*, 120). Corrupt city politics enables and maintains the monstrous network that feeds on the young female souls in Hunter's charge, but at its heart is a single patriarchal figure whom she refers to only as "Starlight."[9] If Hunter sees herself as the matriarchal savior of young black women, she describes "Starlight" as the " 'Great Mogul' of organized vice." He is the epitome of the seducer of young black women, whom he manipulates, betrays, and then drags as "prisoners" down into the depths of "shame and degradation" (*NP*, 122). But although the war is figuratively between these forces of patriarchal power and maternal influence, Hunter's matriarchal power is aimed directly at other women. Black female sexual behavior, because according to Hunter it is degenerate, threatens the progress of the race: threatens to "tumble gutterward," in her words, the "headway which the Negro had made toward the state of good citizenship" (*NP*, 126).

Dance halls and nightclubs are particular targets of Hunter's reformist zeal, and she identifies these cultural spaces, located in the "heart of [the] newly created Negro slum district[s]," as the site of the production of vice as spectacle: "Here, to the tune of St. Louis voodoo blues, half-naked Negro girls dance shameless dances with men in Spanish costumes. . . . The whole atmosphere is one of unrestrained animality, the jungle faintly veneered with civilized trappings" (*NP*, 132–33). Places of amusement and recreation for black people are condemned as morally dangerous and described as being filled with "lewd men and wretched women" (*NP*, 132). Nightclubs where black women perform for a white audience threaten the very foundations of Hunter's definitions of acceptable interracial relations:

> Interracial co-operation built the Phillis Wheatley Association and is carrying on its work; a co-operation of Negroes and whites for worthy purposes; which can gauge the spiritual contribution the Negro has made to American life, since his arrival in America. But in the meeting of blacks and whites in night clubs . . . there is to be found only cause for regret and head-hanging by both races. On the one side an exhibition of unbridled animality, on the other a blase quest for novel sensations, a vicarious gratification of the dark and violent desires of man's nature, a voluntary return to the jungle. (*NP* 133)

There are deep fears being expressed in this passage, in which the exploitation of black women is only one concern among many. These fears haunt the entire narrative and are also embedded in Kellor's account of young black migrating women: fears of a rampant and uncontrolled female sexuality; fears of miscegenation; and fears of the assertion of an independent black female desire that has been unleashed through migration. If a black woman can claim her freedom and migrate to an urban environment, what is to keep her from negotiating her own path through its streets? What are the consequences of the female self-determination evident in such a journey for the establishment of a socially acceptable moral order that defines the boundaries of respectable sexual relations? What, indeed, is to be the framework of discipline and strategies of policing that can contain and limit black female sexuality? These are the grounds of contestation in which black women became the primary targets for the moral panic about urban immorality.

St. Clair Drake and Horace Cayton in their history of Chicago, *Black Metropolis,* describe how the existence of residential restrictive covenants made middle-class neighborhoods in Bronzeville "the beach upon which broke the human flotsam which was tossed into the city streets by successive waves of migration from the South."[10] They also describe the deep ambivalence in the attitudes of the black middle class toward the black working class who, as Drake and Cayton insist, perform "the essential digging, sweeping, and serving which make Metropolitan life tolerable" (*BM*, 523). This ambivalence, they argue, caused the black upper class to live a contradictory existence. On the one hand they defined their social position by emphasizing their *differentness* from the lower class,

> But, as Race Leaders, the upper class must [also] identify itself psychologically with "The Race," and The Race includes a lot of people who would never be accepted socially. Upper-class Negroes, too depend upon the Negro masses for their support if they are business or professional men. The whole orientation of the Negro upper class thus becomes one of trying to speed up the processes by which the lower class can be transformed from a poverty-stricken group, isolated from the general stream of American life, into a counterpart of middle-class America. (*BM*, 563)

Hunter, clearly, lives this contradiction: her self-definition and her right to control her own behavioral boundaries are beyond question. But by positioning herself as part of the emergent black bourgeoisie, Hunter secures her personal autonomy in the process of claiming the right to circumscribe the rights of young black working-class women and to transform their behavior on the grounds of nurturing the progress of the race as a whole.

What Drake and Cayton fail to recognize, however, is the extent to which the behavioral transformation of this lower class was thought to be about transforming the behavior of black working-class women. Hunter's accounts of the women who represented the success stories of the Phillis Wheatley Association, for example, are narratives of the transformation of the behavior of migrant working-class black women to conform to middle-class norms of acceptable sexual behavior while actually being confirmed in their subordinate, working-class status as female domestics. These success stories represented the triumphant fulfillment of the mission of the Phillis Wheatley Association, a mission that declared itself to be "to discover, protect, cherish, and perpetuate the beauty and power of Negro Womanhood," but which was primarily concerned with shaping and disciplining a quiescent urban, black, female, working-class population.

The texts that draw on aspects of this discourse of black female sexuality as a way to respond to northern urban migration are multiple and varied. In two important novels about Harlem during the twenties, Carl Van Vechten's *Nigger Heaven* (1926) and Claude McKay's *Home to Harlem* (1928), both authors use their female characters as the terrain on which to map a relation between the sexual and class politics of urban black life.[11] While neither author appears to be overtly interested in prescribing a program of social engineering, both novels are fictions of black urban classes in formation. Central to the success of the emergent black middle class in these two novels is the evolution of urban codes of black masculinity. In each text, representations of urban black women are used as both the means by which male protagonists will achieve or fail to achieve social mobility and signs of various possible threats to the emergence of the wholesome black masculinity necessary for the establishment of an acceptable black male citizenship in the American social order.

The first part of *Nigger Heaven* focuses on Mary Love, a figure of virginal purity. The failure of Byron Kasson, the male protagonist, to recognize the worth of Mary to the social security of his own future leads directly to his social disintegration. Van Vechten, a white patron of black culture and black artists, describes Mary as "cold":

> She had an instinctive horror of promiscuity, of being handled, even touched, by a man who did not mean a good deal to her. This might, she sometimes argued with herself, have something to do with her white inheritance, but Olive [her friend], who was far whiter, was lacking in this inherent sense of prudery. At any rate, whatever the cause, Mary realized that she was different in this respect from most of the other girls she knew. The Negro blood was there, warm and passionately earnest: all her preferences and prejudices were on the side of the race into which she had been born. She was as capable, she was convinced, of amorous emotion, as any of her friends, but the fact remained that she was more selective. Oh, the others were respectable enough; they did not involve themselves too deeply. On the other hand, they did not flee from a kiss in the dark. A casual kiss in the dark was a repellent idea to Mary. What she wanted was a kiss in the light. (*NH*, 54)

Van Vechten appears to dismiss, or put in doubt, the classic nineteenthcentury literary explanation of blood "admixture" for these opposing aspects of Mary's fictional personality in favor of using a more contemporary, and urban, explanation that uses Mary's "horror of promiscuity" as a sign of her secure class position.

Mary's middle-class existence is initially defined through her job; she works as a museum curator gathering together collections of African art. But Van Vechten also carefully defines her differentness from migrant and working-class black women in a variety of more complex ways. When Mary attends a rent party, for example, she is figuratively defiled by the gin and juice that is spilled over her and stains her clothes. When she regretfully wonders why she danced at this party until two in the morning, Van Vechten has her mentally discipline herself by reflecting on a long, directly quoted passage from Gertrude Stein's "Melanctha." The passage is an extended reflection on the dangers of "colored people" getting excited and "running around and . . . drinking and doing everything bad they can think of" instead of "working hard and caring about their working and living regular with their families and saving up all their money, so they will have some to bring their children up better" (*NH*, 57). Mary carefully differentiates herself culturally and ideologically from the black working class. On the one hand, she defines spirituals, which deeply affect her, as a cultural form produced from "real faith," which has the power to "touch most of us . . . and make us want to cry or shout." But on the other hand, she sees the culture of "servant girls and the poor" as being very different. The latter, she is convinced, don't really "feel faith — except as an escape from the drudgery of their lives. They don't really stop playing Numbers or dancing on Sunday or anything else that their religion forbids them to do. They enjoy themselves in church on Sunday as they do in the cabarets on week-days" (*NH*, 60, 59). Mary's disdain of sexual promiscuity is firmly embedded, by Van Vechten, in a middle-class ideology of endlessly deferred gratification.

The counterpoint to Mary is a character called Lasca Sartoris, who uses her sexuality to negotiate her way through her life. Unlike Mary, who has never even been to the South, Lasca, the daughter of a country preacher, "began by teaching school in the backwoods down in Louisiana" and then migrated north when an uncle left her an inheritance. In the city Lasca is said to "cut loose," dancing, playing the piano, and singing in Harlem clubs all night (*NH*, 83–84). Lasca's sexuality ensnares a rich and much older husband whose death leaves her a rich heiress. Van Vechten uses Lasca as a figure of overt and degenerate sexuality whose behavior is absolutely outside all moral boundaries. She attracts, then physically and emotionally destroys and discards, a series of male lovers, including Byron Kasson, having embroiled them in an intense bacchanalia of alcoholic, drug, and sexual abuse. For Byron, the would-be intellectual and writer, his choice of the influence of Lasca, rather than Mary, brings a certain end to all his hopes and ambition.

Claude McKay has a rather more subtle but, for women, an equally damning approach to the relation between black sexual politics, masculinity, and the securing of social position. McKay's protagonist, Jake, is ultimately saved by Felice, the woman he loves, in an interesting narrative sleight of hand that transforms Felice from the position of prostitute to a figure of wholesome sexuality. Jake arrives in Harlem and meets Felice in a bar. He spends the night with her, pays her, and leaves the following morning thinking he will never see her again. Wondering whether he can afford breakfast, Jake discovers that Felice has returned all his money to his pocket, thus proving that her sex is not for sale. This gesture convinces Jake that he must return to Felice, but he is quickly lost in the unfamiliar city streets, and it takes the whole course of the novel for him to find her again. On the journey back toward this "true" woman, however, Jake has to negotiate the vice and temptations of the city, which are embodied in a series of other women that he meets.

McKay has a much deeper, richer, and more complex understanding of the cultural forms of the black urban landscape on which he draws than Van Vechten. But despite this formal complexity, McKay situates his female figures in a very simplistic manner in various degrees of approximation to an uncontrolled and, therefore, problematic sexual behavior. For Jake's journey is not just a journey to find the right woman; it is, primarily, a journey of black masculinity in formation, a sort of *Pilgrim's Progress* in which a number of threatening embodiments of the female and the feminine have to be negotiated. The most significant of these female figures is Rose, a nightclub singer at a cabaret called the Congo. As its name implies, the Congo is "a real throbbing little Africa in New York. It was an amusement place entirely for the unwashed of the Black Belt. . . . Girls coming from the South to try their future in New York," McKay stresses, "always reached the Congo first" (*HH*, 29–30). These "chippies [that] come up from down home," a male friend of Jake's advises him, represent "the best pickings" in Harlem (*HH*, 35). Felice, of course, is never seen there. At the heart of what McKay describes as the "thick, dark-colorful, and fascinating" Congo, he situates the blues and Rose, the blues singer (*HH*, 36). As far as Jake is concerned, Rose is "a wonderful tissue of throbbing flesh," though he neither loves nor feels "any deep desire for her" (*HH*, 42, 114). The assumption of the novel is that male love and desire could not be generated for, or be sustained by, a woman like Rose, who is characterized as bisexual because she lacks the acceptable feminine qualities of "tenderness . . . timidity . . . [and] aloofness." Indeed, Rose's sexual ambiguity is positioned as a threat to the very existence of black masculinity, reducing Jake to the role of a "big, good slave" (*HH*, 42, 41). McKay proposes that only a pathological and distorted form of masculine power could exist in such a relationship when Rose makes masochistic demands that Jake brutalize her, confirming his belief "that a woman could always go further than a man in coarseness, depravity, and sheer cupidity" (*HH*, 69). Jake's refusal to beat Rose is a triumph of wholesome masculinity over the degenerate female element and allows Jake to proceed on his journey to become a man.

The dance hall and the cabaret, in the texts that I have been discussing, are the most frequently referenced landscapes in which black female promiscuity and sexual degeneracy were described. In William H. Jones's sociological study of black urban recreation and amusement (1927), the dance hall was a complex and contested social space. Jones could not condemn the dance hall as an "essentially antisocial institution" because it was possible that a dance hall could be a place in which "romantic love of the most idealistic type" could blossom. But dance halls encouraged a quick intimacy that could also lead the young "on the downward path to crime."[12] What Jones condemned without compromise was the dancing that took place in the dance halls. He saw modern dances as nothing more than "sexual pantomimes. They are similar to many of the ancient and primitive methods of publicly arousing human passions in preparation for lascivious orgies." He asserted that his "careful investigation disclosed the fact that . . . a large amount of illicit sex behavior is unquestionably the natural sequence of certain modern forms of dancing" (*RA*, 122).

Jones reserved his greatest vehemence for the cabaret, where

> excess in dancing, jungle laughter, and semi-alcoholic beverages are characteristic features of their life. Here, jazz music is carried to extremes. In general, there is more abandon achieved by the dancers than in the formal dance hall, and more of a tendency toward nakedness on the part of the female entertainers. (*RA*, 131)

What Jones particularly feared was what he called "social demoralization." He designated these recreational social spaces as places where "the most powerful human impulses and emotions are functioning," impulses and emotions that threatened the deterioration of the fragile social fabric of the black urban community (*RA*, 122).

The existence of dance halls and cabarets was particularly dangerous to the moral health of the black middle class, Jones maintained, because of "the rapidity and ease with which the anti-social forms of dancing spread upwards into and engross the so-called higher classes." He viewed the social fabric of the black urban community as fragile because of the lack of "adequate bulwarks against the encroachment of such behavior forms upon the life of the more advanced groups of Negroes" (*RA*, 122). "Class stratification" within the black community, Jones continued, only "seems to be strong." If black middle-class public opinion could generate disapproval of "the vulgar, sexually-suggestive modern dances . . . they would be compelled to confine themselves to the lower anti-social cultural groups in which they originated" (*RA*, 123). His appeal to the mobilization of social disapproval appears to be as much about generating a black middle-class ideology of solidarity and coexistence as about challenging threats to the social mores of that group. If middle-class hegemony could be established in the black community, it could more effectively discipline the black working class through the implementation of what Jones refers to as "mechanisms of control whereby forces which tend to disintegrate and demoralize the higher forms of culture may be excluded or annihilated" (*RA*, 123).

Between Kellor's report for *Charities* and Jones's book, the moral panic about the lack of control over the sexual behavior of black women had become absorbed into the fundamental assumptions of the sociological analysis of urban black culture, which thus designated many of its forms of entertainment and leisure "pathological" and in need of greater institutional control.[13] Kathy Peiss, in her recent analysis of white working women's leisure and recreation in New York, describes how white reformers in the early decades of the twentieth century believed that "the primary purpose of reform for working women was to inculcate standards of respectable behavior." Perceptions of "a rising tide of promiscuity and immorality" and panics over "white slavery and commercialized prostitution," she argues, motivated Progressive reformers whose prime target was increasingly "the growing menace of commercial amusements."[14] But the black urban community was constructed as pathological in very specific ways. Black urban life was viewed as being intimately associated with commercialized vice because black migrants to cities were forced to live in or adjacent to areas previously established as red-light districts in which prostitution and gambling had been contained. The existence of restrictive covenants enforced black residential segregation and limited the expansion of what became identified as black urban ghettos.[15] It was within the confines of East St. Louis, the south side of Chicago, the tenderloin in Kansas City, and Harlem in New York that an entertainment industry that served both a white and a black clientele was located and from which an urban blues culture emerged.

On the eve of the Depression, black women who had migrated to urban areas were still overwhelmingly limited to employment in domestic service and as laundresses. In Chicago, for example, between the First World War and the onset of the

Depression, over 40 percent of white women workers but only 5 percent of black women workers who entered the labor force obtained "clean" work (see *BM*, 220–29). The category "clean" work referred to jobs like office secretary and department store clerk; "clean" work was the type of employment from which black women were rigorously excluded. From the biographies and autobiographies of the black women who eventually became entertainers, it is clear that joining a touring vaudeville troupe or tent show was an important avenue of geographic mobility for young black women who were too poor to pay for train fares and for whom hopping a freight car was dangerous. In addition, being a member of a vaudeville show or performing in a nightclub was not attractive primarily because it offered a mythic life of glamor but because it was a rare opportunity to do "clean" work and to reject the life of a domestic servant.

When she was eight years old Josephine Baker started her first job and discovered that working as a maid for a white mistress was not "the happy and human relation" that Jane Edna Hunter maintained it should be. Baker was assured by her mistress, Mrs. Keiser, that she loved children, and she promised Baker the shoes and a coat that her own family was too poor to provide. However, Baker had to start to work at five in the morning so she could be at school by nine, and when she arrived home in the afternoon she had to work again until ten o'clock at night, when she was sent to bed in the cellar to sleep with the dog. One day when Baker made a mistake, Mrs. Keiser punished her by plunging the little girl's arms into boiling water. This story and Baker's account of how she watched white people murder and torture her relatives and neighbors during the East St. Louis riot of 1917 are situated in her autobiography as the preface to her decision to leave St. Louis when she was thirteen and get on a train with a vaudeville troupe called the Dixie Steppers.[16]

Alberta Hunter left Memphis when she was thirteen because she had heard that young girls in Chicago were being paid ten dollars a week to sing.[17] In 1912 she started working in a club called Dago Frank's, singing to an audience of pimps and prostitutes, and then moved to Hugh Hoskins, a club for "confidence men and their girls who were pickpockets." In many ways Alberta Hunter's story of her early years in Chicago epitomizes the life from which Jane Edna Hunter wanted to save young black women in the name of maternal protection. But Alberta Hunter emphasizes how she found maternal care and nurturance from the prostitutes in her audience and describes how "the prostitutes were so wonderful, they'd always make the 'Johns' give me money you know. . . . They'd go out and buy me little dresses and things to put on me so I'd look nice."[18]

Ethel Waters agreed to join the act of two vaudevillians she met in a Philadelphia saloon because she was offered ten dollars a week playing the Lincoln Theatre when she was "getting three fifty a week as a scullion and chambermaid [at the Harrod Apartments] and a dollar and a quarter more for taking home some of the guests' laundry."[19] Waters grew up in the red-light districts of Philadelphia, and in her autobiography she asserts that she "always had great respect for whores" (*H*, 17). Like Alberta Hunter, she utilizes the language of maternal nurturance when she describes how her friendship with a young prostitute blossomed:

Being hardly more than a child herself, Blanche often played with me, read me stories, and sang little songs with me. Her beauty fascinated me. I loved her. There was a great camaraderie between us, and that young prostitute gave me some of the attention and warm affection I was starving for. Whenever I tipped off the sporting world that the cops were just around the corner I felt I was doing it for Blanche and her friends. (*H,* 18)

Waters reveals a consciousness of being part of a world in which women were under surveillance and has little hesitation in declaring her allegiance. The images and figures of the sources of both exploitation and nurturance in the lives of these young black women are in direct contrast to and, indeed, in direct conflict with the attempts of the black middle class to police and discipline female sexuality.

Black women blues singers, musicians, and performers dominated the black recording industry and vaudeville circuit throughout the twenties, and they are the central figures in the emergence and establishment of an urban blues culture. However, in order to acknowledge their roles as the primary cultural mediators of the conditions of transition and the producers of a culture of migration, we have to challenge the contemporary histories of the formation of a black urban culture as a history of the black middle class. The dominance of the conceptual paradigm of the Harlem Renaissance with its emphasis on the practices of literature and fine art relies on a belief that the black middle class did, in fact, accomplish and secure its own cultural and political dominance within black America. However, as Houston A. Baker, Jr., argues, what is called the Renaissance actually marks the historical moment of the failure of the black bourgeoisie to achieve cultural hegemony and to become a dominant social force.[20]

The contradictory nature of the culture that was produced in black urban America between the teens and the Depression has not been retained or absorbed within black urban cultural histories. The twenties must be viewed as a period of ideological, political, and cultural contestation between an emergent black bourgeoisie and an emerging urban black working class. The cultural revolution or successful renaissance that did occur stemmed from this terrain of conflict in which the black women who were so central to the formation of an urban blues culture created a web of connections among working-class migrants. The possibilities of both black female liberation and oppression were voiced through a music that spoke to the desires that were released in the dramatic shift in social relations that occurred in a historical moment of crisis and dislocation.[21]

Women's blues was not only a central mechanism of cultural mediation but also the primary means of the expression of the disrupted social relations associated with urban migration. The blues women did not passively reflect the vast social changes of their time; they provided new ways of thinking about these changes, alternative conceptions of the physical and social world for their audience of migrating and urban women and men, and social models for women who aspired to escape from and improve their conditions of existence. I have already described how hopping freight cars, because of the inherent dangers associated with that form of travel, was not a viable option for women and that traveling tent shows and vaudeville on the

Theater Owner's Booking Association circuit (TOBA) offered an alternative way to achieve mobility for young women — Mamie Smith, for example, started dancing when she was ten, and Ida Cox left home to join the Black and Tan Minstrel Show when she was fourteen. This increase in their physical mobility parallels their musical challenges to sexual conventions and gendered social roles. However, the field of blues history is dominated by the assumption that "authentic" blues forms are entirely rural in origin and are produced by the figure of the wandering, lone male. Thus the formation of mythologies of blues masculinity, which depend on this popular image, have obscured the ways the gendering of women was challenged in the blues. The blues women of the twenties, who recorded primarily in urban centers but who employed and modified the full range of rural and urban blues styles, have come to be regarded as professionalized aberrations who commercialized and adulterated "pure" blues forms. But as Chris Albertson insists, the blues "women were all aggressive women [who] knew what they wanted and went after it."[22] The blues women brought to the black urban working class an awareness of its social existence and acted creatively to vocalize the contradictions and tensions of the terrain of sexual politics in the relation of black working-class culture to the culture of the emergent black middle class.[23] In doing so they inspired other women to claim the "freedom [they] so ardently desired."

NOTES

1. See Daniel M. Johnson and Rex R. Campbell, *Black Migration in America: A Social Demographic History* (Durham, NC, 1981).

2. Carole Marks argues two important points in her recent book. The first is that the majority of migrants at this stage of migration were from urban areas and left not just to "raise their wages but because they were the displaced mudsills of southern industrial development." Second, the level of a laborer's skill was less important "than institutional barriers in determining migrant assimilation and mobility." While there is a dispute about whether the majority of migrants were from rural or urban areas in the South, it is clear that a significant number of migrants were urbanized and had previous experience of wage labor, skilled and unskilled, and that a number were professionals following their clients. Carole Marks, *Farewell — We're Good and Gone: The Great Black Migration* (Bloomington, IN, 1989), 3. See also Johnson and Campbell, *Black Migration in America*, 79.

3. See Stuart Hall et al., *Policing the Crisis: Mugging, the State, and Law and Order* (London, 1978), 16–20. Hall and his coauthors draw on the work of Stanley Cohen, who argues that

> societies appear to be subject, every now and then, to periods of moral panic. A condition, episode, person or group of persons emerges to become defined as a threat to societal values and interests; its nature is presented in a stylized and stereotypical fashion by the mass media; the moral barricades are manned by editors, bishops, politicians and other right-thinking people; socially accredited experts pronounce their diagnoses and solutions; ways of coping are evolved or (more often) resorted to; the condition then disappears, submerges or deteriorates and becomes more visible.

Sometimes the object of the panic is quite novel and at other times it is something which has been in existence long enough, but suddenly appears in the limelight.

Stanley Cohen, *Folk Devils and Moral Panics: The Creation of the Mods and Rockers* (London, 1972), 9.

4. See Frances A. Kellor, "Southern Colored Girls in the North: The Problem of Their Protection," *Charities*, 18 Mar. 1905, 584–85.

5. Ibid., 585.

6. Another unspoken assumption here, of course, is that selling sex is not hard but easy work.

7. Jane Edna Hunter, *A Nickel and a Prayer* (Cleveland, 1940), 67; hereafter abbreviated *NP*. I am very grateful to Darlene Clark Hine for telling me about Hunter, her autobiography, and her papers.

8. Hunter maintains that she was one of only two black professional nurses in Cleveland. See *NP*, 87.

9. This figure was Albert D. "Starlight" Boyd, whom Katrina Hazzard-Gordon refers to as a "political strongman." He owned and operated Woodluff Hall, the dance hall that Hunter felt was so disreputable, and the Starlight Café. Boyd had numerous estate holdings and links to prostitution and gambling and helped to deliver the black votes of the Eleventh Ward to the Republican boss Maurice Maschke. Katrina Hazzard-Gordon, *Jookin': The Rise of Social Dance Formations in African-American Culture* (Philadelphia, 1990), 127; see also 128, 130–32, 136–37.

10. St. Clair Drake and Horace R. Cayton, *Black Metropolis: A Study of Negro Life in a Northern City* (New York, 1946), 577; hereafter abbreviated *BM*.

11. See Carl Van Vechten, *Nigger Heaven* (New York, 1926), hereafter abbreviated *NH*; and Claude McKay, *Home to Harlem* (1928; New York, 1987), hereafter abbreviated *HH*.

12. William H. Jones, *Recreation and Amusement among Negroes in Washington, DC: A Sociological Analysis of the Negro in an Urban Environment* (Washington, DC, 1927), 121; hereafter abbreviated *RA*.

13. Jones acknowledged his greatest debt to Robert E. Park and others of the Department of Sociology at the University of Chicago.

14. Kathy Peiss, *Cheap Amusements: Working Women and Leisure in Turn-of-the-Century New York* (Philadelphia, 1986), 178–79. The focus of my analysis is rather different than Peiss's. She describes her book as "a study of young working women's culture in turn-of-the-century New York City — the customs, values, public styles, and ritualized interactions — expressed in leisure time" (3). Not only am I concentrating on black women rather than white women, but also I am most interested here in the black women for whom the site of leisure was a place of work rather than recreation.

15. See William Barlow, *"Looking Up at Down": The Emergence of Blues Culture* (Philadelphia, 1989), 240–43 (on Kansas City), 250–51 (on St. Louis), and 287–92 (on Chicago). See also *BM*, 174–213.

16. See Josephine Baker and Jo Bouillon, *Josephine*, trans. Mariana Fitzpatrick (New York, 1977), 3–4. See also Phyllis Rose, *Jazz Cleopatra: Josephine Baker in Her Time* (New York, 1989), 12.

17. See Frank C. Taylor and Gerald Cook, *Alberta Hunter: A Celebration in Blues* (New York, 1987), 20–23.

18. Alberta Hunter, quoted in Stuart Goldman (producer), *Alberta Hunter: My Castle's Rockin'* (1988).

19. Ethel Waters and Charles Samuels, *His Eye Is on the Sparrow* (New York, 1951), 72; hereafter abbreviated *H*.

20. See Houston A. Baker, Jr., *Modernism and the Harlem Renaissance* (Chicago, 1987).

21. Virginia Yans-McLaughlin argues that the new scholarship in immigration and migration studies has moved away from questions about

individual and group agency toward the social relations of exchange. So, instead of individuals assimilating or achieving, we have group strategies and networks. What we might call a network-exchange theory seems to be emerging as a potential alternative to assimilation and human-capital theory. In network-exchange theory, an ethnic group's human capital is not simply transported from one place to another by individuals who fold their riches into the American system. Although it is true that the groups are sometimes portrayed as holders of assets, these are transformed to new purposes; indeed, immigrant groups seem capable of creating new advantages for themselves. The network structure that originally functioned as the grid connecting Old World kin might, for example, transform itself in ethnic subeconomies to provide jobs, housing, or even business opportunities.

> Virginia Yans-McLaughlin, introduction to *Immigration Reconsidered: History, Sociology, and Politics*, ed. Yans-McLaughlin (New York, 1990), 12.

Using such a methodology, Suzanne Model argues that because of their very limited access to the job market, black migrants were unable or failed to establish such a system of mutual assistance. Although it is clear that networks of exchange did indeed exist within black urban migrant enclaves, my argument here is that network-exchange theory is unnecessarily limited if it is applied only to access to the labor market and to alternative economies that existed within migrant communities. I would argue that urban blues culture could profitably be regarded as a network of exchange or web of connection rather than as a conglomeration of individual achievement. See Suzanne W. Model, "Work and Family: Blacks and Immigrants from South and East Europe," in ibid., 130–59. It would seem to me that the role of the *Chicago Defender* would be important in a history that documented the system of mutual exchange in black communities that provided information about and access to the job market. See, for example, Emmett J. Scott, "Letters of Negro Migrants of 1916–1918," *Journal of Negro History* 4 (July 1919): 290–340; and; idem, "Additional Letters of Negro Migrants of 1916–1918," *Journal of Negro History* 4 (Oct. 1919): 412–65.

22. Chris Albertson, quoted in Carole van Falkenburg and Christine Dall (producers), *Wild Women Don't Have the Blues* (1989).

23. See my forthcoming book, *Women, Migration, and the Formation of a Blues Culture*.

TEN

Fade to White: Racial Politics and the Troubled Reign of Vanessa Williams

SARAH BANET-WEISER

On 19 September 1983, headlines appeared on hundreds of newspapers across the country celebrating the passing of the crown to Vanessa Williams, the first black woman to win the coveted title Miss America. The *New York Times* headline read, "To First Black Miss America, Victory Is a Means to an End."[1] Other headlines similarly located this unprecedented event in the history of the pageant: "Black Leaders Praise Choice of First Black Miss America,"[2] and, in the *Washington Post*, "Her Crowning Achievement: Vanessa Williams: A New Voice for Miss America."[3] Each of these headlines, and the articles that accompanied them, enthusiastically praised the style and panache that Vanessa Williams brought to the title Miss America. The day had finally come when a black woman had been selected to uphold the values deemed appropriate for "American womanhood" and thus serve as a role model for American women. Vanessa was different, the newspapers claimed, in more ways than her race. She was "outspoken on political issues, race and beauty pageants," and she went public with her support for the Equal Rights Amendment and a woman's right to choose abortion. The executive director of the NAACP, Benjamin Hooks, compared Williams's achievement to Jackie Robinson breaking the color barrier in baseball.[4] Her achievement, like Robinson's, seemed to provide incontrovertible evidence that America was indeed still a land of opportunity, and that anyone could do anything if they but tried.

Ten months into Vanessa Williams's reign, the press had yet another field day with the first black Miss America. The headlines in the same newspapers that less than a year before had applauded the choice of the pageant judges now were somewhat less generous: "Miss America Asked to Resign: Pageant Officials Act after Learning of Nude Photos," and "Miss America Gives Up Her Crown."[5] The opinion columns were perhaps more revealing in their headlines: "Sleaze"; "Missed

America"; "Pageant of Hypocrisy"; and "There She Goes. . ."[6] The ostensible cause of this change? Nude photographs of Williams that were taken in 1981 and that depicted her and a white woman in various sexual acts were published in *Penthouse* magazine. The sales of that issue of *Penthouse* broke all previously held records, generating $5.5 million in profit.[7] Amid much controversy and debate among the Miss America pageant officials, feminist organizations, and the NAACP, among other groups, Vanessa Williams announced that she would resign from her position, claiming that the "potential harm to the pageant and the deep division that a bitter fight may cause has convinced me that I must relinquish my title."[8] The first runner-up, Suzette Charles, also a black woman, was quietly crowned Miss America for the remaining two months of the 1984 reign.

The Miss America Pageant: Celebrating (White) Womanhood

Since 1984, there have been three other black Miss Americas, in 1990, 1991, and 1994. According to the pageant and the general public, the selection of black contestants to this title previously held only by white women attests to the growing understanding that the category "American womanhood" is a diverse one, comprising many different "types" of women.[9] Even *Ebony* magazine, a production targeted to black audiences, quotes Kimberly Aiken, Miss America 1994, on the supposed racial harmony of the pageant: "We [Miss America contestants] all have different backgrounds, but it is as if we are all part of the same sisterhood."[10] From this perspective, the selection of black Miss Americas is viewed as a stabilizing factor in an always precarious racial balance, a final step in achieving "true sisterhood." Viewed from other angles, however, the contradictions and conflicts inherent in this tale of sameness within difference become clearer. Indeed, what happens in beauty pageants when black contestants enter can hardly be told as a story of "racial harmony": the presence of black contestants destabilizes not only the assumptions behind, but the precarious construction of, the category "American womanhood."

In fact, in mainstream U.S. culture generally and in beauty pageants in particular, there is an assumption that an easy and unproblematic correspondence exists between the visible body of a woman and her invisible moral qualities. A woman's appearance is presumed to transparently represent her interior qualities. Indeed, this is the premise behind the pageant's insistent claim that the event is concerned more with "inner beauty" than outward appearance. The ideal woman, embodied in Miss America, is one whose "essence" and appearance are perfectly synchronic. Her self-discipline and commitment to a work ethic are revealed in her athletic body and career goals; her class status (or "good breeding" in pageant parlance) is revealed in her smile, clear skin, and shiny hair; her cultivated creativity or artistry is revealed in her makeup application, her evening gown selection, and her "talent"; while her humility and chastity are revealed in the containment of her movements when sitting, walking, and gesturing.

It is crucial not to overlook the importance of how this notion of "inner beauty" operates within the discourse of the pageant; dismissing it, as many critics of popular culture have done, obscures the ways the pageants work as sites for constructing white American womanhood.[11] The discourse of "inner beauty," I will argue, in effect functions to draw attention away from narratives about sexuality within the pageant. In so doing, it also — and just as importantly — functions as an implicit statement about and affirmation of racial identity. The contestants put it this way:

> I think that not only are [contestants] beautiful, but they are beautiful on the inside and I think that that's important. There's a certain breed of girls that makes it. I mean, occasionally you find a home-town girl that makes it up there, but . . . you don't usually find a girl who just says, "oh I want to be in a pageant" and just enters it without any training.[12]

The language of good "breeding" and "training" used by this contestant makes it clear that beauty pageants are about reading the female body surface as direct, visible evidence of interior, invisible qualities of womanhood.

Reading the body in this way is unproblematic if these invisible qualities of womanhood are uniformly assumed for *every* contestant. But when black women enter beauty pageants, the easy convergence between inside and out that has traditionally been assumed is disrupted. The appearance of the black body is not presumed to correspond so directly to the morality and respectability considered appropriate to a Miss America contestant. The visibly *raced* body serves instead as a signal for the unknown, the threatening, the chaotic. The job for black contestants thus becomes one of "proving" to the audience that they are indeed the moral "sisters" of the white contestants and can occupy (and be occupied by) the abstract category of "American womanhood." This task is exercised in terms of two discursive strategies: a strategy of "*passing*" is performed on the pageant stage, at the same time that a strategy of eroticizing *difference* is enacted.

When "passing," black beauty pageant contestants must authenticate what Wah-neema Lubiano calls a "cover story" in order to "obscure context, fade out subtext, and . . . protect the text of the powerful."[13] "Passing" is enacted, however, not in the conventional sense of passing for a white-skinned person, but engaging in the far more difficult process of controlling and containing the social meaning of blackness, through the discourses of morality and respectability. Since one dominant social narrative is that the morals black women hold are questionable at best, the visible body of the black contestant must pass as a cover for the invisible moral qualities of the white woman. In other words, in the context of the pageant, and in a kind of perverse echoing of Sojourner Truth's question "Ain't I a woman?" black contestants must pass for *women*.

The discursive strategy I identify as passing, however, in the context of black women, is not only the choice of an individual woman to appear to be and thus be regarded as white. In the context of beauty pageants, the practice of passing is also about passing as a particular kind of *sexual* subject, one that is historically, politically, and culturally connected with the racial power of whiteness. So the social narrative that framed the public telling of Vanessa Williams's story is a conventional one about white female heterosexuality. Shaping every part of this discourse was a sometimes implicit but more often explicit theme of homophobia. The *Penthouse* photographs' depiction of Williams engaged in simulated sexual activity with an-other woman not only disrupted the heavily regulated moral boundary of femininity, but also dismantled the even more institutionalized framework of heterosexuality that literally defines the Miss America pageant.

At the same time, however, as passing is exercised as a crucial strategy, the blackness of the black contestants is not to be denied. Indeed, it is precisely this blackness — their *difference* — that is eroticized, celebrated, and made crucial to the pageant's claim to represent diverse womanhood. Despite their seemingly contradic-tory premises, the discourse of passing and the discourse of recognizing and eroticiz-ing diversity function simultaneously *and* successfully within the structure of beauty pageants. Blackness, as a cultural signifier, contains many stories for white audi-ences: stories about laziness, welfare dependence, and overt and uncontrolled sexu-ality.[14] Given the cultural currency of these stories, the beauty pageant's task is to construct a narrative of blackness that obscures the pageant's history of white suprem-acy even while it appears to overcome it. While black contestants are considered living proof of the progressive diversity of the pageant, it remains their job to represent their blackness in a way that does not bring to the foreground those dominant social narratives about the instability of the category "black woman." The pageant, then (like all cultural productions in the United States), must utilize strategies to control this instability, which through public and "spontaneous" perfor-mances of difference can potentially transition into crisis at any moment. In other words, difference must be *managed* within the pageant as it is similarly managed in U.S. culture: black contestants continue to tell the conventional story of racial harmony, and the subjectivities of the black contestants are characterized by the tensions that result from attempting to assert that indeed "black is beautiful," but only when it can be shown to correspond to a historically "white" model of interior womanhood.

In this context, Vanessa Williams's story must be reexamined or reframed in a fashion that foregrounds what was really "exposed" in those *Penthouse* photographs and the public reaction to them. These events seem to suggest that within the site of the beauty pageant, black women cannot fully and simultaneously occupy the social practices of *both* passing and managing difference, even as it is precisely the pre-sumed success of these practices that allows their existence within the pageant. It is the combination of these two practices — containing difference through normative standards of whiteness (or passing) while simultaneously enacting a limited, heavily regulated performance of difference — that characterizes contemporary notions of "diversity" and conservative thoughts on what "multicultural" society should look like. From the story of Vanessa Williams emerge the complex social and cultural practices involved in simultaneously performing, regulating, and containing a poten-tial crisis of diversity.

Passing for Respectable: The "New Black Woman"

In the Miss America pageant, Williams was called to both repress her sexuality through the conventional practices of white womanhood, and eroticize her blackness in a way that called the American public's attention to her diversity — which, of course, functioned as evidence for the diversity of the entire pageant. Consequently, her presence and the presence of African American and other nonwhite contestants in beauty pageants both respond to recent accusations that pageants do not include women of color, and reinscribe the primacy of whiteness celebrated within the pageant.[15] The presence of nonwhite contestants obscures the racist histories and foundations on which beauty pageants rest. At the same time, though, it foregrounds the pageant's "whiteness." A recent study of the Miss America pageant illuminates this history of the pageant: " 'Rule Seven' of the Pageant's bylaws for nearly half a century restricted participation to 'members of the white race.' The first blacks appeared in the contest as 'slaves' in a musical number in 1923, and up until the 1940's contestants were required to list their genealogy as far back as they could."[16] African American women did not even participate in the Miss America pageant until 1970, and not until 1984 was there an African American Miss America.[17] In fact, several contestants I've interviewed unwittingly perpetuated the racism embedded in beauty pageants by discussing recent African American Miss Americas (1990 and 1991) as strategic ploys to incorporate race in the pageants. The crowning of an African American woman was typically viewed by these participants as a purely "political" matter; if it was remarked on at all, the crowning of white women was attributed to their genuine, natural, self-evident beauty. As one contestant put it, "In the Miss America pageant there's always one or two black finalists now and you never saw that before. I don't think that's a coincidence, I really don't."[18] This contestant is claiming that the *presence* of African Americans in beauty pageants is to be understood as noncoincidental, "unnatural," and politically purposeful. The entrance of black women into the pageant, however, both exposes the politics of the event and renders it more vulnerable. What this comment reveals is that pageants have been political all along; the exclusive crowning of white women prior to 1984 *was* overtly political. The inclusion of black women forces awareness and struggle with the implicit definitions of both beauty and national identity, foregrounding the contradictions of the pageant as well as the politics of racial and sexual difference.

Strategies are needed, then, to contain and control the exposure of the kind of race politics that has historically structured and defined the pageant, and that has only recently begun to appear politically untenable. As I've stated, one way that the markers of race are transformed is through the social and cultural practice of passing. In pageants, however, black contestants who must "pass" as versions of white femininity do not erase their mark of racial difference; indeed, this difference is crucial to their success as "black" contestants. By passing in terms of invisible (white) femininity, black contestants do the work of *both confirming and rendering invisible* the particular model of "true womanhood" celebrated in the American pageant. In a curious twist, the "difference" of nonwhite contestants — evidenced by their black or brown skin — actually works favorably in the practice of "passing" through normalizing whiteness. The public focus on Williams's race when she was crowned functioned as a powerful opening for her to deny her difference and to insist that she is simply, and finally, a "person."

Tracing the mass media coverage through which Williams's story was told fore-

grounds the range of currently available narratives about race, sexuality, and nationhood. At the beginning of her reign, she managed to fulfill the expectation of a
"colorless" Miss America (which, of course, meant fulfilling the expectation of a
white Miss America). However, as I will argue later, when she was asked to relinquish her crown because of the public exposure of nude photographs, it became
clear that she succeeded in passing only until it was publicly exposed that she *also*
participated in eroticizing difference. Posing nude with a woman signifies not only a
failure of morals and respectability, but also a failure to occupy a particular definition of white, heterosexual femininity. In the context of eroticizing difference, by the
ostensible evidence of her uncontrollable desire, she does not effectively diffuse and
dilute dominant social stereotypes and narratives about female sexuality, and thus
cannot adequately contain the fears about sexuality that frame the pageant. But
before we get to how Williams ultimately became a site for the simultaneous
mobilization and displacement of dominant racial fears, we need first to examine
how a particular concept of "diversity" was deployed at the beginning of her reign.

Consider the following headline: "Vanessa Williams: A New Voice for Miss
America." The first line of the article is simple and clear: "She is the new black
woman."[19] The article continues by illustrating that what makes the "new black
woman" new is her lack of interest in overt identity claims of blackness. She instead
adopts in effect age-old tropes in American nationalism that recall Horatio Alger and
liberal individualism. As Williams puts it in the article,

> I think I would be doing the same thing if I were Spanish or white or Chinese. I am
> still a person, I still feel the same way about being crowned. I don't think they chose
> me because I was black and it was time for a black Miss America. They chose me
> because they thought I could do the job.[20]

Williams's focus on "doing the job" resonates with anti–affirmative action discourse;
it also constructs the "job" of Miss America as a specific and important one.
Williams denies a racially specific identity, and instead claims that she is first and
foremost simply "a person."[21]

The rhetoric of universalized personhood produces the practice of passing as a
norm for people of color, because it sets up a normative standard of "just people"
without interrogating the racial specificity of that norm. In the case of Vanessa
Williams, at least at the beginning of her reign, she both assuaged and legitimized
white fears about personhood through her constant denials that her crowning had
anything to do with race. Yet at the same time, Williams's election as Miss America
worked to deflect charges that the pageant was a "lily-white" affair by confirming
"America's liberal promise of do-it-yourself political improvement."[22] As feminist
Jackie Goldsby points out, Williams's crowning was situated at a particularly important moment in the history of U.S. race relations, and functioned to provide
answers to questions like these: "How could anyone complain that the contest's
outcome was anything but 'progress'? Didn't the nation have another racial 'first' to
add to the mythic melting pot of American achievement? Wasn't this a fulfillment
of the Civil Rights dream state of affairs — a black woman representing the ideal of
American femininity?"[23] And in fact, Williams's victory was often framed in the

rhetoric of the "Civil Rights dream state of affairs," where specific definitions of diversity — definitions that privileged circumscribed, limited permutations of difference — were applauded and celebrated.

In subsequent press conferences, for example, Williams continued to address the issue of race, and continued to deny that race was a significant factor in her success. This dual strategy of focusing on difference only to insist that "difference" doesn't make a difference served to reassure the Miss America pageant and most of America that selecting a woman of color was not going to disrupt dominant notions of (white) womanhood, but would, at the same time, give it a new twist, spice it up, and make it more accessible to young American women. As one article put it,

> From the first moments of her tenure as Miss America, Williams . . . seemed to accept the inevitable controversy and even crave the distinction of being different. That is one mark of her generation, born in the throes of the civil rights movement, immune from the physical strife of direct racial bias — and taught that a colorless world is the reward the last generation has bequeathed.[24]

The obvious contradiction in this statement, that of "craving the distinction of being different" based on color, and then reveling in the reward of a "colorless world," is one that frames all the media coverage of Williams's crowning.[25] This contradiction precisely captures the tensions characteristic of "diversity" in general and black female subjectivity in particular within the pageant: the strategies of passing (the "colorless world") and eroticizing difference ("craving distinction") are mutually constitutive processes. Of course, employing/deploying both of these strategies simultaneously is an impossible task: one cannot be both other and the same.

"Passing" for white is not only a category of experience defined by race, but also, and in this context more importantly, a clear statement about sexuality, specifically conventional heterosexuality. That is to say, the racial category "white" represents a definition of heterosexuality that is bounded by notions of respectability and morality, and is configured against and in relation to "black," which signifies precisely the opposite: a wanton, insatiable whorishness, as well as a lack of proper discrimination in the choice of object. Thus, in a forum that was conceived on and continues to uphold a rigorous ideology of "respectable" sexuality, black contestants who are actually successful in moving up in the pageant ranks are those women who have shown that they can successfully "pass" as white and are, by consequence, "appropriately" sexual. However, the threat — or perhaps anticipation — of failing to pass is a specter that haunts all black contestants, especially since the "fall" of Vanessa Williams. What happens when that line that is meant to be maintained is crossed? What happens when a person, in this case Vanessa Williams, attempts to occupy conflicting discourses of representation, both passing and eroticization? Neither the pageant nor the American public had at its disposal a dominant narrative that could accommodate Williams's position as *both* Miss America and unapparent porn star.

The Eroticization of Difference, or "Vanessa the Undressa"

> Within commodity culture, ethnicity becomes spice, s-
> easoning that can liven up the dull dish that is main-
> stream white culture.
> — bell hooks, *Black Looks: Race and Representation*

The mere visibility of black contestants on the stage does not erase the ideology of whiteness that defines the pageant; on the contrary, the presence of black contestants serves to foreground whiteness as the only appropriate field of representational power. In contrast to pageants like Miss Black America or other pageants dedicated to a specific ethnic or racial group, the fact that white and nonwhite contestants compete together in the Miss America pageant works to disrupt any presumption that the pageant is an all-white production. Despite her efforts to present herself as "just another person," in other words, Vanessa Williams was simultaneously lauded around the country for her "difference." This difference was marked in a variety of ways, from the omnipresent rephrasing of Williams's title from the simple "Miss America" to the more descriptive "the first black Miss America," to the *Washington Post* news article identifying her as "the new black woman." Vanessa Williams and other popular black female figures are newly considered "all-American," but with an important twist: they are "sultry representatives," representing not necessarily the America that is conjured through conventionally white images such as apple pie and middle-class motherhood, but an America that is characterized by "hip diversity," or "sexy difference."

The question we might want to ask at this point is, how is the social practice of eroticizing difference used in the cultural marketplace? How does the "sexiness" of difference function not only to maintain a racial hierarchy, but also to preserve the ideology that equates the category of "black woman" with aggressive and uncontrollable sexuality? The sexualizing of the black female body, the construction of this body *as* sex, displaces white anxieties concerning female sexuality and allows the maintenance of the social practices and ideologies that make whiteness coextensive with respectability and morality. Feminist theorists Hazel Carby, Patricia Hill Collins, and others have shown how this functioned during slavery: the category of black woman as Jezebel became the repository for fears and fantasies about female sexuality, and constructed black women as sexually aggressive while simultaneously producing white women as chaste and moral.[26] In contemporary times, eroticizing difference works in a similar way. The black female body becomes symbol, metaphor, and literal battleground for the anxiety and anticipation that define sexuality, with the white female body positioned and maintained as the more moral, the more pure, the more respectable.

There are few more illustrative tales of this kind of cultural practice than Vanessa Williams's "fall from grace." In July 1984, *Penthouse* magazine ran an issue that featured Williams engaged in sexual acts with a white woman. Taken three years before the pageant, these photographs led to the decision of the Miss America Pageant Commission to ask Williams to relinquish her crown and title. Although

Williams denied signing a release form for the photos and claimed that they were intended for "private use only," she did not move to sue the magazine or its editor/publisher, Robert Guccione. Rather, she tearfully handed over her crown to her first runner-up, Suzette Charles, also a black woman.

The exposure of these photographs is precisely the kind of event that explodes the contradictions that characterize black female subjectivity. In the context of the pageant, Williams was successfully able to both play the eroticized other and pass as the respectable, straight, white feminine norm. The exposure of the photographs, however, disrupted her performance of passing, seeming to reveal that it was, after all, *only* a performance. The "real" Vanessa Williams, the pictures were read as saying, clearly transgressed the boundaries of femininity so celebrated by the pageant. Her performance in the pageant now seemed merely a hoax; she could not be both pure and sexual, both straight and playfully lesbian. As columnist Richard Cohen argues, as Miss America,

> you cannot have more than just a vague sexuality — maybe one that will ripen only after marriage and then, knock on wood, only in a modest undemanding way.... Vanessa Williams has sullied that myth. Her body, not to mention her simulated sexuality, is available on the newsstands to the enrichment of male fantasies and the coffers of Guccione. He sells one kind of myth; the Miss America pageant sells another. Williams has made the mistake of merging the two — madonna and tart in one woman, although like most women she is neither one.[27]

Although Cohen insightfully points out the contradictions characterizing female sexuality for all women, he fails to extend his point to insist that nonwhite female sexuality, although subject to some of the same cultural constraints as white female sexuality, is nonetheless played out differently and has distinct stakes and consequences. Williams's story cannot be told unless we track the ways race and sexuality are mutually constitutive; indeed, without such tracking, only half of the story can be told. These dynamics of race and sexuality are captured by Jackie Goldsby when she asks how race can condition the terms on which representation occurs, and wonders about the effect of one's agency within the marketplace of sex.[28]

One way that race, or in this specific case, blackness, conditions "the terms on which representation occurs" becomes clear in the way Vanessa Williams is represented in a pornographic magazine and is produced as a symbol of *all* black women. Notwithstanding her efforts at the beginning of her reign to construct herself as simply "an individual," a woman who was selected because of her unique merits, and who could perform the "job" of Miss America just as skillfully if she were "Spanish or white or Chinese," Williams is vilified (by both the black and white communities) as a "bad example" of and for her race with the publication of the porn photos.[29] Her race conditioned the terms of her representation by foregrounding and recalling dominant social narratives of the black female as the "oversexed-black-Jezebel," one who not only signifies sex, but initiates it.[30] Importantly, Vanessa Williams also transgresses the boundary of heterosexuality circumscribing the pageant: not only did she initiate sex, but she (supposedly) initiated lesbian sex, which ultimately proved to be even more disruptive to her construction as Miss America.

While there were outcries from the black community, most notably the NAACP, concerning the racism underpinning the scandal, a sense of shame, a sense that Williams had "let us down," was also expressed by black organizations. This sentiment reflects how whiteness "figures the normative center of political and theoretical debate about sexuality and identity."[31] In an editorial in the *Washington Post* titled "A Sad Lesson," for example, the author writes, "[Williams] had been hailed as a particularly 'exemplary' queen, one who injected new life into the homogeneously bland pageant." She continues, "[this] only makes her fall more keenly felt by black women who are trying hard to exert a sense of self."[32] Of course, the ways nude photos might also "inject new life" into the pageant are, not surprisingly, ignored by this writer. In addition, this "sense of self" does not, apparently, include a sense of sexual self, or sexuality. Instead, a woman's "sense of self" here indicates the self defined by the liberal individual, where sexuality is relegated to the private sphere.

But perhaps more important, this self is, of course, racially specific. When Williams was first crowned, her success at crossing the historically all-white barrier of the Miss America pageant was read as evidence that black women could be included within the parameters of white femininity.[33] Thus, it makes sense that after the photographs were published,

> people have asked her [whether], whereas she once was a credit, she now had become a "disgrace to her race." She replied that she didn't think so and felt black people wouldn't abandon her. It was an ironic answer since Williams herself has played down any racial symbolism when she was first crowned, and some blacks complained that her mulatto looks didn't represent them in a pageant already controversial and slipping in prestige. Now, some of her detractors are embracing Williams as a sister in trouble.[34]

Racial solidarity worked both for and against Williams during this period of her reign; on the one hand, some members of the black community did "embrace [her] as a sister in trouble," a gesture made specifically on behalf of her entire race. On the other hand, her downfall was seen (primarily by the white community, but also by some within the black community) as symbolic of — again — the entire black race. That is, the sexually explicit photographs brought up "old ghosts" about the oversexed black woman — not about the oversexed *Vanessa Williams*.[35] As Goldsby comments in her essay "Queen for 307 Days: Looking B(l)ack at Vanessa Williams and the Sex Wars," Williams could not "revise the racial symbolism of film and the acts depicted in the images, precisely because the historical construction of black sexuality is always already pornographic, if by pornography I mean the writing or technological representation and mass marketing of the body as explicitly sexual."[36] Of course, the question we can put forward at this point is, What would have happened if a white Miss America had posed for *Penthouse*?[37] I would submit that because, as I have been arguing, white female sexuality plays itself out differently in the cultural and social imagination, a white Miss America would also have been asked to relinquish her crown — but her act would have been publicly condemned as an *individual* moral failing. The act of posing in sexually explicit positions would not have been conditioned by and interpreted in terms of the *whiteness* of a white Miss America. With Williams, race was immediately implicated by her representation in *Penthouse*; dominant social narratives about black female sexuality were reinvigorated and once again brought to a public surface.

Nonetheless, the reason for Williams's downfall was insistently read by the majority of the public and the pageant alike as an event not motivated by racism. It was, on the other hand, an incident understood to have everything to do with sex. When the Miss America commission asked Williams to resign, the executive director remarked that "The pageant celebrates the whole woman, and its spirit is intrinsically inconsistent with calculated sexual exploitation."[38] The pageant's suggestion that the "whole"ness of a woman is distinct from her sexual identity or performance is again part of constructing liberal subjects within the pageant. That is, the pageant woman is whole in the sense that the public, liberal individual is whole — she leaves her sexuality at the door, so to speak. And the clear hypocrisy of an event that is dedicated and indebted to an ideology that constructs women *precisely* through the discourses of sexual exploitation did not go unremarked in the media. In other words, the focus on sex was not limited to the pageant officials (as well as many others) who condemned Williams's act as "repulsive," "shocking," or otherwise "indefensible." Advocates of Williams, those feminist critics of the pageant's treatment of her, also singularly located the incident within a discourse of sex. The feminist group Women against Pornography, for example, was quoted as saying that they "deplore the hypocrisy of the Miss America pageant officials for criticizing Miss Williams. The Miss America pageant differs from *Penthouse* in degree, not in kind. Like *Penthouse*, the pageant judges women on the basis of their conformity to a sexist ideal."[39]

The intense focus on Williams as a victim of sexual exploitation or an active agent of sex denies the ways her identity is raced — it denies, in other words, her identity as *intersectional*. Feminist legal scholar Kimberlè Crenshaw argues for a theory of *intersectionality*, or an account of the various ways race and gender interact and intersect. Intersectionality, Crenshaw argues, "captures the way in which the particular location of black women in dominant American social relations is unique and in some senses unassimilable into the discursive paradigms of gender and race domination. . . . black women are in a sense doubly burdened, subject in some ways to the dominating practices of both a sexual hierarchy and a racial one."[40] In the story of Vanessa Williams, the sole narrative both pageant officials and feminists could rely on was a trope of *sexual*, not racial, exploitation. As in the dominant narratives about Anita Hill, the reaction by many in the feminist community about the pageant's treatment of Williams did not take into account the ways that race conditioned both Williams's actions and the pageant's request for her dismissal.[41] As Goldsby comments, "The publication of Vanessa Williams's split images as the beauty-cum-porn queen marked a crucial moment wherein lesbian feminists could — and should — have theorized about the historic workings of race in relation to sexuality because it, and not racism, explains most critically why Williams met the infamous end she did."[42]

Like Goldsby, I am concerned with "locating race in a historical context in order to understand the effective silence which greeted and so defined Williams's fall, to consider why public discourse about colored sexuality remains conventional in its outlook on and response to boundary-shattering incidents such as this." [43] Goldsby argues that the telling and retelling of Vanessa Williams's impressive victory and equally impressive downfall provided an opportunity — a lost opportunity, in her opinion — to open up a public conversation about the various ways race conditions and intersects sexuality, especially lesbian identity. Without an interrogation of the racial specificity of the context in which Williams was positioned, her story could not be told — indeed, there was no available social narrative for the telling. Like the feminist reaction to Anita Hill, the relative silence that greeted the events precipitating Williams's downfall was a result of America "[stumbling] into the place where African-American women live, a political vacuum of erasure and contradiction maintained by the almost routine polarization of 'blacks and women' into separate and competing political camps." [44]

The social narrative that framed the public telling of Vanessa Williams's story is a conventional one about *white* female heterosexuality. Thus, despite the statement by the pageant's chief executive officer, Albert Marks, that the pageant celebrates the "whole woman" in a spirit that is "intrinsically inconsistent with calculated sexual exploitation," many people in the community and in the mass media called Marks to task by implicitly questioning his use of the term "*calculated* sexual exploitation." In other words, many questioned the difference between the pageant and *Penthouse* magazine: were they simply, as WAP (Women against Pornography) claimed, a difference in "degree, not in kind"? Why, many such as Goldsby asked, should the photographs of Williams be seen as anything different from parading down a runway in a swimsuit in front of a panel of judges?

The answer to this question was to be found in the photographs themselves. Apparently unwilling — or perhaps unable — to engage in a debate about whether the pageant *was* sexual exploitation, the pageant commission focused on the content of the photographs, the representation of sexual acts between two women. The specter of lesbianism hangs above almost all the mass-mediated coverage of Williams's resignation, from claims about the "repulsive" nature of the photographs to reports about billboards erected at a shopping area in her hometown, Milltown, New York, with the spray-painted message "Vanessa is a lesbian nudie." [45] Journalists seemed unable to restrain their homophobia when describing the photos; as one writer from the *Washington Post* commented,

> We tell ourselves that, in this day of nude scenes in PG-rated movies, nudity really isn't that big a deal. I might have been tempted to make that argument myself, but then I saw the *Penthouse* photos. I can tell you that nudity is the least of the problems. The thing is indefensible, and we ought to stop confusing our children by suggesting otherwise. [46]

Not surprisingly, Miss America officials shared this journalist's opinion that sexually explicit images involving two women were "indefensible." The pageant commission called attention to the fact that they made the decision about Williams only after "looking at those pictures." The executive director, Marks, was quoted as saying, in response to the public support of Williams, "Now they're supplications . . . 'Please don't do this to that girl' they say. When I talk to them, I tell them to please withhold judgement until they see the pictures."[47] The photographs were the turning point, the moment when the tensions intrinsic to Williams's contradictory subjectivity completely broke down. Apparently it did not matter that these photographs, like all straight pornographic representations that depict same-sex sex, were created precisely for male *heterosexual* desire. As Susan Sontag comments on photography, "photographs furnish evidence. . . . A photograph passes for incontrovertible proof that a given thing happened."[48] The "given thing that happened" for Vanessa Williams was sexual interaction with a woman; the social and cultural stigma of lesbianism within a homophobic society provided justification for Williams's downfall. The heterosexual contract is one that is always assumed in the beauty pageant, an unspoken but omnipresent commitment. When Williams posed nude with a woman, she broke this crucial contract, and thus became the site for crisis within the pageant — a crisis that could be controlled only through her resignation.

Williams herself attempted to "set the record *straight*"[49] in her press conference following the exposure, claiming that

> he [photographer Tom Chaipel] said he wanted to try a new concept of silhouettes with two models. I had no idea what he was talking about. He said it would just be two models, he would tell us how to pose and that you wouldn't be able to recognize us, only shapes and forms. . . . It was not spontaneous. Everything was orchestrated by him.[50]

By claiming that the photo session was "not spontaneous," Williams exempts herself from any connection with lesbian desire, and powerfully reminds us of the patriarchal grid on which straight pornography rests. The photography session, she insistently claimed, was a "mistake," a bad judgment call blamed on youth and inexperience: "I was enraged and I felt a deep sense of personal embarrassment. It is one thing to face up to a mistake one makes in youth, but it is almost totally devastating to have to share it with the American public and the world at large."[51] And, as Goldsby points out, it is clear that Williams's unawareness — "I had no idea what he was talking about" — was contradicted by the photos themselves:

> Once the photos hit the newsstands . . . their value and meaning transformed not around the fact of her ignorance, but around the *representation* of her knowledge. . . . The question of whether Williams knew what she was doing is reflected by what it *looked* like she knew: how to eat snatch, how to please herself. It becomes impossible to classify and so withdraw the images as stock stereotypes from straight pornography precisely because Williams was the paragon of American prenuptial chastity; the beauty queen became, irrevocably, the derivative deviant that is the dyke.[52]

As it has turned out, however, Williams's "fall" from virgin to whore was not irrevocably culturally signified as the "derivative deviant that is the dyke." After Williams relinquished her crown (and after a period of relative invisibility), she found a more tenable position in popular culture, a position where she could more successfully occupy the discourses of passing and eroticizing difference simultaneously. Williams chose the "soft" eroticization of the sexy pop star, where her subjectivity is constituted as both safely white and sexily black.

But it is clear that within the pageant, black women are presented with few options in terms of constructing self-identity. The "exposure" of Vanessa Williams recalled and foregrounded historically powerful narratives about black women and sexuality, and it confirmed racist beliefs embedded within beauty pageants concerning the "questionable morals" purportedly held by all black women. The discourses of passing and eroticizing difference work in the pageant — indeed, in all realms of popular culture — to reinforce a particular construction of the liberal subject as moral, respectable, and white. As Williams's story illustrates, however, the pageant is not and cannot be a seamless production of white supremacy.

What does this story tell us about racism, politics, and the nation? We should consider the story of Vanessa Williams a particularly instructive instance of the ways the discourse of "diversity" works in U.S. culture. It is true that the *Penthouse* photographs functioned to recall to the public's collective memory "old ghosts" about insatiable — and "indefensible" — black female sexuality, but this recollection took place within the context of liberal tales of individual achievement, tolerance, and personhood. The strategies I have identified as passing and eroticizing difference, necessary to "appropriately" position Williams on the pageant stage, resonate with some of the processes and regulatory practices of popular culture that situate black women on the landscape of U.S. political and cultural life. In an increasingly diverse configuration of the nation, accompanied by an increasing absence of the notion of a universal citizen, popular cultural forms in the United States uniquely respond to a moral panic over the current state of national identity. The beauty pageant, for example, offers a performance of feminine subjectivity that functions as a sort of national assurance that despite the threats posed to dominant culture by fluctuating racial and gender codes, the pageant successfully manages and disciplines the construction of national identity, femininity, and racial identity.

This kind of management emerges in pageants through the forced confrontation between a history of celebrating universal whiteness and contemporary demands that pageants reflect racial and ethnic diversity. In the 1990s, pageants function to assuage nationwide fears and anxieties about multiculturalism and "political correctness" through both a reinvention of this hysteria and a simultaneous retrenchment of racist "moral" values. Appropriating the terms and language of diversity, the beauty pageant valiantly fights in what has been called the "Battle for America's Future"[53] by accommodating diversity, performing and exercising toleration, and simultaneously managing to efface any obvious signs of particular ethnicities or races. This strategy relies on representation or recognition of diversity — achieved simply through the literal presence of nonwhite bodies — where the physical representation of the few black and brown women on the pageant stage serves as testimony to the pageant's claim that it does indeed represent *all* American womanhood. The nationwide political crisis on diversity, which is situated centrally in fears about identity politics, is then reinvented in the beauty pageant as a classic liberal tale about individual achievement in a land of opportunity.

Within this "land of opportunity," social narratives of individual difference work alongside other classic liberal tales of achievement and assimilation in a broader political context that affirms the basic logic of competition between whites and people of color. Just as competition for points and glory on the "playing fields" of the baseball diamond, the job market, or the educational system is understood as the "natural" quest of an individual for self-fulfillment and "success," women in competition with each other in the beauty pageant are presumed to compete on a level "playing field" of beauty. However, this status of the liberal female subject — as equal participant, as "unmarked" — excludes black women, who are "doubly burdened" by the markers of race and gender. Within liberal society, the self-representation of black women thus takes place in a context of double exclusion. However, as Crenshaw argues, "the problems of exclusion cannot be solved simply by including Black women within an already established analytical structure."[54] Feminist historian Joan Scott has called our attention to the theoretical inadequacy of "gender by addition," which merely inserts gender as a factor in an existing theoretical structure that is not intended to truly and richly account for gender as an analytical category.[55] In a similar way, Crenshaw's theory of intersectionality allows us to account for the various ways gender and race interact and intersect. It is only in an intersectional framework that the complexities of Vanessa Williams's story become clearer, so that we can better understand how the Miss America pageant was an ideal site for simultaneously domesticating her difference while exploiting dominant narratives about black female sexuality. As Miss America, Vanessa Williams may have been the "new black woman," but the cultural and political forces that shaped her "downfall" were all too familiar.

NOTES

1. Susan Chira, "To First Black Miss America, Victory Is a Means to an End," *New York Times*, 19 September 1983.

2. "Black Leaders Praise Choice of First Black Miss America," *New York Times*, 19 September 1983.

3. Jacqueline Trescott, "Her Crowning Achievement, Vanessa Williams: A New Voice for Miss America," *Washington Post*, 20 September 1983.

4. Ibid.

5. Elizabeth Kastor, "Miss America Asked to Resign: Pageant Officials Act after Learning of Nude Photos," *Washington Post*, 21 July 1984; Esther B. Fein, "Miss America Gives Up Her Crown," *New York Times*, 24 July 1984.

6. Judy Mann, "Sleaze," *Washington Post*, 25 July 1984; William Raspberry, "Missed America," *Washington Post*, 23 July 1984; Richard Cohen, "Pageant of Hypocrisy," *New York Times*, 25 July 1984; William Safire, "There She Goes. . . ," *New York Times*, 23 July 1984.

7. Esther Fein, "Miss America Denies Giving Consent to Run Nude Photos," *New York Times*, 23 July 1984.

8. Fein, "Miss America Gives Up Her Crown."

9. For more on "types" of people, see Kathy Peiss, "Making Faces: The Cosmetics Industry and the Cultural Construction of Gender, 1890–1930," *Genders* 7 (spring 1990): 143–69. See also Liisa Malkki, "Citizens of Humanity: Internationalism and the Imagined Community of Nations," *Diaspora* 1 (1994): 41–68.

10. Karima A. Haynes, "Miss America from Vanessa Williams to Kimberly Aiken: Is the Crown a Stumbling Block or Steppingstone?" *Ebony* 3 (January 1994): 42–46, 42.

11. For an example of these critics, see Richard Wightman Fox, "The Miss America Pageant: A Scholarship Organization," Z *Magazine*, December 1990, as well as many examples in the popular press.

12. Alice [pseud.], interview by author, San Diego, 15 April 1991 (names of those interviewed have been changed to insure confidentiality).

13. Lubiano defines cover stories as narratives that "cover or mask what they make invisible with an alternative presence; a presence that redirects our attention, that covers or makes absent what has to remain unseen if the *seen* is to function as the *scene* for a different drama. One story provides a cover that allows another story (or stories) to slink out of sight." Wahneema Lubiano, "Black Ladies, Welfare Queens, and State Minstrels: Ideological War by Narrative Means," in *Race-ing Justice, En-gendering Power: Essays on Anita Hill, Clarence Thomas, and the Construction of Social Reality*, ed. Toni Morrison (New York: Pantheon, 1992), 323–63, 324.

14. Ibid. Also see Patricia Hill Collins, *Black Feminist Thought: Knowledge, Consciousness, and the Politics of Empowerment* (New York: Routledge, 1990) for more on the social narratives of black women.

15. See, for example, the highly publicized protests of the Miss California pageant during 1980–1990; or A. [pseud.] interview by author, Santa Cruz, California, December 1991. See also Frank Deford, *There She Is: The Life and Times of Miss America* (New York: Penguin, 1971).

16. Fox, "Miss America Pageant," 66.

17. Deford, *There She Is.*

18. Mary [pseud.], interview by author, San Diego, 26 September 1991.

19. Trescott, "Her Crowning Achievement."

20. Ibid.

21. The performance of passing that lays claim to "personhood" works to reinforce white supremacy; claiming that everyone is a "person" serves only to further the successes of those who construct the concept of personhood as an identity claim, a construction that celebrates the invisible power of whiteness at the expense of all other ethnic groups.

22. Jackie Goldsby, "Queen for 307 Days: Looking B(l)ack at Vanessa Williams and the Sex Wars," in *Sisters, Sexperts, Queers: Beyond the Lesbian Nation*, ed. A. Stein (New York: Plume Books, 1993), 119.

23. Ibid.

24. Trescott, "Her Crowning Achievement."

25. In addition, the word "crave" is interesting in itself. It suggests that her difference is itself a choice, something she wants or lusts after, rather than something she is. Again, this notion of "choosing" identity emerges from liberal discourse and the idealized concept of meritocracy: one can be anything, as long as the desire (or craving) and effort are there.

26. Hazel V. Carby, *Reconstructing Womanhood: The Emergence of the Afro-American Woman Novelist* (New York: Oxford University Press, 1987). Jacqueline Dowd Hall, " 'The Mind That Burns in Each Body': Women, Rape, and Racial Violence," in *Powers of Desire: The Politics of Sexuality*, ed. Ann Snitow et al. (New York: Monthly Review, 1983), 328–49.

27. Cohen, "Pageant of Hypocrisy."

28. Goldsby, "Queen for 307 Days," 120.

29. Interestingly, this is the same discursive process that shaped the social construction of

Clarence Thomas as a particular kind of raced being during the Hill/Thomas hearings — although with very different effects. Thomas, after vigorously (and viciously) constructing himself as an individual who "made it" without the help of affirmative action or welfare (apparently the only ways other black Americans "make it"), then "played the race card" to establish himself as a victim of racial discrimination, and more specifically, the victim of a "high tech lynching." See Morrison, *Race-ing Justice, En-gendering Power.*

30. Nell Irvin Painter, "Hill, Thomas, and the Use of Racial Stereotype," in *Race-ing Justice, En-gendering Power,* ed. Morrison.

31. Goldsby, "Queen for 307 Days," 116.

32. Dorothy Gilliam, "A Sad Lesson," *Washington Post,* 26 July 1984.

33. I emphasize "included within" these parameters here; at no time did the pageant actually reorganize or restructure those barriers of femininity; rather, the parameters remained intact and black women were admitted within them, as long as they constructed themselves according to the terms and limitations of white femininity.

34. Gilliam, "A Sad Lesson."

35. Campbell, "A New Black Freedom to Fail," *Washington Post,* 29 July 1984. Campbell has more to say:

> Unlike Thurgood Marshall, the first black Supreme Court Justice, there was no background check of Williams. So when she took on the mantle of Miss America — unlike many other Firsts — she brought to the position a damaging flaw. It was created by an error in judgment, a human error. Williams wasn't careful. And that was her downfall. Hers alone. . . . Yet, some blacks seemingly feel themselves a part of her disgrace. Is that racial solidarity or foolishness? If blacks swell with pride at the achievement, must we then feel shame at the failure? . . . Lucy Heim, of Melbourne, Fla., the white executive director of the pageant's Brevard County Contest: "I really felt like this was the time for a young black woman. . . . She [Williams] was very charming, very aware. She deserved to win, and frankly, she blew it."

36. Goldsby, "Queen for 307 Days," 121.

37. And in fact, this is the most commonly asked question whenever I relate my retelling of Vanessa Williams.

38. Donald Janson, "Miss America Asked to Quit over Photos Showing Her Nude," *New York Times,* 21 July 1984.

39. Kastor, "Miss America Asked to Resign."

40. Kimberlè Crenshaw, "Whose Story Is It, Anyway? Feminist and Antiracist Appropriations of Anita Hill," in *Rac-ing Justice, En-gendering Power,* ed. Morrison, 404.

41. For more on the Anita Hill/Clarence Thomas hearings, see Morrison, *Race-ing Justice, En-gendering Power.*

42. Goldsby, "Queen for 307 Days," 117.

43. Ibid., 116.

44. Crenshaw, "Whose Story Is It, Anyway?" 403.

45. Kastor, "Miss America Asked to Resign."

46. Raspberry, "Missed America."

47. Kastor, "Miss America Asked to Resign."

48. Susan Sontag, *On Photography* (New York: Anchor Books/Doubleday, 1977), 5.

49. Elizabeth Kastor, "Miss America Says Photos Were Private," *Washington Post,* 23 July 1984. My emphasis.

50. Ibid.

51. Elizabeth Kastor, "Miss America Resigns amid Controversy," *Washington Post*, 24 July 1984.

52. Goldsby, "Queen for 307 Days," 119–20.

53. Richard Bernstein, *Dictatorship of Virtue: Multiculturalism and the Battle for America's Future* (New York: Knopf, 1994).

54. Crenshaw, "Whose Story Is It, Anyway?" 424.

55. Joan Scott, *Gender and the Politics of History* (New York: Columbia University Press, 1988).

PART TWO

Consciousness Raising, Cultural Politics, and Grassroots Organizing

ELEVEN

Education, Cultural Rights, and Citizenship

RINA BENMAYOR
AND ROSA M. TORRUELLAS

In the late 1980s, the Inter-University Program for Latino Research (IUP), a national consortium of Latino research centers, brought together a Cultural Studies Working Group comprising Puerto Rican and Chicano scholars from the Northeast, West, and Southwest regions. Our common agenda was to examine local movements for empowerment in Latino communities, using our work in East Harlem (New York City), Watsonville (California), San Jose (California), Huntington Park (Los Angeles), and San Antonio (Texas).[1] Our common questions concerned the issues of why and how Latinos mobilized to claim cultural identity and civil rights. These collective discussions led us to acknowledge the following:

- Small-scale, local struggles of cultural affirmation in Latino and other marginalized communities were taking place throughout the country.
- Many of these struggles were articulated in terms of culturally specific interpretations of rights and entitlement not necessarily reflected in the dominant legal and political canons.
- These actions, which constituted an oppositional discourse, did not receive widespread media coverage and almost never became collective public knowledge. For example, women in East Harlem engaged in a struggle for educational empowerment and Mexicana cannery workers in Watsonville striking for better wages and working conditions knew nothing about each other's actions and efforts.
- Mainstream paradigms of assimilation, acculturation, and integration did not illuminate the new demographic, economic, and cultural formations emerging on a national and global scale.

Our discussions confirmed that assimilation and superficial interpretations of diversity and multiculturalism did not adequately represent the claims being made in many Latino communities. Rather, we postulated that the dynamics of struggle might be better captured through the concept of "cultural citizenship," affirming the right to full membership and participation in society *through* cultural rights.[2] Culturally specific beliefs and practices were at the core of the demands for equality we saw emerging in our class, national, gender, and racially marked communities.

What follows is a discussion of cultural citizenship and its relevance to empowerment through two examples — a program for native Spanish literacy and education for Puerto Rican and other Latina women in East Harlem, and recent mobilizations for educational rights among students at the City University of New York. Although the latter example was not part of the initial IUP study, it illustrates the potential of cultural citizenship as an interpretive concept.

Cultural Citizenship as a Theoretical Tool

Our framing concept brings together two fields of analysis — culture and citizenship — that are not linked traditionally. They can almost be thought of as inimical to one another. Cultural citizenship implies that citizenship is defined not simply by law but also by culturally specific understandings and practices. In fact, culturally constructed understandings of citizenship challenge the narrow legal description of what it means to be a participating and contributing member of a community, a nation-state, and a society, and consequently, what it means to have rights.

For example, in response to the attempt to deny education and health care to the undocumented, including their children (as in the case of California's Proposition 187), many Latinos collectively and publicly affirm the right of the undocumented to health and well-being. These affirmations are often rooted in the belief in universal human rights and community practices of social responsibility, which are highly valued in Latino cultures. At the same time, such affirmations challenge the myth that the undocumented are social parasites, when in fact they are usually the working poor relegated to the lowest echelons of the agricultural, manufacturing, and service economies. Although they cannot vote, the undocumented contribute to the social good in much greater proportion than the cost of services they receive. In practice they are social and cultural, if not legal, citizens.

The concept of cultural citizenship takes on even sharper contours when related to the struggles for bilingual education. In response to anglocentrist movements that see public support of linguistic diversity as a threat to cultural unity, Latinos, Asians, and other immigrant groups affirm this diversity not only as a cultural right, but as a resource, contribution, and enrichment of the cultural fabric as a whole. Thus, cultural citizenship becomes a framework for understanding culturally specific modalities and practices of both the rights and responsibilities of citizenship.

Affirming cultural citizenship implies something broader and deeper than what is often referred to as empowerment. Although we have used "empowerment" to describe the process of transformation and community building in the case of the Barrio Program described below, empowerment itself does not necessarily propose a radical theory of change. Within mainstream discourse empowerment is often used to describe authorization: "The president was empowered by Congress to act. . ." Other uses of the term may refer to individual processes of growth and increased self-confidence. When associated with a group process, it often denotes the acquisition of power through electoral or other existing institutional processes.

None of these usages suggests challenging the system of power, but may simply mean wanting access to one's own piece of the status quo pie. Thus, the conventional use of the term "empowerment" does not necessarily describe the efforts of people to bind together in collective struggles waged outside existing institutional frameworks. It does not necessarily signal the more intangible roles culture and identity play in the transformation process. It does not necessarily require us, on an analytical level, to discover the imagined or invisible sense of community and solidarity that underpins visible acts of resistance, demands, and affirmation. As Patricia Hill Collins states, "revealing new ways of knowing that allow subordinate groups to define their own reality has far greater implications."[3]

Within activist discourse in the United States, empowerment relates to a family of liberatory concepts, including grassroots democracy, human rights, and the Freirian notion of "concientización."[4] Empowerment in its Freirian uses expresses *collective processes* of resistance to social disenfranchisement and claims to entitlement and rights not acknowledged in preexisting institutions and definitions. However, the historical context of the United States in the latter half of the twentieth century is one in which new waves of im/migration and economic polarization challenge the ideology of assimilation and cultural unity ("e pluribus unum"), as traditionally defined. For this reason, the intent of our IUP collaboration was not only to identify collective processes of empowerment but also to understand more clearly how specific cultural values and practices inform struggles for equality and democracy and challenge traditional national definitions of citizenship. In the context of late twentieth-century global migrations (of the documented and undocumented), the vibrancy of transnational and multinational identities, and the persistence of neocolonial arrangements of power, cultural citizenship invites us to conduct a reality check. What do we want citizenship to mean in the twenty-first century, vis-à-vis membership, participation, contribution, and rights?

Cultural citizenship expresses "a process through which a subordinated group of people arrives at a common identity, establishes solidarity, and defines a common set of interests" that binds the group together in collective action.[5] Critical to this process is the affirmation and assertion of perceived *collective* identities and rights that have been ignored or denied by the dominant society and its legal canon. Defined in this way, cultural citizenship is clearly oppositional, articulating the needs of peoples who do not hold state power. Moreover, cultural citizenship seeks to interpret people's experience from the standpoint of agency: protagonizing people as active participants in a struggle for advancement, as exercisers of rights and responsibilities. Our usage of the term "citizenship" is not synonymous with legal membership in the nation-state. Rather, it is based on a broader notion of human citizenship and rights.

In contrast, state citizenship is a restrictive concept, limiting who can belong to the polity: "The large numbers of undocumented Latinos in the United States, the longstanding colonial subordination of Puerto Rico, and the widespread experience of second-class citizenship in the country significantly complicate the relationship between membership and rights."[6] Moreover, contemporary global migrations to the United States and other postindustrial countries are profoundly transforming the concept of state citizenship. The reality of transnational economies and migration circuits has compelled countries like Mexico to reconsider their citizenship laws and grant dual citizenship. Similarly, forward-thinking scholars and policy makers are beginning to pose the notion of formal transnational citizenship.[7]

Examined from a cultural perspective, the concept of cultural citizenship allows us to see the notion of rights as it is defined not by the legal code but by the cultural foundations and vernacular practices of people themselves, in their own philosophical and political terms. These forms of cultural affirmation challenge the terms of association and constitution of the polity in fundamental ways. They question the claim that the "American" nation must express itself and act in a culturally homogeneous and monolithic fashion. Cultural citizenship articulates a dialectic between the politics of difference and the politics of inclusion. It allows us to relate major demographic and cultural changes to the demand for new terms of affiliation that validate diverse cultural identities and resources. The right to cultural difference, then, becomes the basis and the arena for challenging marginalized status and demanding full inclusion. In short, to affirm cultural citizenship is to collectively come to consciousness around the denial of human, civil and cultural rights; to articulate new visions — new cultural "imaginings" — of equality; and, through culturally specific practices, to act collectively for change.

Cultural Citizenship in El Barrio

The Context

The New York–based part of the IUP comparative project was directed by a team of researchers from the Centro de Estudios Puertorriqueños at Hunter College of the City University of New York. Unlike the other research teams in the project, the New York team focused on a research-intervention project that the Centro had initiated and was directing.[8] The Barrio Popular Education Program, located in East Harlem, provided an unusual opportunity for native-language literacy and basic education to Latino adults. We have published more extensive descriptions and analyses of various aspects of this program from 1986 to 1992.[9] The majority of the participants in this program were first-generation Puerto Rican women. Most fell within the thirty to sixty age range. With few exceptions, they were mothers and single heads of household (including never married, separated, or divorced). Their documented yearly income was well below $10,000. Most of them received public assistance and had fluctuating participation in the labor market. A good number of them had no formal schooling whatsoever. Others had completed the first few years of elementary school. Several managed to attain some high school education. Most did not have a functional command of English.

Economically and culturally, the women in the Barrio Program represented a sector of the Puerto Rican and Latino im/migrant community in New York City that has experienced intensified social marginalization and persistent poverty, especially in the past two decades. The flight of the manufacturing sector, limited access to service jobs, the current fiscal crisis in the city, coupled with cuts in federal funding all forecast even harder times. Roughly half of the women lived in public housing projects in *el barrio* (East Harlem), the Bronx, the Lower East Side, or poorer parts of Queens. These neighborhoods have a marked Puerto Rican and Latino character. In Mrs. Tavárez's words, "I've lived in El Barrio for many years now, and life here is easier. . . . Here you have everything within reach. It's not like going to another place where you don't know anybody. And besides, when you are raising children and you have them in school. . . . as long as I can, I will stay right here."[10]

The institutional, organizational, and political entities in the "barrios" are connected to the identity of the community. Cultural practices embodied in lifestyles, values, and perspectives, all lived within the social interaction of neighbors, family, friends, and strangers contribute to this feeling. In addition, commercial establishments cater to Latinos in language, custom, and taste. This milieu offers residents a feeling of familiarity and control in the urban social landscape. At the same time,

> The "barrios" are among the poorest sectors of New York City. City service agencies blatantly ignore their environmental and economic needs. They tend to be dirty, polluted neighborhoods in which drug dealing, substance abuse, and hard-core crime abound. The unavailability of jobs is one of the most significant defining features of the present difficult situation, unrelieved since the late sixties in intensity. All these factors convert daily existence into a constant struggle for survival.[11]

One woman's essay for class effectively captured the stressful circumstances in which many poor Latinos are forced to live:

> This morning I went to take out money to pay my rent and when I got into the elevator, on the fourth floor two people got on. The man pressed a knife to my back and the woman took all that I had. . . . I was so scared! And now, what am I going to do to pay the rent and the telephone and to feed my kids? I'll have to borrow money until my next check comes. Someone will lend me the money because they know I will pay them back. I have so many problems to deal with that one more doesn't make a difference. . . . Why do these things happen to me?[12]

Within this difficult and often hostile environment, the Barrio Popular Education Program became a positive refuge where participants could aspire and grow. The pedagogy of the classroom prioritized experiential knowledge as the basis for literacy acquisition. *Testimonio*, or the sharing of life histories and experiences openly in the classroom setting, was a particularly important catalyst in establishing a collective identification and a sense of "safe space."

Premises

Through participant observation, classroom ethnographies, and recorded life histories, our investigation sought to identify factors driving this particular group of

Puerto Rican and other Latina women to confront a condition of poverty in a proactive way. In other words, how did women contribute to their self-empowerment and community empowerment and in what ways did they affirm cultural citizenship? The study drew out the connections between concrete responses to marginality and subordination, and frameworks of cultural practice, identity, and thought.

We started from the premise that participation in the Barrio Popular Education Program was one such concrete response. It constituted a new and empowering social practice for the women through the affirmation of their right to education. This practice generated conflict and change in many spheres of the women's daily lives. It also brought long-held ideological notions of the self and society into question, particularly with reference to gender and class arrangements of power. The educational experience promoted a process of internal transformation. Going to school became an essential part of each of their lives. Although the women identified the program as a space for learning, it came to signify much more than an institution where one could acquire skills. The program provided an opportunity for each to transcend the realities of social isolation and powerlessness. It offered a social network and source of support for "coping" on a daily level and for daring to take a look beyond: "I am very happy here because I have learned a lot. I like this school because I appreciate the way you treat us. You treat us like family." [13]

A second working premise was that transformations at the personal level were influenced by and had to be understood in the context of collective interaction and identification. Community networks and affective ties (understood broadly to include family, religious, educational, and other social groupings) provided crucial supports. The Barrio Popular Education Program became an important network in the lives of its participants. It provided each individual with the collective referent for claiming educational rights. They recognized deep commonalities in terms of history, class, and gender, and articulated demands that were both personal and collective.

Culture and Constructing Identity

Much of the existing literature on Puerto Rican women, both on the island and in the United States, has explored and described their labor experience and its class dimensions. [14] The women in this study expressed a well-defined class identity, recounting a long history of proletarian work. However, this identity was particularly marked by their *exclusion* from the labor market. Their status as welfare recipients redefined their identity as "poor" in decisive ways.

In their relationship with the state, the women opened up a negotiating space. Despite the many disempowering aspects of this relationship, they learned to use the system strategically to advance their goals. Originally, they used welfare as a resource for raising their families. This time, the focus of their claim was on their own educational development. Instead of taking on the limiting types of jobs available through workfare, the women opted for going to school. This decision placed them in an active mode, turning an oppressive situation into an advantageous one. In this way, they challenged an ascribed status as "dependent poor," affirming a self-generated identity as "resource strategists."

Analysis of life histories suggested that class position was not limited to structural factors, but that gender permeated the work experience and the women's location within relations of production. A culturally informed commitment to family often influenced their decision to stay home and raise their children. The dominant patriarchal ideology legitimized this arrangement. At the same time, they were stigmatized for having to rely on welfare to do so.

Gender expectations also mediated and were affected by the women's connection to the welfare state. Confrontations with the system were framed in terms of their being able to fulfill their reproductive roles. At the same time, the women claimed the right, as single mothers, to be able to provide their children with decent housing, nutrition, clothing, and other basic necessities. Thus a dual process occurred. The commitment to raising their families reinforced the nurturing aspect of the women's gender identity. Yet becoming the main sustainers of the household forced a redefinition of that identity, since the role of provider was culturally perceived to be a central aspect of "maleness."

Gender identity, however, did more than negotiate the women's class experience. Rather, it emerged in their life stories as a key expression of their overall identification. *Familia*, as a cultural resource and a form of social interaction, was central in the process of affirmation of self. It gave strength, influenced choices, and provided direction to the women's actions. It was in this arena that they felt most at ease. By extending family values to the educational context, for example, they were able to situate themselves as active agents, defining their own interests and terms of action.

Paradoxically, their practice and self-representation as women also expressed a subordinate social identity. This phenomenon needs to be understood in the context of a patriarchal ideology and practices of female socialization that assign a dominant role to males. The women's advancement, then, was not smooth and linear, but was characterized by struggle and conflict. Nowhere was this dialectical process more evident than in the domestic sphere, where women were forced to confront expectations of subordinate gender status head-on. Although not included in the scope of this discussion, their testimonies were full of references to conflict in this domain. Since gender was such an important part of these women's overall identity, we can expect the difficulties they experienced in this realm to have affected the way they approached relations in other arenas. Changes in this primordial set of relationships and identity, then, became a key element in the process of personal empowerment.

National identity was most clearly manifested in the importance the women attached to the maintenance and usage of Spanish in the U.S. context. Their assertion of their right to receive an education in their mother tongue could be interpreted as an affirmation of membership in a linguistic and cultural community. It was also a way of asserting cultural difference as the basis for contributing to and fully participating in U.S. society. Significantly, we did not find among this group of women a discourse of national independence, colonialism, and Puerto Rican sovereignty. In fact, preliminary analysis suggested that they had limited knowledge of contemporary political debates in Puerto Rico, including, for example, efforts to hold a plebiscite to define the political status of the island. They did not express a clear understanding of the colonial dimension of the U.S.-Puerto Rico relationship either.

Although the women did not mobilize politically around the national question, they have always lived the consequences of colonialism in their daily lives.[15] Given Puerto Rico's history of subordination, cultural expression became the fulcrum for affirming a national identity. Our observations in the program corroborated many ways cultural practices rooted in national identity were being asserted in response to the minority status of the Puerto Rican community in this country. Understood in these ways, the women's discourse around their *"puertorriqueñidad"* (Puerto Ricanness) was eminently political. The discourse ranged from expressive language — *"¡Yo soy puertorriqueña!"* — to visual symbols, such as wearing T-shirts with the Puerto Rican flag. The women spoke proudly of the ways they have transmitted their Puerto Rican heritage to their children. The entire fabric of their daily lives — from food to language, interpersonal relations, and forms of recreation — embodied a Puerto Rican identity. And still they did not see a contradiction between maintaining and affirming their national identity and being U.S. citizens.

Citizenship as Affirmation of Cultural Rights

Throughout this study, we marked instances in which the women articulated claims to rights. The ways they conceived of and expressed these claims were intimately linked to the multiplicity of identities they affirmed. The women's relationship to the state provided one of the clearest examples of how gender, class, and national identification formed the basis for their sense of rights. The women expressed indignation over the discrimination they encountered in receiving welfare entitlements. This ranged from being treated poorly because they spoke Spanish, having to wait endless hours to see a case worker, and having to "plead" for the monthly check when it didn't come, to being assigned demeaning workfare assignments instead of more dignified jobs that they were qualified to hold. Faced with a constricted labor market and their inability to obtain well-paid work, they nevertheless felt entitled to an income. They perceived this as a basic human right. Moreover, this sense of economic entitlement was more specifically linked to their widespread commitment to motherhood, family values, and their responsibility to provide for and raise their children. Thus, in their relationship with the state, the women came to assert economic, reproductive, and human rights all at once.

Our life histories and participant observations revealed how, in the face of systemic power, the values and practices the women held dear became meaningful, if not always effective, vehicles for striking back. Hence, we heard them invoke a "vernacular" understanding of rights, based on their conception of human entitlement: "We are poor, but we have our dignity." *Dignidad* and *respeto* (dignity and respect) were cornerstones of the women's shared cultural code.

The frustration the women experienced in their dealings with the state was in part due to the fact that they generally faced these conflicts alone. They were aware that the problems each of them confronted were also shared by many others in the community. In this respect, their claims had a collective class, gender, and national base. However, the state required them to make their claims as individuals, enhancing a sense of isolation. As Blanca Silvestrini (1990) points out, in the U.S. legal system, the concept of rights is divorced from a cultural and group base. Before the law, "claimants are viewed as individuals.... Once separated from their group ... they lose the strength that the community provided, because they had originally defined their claim as mediated by their participation in a cultural community."[16]

The majority of the program's participants were Puerto Rican, which lends unique dimensions to the concept of citizenship and rights. As U.S. citizens, Puerto Ricans may tend to have more concrete knowledge of their legal rights, particularly as compared to immigrant groups. The women in our project knew, for example, that legally they could not be detained and deported by the *migra*, (Immigration and Naturalization Service). They knew that they were eligible for certain entitlements as a consequence of being poor or left without employment. However, the Puerto Rican case especially illustrates the paradox that having citizenship does not in itself confer on them or imply that they enjoy full and equal rights in the U.S. context. As one of our IUP working concept papers stated, "while all inhabitants in a country contribute to the society, pay taxes, serve in the military, send their children to school and are subject to the laws of the nation, not all are protected by it or enjoy the benefits of their contribution."[17]

Interestingly enough, one of the arguments put forth by recent neoconservative onslaughts on Puerto Rican women is that citizenship has been a liability rather than an advantage in social and economic mobility. The contention is that, as citizens, Puerto Ricans have automatic entitlements to welfare, and these very rights have led them to become dependent; but in fact, citizenship has nothing to do with welfare entitlement. Neoconservatives claim that in contrast to Puerto Ricans, all other Hispanics are "following the upwardly mobile path of previous immigrant groups."[18] By this logic, it is more beneficial to be denied legal rights, as an incentive to work hard and to prosper. What this view fails to appreciate is that the struggles in Latino and other subordinated communities illustrate a very different concept of citizenship. Through cultural community rather than legal canon, Puerto Ricans and other Latinos affirmed national, cultural, and human citizenship as the basis for their claims for equity and full participation in the society.

Rather than accepting the marginal position to which they were relegated, rather than perceiving themselves as social dependents, deviants, or an "underclass," the women of the Barrio Program placed themselves at the center of action, affirming as well as redefining their own cultural values, identity, and practices. From the perspective of their own cultural center, the women also challenged the assumption that assimilation leads to equality. First of all, they were well aware of the racial, class, and language prejudices that excluded them from entry into the "mainstream." More important, from their own perspective, the move toward *superación* (advancement) was not an effort to become *americanas*, but rather an attempt to fulfill their human potential. They did not contemplate the need to modify or even hyphenate their Puerto Rican identity. Mrs. González expressed a sense of pride common among the women:

"I thank God for having been born Puerto Rican, because the truth is that I feel very, very proud. . . . and to those who paint an ugly and maligning image of Puerto Rico, [I would like] to hear them say instead, 'Puerto Ricans, a fine people.' " [19]

The liberal "salad bowl" and the multicultural "gorgeous mosaic" metaphorically acknowledge the existence of cultural diversity. However, within these conceptions, Puerto Rican/Latino identity is posed as cultural patrimony, as a surface or private form of difference and not as an arena of social struggle. These models fall short of explaining the full import of cultural affirmation for the women in the Barrio Program. Language, values, spiritual traditions, forms of work and cooperation, and gender commitments to family — as we have addressed in our study — were the precise cultural terrains through which the women contested oppression. These practices were not neutral markers of difference. They were vital strategies in the daily struggle, on the streets and in the home, for equity and rights. Consequently, citizenship also means the right to cultural belonging, the common right to exercise cultural difference.

In many ways, the Barrio Program created a space in which the women could articulate what Brazilian scholars concerned with concepts of new citizenship call "the right to have rights." [20] The women came to the program with an essential ingredient for change already firmly in hand: the recognition that they were systematically excluded from the economic and social opportunities for which they came to the United States. The program's particular contribution was to move the perception and the discourse forward, acknowledging the collective dimensions of their experience. Because the program validated and strengthened their culturally derived "vernacular" conceptions of entitlement, women could more forcefully speak of education, income, and health care as rights. How did the recognition of rights enable citizenship as action?

Forms of Affirmation

As stated in our monographic study, *Responses to Poverty*, when we began this investigation, one of our assumptions was that the process of educational empowerment would lead participants to go out into the community and organize their own collective mobilizations around community problems and issues. This did not happen. The women in the program did not spontaneously take to the streets, organize the neighborhood, or engage in other traditional forms of political protest and organization. They were, however, deeply engaged in another type of action. Instead of seeing the Barrio Program as a catalyst for political activity on a mass scale, we came to realize that the women's sustained struggle for education and participation in the program in itself constituted a mobilization. Smaller in scope, this movement reflected the women's definition of *their* needs, *their* issues, and *their* conception of social change. It suggested that empowerment processes had to be analyzed from within and that models of mass political action did not constitute the full range of oppositional strategies and practices existing in subordinated communities. Moreover, the collective recognition of shared need implies that we were dealing with culturally defined issues and forms of response.

"Education Is a Right"

The 1991 struggles around education in New York City illustrated the ways the women defined their own forms of action. Faced with severe budget cuts and the lack of policy commitments to alternative, native-language literacy, the Barrio Popular Education Program became almost entirely dependent on short-term grants. The women became engaged in the defense of the program's right to exist and to grow. Redressive efforts were both spontaneous and organized within the program itself. Fearing the loss of their program, the women immediately suggested mounting a letter-writing campaign to public officials and the press. Letter writing was both an act of political expression and an act of literacy, consistent with their educational effort. The staff then escalated the action by organizing group visits to local legislative representatives and bringing newspaper reporters to the program to interview the women. An article in a Spanish-language newspaper about the precarious status of the program and of Spanish literacy education for adults included the following quote, among many offered by the women:

> This program has been very important in my life. Here I have learned how to read and write, and that has made it easier for me to learn English. Before coming to this program, I did not know that I could get ahead. If the [budget] cuts cause this program to disappear, it will be very sad for us, because we will be left illiterate.[21]

Their claims were posed in class, gender, and national terms. They understood the conflict as a class issue of poor people being deprived of their educational and cultural rights. Their chosen title for the 1991 student publication, *Progresando en español porque es nuestro idioma* (Progressing in Spanish, because it is our language), was one among many examples of how national culture intersected with their educational demands.

The women's educational claims sharpened their awareness of gender rights as well — the right of women to education, regardless of the constraints of poverty or parenting. The fact that most of the program participants were female was a vivid reminder of the role gender played in being denied an education in the first place. The many ways the women had to assert their choice to go to school profoundly redefined the way they saw themselves. Interestingly, however, this awareness did not translate into an easy or immediate participation in certain other forms of mass political action. When informed that there would be a massive afternoon and evening rally at City Hall in protest over the budget cuts, some of the women were eager to participate, but for the majority, this was an unfamiliar and perhaps uncomfortable form of action that also conflicted with their responsibilities in the home. It fell to the program teachers and staff to organize the making of banners and picket signs, and to encourage and orchestrate the women's participation in the rally. For those who went, it was the first time they had taken part in such an event. Mass protests would not be a spontaneous form of organizing in the defense of rights. And yet, as they marched in front of City Hall, carrying banners and signs, the women affirmed their culturally defined right to become literate in their native language, an educational right that is usually understood to be a necessary ingredient of good citizenship.

Around that time, another culturally marked action took place, this time around CUNY students. More specifically, at Hunter College a multiethnic, multiracial, and multigendered coalition of students struck and took over the administrative building and offices. Latino students were a significant force in this coalition. When the women in the program learned from staff members who worked and taught at Hunter College that students were spending day and night in the building, they decided to send food down to them. They cooked large pots of rice and beans, mashed plantains, and chicken stew and delivered these to the striking students. While this was an obviously cultural and engendered act, the women also understood the struggle in class, racial, and national terms. The students could be their own children and grandchildren, the generations they had worked so hard to put through school and who embodied the collective hope for improved life chances for Latino communities. Consequently, their support of the CUNY students was a familial, cultural, and gendered response of class and ethnic/racial solidarity.

Cultural Citizenship and CUNY Students

Although it was our intention to eventually extend the study of cultural citizenship to include the children of the women in the Barrio Program, we were unable to develop that next phase of research. Nevertheless, the escalation of attacks on higher education in New York and the student responses present an instance for reflection on the intergenerational relevance of cultural citizenship as a concept. If first-generation migrant women conceptualized their education as a class and cultural right, how did CUNY students — first-, second-, third-generation and beyond — interpret their situation?

The 1991 strikes and protests were the beginning of an intense and ongoing fiscal retrenchment process that would have disproportionate effects on working-class students, immigrant students, and students of color. Two decades earlier, in 1975, the country's historic public university went through a similar fiscal and policy crisis over admissions, access, and commitment to "minority" students. In November 1994, in an election with one of the lowest voting turnouts, New York state elected a Republican governor. This act was to have immediate and profound repercussions for the City University of New York, whose historic mission has been to provide free quality education to the poor, blue collar, and immigrant populations make up the majority of the city's inhabitants. One of the first acts of the new governor was to announce a new budget (during the semester break of January 1995). This budget included draconian cutbacks in funding to CUNY, unprecedented in size and impact, resulting in a "state of fiscal exigency" for the university that converged with internal plans for downsizing and restructuring. The university moved swiftly from February to June 1995 to eliminate programs, retrench tenured and nontenured faculty, decline to reappoint adjunct faculty, lay off staff, and impose a substantial tuition increase on students who at the same time saw massive shrinkage in financial aid opportunities.

The events of the spring of 1995 in CUNY convulsed higher education nationwide, but where they were most acutely felt was among the overwhelmingly poor, working-class student body of CUNY and its thousands of students of color. Largely of African American, West Indian, Puerto Rican, Dominican, Haitian, South American, Korean, Chinese, and many other "third world" origins, these and other economically disadvantaged students, many of whom are women and most of whom work and support families, are facing a dramatic shutout from higher education. Here, the paraphrased words of a Puerto Rican/Dominican sophomore ring clear:

> I was a teen mom. I had my child in my last year of high school, but my parents, especially my father, would not let me drop out. He is Puerto Rican and did not get much of an education and he would have killed me if I had dropped out. He was on my case all the time. So here I am in college, working and raising my two-year-old daughter, and struggling to do what they say you have to do to get ahead in this country — get an education. And now they make it impossible for us to continue in school. They are going to cut my financial aid and raise the tuition and I won't be in class next year. There's no way I can afford it. So you won't be seeing me next year. And what kind of future do I have without a college diploma?[22]

Returning from semester break, students responded to the governor's budget with vigor. They were acutely aware of their own imminent educational disenfranchisement and social expendability, not to mention long-term exclusion from the "American dream." They began by mounting a massive letter-writing campaign to the governor and state assemblymen. Then, along with CUNY faculty, they descended by the busloads on Albany, joining faculty and students from SUNY (the state university system). They held mass rallies and targeted office visits to local representatives. Students began to take their role as citizens seriously. Through conventional practices, but ones not largely used by younger generations, they began a process of coming to consciousness and unity to defend what they identified as common rights. As the large button they produced stated, "The Budget Crisis: Not a Force of Nature but an Attack on People's Rights."

The letter-writing campaign and the visits to Albany were the first step. Students began holding regular meetings to plan more creative and unconventional actions. They visited classrooms to explain the effects of policy changes on all students' future. They planned rallies at the various CUNY campuses. At Hunter, they met with concerned faculty to erect a mock education graveyard on the corner of 68th Street and Lexington Avenue, attracting wide media attention. With the tombstones as a setting, a mass rally was held that ended in the arrest of eight students for "disorderly conduct," when as part of the guerrilla theater, they sat down in the street and stopped traffic.

The unnecessary arrest of students sparked outrage at the university as well as at the powers in Albany, escalating the sense of resolve to fight. Days later, students, faculty, and supporters marched on City Hall in protest. They came from all directions, with banners, flags, drums, and effigies, marching across the Brooklyn Bridge, from uptown and the boroughs on the subway, to converge on the park in front of City Hall. Once they were gathered, speakers began to address the crowd from a distant podium. Suddenly, toward the back of the park, one student shimmied up one of several flagpoles in their midst, removed the American flag, and replaced it with the Puerto Rican flag; cries and chants of approval rose from the crowd.

Almost immediately, the same process was repeated and at the end the Puerto Rican, Dominican, and Jamaican flags were flying.

Flag raising is conventional symbolic action. Loyalty, citizenship, responsibility, rights, and national pride are all invoked. However, in this context, what did it mean? Representationally, the students constructed their cultural identity not only as students, but specifically as im/migrant students, poor students, and students of color. Flag raising exhibited the profound sense of dual and transnational identities that inhabits New York City; it was a historical reminder of the experience of economic, racial, and linguistic discrimination; it brought national and cultural pride into the picture; and through convention, it signified oppositional resistance to policies that would disproportionately affect the city's poor people of color and the life chances of their families for generations to come. The fact that the Puerto Rican flag was the first to be hoisted underscored the irony that state citizenship does not imply greater access or life chances, or diminished risk; state citizenship attempts to rewrite the culture of a people as one of deficit rather than to acknowledge and support its unique resources and strengths.

At the same time, students were openly and collectively affirming their cultural citizenship, that is, their right to education as students, as the providers of future generations, as im/migrants and children of im/migrants, as students of color, and as progressive and socially responsible students. Ultimately, it was through the solidarity of collective action and recognition of a larger than individual picture — of the widespread effects of neoliberal policies on all — that students changed their understanding of citizenship. Citizenship was no longer an abstraction in political science textbooks, nor was it reduced to writing to one's congressional representative. It became a collective reality, defined by the defense of common interests and a redefinition of rights. As one of the slogans put it, "Education is a right. Fight, fight, fight!" Using culturally specific forms of real and symbolic actions (marching in protest and hoisting national flags), students connected their individual plights to a collective condition. Defending the right to a college education was not a matter of individual freedoms but a question of collective rights. Students demonstrated a broader historical and cultural understanding of the meaning of education for all.

This latter point brings us back to the women in the Barrio Program, whose struggle was for native-language literacy, for linguistic rights from the perspective of active workers and nurturers in U.S. society. Interestingly, the process of affirmation for women in the Barrio Program and for students at CUNY was different. Whereas mass mobilization was a cultural strategy for the students, one they conceived and organized, for the women in East Harlem taking to the streets was strange, uncomfortable, a learned activity that had to be organized and guided by others. On the other hand, the atmosphere of *familia* that the women established was culturally rooted and felt as their domain of expertise. Students would have to face the struggle of maintaining cohesion and sustained awareness in the midst of classes, exams, and summer vacations.

One of the contributions of cultural citizenship is affirming that membership in a cultural community in no way negates the desire and claim to be a full member of society. As we noted earlier, the women in East Harlem did not see a contradiction between maintaining their Puerto Rican identity and being U.S. citizens. They did not see their affirmation of cultural rights to be in conflict with their rights as members of U.S. society: "The term cultural citizenship reflects this dilemma. On the one hand, subordinate racial and ethnic groups such as Latinos seek cultural rights. On the other hand, they seek to be accepted as equal participants in society, as full citizens."[23] Similarly, the students of CUNY were affirming a hallmark of the American dream from their own particular social and cultural positions. That the "mainstream" is unable to recognize and validate a range of resources and positive contributions different peoples can make to the common good is a statement about its own racism and myopia. The women in the program rightfully asked, why was the opportunity to become educated in their own language not adequately funded at the same time that the private sector, the government, and the press were giving widespread recognition to the serious future consequences of illiteracy for the country? Why was becoming educated in Spanish seen as a liability and an unnecessary expense rather than a resource to be cultivated and harnessed to the development of the Latino community? Similarly, the students questioned the commitment of the university and the state to educate all its citizens, and resisted policies of downward tracking.

These issues raise the larger political question of the kind of society envisioned for the future. Mixed messages from the cultural "mainstream," like those exemplified above, are often accompanied by a view that to affirm citizenship through cultural difference is inimical to this country's ethos. Thus, the affirmation of cultural rights is seen as antithetical to the liberal democratic concept of national citizenship. However, affirming cultural citizenship can be viewed from a different angle: not as static preservation of culture but as infusion that brings new meaning to the practice of citizenship. The choice is not black or white — between preserving tradition or becoming "assimilated" into a common mainstream. Rather, the challenge is to recognize and value the infusion of cultural difference as vital to the preservation of democracy. In this way, the affirmation of the right to native-language literacy was not a special interest but a common interest, strengthening and revitalizing the cultural terrain. Despite the English-only movement, many in this country would see multilingualism as a valuable resource for the country as a whole. Similarly, the hope of the future lies in extending and insuring quality education to all who desire it. To act otherwise, to create consciously an expendable population, is to commit cultural suicide.

The collective affirmations we have cited here cannot be fully understood through a simple empowerment paradigm, for we lose the dynamic relationship between citizenship and culture. Rather than threatening to disunite the society, cultural affirmation expands the meaning of citizenship and democracy to be inclusive and embracing of cultural difference. Continuing to stigmatize certain communities in terms of deficits, and denying them access to quality education does not promise to yield any more equitable arrangement than that which prevails today. Conversely, acknowledging diversity as an asset opens the way to discovering the resources different cultural communities have to offer. Recognizing respect for difference as the basis for social unity expands the meaning of democracy and citizenship. As concerned and engaged scholars, we must ask, How will the "new world order" respond to this dual sense of belonging, and to the claim to culture as a contribution and a right?

NOTES

A substantial portion of this essay is derived from a longer monograph titled *Responses to Poverty among Puerto Rican Women: Identity, Community, and Cultural Citizenship*. Dr. Rosa M. Torruellas and I wrote that monograph, in collaboration with Ana L. Juarbe, when we were team researchers at the Centro de Estudios Puertorriqueños, Hunter College. Dr. Torruellas passed away in 1993, and though she could not participate in crafting this article, her ideas and writing are embedded in every subsequent derivation from that central work.

1. The Inter-University Program for Latino Research was formed in 1984, bringing together Puerto Rican, Chicano, Cuban, and other Latino research centers in universities around the country. Growing from four to nine affiliated centers, the IUP seeds comparative research teams in areas ranging from political economy, electoral participation, labor studies, and health, to religion, culture, and feminist research. Our Cultural Studies Working Group comprised Renato Rosaldo (Stanford University), William Flores (California State University at Fresno), Blanca Silvestrini (University of Puerto Rico), Richard Flores (University of Wisconsin, Madison), Richard Chabran (UCLA), Luis Ruvalcava (California State Northridge), Rosa Torruellas, Pedro Pedraza, Ana Juarbe, and myself (Centro de Estudios Puertorriqueños, Hunter College, CUNY).

2. The term "cultural citizenship" was first introduced to our group by anthropologist Renato Rosaldo. In elaborating our own conceptual interpretation of the term, we referred to the ethnographic case studies that each individual or site team was conducting at the time. We developed several working concept papers that guided the analysis of the various ethnographic studies. Citations from these unpublished papers are indicated throughout this piece.

The IUP Working Group is currently compiling the collected ethnographic studies in cultural citizenship, with the working title *Struggles for Latino Cultural Citizenship: Claiming Memory, Space, and Rights* (Boston: Beacon Press, 1997, in press).

3. Patricia Hill Collins, *Black Feminist Thought: Knowledge, Consciousness, and the Politics of Empowerment* (Boston: Unwin Hyman, 1990), 222.

4. Paulo Freire, *Pedagogy of the Oppressed* (New York: Seabury Press, 1970).

5. Quotation from unpublished IUP Concept Paper no. 3, 1989.

6. From unpublished IUP Concept Paper no. 4, 1991.

7. Among others, recent proposals emerging from the Center for Migration Studies at the New School for Social Research suggest the need for radical revision of legal citizenship to reflect transnational global realities. For example, the new and growing Mexican communities in New York City practice dual citizenship; while living in the United States, they are intricately involved in the development of their home communities in Mexico, influencing the economies and political leadership of these towns. At the same time, they live, work, and develop strong communities in the New York metropolitan area, participating and contributing to Latino community development in the United States.

8. This case study was different from the others in that the intervention of an advocacy research institution set the context for examining affirmation of cultural citizenship. In the other site projects, instances ranged from the organization of a labor strike, demands for access to public space, and the politics of cultural performance. The richness of the comparative project derives in part from its examination of different forms of mobilization for cultural citizenship.

9. For a full description of the program and the research project we developed, see Rina Benmayor, Rosa M. Torruellas, and Ana L. Juarbe, *Responses to Poverty among Puerto Rican Women: Identity, Community, and Cultural Citizenship* (New York: Centro de Estudios Puertorriqueños, Hunter College, 1992), and the following articles: Rosa M. Torruellas, Rina Benmayor, Anneris Goris, and Ana L. Juarbe, "Affirming Cultural Citizenship in the Puerto Rican Community: Critical Literacy and the El Barrio Popular Education Program," in *Literacy as Praxis: Culture, Language, and Pedagogy*, ed. Catherine E. Walsh (Norwood, NJ: Ablex, 1991); Rina Benmayor, "Testimony, Action Research, and Empowerment: Puerto Rican Women and Popular Education," in *Women's Words: The Feminist Practice of Oral History*, ed. Sherna Berger Gluck and Daphne Patai (New York: Routledge, 1991); and Rosa M. Torruellas, Rina Benmayor, and Ana L. Juarbe, "Negotiating Gender, Work, and Welfare: *Familia* as Productive Labor," in *Puerto Rican Women and Work*, ed. Altagracia Ortiz (Philadelphia: Temple University Press, 1996).

10. For the original Spanish, see Benmayor, Torruellas, and Juarbe, *Responses to Poverty*, appendix, no. 2.

11. Pedro Pedraza in ibid., 9–10.

12. For the original Spanish, see ibid., appendix, no. 3.

13. For the original Spanish, see ibid., appendix, no. 4.

14. See History Task Force, *Labor Migration under Capitalism: The Puerto Rican Experience* (New York: Monthly Review Press, 1979); Palmira Ríos, "Puerto Rican Women in the United States Labor Market," *Line of March* 18 (fall 1985); Alice Colón Warren, "Competition, Segregation, and Succession of Minorities and White Women in the Middle Atlantic Region's Central Cities Labor Market, 1960–1970" (Ph.D. diss., Fordham University, 1984); and Edwin Meléndez, Clara Rodríguez, and Janis Barry Figueroa, eds., *Hispanics in the Labor Force: Issues and Policies* (New York: Plenum Press, 1991).

15. As we were dealing with Puerto Rican women in the United States, national dimensions of culture figured prominently in the expression of identity. Although we have not addressed the complex aspects of race in this essay, it is important to note that for Puerto Ricans, national identity overshadows race as a basis of self-identification. The difficulty Puerto Ricans have with North American categorizations of race through the black/white dichotomy has been documented in several studies. See Clara Rodríguez, "Racial Classification among Puerto Rican Men and Women in New York," *Hispanic Journal of Behaviorial Sciences* 12:4 (1990). The women's discourse on this subject was contradictory. On the one hand, they denied suffering racism. On the other, they clearly identified discrimination against *la raza hispana* (the Hispanic "race"), used here to identify a cultural group, as a factor that impeded their children's job advancement. At the same time that they subscribed to the view that there was no racism in Puerto Rico, they used a descriptive vocabulary clearly marked by race — *negrito* (black), *blanquito* (white), *trigueño* (brown), *los morenos* (dark brown, the Blacks) — suggesting a social classification based on skin color.

16. Blanca Silvestrini, "The World We Enter When Claiming Rights: Latinos and the Quest for Culture," unpublished manuscript, 1990, 8.

17. From unpublished IUP Concept Paper no. 4, 1991.

18. Linda Chávez, *Out of the Barrio: Toward a New Politics of Hispanic Assimilation* (New York: Basic Books, 1991).

19. For the original Spanish, see Benmayor, Torruellas, and Juarbe, *Responses to Poverty*, appendix, no. 62.

20. Evelina Dagnino, "Citizenship and Popular Participation in Brazil" (paper presented at the Eighteenth International Congress of Latin American Studies, Atlanta, March 1994).

21. For the original Spanish, see Benmayor, Torruellas, and Juarbe, *Reponses to Poverty*, appendix, no. 63.

22. I am paraphrasing the words of a nineteen-year-old Hunter College student of mixed Puerto Rican and Dominican heritage, who is herself raising her two-year-old child.

23. Unpublished IUP Concept Paper no. 3, 1989.

TWELVE

Exemplars of Indigenism: Native North American Women for De/Colonization and Liberation

M. A. JAIMES * GUERRERO

Pockets of third world oppression exist among Native American peoples in the United States and Canada, creating a theater for indigenous struggles for liberation within these first world countries. Poor living conditions can be found on Indian reservations in the United States and Aboriginal reserves in Canada, as well as in marginal rural settings and the urban ghettos in metropolitan cities. The largest Indian populations are found in cities, the result of imposed government programs that aim to assimilate traditional indigenous cultures.[1] This essay is focused on the Native women of North America and how their traditional consciousness and cultures have survived such colonizing experiences. It illustrates their sociopolitical perspectives and positions, as both activists and critics of government American Indian/Aboriginal policy. Native women have formed organizations at all levels: local, regional, national, international, and transnational (since the 1995 Fourth World Conference on Women in Beijing). The shape of these organizations has been influenced by Native women's early disempowerment in the process of Euroamerican conquest and colonization. Their success can be seen in the growing number of strong Native women's voices, as well as in the reemergence of women activists and tribal leaders (Bataille and Sands 1984; Green 1983, 1992). Native women leaders can still draw inspiration from the traditions of matrilineal societies and matrifocal spheres of female power bases. However, these are also very troubled times for Native women, since sexism in Indian tribal politics compounds the racism they experience in the mainstream societies. In what can be termed "trickle-down patriarchy" (Elliot 1992; see also Jaimes with Halsey 1992), Indian women are sometimes forced to choose between being loyal to their male-dominated tribal group and acting to allay their subjugated experience as "third world" women.

These bicultural conflicts raise critical questions about how best to engage in liberation struggles for gender equality as well as Native rights among Native peoples and their communities.

Many Native women find themselves a distinct oppressed group: because they are both Indian and female, they experience "engendered racism." Current census data (1980 and 1990) indicate that reservation-based males live to be about forty-seven, while their female counterparts live about three years longer. In 1980, nearly one in four American Indian families were maintained by a woman, over twice the rate for non-Indians, and 47 percent of these single-mother families were considered poor by federal guidelines. In addition, the poverty rate for Indian women with children under six has been a shocking 82 percent (Stiffarm and Lane 1992; Jaimes with Halsey 1992; Amott and Matthei 1991; on infant mortality see WREE 1991). Among Native women, 23 percent are single heads of households, compared to 14 percent of the general population in the United States. These patterns exist both on and off the reservations, but rates of poverty are higher in rural areas. There is a poverty rate of approximately 27.5 percent on the reservation, compared to 12.4 percent in the mainstream population of the United States. Almost two-thirds of the 1.9 million census-reported American Indians, as individuals and families, live off the reservation and in urban centers. Los Angeles has the largest Indian population, followed by Chicago and Minneapolis. The U.S. census indicated that for 1990, four out of ten of the 1.9 million self-identified American Indians are members of the largest groups: the Cherokee in the Southeast, Navajo (Dineh) in the Southwest, and Chippewas and the Sioux tribes (Dakota and Lakota) in the Plains region. Other large groups include the Choctaw and Creek, mostly in the Southeast states, the Pueblos and Apache in the Southwest, the Iroquois in New York state, and the nonfederal- but state-recognized Lumbee in North Carolina. The smallest groups include the Cayuse in Washington state (126 members), the Croatan in the Carolinas (111 members), and the Siuslaw (44 members) (Communicator 1993; 1980 U.S. census data).

In this essay I will first describe the numerous ways the U.S. government has shaped Native American experience into its current colonial status. Then I will describe how Native American women have tried to respond within this complex structure of colonial treatment to create conditions for their own liberation. I will argue that the seeming contradictions that divide Native Americans in making strategic political decisions (for example, in such choices as " 'civil rights' versus 'sovereignty' " and "feminism or indigenism") result from this colonial context. The first contrast takes the existing colonial structures as a given in its attempt to explain how Native people might respond to political oppression. The second contrast expresses the view of Native women activists that the priorities and sociopolitical agendas of the "women's" movement in general, led by predominantly "white" feminists, is not necessarily the same for Native women in their liberation struggles. Against these artificial choices, I will argue that indigenism holds more promise as a way to describe Native American women's consciousness and their political project. Native women among indigenous peoples perceive their liberation from American colonization in the context not of individual rights, but of human rights as traditionally communal peoples. This commitment to *indigenism* makes Native women's activities part of the global indigenist movement (LaDuke 1995; Jaimes 1995b).

"Civil" versus "Sovereignty" Rights: Constructs in Legal Conflict

The U.S. government has used a number of means to subordinate Native people. As a whole, the relationship between the U.S. government and Native people can be described as one between dominant and subordinate powers. From its position of dominance, the U.S. government has been able to force American Indian activities and relations into patterns that copy those of the dominant cultures; change the internal structures of tribal governance; and control the membership of tribes. In addition, a history of attempts at physical and cultural genocide have greatly damaged the Native people and their respective cultures.

Although it is beyond the scope of this essay to retell this entire history, a few examples make the point. This section will focus on the legal discourse used by the U.S. government to subordinate Indian populations under the paternalistic guise of the "trust responsibility" or "guardianship" of Indians, who are thus understood as "wards" of the U.S. government. In the next section, questions of genocide and the health of the Native North American populations, especially women, will be discussed.

The U.S. government has unilaterally reinterpreted its legal relationship with Indian nations to make those nations subordinate to Euroamerican and patriarchal nationalist will. In the 1830s Chief Justice John Marshall made the determination that Indian tribes in the United States were "domestic dependent nations" (*Cherokee Nation v. Georgia*, 5 Pet. 1, 17–18 [1831]). In this major decision, the original *bilateral* relationship that required treaties between tribes as nations and the U.S. government as another nation was converted to a *unilateral* arrangement in which the United States would no longer think of Indian tribes as separate and sovereign nations. The result has been to keep Native peoples in perpetual subordination as a conquered people and in what has been called a "settler state" (Stock 1990–91). Another statement of this view appears in *Native American Church v. Navajo Tribal Council* (272 F.2d 131, [C.A. 10, 1959]), a legal decision about whether the council had the jurisdiction to prohibit the use of peyote by members of the church. The court declared, "But as declared in the decisions hereinbefore discussed, Indian tribes are not states. They have a status higher than that of states. They are subordinant and dependent nations possessed of all powers as such *only* [italics added] to the extent that they have expressly been required to surrender them by the superior sovereign, the United States" (272 F.2d 131, 134).[2] From this position of legal domination, the U.S. government has constantly set and reset the conditions of citizenship for Indians (for example, in the Indian Citizenship Act of 1924) and dictated forms for tribal governance (in the Indian Reorganization Act of 1934 and the Indian Civil Rights Act of 1968) (Churchill and Morris 1992).

These legal reworkings have been grafted on to traditional Indian cultures, with disastrous consequences. As Deloria and Lytle stated, "Civil rights depend first of all upon a social contract theory of government, which Indian tribes do not possess, but they also depend upon a kind of government that allocates the political powers to branches, and then separates the branches of government to act as a check-and-balance protection for the citizenry." Thus, they conclude, the real impact of the Indian Civil Rights Act (ICRA)

> was to require one aspect of tribal *government* — the tribal court — to become a formal institution more completely resembling the federal judiciary than the tribal govern-ment itself resembled. . . . The informality of Indian life that had been the repository of cultural traditions and customs was suddenly abolished. . . . The ICRA basically distorted reservation life . . . [with] impositions of rules and procedures . . . in philo-sophical terms. Traditional Indian society understood itself as a complex of responsibili-ties and duties [to its members]. . . . The ICRA merely transposed this belief into a society based on rights against government and eliminated any sense of responsibility. . . . [Thus] People did not have to confront one another before their community [to] resolve their problems; they had only to file suit in tribal court. (Deloria and Lytle 1984, 212–13)

Native people find themselves in difficult situations as they try to respond to their current circumstances. Resources for communal self-renewal have often been stripped away by one or another historical act of intervention by the U.S. govern-ment. Yet reliance on formal U.S. legal institutions, such as the assertion of "civil" versus "sovereignty" rights, is also problematic.

Civil rights pose a problem because, prior to European contact, "Indian tribal societies had no concept of civil rights since every member of the society was related, by blood or clan responsibilities, to every other member . . . Indians understood fully that injury is personal. . . . [Hence] . . . historically and *at least* in theory Indian tribes derived their basic powers from that primordial contract era when they enjoyed perfect political freedom" (Deloria and Lytle 1984, 200–204, 212).[3]

Among many tribes, federally mandated reorganization has created a confusing clash of two societal systems. When a tribe's "sovereignty" comes into conflict with "civil rights" issues, which often happens in complex jurisdictional problems, the resulting scenarios often pit Native women and their offspring as individuals against a predominantly male tribal group authority that asserts such "sovereignty" over the woman's "civil rights" grievances. The first modern case of a "civil rights" nature was *Martinez v. Southern Ute Tribe* (151 F. Supp. 476 [Dist. Colo. 1957], affirmed 249 F.2d 915 [10th Cir. 1957], 356 U.S. 960 [1958] and 357 U.S. 924 [1958]), which dealt with the power of a tribe to determine its own membership. In this case, Martinez lost her case regarding her tribal membership status. A later case, *Martinez v. Santa Clara Pueblo* (436 U.S. 49 [1978]), involved an unrelated Indian woman who was also named Martinez (Jaimes with Halsey 1992, 341). In this second case, Martinez sued the male-dominated Pueblo council in a civil rights grievance that involved her children's loss of intertribal status. This particular case involved the question of the power of the predominantly male-dominated tribal government, created by the Indian Reorganization Act of 1934, to determine the right of an Indian woman's children to membership in the tribe. Martinez's children were, not unusually, offspring from an intertribal marital union. She lost her case on the grounds that the district court would not intervene in the decision of the tribe not to grant her membership, citing the tribe's sovereignty in its internal affairs. What complicated this particular case, and still confounds such questions today, is that the Pueblo governance and its court system had been reconstructed by the Indian Reorganization Act as an extension of the federal government. An ethnologist on the Pueblo's traditional society provided evidence in court that it had been a matrilineal society before the IRA. Therefore, this case would not have even materialized in the traditional matrilineal kinship society. Further, Martinez had also married a Navajo (Dineh) man who was from a non-IRA tribe that still practiced its quasimatrilineal customs. Hence, this particular case was even more entangled in sovereignty and jurisdictional issues. Martinez herself was told and even pressured by tribal council members to move her family to the Navajo reservation. Therefore, her case revealed a clear illustration of the three-sided triangle that caused this woman's children to be denied both their IRA "civil rights" and their tribal membership in *either* the Santa Clara Pueblo or Navajo societies.

From these cases it seems that any Native woman's individual rights are constrained within the context of a kind of internal colonialism. Indeed, most tribes now politically favor patrilineal descent. A recent, brief survey of about a hundred responses from three hundred inquiries on how tribal governments throughout the United States determine membership has indicated that most tribal nations who responded do implement patrilineal descendancy; this is despite matrilineal traditions in pre-Columbian to pre-IRA times. These data, therefore, substantiate a "trickle-down patriarchy" resulting from the imposition of federal control and regulations in these matters of tribal membership status and Indian identification determination (Elliot 1992).

In this oppressive schematic, Native peoples will always be under the control and domination of their colonizers, while Native women will find themselves second-class citizens at best, and in the worst case scenario third-class refugees in their own homelands. In these cases, it is Native American women and their mixed offspring who have the most to lose. In these colonizing circumstances, then, many Native North American women find themselves "third world" women in "ethnic-minority" populations, single parents with small children who no longer have the traditional support of extended family networks and kinship structures. The conditions confronting those women (and their children of both genders) who have left the reservation community and married outside the tribe are especially problematic and legally harrowing. By contrast, any Indian male who has married outside the tribe and a non-Indian is more likely to maintain his status and include his wife and any offspring on the tribal rolls. This is, of course, a generalization; a given situation is greatly affected by the prevailing partisan political situation of the tribe itself, since tribal council leadership is predominantly male. A common alternative for a Native woman is to marry a white male and give up her Indian identity and tribal membership. There are exceptions to this general rule, but this depends on who and what families have control of the tribal politics on the reservations. In these advanced stages of our Euroamerican colonialism, it is a tragedy that Indian peoples are oppressing other Indian peoples, in what can be called an "internal psychology of colonization," when colonized persons become colonizers among their own people, as a "broken class" (compare Fanon 1963 and 1967; Hechter 1977; Acuña 1988).

This convoluted situation also creates a "dual citizenry" status, in theory if not in practice, between tribal nations and the U.S. nation-state, which in turn poses legal questions in both the domestic and international arenas. The federal government has a long history of legislating the criteria with which to determine who is an "American Indian." These criteria stimulate a racialized policy that involves a "blood quantum" formula for defining tribal membership, which is created and used by the Bureau of Indian Affairs to provide federal services. For example, this racial coding in tribal membership creates a narrow identification process, one that Susan Lobo (cited in Anner 1992) has criticized in census procedures as a racist policy for "statistical genocide" (also Jaimes 1992a; Forbes 1990). This system of codification is in contrast to the kinship systems and cultural traditions that have prevailed among many documented indigenous societies (i.e., the traditional Lakotas, Navajo/Dineh, Southwest Pueblos, and Yaqui, among others), which did not previously hold to a "race" construct to determine tribal membership.[4] The results of this criterion are to create the abstraction of "Indian identity" for identification politics, and to deny those Native persons not certified by the Bureau of Indian Affairs (BIA) their indigenous recognition for federal status as "American Indians."

Native peoples had been intermarrying with non-Indians years before the onset and establishment of Euroamerican colonialism. Traditionally this intermarriage, or what has derogatorily been called miscegenation (intermarriage between the races) was not a problem in an indigenous society that based its membership on kinship systems (or moities) and cultural criteria, including naturalization of non-Indians by way of intermarriage and other means.[5] It was not unusual for Native societies to practice exogamy as a traditional custom or law. Nevertheless, such practices did become problematic when Eurocentric males took Native women as their "squaws" (a Eurosexist term), often without legal license or tribal sanction, and began to mistreat them as subservient women under their domination (Weatherford 1991, chap. 3; Green 1992, chap. 3).

It is evident that the dominant authorities in North American societies hold to restrictive "race" categories that reject "interracial" categories of "mixed-blood" offspring. Therefore, the reality of "mixed-bloods" among Native peoples, defined as *mestizos*, mulattos, and/or metis, is not well represented in restrictive "race" categories used by the U.S. Census Bureau. In fact, the Census Bureau discourages, if not actually prohibits, the use of any "mixed-blood" categories among the federally constructed racial categories of "American Indians" or "Native Americans" (see Forbes 1990, 1988; Price 1958; Green 1992, chap. 2; Gonzales 1992).[6]

The differences between determining Indian status and tribal membership within the context of elaborate traditional kinship systems, with clan structures determining kinship relations within extended families and the communal society as a whole, in contrast to the colonial categories and laws for defining "race" are stark. In Lakota society, women who were taken in (or raided) from other Native nations could be considered Lakota members only after they learned the native language and cultural ways. In the context of the traditional matrilineality of the Great Plains Nations, their children would be considered Lakota by birth regardless of "mixed-blood" biology (Walker 1982).[7] Today, however, the "mixed blood" situation has become a critical issue and even a ruthlessly divisive federal government political tool adopted among Native peoples themselves. Some tribal leaderships, mostly among men, have even called for the prohibition of marriage outside the tribe if one wants to continue holding tribal membership. This agenda could have dire consequences, including the destructive possibility of breaking customs of incest taboos in clan structures within kinship systems that were meant to avoid these situations.

Beyond questions of membership, the tension between individual civil rights and tribal sovereignty also complicates the possibilities for political action for Indian activists engaged in land and life struggles. The case of Ramona Bennett (Puyallup), an Indian woman activist in the Northwest, brings to light the hidden complexity in the "dual-citizen" status that many Indians, both male and female, traditionally assert. Bennett was arrested by state authorities in a case of civil disobedience when she was representing her tribe, as a tribal council member, in an Indian fishing rights demonstration. In her testimony, she describes how and why she and other demonstrators had been arrested, and how they saw their actions as an exercise of Native rights:

> They [the police] came right on the reservation. . . . They gassed us, they clubbed people around, (and) they laid a $125,000 bail on us. At that time I was a member of the Puyallup Tribal Council, and I was spokes(person) for the camp [of local fishing rights activists]. And I told them what our policy was, that we were there to protect our Indian fishermen. And because I used a voice-gun, I'm charged with inciting a riot. I'm now faced with an eight year sentence. This was happening while Indian fish-ermen's lives, among husbands, brothers and sons, were being harassed by federal and state authorities for practicing their traditional fishing ways, as stipulated in Indian treaty rights of tribal members. (Jaimes with Halsey 1992, 311–12)

Bennett, who had been shot and wounded by "white vigilantes" while seven months pregnant, was eventually acquitted of any wrongdoing.[8] This case brings out the more complex entanglements between a tribal member's struggle for individual rights, as in the case of Bennett, who was asserting her "civil rights" as a part of her Native rights. At the same time, she was asserting her Native rights that were premised on treaty law, as a member of a tribal society in Washington state. What becomes clear here is that the concept of "sovereignty" has to be construed for a communally based people and their tribal society in contrast to the patriarchal hierarchy of a colonialist legacy, in which governments established under the Indian Reorganization Act of 1930 operate as extensions of the U.S. government.

Exercises in Native rights, as illustrated in the above case, are understood to be collectively oriented in the context of *nationhood*, as exercised by a tribal people with traditions of egalitarianism (Jaimes with Halsey 1992). Many traditionally ori-ented leaders, both men and women, in grassroots movements find it difficult to assert such Native rights, individually and collectively, given the way the federal law constructs such rights. Indian-hate groups' tactics escalate these conflicts and confrontations when aggressively asserting their own non-Indian self-interests.

Within contemporary Indian communities, a tribal group with a collective agenda is criticized for presumedly undermining a member's individual rights. Such issues need to be understood in the context of the restoration of a cultural canon of indigenous law, with its emerging implications for which individual rights are met within the collective group as part of an egalitarian tradition.

The legal discourse of the United States has shaped Indian relationships, but this canon of federal Indian law is not neutral with respect to Native peoples and tribes and the U.S. government. Despite the fact that the law used the paternalistic guise of a "trust responsibility" toward Indians, this canon works to the advantage of the nation-state in its relations with Indians as tribal peoples and at the expense of the original inhabitants (see, among others, Deloria and Lytle 1983, 1984). Since these effects are not immediately illegitimate, they have the more serious negative effect of making Indian groups accept them, with destructive consequences. In an advanced stage of colonialism, the original inhabitants succumb to a racialized experience as they accept the various federally constructed classifications of the dispossessed and disenfranchised (i.e., "relocated Indians," "ethnic/minorities," "federally recognized" tribes, and so on). In this colonialist experience, these "subcultural" groups even start to advocate the perceived advantages of referring to themselves as a disadvantaged population, forgetting their original status as independent and sovereign (that is, autonomous) nations. Such subordinate positioning as "disadvantaged" people and "victims" might bring monetary and economic gain in the short term, but in the long run it often establishes federal dependency, which thwarts longer-term goals of communal self-determination and self-sufficiency as well as the further disempowerment of Native women by erosion of traditional indigenous egalitarianism.

Genocide against Native Americans and Native Women in Resistance

Episodes of indigenous genocide were covert U.S. policy during periods of removal and containment on designated reservations by the U.S. government. If a Native group refused to move (thus understood as "hostile" Indians in contrast to "pacified" ones), or if they got caught in the ensuing fights, they found themselves victims of a brutal military force exercised by state militias and the U.S. cavalry. The Colorado militia is recorded as proudly displaying bloody female parts, taken from the Native women victims they murdered, while parading in the streets of Denver (Jaimes 1992c). Such inhumane wartime operations took place throughout the late 1800s and into the 1900s, in order to keep the "natives" corralled on what have been referred to as prototypes of concentration camps (Churchill 1986; also Jaimes 1992c). Historically, there have been cases of both physical and cultural genocide that has targeted Native women as a distinct racial and gendered group. In some areas, they have been subjected to coerced marriages with "white" males in order for the latter to obtain their allotment annuities and other Indian claims (Weatherford 1991, chap. 3; Hogan 1991). This is different from the marital and common law alliances that

were made between Indian leaders and early non-Indian traders, which were voluntary liaisons for commerce between the women and men involved. Abuses are
documented in military-regimented mission schools as well as private institutions
that subjected young Indian women (and men) to indentured servitude as domestic
servants or factory workers (Noriega 1992). Consequently, there was little actual
education taking place, but rather a heavy socialization process calling for the
"civilization" of the "primitive" and the eradication of their respective indigenous
cultures (Szasz 1992). At times Native women and children were abducted into
virtual slavery or raped by non-Indian men, as in the case of Pit River Indian women
in Northern California, from 1852 to 1867.[9]

Such charges of physical genocide correlate with the charge of cultural genocide.
A classic case of this mode of government abuse was the taking of Indian children
into "foster" homes to ameliorate the (federally wrought) dire economic conditions
on the Indian reservations. After a protest in which Native women were in the
vanguard, this policy was changed by the passage of the Indian Child Welfare Act of
1978 (P.L. 95608; 25 U.S.C., 1901; Churchill and Morris 1992).

A series of sterilization cases also raise the specter of physical genocide committed
against a group of Native women. These documented cases targeted Native women
among other ghettoized groups such as Chicana women in Los Angeles, mainly
from 1968 to 1970, and the birth control experimentation on women in Puerto Rico
in the 1930s to 1960s (Del Castillo 1980; Jaimes with Halsey 1992, nn. 102, 104).
Hence, these cases also involved the violation of civil rights of female members of
designated "minority" groups, women of color, and "ethnic" cultures. In 1972, Dr.
Connie Uri, a physician and Native woman, found documentation that the federal
Indian Health Service(s) (IHS) was sterilizing American Indian women, both on
and off the reservations. The U.S. General Accounting Office (GAO), at the request
of Senator James Abourezk (Dem., S.D.), announced in a 1976 report that more
than 3,400 American Indians, mostly women, had been sterilized by the IHS from
1973 to 1976. This report also stated that there had been thirty-six violations of
a court-ordered moratorium on sterilizing persons under the age of twenty-one
(Dillingham 1977). Uri and others also found that during fiscal year 1973, 132 Native
women were sterilized at the IHS hospital in Claremore, Oklahoma. One hundred
of these sterilizations were nontherapeutic, that is, they had the sole purpose of
rendering a young woman incapable of reproduction. Most of these cases were
performed by physicians or nurses on women who were not aware of or prepared for
the long-term consequences of sterilization. Some of them believed they were being
treated for an ailment, while others thought that their sterilization was not a permanent condition. It was discovered, in many of these cases, that these women did not
consent to these operations ("Oklahoma" 1989). Native women and their supporters,
especially WARN (Women of All Red Nations), have continued to conduct their
own research into such abuses as genocidal practices. This organization concluded
that since 1972 approximately 42 percent of Native women of childbearing age had
been sterilized by IHS programs without their consent. After a protest led by WARN
the IHS was transferred from the Bureau of Indian Affairs (BIA) to the Department

of Health and Human Services in 1978, supposedly for more IHS accountability, to deter such practices in the future (WARN 1975, 1978; Jaimes with Halsey 1992).

In its April 1992 news bulletin, WARN reviewed findings presented at its conference on "Genocide of Indigenous Peoples in North America," calling attention to some of the worst scenarios of these genocidal campaigns. The issues ranged from "environmental policies on Indian lands," such as the case of the Nevada test site, where the Dann sisters have been attempting to defend their right to raise cattle on their Shoshone ancestral lands, traditionally called *Newe Segobia*, to the Columbia River Project, which targets the Hanford nuclear reactor because of the environmental destruction it has wrought. In this last case, for example, nuclear wastes from the reactor were placed in unstable containers that have since leaked into the Columbia River in Washington state, and that are threatening the water table for the Yakima Nation. In the case of James Bay, located in Quebec province, a U.S. collaboration with Canada planned to build a $60 million hydroelectric plant, which would destroy four major river systems and involve the deforestation of 356,000 square miles. The first phase of this project has caused extensive environmental damage to the surrounding Cree and Innuit lands, and mercury poisoning throughout the rivers and lakes of the Eastern Woodlands, causing damage to soil and the endangered caribou. This project was planned to provide energy for the markets of forty-eight U.S. states, at the expense of the indigenous populations on both sides of the U.S.-Canada border. WARN also cited blatant violations of the American Indian Religious Freedom Act of 1978 in its grievance against the Columbus Project, and in its protest of the collaboration between the Catholic Church and the University of Arizona to build a $200 million observatory on Mount Graham in the area. This location is a known sacred site to the San Carlos Apache and other Native groups in the area, who are the major protesters, in alliance with other environmentalists (WARN 1992).

Of more recent concern among indigenous peoples worldwide is the corporate and privately sponsored Human Genome Diversity Project, which has a profit-motivated interest in collecting samples for DNA banks from targeted indigenous peoples. This is a separate research plan from the Human Genome Project, which is sampling the human populations globally. Both projects are promoted in the name of health for medical cures of diseases as well as genetic engineering by way of "gene tinkering" for a hardier human species. Indigenous nongovernmental organizations (NGOs) that go before the United Nations with grievances of human rights violations have raised an outcry against the Diversity Project, which is sometimes called "the Vampire Project" (Harry 1995). These international organizations object to the collection methods (preferably blood samples, as well as cheek scrapings and hair analysis) as well as to the reasons indigenous peoples are being targeted for these data. According to a Stanford University report, the initial research design targeted over six hundred designated groups as "subjects" of the Diversity Project, with more than sixty in the United States alone. This Stanford report itself acknowledges the public concerns addressed by geneticists as well as project designers regarding the lack of ethical and moral considerations in this global plan.[10]

Native North American Women's Activism for Indigenism

The Native North American woman has a long and life-sustaining legacy of respect and empowerment among her own people, in her traditional indigenous societies. In the context of indigenous values and belief systems, the concept of tradition has a very different meaning than its Eurocentric connotation of being in the past and therefore "backwards," that is, holding back the Euroamerican idea of "progress." Traditionally, Native women have always held important and influential positions in their communal societies; some examples are the Creek and Cherokee Nations and the Haudenosaunee's Iroquois Confederacy in New York state, where "clan mothers" selected male council leaders in their traditional longhouse form of government. Others included the Narragansett of Rhode Island and the Delawares, among the Algonquin peoples along the Atlantic coast; the latter generically referred to themselves as "women," which was meant to be supremely complimentary (Jaimes with Halsey 1992, 311–19). This same government tradition, albeit in varied forms, can also be found among the Southwest tribal peoples, such as the Navajos (Dineh) and Pueblos, and among the Great Plains Nations as well as in the Northwest. These indigenous cultures were more often matrilineal than patrilineal. In addition, these systems included matrifocal or patrifocal spheres of influence, as power bases, in what was more likely the closest state of egalitarianism in any human society. Hence, sociocultural *communal* structures, based on long-standing kinship customs, were designed to balance out any internal conflicts, including gender differences among the membership.

Despite this post-conquest disempowerment by European chauvinism, North American Native women have continued to denounce their negation from, if not oblivion within, American history. Native women have been in the vanguard of decolonization movements in resistance to the European encroachment, and they have acted as warrior women in their own indigenous liberation struggles in North America. They have indeed formed the backbone of indigenous nations on this Northern Hemisphere, and have continued to be at the center of their people's protest against Euroamerican domination as well as the male chauvinism prevailing in the Indian world (Jaimes with Halsey 1992).

Today, this tradition is continuing with the reemergence of Native women as tribal leaders. In addition, Native women in the United States and Canada have been in other not-so-visible leadership positions throughout the twentieth century, especially in the areas of education and community development and land and resource reclamation and restoration. Nevertheless, there remain critical problems of poverty, illness, unemployment, and other social ills, as well as having to deal with misogynist men.

This structural sexism, as well as racism, is the result of the intervention by and the encroachment of the mainstream society. In response to this U.S. colonialism with its internalized chauvinism, indigenous women's organizations have been established throughout North America. Native women have been at the forefront of grassroots movements for what I have termed life and land struggles, and have assumed leadership for a way of life focused on health and healing, which involves the restoration of land and natural resources as a method of control over the environment. Many of these Native warrior women activists are asserting these issues as basic human rights, and are engaged in international forums (e.g., the United Nations) as well as regional, state, and national agendas. The 1995 Fourth World Conference on Women in Beijing, China, was the first time that this international forum has recognized an indigenous women's liberation agenda. Such concerns revolve around the question of "to develop or not to develop" in Native communities as cultural enclaves in urban settings and land-based reservations in rural settings. They are also concerned with the preservation and restoration or repatriation of sacred sites and burial grounds. Marie Legos, an elder of the Achumawi band in Northern California, provided crucial leadership in the Pit River Indian Land Claims Settlement, a federal land fraud dispute in the 1970s. Her family and supporters protested the "settlement" by occupying their ancestral lands, claimed by Peabody Coal Company, until they were starved off the area. In Washington state, women such as Janet McCloud (Tulalip) amd Ramona Bennett (Puyallup) had leading roles in the "fish-in" demonstrations of the 1960s, initially pursued within a framework of "civil disobedience" and "principled nonviolence." The same sort of dynamic was involved during the early 1970s, when elder Oglala Lakota women, Ellen Moves Camp and Gladys Bissonette, assumed the leadership in establishing the Oglala Sioux Civil Rights Organization (OSCRO) on the Pine Ridge Reservation in South Dakota. It is not well known that among the founders of the American Indian Movement (AIM) in 1968, two were Native American women, Mary Jane Wilson (Anishinabe) and Betty Banks (Jaimes with Halsey, 1992, 341).

In addition to individuals who have been outstanding activists, Native women have also created organizations that have been asserting women's rights and demanding self-determination in regaining our lost traditional sociopolitical status. Among these organizations are the Women of All Red Nations (WARN) and the Indigenous Women's Network, both in the United States and Canada. The Native Women's Association of Canada as well as the Women of the Metis Nations, in the Alberta province, have issued statements on "gender equality"; they are ahead of U.S. organizations on this issue.

In this arena, Native women's health is linked with environmental issues, and problems should be described in terms of resistance to being "national sacrifice peoples" for unbridled "development-for-profit-motive-only" (Churchill and LaDuke 1992; Jaimes 1995b). No matter what her age, the more traditionally value-oriented a Native woman is, the less she will be willing to separate her health, well-being, and healing from that of the Earth Mother Herself. These indigenous societies as nations were often based on matrilineal kinship systems that were egalitarian models of gender equity, since patrilineality was rare and patriarchy unknown. Therefore, one's ecocultural identity was derived from these land-based cultures and religions in a bioregional homeland, in which Native women had spheres of matrifocal authority over men in kinship traditions.[11] Native men had their own patrifocal spheres of authority in religious matters and activities outside the communities, but these have received a distorted importance since they were more visible to chauvinistic Europeans. These indigenous ecocultures were engaged in agricultural practices that utilized organic food sources and farming practices, and created sustainable natural environments that were models of egalitarianism among the Native inhabitants in reciprocal relationship with their habitat. There is also the significance of ritual and ceremony, and what is being called *geomythology*, which is based on "female organic archetypes" (i.e., Corn Daughter among the Pueblos; Buffalo Calf Woman among the Plains peoples, and numerous others), that spiritually inspired both a distinct ecocultural locale in a national habitat, and traditionally oriented health and healing practices.

Indigenism is a decolonizing movement among third world peoples throughout the globe. This movement recognizes third world living conditions among Native peoples in the United States, both on and off the reservations and in urban as well as rural settings. Among these groups, headed by Native women spokespersons, many are reclaiming their precolonialist traditions that espouse a land-based culture and identity derived from and in reciprocity with a particular bioregion. This indigenous worldview is inherent in the meaning of what I called ecoculturalism, in which the significance of biology and culture determining one's identity are derived from *a sense of being with a sense of place*. Biodiversity calls for economic self-sufficiency with environmental sustainability, in contrast to a corporate-privileged economic system that is interested in "development-for-profit-only," at the expense of a quality way of life for its inhabitants and ecological habitat (Vandana 1993; Jaimes 1995b).

For Native groups, the issues of land and the environment are very much connected with issues of health, well-being, and healing, or "life and land struggles." Concern for such issues has brought forth resistance in the form of grassroots movements that are international in scope. Native women are always in the vanguard of this resistance against genocide, ethnocide, and ecocide. The destruction of a natural habitat (ecocide) and a land-based culture (ethnocide) erases the biodiversity of traditionally oriented inhabitants in their own bioregional homelands. Such destruction has led to certain areas being designated "national sacrifice zones" since the 1970s. The phrase "national sacrifice zones" implies that human inhabitants in that area are considered expendable in the face of the imperatives of developing corporate enterprises. In international circles such acts are called genocide, and often operate in conjunction with ethnocide and ecocide (see Harry 1995).[12]

This essay has noted two ways the U.S. government treats Native American peoples: as its wards, and as dispensable peoples. Native Americans respond to these oppressions both through the use of the law and through other creative forms of activism. What becomes clear, though, is that neither form of response is adequate unless it is placed within the context of the maintenance of the traditional ways of life of Native North American peoples. These traditions place individuals in a respectful relationship to others and to their world, creating a pattern of reciprocal relations. Such an analysis of indigenism makes sense out of the legal quagmires and the struggles for survival of Native peoples throughout North America as we enter the twenty-first century.[13]

The only way to reverse the dominant colonialist mentality and pro-development agenda is for traditionally oriented Native peoples to reclaim their birthright, internally as well as outwardly. In such a liberation movement, Native women can be seen as proactive agents of change leading the way as "exemplars of indigenism." This indigenous movement is about our decolonization; it is focused on the recovery of our health and respective cultures, the healing of our mind, body, and spirit among our kinship relations of both genders and all ages. Such a movement exists in reciprocity with our natural environment, and is part of our reclaiming our respective homelands for our liberation through decolonization. This is the significance of an ecocultural connection with the Earth, as the archetypal Feminine Principle, and as a living organic presence that we Native Daughters love, honor, and respect as the Mother of Us All.

NOTES

1. Deloria and Lytle (1983, chap. 1) describe the federal Indian "policy periods" as allotment (mid-1880s), relocation (1940s to present), and termination (1950s). See also Jaimes 1990.

2. Deloria (1992) provides the following analysis of this case:

> although tribes are comparable to states, they have a higher status than states because they are dependent domestic nations, not the originators of the constitutional social contract or creatures of the national government. The principle announced by the Senate Judiciary Committee in 1870, in finding that Indian nations were excluded from the operation of the [Fourteenth] Amendment, was that it would be unfair and unjust to subject them to a rule or law to which they had not consented. . . . Consent, the basis of modern Western social contract theory, can only be found in the Indian treaty relationship with the U.S. (314–15)

Deloria does not, however, address the relevant political position some nontreaty (as well as nonratified) Indian groups hold, among them the Abenaki of Vermont and "California Mission Bands" (as they are called throughout the state). These groups hold that since they never signed a treaty with the U.S. authorities in the first place, they still hold title and its attendant sovereignty to their traditional lands and sovereignty in their internal affairs. In this scenario, the Abenaki of Vermont have asserted their claim of a significant proportion of that particular state.

It should also be noted that the Mohawk and Lyons edited text in which Deloria 1992 appears has a conspicuous absence of Native women contributors. The essays here downplay or ignore the importance of the societies of the matrifocal Clan Mothers among the Six Nations in the Iroquois Confederacy.

3. In the historical background, they note that the question of individual civil rights arose in the 1950s, motivated by an effort to record the development of case law pertaining to the articulation of the list of inherent powers (still) possessed by tribes; such cases involved the power of tribes to tax (or be taxed, a crucial Indian gambling issue today), to lease or consolidate lands, to give rights of way, and other functions (204). In a related issue about "tribal taxation" by the federal or state entities, see M. A. Jaimes 1992b and 1993. On traditional tribal membership rights for "political freedom," see Deloria and Lytle 1984, 204.

4. This "race construct" is a basic premise of comparison between cultures that are European and those cultures that are indigenous to the Americas. See Jaimes 1995a.

The recent BIA Certification Act (P.L. 101–644–1104 Stat. 4662) has set a blanket policy that imposes "blood quantum" as well as other criteria in the U.S. government's determination of who is an "American Indian" (which the author calls a sociopolitical construct) while it criminalizes any "noncertified" Indian or art gallery that sells their art and subjects them to penalty of fraud; this congressional legislation, which does have support from the political leadership of some "federally recognized" groups of Indians/Tribes, results in denying many "nonfederally recognized" Indians access to this federal determination via the BIA, under the Department of Interior. The author sees such political strategies as the result of federal constructions.

5. See Jaimes 1990, chaps. 5 and 6. My current research indicates that clan societies in traditional kinship systems actually established taboos that prohibited incestuous practices, in order to protect against biological disabilities. In addition, the practice of *exogamy*, intermarriage by custom and law outside the nation, was encouraged and even resulted in raiding parties in some cases for women and children when there was a survival need for a society to increase its membership. This was not seen as morally abhorrent in those times, however. See also Shepardson 1963.

6. Regarding the "mixed-blood" experience among Native women, this is poignantly illustrated in the historical fiction of Louise Erdrich, a Turtle Mountain Chippewa meti (*Love Medicine* [1984] and *Tracks* [1988]). See also Linda Hogan's historical novel *Mean Spirit* (1991), where she describes the predicament of allotment years for "full-blood" ' Indians who were determined "incompetent" to hold land and "mixed-blood" Indians who were declared "unqualified" for their allotments. In Canada, there is also the autobiography *Halfbreed* (1973) by Marie Campbell, a Canadian meti, that highlights the marginalization of "mixed-bloods" both on and off the reservations.

7. Thanks to Ed Valandra (Lakota) for calling this citation to my attention.

8. Since the Bennett episode Indian men have been imprisoned, among them the elder David Sohappy (who died soon after his release from prison) for his leadership in the fish-in protests that took place in Washington state.

9.

Laws provided the cover for virtual kidnap and slavery of Indians. . . . Perhaps the most terrible outrage against the California Indians was the practice of kidnapping children. . . . Sherbourne Cook estimates from reports written in California at the time, that from 1852 to 1867, three or four thousand children were stolen. Cook is a careful scholar who admits that his statistics are conservative. . . . The number of women abducted and raped is enormous. Whenever a miner or soldier took a fancy to an Indian woman, he did not meet any resistance from the law. Indian men, however did resist and were often killed in the effort. (Bancroft 1882)

10. On the Human Genome Diversity Project, see "Summary of Planning Workshop 3(B)" on "Ethical and Human Rights Implications," regarding the methods of research sampling, Stanford University, Stanford, CA; cover letter dated May 17, 1994, and signed by Jean Dobie, Assistant Director, Morrison Institute for Populations and Resources Studies (involved in "selected dissemination of the report"). The Stanford report is an inside document by a group of geneticists who are both key designers and implementers of the Human Genome Diversity Project.

11. I conceptualize "ecocultural" to denote land-based cultures that derive and have their sense of cultural identity from the environment.

12. International NGOs (nongovernmental organizations) have been making these linkages and presenting them in such forums as the United Nations Human Rights Committee,

Working Group on Indigenous Populations/Peoples. There they challenge destructive practices to human populations (as genocide), cultures (as ethocide), and the environment (as ecocide). See also Churchill and LaDuke 1992.

The author is currently engaged in research on the disproportionate levels and impact of cancer in Native groups in North America among Yaqui communities in Arizona.

13. Space limitations have required the omission of an extended treatment of Canadian policy toward Native peoples.

REFERENCES

Acuña, Rodolfo. 1988. *Occupied America: A History of Chicanos*. 3d ed. New York: Harper and Row.

Amott, T. L., and J. A. Matthaei. 1991. *Race, Gender and Work: A Multicultural Economic History of Women in the U.S.* Boston: South End.

Anner, John. 1992. "To the U.S. Census Bureau, Native Americans Are Practically Invisible." In *1492–1992: Commemorating 500 Years of Indigenous Resistance: A Community Reader*, ed. Donna Nicolono, 143–46. Santa Cruz: Resource Center for Nonviolence with Santa Cruz Resistance 500 and the Central Coast Quincentennial Indigenous Council.

Bancroft, H. H. 1882. *The Works of Hubert Howe Bancroft*. San Francisco: A. L. Bancroft and Co.

Bataille, G. M., and K. M. Sands. 1984. *American Indian Women: Telling Their Lives*. Lincoln: University of Nebraska Press.

Campbell, Marie. 1973. *Halfbreed*. New York: Saturday Review Press.

Churchill, Ward. 1986. "Genocide: Towards a Functional Definition." *Alternatives: Social Transformation and Humane Governance* 11, 2 (July): 403–30.

———. 1992. "Perversions of Justice: Examining the Doctrine of U.S. Rights to Occupancy in North America." In *Struggle for the Land: Indigenous Resistance to Genocide, Ecocide and Expropriation in Contemporary America*, 33–83. Monroe, ME: Common Courage Press.

———. 1992–93. "I Am Indigenist: Notes on the Ideology of the Fourth World." In *Struggle for the Land: Indigenous Resistance to Genocide, Ecocide and Expropriation in Contemporary America*, pt. 4. Monroe, ME: Common Courage Press.

———. 1993. "Naming Our Destiny: Towards a Language of American Indian Liberation." *Global Justice: Bulletin from the Center on Rights Development*, spring.

Churchill, Ward, and W. LaDuke. 1992. "Native North America: The Political Economy of Radioactive Colonialism." In *The State of Native America*, ed. Jaimes, 241–66.

Churchill, Ward, and Glenn Morris. 1992. "Key Indian Laws and Cases." In *The State of Native America*, ed. Jaimes, 13–17.

Communicator (Minneapolis). 1993. May–June, 1–4.

Del Castillo, Adelaida R. 1980. "Sterilization: An Overview." In *Mexican Women in the United States: Struggles Past and Present*, ed. Magdalena Mora and A. R. Del Castillo. Los Angeles: Chicano Studies Research Center, University of California.

Deloria, Vine, Jr. 1992. "The Application of the U.S. Constitution to American Indians." In *Exiled in the Land of the Free: Democracy, Indian Nations, and the U.S. Constitution*, ed. Oren Lyons, John Mohawk et al., 282–315. Santa Fe: Clear Light Publishers.

Deloria, Vine, Jr., and Clifford M. Lytle. 1983. *American Indians, American Justice*. Austin: University of Texas Press.

———. 1984. *The Nations Within: The Past and Future of American Indian Sovereignty*. New York: Pantheon.

Dillingham, Brint. 1977. "Indian Women and IHS Sterilization Practices." *American Indian Journal* 3, 1 (January): 27–28.

Elliot. 1992. "Once Upon a Conquest: The Legacy of Five Hundred Years of Survival and Resistance." *Labyrinth* (Philadelphia), October, 2–3.

Erdrich, Louise. 1984. *Love Medicine.* New York: Bantam.

———. 1988. *Tracks.* New York: Henry Holt.

Fanon, Frantz. 1963. *The Wretched of the Earth.* New York: Grove.

———. 1967. *Black Skin, White Masks.* New York: Grove.

Forbes, Jack. 1988. *Black Africans and Native Americans: Color, Race, and Caste in the Evolution of Red-Black Peoples.* Oxford: Basil Blackwell.

———. 1990. "Undercounting Native Americans: The 1980 Census and the Manipulation of Racial Identity in the (U.S.)." *Wicazo Sa Review* 6, 1 (spring): 2–26.

Gonzales, Sandra. 1992. "Intermarriage and Assimilation: The Beginning or the End?" *Wicazosa Review* 8, 2 (fall): 48–52.

Green, Rayna, ed. 1983. *Native American Women: A Contextual Bibliography.* Bloomington: University of Indiana Press.

———. 1992. *Women in American Indian Society.* Indians of North America Series. New York: Chelsea House.

Harry, Debra. 1995. "The Human Genome Diversity Project and Its Implications for Indigenous Peoples." *Indigenous Women* 2, 11: 30–32.

Hechter, Michael. 1977. *Internal Colonization: The Celtic Fringe in British National Development, 1536–1966.* Berkeley: University of California Press.

Hogan, Linda. 1991. *Mean Spirit.* New York: Atheneum.

Jaimes, M. A. 1990. "American Indian Identification-Eligibility Policy in Federal Indian Education Service Programs." Ph.D. diss., Arizona State University, Tempe.

———. 1992a. "Federal Indian Identification Policy." In *The State of Native America,* ed. Jaimes.

———. 1992b. "Gambling Wars: An Assault on American Indian Sovereignty," *New World Times* (Santa Fe), August, 17, 30.

———. 1992c. "Sand Creek: The Morning After." In *The State of Native America,* ed. Jaimes, 1–12.

———. 1993. "Our Brother's Keeper." *Turtle Mountain Quarterly,* winter, 39–42.

———. 1995a. "American Racism: The Impact on American Indian Identity and Survival." In *Race,* ed. Steven Gregory and Roger Sanjek. New Brunswick: Rutgers University Press.

———. 1995b. "Native American Identity and Survival: Indigenism and Environmental Ethics." *Issues in Native American Cultural Identity* 2:273–96.

———. 1992d. *The State of Native America: Genocide, Colonization, and Resistance.* Boston: South End.

Jaimes, M. A., with Theresa Halsey. 1992. "American Indian Women: At the Center of Indigenous Resistance in Contemporary North America." In *The State of Native America,* ed. Jaimes, 311–44.

LaDuke, Winona. 1995. "Indigenous Women: Our Future, Our Responsibility." Plenary Statement at Fourth World International Conference on Women, Beijing, China. Typescript, in author's possession.

Martinez, Elizabeth. 1992. "Defending the Earth in '92: A People's Challenge to the EPA." *Social Justice* (special issue, "Columbus on Trial") 19, 2 (summer): 95–105.

Noriega, Jorge. 1992. "American Indian Education in the United States: Indoctrination for Subordination to Colonization." In *The State of Native America,* ed. Jaimes, 371–402.

"Oklahoma: Sterilization of Native Women Charged to I.H.S." 1989. *Akwesasne Notes* (Roosevelttown, NY: Mohawk Nation), midwinter, 11–30.

Price, E. T. 1958. "A Geographic Analysis of White-Negro-Indian Racial Mixtures in Eastern United States." *Association of American Geographers Annals* 43 (June): 138–55.

Shepardson, Mary. 1963. "Navajo Ways in Government: A Study in Political Process." *American Anthropologist, Memoir* 96 3, pt. 2 (June): 65.

Stanford University. [1994]. "Summary of Planning Workshop 3 (B)." Personal copy in the possession of the author.

Stiffarm, L. S., and Phil Lane, Jr. 1992. "The Demography of Native North America: A Question of American Indian Survival." In *The State of Native America*, ed. Jaimes, 23–53.

Stock, Robert. 1990–91. "The Settler State and the American Left." *New Studies on the Left* 154, 3 (winter): 72–78.

Szasz, Margaret. 1992. " 'Poor Richard' Meets the Native American: Schooling for Young Indian Women in Eighteenth Century Connecticut." In *The American Past and Present*, ed. R. L. Nichols. 4th ed., 76–86. New York: McGraw-Hill.

Vandana, Shiva. 1993. *The Monocultures of the Mind*. Atlantic Highlands, NJ: Zed Books.

Walker, J. R. 1982. *Lakota Society*. Lincoln: University of Nebraska Press.

Women of All Red Nations (WARN). 1975. "WARN News Bulletin." In *Native American Women*. New York: International Treaty Council.

———. 1992. "WARN News Bulletin." Special edition. Chicago, April.

———. 1978. *We Will Remember Group*. Porcupine, SD: n.p.

Weatherford, Jack. 1991. *Native Roots: How the Indians Enriched America*. New York: Fawcett Columbine.

Women for Racial and Economic Equality (WREE). 1991. *One Hundred Ninety One Facts about U.S. Women*. New York: Women for Racial and Economic Equality.

———. 1992. *Bulletin*.

THIRTEEN

Latina Women and Political Consciousness: *La Chispa Que Prende*

CAROL HARDY-FANTA

Es como una chispa que prende ¿verdad? y, que el espíritu de la persona en ese momento está listo. [It's like a spark that ignites, right? and, at that moment, the spirit of the person is ready.]

— Aracelis Guzmán

Central to the study of gender, culture, and Latina politics are questions about the ways political socialization occurs: How do women of color, specifically Latinas, become active in politics? What is the impact of cultural background on their political development? How do experiences gained in adulthood shape their sense of themselves as political actors? How does gender affect the political development of Latina women? Embedded in all these questions is one central issue: What role does political consciousness play in the development of a "political self"?

In the literature on Latino politics there has been remarkably little research on the political development of Latina women. The bulk of research on *Latino* political consciousness centers on the effects of the Chicano movement on political participation and access to political power (Garcia and de la Garza 1977; Guzmán 1976) or on the development of *ethnic* consciousness in multiethnic Latino communities (Padilla 1985; Uriarte-Gaston 1988) — and thus misses or downplays the experiences of Latina women. Specific research on Latino political socialization also has tended to study Mexican American children (Garcia 1971; Howell-Martinez 1982), and the literature on Latina political consciousness is, with few exceptions, limited to Chicanas/Mexican Americans (Campos Carr 1989; Mota 1976).[1]

In general, most writings on Latina women focus on women in their reproductive, social, or labor market roles.[2] Latina women are portrayed in this literature as "three times oppressed" — by racism, sexism, and cultural traditions (Mirandé and Enríquez 1979; Barragán 1980; Melville 1980). The stereotype of Puerto Rican and Mexican women, in particular, is that of passivity and submissiveness. *Marianismo*, the feminine correlate to and opposite of *machismo*, derives from the image of the Virgin Mary — meek, mild, and supportive of men. Assertiveness in social, public, and political arenas by Latina women supposedly runs counter to these cultural traditions. Garcia and de la Garza (1977) refer to a Latino tradition of "strong women," but these women are mythical figures; from these examples one would have to conclude that mainstream social and political science is comfortable with women only in their reproductive roles — or as goddesses.

In this chapter I propose to challenge these traditional political theories that view Latina women as "passive" and "apolitical." While Latina women do indeed face barriers to political participation that stem from sexism and cultural traditions, empirical research suggests that, for Latina women, political participation is inextricably linked with the development of the political self. At the same time, the political self evolves in conjunction with *personal* self-development. In a reciprocal fashion, political consciousness — a sense of "becoming political" — contributes to and emerges from personal and political self-development.

Latina Women in Boston

This chapter is based on a study of the Latino community in Boston, Massachusetts. The community is a relatively small one: Latinos now make up 11 percent of the city's population (1990 census). The community is also characterized by considerable diversity. Forty-two percent of the Latinos in Boston are Puerto Rican; the rest of the community is made up of Central and South Americans (approximately 30 percent), a rapidly increasing Dominican population (13.1 percent), Cubans (3.5 percent), and Mexican Americans (3.5 percent).[3]

In this study I conducted in-depth interviews with twenty-nine Latina women and twenty-four Latino men — community activists, influential Latinos, and *la gente del pueblo*.[4] I also participated in numerous community events: protest marches, election campaigns, voter registration, community forums, workshops, and conferences, and formal and informal discussions throughout the community. In all the observations and interviews conducted over the two-year research period, a recurrent theme emerged: Latina women are political actors and play crucial roles in Latino community mobilization. Of particular interest to the study of political development is the way Latina women revealed the interaction of personal development, political consciousness, and political and social change.

While in the overall study, interviews were conducted with men as well as women, specific gender differences will not be discussed here; the focus of the chapter will be on the experiences of Puerto Rican, Dominican, Mexican American, and Central and South American women. For a complete discussion of gender differences, see chapter 5 in Hardy-Fanta 1993. Of primary importance for the current discussion is that virtually all the Latina women in Boston identified personal development with political consciousness and political change, while the men who were interviewed had little or nothing to say on political consciousness or the development of the political self.

As I sorted out the threads of many different life experiences, it became clear that all the women's stories had in common a theme: "becoming political." There is a *process*, for many a contemplative process, of political development. For some, this process is quick — a sudden *¡chispa!* of recognition that a change is needed. For others, there is a slow emergence of political consciousness, a questioning of the conditions of life, and a searching for alternatives within themselves and with others.[5]

"Becoming Political"

The women I interviewed formally and talked with during community observations offered many perspectives on how they became politicized. For some Puerto Ricans, the status options for Puerto Rico — statehood, independence, socialism — created a political issue that formed their political identity and molded their activism. For others, and for those of other Latino groups, it was *la necesidad*, being confronted by the needs of the community, crushing problems such as a lack of decent housing, AIDS, and a high dropout rate for Latino public school children. A few *decided* to become political, others would have liked to be allowed into politics but felt shut out, and still more felt they emerged gradually despite personal and structural barriers.

Questions about the development of the political self (Dawson and Prewitt 1969, 15–24) and the sources of politicization have concerned political scientists for decades.[6] Traditional theories of political socialization generally focus on (1) child-hood socialization,[7] (2) adult resocialization and countersocialization (especially through structural changes such as the civil rights movement and the women's movement),[8] and (3) political consciousness.[9] Unfortunately, these theories have paid scant attention to the political development of Latina women. However, as in the traditional literature, the role of the family in the political socialization process emerges in the stories of some Latinas.

Childhood Socialization: The Role of the Family

Family background is frequently cited as one of the most influential factors in political development (Dawson and Prewitt 1969). "*Political socialization* assumes that the political habits of people are formed primarily before adulthood" (Orum et al. 1974, 198; emphasis in original). Political learning in the family supposedly develops partisan attachment, ideology, national loyalty, orientations toward author-ity, sense of regime legitimacy, and recruitment to bureaucratic and governmental roles (Hirsch 1971, 4). The family, according to theories of childhood socialization, affects the acquisition of participant values; these values then determine subsequent levels of political activism, party identification, political knowledge, and sense of political efficacy. Exposure in the home to political talk and activism thus is linked to future political behavior. Gender differences in adult women's (supposedly lower) levels of political participation are attributed to sex-linked restrictions, male dominance of the political domain (Campbell et al. 1960; Lane 1959), and feminine characteristics learned as children.[10]

Family traditions of "being political" *do* affect some Latinas in the predicted way.[11] Josefina Ortega, for example, agrees with earlier researchers that family background is an important component to political socialization. "*Vengo de una familia muy política*" [I come from a very political family], she says. Josefina Ortega locates the roots of her "becoming political" in her family of origin: "*Está en la sangre*" [It's in the blood].

Becoming political also may come from following a long tradition of activism in the family. Dalia Ruiz, for example, is a Puerto Rican woman of very humble background. She attributes her enjoyment of politics to her family: "*A mi mamá le gusta muchísimo la política. Porque ella se vuelve loca con las elecciones. ¡Ella se vuelve loca! A ella le encantaba la política.*" [My mother likes politics a lot. She goes nuts about the elections, she just goes nuts! She adored politics.]

Gender, Political Socialization, and the "Ethics of Care"

The stories of many Latina women from a variety of backgrounds and countries of origin revealed a vision of politics that is different from that of traditional political theorists, Latino and non-Latino alike. They seemed to emerge from their families with a view of politics imbued with what feminist theorists call an "ethics of care" (Flanagan and Jackson 1990). Politics, for them, consists of "helping others," "fulfilling an obligation," "sharing and giving," and "providing support." The women stated that this view of politics derived from values taught by their families.

For example, Marta Correa is a woman from Ecuador who sees politics as a way of helping members of her community get jobs and improve neighborhood services. The value Marta Correa places on political participation clearly comes from her family. As can be seen in the following quote, her family is the source of her political interest and her desire to help others:

> Es la forma en que nos han criado — así me criaron a mí. Yo soy de Ecuador; nos criaron con un respeto; nos criaron muy diferente. . . . Mi abuela me decía siempre, "Respeta para que te respeten." . . . O sea, tu cooperas con las personas siempre que te necesiten. Porque en el futuro — esa persona no te va a ayudar a tí pero otra persona te puede dar ayuda. Entonces, a mí me criaron en esa forma — ese respeto — esa ayuda. [It's the way that we were raised — that's the way they raised me. I am from Ecuador; we were raised with the value of respecting others; we were raised very different. . . . My grandmother always told me, "Respect others so they'll respect you." . . . In other words, you help others whenever they need you. Because, in the future, that person is not going to help you, but another person may give you help. So, that's the way I was raised — with that kind of respect — that kind of help.]

For many Latinas, a sense of family tradition had a major impact on the politicization process. The women recalled an ethos of sharing and giving in their families.

For example, Latinas who come from political or politically supportive families describe the impetus to *compartir* — to share — as the basis of working with people. Josefina Ortega talks about how her family communicated the idea that, if they had only one piece of bread, they would share it with others. Catalina Torres, a Mexican American woman who moved to Boston from the West, is now in a position relatively high up in the city power structure. She says,

> My parents had been migrants — we call them *braceros*.[12] My parents, both of them — although we were very poor — whatever we grew, you could always count on us to get you a hundred pounds of potatoes, a hundred pounds of beans, a hundred pounds of flour, what you needed — staples — to get you through the winter if you didn't have anything, because my dad had a year-round job and it wasn't seasonal, and he always would help somebody else, always. I would always say, "Why do you do that? You don't know those people, we need it too." That was my thing, and I was always told, "*Favores no se cobran*"[13] — don't ever look at a favor and expect that favor to be repaid. Someone else will pay you back and it's a *sin* to ask to be paid back! So, all right, I grew up like that.

Jovita Fonseca, a longtime activist who, at the time of the study, worked in the Elections Division at Boston City Hall, states, "I could always remember somehow, somebody always saying things like — my family — we had an obligation." She recalls the network of Central American women who circulated through her house, helping each other become adjusted to this country, and providing both a source of inspiration to her and training in politics. Her first exposure to government institutions came when she served as a translator for these women. Another woman traces her interest in influencing political decisions at the governmental level to her anger at injustice — and to the fact that she comes from a family of social workers.

In these examples, Latinas did not say that their political activism derived from cultural or family traditions but that they drew on certain family traditions and values once they became active politically. The sense of politics as caring, giving, and helping was, at least among the men and women interviewed in Boston, uniquely expressed in the interviews of Latina women.

The role of family has another, equally gendered, impact on Latina political development: families often provide support to women as they move into the more formal political arenas. Marta Rosa, for example, is a Puerto Rican woman who was first elected to the school committee of a town across the river from Boston in 1989; she was reelected in 1991 and 1993. In 1994 she ran for city council in that town; she narrowly made it into office. She felt that the supportiveness of her family gave her the practical means and the emotional strength to weather the demands of her election campaigns: "My mother lives in the basement apartment I built for her and my sister lives on the first floor. I've always had babysitters, . . . It's always been my mother, my husband, my sisters — and they're *really* supportive of what I do, the work that I do. They know it's for a good cause" (emphasis in original). Her family, including her husband and her children, worked on her campaign.

Despite these testimonies in support of the family as the primary source of participatory political orientations, there are many examples of Latinas who illustrate how politicization can occur without a family tradition of political involvement and *despite* inactive and oppressive family conditions. Latina women in Boston, in particular, describe many experiences of adult resocialization — "a fundamental reorientation of an *adult* woman's political self" (Rinehart 1986, 13; emphasis in original). These women who, as adults, participate in experiences that run counter to female or cultural role expectations emerge from these experiences as political activists.

Rising from Oppression: Latina Women and Adult Resocialization

One of the barriers to political participation discussed in much of the literature on politics, and in the interviews conducted for this study, is the grinding down effects of poverty. Virtually all the Latina women talked about how difficult it is to think of going to a meeting, challenging a landlord, protesting, or even voting when just trying to survive consumes all your energy. The participation of poor people — poor Latinos in Boston — hinges on having a reason to participate, whether through personal relationships, the personal appeal of a Latino candidate or friend, or some combination of factors that pulls one into taking action on one's own behalf. For Latina women, "the triple oppression suffered by many women of color has fostered innovative methods and approaches to political organizing" (Morgen and Bookman 1988, 11). To discover how people who are poor, who are oppressed by life and larger socioeconomic structures, become political, one must examine the life experiences of people who have been there themselves.

María Luisa Soto is a housing activist in a Latino neighborhood in Boston. She is a woman who makes a clear connection between her personal development, her political consciousness, and her emergence into the arena of political activism. Her early life in Puerto Rico and New York City was lived within a very "traditional" Latina woman's role, restricted to the home under the watchful eye of first her father, then her husband. When asked about the roots of her community-based politics, María Luisa Soto focused on social and affiliative needs. Being a political person dates to her arrival in Boston. She recalls that, after hearing about a meeting on the problem of housing, "I went and I said to myself, 'This seems interesting.'" Meeting people and expanding her horizons outside the home created new thoughts and provided new opportunities for María Luisa Soto. As she connected with other women, she began to see the vacuum in leadership, and began to take action.

María Luisa Soto is eager to point out that she did all this while raising her two children in the projects, going to college, and working full-time — her pride in her personal development permeates her story. Her story also reveals that her politicization ran counter to her upbringing. Leaving her husband seems to have been a beginning marker for branching out into a broader lifestyle. While male researchers like Lane pay scant attention to the need for affiliation in political development, the fulfillment of social, affiliative needs — meeting other people — contributed substantially to the politicization of María Luisa Soto. She ended her interview by making a connection between her personal and political self-development. With great force and feeling she said that it was *"parte de mi desarrollo como una mujer"* [part of my development as a woman]. What is important about the story of María Luisa Soto is the way her childhood socialization was challenged in adulthood; she moved from a noninvolved, traditional woman's role to become one of the most politically active and influential people in Boston.

This process of adult resocialization is somewhat different, although the result may be the same, from childhood experiences that challenge female and cultural role expectations (countersocialization). For example, when, as a child, Jovita Fonseca acted as a translator for adult Central American women, her exposure to governmental institutions, the proactive role involved, and a sense of competence in the outside world created a socialization experience *during her childhood* that ran counter to the more traditional childhoods of many Latina girls. María Luisa Soto, on the other hand, had a very traditional childhood and was kept at home; she was challenged to become political only when adult circumstances opened up opportunities beyond those of her childhood and cultural expectations. The dynamics of adult resocialization (separate from childhood countersocialization) raise an important question: What is the *process* by which poor women of color become politicized as adults?

Whereas many influential, activist Latinas describe the impact of family background, opportunities for activism, and issues such as the status of Puerto Rico as stimulators of their political involvement, non-activists, *la gente del pueblo*, describe a more personal struggle against oppression. For Aracelis Guzmán, the politicization process began when she started working for the Department of Public Health as a nursing outreach worker. She described the debilitating effects of the poverty she saw when she went into the homes of poor Latina women:

> Creo que lo que yo estaba aprendiendo era que . . . cuando tu no tienes suficiente dinero para tu renta, para alimentar a tus hijos, cuando no tienes dinero para salir ni a un cine o ir a un baile, que estás todo el día encerrada en la casa, cuando tu no estás consciente de que hay otras alternativas en la vida aparte de ser mamá, que puedes ir a la escuela, que puedes sacar un inglés ¿verdad? es muy difícil dar educación preventiva. Que la mente no está abierta para recibir ese conocimiento, está uno embotado — unos lloran, unos tienen diarrea — si están en una relación abusiva con el marido o con el novio, es que . . . son demasiadas presiones. [I believe that what I was learning was that . . . when you don't have enough money for rent, to feed your children, when you don't have money to even go out to a movie or go to a dance, when you are locked in the house all day long, when you aren't conscious of having other alternatives in life other than being a mother, that you can go to school, that you can learn English, right? it's very difficult to do preventive education. Because the mind isn't open to receiving that knowledge — one is dulled (enervated) — some cry, some have diarrhea — if they are in an abusive relationship with a husband or boyfriend . . . there are too many pressures.]

Aracelis Guzmán goes on to describe how the spark of political awareness transforms poverty and a sense of debilitating oppression into a potential for political participation:

> Entonces yo creo que para uno poder envolverse políticamente — ¿verdad? — tiene que en primer lugar sentir esa necesidad de decir, "Bueno, ¿por qué es que yo estoy así?

¿cómo es que yo puedo cambiar esto? . . . Yo tengo que hacer algo," y entonces uno empieza a preguntar, ¿verdad? o a la vecina, o si hay una agencia dos cuadras acerca de mi casa. . . . Es como una *chispa que prende* ¿verdad? y que el espíritu de la persona en ese momento está listo. (Emphasis added.) [So I believe that, for one to get involved politically — right? — one has to first feel that need to say to oneself, "Well, why is it that I'm like this? What can I do to change this? I have to do something," and then one begins to ask, right? your neighbor, or if there's an agency two blocks away from my house. . . . It's like *a spark that ignites,* right? and, at that moment, the spirit of the person is ready. (Emphasis added.)]

For Aracelis Guzmán, making the initial connection between one's daily problems and larger political issues is the beginning step toward participation.

The feminist theme of the idea that the personal is political cannot have a stronger argument than this. Aracelis Guzmán describes this moment as a spark — *una chispa* — a critical moment in which one begins to question the nature of one's existence. Crucial to the present study of political consciousness is that the spark drives one to venture outward — to other people, other places, first for help, later with others in action for change. This spark can come from a *charla* ("chat" — a type of discussion group) for women at local community organizations, from interaction with a new friend, or from a slow process of questioning within the self, as the following example demonstrates. The story of Julia Santiago shows how, after the spark, there is a slower emergence of increasingly politicized consciousness and behavior.

Julia Santiago: From Oppression to "Being Political"

I first met Julia Santiago at the National Puerto Rican Congress Convention, Memorial Day weekend, 1989. She was one of a panel of women in a workshop called "The Vision of the Woman: Head of the Family, Administrative Tasks of the Household — The Socio-political Struggle."[14] At this workshop I heard Julia Santiago tell the story of her development from *una jibarita* to a political activist.

A *jíbaro* is one of the country folk of Puerto Rico, a "worker of the cane," a peasant. Julia Santiago uses the term *jibarita* in its (affectionate) diminutive and feminine form to describe her naïveté, her youth, and her oppressive, traditional family. It is important to keep in mind that this is not a woman who comes from the middle class or even the working class. She very much typifies the poor women who make up much of the Latino community. In her language and demeanor, she has not changed into a professional or middle-class person, despite the fact that she now works in an organization for women and has studied theories of oppression. There, as an adult, she has been able to reevaluate her life and conclude, "Yo *siempre he estado cuestionando la situación patriarcal*" [I have always been challenging the patriarchal system].

What is striking about the story of Julia Santiago is how similar her early life is to that of many Latino people who are the least active politically. In many ways her experiences as a child and young adult sound similar to the description given by Aracelis Guzmán in the previous example — someone too enervated to think beyond surviving day by day. Julia Santiago came from a family with a rigid, authoritarian father. She left Puerto Rico to *"salir de la dictadura de mi padre"* [leave the dictatorship of my father], but "like many young women, came to live in a house very similar to that of my father." Her husband made her lie to get welfare; Julia said, "You have to lie so that they'll serve you." She recalls how alienating and intimidating the experience of "seeking help" was; she describes the welfare workers as *"majadores,"* real bruisers. After ten months she went to work in a factory and went from *mal en peor* (from bad to worse). She finally decided to put an end to her marriage because *"mejor ir sola, que mal acompañada"* [better to go it alone than in bad company].

With the decision to leave her husband began a new period in her life. She moved to Boston with her children and got a job as a hospital aide. At first she enjoyed the job so much that she believed she would stay as long as they would keep her. After a while, however, she began to be aware of discrimination and was the brunt of demeaning jokes against Latinos. At the same time, problems with her landlord and her children led her to seek solutions in ways she had not thought of before.

During the workshop Julia Santiago passed quickly over how she changed from a woman suffering quietly — alone — to one leading a tenant action, attending college classes, and *"haciendo trabajo político"* [doing political work]. Only in a later interview were we able to explore the process of her politicization.

Julia Santiago confirms, in many ways, the route to becoming political discussed in Aviel (1981) — through her daily life and the needs of her children:

> Es bien curioso, precisamente es que todo de momento te encuentras que los hijos te lleguen a tener problemas y tu no sabes que hacer. Porque no importa que tu estás trabajando, cuan honesta tu eres, no se te — no es lo mismo. Tu, como los niños no entienden y lo único que te queda por él es tirarte por la calle buscar información — de momento. [It's really curious, it's just like, all at once you find that your children begin to have problems and you don't know what to do. Because it doesn't matter that you're working, how honest you are, it doesn't — it's not the same. Your children don't understand, and the only thing left to you is to throw yourself out into the street looking for help — all of a sudden.]

In the process of seeking help for her children, Julia Santiago developed relationships that brought her out of the social isolation common to many Latina women and created social connections and opportunities to go beyond her personal experience into questioning why things had to be the way they were. She says, *"De momento me encuentro con gente que sabían tanto más que yo, de momento, digo, 'Pero, ¡¿qué es lo que pasa conmigo?!'"* [All of a sudden I find myself with people who knew so much more than me, all of a sudden, I say, "But what's going on with me?!"]. Like Aracelis Guzmán, Julia Santiago experienced the *spark*, the moment of being conscious of the need for change. This consciousness, together with greater social connectedness, is the crucial ingredient in the politicization process of Latina women who move from oppressed backgrounds to political involvement.

Later in the interview Julia Santiago discussed her tenant organizing experiences;

how her new role evolved reveals much about the theme of "becoming political." She is able to describe the fine line between the "not-conscious" to the "consciously political" as she describes her early days in New York:

> Es que *tu misma* no lo sabes que es algo político. Por ejemplo, . . . yo vivía en New York, yo siempre ayudaba la gente. Yo estaba en welfare y las mujeres, muchas veces me decían: ¿qué yo podría hacer en tal y cual situación? y siempre yo estaba aclarandoles a ellas, cómo era una manera de saber defenderse — y a la misma vez luchar por lo que *ellas* querían. [It's that *you yourself* don't know that it's political. For example, . . . I lived in New York, I was always helping people. I was on welfare, and the women would often come to me asking what I could do to help them with this and that situation, and I was always explaining things to them how there was a way to stick up for oneself — and at the same time fight for what *they* wanted (emphasis in original).]

Julia Santiago then goes on to link this experience to a point she made at the workshop:

> Parte de lo que yo dije en mi presentación — que en mi trabajo ahora yo siempre me considero político; yo lo veo como el mismo — de eso de sobrevivir — y no, tu sabes — tu siempre estás haciendo trabajo político y tu no lo sabes. [Part of what I was saying in my presentation (at the workshop) — that in the work I do now I always consider myself political; I see them as the same thing — that of surviving — and not, you know — you're always working politically and you don't (even) know it.

Julia Santiago's life illustrates that adult resocializing experiences are as important as childhood socialization in the development of the political self. Julia Santiago became political as an adult through a network of personal relationships in her daily life. Her radical feminist ideology is thoroughly entrenched in her worldview but is an ideology clearly learned in adulthood. Her family was part of her oppression, not a source of political strength.

Julia Santiago sees the fine line between political unawareness and political consciousness; she also connects daily survival with politics. Political development is not a fixed characteristic, handed down through the family; it is a process that occurs in interaction with others. In addition, being political and becoming political may develop out of actions begun within women's traditional roles. Latina women's decisions to protest or take other forms of political action may first be stimulated by concerns for children and family needs. However, the internal and collective process that occurs by participating in such activities can itself be politicizing.

Pardo, for example, describes a similar "transformation" process for Mexican American women in East Los Angeles. She states that "women have transformed organizing experiences and social networks arising from gender-related responsibilities into political resources"; she traces this political development to women's concerns (Pardo 1990, 2). "In these processes, women meet other mothers and begin developing a network of acquaintanceships and friendships based on mutual concern for the welfare of their children." This concept of transformation suggests that, in contrast to earlier theories that saw motherhood as a constraint on participation, many poor women are motivated to action precisely out of concern for their children. In other words, political development begins with concerns rooted in their roles as mothers, but personal empowerment leads to political action with wide-reaching impact. Marisela Pena, a teacher at a local community organization, for example, sees the political education of Latina women as having a greater impact than the education of men because of women's socializing effect on children. She quoted a Latino saying: *"Educar un hombre es educar una persona; educar una mujer es educar una familia"* [To educate a man is to educate one person; to educate a woman is to educate a family].

Latina Women, Marriage, and the Politicization Process

Julia Santiago is one of several Latina women who marked her entrance into a political life with the decision to leave her husband. María Luisa Soto, an activist discussed earlier, is another woman who became involved in politics only after she moved away from her husband. I did not specifically collect marital status information on the people interviewed. However, only nine (37 percent) of the twenty-four women for whom I had marital status information were married. The rest were divorced or separated. Three of the nine married women portrayed their husbands as supportive of their political activism; these three were women with higher educational levels and income. For the poorer women, not having a husband seemed associated with a higher degree of politicization that began after separation from their husbands. The Latino men interviewed as part of the study did not mention marriage as having an impact on their degree of political participation or their path to becoming political.

Why poorer Latina women may become more political after separation is a tantalizing question that deserves future research. There is a wide-ranging debate about whether child-rearing and homemaking responsibilities limit the time or energy women have available for political participation (Jaros 1973; Lipset 1963; Pomper 1975; for a feminist perspective, see Randall 1987, 85–88). Since the Latina women who were poor but who had become politicized as adults all had children, worked, and often went back to school as adults, it may be marriage, not child and home responsibilities per se, that constrains certain groups of women.[15]

Gender, Consciousness, and Political Participation

The political development of Latina women in Boston demonstrates that political consciousness emerges within the social context — in connection with others. The image of political socialization and political consciousness that exists in mainstream literature is revealed to reflect male concerns for power and autonomy, the assertion of the self, and competition — concerns that overshadow what feminists suggest are equally valid political needs: the needs for affiliation, caring, connection, and community.

The process of coming to political consciousness seems to be a process of making connections — between their own lives and those of others, between issues that affect them and their families in the neighborhood or community and those that affect them in the workplace. Latina women who become politicized do so, therefore, by making connections between the so-called differing spheres of their lives, between the apparently private sphere of family and home and the supposedly public sphere of formal politics. Rather than the "fragmented consciousness" that, in Katznelson's view, constrains political action in the United States (Ackelsberg 1988, 305), Latina women's political consciousness is made up of a seamless cloth in which their personal development as women is intertwined with their roles as mothers and their emergence as political activists.

NOTES

1. Mota is particularly relevant to my study because she explored the interaction of class and feminism in the Dominican Republic.

2. See the discussion in Hardy-Fanta 1993, 18–23 and n. 9. This paragraph is taken from Hardy-Fanta 1993, 19.

3. My source for the Puerto Rican data is the 1990 census; other data are from Osterman 1992. Please note that the Puerto Rican population data in the census differ from Osterman's data; I utilize Osterman because the census data for Latinos other than Puerto Ricans, Cubans, and Mexican Americans are not available for Boston.

4. *La gente del pueblo* literally translates as "the people of the village." The term is generally used to mean "the common folk" or "the masses."

5. Chapman describes how "out-groups" (such as women and minorities) need to develop "political consciousness and the commitment which gives courage to confront their marginality" (1987, 318).

6. Herbert Hyman (1959), the "originator of the concept of political socialization" (Walton 1985, 43), began to systematically review the process of political learning over thirty years ago.

7. See, for example, Jaros 1973 and Dawson and Prewitt 1969; for a review of early literature on black political socialization in childhood, see Morris and Cabe 1972 and Abramson 1977. There are a few studies that compare the interaction of gender and race in the political socialization of children; see, for example, Orum et al. 1974.

8. See, for example, the articles in Sigel 1989; for an example of the adult socialization of immigrants, see Hoskin 1989. For the impact of the civil rights movement on black political socialization, see Walton 1985, chap. 3; and Morris, Hatchett, and Brown 1989. There are many works that focus on the women's movement as a socializing force; see, for example, Klein 1984, chap. 5; and Carroll 1989.

9. Robert Lane has played a major role in shaping the study of political consciousness; see Lane 1959, 1962, 1969, and 1972. For a discussion of the role of black consciousness on political thinking, see Morris, Hatchett, and Brown 1989, 283–92; Jackson 1987; and Shingles 1981. It would be impossible to note all the research and writings on political consciousness and the women's movement; see, for example, Klein 1984; Kelly and Burgess 1989; Conover 1988; and Chapman 1987.

10. These characteristics supposedly include passivity, less interest in politics, beliefs that politics is for men, and, in the infamous words of Duverger, the "mentality of minors" (1955, 129). For a review of the literature on gender differences in political socialization, see, for example, Randall 1987; Bourque and Grossholtz 1974; and Orum et al. 1974. For examples of research dismissing gender differences in children on scales of political efficacy, see, for example, Easton and Dennis 1967 and Orum et al. 1974.

11. Twelve of my total sample of fifty-three mentioned family background as playing a role in their political development.

12. The *bracero* program was a U.S. government labor agreement with Mexico to import Mexican agricultural laborers during the 1940s and 1950s.

13. This phrase is hard to translate directly. It means that one does not ask to be repaid for a favor: no "tit for tat"; one is not owed something in return. Doing things for others may result in others helping when one is in need; however, there is no *exchange* or *promise* of repayment.

14. "La Visión de la Mujer: Jefe de la Familia, las Tareas Administradores del Hogar — La Lucha Política-Social."

15. Rinehart suggests that "the expected constraints [of marriage and child rearing] on adult women's political development may be overemphasized" (1986, 23). Data in Flora 1977 suggest, however, that marriage does constrain political efficacy in (nonindustrial) blue-collar women (90). There was a twenty percentage point drop in the number of married women who scored high on a political efficacy scale compared to men. However, divorced women and men showed an opposite tendency: 14.3 percent of divorced blue-collar (nonindustrial) women had high political efficacy scores, compared to only 7.1 percent of the men. This difference was not true for white-collar workers or industrial workers.

REFERENCES

Abramson, Paul R. 1977. *The political socialization of black Americans: A critical evaluation of research on efficacy and trust.* New York: Free Press.

Ackelsberg, Martha A. 1988. Communities, resistance, and women's activism: Some implications for a democratic polity. In *Women and the politics of empowerment,* ed. Ann Bookman and Sandra Morgen, 297–313. Philadelphia: Temple University Press.

Aviel, JoAnn Fagot. 1981. Political participation of women in Latin America. *Western Political Quarterly* 34, no. 1 (March): 156–73.

Barragán, Polly Baca. 1980. The lack of political involvement of Hispanic women as it relates to their educational background and occupational opportunities. In *Conference on the educational and occupational needs of Hispanic women,* ed. National Institute of Education, 39–46. Washington, DC: National Institute of Education.

Bourque, Susan C., and Jean Grossholtz. 1974. Politics an unnatural practice: Political science looks at female participation. *Politics and Society,* winter, 225–66.

Campbell, Angus, Philip E. Converse, Warren E. Miller, and Donald E. Stokes. 1960. *The American voter.* New York: Wiley.

Campos Carr, Irene. 1989. Proyecto la mujer: Latina women shaping consciousness. *Women's Studies International Forum* 12, no. 1: 45–49.

Carroll, Susan J. 1989. Gender politics and the socializing impact of the women's movement. In *Political learning in adulthood,* ed. Roberta S. Sigel, 306–39. Chicago: University of Chicago Press.

Chapman, Jenny. 1987. Adult socialization and out-group politicization: An empirical study of consciousness-raising. *British Journal of Political Science* 17, pt. 3 (July): 315–40.

Conover, Pamela Johnston. 1988. The role of social groups in political thinking. *British Journal of Political Science* 18, pt. 1 (January): 51–76.

Dawson, Richard E., and Kenneth Prewitt. 1969. *Political socialization.* Boston: Little, Brown.

Duverger, Maurice. 1955. *The political role of women.* New York: UNESCO.

Easton, David, and Jack Dennis. 1967. The child's acquisition of regime norms: Political efficacy. *American Political Science Review* 61 (March): 25–38.

Flanagan, Owen, and Kathryn Jackson. 1990. Justice, care, and gender: The Kohlberg-Gilligan debate revisited. In *Feminism and political theory*, ed. Cass R. Sunstein, 37–52. Chicago: University of Chicago Press.

Flora, Cornelia Butler. 1977. Working-class women's political participation: Its potential in developed countries. In *A portrait of marginality*, ed. Marianne Githens and Jewel L. Prestage, 75–95. New York: David McKay.

Garcia, F. Chris. 1971. *The political life of Chicano children*. New York: Free Press.

Garcia, F. Chris, and Rudolph O. de la Garza. 1977. *The Chicano political experience: Three perspectives*. N. Scituate, MA: Duxbury Press.

Guzmán, Ralph C. 1976. *The political socialization of the Mexican American people*. New York: Arno Press.

Hardy-Fanta, Carol. 1993. *Latina politics, Latino politics: Gender, culture, and political participation in Boston*. Philadelphia: Temple University Press.

Hirsch, Herbert. 1971. *Poverty and politicization: Political socialization in an American subculture*. New York: Free Press.

Hoskin, Marilyn. 1989. Socialization and anti-socialization: The case of immigrants. In *Political learning in adulthood*, ed. Roberta S. Sigel, 340–77. Chicago: University of Chicago Press.

Howell-Martinez, Vicky. 1982. The influence of gender roles on political socialization: An experimental study of Mexican-American children. *Women and Politics* 2, no. 3 (fall): 33–46.

Hyman, Herbert. 1959. *Political socialization*. New York: Free Press.

Jackson, Byran O. 1987. The effects of racial group consciousness on political mobilization in American cities. *Western Political Quarterly* 40, no. 4 (December): 631–46.

Jaros, Dean. 1973. *Socialization to politics*. New York: Praeger.

Kelly, Rita Mae, and Jayne Burgess. 1989. Gender and the meaning of power and politics. *Women and Politics* 9, no. 1 (winter): 47–82.

Klein, Ethel. 1984. *Gender politics: From consciousness to mass politics*. Cambridge: Harvard University Press.

Lane, Robert E. 1959. *Political life: Why people get involved in politics*. Glencoe, IL: Free Press.

———. 1962. *Political ideology: Why the American common man believes what he does*. New York: Free Press.

———. 1969. *Political thinking and consciousness: The private life of the political mind*. Chicago: Markham.

———. 1972. *Political man*. New York: Free Press.

Lipset, Seymour M. 1963. *Political man*. New York: Anchor Books.

Melville, Margarita B., ed. 1980. *Twice a minority: Mexican American women*. St. Louis: C. V. Mosby.

Mirandé, Alfredo, and Evangelina Enríquez. 1979. *La Chicana: The Mexican American woman*. Chicago: University of Chicago Press.

Morgen, Sandra, and Ann Bookman. 1988. Rethinking women and politics: An introductory essay. In *Women and the politics of empowerment*, ed. Ann Bookman and Sandra Morgen, 3–29. Philadelphia: Temple University Press.

Morris, Aldon D., Shirley J. Hatchett, and Ronald E. Brown. 1989. The civil rights movement and black political socialization. In *Political learning in adulthood*, ed. Roberta S. Sigel, 272–305. Chicago: University of Chicago Press.

Morris, Milton, and Carolyn Cabe. 1972. The political socialization of black youth: A survey of research findings. *Public Affairs Bulletin*, May–June.

Mota, Vivian M. 1976. Politics and feminism in the Dominican Republic: 1931–1945 and 1966–1974. In *Sex and class in Latin America*, ed. June Nash and Helen Safa, 265–78. New York: Praeger.

Orum, Anthony M., Roberta S. Cohen, Sherri Grasmuck, and Amy W. Orum. 1974. Sex, socialization and politics. *American Political Science Review* 39, no. 2 (April): 197–209.

Osterman, Paul. 1992. Latinos in the midst of plenty. In *Beyond poverty: Building community through new perspectives*, background paper for the Boston Persistent Poverty Project, 37–71. Boston: Boston Foundation, March.

Padilla, Felix M. 1985. *Latino ethnic consciousness: The case of Mexican Americans and Puerto Ricans in Chicago*. Notre Dame: University of Notre Dame Press.

Pardo, Mary. 1990. Mexican American women grassroots community activists: "Mothers of East Los Angeles." *Frontiers* 11, no. 1: 1–7.

Pomper, Gerald. 1975. *Voter's choice*. New York: Dodd Mead.

Randall, Vicky. 1987. *Women and politics: An international perspective*. 2d ed. Chicago: University of Chicago Press.

Rinehart, Sue Tolleson. 1986. Toward women's political resocialization: Patterns of predisposition in the learning of feminist attitudes. In *Gender and socialization to power and politics*, ed. Rita Mae Kelly, 11–26. New York: Haworth.

Shingles, Richard. 1981. Black consciousness and political participation: The missing link. *American Political Science Review* 75, no. 1 (March): 76–91.

Sigel, Roberta S., ed. 1989. *Political learning in adulthood*. Chicago: University of Chicago Press.

Uriarte-Gaston, Miren. 1988. Organizing for survival: The emergence of a Puerto Rican community. Ph.D. diss., Boston University.

Walton, Hanes. 1985. *Invisible politics: Black political behavior*. SUNY series in Afro American Society. Albany: State University of New York Press.

FOURTEEN

Ritual and Sacrifice at Tailhook '91
A Documentary Exhibition
and Political Action

FRANCES K. POHL

In 1956 groups of naval aviators, Defense Department contractors, and others associated with naval aviation traveled to San Diego to attend the first annual Tailhook Symposium ("tailhook" refers to the hook on fighter planes that snags the cable on aircraft carriers during landings). Conceived as a reunion of naval aviators, it soon expanded to include a number of seminar sessions relating to naval aviation, as well as other professional development activities. In 1963 the annual convention moved to Las Vegas, where it remained until 1991, the year one female naval aviator began a process that exposed the physical assaults and verbal harassment experienced by female naval aviators and civilians at these reunions that had become an accepted part of Tailhook "tradition." This essay examines the nature of this "tradition," the events surrounding the 1991 Tailhook convention, and the efforts of one radical feminist group, the Women's Action Coalition (WAC), to prevent such events from happening again.

From its inception in 1956, the Tailhook Association relied heavily on support from the Navy and from contractors doing business with the Navy. Senior aviation leaders also regarded the association as an integral part of naval aviation and, until the aftermath of the 1991 Tailhook convention, felt justified in lending Navy support. This support included free office space at Naval Air Station Miramar, transportation of officers, civilian staff, and spouses and friends to the annual conventions, and use of Navy time to plan these conventions. Transportation in military aircraft to the Tailhook 1991 convention in Las Vegas cost the Navy nearly $400,000 for fuel and contract maintenance. The Navy has also been the primary source of seminar speakers and has played an integral role in determining the agenda for each year's symposium. The Tailhook Association, therefore, was seen by the majority of its members and by those outside the association as a government-sanctioned organization.

The Tailhook Association was also closely connected to the defense industry. According to Derek J. Vander Schaaf, the deputy inspector general of the U.S. Department of Defense who led the government's investigation of Tailhook '91, "in the early years of Tailhook, the conventions revolved around social gatherings and parties held in various hospitality suites that were funded and operated by Defense contractors. Those suites offered free food and beverages to all Tailhook attendees."[1] In the late 1970s the Department of Defense informed the Tailhook Association that it would no longer condone the hospitality suites sponsored by the defense industry because of potential conflict of interest. As a result of this directive, the hospitality suites became the responsibility of individual squadrons. Defense contractors still attended the conventions, however, and were provided with another forum in which to socialize with senior naval leadership, the "President's Dinner."

In addition, an important aspect of Tailhook conventions was the exhibition hall set up by defense contractors. According to a Tailhook Association document, "the exhibit hall housing defense contractor exhibits and Navy informational booths [at Tailhook '91] . . . numbered a record 172 booths in what has become one of the largest aerospace industry trade shows in the nation." The document goes on: "At no time in the Association's 35-year history had there been a better illustration of the unique triumvirate that is Tailhook as a symbiotic relationship among aviators, admirals and industry, each giving and receiving information from the other."[2]

This was obviously a beneficial arrangement for the defense industry, but was it as beneficial for the majority of naval aviators? What did these junior officers expect to get out of their membership in Tailhook? What came up often in newspaper and Defense Department interviews with naval aviators who attended Tailhook '91 was their perception of the convention as a place where rank was dropped, where junior grade officers could socialize and speak frankly with senior officers as well as with defense industry representatives. According to a report issued by the Tailhook Association on November 30, 1992,

> nowhere else is so objective and relaxed an atmosphere possible in a military context. A lieutenant (jg) can tell a vice admiral what's wrong with a piece of equipment, and five minutes later that admiral can ask an industry representative how to fix it. Conversely, the admirals can explain policy directives or tactical changes to junior officers with a directness that otherwise probably would be impossible. And simultaneously, an aircraft designer or ordnance engineer can tell a Navy program manager what to expect from a new procurement item without an onerous paperwork burden.[3]

As we will see, this "relaxed atmosphere" also included the consumption of large quantities of alcohol, which helped create an atmosphere that was far from relaxed for most women. In addition, women's presence at the conference as aviators rather than as wives or girlfriends or hired prostitutes altered the "men's club" atmosphere of earlier Tailhook conventions.

Tailhook '91 took place in Las Vegas, Nevada, from Thursday, September 5 to Sunday, September 8. At least 4,000 people attended — some estimates go as high as

7,000 — although at most 2,100 were actually registered for the professional aspects of the convention, and even fewer attended the professional events. Most interviewed agreed that the primary reason officers attended Tailhook was to "socialize" or party.

Vander Schaaf's report for the Department of Defense is the most complete account of this event available at the moment. Over 2,900 individuals were interviewed, and some 800 pictures of events at Tailhook were obtained. That this report is not as complete as it could be is due to the fact that many of the convention attendees involved in or witness to the attacks on women decided to cooperate only minimally with the investigation. Very few officers named names. Instead, they abided by an unofficial "code of silence" in order to protect those who had engaged in behavior that ranged from dereliction of duty to indecent assault.[4] In the words of Vander Schaaf, "collective 'stonewalling' significantly increased the difficulty of the investigation and adversely affected our ability to identify many of those officers who had committed assaults" (IV-1, IV-2). Some officers also reported to Vander Schaaf the existence of a "Lieutenants' Protective Association (LPA)" and a "Junior Officers' Protective Association (JOPA)," both of which were described as allegiances among officers. According to LPA and JOPA rules, "a junior officer will not 'give up' another junior officer just because he has done 'something stupid' " (IV-2).

Despite the stonewalling and code of silence, Vander Schaaf was able to identify ninety instances of indecent assault (eighty-three against women, seven against men) and numerous other incidents involving "indecent exposure and other types of sexual misconduct, as well as other improprieties by Navy and Marine Corps officers." Forty-nine of the women assaulted were civilian, twenty-four were military officers, six were military spouses, and six were government employees. All seven men were Navy or Marine Corps (their assaults involved, primarily, being pinched on the buttocks by a woman or by a person they did not see). The "other improprieties" included the hiring of strippers and prostitutes to perform in the hospitality suites and the display of pornographic photographs and videos, also in the hospitality suites. Prostitution, while legal in some counties in Nevada, is not legal within the city limits of Las Vegas.

The files of 140 officers were referred by Vander Schaaf to the acting secretary of the Navy for consideration of appropriate action. Of these officers, twenty-three were determined to warrant referral to the Navy for having participated in indecent assaults. Indecent assault is a crime under Article 134 of the Uniform Code of Military Justice (UCMJ). The files of an additional thirty-five flag, or senior, officers were also forwarded to the acting secretary so that he could determine whether action was warranted "with respect to the responsibility of each flag officer for the overall leadership failure that culminated in the events of Tailhook 91." Finally, fifty-one officers were discovered to have made false statements during the investigation.

Vander Schaaf's report included two parts: the first reviewed the Navy's initial investigation of Tailhook '91 and found it lacking; the second looked into Tailhook '91 itself. Almost all the assaults and indecent exposures took place on the third floor of the Las Vegas Hilton, in the area of the twenty-two squadron-sponsored hospitality suites, including the adjoining patio. These suites were ostensibly set up for the members of various squadrons to meet and relax during the convention. In reality, they were the sites of excessive drinking and rowdy behavior. Such behavior included streaking, mooning, butt-biting, and ballwalking.

"Butt-biting" is just that — one individual biting the buttocks of another. In almost all the cases reported at Tailhook '91, men bit women. This activity appears to have had a long history within the Navy, going back, according to one marine major, at least twenty years. Many interviewed tried to pass it off as good-natured fun and, for the most part, consensual. Vander Schaaf identified eight individuals (seven women and one man), four of whom were officers, who had been subjected to nonconsensual "butt-biting." One woman described her experience as follows: "A British pilot came up to me and bit me on the left hip. He bit me hard enough that his one tooth went through my cloths [sic] and broke the skin. The bite hurt me but I did not know I was bleeding until I lifted up my clothes to look. I could smell alcohol and I think he was very drunk" (F-2). The same man returned later and bit her again, leaving a large welt and bruise.

Ballwalking involved men walking around with their testicles exposed. The origins of this "ritual" are unclear, but some officers remembered observing ballwalking among naval officers in Korea or the Philippines, while another noted that he first came across it at a squadron golf game. "Those golfers who failed to reach the point of the women's tee, when teeing off, were required to play the remainder of the hole while ballwalking" (VII-3). A number of aviators described ballwalking as a "manly thing" to do with the guys. It was also described as an "act of defiance" or an activity that would allow a person to get one up on the other guy by being "ruder and wilder." One of the T-shirts sold at the convention referred to ballwalking with the phrase "Hang em if you got em." Hospitality suite organizers also engaged in this competitiveness for the honor of hosting the "rudest," "wildest," or "manliest" suite, which contributed, according to one officer, to the increasing rowdiness at the Tailhook conventions.

Another "ritual" that occurred at Tailhook '91 took place in the "Rhino" suite, named after the mascot of the suite squadron. To a large painting of a rhinoceros was attached an equally large dildo, which functioned as a drink dispenser, dispensing a mixture of Kahlua and cream called "Rhino spunk." Women who entered the room were shoved toward the rhino dildo as the men chanted loudly the woman's name, along with "suck the rhino" or "please the rhino." Those who complied were cheered. Those who refused were booed. A number of women told Vander Schaaf that they found the behavior of the men "unnerving." At least five stated that they were physically restrained from leaving the suite and forced toward the rhino against their will. Some were rescued by friends; others managed to escape on their own.

Little had been done in prior years to condemn or prevent such behavior, despite the fact that complaints had been lodged with the board of directors of Tailhook in 1985 and 1989. Prior to Tailhook '91 the board did issue a letter warning against such things as "gang mentality," underage drinking, and damage to Hilton property (the bill for damage after the 1991 convention was $23,000). In both April 1985 and July 1990 the secretary of the Navy issued instructions on alcohol and drug abuse that outlined the goal of the Department of Navy "to be free of the effects of alcohol abuse." Needless to say, these instructions were not followed at Tailhook '91. According to Vander Schaaf's report, a total of $33,500 was spent on alcohol at the convention, a figure that did not include much of the alcohol bought when initial supplies ran out. Two hundred seventy-one kegs, or 4,200 gallons, of beer were delivered to the hospitality suites over the course of the weekend. This did not include the ninety-seven kegs of beer ordered for consumption in the exhibition area (V-8).

Those who consumed large quantities of alcohol did not remain inside the hospitality suites. Many congregated in the hallway outside the suites, forming the infamous "gauntlet." Drunken male aviators, at times numbering close to a hundred, would mill about as if socializing, until a woman approached, usually from the direction of the elevators. As soon as she entered the group, the men would line up on either side of the hallway and start grabbing her breasts, buttocks, and crotch area as she tried to make her way down the hallway. Women described men pulling their tops down, ripping their clothes, reaching inside their underwear, and grabbing their breasts and buttocks. Many fought back, kicking, biting, hitting, and, in at least one instance, threatening to use a tazer gun. Many others said they felt "helpless, angry, violated and humiliated." At least one woman, an eighteen-year-old student from the University of Nevada, Las Vegas who had been drinking heavily, was lifted up, stripped of her jeans and underwear, passed along the hallway, and dumped on the floor at the other end. When the executive director of Tailhook, who knew what had happened, was asked how he viewed the matter, he responded, "I looked at it as a spontaneous incident, more along the line of a prank, not a prank in good taste, but . . . that's my view of the situation at the time" (VI-11). The general state of the hallway was described by one officer as follows: "the hallway was gross. . . . People — I'm sure they peed in the corners or wherever they happened to be standing. . . . They puked there. It was terrible" (VI-4, IV-6). Others said the hallway carpet was saturated with spilled beer to the point that it "squished" when walked on. The Hilton had to replace or repair the carpet on the floor containing the hospitality suites every year after the Tailhook convention.[5]

And where was hotel security during all this? According to witnesses interviewed by Vander Schaaf, "many assaults occurred in the presence of hotel security staff and those officers failed to act in the absence of specific complaint by the victims" (IX-3). Another witness stated that he saw approximately ten women attacked in the gauntlet and that, although the women were protesting the attacks, the "two security guards or police officers standing there [were] laughing while watching the assaults" (IX-3). Several other "witnesses reported seeing hotel security officers in the hospitality suites watching strip shows and pornographic movies" (IX-3). Vander Schaaf concluded that

> the relationship between the Tailhook Association committee members and the hotel was such that both parties approached the security function simply as an issue of containment. Neither party sought to control improper activities unless severe bodily harm or significant property damage appeared imminent. . . . The general opinion stated by countless witnesses was that, within the confines of the Tailhook convention, the aviators could act with impunity. (IX-4)

Those interviewed said that the gauntlet was a Tailhook tradition and had existed for at least fifteen years, but had not always been so violent. The move from catcalls and joking to grabbing and pinching occurred at the same time that increasing numbers of women entered the military. Early Tailhook conventions were mostly "stag" affairs. Unwritten rules discouraged officers from bringing spouses (or cameras), and the majority of the women in attendance were either prostitutes or "groupies." Since the early 1980s increasing numbers of female naval officers and male officers' wives had begun attending the conventions.

The appearance of these "respectable" women obviously cramped the male naval aviators' style and, correspondingly, increased their hostility toward these women. Alcohol aggravated this hostility and created a heightened sense of territoriality. These women should not be here. If they do attend, then they must accept the consequences. Many of those interviewed in the press about Tailhook '91 said that the women assaulted knew what was going on on the third floor and shouldn't have gone there. Yet the third floor was also where the majority of the "socializing" and "informal behavior" praised as such a valuable part of Tailhook took place.

The hostility toward female aviators in 1991 was particularly intense because of three additional factors: the Gulf War, the downsizing of the military, and women in combat. Tailhook '91 was seen as a celebration of the U.S. "liberation" of Kuwait and defeat of Iraqi forces earlier that year. Those who attended felt particularly entitled, therefore, to "blow off a little steam" (one officer referred to the convention as a "free fire zone"). At the same time, however, the futures of many of these military heroes were jeopardized by the pressures on the U.S. government to cut back on military expenditures in the face of the end of the Cold War. And finally, the possibility of women flying combat aircraft had been placed on the table, and arose during the symposium part of the convention. Vander Schaaf's report notes that when a female officer asked the panel of flag officers whether women would be allowed to fly aircraft in combat, the response was an uncomfortable acknowledgment that if Congress directed them to allow women to take on this role, then such a direction would be carried out. A male officer in the audience offered a different opinion, standing up and forcibly stating his personal objections to women in combat. The audience responded with loud cheers and applause (III-2).

According to one female Navy commander, the combination of heightened emotions from the Gulf War, the downsizing of the military, the fear of the loss of not only a job but a lifestyle, and the large quantities of alcohol led to

> an animosity in this Tailhook that . . . was telling the women that "We don't have any respect for you now as humans." . . . This was the woman that was making you, you know, change your ways. This was the woman that was threatening your livelihood. This was the woman that was threatening your lifestyle. This was the woman that wanted to take your spot in that combat aircraft. (X-2)

The male aviators displayed this attitude not only through their actions but also through their choice of clothing (or lack of it). One of the T-shirts worn by the men at Tailhook '91 read "He-man woman hater club" on the front and "Women are property" on the back.

A female aviator also reported that, immediately following the flag panel, she was verbally harassed by male aviators who expressed to her their belief that women should not be employed in naval aviation. They also accused her of having sexual relations with senior officers while deployed on carrier assignment (III-2). This tactic of discrediting female aviators through accusations of sexual impropriety was used time and again against those women who spoke out about the sexual assaults at Tailhook '91. The best-known case involved Lieutenant Paula Coughlin, the naval aviator who broke the story of Tailhook '91 to the press in June 1992. Here is Coughlin's description of what happened to her at approximately 11:30 p.m. on September 7, 1991, as she entered the third floor hallway:

> The man . . . moved in immediately behind me with his body pressed against mine. He was bumping me, pushing me forward down the passageway where the group on either side was pinching and then pulling at my clothing. The man then put both his hands down the front of my tanktop and inside my bra where he grabbed my breasts. I dropped to a forward crouch position and placed my hands on the wrists of my attacker in an attempt to remove his hands. . . . I sank my teeth into the fleshy part of the man's left forearm, biting hard. I thought I drew blood. I then turned and bit the man on the right hand. . . . [The man removed his hands], and another individual reached up under my skirt and grabbed the crotch of my panties. I kicked one of my attackers . . . I felt as though the group was trying to rape me. I was terrified and had no idea what was going to happen next. (F-27)

When she finally broke free she ran into one of the administrative suites. She sat in the dark, attempting, in her words, "to understand what had happened to me. . . . I was appalled not only by the brutality of the incident, but the fact that the group did that to me knowing I was both a fellow officer and an admiral's aide" (F-27).

Paula Coughlin was aide to Rear Admiral John W. Snyder at the time of the 1991 Tailhook convention. In reporting to Snyder what had happened to her, she opened herself up to accusations of having "broken rank," of having dared to call into question the "boys will be boys" mentality and activities of the Tailhook conventions. Shortly after the convention, the Navy began an internal investigation into Tailhook '91. At the same time, rumors were circulated about Coughlin in an attempt to discredit her — for example, that she was seen in the Rhino suite collecting souvenirs or she willingly had her legs shaved at the leg shaving booth set up in one of the suites (many of these claims were investigated later by Vander Schaaf and proven false).[6] In May 1992 the Navy issued its report stating that fourteen female officers and twelve civilian women had been assaulted by mostly junior Navy officers; only two men were identified. The following month Coughlin went to the press with her story, knowing that what had been identified in the Navy's report was only the tip of the iceberg. She also had further reason to suspect the accuracy of the report: the civilian hired by the Naval Investigative Service to interview her had pressured her to see him socially (his punishment, when Coughlin reported his actions, was a three-day suspension without pay).

Coughlin's statements to the press forced the Pentagon to initiate its own investigation, headed by Vander Schaaf, into the Navy's investigation of Tailhook '91. The first head to roll was that of naval secretary H. Lawrence Garrett III, who resigned in June 1992, shortly after Coughlin went to the press, amid questions about his involvement in Tailhook '91. Not only did he attend the convention, but he was in at least one of the third-floor hospitality suites. In his letter of resignation he took full responsibility for the Navy's handling of the incident. That same month, two top naval officers were relieved of their commands for failing to keep subordinates from displaying lewd banners about Representative Patricia Schroeder at a naval aviators' banquet in June 1992. Schroeder had been a vocal critic of Tailhook '91 and had lobbied for the new investigation.

In September 1992 three admirals in charge of the Navy's investigation of Tailhook '91 were relieved of their commands. Two, including Rear Admiral Duvall M. Williams, Jr., were forced to take early retirement, while a third, the naval inspector general, was reassigned. Witnesses reported that Williams, the commander of the Naval Investigative Service, had engaged in a "screaming match" in a Pentagon corridor with the assistant Navy secretary for manpower and reserve affairs, Barbara S. Pope. During this altercation Williams compared female Navy pilots to "go-go dancers, topless dancers or hookers."[7] In September four civilian women also sued the Tailhook Association and the Las Vegas Hilton over sexual assaults that occurred in both 1990 and 1991.[8]

The fallout from Vander Schaaf's investigation continued into the following year. In May 1993, six senior officers were reassigned; in October, three admirals were censured, and thirty were reprimanded. Navy secretary John H. Dalton also recommended the removal of Admiral Frank B. Kelso, the nation's top naval officer, but defense secretary Les Aspin refused to follow the recommendation. It was only continued pressure on Kelso from outside the military establishment that forced him to resign in February 1994. Thus, while a number of junior and senior officers received various forms of reprimands and Admiral Kelso succumbed to pressures to resign a few months before his planned retirement, not one person was court-martialed or found guilty of a criminal act. Only four men were officially charged with any criminal wrongdoing: Lieutenant Cole V. Cowden was charged with conduct unbecoming an officer; Marine Captain Gregory J. Bonam, Lieutenant David Samples, and Commander Gregory E. Tritt were charged with indecent assault. The cases against all four were eventually dismissed. Bonam made front-page news because he was the one identified by Coughlin. Two witnesses for the defense claimed they were with Bonam elsewhere at the time of the assault; another said he saw the assault, but the man who attacked Coughlin was not Bonam's height (he could not say who the man was). And Coughlin, having suffered not only the initial assault, but over two years of what she terms "covert and overt attacks," resigned from what had promised to be a successful career as a naval aviator on February 11, 1994, the day after the case against the last officer facing Tailhook charges was dismissed.[9]

Certainly nobody wants to send the wrong man to jail. But that is not the issue here. Vander Schaaf's report states that at least eighty-three women, and probably more, were assaulted at Tailhook '91. The male naval aviators hanging out on the third floor of the Hilton know who did it. And they are not talking. Why should they? What they did was engage in the time-honored and government-sanctioned activity of sacrificing women in rituals meant to prove their manhood and their right to define the rules and regulations of the military order.[10]

The decision of a military judge in February 1994 only confirmed this right. Captain William Vest, Jr., dismissed the cases against three officers who had been charged with failing to stop misconduct by junior officers at the convention; Vest argued that Kelso had indeed been privy to the sexual misconduct at the convention and had tried to cover it up when he "manipulated" an initial investigation. His actions thus compromised the cases against the three officers.[11] Yet the findings of this judge were not enough to convince the U.S. Senate two months later to vote to demote Kelso to the rank of two-star admiral because of his involvement in the Tailhook scandal, a move that would have cut his retirement pay by approximately $17,000 a year. Instead, they followed President Clinton's recommendation that Kelso be allowed to retire without a demotion, at the rank of four-star admiral. Clinton argued that the "evidence is not sufficiently compelling" to deny Kelso retirement at full rank.[12] This was the same evidence that was "compelling" enough to allow Vest to dismiss the cases against the three officers. Thus, through a legal sleight of hand and a selective questioning of credibility, all parties escaped punishment, although the seven female senators made certain their male colleagues took part in a full discussion of sexual harassment before the vote on Kelso's retirement.[13]

At the end of the summer of 1993 I was sitting in my office feeling the inevitable sense of excitement and dread that precedes the beginning of yet another semester of teaching and administrative work. I looked at the texts for my class on art and labor — Harry Braverman's *Labor and Monopoly Capital: The Degradation of Work in the Twentieth Century*, Barbara Melosh's *Engendering Culture: Manhood and Womanhood in New Deal Public Art and Theater*[14] — and wondered whether simply teaching about politics was enough, whether I ought not to be out actually doing something political. Acting on this sense of dissatisfaction, I called a friend known for her combination of intellectual and political activity and accompanied her to my first Women's Action Coalition (WAC) meeting in downtown Los Angeles.[15]

WAC identifies itself on one of its many flyers as "an open alliance of women committed to direct action on issues affecting the rights of all women. . . . WAC insists on economic parity and representation for all women, and an end to homophobia, racism, religious prejudice, and violence against women. We insist on every woman's right to quality health care, child care and reproductive freedom." The organization was formed in New York in January 1992, less than three months after the interrogation of Anita Hill by the all-white male Senate Judiciary Committee during the course of the hearings on Clarence Thomas's nomination to the Supreme Court.[16] This interrogation made blatantly clear over national television what many women in this country already knew — that the current political and legal system fails to adequately represent or reflect the experiences and concerns of women.

The hundred or so women who gathered in New York, many of them artists, committed themselves to resisting attempts to limit the gains made over the last two decades in the area of women's rights. They also committed themselves to advocating for substantial changes in the way the political and legal systems currently operate. WAC's goal is to keep issues of concern to all women in the public eye, and, whenever possible, to make alliances with other organizations who are attempting to achieve similar goals.[17] Since January 1992 WAC chapters have been set up in nearly every major city in the United States, as well as in Europe and Canada.

One of the upcoming actions discussed at the first WAC meeting I attended was a demonstration in San Diego on October 8 to protest the 1993 Tailhook Association convention. WAC had organized a highly successful demonstration the previous summer at Naval Air Station Miramar in San Diego that contributed to the cancellation of Tailhook '92. This year the Tailhook Association, a group composed primarily of Navy and marine aviators, obviously felt that the controversy had died down enough to allow them to resume their annual conventions without attracting any attention. I had vague memories of reading about the 1991 Tailhook convention in the newspapers the previous year, but had not heard much about it since. I volunteered to work on the committee organizing the action. One idea being tossed around at the first committee meeting I attended was the inclusion of some kind of exhibition — a "museum of horrors" perhaps — for the conference room WAC was renting at the convention hotel. The space was to be used as a press room, so the group felt there should be something strikingly visual for the press to photograph. This seemed to be an area where my art historical talents could be put to good use, so I offered to help organize the exhibition.

One of my first tasks was to familiarize myself with the Department of Defense inspector general's report on the 1991 Tailhook convention, which had been released in April 1993. Reading this report was like reading an anthropological account of another culture. Even though I recognized all too well the various forms of sexual harassment and sexual assault that occurred on the premises of the Las Vegas Hilton, they still appeared to me as foreign rituals, part of a social order far different from the one in which I lived. It struck me, therefore, that the exhibition would be more effective if it avoided sensationalizing or caricaturing the events of the 1991 convention, but instead "played it straight." What resulted was *Ritual and Sacrifice at Tailhook '91: A Documentary Exhibition*, composed of enlarged excerpts from the inspector general's report, drymounted on foam core, and replicas of various objects that had been part of Tailhook '91 and mentioned in the report, including the infamous "Rhino mural," T-shirts reading "Women are property" and "He-man woman hater's club," a toy tazer gun, and a can of shaving cream and razor (see figs. 14.1 and 14.2).[18]

In a short introductory panel I attempted to provide a framework for viewing the exhibition. Ritual is an essential aspect of every social order. Through rituals belief systems and modes of behavior are confirmed. Rituals often include sacrifice, either literal or symbolic. A victim is offered up so that the power of one segment of the social order over another is confirmed. Such rituals tend to multiply when established power relations are threatened. They are also the hallmark of highly militarized societies in which male warriors attempt to assert their dominance within the

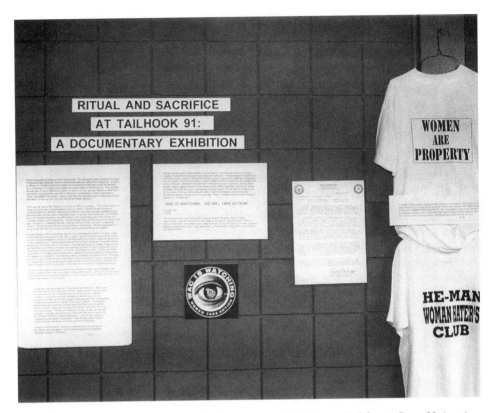

Ritual and Sacrifice at Tailhook '91: A Documentary Exhibition, California State University, Dominguez Hills, November 2, 1993 (photo by Frances Pohl).

social order, as well as their right to determine membership in military organizations. Those most different from them — women — are often the sacrificial victims, particularly women who dare to attempt entry into the sacred military domain.

It is in this light, I argued, that the 1991 Tailhook Association convention in Las Vegas must be understood. The multiple attacks on women documented in the investigative report of Derek J. Vander Schaaf, the deputy inspector general of the U.S. Department of Defense, were part of a well-orchestrated series of rituals, ones not new to the 1991 convention. These rituals were intended to put women "in their place," particularly those women who had become a part of this elite military order. Vander Schaaf notes in the foreword to his report that it was "important to understand that the events at Tailhook 91 did not occur in a historical vacuum. Similar behavior had occurred at previous conventions. The emerging pattern of some of the activities, such as the gauntlet, began to assume the aura of 'tradition' " (i).

Ritual and Sacrifice at Tailhook '91 was intended as a challenge to this "tradition." We hoped that the exhibition would bring to the public's attention the gruesome, often criminal nature of Tailhook rituals, and inspire people to call for an end to sexual harassment carried out with the implicit, if not explicit, approval of the U.S. military establishment. Vander Schaaf left no doubt as to who he felt should be held accountable for the events of Tailhook '91:

There was a serious breakdown of leadership at Tailhook 91. Misconduct went far beyond the "treatment of women" issues for which the Navy had enacted new policies in the years preceding Tailhook 91. Tailhook "traditions" such as the gauntlet, ballwalking, leg shaving, mooning, streaking and lewd sexual conduct significantly deviated from the standards of behavior that the Nation expects of its military officers. The disparity between the espoused Navy policies regarding officer conduct and the actual conduct of significant numbers of officers at Tailhook 91 could not have been greater. Officers who assaulted women, as well as those who engaged in improper sexual behavior, knew that their actions would not be condoned under any objective standard. These officers needed no "policeman at the elbow" to warn them of the wrongful nature of their actions and they, therefore, must bear a portion of the blame. Leaders in naval aviation, ranging from the squadron commanders to flag officers who tolerated a culture that engendered the misconduct also bear a portion of the blame. (XI-1)

Ritual and Sacrifice at Tailhook '91: A Documentary Exhibition, University of Nevada, Las Vegas, Nidech Women's Center, October 21, 1994 (Photo by Frances Pohl).

Yet Vander Schaaf also warned that the Navy would face many difficulties in dealing with the issues raised in his report. "Personal friendship, knowledge of past service and sacrifice by the officers involved, and a general reluctance to end or adversely impact otherwise promising military careers will further complicate the matter" (XI-1). He had "every expectation," however, "that the Navy [would] address the causes and conduct that combined to produce the disgrace of Tailhook 91," and therefore offered no specific recommendations. The Navy did not live up to Vander Schaaf's expectations. By October 1993, despite the fact that Vander Schaaf had referred 140 officers to the acting secretary of the Navy for consideration of appropriate action, only two male aviators had criminal charges pending against them; only four had been charged with any criminal wrongdoing.

Vander Schaaf's report helped break a "code of silence" that had been entered into by the majority of aviators who took part in the attacks at Tailhook '91. His investigation would never have taken place, however, without the testimony of one of the women assaulted, Lieutenant Paula Coughlin. WAC wanted to honor Coughlin for her courage (an "altar" to Coughlin was part of the exhibition). WAC also wanted to encourage others to follow her lead in refusing to be silent. Sexual violence against women in the military, and in society in general, will not end unless people express publicly an unwillingness to accept such violence as a "normal" part of daily life.

The WAC demonstration was a success. By publicizing the upcoming convention and staging a demonstration of 150 to 200 people on the night of October 8, WAC spoiled Tailhook's party. Only approximately 700 people attended, mostly retired Navy men and their spouses or girlfriends, who were treated to chanting protesters and television cameras.[19] This vastly reduced number was undoubtedly the result, in large part, of the Navy's decision to officially dissociate itself from the organization and to forbid officers from attending Tailhook conventions on Navy time. In addition, by October 1993 Tailhook had lost 80 percent of its corporate sponsors, membership had dropped 15 percent, and insurance premiums had skyrocketed, primarily because of the twelve lawsuits filed by women who claim they were sexually assaulted at Tailhook '91.

The exhibition was also a success.[20] One of the many press people who viewed it told me he felt the black and white text, the lack of editorializing, and the general understatement of the exhibition as a whole conveyed very effectively the violent nature of the events that had taken place. The four Tailhook convention participants who ventured into the press room (three women and one man) also appeared to realize the serious nature of the material, judging from the tense expressions on their faces. When I asked the man his reaction, he said that the exhibition was obviously based on "biased" information. The demonstrators who poured into the room once the march was over were much more willing to accept as valid the information drawn from the Department of Defense inspector general's report.

As the crowds thinned out and we prepared to dismantle the exhibition, it struck me that so much work and such a powerful visual display should not simply end up in someone's garage until the next demonstration. I had already been inspired enough during my initial involvement in the exhibition to put together a faculty research lecture about Tailhook '91 at Pomona College, so it seemed only logical to install the exhibition on campus for the week of my lecture. From that moment on the exhibition appeared to develop a life of its own, although one that certainly required considerable nurturing on my part. Over the next six months it appeared at California State University, Domingues Hills; California State University, Long Beach; and the University of California, Irvine. At each campus it was housed in the women's resource center, and at each campus the student response was the same: anger, sadness, disbelief, and a desire to see the exhibition continue to travel so others could be equally enlightened and enraged.

During the exhibition's Southern California sojourn, I also began to feel that the information on Tailhook needed to be presented more completely and in a different format so that it could reach a wider audience. Therefore, I began doing further research on the 1991 Tailhook convention and on the history of the Tailhook Association, reworking the material I had already gathered and following the continuing developments in the Tailhook saga in the local press.

Having spent many months after the San Diego Tailhook demonstration gathering and writing up the above information, I decided to submit the results to Z *Magazine*, which describes itself as "an independent political magazine of critical thinking on political, cultural, social and economic life in the United States." As the article had arisen out of a political action, I thought it appropriate that I should submit it to a political, rather than academic, journal. It appeared in the June 1994 issue under the title "Tailhook '91: Women, Violence and the U.S. Navy."[21] That same month I took the Tailhook exhibition on the road to the National Women's Studies Association's (NWSA) annual meeting in Ames, Iowa. As a result of its appearance at this meeting, many women's studies professors contacted me and asked to have the exhibition shown on their campus.

The site of the first showing of the exhibition after the NWSA meeting could not have been more fitting: Las Vegas, Nevada.[22] Paula Coughlin's federal suit against the Las Vegas Hilton for failing to provide adequate security during the Tailhook convention had gone to trial September 12 and, fortunately, was still in progress when the exhibition opened at the Nidech Women's Center at the University of Nevada, Las Vegas, on October 21.[23] Because of the trial, the local media were particularly interested in the exhibition and in the talk I presented at the opening. Articles appeared in the local newspapers, and the local television station devoted a portion of its six o'clock news to the event, although its "coverage" of the exhibition included digitally erasing the dildo on the replica of the "Rhino mural" included in the show.

The audience for my talk was also much more varied than at previous venues. It included not only a former Navy officer and a paralegal for the law firm representing the Tailhook Association's insurance company,[24] but also the wife, daughter, and mother of the judge in the Coughlin trial. U.S. district judge Philip Pro was, of course, unable to attend my afternoon lecture, but wrote to me after the trial was over. I was, needless to say, somewhat nervous when I saw the return address on the envelope. Had I broken a law or libeled someone during my presentation? He wrote, however, simply to correct a misperception of mine regarding the reasons he had refused to permit Vander Schaaf's report from being entered as evidence in the case. In my talk I had quoted a *Los Angeles Times* reporter, who had written that Judge Pro had not allowed the report to be entered as evidence because he found it to be too "flimsy." Rather, according to Judge Pro, his decision had been based on the federal rules of evidence regarding hearsay. While the report itself could not be used as evidence, both sides in the case could, and did, introduce testimony or evidence from the report where hearsay was not an issue.[25]

On October 28 the jury in the Coughlin trial handed down its decision ordering the Las Vegas Hilton to pay Coughlin $1.7 million in compensatory damages. Three days later it awarded her a further $5 million in punitive damages, having determined that the Hilton had acted with malice. Of course, the Hilton is appealing these decisions, which somewhat dampens Coughlin's victory. Yet an even greater pall was cast over this victory by the death of Lieutenant Kara Hultgreen, the first female F-14 combat pilot, on October 26, two days before the end of the trial. Hultgreen was killed when her plane crashed during a training mission off Southern California.[26] Equal rights for women in the military also means equal risks in what is ultimately a dangerous profession. Women who are willing to die for their country certainly deserve to be treated with courtesy and respect while they are alive.

The events surrounding Tailhook '91 raise many questions. Given the way the U.S. military trains its soldiers, could we have expected the naval aviators who congregated in Las Vegas in September 1991 to have acted in any other way? Will the lifting of the ban on women flying combat duty result in a kinder, gentler military? Has the sensitivity training organized for male aviators and the toll-free telephone line set up for advice and counseling for victims of sexual harassment made any difference?[27] Is there any connection between male heterosexual misconduct and homophobia in the military (is it just a coincidence that the public controversy surrounding Tailhook '91 occurred at the same time as the controversy around gays and lesbians in the military)?

I am not going to attempt to answer these questions here. Instead, I would like to end this essay with a brief account of a telephone conversation I had the morning of October 13, 1993. A man named Vincent called after having read an article on the San Diego demonstration in the *Los Angeles Times*.[28] He wanted to know what *Heterodoxy* was. The *Los Angeles Times* article had mentioned that *Heterodoxy* had printed an article on the "Tailhook Witchhunt."[29] I gave him a lengthy description of the journal as a right-wing publication run by two neoleftists turned neoconservatives that often attacked attempts by educational institutions to diversify their curriculum and institute things such as sexual harassment policies. There was silence at the other end of the line. "Were you thinking of subscribing?" I asked. "Well, I don't think so," he responded. "I subscribe to the *Hook*." The *Hook* is the Tailhook Association publication. Vincent was, as I discovered, a Navy pilot and a member of Tailhook. It appears he thought *Heterodoxy* was a Navy publication, or, as a colleague of mine suggested, perhaps he thought it had something to do with heterosexuality. Or perhaps he only used this as an excuse to call me, because after I had told him what *Heterodoxy* was, he asked whether he could talk to me a little bit about women in the military.

Forty-five minutes later we ended our conversation. He was not hostile. Rather, he seemed confused. The Navy is a man's world, he said. The raunchy mentality that soldiers develop is necessary for their survival in combat situations. Women and men are just different. Women are supposed to be feminine, to wear skirts and high heels and perfume. If they stop wearing these clothes and start doing things that guys do, how are we going to be able to tell men and women apart? War has been a male thing for thousands of years. How can women do what needs to be done in the military? They aren't strong enough.

I suggested that all men and all women don't have to be the same; that diversity is a positive factor; that women are as strong as, or even stronger than, men in many ways; that being a "man" did not have to entail proving that you were not a "woman"; and that teaching his teenage sons that being called a "girl" was not an insult might begin to help change things. But this seemed only to confuse Vincent even more. He just could not conceive of relationships between men and women, girls and boys, being any different than they are now. "The guys have been talking a lot about this," he said. "They're hunkering down. They're drawing a line. They don't want any more women trying to be men."

I hung up the phone, feeling that I had spent too long in academia speaking a language and living a life that had little relevance to the language and lives of men like Vincent and his friends. What will it take, I wondered, to draw them out of their corner? What will it take to help them erase the line they have drawn between men and women? Certainly not another Tailhook convention.

NOTES

1. Derek J. Vander Schaaf, *Tailhook 91 — Part 2: Events at the 35th Annual Tailhook Symposium* (Washington, DC: Department of Defense, Inspector General, 1993), V-1. All subsequent quotations from the body of this report will be indicated by a page reference after the quotation. St. Martin's Press also issued a trade version, *The Tailhook Report*, in 1993.

2. "Appendix B: Tailhook Association Submittal," in Vander Schaaf, *Tailhook 91*, B5–B6.

3. Ibid., B6.

4. According to a *Sixty Minutes* segment on the Tailhook incident in the fall of 1993, certain officers who admitted assaulting women were granted immunity so that they would testify against others. Gregory Geiss, who admitted to organizing the gauntlet and participating in one particular assault on an eighteen-year-old woman, was one such officer granted immunity. He said on camera that the convention was basically a "three-day bachelor party."

5. During my visit to Las Vegas to install the exhibition in the Women's Center at the University of Nevada, I was told that, according to a woman who worked at the Hilton, the hotel knew that the Tailhook Association would be paying to have the carpet replaced after each convention.

6. Probably the most vicious attacks on Coughlin appeared in the October 1993 issue of *Heterodoxy* in a front-page article entitled "Tailhook Witch-Hunt," by David Horowitz and Michael Kitchen. Horowitz is one of the founding editors of *Heterodoxy*, a conservative publication that takes particular pleasure in attacking feminist scholarship and political campaigns. Michael Kitchen is a former Navy officer and, in 1993, editor of a publication titled the *Gauntlet*.

7. See Eric Schmitt, "Senior Navy Officers Suppressed Sex Investigation, Pentagon Says: Scathing Report Cites Hostility Toward Women," *New York Times*, September 25, 1992, A1, A20.

8. See "4 Sue Navy Flier Group over Sexual Assaults," *New York Times*, September 11, 1992, A24.

9. See "Case against Last Officer Facing Tailhook Charges Is Dismissed," *Los Angeles Times*, February 10, 1994, A2; "Woman Who First Reported Tailhook Sex Scandal Resigns," *Los Angeles Times*, February 11, 1994, A18.

10. Vander Schaaf notes in his report that during interviews conducted by himself and his investigative team, "many senior officers repeatedly referred to the aviation lieutenants and lieutenant commanders as 'the kids.' To us, their use of this term, in context, symbolized an attitude where irresponsible behavior and conduct were accepted manifestations of high-spirited youth" (X-2).

11. See "Military Judge Says Adm. Kelso Saw Misconduct, Covered It Up," *Los Angeles Times*, February 9, 1994, A12.

12. Quoted in Michael Ross and Karen Tumulty, "Senate to Retire Kelso at 4 Stars, after Fiery Debate," *Los Angeles Times*, April 20, 1994, A28.

13. Ibid.

14. Harry Braverman, *Labor and Monopoly Capital: The Degradation of Work in the Twentieth Century* (New York: Monthly Review Press, 1974); Barbara Melosh, *Engendering Culture: Manhood and Womanhood in New Deal Public Art and Theater* (Washington, DC: Smithsonian Institution Press, 1991).

15. This scholar/activist was Jennifer Rycenga, certainly a role model of political integrity and activism if there ever was one.

16. For further information on the founding of the Women's Action Coalition, see Margo Mifflin, "Feminism's New Face," *Artnews* 91 (November 1992): 120–25. See also Charleen Touchette, "Multicultural Strategies for Aesthetic Revolution in the Twenty-first Century," in *New Feminist Criticism: Art, Identity, Action*, ed. Joanna Frueh et al. (New York: HarperCollins, 1994), 202–4.

17. For example, the Los Angeles chapter of WAC has taken part in demonstrations organized by labor groups like Justice for Janitors and AIDS organizations like AIDS Project Los Angeles.

18. The exhibition came together as the result of the collaborative efforts of Kate Coyer, Sean Duffy, Lynne Kaneshiro, Molly Reid, Anne Summa, Steve Comba, and myself.

19. See Ed Jahn, "Tailhook Meeting in San Diego Feels Chill: Women's Action Coalition Stages a Protest March," *San Diego Union-Tribune*, October 9, 1993, B3, B8; and Michael Granberry, "No Retreat, No Surrender at Tailhook '93," *Los Angeles Times*, October 10, 1993, A1, A42.

20. See Robin Abcarian, "Tailhook 1993: Guys in the Grip of Denial," *Los Angeles Times*, October 13, 1993, E1, E2.

21. Frances K. Pohl, "Tailhook '91: Women, Violence and the U.S. Navy," *Z Magazine*, June 1994, 40–46. This essay is an expanded version of the *Z Magazine* piece.

22. After Las Vegas, the exhibition traveled to Colorado Springs to be included in the Colorado College Symposium "Sexuality and Gender" (January 18–21, 1995) and to Denver, Colorado, for a two-week showing in early March at the Auraria campus of the Community College of Denver (Metropolitan State College of Denver cosponsored this venue).

23. Coughlin had settled her suit against the Tailhook Association out of court, just before her case against the Las Vegas Hilton went to trial.

24. Susan Greene, "Tailhook Scandal the Focus of Traveling Exhibit at UNLV," *Las Vegas Review-Journal*, October 22, 1994, 1B–2B. Greene notes that the two individuals "shook their heads in disapproval, but declined to comment on Pohl's speech."

25. U.S. District Judge Philip M. Pro to Frances Pohl, October 28, 1994. Judge Pro included a copy of his order regarding the defendant Hilton's motion to exclude from evidence at trial the Department of Defense Inspector General's report regarding Tailhook '91, parts 1 and 2. I wrote to thank Judge Pro for taking the time to write to me and to ask whether he knew of any good summaries of the trial. Unfortunately, he didn't, but he did let me know that he had had a chance to see the Tailhook exhibition and thought it was well done (Judge Philip Pro to Frances Pohl, November 7, 1994).

26. See Tony Perry, "Crash Kills First Female F-14 Combat Pilot," *Los Angeles Times*, October 27, 1994, A1, A33.

27. Not according to the statements of four servicewomen representing each of the military services, who testified in March 1994 in front of the House Armed Services Committee. These women described having suffered sexual harassment ranging from unwanted kisses to verbal abuse during basic training. They also described how they were then punished or put in dead-end jobs for complaining, while those who harassed them went unpunished or received only mild reprimands. "I began my naval career on a fast track toward advancement," stated Navy Lieutenant Darlene Simmons. "These events have completely derailed my ambitions. Despite the rhetoric, the Navy will not tolerate those who report sexual harassment." "Servicewomen Tell Panel of Sex Harassment," *Los Angeles Times*, March 10, 1994, A12.

28. Abcarian, "Tailhook 1993."

29. See n. 6.

FIFTEEN

No Cultural Icon: Marisela Norte

MICHELLE HABELL-PALLÁN

> I am no cultural icon
> not one of the ten most beautiful poets in Los Angeles
> I am not your worst enemy
> Not your urban nightmare
> I don't even have my license yet
> I am the one that cut the label out
> — Marisela Norte, "976–LOCA"

Although spoken-word artist Marisela Norte's Latina/Chicana narrator rejects the title of "cultural icon" and in the process, rejects the burden of representing an unchanging notion of Chicana identity, local Los Angelinos call Norte the "East L.A. Ambassador of Culture." Born in 1955 to Mexican parents who immigrated to Southern California in the late 1930s and early 1940s, Norte recalls that her father banned English from their home. But growing up during the 1950s and 1960s, Norte learned to speak impeccable standard English at public schools and from television, radio, and films.

Often praised for her cinematic depiction of Los Angeles cityscapes, Norte skillfully constructs sweeping takes of Los Angeles public spaces. Her forte, however, lies in her ability to focus her audience's attention on images that usually get panned over by less keen observers. Generally, her body of work thematizes the tensions many working-class women feel about their lives, specifically the tension generated between the desire for forward movement in the struggle for both economic and social equality and an immobility that seems at times impossible to break. The ribbon that ties these different components of her writing together (to make Norte the consummate storyteller she has become) is her gift of humor and mastery of irony, which work in combination to create countermeaning. As such, she is "no cultural icon." She demands to be known as an important writer and spoken-word artist who struggles to make visible the practices of social inequality in everyday life in Los Angeles by seizing "the most advanced forms of modern technology to present [her] experiences and aspirations to a wider world."[1] What emerges from her struggle is a particularly useful form of cultural politics, one that wages its battle on the terrain of popular culture.

What sets her writing apart is that for approximately the last ten years, it has tended to circulate more often in spoken-word form — in live performances, on compact discs and cassettes — than as written text.[2] In fact, her best-known collection of spoken-word narratives is a compact disc entitled *Norte/word*.[3]

What is the significance of Marisela Norte using one of the most advanced forms of audio technology to present her experience? Those who have limited access to the production and distribution of the dominant modes of representation such as commercial film, popular music, and so forth find more accessible formats, such as live performance and compact discs, to intervene in discussions about everyday life in the United States and to represent themselves and their concerns, fears, and hopes about and for the future. Formats such as spoken-word compact discs are crucial in the construction of new subjects for political identification because they open a space, a countersite, a condition of possibility where writers like Norte can publicly imagine new ways of constructing racial, ethnic, gendered, and economic identities and where the struggle for social equality can be articulated.[4]

Cultural Politics

What is at stake when Norte's narratives describe the experiences of Chicanas living in Los Angeles, experiences the dominant culture rarely depicts with depth or complexity? Norte's narratives engage in cultural politics. This "politics" is not conceptualized in the traditional way we have come to understand the term, as in relation to voting and governmental policy making. Cultural politics — the struggle to acquire, maintain, or resist power — instead emerges most often as a struggle over the supposed superiority or inferiority of a culture, over what is a "central" or "marginal" social group, over official and "forgotten" histories, and over external and internal representations of social relations. In general, cultural politics engages in the struggle over meaning within a context of inequality.[5] For instance, Norte's narrators struggle to define on their own terms — from an unprivileged perspective — the meanings of particular places like Los Angeles and the U.S.-Mexico border and the function of institutions such as family and marriage, and to critique the practices of violence against women.

In the process of describing the contradictions contained in these places, institutions, and practices from the perspective of a working-class Chicana, Norte's narratives contest the meaning and function of these formations. Her narrator's point of view often opposes that of the dominant culture; yet her narratives are more complex than a simple reversal of negative stereotypes. They counter images of working class and poor immigrant Latinas formed by anti-immigrant campaigns, and they refuse to represent Chicana poets in the standard terms: as earthy goddesses, holders of uncomplicated mythic pasts. Instead, her narratives represent the conflicts and ambivalence that arise around cultural identity and in relation to places, institutions, and practices.[6] In doing so, they open a space — although imaginary — where the possibility of life without hierarchy and exploitation can emerge.

Since cultural politics determines both the meanings of social practices and the groups that will define these meanings, and because cultural politics involves the struggle over what and whose images of social life will be validated on mainstream television and radio and what images should remain unseen, it becomes especially important for those who come from traditionally aggrieved groups, and who are determined to transform relations of social inequality, to pay attention to it. As Glenn Jordan and Chris Weedon explain,

> Cultural politics are also concerned with subjectivity and identity, since culture plays a central role in constituting our sense of ourselves. . . . The forms of subjectivity that we inhabit play a crucial part in determining whether we accept or contest existing power relations. Moreover, for marginalized and oppressed groups, the construction of new and resistant identities is a key dimension of a wider political struggle to transform society.[7]

Questions of subjectivity and identity also invoke thorny questions of cultural authenticity. Put simply, "identity" can be understood as how one perceives oneself, while "subjectivity" can be seen as how one imagines oneself in relation to others. In her ground-breaking writing on Chicana/o representational practices, Rosa Linda Fregoso questions the existence of "authentic," immutable cultural identity and argues against the production of ethnic (specifically Chicano) identity built on "a political model of subjectivity grounded in a notion of a fixed self. In this formulation, cultural identity appears as an authentic essence, located in a core subject, whose identity is one of 'being,'"[8] an identity that was the basis for the male-centered subject of Chicano cultural nationalism.

In contrast, Fregoso understands identity as a formation — one becomes a "subject in process" and is never a "fixed self." This understanding allows one to recognize that the production of cultural identity is one that is dynamic and subject to historical, geographical, and political change. Thus, what was once considered to constitute Chicana and Chicano identity is not completely lost in the past, but does in some way inform the construction of a future identity, though it does not necessarily determine it. Fregoso's argument assumes that categories of race/ethnicity, gender, sexuality, and nationality are never biologically given or inborn, immutable characteristics, but are instead shaped by history and constructed through the stories people tell about them. This assumption allows people (subjects) in their capacity as artists (and as everyday people) to reshape cultural, gendered, and political identity. Norte's narratives reshape Chicana identity by figuratively "cutting old labels out."

The protagonists of Norte's spoken-word narratives are subjects in the process of "becoming." As they inhabit multiple subject positions as women who refuse traditional marriage and as border-crossing laborers, they enact what Fregoso discusses at length, "an alternative formulation of cultural identity."[9] This alternative formulation resists a strictly defined Chicana identity. The tension Norte writes about as her protagonists resist the pushes and pulls of the Chicano and the dominant culture fuels their ambivalence about the two, yet their identification with aspects of multiple cultures (Latino, Chicano, Mexican, and African American) allows them to turn, as Fregoso so aptly describes it, "the ambivalence of cultural identity into a politics of political identification." That ambivalence leaves room for the construction of something else.

Irony as Cultural Politics

Cultural politics is equally important as a more traditional form of political struggle, in that it helps to construct a space, often in the realm of popular culture, where the imagining of new identities based on new forms of social relations can take place. Because of its accessibility, most people have investments in popular culture, hence its importance in the transformation of daily life.

Norte's narratives use complex irony to call attention to gaps in the logic of the status quo where meaning and countermeanings can be produced and where new political formation might emerge. Irony, defined in traditional terms, is a rhetorical technique used to hide "what is actually the case, however, not in order to deceive, but achieve rhetorical or artistic effect."[10] In Norte's work, and in the work of many artists from marginalized communities, the use of irony not only aspires to a "rhetorical or artistic effect," but also strives to make apparent relations of power. Irony and understatement require audiences to read between the lines. In the gap between the lines, a space emerges where the possibility of imagining the future based on economic and gender equality exists. By asking her audience to read between the lines, she does not dictate what the future should be, but invites them to help imagine it.

The struggle to produce countermeaning takes place most visibly and immediately in the titles of Norte's spoken-word narratives. Titles such as "Peeping Tom Tom Girl," "Act of the Faithless," and "Three Little Words" reverse readers' expectations. With slight alterations — faithless instead of faithful, words instead of pigs — and new combinations, such as peeping Tom with tom girl instead of tom boy, these titles subvert standard meanings. As we shall see in the following discussion, these subtle ironic reversals — commentaries in themselves — critique the status quo while provocatively suggesting the content of the narratives.

Situatedness in the Chicano Community

Even though Norte's narratives take issues of race, ethnicity, class, and gender as inextricably intertwined, Norte's cultural production is compelling because her situated experiences as a working-class Chicana enable her to represent general social problems. For instance, her narratives represent the way violence against women is experienced in particular communities but also exists as a practice sanctioned by patriarchal culture in general. Class position, however, does have a certain effect on her work. That she rides and writes on the bus — out of necessity, not by choice — impacts the form and content of her writing enormously. Never having owned a car, she has ridden public transportation for the last ten years back and forth to work and to readings.[11] In the liner notes of her compact disc titled *Norte/word*, Norte describes the conditions under which she produces her narratives most of the time: "I write on the bus, the No. 18 bus especially. That's the bus that's taken me from East Los Angeles over the bridge into downtown L.A. for most of my life." For the most part, Norte explains, her narratives are as long "as it takes to get from one bus stop to another."

Norte's narrative entitled "Peeping Tom Tom Girl" introduces her listeners to the point of view of her narrators and to the larger issues in Norte's poetry. The title itself complicates the meaning of voyeurism. "Peeping Tom," in most cases, describes a man who gets pleasure from watching women without their permission. "Tom Girl" used in place of "Tom Boy" suggests that the narrator is a "femme" female rebel. Norte combines "Peeping Tom" with "Tom Girl" to imply that her narrator watches women, not for voyeuristic pleasure, but in an empathetic way. Because the narrator identifies with the women, we do not see the women through the male's eyes — they are not viewed as sexual objects — nor does she see them as racial, ethnic, or economic threats. Shifting the perspective from a "Peeping Tom's" to a "Tom Girl's" is just one example of how cultural politics is employed.

What Norte's narrators see from the bus happening to women on the streets of East and downtown Los Angeles are scenes perhaps not visible from a room on the city's (wealthy) west side. Moving through economically marginalized sections of the east side and downtown, the narrator in "Peeping Tom Tom Girl" critiques the social practices that force working-class single women to live at the edge of society, on the street, and/or without a job. The character who narrates "Peeping Tom Tom Girl" is no longer the object of another's representation; she claims her own position as subject.[12] She is at once both the Chicana "I" and the "eye" who experiences, witnesses, interprets, constructs, and transcodes into images events as they occur in her everyday life. The narrative takes place on the bus and describes the lives of several women:

> I am a peeping tom girl / and from my seat on the downtown bus / I have been driven through, been witness to, invaded by las vidas de ellas / I've made myself up to be the girl who sits in the back with a black mask over her eyes / the high school doll too anxious to experiment / la muchachita stuffed into the pink lampshade dress / who listens as her parents argue through different neighborhoods / she shuts her eyes and tries to memorize / the menus on the chalkboards outside / and then there is this woman.[13]

As a spectator "peeping" from the window of the "downtown" bus, the narrator is drawn to "las vidas de ellas" (the women's lives). Riding the bus through different Los Angeles neighborhoods, the narrator witnesses the economic stratification of Chicanas and Latinas.[14] She also shows that there is more to Latina experiences than California governor Pete Wilson's infamous anti-immigrant campaign wants us to see. For instance, she passes "The widow with the gladiolus / who never misses a day of forgiveness" and "the countess," who "sleeps in doorways / hefty bag wardrobe / broken tiara / and too much rouge." This countess "counts todos los dias en ingles y español [she counts each/every day in English and Spanish], she is nuestra señora de la reina perdida que cayó en Los Angeles." Using this phrase to describe both the homeless woman and the city's east side, the narrator ironically twists the meaning of the original name of Los Angeles — El Pueblo de Nuestra Señora la Reina de los Angeles de Porciúncula (The Town of Our Lady the Queen of Angels of Porciúncula) becomes "nuestra señora de la reina perdida que cayó en Los Angeles" (Our Lady of the Lost Queen Who Fell in Los Angeles) — in order to comment critically on the living conditions of women surviving in the city. This pun on the Spanish name of Los Angeles is characteristic of the linguistic strategies Norte uses to articulate social criticism. She gives new meaning to the name, making it describe more accurately the women's lives. The Spanish pastoral myth of Los Angeles's limitless abundance is contrasted with the dwindling chances of survival of many Latinas in the city.[15] On the same bus ride, the narrator shares a different view of the city with her friend "Silent, who taught a friend of mine how to flick her cigarette out of a car window and be so bad in the process / Silent who spends a lot of time in the welfare office now filling out those pink and blue forms / Can't find a baby-sitter, a good man, a job . . . she rides those buses I do / balancing boxes of Pampers marked half-price / and pulling two kids / a pink one and a blue one / behind her on a string.[16]

The unifying component of the narrative is its theme: single women facing economic hardship in Los Angeles. The sympathetic representation of the women and their living conditions in "Peeping Tom Tom Girl" — the widow, the homeless "countess," and the "Silent" single mother — generally falls to the margins of mainstream cultural expression.

She Cleaned Up

Norte's construction of a space within the imaginary where she can represent "real sites," or places, from a Chicana vantage point is an important intervention. As "countersites," her narratives are a space where an alternative to the representation of Chicana and Latina identity maintained by U.S. mainstream culture can be imagined and articulated. In addition to showing that different women share common ground in their struggle to survive in the face of economic hardship and constantly negotiate representations of sexuality in their everyday lives, Norte's work illustrates that place also shapes Chicana experiences. The urban spaces the narrator in "Peeping Tom Tom Girl" travels through are contrasted with the U.S.-Mexico border-crossing experience in "Act of the Faithless." The title itself, "Act of the Faithless," makes a pun on the institution of marriage, which ideally functions as an "Act of the Faithful." It also articulates one way geopolitical lines drawn between national and economic communities are negotiated by women who live and work across national borders:

It was a Holiday Inn / downtown El Paso / where she crossed the line daily / paso por paso / mal paso que das / al cruzar la Frontera / [step by step, mis-stepping as you cross the border] / There was the work permit / sealed in plastic / like the smile / she flashed every morning / to the same uniformed eyes / She cleaned up / decorated her home with objects of rejection / souvenirs turistas left behind / salt and pepper shakers / shaped like ten gallon hats / Lone Star state of the art back scratchers / all the way from Taiwan / She cleaned up / after everyone else / leaving her mess at home / in neat piles / like his laundry / waiting to be washed / cleansed / delivered from evil.[17]

Considering that Norte herself travels across unfriendly urban terrains to reach her job, it is not surprising that many of Norte's narratives recognize and pay tribute to the lives of the women who must constantly travel across unfriendly terrains such as those of the U.S.-Mexico border to reach their places of employment. Though similar in this respect, Norte's urban experience is significantly different from the woman's border experience: Norte does not have to flash documentation "sealed in plastic" to travel and to and from work.

Employed as a domestic worker who crosses the U.S.-Mexico border, the woman in the text — who we find later to be the narrator's aunt — crosses the borderlands every day to get to her place of employment. For people like the narrator's aunt, this borderland space, among other things, is a threatening social space. The aunt can cross the U.S.-Mexico border because she possesses the documents, "the work permit / sealed in plastic . . . she flashed . . . to the same uniformed eyes," that she requires to make a living on the U.S. side of the border. But for those left without documentation, the national borders are a site of exclusion and many times death.

"Act of the Faithless" represents the ways private spaces are affected by public spaces. Narrated in the past tense, the niece describes what her aunt did on the U.S. side of the border: "She cleaned up," literally and figuratively. That is, "she cleaned up" literally by performing her job at the Holiday Inn and cleaning up after her husband in their home in the Ciudad Juarez, while the narrator uses the figurative expression "she cleaned up" to make an ironic comment about the goods she collected. With the discarded objects the tourists have left behind at the Holiday Inn, the narrator's aunt practices a type of Chicana *rasquache*. Norte's description of the aunt's home illustrates what Jennifer González describes as "the practice of 'domesticana.' "[18] In this narrative, the objects the aunt gathers and arranges are not, as González explains, merely a "collection of things," but are rather a symbolic representation of a life lived across the U.S.-Mexico border. The aunt situates the discarded objects in a new context — her home — in which they signify differently. No longer "objects of rejection," the souvenirs become concrete representations of her life, her relation to other people and other places.

The objects the aunt collects, like the "Lone Star state of the art back scratchers / all the way from Taiwan," are themselves culturally hybrid, given that they are manufactured in Taiwan and sold to tourists as authentic Texan artifacts. These souvenirs, like the people who are paid to make them, play their part in a late twentieth-century international tourist economy. These objects too, like the aunt, cross national borders according to the demands of the tourist market. The identity the aunt constructs with these objects is determined in part by the market that brings those "Lone Star back scratchers . . . from Taiwan" to the El Paso/Ciudad Juarez border.

By chronicling the experiences of her aunt, and of many women who must cross the border daily to earn wages, Norte's text critiques the constructions of space that privilege patriarchal practices. Though "uniformed eyes" fail to see the complexity of the aunt's identity, she is more than a "smile" with a work permit. On the Mexican side of the border, she constructs different identities for herself — one of which is that of wife. Juxtaposing the image of the aunt who works as a maid on the U.S. side with the image of her as devoted Mexican wife, Norte demonstrates how this woman must negotiate different systems of patriarchal practice. If on the U.S. side she is seen only as labor for the turistas, she also must serve her husband at home, who leaves "his laundry / waiting to be washed / cleansed / delivered from evil." Though she may not be "othered" by her citizen status in Mexico, she is discriminated against because of her gender.

Besides articulating a narrative about a woman's experience on the U.S.-Mexico border, "Act of the Faithless" also critiques the double standard that women are subjected to in traditional Latino culture. As a child the narrator had romanticized both the marriage of her aunt and uncle and marriage in general. The young narrator dreams of home life "in Ciudad Juarez, on the corner of Revolución and Eternidad" where she "wanted to be the child bride, mixing up Martinis in [her] ten gallon hat." But the narrative goes on to explain how her aunt and uncle's marriage was anything but ideal. Years later, after his death, the narrator realizes the uncle was a womanizer, and she reflects on his life.

> I thought of my Uncle / wondering how many times / he had snuck up the back way / for a dip in this luxury sized pool of regret / knowing that after his swim / there would be food and clean clothes / waiting at home / clothes that would surely take him / into the night and possibly / the next couple of days.

After the narrator realizes the marital situation her aunt had to negotiate, knowing that her aunt was required to prepare the "food and clean clothes" for her unfaithful husband, she takes on a different view of marriage. She recognizes how relations between men and women in traditional patriarchal cultures favor the subordination of women and how patriarchal ideology supports and reproduces that inequality. Despite the fact that her marriage did not correspond to romanticized images of matrimony found in women's magazines and romance novels, the aunt endures. While watching her aunt clean at the Holiday Inn, the niece listens to the advice she offers. Handing the niece a pair of women's sunglasses she found in her husband's jacket, the aunt tells her to "cuidate los ojos" — take care of her eyes — because there is "too much you should see." The aunt's advice is double edged: she seems to be both warning her young niece to be aware of possibly harmful situations and giving her hope that there is something worth looking forward to. Leaving unspoken exactly what she herself sees and what the niece "should see," their exchange is interrupted by a lounging Holiday Inn tourist. Displaying a complete lack of cultural consciousness, the tourist yells — American accent and all — "[e]x-cuse me . . . um . . . Senorita, can you come over here por favor?" The narrative articulates for the aunt and niece what they cannot say to him directly:

> Senorita / and the name stings like the sun / and my aunt / she cusses him out real good in Spanish / under her breath. . . . The man in the chair / is still trying to get her attention / "Maria . . . Marrria! / only I can't hear it anymore / only his lips are moving / I tug on her arm / I point at the man / now gone silent / there is too much to see / she said / too much to remember.

This concluding segment of "Act of the Faithless" critiques the dominant culture's narrow vision of Latinas. The aunt knows that the tourist with uninformed eyes mistakes her for a servant. Though Maria isn't her name, he sees her as he probably sees most Latina women — as a homogeneous group and as indistinguishable. And though the aunt's defiant gesture (she cannot "cuss him out" aloud because if she does, she will jeopardize her job) may not be considered radical, it does demonstrate her self-pride and self-knowledge and her dissatisfaction with the status quo. How-ever, the narrative ends more realistically than idealistically: the tourist remains ignorant of his offensive racist and classist actions, demonstrating that there may be too much "to see." Also, the aunt, who is restricted by her own cultural system, fails to tell the niece not to idealize the institution of marriage. It is rather through her acute observations that the narrator arrives at this conclusion. Thus Norte's narrative does not characterize women as victims, but instead critiques the cultural restrictions they constantly negotiate.

Estoy Destroyed

By discussing Norte's work in the context of patriarchy, I do not intend to "universal-ize" the term. Instead, I want to emphasize that there are different formations of patriarchy operating in different cultures across the globe and within U.S. contempo-rary culture. "Three Little Words," Norte's narrative about childhood summers at the movies, demonstrates the specific ways patriarchal practices of the dominant culture converge on the bodies of Chicanas and others. To make visible these practices, Norte incorporates samples from mass culture into her narratives. Like rap artists, Norte strategically appropriates "the tools used against [her] to inject [herself] into the venues from which [she has] been excluded."[19] Those "tools" include images found in mass popular culture such as Mexican and American television, movies, music, magazines, and newspapers. Although mass culture tends to misrep-resent women and people of color, Norte self-consciously ironizes, inverts, and subverts popular culture stories by sampling them into a new hybrid reflective of her multiply inflected subjectivity. Her dialogue with mass culture brings to the forefront her situatedness as a gendered subject, citizen, and member of an aggrieved ethnic group.

Using images from mass culture allows Norte to critique sexist practices as they manifest themselves in U.S. popular culture. Her text suggests that these practices constantly work against women's attempt to construct themselves as subjects and to construct their identity outside limited gender roles. "Three Little Words" highlights the objectification of women by defamiliarizing the image of mutilated and dismembered female bodies found in the realm of popular movies. Norte's work situates the image of violence against women in a new context in order to combat the ease with which representations of violence against women are consumed and asks the audience to question the representations of violence against women.

"Three Little Words" sounds like the title of the well-known children's story "Three Little Pigs." In what follows, however, Norte's narrator describes a story no child should have to see. In "Three Little Words," Norte suggests that popular culture, through horror films, "normalizes" the image of a bloody, dismembered female body:

> It was my cousins' grandmother who took us to the movies and fell asleep during Bloodfeast / so we got to sit through it twice / and for weeks after all we could talk about was the gigantic horse's tongue / that was extracted from the pink lipped mouth of / another buxom blonde / and there is a picture of her / laying across / a fuzzy white bedspread / in a Florida motel room / and there is blood everywhere / enough for all of us / five cousins / to remember her by / this is the image that falls under childhood memory / it is not the smell of grandmother's tamales cooking on a wooden stove.[20]

In other words, Norte's text defamiliarizes the representation of violence against women by situating the image in a familial context. The image of the grandmother sleeping through the horror film is at once funny and frightening. Although the audience can never know the cause of the grandmother's slumber, what speaks in this image is that the grandmother is unable to protect the cousins from the grotesque images. In "Three Little Words," Norte constructs images that represent Latino childhood in a U.S. urban context. What the narrator remembers are not clichéd images of "grandmother's tamales cooking on a wooden stove." Instead, she remembers the grandmother who took her and her cousins to see the "gigantic horse's tongue / that was extracted from the pink lipped mouth of / another buxom blonde." Although mainstream expressions tend to represent childhood in idyllic terms, Norte, like writers Ana Castillo, Luis Alfaro, and Sandra Cisneros, represents "lived" experiences that have remained unrepresented in mainstream culture. Equally as important, this image of childhood memories expresses the ways the articulation of female sexual identity is associated with violence in patriarchal cultures. By shifting the point of view to that of a young Latina girl, the image also illustrates that it is not the traditional Latino patriarchal culture alone that objectifies women. Norte's text demonstrates again that the dominant culture also violently objectifies women.

Ultimately, Norte's narratives attempt to make way for new ways of "becoming" a gendered, racialized, and classed subject. In a recent spoken-word narrative entitled "untitled," written specifically for a live performance "Diva L.A.: A Salute to L.A.'s Latinas in the Tanda Style" (1995),[21] Norte's narrator enumerates a series of stereotypical labels used to define Chicanas/Latinas, then turns the list on its head by boldly (un)defining them. She asserts,

Soy
I am
Woman of Power
Poder
Fuerza
Fire
Mujer
Cactus Woman
Nopalera
Mujer
Madre
Sol
y Tierra
Mujer
Poder
Fuerza
Mujer
Mujer
Joder

For the record
I am not
Woman Mujer of power poder
cactus flower eating
Goddess of whatever?
No

The narrative then continues to resist the stereotypical labeling of Chicanas/Latinas by telling several stories to represent the diverse experiences of Chicanas/Latinas. By resisting stereotypical labels, Norte's narrative opens up a space within the imaginary to create new images of Chicanas/Latinas and new ways of being Chicana/Latina.

Although her narratives do not circulate in the mainstream media, the grassroots nature of their distribution allows them to reach people both outside and inside the university who do not have easy access to feminist discourse. Producing spoken-word narratives — which are performed and heard at coffee shops, high schools, community centers, performance spaces, universities, and the homes of her listeners in their CD/cassette form — transforms the social space in which Norte moves and momentarily produces a discourse that unfixes, displaces, and refigures images of Chicanas, Los Angeles, and the border. Norte's narratives offer not only a new vision of cultural identities, mapped across local and global economies and cultural practices, but also the power and imagination to redefine these "geographies." They change space by making new spaces — in the world and in the imagination — where oppressive social practices based on structures of racism, sexism, and nationalism can be exposed, critiqued, and transformed.

The analysis of Marisela Norte's spoken word helps make clear the role of culture in the struggle to acquire, maintain, or resist power. When Norte reconstructs the images of Chicanas, she is struggling for the power to define herself and her own interests, interests that often go against exploitative and unjust formation of places, institutions, and practices. Critique in and of itself will not make change. However, critique opens up a space for imagining a way of life based on social equality, a place where all women have access to health care, education, and safe jobs. In other words, it opens a space where new political projects may be imagined and emerge, where no one, especially women and children of color and undocumented workers, will bear the burden of poor health care policies, poor education, and poor living conditions. While the production of spoken word may not be considered a traditional mode of political action, and is only one place of many to engage in cultural politics, Norte's work, like all cultural production, "plays a constitutive, not merely a reflective role" in the culture of everyday life.[22] In other words, representations of life constructed in forms like literature, popular music, and spoken word do not merely reflect what everyday life is, but work to imagine and construct what it could be in the future. Because Norte articulates a multifold critique of the ways patriarchal institutions attempt to impose a cultural and gendered identity on working-class Latina bodies, she produces a countermeaning about Latina identity and subjectivity, one that constructs women as active subjects ready to critique relations of power instead of passive, accepting objects.

NOTES

Portions of this essay also appear in *Inscriptions* 7 (1994) and *Latinas on Stage* (Berkeley: Third Woman Press, in press).

1. See George Lipsitz's insightful article, "We Know What Time It Is: Race, Class and Youth Culture in the Nineties," in *Microphone Fiends: Youth Music and Youth Culture*, ed. Andrew Ross and Tricia Rose (New York: Routledge, 1994).

2. Considering that Norte composed her spoken-word narratives with the intent to perform them, compact discs and cassettes are ideal and appropriate mediums for her writing. However, they are particularly engrossing in the written form.

3. *Norte/word*, New Alliance Record Company 062/Cr02, 1991.

4. For an invaluable discussion concerning the formation of "new subjects for political identification," see Angie Chabram, "I Throw Punches for My Race but I Don't Want to Be a Man: Chica(Girls)/Nos(Us)," in *Cultural Studies*, ed. Lawence Grossberg, Cary Nelson, and Paula Treichler (New York: Routledge, 1992), 81–95.

5. Cultural politics in and of itself is not necessarily progressive. A clear example of a conservative engagement of cultural politics is California governor Pete Wilson's Proposition 187 anti-immigrant campaign. For instance, the campaign's infamous television advertisements dehumanized people I recognize as "undocumented workers" and constructed them as "illegal aliens," thus framing border-crossing job-seekers in such a way that erases the vital role they play in the California economy. Instead of featuring the undocumented workers picking crops in our agricultural fields, keeping houses and caring for children not their own, sewing in unsafe shops, or washing dishes in the back of restaurants — typical employment sites where they commonly work for below standard wages — the ads instead show helicopter footage of these workers running for their lives, across an interstate freeway located near the border checkpoint. Designed to play on the economic insecurities of "legal citizens," the

image suggests that California's economic crisis is caused by assumed "parasitic aliens," omitting the fact that people do not take jobs, but instead are given them. The ad also ignores the larger reasons for the crisis: a major one being the defunding of federally supported defense contracts, contracts that once upheld California's economy.

6. Other writers such as Gloria Anzaldúa, Ana Castillo, Gina Valdez, and Helena Viramontes, to name a few, make similar moves in their writing.

7. Glenn Jordan and Chris Weedon, eds., *Cultural Politics: Class, Gender, Race and the Postmodern World* (Cambridge: Blackwell, 1995), 5.

8. Rosa Linda Fregoso, *The Bronze Screen* (Minneapolis: University of Minnesota Press, 1993), 31.

9. Ibid., 31.

10. M. H. Abrams, *A Glossary of Literary Terms*, 5th ed. (San Diego: Harcourt Brace Jovanovich, 1988), 91.

11. In fact, Norte has recently joined the Bus Riders Union of Los Angeles to reform the city's remiss bus service.

12. For examples of the way the dominant culture has represented Chicanos, see A. C. Pettit, *Image of Mexican-Americans in Fiction and Film* (College Station: Texas A&M University Press, 1980).

13. Marisela Norte, "Peeping Tom Tom Girl," in *Norte/word*. Page numbers are not cited, since the poem is transcribed from the word recording.

14. My use of the term "Latina" refers to Mexicana, Central American, South American, and Puerto Rican women, all of whom can be found — in varying degrees — working in Los Angeles's industrial sections. Because it is not my intention to flatten and uncomplicate Latina identity, I use the terms "Chicana" and "Mexicana" when describing geopolitical particulars.

15. Douglas Monroy, *Thrown among Strangers* (Berkeley: University of California Press, 1990).

16. Norte, "Peeping Tom Tom Girl."

17. Marisela Norte, "Act of the Faithless," in *Norte/word.*

18. See Jennifer González and Michelle Habell-Pallán, "Heterotopias and Shared Methods of Resistance," *Inscriptions* 7 (1994): 87.

19. George Lipsitz, *Time Passages: Popular Memory in American Culture* (Minneapolis: University of Minnesota Press, 1990), 265.

20. "Three Little Words," in *Dis Closure*, New Alliance Record Company, 1992.

21. The Tandas de Varidad were the Mexican equivalent of American vaudeville shows. Popular during the 1920s and 1930s, they entertained the U.S. Spanish-speaking population until Depression-era deportation and repatriation policies eroded their audience base.

22. Stuart Hall, "New Ethnicities," *ICA Documents* (Institute of Contemporary Arts) 7 (1988): 27–31.

SIXTEEN

Feminisms of the Diaspora Both Local and Global: The Politics of South Asian Women against Domestic Violence

SANDYHA SHUKLA

Recent feminist writings have engaged in many important efforts to theorize issues of diversity and difference for two ends: first, to be relevant to a wide range of women (and men) at a time when there is a perceived decline in the solidarities of gender politics; and second, to respond to the material realities of a global economy that effects dramatic forms of female exploitation at each of its operating sites.[1] Theorists and practitioners alike have posed a "local-global" problematic to illuminate the pleasures and difficulties of developing an integrated feminist politics across borders of nation, race, and culture, and through a number of highly unstable economic and social contexts around the world.

Women from India, Pakistan, and Bangladesh[2] who reside in the United States or Britain have lived that oft-cited local-global paradox and have developed a wide range of critical apparati and political practices both to contest facile analytic binarisms between the "third world" and the "first world" and also to effectively address the daily lives of immigrant women. They have devised new feminisms to contest the ways "Indian culture" has generally been constructed and to address specific issues of domestic violence in the community. By building organizations such as Manavi and Sakhi for South Asian Women to combat violence against women, activists in the New York area foreground the subjectivity of the "South Asian woman," and in so doing, give life to a feminism that is diasporic, with an international set of reference points, and yet highly localized with respect to actual communities. It is this multiple set of articulations, in both the "local" and the "global," that marks the important contributions that South Asian activists against domestic violence have made to the broader field of feminist praxis.

Groups like Sakhi and Manavi evolve in a context of an explosion of "ethnic" organizations and associations serving and being constituted by the increased numbers of immigrants from the Indian subcontinent in the United States. The Indian American community in particular currently has a number of economic and business groups that concern Indian merchants, a multitude of religious places of worship, professional associations for lawyers and doctors, student groups at major university campuses, and other culturally based organizations. The great majority of these organizations define themselves as "mainstream" and cater primarily to a professional class. They develop a politics to establish themselves in social terms, as a group with a hyphenated ethnicity, Indian-American, in the tradition of white ethnicities like Jewish, Italian, and Irish Americans, those groups that have attained a measure of legitimacy in U.S. political life while at the same time being recognized as discrete groups. Consequently, many Indian American groups are directed toward the ends of economic and political assimilation and act to concretize middle-class status and gain visibility and representation within the U.S. electoral system.

Such groups also develop ethnic self-identifications that focus on the country of origin, India, as a source of cultural traditions. The India that they construct, at a moment of rapid social and economic changes in the nation-state itself, nonetheless relies on older visions of a country that are vigorously and romantically nationalist and anticolonial, and also steeped in images of the traditional nuclear family with its specified gender roles as a metaphor for distinctive cultural values in the face of Western change. A kind of cultural nostalgia greatly determines the constitution of "Indian groups" in the associations themselves and has broader social effects outside formal political activities.

The formation of these mainstream immigrant associations proceeds apace alongside the development of first, needs and desires of the communities *they* serve, and second, material and ideological affinities with political struggles in the homeland. These two components, group needs and political affiliations, are integrally linked. The anxiety of displacement, the presumed lack of a "home," and the implicit and explicit discrimination faced by a large majority of imigrants are to some degree assuaged by the act of coming together under specific labels deemed legitimate in the U.S. cultural landscape (like "Indian American," for its resonance with other palatable ethnic selfnamings like "Italian American" or "Jewish American"). And the aggressive and often religiously fundamentalist nationalisms that come out of countries like India speak to the desire of immigrants to keep "home" a pristine and fixed entity.

The perspectives from some sectors of the immigrant population betray altogether different lived realities. As immigrant communities themselves diversify and change, the need for a new set of identifications, to address complicated subject-positions and contradictory experiences of being "othered" in the first world, arises with a vengeance. Certain formulations, of "Indian-ness," and to a lesser extent "Pakistani-ness" and "Bangladeshi-ness,"[3] close down any space that would exist to formulate a more dynamic sense of community in dialogue with new interests that include

gender, sexuality, bicultural and/or biracial loyalties, and most especially generational differences. Indeed, most of the politics of mainstream Indian American
and Pakistani American/nationalist organizations are in direct conflict with the
perspectives emerging from new and marginal quarters.

A range of political interests locates new sources of oppression by developing new
definitions and possibilities for ethnicity, outside purely nationalist-based accounts
of group identity. The alternative political space created by these interests provides
the backdrop for the development of organizations such as Sakhi and Manavi, which
convey an ethnically and culturally based politics around gender by addressing
issues that are relevant to all Indian, Bangladeshi, Pakistani, Sri Lankan, Nepali, and
other populations hailing from what is known as the Indian subcontinent.

Sakhi and Manavi, like many progressive organizations both in the Indian subcontinent and in the diaspora currently, use the category "South Asian" to actively
work against nationalist/fundamentalist tendencies and to propose a racial group out
of the many peoples that were colonized by Britain as "Indians." Even more important, by fighting against domestic violence in Indian, Pakistani, and Bangladeshi
communities, the women in Sakhi and Manavi may be seen as constituting the
South Asian woman as a political subject and as a figure to organize around. This in
no way is to diminish the fact that the individual women served by the organizations
have complicated and rich identities of their own, but only to point out that one
staging of their ethnic identity in the public sphere has been constructed through
the politics around the category of the "South Asian woman."

It is in the very process of negotiating the political space that embraces gender,
sexuality, and transnationality, then, that we can see the emergence of what can
legitimately be called a "new ethnic politics." New South Asian communities produce cultures of solidarity that are different from the ones that scholars of leftist and
progressive politics have studied in the past; in this case, *middle*-class immigrants
have largely created cohesive interests, and middle-class formation deeply structures
the political processes they engage in. Understandings of oppression come out of
the private space but evoke more public understandings of ethnicity. Significantly,
the groups Sakhi and Manavi ground their "ethnic politics" in a number of particular circumstances that many South Asian women face, including a lack of familiarity
with the United States and the English language, the isolation and alienation that
comes from being separated from family networks in the home country, issues with
money and legal residency, and extreme vulnerability in marriages that serve as
singular sources of support. Largely because of the translatability of some of these
experiences across the boundaries of first world countries, a number of feminist
organizations all over the United States, as well as in Britain, Canada, and Australia
(all points of the Indian "diaspora") have first come together around domestic
violence, an issue that strikes deep at the heart of immigrant communities because
it speaks to the construction of the nuclear family.[4]

One of the first groups to come together in this way was Manavi (meaning
"woman" in Sanskrit). In 1985, six Asian Indian women in New Jersey began
discussing issues of feminism and in particular their dissatisfaction with the mainstream women's movement in which they had been participating for many years.

The women had been involved in a range of activities that included women's collectives, university groups, and the National Organization for Women. These six women came together around the belief that established organizations and political efforts had somehow successfully elided what they felt to be the issues and problems of Asian Indian women. Together they decided to form an Asian Indian women's feminist group, the first of its kind in the United States, and called it Manavi.

The group started, then, as a specifically Asian Indian organization, to consider the political and "actual" borders of a feminist constituency. At first the women chiefly engaged in what they termed "consciousness raising," but within a few months the organization began to receive calls from women who were victims of domestic violence. The women in the group had always been interested in practically addressing the needs of other women in their community and consequently shifted their focus to violence against women, to preventing it in the community through education and to helping individual women cope with and leave violent situations in the home. In the stories that founding members tell, then, the yoking of the issue of domestic violence to larger questions of Asian Indian feminism came about quasi-organically; this implies that the collective assertions of a commitment to equality for women opened up a space to address practical (and at times individual) issues of women's suffering at the hands of men within the structures of a marriage, and more generally within the institution of the nuclear family. After further discussions of and awareness of both the changing immigrant populations in the area and the violence intrinsic to the maintenance of borders between countries in the Indian subcontinent, Manavi became a self-consciously South Asian organization.

The parameters of the constitution of Manavi today reflect the ways violence against women is a practical manifestation of broader issues of inequality, and stands as testament to the founding moment of the organization, when the intersection of these issues and problems was realized. But the group does not simply see domestic violence as the only element of its struggle; members employ broad and flexible definitions of violence to constitute the group's ideology. In literature from Manavi, the members note, "Manavi believes that attitudes, conditions, and behaviours that perpetuate women's subordination in society constitute violence toward them."[5] The group evinces an understanding of gender oppression as a rather complicated process and endeavors to explore forms of violence through social, political, and economic analysis. Their mission statement clarifies this point: "issues related to violence against women should not be looked at in a vacuum. The different manifestations of violence affect women in all spheres of their life."[6] By engaging an understanding of violence that is broader than the symptom of domestic abuse, Manavi deviates from those organizations more oriented toward social service. Emblematically, Manavi does not seek or receive any government monies because, its members assert, accepting such funds would prevent them from being able to express opposition to all systems of oppression. They consciously define themselves as a feminist organization whose goals overlap but extend beyond the social service models that deal only with short-term solutions and eschew broader or more general analyses of oppression.

Manavi develops the idea of a "feminist organization" in a rather unorthodox way by not being exclusively female. After the group was in existence for three years, the members decided to include men on the board and in all other functions except for advocacy. Employing a broader model for "feminist" activities — in effect, not simply being a "group of radical women" — has enabled Manavi to situate itself, on the first level at least, within a network of ethnic-based organizations in South Asian communities themselves that are not gender-based, but cultural and political as well. In this form, the group also draws on the experiences of political activities of the diaspora, in particular those back home in India. Sujata Warrier, an active core volunteer, suggests that the tendency to limit the membership of organizations like these to women is far more common in the United States than in places like India; she notes, "in India women's survival is linked to men's survival because of broader things . . . you see them fighting together and if not [the movement] fails."[7]

Inherent in Manavi's guiding philosophies is a particular notion of international feminism; the links to women and women's projects in South Asian countries are a very important part of the group's efforts. In one recent newsletter, for example, the "News" included an update on the legal case of Taslima Nasrin, a censored feminist writer in Bangladesh, a report on violence against women in Calcutta, and a discussion of "role model" Kiran Bedi, a popular female police officer in India.[8] Manavi also sends funds to countries in South Asia; the group has raised money for a rural women's development project in Bengal and supported other emerging women's collectives.

Although the women served by Manavi span regions and classes, there is a great deal of ethnic, class, and geographic homogeneity in the membership of the organization; the majority of members continue to be Indian and Hindu. A variety of factors contribute to this tendency, including the specifics of the formation of South Asian communities in the New Jersey suburban area, where the more credentialed and economically secure people, with histories of political activism, in fact are Indian. One woman noted that all the core female members of Manavi are married to men who work at Bell Laboratories, a large employer of Indian engineers, physicists, and other scientists in the area.

The distance between the class and cultural characteristics of alternative political organizations and the people they serve is of course an issue not unique to Manavi, but the problem does have a different spin here, given that this is an explicitly South Asian progressive group and not a mainstream women's organization. The founders of Manavi indeed had cited the racial exclusions, both intended and otherwise, of women's organizations they had been involved in during the 1970s and 1980s as being formative in their desire to build different kinds of groups to speak to other constituencies; and for that matter they too are conscious of the difficulties (and importance) of the practical project of "inclusion" in class terms as well.

The group constitutes itself as South Asian and maintains that it is an alternative political space, particularly to women's organizations that are majority white American. Manavi has emerged from and remains committed to an analysis of and sensitivity to issues having to do with being South Asian in the United States. Warrier notes, "Mainstream feminist organizations are unable to see the nexus of race, class, and gender."[9] Although this kind of political articulation, which investigates the intersections of race, class, and gender, might have a variety of implications and possible identifications in the sphere of progressive political ideologies, Manavi as a group seems reluctant to define itself in Marxist, socialist, or even leftist terms. Shamita Das Dasgupta notes,

> We do recognize an economic analysis of problems but we don't adhere to the standard Marxist point of view that if we change economic relationships things will be better. . . . we've tried to break away from those standard traditional rhetorics (Marxist, leftist, progressive), and instead say what it is . . . (we would) like to define our work as pertaining to people's lives.[10]

In discussions about the group, members refer to "systems of oppression" but do not describe, in theoretical or material terms, the process by which such oppression is carried out and therefore do not seem to be in any obvious way leftist. They do not, for example, specifically identify capitalism as a major exploitative "system." This tendency is described by members as coming out of the practical emphasis of the project; they see the focus on everyday concerns ("pertaining to people's lives") as deviating from specific political ideologies, though it is not always clear why.

In the group's literature and in members' comments, the language used to describe Manavi's work refers back to the group's initial formation as a consciousness-raising group that diverges from but also comes out of the women's movement of the 1970s. Words like "patriarchy" and references to members of other women's movements as "sisters" in the literature reveal the dominance of older women trained in the lexicons of a 1960s/1970s generation of feminism. Articles in the newsletters by the few younger women in the group (college students and women in their early twenties), by contrast, are marked by the presence of new terms like identity, subalternity, and discourses of oppression. The feminisms of the 1980s and 1990s are to some degree informed by critiques of "patriarchy" as an organizing principle and by post-Marxist and postmodern theories that use a different language to describe gender inequalities. So far, however, while the very different languages used to describe the goals and work of the organization appear as markers of either older or younger generations, they do not necessarily reflect an ideological split in the group, as neither the younger nor the older women describe serious disagreements on strategies or overall objectives of the group. This may of course change over time as a new generation of women comes to dominate the group.

A slightly younger generation of feminist women forms the core group of Sakhi for South Asian Women in New York City. In 1989 a small group of women from India who had come to the United States for graduate or professional school heard about the work that Manavi was doing in New Jersey and decided that working on domestic violence would be an excellent springboard for a South Asian women's organization in New York; they named their group Sakhi, which means female friend in Hindi. Though none of the women had any formal experience in this sort of work, they consulted people in Manavi and the Asian Women's Center and learned about the court system and shelters around the city as they began to help South Asian women from a variety of communities. Their initial activities were helping battered women find shelter and develop strategies of self-empowerment, and eventually accompanying them through the legal system. During the first eight months, all of the ten to twelve women involved had full-time jobs and helped fund the organization by themselves. Before long they had put together a training manual, solicited new volunteers, and supported a number of women through domestic violence situations.

As quickly as it formed, Sakhi had also developed a sense of its own political orientations and had begun to locate itself in a landscape of progressive activist politics. As Romita Shetty, a founding member, notes, "The conscious principle was to create a democratic, nonhierarchical organization."[11] From the very beginning, then, the women of Sakhi were conscious of the need to be dynamic in terms of membership and philosophy, and also to ground the organization itself in the very rapidly developing social formations of South Asian communities. Since 1989, the organization has expanded by leaps and bounds and now has sixty to seventy active volunteers as well as an executive board. In the first couple of years of Sakhi's existence, members also obtained several large foundation grants that enabled the continued employment of two full-time staff people in an office in Manhattan.

Like Manavi, Sakhi proposed rather complex understandings of violence against women that emerged from both a well-theorized feminist ideology and the realities of women's alienation and isolation in a South Asian–United States cultural context; both groups can be said to have been constituted by and through a relationship with actual communities of women. Sakhi saw itself as a progressive South Asian women's organization to empower the women it served, rather than to simply provide "social services." Sakhi has never sought to have a shelter, as many in the organization have felt that the focus would instantly change because of the energy and finances needed to maintain a residential space.

Today women in Sakhi seem deeply aware of the importance of language. Calling the women they work with "battered women" rather than "clients" or "cases" and the person who works with them the "advocate" and not the "counselor" is a stated commitment of the organization. In so doing, members reveal a very sophisticated understanding of the ways that political activities are discursively represented (and misrepresented) and the vast number of issues at stake in the development of these feminist languages about oppression.

Sakhi also maintains a commitment to encouraging the women they work with to become part of the organization. One woman who was helped out of a troubled and abusive marriage and now speaks at outreach events said, "I was afraid to talk about myself in front of other people but I kept being encouraged to come to support group meeting and there I felt such a release of tension . . . now I feel like I can help other people."[12] While one Pakistani woman who was formerly served by Sakhi is now on the board of directors and there are a few other Pakistani and Bangladeshi women in the volunteer corps, the organization continue to comprise largely Indian (and perhaps even more North Indian than South Indian) women who have not come into the organization by being served by it. Again, this is not unusual and is in fact a recurring problem for organizations of this nature.

In some progressive-activist circles, Sakhi has an upper-middle-class or "bourgeois" reputation.[13] The core group of women are all known to be highly educated and economically secure, and Sakhi periodically sponsors expensive fund-raisers. The narrow class and geographic representation, however, is considered a serious problem for many in the organization itself, particularly as it tries to develop an alternative political space to the existing social service models for community activism.

Such class (and ethnic) markings may also come out of a special focus on domestic violence, which in and of itself does not illuminate economic cleavages. However, a range of new activities of the organization includes literacy classes, work around immigrant bills, and a domestic workers' initiative. The domestic workers' project informs South Asian female domestics who have recently come to this country of their rights as employees; women in Sakhi also serve as advocates for the workers who seek the protection of their rights. A project like this could be approached with many possible philosophies; economic, legalistic, and social analyses could all illuminate these forms of exploitation. Sakhi's governing ideology with respect to these issues is openly acknowledged to be in formation. Indeed, the domestic workers program, say many members, may move the group in new political directions.[14] Finally, because many of the South Asian domestic workers are employed by other, wealthy South Asians, the initiative may produce new and interesting self-questionings within the group.

Sakhi and Manavi are but two of the many South Asian women's groups in the United States that have chosen to organize around domestic violence, and it is important to consider why this issue seems "a good introductory topic."[15] By challenging the "naturalness" of gender relations and the glorification of the nuclear family, women struggling to eliminate violence in other women's private lives create a cultural space that is different from that in more mainstream South Asian groups; and in saying that what they do is "political," female activists redefine the actual space of politics. By resisting the "liberalizing" influence of government funds and not operating shelters, these two groups also adhere to more progressive ideologies as defining features of their work; they say, in effect, that they refuse to be *read* and implicated as social service arms of the state.

The critique of gender relations and "the family" also makes an intervention in the contentious debates on nationhood. In an article about Sakhi and issues of gender and nationality, Sakhi cofounder Anannya Bhattacharjee notes,

> any challenge to the family in the Indian community translates for the national bourgeoisie into a betrayal of national cultural values. For a woman . . . to disown her role(s) is to betray not just the family but also the nation. . . . the woman who occupies the space outside the heterosexual, patriarchal family is in a space unrecognized by the nation, currently a highly valued construct.[16]

Bhattacharjee argues that the formation of nationalism and nationhood, both within India and through the diasporic Indian community, is premised on the specific gender and sexual roles that constitute a nuclear family, for reproduction's sake and also for the construction of cultural traditions through a disparate group of ethnic and regional entities. Both Sakhi and Manavi, in stressing that violence in women's lives is the result of much more than a "husband gone crazy," gesture at critiques of the very circumscribed roles of women in so-called national communities.

The term "South Asian" itself challenges the boundaries of the nation in rather obvious ways. Manavi and Sakhi are consciously South Asian, as are a number of progressive organizations throughout the United States; indeed, that label marks organizations that actively define themselves against immigrant culture based in nationalist politics of the homeland. The ostensible truism of "Indian means Hindu, means middle class, means nationalist" falls to the wayside as groups articulate a commitment to the South Asian identity through the diaspora. Relatively recent in this country, the term originates in progressive circles in India in the context of communalist politics.

Constructing organizations around "South Asian" peoples and identities determines a politics of ethnicity based not in the state (of India or Pakistan) but in a culture that those populations share. The investment in culture can be seen in the very commitment to the term; similarities in family relationships, domestic arrangements, language, and customs purportedly provide the glue that holds these divergent groups of people together for some political end. Thus the stuff of ethnicity — language, kinship, and culture — can be found in these spaces as well as in mainstream "Indian" or "Pakistani" organizations, and the women in these groups engage in the process of "making" an ethnic/cultural identity that has a rather brief history in the United States.

People from countries in the Indian subcontinent experience residence in the United States through histories of colonialism and postcolonialism and have a set of racial identities not commonly acknowledged within U.S. racial paradigms. Asian American as a category has only recently broadened its scope to include peoples from India, Pakistan, Bangladesh, and elsewhere in the region called South Asia. Large South Asian populations are recent and recently visible, and there is no immediate acknowledgment of their presence in popular culture. Such open issues of categorization and political organizing help to form identities, be they "Indian," "Pakistani," or "South Asian." While a number of regional alliances exist in the Indian subcontinent, the postcolonial history of that area is marked more by conflict than cooperation. And recent generations of people in the era following Indian independence in 1947 have developed cultural as well as political affiliations to their region, religion, and national state. These people tend to say that they are, for example, Indian, Bengali, Muslim, or Pakistani; very rarely do they see or call themselves South Asian. The title "South Asian" is a political term, used for particular ends. South Asian-ness challenges Indian-ness more than identities arising from other national affiliations (like Pakistani or Sri Lankan, for example) because of the majority Indian population among those groups in the United States and because of the aggressiveness of both those Indian identities and the nation-state of India in the subcontinent. The very fact that the label of identity seems inorganic may make it a different kind of term in an alternative lexicon.

The political process that South Asian women activists engage in creates new categories of identity and challenges old formulations of ethnicity. The ethnic/racial identity of "South Asian," like any other, relies on some conscious sense of shared cultural experiences. The "culture" that it asserts may be a matter of some debate, particularly given the ways conservative political forces have conjured up very problematic uses for that entity. Because the common understandings of South Asian identity emerge from contemporary political formations rather than intrinsic meaning, we might also interrogate the ways such groupings are potentially *un*meaningful and limited. The term "South Asian" does not necessarily, for example, move toward greater shared identities between women of color or toward new inclusive categories of race. In some ways the discussions of the South Asian label take place outside the predominant structures of race in the United States (and the world), usually discussed in terms of "blackness." The trajectory of this terminology leads not toward something like "third world women" but in the direction of more ethnically defined groups. Manavi and Sakhi do work with other groups (Asian, women of color, immigrant, etc.) but in coalition, rather than beneath umbrella identities. Such developments may be the product of the particular sociopolitical moment and may change very rapidly toward something else. As younger Indian, Bangladeshi, and Pakistani women imbibe a wide variety of racial and cultural influences, we may see a shift toward other types of identifications. Generational differences may play a leading role in redefining these organizations themselves, as well as in building new organizations to challenge the importance of older political formations.

Yet organizations like Sakhi and Manavi, as they exist now, provide a space for women of many generations to come together around political objectives. The first/second/third generation issues are negotiated in a venue that is rather different from the nuclear family or the local Indian community function. One college woman in Sakhi notes that many of the older women are role models for her.[17] The work of these organizations, however, remains specifically political; rarely if ever do the members describe Sakhi or Manavi as social spaces.

Women in Sakhi and Manavi build a progressive politics around gender and not class. The middle-class formation of the South Asian (and here really the Indian) population in the United States gives rise to groups like these and also to the next generation of mostly college-educated young woman who derive political understandings of oppression from those representations of abuse and exploitation in the private sphere. In contrast to the experiences of largely working-class immigrant groups in the past (Jewish or Irish, for example),[18] for the most part, the workplace is not the site of political activity for middle-class South Asian immigrants or their children.

The challenge, then, to existing political organizations is multifaceted. Sakhi and Manavi cannot be interpreted through models of working-class organization, patterns of middle-class ethnic politics, or largely white feminist strategies. The space negotiated here is alternative and should be read that way. Organizations like Sakhi and Manavi occupy a contradictory and complicated position with regard to a set of established political interests because of their position that is at once racialized and gendered. As advocates of women in oppressive family situations in South Asian communities and of women's struggles for a political space, they work without an established model for political action.

While Sakhi and Manavi face censure from Indian organizations bent on preserving essential and traditional notions of the Indian family, the articulation of domestic violence as a problem in South Asian communities need not be antagonistic to the interests of the more conservative elements of the Indian immigrant middle class. Another domestic violence organization, Apna Ghar in Chicago, provides an interesting counterpoint. Caitrin Lynch argues that Apna Ghar utilizes a South Asian identity, fights violence against women, and preserves a sense of "Indian-ness" all at the same time, by implying that domestic violence is a product of the process of Westernization. Lynch notes,

> The founders are all well established in the Asian community and have lived in the United States for many years. . . . Many wear "traditional" South Asian clothing. They speak a language other than English. In being wives and mothers . . . the founders and staff of Apna Ghar implicitly reassure their community that they are not antifamily or anti-Indian but concerned about people getting hurt in a hostile immigrant environment.[19]

We can read this example in a number of ways. First, it suggests not only that there are more mainstream versions of domestic violence organizations, but also that there is a more politically conservative interpretation of domestic violence itself. Second, it is also possible that the group uses an explicitly pro-family rhetoric to make its ideas less threatening to community members whose support they need. The effects and perhaps limits of such a strategy may yet be seen.

There is a complicated field here of acceptance and marginality, and it absolutely depends on the particular issue and if and how it threatens the boundary of what is deemed politically acceptable. Even Sakhi and Manavi, who are more consciously left of center, receive a good deal of support from the mainstream Indian community, both financial and otherwise, and must therefore wage their struggles through some kind of relationship with national and religious groups, because of the centrality of some of those interests in the lives of the women they serve as well as perhaps in their own. On the first level, there is some external acknowledgment of the relationship between a number of different interests. All the major immigrant newspapers that espouse mostly mainstream if not conservative viewpoints like *India Abroad*, *News-India*, and *Hinduism Today*, as well as *India Today* and *Far Eastern Economic Review*, have had major stories on domestic violence and have lauded the accomplishments of Sakhi and Manavi. Very simply, as Sakhi co-coordinator Prema Vohra says, "No one is going to say it is right to beat your wife."[20] Even religious organizations such as the Long Island Islamic Center call in Sakhi to produce workshops for their domestic harmony programs.

Nonetheless, because of the group's political orientation, which is both feminist and antinationalist, negotiations with established interests are sometimes difficult if not impossible, and the delicate "in-between" space does not always exist. Sakhi and Manavi support other progressive South Asian groups; Manavi's newsletter recently published a letter from Trikone, a South Asian gay and lesbian group, congratulating Manavi on its tenth anniversary and explicitly linking the types of political struggles that each group has waged over the last ten years.[21] Sakhi has over the years maintained cordial working relations with the South Asian Lesbian and Gay Association (SALGA). This support of SALGA has led to a number of complicated confrontations with more mainstream organizations in the community.

Until recently, Sakhi has never had a problem marching in the India Day Parade, an August celebration in Manhattan to mark the anniversary of India's independence from British colonial rule. The parade is organized by a mainstream organization, the Federation of Indian Associations (FIA), and is commonly seen to be a demonstration of Indian nationalism. Quite the opposite has been true, however, for SALGA. Like gay and lesbian Irish American groups trying to march in the St. Patrick's Day parades in New York and Boston,[22] SALGA encountered a host of justifications for denial, including the tardiness of its application, its refusal to carry nationalist banners, and its disruptive activities.[23] Mostly, the FIA has maintained publicly, at least, that because SALGA is a South Asian group, it should not march in the India Day parade. The first couple of years that this happened, women in Sakhi invited SALGA to march with them, explicitly supporting SALGA's right to be part of the larger Indian American community, as a right it asserted for themselves. In 1995, however, when SALGA pointed out the hypocrisy of letting some South Asian groups (including Sakhi) march and prohibiting others from doing so, the FIA also denied Sakhi permission. In response to this, Sakhi and SALGA with other progressive groups in the city protested at the parade. Unlike SALGA, however, which sees itself as deeply marginalized and simply unassimilable into more mainstream interests, Sakhi can and must return to negotiations with the very communities that excluded it. It depends on financial support from the immigrant community and has an interest in working on relations with its quite diverse members.

The relationships of Sakhi and Manavi to either mainstream or alternative political groups do not fully constitute the transgressive potential of the organizing of a feminist politics around domestic violence. Precisely because of the critiques of family and culture that anti–domestic violence groups advance, the efforts to construct a seamless community, in a variety of spaces, are interrupted and punctuated. Proposing that violence against a person, particularly against a woman, is wrong is to assert individual rights within the group. New identities, then, may find room in what were once closed spaces, of nation, family, ethnic culture, and religion.

The South Asian woman, both as an actual being and as a figure for a new set of identities, emerges in the space created by groups like Sakhi and Manavi. In a context where people are living important contradictions that include the transnationality of economic interests, the resurgence of ethnic nationalisms, the coalescing of the "traditional" and the "modern," and increased economic, political, and social difficulties of migrating to countries like the United States, the politicized figure of the South Asian woman serves as a symbol for political possibilities, and as a category that is *diasporic*, with a relationship to the "local" everyday lives of people.

Diasporic South Asian feminism, of the kind evidenced here, has an ambivalent position with regard to both what has been constructed as "international feminism" and national versions of feminism. While Manavi stresses the importance of links to women's projects in South Asia, it does not necessarily or explicitly promote such efforts in other parts of the world; its focus is on South Asian women. And while

Sakhi maintains strong relationships with other progressive organizations in New York City, it does not do much work in coalitions of "women of color," a recently popular organizing principle for young African American, Asian American, and Latina women.[24] All of this suggests that some established models of "global sisterhood" and/or "third world feminism" may not be the most appropriate ones in which to consider groups like Sakhi and Manavi, or that they may not be the political narratives that are being currently chosen by women in these organizations.

Sakhi and Manavi have arisen out of new (and perhaps postmodern) political and social arrangements whereby the third world is now in the first world and retains cultural links with the "homeland." The women who work in and with Sakhi and Manavi do not always explicitly see themselves as minority women, in the language of contemporary progressive politics; their immigrant affiliations often fall outside established categories. They rework general notions of feminism through the expansive ways they discuss gender issues. Sakhi and Manavi remain explicitly feminist groups in an age when this is not altogether common. And as their feminism is part and parcel of the negotiation not only of race and ethnicity but of immigration, economic dislocation, and politics of the home country, any identification with idealized notions of womanhood or any essential "femaleness" could not be farther from the visions expounded by these women. In short, there is no easy answer to the question of how to interpret these South Asian women, both as subjects and as political actors.

What is clear is that the women in Sakhi and Manavi are articulating their objectives and their politics of gender with actual changes in the immigrant communities themselves. While most of the examples cited arise out of the organization and development of the middle and upper middle classes of South Asian communities, there is a critical mass of students, activists, and scholars in formation that is contending with changes in their referent populations, such as the increase in more recent and working-class Indians, Pakistanis, and Bangladeshis in this country. Sakhi's domestic workers' initiative may be a harbinger of future developments, and other possibilities may soon emerge.

Finally, "cultures" will change. The development of the political category of "South Asian" seems provisional and not an end in itself. As the social worlds of second- and third-generation Americans who trace their ancestry to the Indian subcontinent change and become even more complicated and hybrid, "South Asian" may not mean the same thing, have the same effect, or be as important in a progressive or left political landscape in the future. Changing patterns of gender relations and the increasingly sophisticated embodiments of sexism are influenced by changes in the global economy; in the age of multinational capitalism women and men may need to militate for different issues in different ways. And they may need to build broader coalitions with other political strategies, be they "minority feminist," "international feminist," "progressive/left-postcolonial," or something else altogether.

The increased migration of peoples to the United States from countries such as India, Pakistan, and Bangladesh in recent years has made the South Asian subject highly visible at a time when new models for class and ethnicity are pitted against older stories of racial formation. The pace and magnitude of immigration from Asia, Africa, and Latin America in recent years highlight the need for a new set of languages for identity and politics. Middle-class Asian American, Latino, and African American groups have all stepped up efforts to control the representation of their "ethnicity" just as "race" has been rendered invisible or has been relegated to the urban poor. It is in this context that women in groups like Manavi and Sakhi shape political life by organizing new communities. South Asian women activists appear at the confluent and recent historical developments of postcolonialism and post-1965 immigration to the United States; as such they are precariously situated within already existing discourses on national, racial, and ethnic identities. As they work for goals that transgress the national, gender, and sexual boundaries of their more conservative counterparts, these "new (female) ethnics" do cultural work that re-imagines the political (and feminist) future of international immigrant communities.

NOTES

I would like to thank all the women of Sakhi, Manavi, and SALGA who agreed to speak with me and offer their perspectives on this important work in which they are engaged.

1. *Third World Women and the Politics of Feminism*, ed. Chandra Talpade Mohanty, Ann Russo, and Lourdes Torres (Bloomington: Indiana University Press, 1991) has become a seminal text in this regard; *Scattered Geographies*; *Postmodernity and Transnational Feminist Practices*, ed. Inderpal Grewal and Caren Kaplan (Minneapolis: University of Minnesota Press, 1994) is a more recent text that rigorously comes to terms with some of the complications of feminism beyond the nation-state.

2. I would name the countries of India, Pakistan, Bangladesh, Sri Lanka, Nepal, and Bhutan as constituting the category of "South Asian." This delineation arises out of common usage and is for that matter relatively arbitrary in its "actual" meaning; I hope not to foreclose the inclusion of other regions into that grouping. Within that group, India, Pakistan, and Bangladesh are the most prominent in the work of immigrant organizations because of the numbers of people in this country as well as their time here.

3. Though all the major South Asian groups (Indian, Bangladeshi, Pakistani, Sri Lankan, etc.) have middle-class organizations that exhibit the tendencies I am referring to, it is the Indian groups that are most numerous, most politically powerful, and most influential in establishing themselves as "ethnic groups." And it is their formulation of nationally based ethnicities that is most germane to such questions in a first world context because of the way "India" (and not Pakistan or Bangladesh) both signifies a set of colonial and imperial relationships in the popular imagination and also projects itself as an emerging economic force to be contended with.

4. In London, for example, one of the most public (and famous) women's groups to emerge in recent years has been the Southall Black Sisters, which focuses also on domestic violence in the local community.

5. From official pamphlet about the organization, under the heading "About Manavi . . ."

6. From section entitled "Domestic Violence in the South Asian Context: Understanding the Work of Manavi."

7. Sujata Warrier, interview by author, February 21, 1995.

8. *Manavi Newsletter* 6, no. 2 (fall 1994).

9. Warrier, interview.

10. Shamita Das Dasgupta, interview by author, February 21, 1995.

11. Romita Shetty (one of the founding members of Sakhi), interview by author, February 15, 1995.

12. Interview by author, February 22, 1995. The woman asked to remain unnamed for reasons of privacy.

13. From informal conversations with South Asian activists in organizations other than Sakhi.

14. Neena Das, interview by author, February 16, 1995.

15. Shetty, interview.

16. Anannya Bhattacharjee, "The Habit of Ex-Nomination: Nation, Woman and the Indian Immigrant Bourgeoisie," *Public Culture* 5, no. 1 (fall 1992): 19–44.

17. Sharmila Desai, interview by author, February 20, 1995.

18. See studies like Elizabeth Ewen, *Immigrant Women in the Land of Dollars: Life and Culture on the Lower East Side* (New York: Monthly Review Press, 1985); and John Bodnar, *The Transplanted: A History of Immigrants in Urban America* (Bloomington: Indiana University Press, 1985).

19. Caitrin Lynch, "Nation, Woman, and the Indian Immigrant Bourgeoisie: An Alternative Formulation," in *Public Culture* 6, no. 2 (1994): 425–37. This piece dialogues with Bhattacharjee's essay "The Habit of Ex-Nomination."

20. Prema Vohra, interview by author February 22, 1995.

21. *Manavi Newsletter* 7, no. 2 (winter 1995): 1.

22. Andrew Hsiao, "Gays Get Marching Orders," *Village Voice*, August 30, 1994.

23. Some of this information has been culled from conversations with Gayatri Gopinath, a longtime member of SALGA who also writes on issues of queer culture in the South Asian diaspora, and Priyamvada Sinha, a more recent member.

24. See the collection *Making Face, Making Soul: Haciendo Caras*, ed. Gloria Anzaldúa (San Francisco: Aunt Lute Foundation, 1990) as an example of this feminist tendency; see also the recent magazine *Hues* (Hear Us Emerging Sisters) from college-aged women in Ann Arbor, Michigan, as an attempt to constitute a progressive politics around the category of "women of color."

SEVENTEEN

The Marginalized Uses of Power and Identity: Lesbians' Participation in Breast Cancer and AIDS Activism

ANDREA DENSHAM

> my fullest concentration of energy is available to me only when I integrate all the parts of who I am openly, allowing power from particular sources of my living to flow back and forth freely through all my different selves, without the restrictions of externally imposed definition. Only then can I bring myself and my energies as a whole to the service of those struggles which I embrace as part of my living.
>
> — Audre Lorde

Marginalized Communities' Political Participation

Lesbians have played an increasingly visible role in American politics over the past ten years. Particularly significant to this increased visibility has been the role of lesbians in AIDS and breast cancer activism. The activism that emerged during the 1980s in response to the AIDS epidemic has drastically changed the topology of urban politics in the United States; AIDS activists and, in the 1990s, breast cancer activists have challenged the basic notions of what is political and how people mobilize politically. For those of us concerned with the political participation of marginalized communities, studying the role of lesbian activists in the politics of both AIDS and breast cancer provides an opportunity to better understand what shapes the form, content, and trajectory of efforts by marginalized communities to participate politically.

This essay is an attempt to enter into the discourse on political participation by presenting a theory of marginalization that examines the influences of power, identity, and ideology on marginalized communities' political participation. The political work of lesbians and gay men has often been made invisible in the study of politics in the United States.[1] Even as progressive scholars within the field of political science have recently engaged in the study of other marginalized communities — blacks, Latinos, the poor, and women — there has been virtual silence when it comes to the efforts of lesbians and gay men to create social and political change. The absence of such thoughtful investigations is particularly conspicuous in light of the recent increase in lesbian and gay political activism, the impact such organizing has had on the greater body politic, and the emergence of a politics of AIDS.

Similarly, there continues to be an observable gap in much political science research between the theoretical assertions of scholars and the political realities of societal actors. Particularly ill-fitting have been the notions of static and essential identities. At the heart of much contemporary scholarship has been the assertion that identities are permanent, unchanging entities — a theoretical position that fails to recognize the far more complex and multifaceted nature of identity. While I argue that identity is not a biologically determined or essential entity, I am not asserting that identities, due to their malleable state, are of little consequence to politics. To the contrary, I contend that identities have serious effects on the structure of political debate as well as on people's lives. One's identity insures one's access to societal benefits or can restrict one from social and political resources. We can see this process at work in the historical struggles between dominant societal actors, such as government or the press, and marginalized communities, such as people of African descent or women who primarily have emotional and sexual relationships with women, to control the public presentation of what it means to be black or lesbian. Identity is the site of heated and enormously important political debates precisely because the stakes surrounding determination of identity are so high. Challenges come, however, not only from external forces but also from internal forces, including conflicts within a community about the purposes of self-determination and about the public presentation of a group's identity.

Like a number of scholars, I focus my examination of political participation on marginalized communities and individuals (Cohen 1993; Mitra 1992; Mohanty et al. 1991; Alexander 1991). In doing so I am asserting an important methodological break with the canonical work of traditional political scientists. By moving away from the normative focus on elites and dominant institutions, I refocus my theoretical lens onto the efforts of those formerly understood as "powerless" to participate politically and to reveal their historical and contemporary employment of power. Indeed, a more critical examination should be made of what I would call the internally developed identities of marginalized communities. It is through the construction of internally developed identities that marginalized communities establish membership and project an alternative presentation of a given identity. By more closely examining this process we can better illuminate the entirety of the process of group political participation. Although dominant societies do repress and suppress the efforts of individuals and groups that they identify as "other," "deviant," or "dangerous," such efforts do not eliminate the ability of marginalized individuals (or groups) to marshal their own resources in resistance. It is this process of resistance, an important part of which is the internal development of identity, that my theoretical framework is constructed to recognize and further examine.

Marginalization is the process by which dominant societies identify groups and individuals who are deemed deviant, dangerous, or "other" (Cohen 1993, 15–16). By so marking groups and individuals, dominant society constitutes such identities as a repressive tool used to limit specific individuals' and groups' access to resources. As many scholars have described it, marginalization highlights the role of the state or dominant societal institutions in the construction of externally imposed identities of marginalized groups and the resulting delimitation of resources. Although this story has been well told by many scholars, what happens after groups have been marginalized (and thus restricted access to resources) remains less well investigated. In this essay I analyze how both the process and ramifications of marginalization have an impact on groups and individuals around such issues as self-identification, conceptualization of community, establishment of priorities, and the form and content of political participation. I extend the theory of marginalization into an investigation of the means by which marginalized communities construct internally developed resistant identities and employ particular ideologies in an effort to participate politically.

This framework presumes the inscription of power in a diversity of ever-changing relationships. Central to this formation is a recognition of the concomitant effort of marginalized communities and dominant society to ascribe meaning to publicly presented identities and to employ power in order to shape and reshape the form and content of public political discourse and political and economic operations to their advantage. Although my framework acknowledges that identity can be constructed resistantly by way of internally developed identities, it also recognizes that these identities are not created in a void, but rather are the result of an interaction between marginalized community members' self-identification and the hegemonic societal description of these individuals as "other."

It is in this context that communities produce internally constructed identities, ideologies, and, ultimately, agendas and tactics for political participation. But what constitutes political participation? Within my theoretical framework, political participation is broadly conceived, but it is primarily confined to the activities of groups or individuals who are engaged in contemporary political institutions, who challenge these institutions, or who insert themselves into formerly restricted venues of political, economic, or social commerce. Examples of such activities include participation in political institutions (e.g., electoral politics and congressional lobbying); political challenges to such institutions (e.g., grassroots political action such as protests over the National Institutes of Health's breast cancer research priorities); and marginal groups' political insertion into formally restricted venues (e.g., AIDS activists' insistence that school boards create informative AIDS education programs for public schools). Although there is no singular formula to test whether an activity is political participation, I contend that participation should be directed at a public audience (or quasi-public audience, thus including venues formerly protected from the public gaze) and should be part of a larger ideological agenda.

Lastly, my framework is constructed to recognize the diversity of implications of power in the activities of political participation. Especially important is identifying how marginalized communities employ the tools available to them in the implementation of power. That is, how do resource-poor communities, in the process of identifying their political goals and agendas, also identify the resources necessary for their political participation? Identifying resources and the later creation of alternative resources and tools is, for resource-poor communities, essential to effective employment of power.

My framework, then, adjusts its lens to examine the reciprocal relationship between ideology production and the internal construction of identity. Although it is difficult to describe a universal causal equation for this interaction, it is possible to examine how each component affects the other — how internally developed identity affects the process of ideology production, community formation, individual agenda creation, and the resulting political participation within marginalized communities. Similarly, it is important to examine how the ideological position taken up by a community shapes the boundaries of its internally developed identity. This framework breaks new theoretical ground in its bridging of a number of different methodological and theoretical efforts. It brings together examinations of political participation and the employment of power within marginalized communities by political scientists Cathy Cohen (1993) and Subrata Mitra (1992); theoretical examinations of identity and ideology construction among marginalized communities by sociologist Chandra Talpade Mohanty (Mohanty et al. 1991); investigations of the impact of dominant society's construction of identity and individuals' response to such constructions by sociologist Jacqui Alexander (1991); and investigations of power and ideology construction by political scientist Michael Dawson (1995). By bridging these diverse and intersecting works I hope to construct a strong framework on which to build an examination of the complexities and diversity of political participation among marginal communities — in particular, the different means by which lesbian activists involved in breast cancer and AIDS activism were able to mobilize resources and thereby effect change.

Compared to traditional theories of political participation, marginalization theory represents a rejection of the tendency to dichotomize political realities. Instead, marginalization requires that the political terrain, and individuals' interactions within it, be understood in all their dynamic complexity. Those working within this body of ideas assert that, in order to understand better why people and groups participate as they do, social scientists must examine the complex interactions among power, political participation, and identity.

A History of Movements: AIDS and Breast Cancer Activism

In many ways the histories of medical crises are much more about the contemporary social, political, and economic climate and configuration of the period in which they occurred than they are about the particular medical conditions themselves. Responses to tuberculosis, the black plague, and other medical crises in history have provided windows into the heart of the societies they have struck (Hansell 1993;

Hardy and Rosenberg 1995). Such medical crises often expose the deepest fears, hatreds, and prejudices of a society. This is true for the contemporary illnesses of breast cancer and AIDS.

Knowledge about the insidious nature of heterosexism, racism, sexism, and class oppression throughout U.S. society and U.S. political structures is similarly important; when we examine the agenda and strategy of breast cancer activists, it is important to understand what causes the relative lack of medical research on women and the lack of significant advances in breast cancer treatment and treatment of other medical conditions affecting women, including HIV/AIDS.[2] Thus, although the epidemiological specifics of these two medical crises outline the parameters of discourse, the content of political activism is directly shaped by the political and social terrain of the contemporary moment.

As noted above, AIDS activist organizations have broken new ground in the form and content of community political participation. In the mid-1980s AIDS activists, particularly the members of the organization ACT UP, were able to integrate protest tactics with formal negotiations, in large measure due to the work of the many political protest movements that came before them. One example of this integration of tactics can be seen in ACT UP's employment of both protest and negotiation strategies with the Food and Drug Administration in the late 1980s (Schulman 1994, 12). This integration of tactics reflected the influence of organizations like the Student Non-Violent Coordinating Committee (SNCC), which in the mid- to late 1960s employed such a strategy in its civil rights efforts, on current AIDS activist strategies.

ACT UP is a network of locally based activist groups that started in the early 1980s in New York City and soon spread to include local chapters in San Francisco, Boston, Chicago, and later, numerous smaller cities and towns. At its founding, the organization committed itself to develop quick, well-produced, and well-publicized political protests, to encourage self-education regarding the HIV virus and political institutions, and to employ that knowledge in an effort to challenge the status quo.

ACT UP, however, has never been free of controversy, even within lesbian and gay communities. Much of the controversy within lesbian and gay communities regarding ACT UP has been centered around the goals and agendas of the organization. AIDS activists such as Sue Hyde and Sarah Schulman have argued, for instance, that issues of importance to Latinas/os, African Americans, women, and poor people with AIDS have at times been ignored or dismissed. This rift is especially important to my examination of political activism among marginal communities, because it speaks to the diversity of priorities within such communities. Earlier theories of political participation have argued that groups often operate in a monolithic manner, with a common identity creating a common political agenda. I contend, however, that people are marginalized in a diversity of intersecting ways, and as a result, individuals and groups develop a multilayered approach to the establishment of group political priorities. Said more simply, a lesbian, because of her experiences with barriers based on gender, may prioritize different components of the AIDS crisis than a gay man who has never had to face, and may have yet to recognize, the barriers facing women.

Similarly, cancer activists have become ever more vigilant in their fight against this increasingly common disease, by challenging the authority of national cancer associations and the research priorities of federal agencies. Activists from Boston's Women's Community Cancer Project (WCCP), for instance, have been in the forefront in publicly challenging the American Cancer Society (ACS) and in forging new alliances with organizations like Greenpeace. This organization has increased its pressure on the ACS as well as the National Cancer Institute (NCI) to acknowledge the threat that pollution poses in the continually increasing risk of cancer, and to adjust their research and funding priorities accordingly.[3] Breast cancer activists have also, however, faced controversy as they have struggled with questions such as whether to challenge large cancer institutions like the ACS, or how to address the needs of lesbians and their families in terms of direct-care services.[4] Thus, like AIDS activists, breast cancer activists have struggled over the goals, tactics, and agendas of their organizations. Lesbian activists have inserted themselves into AIDS and breast cancer activism and have become important actors in shaping these organizations.

Engaged, provocative, and effective breast cancer activism began to emerge on the public scene in the late 1980s. In Boston, fervent public discussion of breast cancer can be traced to a 1989 article in the monthly feminist publication *Sojourner*, which published Susan Shapiro's article "Cancer as a Feminist Issue." That same year the Women's Community Cancer Project (WCCP) was formed in Boston and began instigating some of the first direct action protests targeted at issues relating to women's cancers.

It was during the early 1990s that lesbians began to present the issue of breast cancer to lesbian and gay communities. One of the first articles to appear on breast cancer in the gay press was published in June 1990 in the *Gay Community News* (GCN), an influential Boston lesbian and gay biweekly with national distribution. Many lesbians and some gay men had, however, first been confronted with the realities of breast cancer in Audre Lorde's 1980 book *The Cancer Journals*.[5] Yet it was not until African American lesbian, poet, and women's health activist Pat Parker's death from breast cancer in the fall of 1989 that a collective sense of urgency regarding cancer and cancer deaths struck a number of lesbians and resulted in the creation of lesbian-specific cancer projects, including the Seattle Lesbian Cancer Project, Chicago's Lesbian Community Cancer Project, and Washington, D.C.'s Susan Hester Mautner Project for Lesbians with Cancer.

By the time breast cancer activism had come into full swing in 1991, AIDS activism was, by some accounts, ten years old. Within the lesbian and gay community, political activism around AIDS during the mid- to late 1980s brought about a significant change in the relationship between lesbian and gay male activists, and the birth of a new form of lesbian and gay coalition politics. As the AIDS movement developed, lesbians played an important role in shaping the trajectory of discussion and action (GCN, 18–24 September 1988). From early on, a number of women argued for attention to be paid to both the cross-section of individuals affected by the pandemic and the diversity of issues particularly relevant to the lives of those living with the disease (in particular, housing, food, and other basic needs) (ACT

UP/NY Women and AIDS 1990). Sarah Schulman, lesbian journalist, novelist, and activist, described the politics of the period this way:

> After ten years of the feminist movement while most gay men were apolitical, lesbians had a more sophisticated analysis of the state and a clearer impetus towards direct action. Although gay men had access to significantly more resources and power than lesbians, they were just realizing that the state did not care whether they lived or died. This process of revelation was an obstacle that lesbians did not have to overcome, having been clear on their exclusion from the beginning. (1994, 123–24)

By the late 1980s and early 1990s, increasing numbers of lesbians were actively a part of the many ACT UP organizations across the country (ACT UP/NY Women and AIDS 1990, vii–5). Yet although a united front was presented during protests, the men and women in these organizations had many tense moments. Much of the tension was centered around the goals and agendas of ACT UP (6–15). During the early 1980s, internal debates within ACT UP chapters were often framed as treatment versus housing, food, or access to health care. Generally speaking, primarily white gay men argued for ACT UP to commit its energies to issues relating to treatment and a cure, while many lesbians and a number of gay men of color argued for more attention to be paid to the day-to-day needs of people living with AIDS (PWAs), such as housing, food, and access to health care. In many ways this split may have been as much a function of race and gender (inasmuch as such identities may shape one's political priorities) as it was of class and thus access to financial resources.

At the heart of such debates were issues of ideology — What are the ultimate goals of the work? Or said differently, what kind of societal change are these particular forms of political participation trying to elicit? Nancy Wechsler, a lesbian AIDS activist, described her ideological location this way in a 1988 diary entry:

> I have questions about the direction this movement is taking. With most of the news coverage being limited to demands for release of new AIDS drugs, I'm worried about whether or not it will be possible to broaden the agenda. . . . We need to draw attention to the need for sexually explicit, culturally sensitive safe sex education/brochures. . . . And it doesn't even get us into the issues of national health care, or housing, child care, good nutrition, etc. that some PWAs need and can't afford. . . . We can't be afraid to challenge each other . . . nor should we be afraid to listen. (GCN, 16–22 October 1988)

Another lesbian activist, Boston's Sue Hyde, played an important role in the early development of AIDS activism by helping to develop a coalition among progressive grassroots AIDS organizations, out of which grew ACT NOW. The work of ACT NOW challenged ACT UP and other organizations to understand the medical crisis of AIDS in a larger economic, political, and social context. Hyde has argued that one of the most important roles of ACT NOW was to insure that inclusiveness was a key priority in the AIDS movement (GCN, 15–21 May 1988). Hyde worked with Urvashi Vaid, the former director of the National Gay and Lesbian Task Force and a founding member of ACT NOW, to ensure that AIDS organizations began to dialogue with each other about their respective goals and agendas for future activism.

One of the first such meetings was held in Boston in September 1988 (GCN, 1 October 1988). This meeting and others that followed were symbolic of the efforts of a number of lesbian AIDS activists to broaden the political agenda of AIDS activism. The diversification of the agenda of AIDS activism came slowly and only after many heated debates. The efforts of activists like Hyde and Vaid exposed the ideological roots of political protest and required that, at least intermittently, AIDS activists overtly discuss their larger political agendas and ideological roots.

Importantly, lesbian participation in AIDS activism highlights both the power of marginalization to have an impact on the goals and agendas of those marginalized and the ability of groups to coalesce politically around internally developed identities. In a 1988 speech Cindy Patton, a public health professional, academic, AIDS activist, and lesbian, accurately described the political terrain on which AIDS activism has evolved:

> The different ways in which lesbians identify with or deny AIDS as a political, personal, and health issue and the reluctance of gay men to acknowledge the contributions of lesbians in AIDS organizing, and the reality that women and lesbians are also people living with AIDS, have provoked complicated and bitter battles over sexism. Lesbians and gay men have differing degrees of social visibility and different health care needs. ... At this same time, lesbians were (they continue to be) concerned about their health care needs as women — cervical and breast cancer, and the role we found ourselves playing in the lives of lesbian friends with terminal illnesses who needed care outside traditional family structure. (GCN, 18–24 September 1988)

Patton's speech not only highlighted the role of lesbians as AIDS activists, but also reminded her audience that lesbians themselves faced medical crises and were struggling to find a balance between AIDS activism and activism around issues that directly impacted their own lives. Despite her recognition of the lack of research and treatment targeted at women's health care issues, Patton continues to work hard on issues relating to AIDS while supporting those fighting breast cancer.

The Making of an Identity

Important to the theoretical construction of marginalization is the assertion that a marginalized group's outlook and experience of the world are informed by its members' marked status as "other," which shapes the contours of their political, social, and economic interactions. Similarly important are the definitions of "self" that are developed within marginalized communities. Internally developed identities, such as "lesbian," are created to project particular political and ethical images, and the employment of such identities in this manner often directs the trajectory of marginalized communities' activism. It is through the construction of internally developed identities that marginalized communities establish membership and project an alternative presentation of a given identity. Marginalized communities, through this process of remaking an identity, are also acting to transform the parameters of political debate by, for example, actively challenging the status quo's construction of their own identity. Such a challenge opens a public discussion of who can legitimately construct a group's identity.

As was noted earlier, tensions between gay men and lesbians have persisted throughout the AIDS crisis. As Sarah Schulman explains,

> [C]oming to ACT UP also meant working with men who had never supported women's struggle for autonomy. Men who had never fought rape, marched for abortion rights, contributed financial support, or simply informed themselves about women's lives. And for many, but not all, gay men this is still true today. In fact, it sometimes seems that the reason some gay men who once ignored us [lesbians], now praise us, is only because of our contribution to AIDS activism and not a recognition of our personhood. (1994, 216)

Part of Schulman's larger argument is that lesbians, due to our status as "other," have experienced discrimination in ways that are unique and can provide insights that are important to expansive political agendas. Sandra Steingraber, a cancer activist working with the Women's Community Cancer Project in Boston, echoes this sentiment when, as a breast cancer survivor, she argues that "I certainly believe that our experience of illness is inscribed by all of our particular identities" (Stocker 1991, 102). In these ways, identity is employed to explain differences in political activism and in the ideological positions of lesbian activists as compared to nonlesbians.

Although tensions between lesbians and nonlesbians are important for an understanding of the form and content of lesbian activists' activities, tensions among lesbians regarding the diversity of internal constructions of the category "lesbian" are also important for an understanding of lesbian activism. There tend to be, for instance, important generational differences between young lesbian AIDS activists and older breast cancer activists. Although some of these differences are grounded in political ideology (ideology here is understood to be a group of organizing principles that shape individuals' and groups' ultimate political and social objectives), others may be due to divergent understandings of "lesbian" identity (Dawson 1995). An activist and researcher from the Mautner Project for Lesbians with Cancer in Washington, D.C., conducting research comparing lesbian AIDS activists and lesbian breast cancer activists, found a generation gap that correlated with the individual activist's different constructions of the category "lesbian." She found that younger lesbians (those in their teens and twenties) were more likely to identify strongly with a lesbian and gay or "queer" identity than were their older counterparts, who were more likely to identify with a women-centered lesbian identity. Similarly, younger lesbians were more likely to be AIDS activists, while older lesbians were more likely to be breast cancer activists. The association of younger lesbians with queer politics and AIDS activism, and older lesbians with feminist politics and breast cancer activism reaffirms the existence of a symbiotic relationship between identity and ideology in the context of political participation.

The Mautner researcher found another area of divergence: lesbians of different races and ethnicities have different political goals and agendas. This finding resonates in Chicago's lesbian and gay community, where the political agendas of African American lesbians are often contrary to the agendas promoted by the increasingly politically powerful white gay male and lesbian leadership. The conflicts are most often publicly displayed during elections when different political action coalitions (PACs) endorse candidates (*Outlines*, October 1994). In recent years the city's mainstream lesbian and gay PAC has been challenged by African American lesbians and gay men for not taking into account issues relevant to their lives or the lives of other nonmajority lesbians and gay men. These conflicts have led some African American lesbians and gay men to develop their own PAC. In creating this coalition, these activists are asserting that their identity as black lesbians and gay men impacts not only their personal experiences but also their political priorities.

Indeed, identity is an important factor in the shaping of political agendas, the development of community cohesion, and the construction of coalitions. In the following section I examine how ideology operates in the process of constructing political priorities and conceiving of the political landscape.

Ideology and Lesbian Activism

Lesbians who participate in breast cancer and AIDS activism come to that work for an assortment of reasons. Many facets of their backgrounds may affect the activities in which they engage. Particularly relevant to an examination of the role of lesbians in AIDS and breast cancer activism is an understanding of the diversity of ideological locations that shape their participation. Internally developed ideologies and an internal infrastructure operate as important tools in the active resistance against dominant society's repression and as means of developing internal cohesion. It is important to recognize how ideology and identity operate differently in the process of group political participation. Here I understand identity to be a category that establishes an individual's membership in or exclusion from a community or group of individuals. Ideology, on the other hand, is understood to be a group of organizing principles that shape individuals' and groups' ultimate political and social objectives. Ideology, then, provides a group of principles around which groups of individuals can develop political strategy. As is true with identity, there are a number of different ideological positions to which lesbian activists adhere. These different ideologies have been constructed to provide an alternative to other ideological traditions in the United States that, in the eyes of some lesbians, do not present a group of principles around which they feel they can coalesce, form coalitions, and organize politically.

As we have seen, one important effect of marginalization is that marginalized people will have different priorities than those not similarly marginalized, and they will use different means to carry out those priorities. Marginalization creates barriers and limitations to resources to those marginalized. Experiencing these barriers can result in a marginalized person's adherence to a different set of organizing principles than a person who has never faced such barriers. Lesbian AIDS activist Cindy Patton has argued that in the realm of AIDS activism, lesbians bring a different group of primary concerns to the table than do gay men. She contends that these differences are not merely about strategy, but are about the respective ideological locations of lesbians and gay men (GCN, 18–24 September 1988). What Patton's observations reveal is that marginalization, while not determining the boundaries of ideology as it does for identity, does affect the construction of political priorities and the adherence to different ideologies. Indeed, as individuals and groups choose (or create) the organizing principles — ideology — that will shape their political priorities, factors such as the barriers they have faced and the deficit of resources they may work within will undoubtedly affect their ultimate choice of goals. It is for these reasons that the impact of marginalization is important for an understanding of those factors that determine groups' political participation. In this section I will examine how ideological differences have been greatly limited by the political, social, and economic context.

By the early 1990s, the late lesbian breast cancer and AIDS activist Jackie Winnow believed that women, especially lesbians, were spending too much of their time and energy on AIDS and too little on issues that directly affected large numbers of lesbians. Winnow argued, "We need to take the skills we have learned as feminists and apply them to our work on AIDS and to our work with women. And then take the skills we have from working with AIDS and apply them to working in women's health care. Let's bring it back home" (Stocker 1991, 34). What Winnow is asserting, then, is that one's identity should direct one's political ideology. For Winnow, politics should originate in the "home" — defined by one's identity — and move outward. The AIDS activist community, she argued, was not home; rather, home is where lesbian-centered activism is happening. Lesbian breast cancer activist Susan Liroff has echoed these sentiments:

> [During the seventies] lesbians everywhere were starting to deal with the fact that we need to take responsibility for our own bodies and each other's bodies. [But] once abortion rights and access to birth control became politicized, that whole self-help movement ... got pre-empted by the reproductive rights movement. And lesbians hopped on that bandwagon, whether it had anything to do with us or not, [because] it was a women's issue. Then the AIDS pandemic happened, and once again lesbians, by and large, went from reproductive rights to the AIDS movement. And we're really coming back to our own health. We're coming full circle, because we're dying in large numbers. (Brandt 1993, 36)

Lesbian AIDS activist Sarah Schulman has argued differently. An important part of her community has been found among AIDS activists, and she has often argued that some of the best activism has come from a cross-pollination of the skills of lesbians and the relative privilege of gay men. For Schulman, taking skills and knowledge learned from doing feminist organizing and applying it to AIDS activism was bringing that knowledge home. For her, this combination of efforts was a positive development, not a step away from a commitment to lesbians. Schulman writes,

> Beyond the deaths of personal friends to AIDS I also came to ACT UP, over three years ago, because lesbians were no longer doing activist work. ACT UP was the only movement I could agitate in that permitted me to affirm my homosexuality. And it was the only organization addressing AIDS that was truly activist. I also came to ACT UP because AIDS is an event, which like abortion, encompasses social and personal liberation issues that are consistent with my vision of what we need to have freedom. (1994, 216)

The ideological differences represented in the concerns of lesbian activists Winnow, Liroff, and Schulman have not developed in a vacuum. They have been greatly affected by the political, social, and economic context. In the next section I will further explore this context.

CDC, NIH, ACS, FDA — Alphabet City: The Institutional and Organizational Terrain of Breast Cancer and AIDS Activism

Although dominant and resistant relations to gender, sexuality, race, and class are important components of AIDS and breast cancer activism, the role of the country's most powerful medical organizations and institutions must also be investigated. Such institutions, due in part to their political and economic positions, have delimited citizens' access to the various discourses regarding medical conditions. Thus, in order to understand why breast cancer and AIDS activists choose the targets and tactics they do, we must further explore the role and influence of medical organizations and governmental institutions, and how they determine the distribution of resources.

The federal government plays a pivotal role in codifying identities of otherness and perpetuating marginalization.[6] Federal agencies, by way of policy, and Congress, by way of legislation, categorize groups as "undeserving" or "deviant" and restrict their access to the goods they distribute. Such goods include, but are not limited to, monetary goods, whether they be tax breaks or cash stipends; noncash goods, such as medical care; and legislative or governmental goods, such as control over construction of federal voting districts. At the same time, governments level sanctions against prohibited actions. For example, lesbians and gay men can be restricted from filing joint federal taxes with their partners; they can also be prohibited from adopting children. Importantly, it is these two branches of government that have set the agenda for federally funded research and treatment, and all federal laws regarding HIV and breast cancer.[7] In doing so, these two branches of government are able to marshal the resources and authority of the federal government in the implementation and enforcement of marginalization.

AIDS activists in the mid-1990s made historic strides in subjecting federal health organizations and medical research institutions to public scrutiny and protest. These activists did so, however, in the wake of efforts by women health activists of the late 1960s and 1970s who forced public discussion of the government's and private industry's role in the creation of dangerous birth control devices (see Gordon 1990). Some of the most important outcomes of AIDS activism has been the opening up of formerly private processes to public scrutiny and the forced acknowledgment that laypeople have an important role to play in shaping policies and agendas. As activists attempted to learn more about potential AIDS treatments, they found that the public was entirely restricted from the drug approval process. In response, AIDS activists insisted that pharmaceutical companies prioritize AIDS research and that governmental agencies move quickly and diligently through the drug approval process.

By directly confronting the FDA's drug approval policy, AIDS activists brought to the public spotlight the formerly private interactions between the FDA and private pharmaceutical companies in the approval process (ACT UP/NY Women and AIDS 1990, 69–79). In a similar manner, breast cancer activists have called into question the NIH's research priorities and relationship with the ACS (American Cancer Society) (*Canswers* 3, nos. 1–2, 1995). They have exposed the private and exclusive nature of the relationship between the ACS and the NIH: as a result of extensive lobbying by the ACS, the NIH consults the ACS — and almost no on else — before constructing policy announcements.[8]

A particularly significant example of the impact of activism on federal institutions' policy is the recent change in the Center for Disease Control's (CDC) definition of AIDS — a change due, in part, to the role of lesbian AIDS activists. The definition of AIDS (as distinguished from an HIV-positive status) is actually a checklist of symptoms. For a person to be diagnosed with AIDS (a prerequisite for qualifying for most federal assistance), they must exhibit a combination of symptoms from the official checklist (ACT UP/NY Women and AIDS 1990, 32–41). Until 1994, nearly all medical research and diagnostic categories were based on male subjects (not unlike nearly all other medical research, including cancer research) (Schulman 1994, 211–15). The result was that some women living with the HIV virus were becoming terminally ill and in some cases dying before being diagnosed as having AIDS. Such women were not receiving federal assistance and, in some cases, were dying prematurely due to lack of medical services. In the early 1990s AIDS activists from ACT UP women's committee began lobbying the CDC to change its definition of AIDS to better represent the actual medical conditions of the diversity of HIV-positive people (Schulman 1994, 211–15).

After years of intense lobbying and other political pressure (including phone-zaps and protests), in the spring of 1994 the CDC changed its definition. An important victory for AIDS activists, this change in policy also represented an important shift in relations between citizens and federal agencies. The discussions that occurred between ACT UP women's committee and the CDC did not occur as result of the work of influential lobbyists. Rather, the needed change in policy came as a result of the insistence of self-educated activists that the right public health discussion was different from the former CDC policy.

Similarly, breast cancer activists have noted that treatments for cancer are tested primarily on men despite the fact that gender-linked cancers are more prevalent among women (Stocker 1991, 5). The medical industry has, in other words, continued to operate with a presumption of the male body as the norm. Such an assumption, as Sharon Batt has noted, results in cancer research that continues to systematically exclude women from clinical tests and case studies (Batt 1994). In this way, the biased research priorities of much of the medical industry predetermine some of the areas of organizing for AIDS and breast cancer activism. Research on medical conditions that affect women — including breast cancer and AIDS — has been sparse to nonexistent. Because of this research bias, there is little good information on the impact of the diversity of protocols being employed to address both of these medical conditions in women. Although such biased research and treatment continue, they have been challenged by breast cancer and AIDS activists who have called into question the arbitrary ranking of the health of some of society's members over others.

As we have already seen, the functions and actions of private organizations and businesses such as the ACS, the AMA (American Medical Association), and pharmaceutical companies have also had a critical impact on the day-to-day lives of individuals while operating entirely outside the public gaze. Many activists, including those at the Women's Community Cancer Project in Boston, have questioned the ACS's agenda and priorities. Monies devoted to cancer through organizations like the ACS have historically been allocated to early detection and to education regarding early detection and personal habits (for example, encouraging people to stop smoking and to eat a balanced diet), while very few resources have been dedicated to locating the causes of cancer and improvements in treatment. Jean Hardisty of WCCP discusses their targeting of ACS:

> The other part of the protest was over the American Cancer Society's reluctance to pay attention to the relationship between environmental pollution and cancer, to the point that they have actually not signed on to environmental legislation, which seems such a scandal. We were demonstrating to demand some kind of explanation. I think the explanation probably is that half of the polluters sit on the board of the American Cancer Society! (Brandt 1993)

In targeting ACS and others, WCCP and other breast cancer organizations have begun to open to public view and scrutiny the operations of large institutions, with the goal of making such institutions more responsible to the citizens they assert they are serving and representing.

As alluded to earlier, it is an individual's marginal status rather than their medical condition that dictates how a society and economic polity will react to their condition. At the same time, a marginalized community's indigenous identity and ideological position deeply shape their construction of goals and choice of tactics, as well as their political participation. It is through a comprehensive examination of the terrain on which lesbians participate politically that insights into some of the causal agents will arise. The impact of marginalization on the provision of medical care, the distribution of societal goods by governmental bodies, the construction of ideological positions, and the indigenous construction of identity by marginalized communities all have important consequences for marginalized communities' political participation and thereby remain an important area for future research by social scientists.

The Marginalized Uses of Power and Identity

This examination of lesbian activists lends credence to the assertion that marginalization does indeed shape the political participation of individuals and groups. In the context of AIDS organizing, many lesbian activists have persistently argued for a more expansive conceptualization of the goals than that articulated by many of their gay male counterparts. This suggests no inherent differences between lesbians and gay men, but rather that lesbians and gay men are marginalized in significantly different ways, a fact that affects their relative access to resources and, consequently, the definition of their respective political goals.

Most centrally this project has been aimed at constructing tools that will help social scientists better understand what factors shape citizens' participation in politics. My focus has been on the political participation of marginal community members, thus taking seriously their role in and impact on the polity, and on the importance of a number of intersecting factors influencing such participation, including ideology, governmental and societal structures, and — most importantly for my work around marginalization — identity. Such examinations provide additional insights into boundaries of participation — that is, the domains in which citizens can engage politically to effect change in societal and governmental structures. The efforts of communities to resist dominant society's repression and exclusion can provide scholars (as well as those outside the academy) with important information about the contemporary operation of the democratic process in the United States, the impact of the political economy on this operation, and effective (or ineffective) ways communities can attempt to resist such domination.

AIDS and breast cancer activists serve as useful case studies of the important role that community political participation can have on the greater polity. By forcing public debate around important medical issues, breast cancer and AIDS activists have substantially altered the way the medical industry and governmental bodies make important epidemiological and medical decisions. Specifically, they have forced open the certification process for experimental drugs and have challenged and demanded a reconsideration of the protocol employed by researchers in longitudinal research and for treatment of breast cancer and AIDS patients more generally. Most centrally, these activists have helped to continue to politicize a realm of the society that was formerly shielded from public scrutiny and political debate. By opening these areas to political debate, these activists have challenged the former notions of public and private spheres in the American polity, and have thereby reopened debate regarding the boundaries of political discourse.

Particularly relevant to this study have been the insights gained by examining the influence lesbian activists have had both on expanding the range of issues AIDS activists address to include issues pertaining to women and impoverished PWAs, and on ensuring the provision of direct-care services to lesbians battling breast cancer. The theoretical framework employed here allows for a further examination of how the intersection of ideology and identity results in the use by some lesbian activists of different tactics to achieve different goals. This framework also highlights the importance of understanding how societies and governments marginalize groups of individuals and how that process shapes resistance to such domination. Those most disenfranchised from institutional resources will most heavily rely on internally developed institutions, such as media (alternative newspapers), philanthropic organizations (the Aestra Foundation), or service organizations (programs like Meals on Wheels for HIV-positive people or women living with cancer), and will be less likely to look to traditional avenues for effecting change.

This project opens the door to further examination of the impact of marginalization on political participation. As research continues in this area, social scientists will be provided important information into the full range of restrictions imposed on marginal groups, the areas in which such communities can create their own indigenous resources, the effectiveness of such resources, and the possibilities available for a broad, societal reconfiguration of power relations.

NOTES

1. The exceptions are the work of a group of primarily lesbian and gay political scientists: Martha Acklesberg, Robert Bailey, Ann Marie Smith, Paisley Currah, and Cathy Cohen, to name a few. However, the majority of political scientists studying U.S. politics have failed to incorporate lesbians and gay men into their examinations of the American polity.

2. Until 1994 almost none of the experimental drug trials were being conducted on women. Researchers argued that women's bodies are too complex and make "conclusive" findings harder to achieve. Women are, indeed, different biologically from men, and the HIV virus (as is the case with reproductive cancers) expresses itself differently in women than in men. Thus, medical research on women subjects (beyond pregnant mothers) is an important venue for political activity. See the ACT UP/NY Women and AIDS Book Group 1990, 1–3; "Lesbians Get AIDS, Too" 1990; "Women and HIV" 1993; Schneider and Stoller 1995, 36–37.

3. A good example of this new coalition was the conference in Garden City, New York, entitled "Breast Cancer and the Environment: What We Know, What We Don't Know, What We Need to Know," in which Greenpeace, WCCP, and the Women's Environment Development Organization (WEDO), among others, came together to discuss the connection between breast cancer and the environment and to form a political coalition (*Women's Community Cancer Project Newsletter*, no. 4 [winter 1994]).

4. A good example in the Massachusetts context is the different tactics employed by two Boston-based organizations regarding NIH and ACS policies. The Massachusetts Breast Cancer Coalition (MBCC) has more institutional roots, and its relationship with the NIH and the ACS is based more on negotiation, whereas its sister organization, WCCP, is more confrontational, and its members have less direct ties to either the ACS or the NIH.

5. Audre Lorde died of breast cancer in February 1993.

6. For a further examination of the role of government in the codification of otherness, see Alexander 1991.

7. These laws include the regulation of mammography for breast cancer screening and the regulation of the HIV testing process. It is also important to remember the role of industrial representatives in shaping legislation and directing the trajectory of the legislative process. Breast cancer and AIDS disproportionately affect communities that have faced decades upon decades of legislated discrimination.

8. While the ACS maintains an exclusive relationship with the NIH, a number of cancer activists, including NBCC, due to persistent efforts, have begun to meet with NIH representatives and testify at a variety of NIH hearings.

BIBLIOGRAPHY

Abelove, Henry, Michele Aina Barale, and David Halperin. 1993. *The Lesbian and Gay Studies Reader*. New York: Routledge.

ACT UP/NY Women and AIDS Book Group. 1990. *Women, AIDS, and Activism*. Boston: South End.

Alexander, Jacqui. 1991. "Redrafting Morality: The Postcolonial State and the Sexual Offenses Bill of Trinidad and Tobago." In *Third World Women and the Politics of Feminism*, ed. Chandra Mohanty et al. Bloomington: Indiana University Press.

Anthias, Floya, and Nira Yuval-Davis. 1992. *Radicalized Boundaries: Race, Nation, Gender, Colour and Class and the Anti-Racist Struggle*. London: Routledge.

Batt, Sharon. 1994. *Patient No More: The Politics of Breast Cancer*. Charlottetown: Gynergy.

Blasius, Mark. 1994. *Gay and Lesbian Politics: Sexuality and the Emergence of a New Ethic*. Philadelphia: Temple University Press.

Brady, Judy. 1991. *One in Three: Women with Cancer Confront an Epidemic*. San Francisco: Cleis.

Brandt, Kate. 1993. "Lesbians at Risk: Breast Cancer." *Deneuve*, September–October, 34–37.

Butler, Judith, and Joan Scott. 1992. *Feminists Theorize the Political*. London: Routledge.

Calhoun, Craig. 1994. *Social Theory and the Politics of Identity*. Cambridge, MA: Blackwell.

Cant, Bob, and Susan Hemmings. 1988. *Radical Records: Thirty Years of Lesbian and Gay History*. London: Routledge.

Castells, Manuel. 1983. *The City and the Grassroots*. Berkeley: University of California Press.

Cohen, Cathy. 1993. "Power, Resistance and the Construction of Crisis: Marginalized Communities' Response to AIDS." Ph.D. diss., University of Michigan.

———. 1996. "Contested Membership: Black Gay Identities and the Politics of AIDS." In *Queer Theory/Sociology*, ed. Steven Seidman. London: Blackwell.

Dahl, Robert. 1961. *Who Governs?* New Haven: Yale University Press.

Davis, Angela. 1983. *Women, Race and Class*. New York: Random House.

Dawson, Michael. 1995. "Structure and Ideology: The Shaping of Black Public Opinion." Presented at the Race, Ethnicity and Urban Poverty Workshop, University of Chicago, January 26.

Echols, Alice. 1989. *Daring to Be Bad: Radical Feminism in America, 1967–1975*. Minneapolis: University of Minnesota Press.

Gallagher, John. 1993. "Lesbian Health Comes Out of the Closet." *Advocate* 643:30–32.

Goodman, Gerre et al. 1983. *No Turning Back: Lesbian and Gay Liberation for the '80s*. Philadelphia: New Society Press.

Gordon, Linda. 1990. *Woman's Body, Woman's Right*. Rev. ed. New York: Penguin Books.

Gunew, Sneja. 1990. *Feminist Knowledge*. New York: Routledge.

Habermas, Jurgen. 1991. *The Structural Transformation of the Public Sphere*. Cambridge: MIT Press.

Hansell, David A. 1993. "Comment: The TB and HIV Epidemics: History Learned and Unlearned." *Law, Medicine and Health Care* 21:376.

Hardy, Anne, and Charles E. Rosenberg. 1995. "Explaining Epidemics and Other Studies in the History of Medicine." *Journal of the History of the Behavioral Sciences* 31:162.

Harper, Philip Brian. 1995. *Gender Politics and the "Passing" Fancy: Black Masculinity as Societal Problem*. Chicago Humanities Institute. Photocopy.

Hull, Gloria, Patricia Bell Scott, and Barbara Smith. 1982. *All the Women Are White, All the Blacks Are Men, but Some of Us Are Brave*. New York: Feminist Press.

Jennings, James. 1993. *The Politics of Black Empowerment*. Detroit: Wayne State University.

Jones, J. H. 1993. *Bad Blood: The Tuskegee Syphilis Experiment*. Rev. ed. New York: Free Press.

Kayal, Philip. 1993. *Bearing Witness: Gay Men's Health Crisis and the Politics of AIDS*. Boulder: Westview.

Laraña, Enrique, Hank Johnston, and Joseph Gusfield. 1994. *New Social Movement: From Ideology to Identity*. Philadelphia: Temple University Press.

"Lesbians Get AIDS, Too." 1990. *Sojourner*, November.

Lorde, Audre. 1980. *The Cancer Journals*. San Francisco: Spinsters/Aunt Lute.

———. 1986. *Our Dead behind Us*. New York: Norton.

Love, Susan. 1990. *Dr. Susan Love's Breast Book*. New York: Addison Wesley.

McEwen, Christian, and Sue O'Sullivan. 1989. *Out the Other Side*. Freedom, CA: Crossing.

Mitra, Subrata. 1992. *Power, Protest and Participation*. London: Routledge.

Mohanty, Chandra, Ann Russo, and Lourdes Torres. 1991. *Third World Women and the Politics of Feminism*. Bloomington: Indiana University Press.

Mueller, Carol. 1994. "Conflict Networks and the Origins of Women's Liberation." In *New Social Movement: From Ideology to Identity*, ed. Laraña, Johnston, and Gusfield.

National Cancer Institute. 1994. *SEER Cancer Statistics Review 1973–1991*. Washington, DC: National Institutes of Health.

O'Hanlan, Katherine. 1995. "Homophobia in Lesbian Health Care." *Advocate* 676:47–49.

O'Malley, Padraig. 1988. *The AIDS Epidemic: Private Rights and Public Interest*. Boston: Beacon Press.

Patton, Cindy. 1990. *Inventing AIDS*. New York: Routledge.

Phelan, Shane. 1994. *Getting Specific: Postmodern Lesbian Politics*. Minneapolis: University of Minnesota Press.

Rubenstein, William. 1993. *Lesbians, Gay Men, and the Law*. New York: New Press.

Schneider, Beth, and Nancy Stoller. 1995. *Women Resisting AIDS: Feminist Strategies of Empowerment*. Philadelphia: Temple University Press.

Schulman, Sarah. 1994. *My American History: Lesbian and Gay Life during the Reagan/Bush Years*. New York: Routledge.

Stocker, Midge. 1991. *Cancer as a Women's Issue: Scratching the Surface*. Chicago: Third Side Press.

———. 1993. *Confronting Cancer, Constructing Change*. Chicago: Third Side Press.

Thomas, S. B., and S. C. Quinn. 1991. "The Tuskegee Syphilis Study, 1932 to 1972." *American Journal of Public Health* 81:1498–1504.

What a Lesbian Looks Like: Writings by Lesbians and Their Lives and Lifestyles from the Archives of the National Lesbian and Gay Survey. 1992. London: Routledge.

"Women and HIV." 1993. *Sojourner*, March.

EIGHTEEN

Winning Action for Gender Equity
A Plan for Organizing
Communities of Color

RINKU SEN

The average American woman of color finds life difficult and getting harder every day. She works for poverty wages, without health or pension benefits, and in physically dangerous conditions. If she is injured on her job, or she gets pregnant, or the company she works for decides to move operations to a more hospitable environment, she is likely to lose her irreplaceable job. She finds herself under investigation or arrested for any number of sins — smoking the occasional joint, receiving food stamps she "doesn't deserve," being unable to keep her teenager in school every day, bouncing too many checks, or behaving in a manner thought inappropriate to women and labeled "solicitation."

All things considered, though, she knows that the worst is coming. By the year 2000, she'll be unable to rely on standard public services, forced to bargain for health care, food, housing, and education on the free market, or count entirely on the whims of private charity. She sees that the available decent jobs are moving further away from her community, and their decency seems to be quickly eroding. She hopes that her friends and family will be around, but expects to see them in juvenile and adult prisons. She may find herself on her way to deportation if she cannot document her citizenship. She will find herself the victim of escalating, and not so random, violence.

These horrific images of women's lives evoke the need for a vibrant, large, strategic movement to reverse the victories of the Right Wing. The victories of the Left in civil rights, anti-imperialist, feminist, and labor movements have spurred a well-planned backlash by a resurgent Right Wing (the New Right) that gains power daily. These are not our grandmothers' conservatives, who had their heyday in the 1950s. The New Right also relies on scapegoating for its divide and conquer strategy, most frequently to protect capitalist privileges, and is profoundly racist and patriarchal. But unlike the Old Right, the New Right views government as its enemy, rather than its ally, and it is well organized. The New Right is as much a men's movement as it is white supremacist and capitalist, and it is global. From Rush Limbaugh's hatemongering radio shows, through attacks on affirmative action that target women and people of color for causing economic problems, to the increasing monopolization of American industry and its downsizing of the U.S. workforce, the New Right pushes the levers of economic, political, and cultural power that shape and direct public opinion.

Progressive organizers of color agree that the justice movement has the potential to unify despite our current state of fragmentation. That potential depends on a full analysis, grounded in fact and experience, and the ability, freedom, and infrastructure to act. The elements of such analysis and action already exist abundantly in local, often small community organizations of color, and this is a promising location for movement building over the next twenty years. Women working in these organizations offer seasoned leadership, plenty of experience living with and subverting oppressive systems, and the drive to imagine and fight for transformed social systems. To nurture and consolidate this source of power, community organizations will need to integrate gender analysis and fights for gender equity into their racial and economic justice work.

These assertions emerge from my own organizing experience in Black, Asian, Latino, and Native American communities for the last eleven years. For eight years I have been on the staff of the Center for Third World Organizing (CTWO, pronounced C2), a national training and organizing institute owned and operated by people of color. Organizers of color founded CTWO in 1980 to meet the interests of our communities by increasing our capacity to build constituency-led, direct action organizations as independent fighting machines. CTWO's programs include training and recruiting organizers of color, testing multiracial models that define new issues, convening discussions and collaborative campaigns, pursuing research, and producing publications.

CTWO is driven by a primary constituency of women of color who lead investigations into the gender question. Seventy-five percent of the graduates of our most famous organizer training program, the eleven-year-old Minority Activist Apprenticeship Program, are women aged eighteen to thirty. Seventy-five percent of the members and volunteer leaders of our three local organizations, and most of the other organizations we work with, are women, usually mothers between twenty-five and fifty-five years old. The majority of our staff, fed directly by our training programs in a grow-your-own model of staff development, are women. Any realistic assessment of our own power reveals that much of our best leadership comes from women and that the roles patriarchy has assigned to women fuel our attraction to organizing. With this understanding, we have designed a program to support gender analysis and gender equity campaigns in community organizations of color. The program, Winning Action for Gender Equity (WAGE), incorporates a Budget Equity Project, which will analyze public budgets to reveal their discriminatory racial and gender dimensions, and a Model Campaigns Program that will provide technical

assistance and documentation to organizations challenging sexist institutional practices. Our design has been informed primarily by a thorough examination of the
New Right and a gendered assessment of our own movement's strengths and weaknesses.

Examining the New Right's leaders, motivations, strategies, and weaknesses constitutes more than a conspiracy theory exercise; we want to understand the forces
exploiting our constituencies in order to create effective strategies. The New Right's
strategy encompasses three broad institutional trends: the globalization of free market capitalism, the abolition of government for all purposes other than criminal
prosecution and national defense, and the creation of a national culture that is white
supremacist and patriarchal to its core. These trends already have hurt women of
color deeply. Global capitalism gives corporations free rein and severely restricts
women's rights in the workplace and market. The reduction of government manifests
itself through the privatization of public social service systems that women predominantly rely on, work in, pay for, and replace. The Right's cultural agenda appears to
challenge the socially liberal corporate media, yet both the Right and corporate
America portray women as subservient sexual objects for men, and feed a culture of
misogyny (hatred of women) that kills women daily.

In truth, we have been fighting the conservative wave for many years. Throughout
the 1970s and 1980s, community organizing grew in size and shape, as organizations
defined and won all kinds of struggles, the majority related to social arenas dominated by women's labor: health care, education, housing, environment, and food.
These victories include shutting down welfare hotels and winning permanent housing for homeless families, getting multiracial social studies curricula implemented
in public high schools, preventing the siting of toxic dumps in low-income communities. Despite our successes, community organizing, like its counterparts in labor,
feminism, and other movements, faces a turning point, partly because the New
Right is clearly on the verge of a massive victory. The future of community organizations depends entirely on our ability to understand our opponents, develop our
strengths, attack oppressive systems where they are most vulnerable, and design new
social systems that transform power relations from those of domination to those of
community and fairness.

Because women are central to the New Right's success and because women make
up the liveliest contingent of our activist base, community organizations wishing to
expand their reach and effectiveness have to build an active feminist constituency
among women of color. We believe that community organizations need to start these
efforts with a systematic popular examination of gender dynamics in political,
economic, and social life. Such an investigation will force organizations to consider
the gender question in relation to all available institutions — prisons, courts, hospitals, schools, factories, social service providers — that oppress us. That analysis has to
inform our collective attack on the racist, sexist, patriarchal policies of the New
Right, and to equip us to implement equitable and just social structures. The ability
of organizers to do gender analysis and generate effective action for gender equity
rests on our ability to remove three barriers from community organizing practice.
These barriers — nationalism, an anti-ideological definition of the role of the orga-

nizer, and the sexual division of labor within our organizations — present distinct challenges to organizers of color.

Our ultimate goal is to enable organizations to act together on a common agenda. The ability to take collective action is our single greatest source of power; it can be expanded only by further action and reflection. Because women share so many roles across culture and class, explicit gender analysis has the potential to draw together women of color to collectivize our issues, a necessary precursor to taking action together. If our agenda is grounded also in the standards of racial and economic justice, because it is led by women who have the most to gain from a complete overhaul of all three systems, we may avoid the fragmentation of feminism's second wave, frequently criticized by women of color as catering to the interests of racially and economically privileged women. We may also avoid the mistakes of male-dominated race- and class-based organizations whose memberships are dying out because they did not organize women; these include the less progressive AFL-CIO unions and mainstream civil rights organizations like the NAACP.

What We're Up Against: Global Capitalism, Abolition of Government, and a Misogynist Culture

The institutions and tactics of the New Right shape political, economic and cultural life in the United States. The policy initiatives we encounter today — the resistance to a woman's right to an abortion, scapegoating of immigrants of color as job stealers and welfare queens, attacks on gay men and lesbians as leeches preying on the legacy of the civil rights movement — divide Americans by race and gender interests. This movement results from a carefully implemented thirty-year plan conceived by New Right leaders after the failed Barry Goldwater presidential campaign.[1] Jean Hardisty, director of the Political Research Associates in Boston, attributes the success of the New Right agenda as much to its high level of infrastructure as to its ability to gauge the mood of the American public:

> These goals were achieved not simply because of a spontaneous expression of backlash social sentiments, racial resentments, or economic anger. They were accomplished by capturing decision-making positions (winning elected office), mobilizing resources (getting control of bureaucracies), and swaying public opinion (activating political ideologues through a network of organizations, publications, conferences, television and radio); voter education and activist training.[2]

Right Wing institutions are carrying out a plan for globalizing capitalism, privatizing social services, and producing a culture of misogyny. These institutions often engage the same people in multiple formations, including Concerned Women of America, Operation Rescue, the California Business PAC, and Focus on the Family.

Globalizing the Free Market

The New Right's approach to the goals of capitalism and its hatred of government distinguish the New Right from its predecessors. While the Old Right willingly made labor and environmental concessions to preserve stability for capital, the New Right is dominated by a younger generation of capitalists, usually independent, smaller venturers in high-risk industries.[3] These venture capitalists value fast growth more than stability, and they have absorbed the stability capitalists. The New Right's allegiance to venture capitalists has created a global economy whose fastest growing sectors are hi-tech companies (oil, electronics, software, pharmaceuticals) and service operations (restaurants, hotels, clerical, tourism). Women are heavily concentrated in the bottom rungs of the former, for example, as microchip assemblers, and the nonmanagement role of the latter, for example, as hotel maids.[4] Using the tools of free trade agreements, temporary employment, and subcontracting, the New Right capitalists have successfully turned the entire world into "an economic environment that was hospitable for fast growth. Deregulation, deunionization, and lower corporate taxes were the agenda. . . . The result has been the preservation (even inflation) of profits, but at a high social cost."[5]

Contingent work and subcontracting in the industries dominated by women workers encourage widespread corporate irresponsibility toward workers. Both devices rely heavily on the devaluation of women's labor. In the United States, the use of temporary workers and part-time workers is growing much faster than total employment, and many employers are beginning to replace permanent staff with contingent workers.[6] Temporary and part-time workers, 70 percent of whom are women, have very little job security, endure frequent wage and hour abuses, and have no recourse when they are abused at work — a potential worker stands ready to take the job they vacate.[7]

For example, Myrna Major, an African American food service worker at the Citadel — a South Carolina public all-male military college — has watched the degeneration of working conditions there for twenty-seven years. Major notes that "we never considered anybody part time workers before, but the new management told us last year that workers who did not work during the summer, when the school is closed and we are laid off for lack of work, will be considered part time and cannot get health insurance."[8] Major's coworkers have also felt the harsh realities of subcontracting, as the Citadel contracts these workers through Aramark, a private national food service company. The Citadel contracts out much of its operations, from janitorial to food services, and awards contracts to the lowest bidders, who are most likely to be large, even multinational companies whose established infrastructure and regressive labor policies allow them to bid cheaply on contracts. Major says that in their battle to unionize food service workers, subcontracting allows both institutions to pass the buck. "The Citadel denies that we are employed by them, and Aramark also denies it in the sense that we serve the Citadel, not Aramark. We don't really know who employs us, though Aramark writes our checks." Major and her coworkers are now organizing their union through the Carolina Alliance for Fair Employment (CAFE), a community workers' organization.

Global capitalism devastates workers of color and poor people in general. The United States has the widest gap among the industrialized countries of the world between the population's richest 10 percent and poorest 10 percent, an almost 600 percent difference.[9] Although corporate profits rose 40 percent in 1994, stockholders, rather than workers, see the benefits of higher production and higher profits. Stock-holder dividends increased 250 percent from 1980 to 1993, while real wages have decreased by 20 percent since 1973.[10] Because real wages are so low, even working full-time at minimum wage does not guarantee freedom from poverty. Nearly 75 percent of full-time working women and 37 percent of full-time working men earn less than $20,000 per year.[11] One-third of women-headed families live in poverty.[12]

Privatization and the Abolition of Government

A move to the right usually means reinforcing the position of the establishment, "but the contemporary U.S. Right's conservatism is not of the system-supporting type. . . . The right, both religious and secular, is more extreme in its ideology. It fosters suspicion, even hatred of government."[13] Nowhere is that more evident than in the current public policy debates over social service budget cuts and public reinvestment into society.

Today's reduction of government was launched by Ronald Reagan, continued by George Bush, and reaches new success under the leadership of Republican Congressmen Newt Gingrich and Bob Dole. Reagan's trickle-down theory argued that the wealthy would manage their own reinvestment in the U.S. economy, and Bush's Thousand Points of Light plan expected volunteerism to replace publicly funded services. The ultimate goal of reducing the U.S. government is to privatize most governmental functions (except incarceration, policing, and military) and return to a laissez-faire economic system in which government does not regulate business. The reduction appears in social service budget cuts and in the privatization of social investment, which becomes voluntary rather than mandated through tax policy.

The New Right justifies reducing government by laying the blame for budget deficits squarely at the door of poor people, citing domination of the federal budget by entitlements — "benefits programs in which eligible beneficiaries are automatically entitled to their payments without annual appropriations by Congress or any control by the President."[14] The authors of *The People's Budget* — a widely circulated New Right text outlining a rationale for reducing the federal government's involvement in antipoverty and other social programs — argue that entitlement programs actually encourage poverty by producing antisocial behavior, particularly in women:

> [The decline in poverty] stopped at 13–14 percent of the population . . . just as spending on Federal anti-poverty programs was beginning to rise rapidly. The U.S. saw a sustained, if not spectacular, growth of the economy in the 1980's, and the creation of more than 2 million jobs a year — but the poverty rate barely budged. At about the same time the War on Poverty was getting underway, there was a dramatic increase in births out of wedlock . . . the public is correct in perceiving that the government poverty programs subsidize anti-social behavior . . . the statistics on out-of-wedlock births directly related to crime rates are not fantasies."[15]

The authors do not mention that the jobs created are mainly low-wage, part-time, and devoid of benefits, nor that the average family on AFDC has fewer children than other American families.[16]

Privatization, or the transferral of previously government-funded programs in health care, education, and other social services to the private sector, opens new markets for corporate profit. Privatization is, in turn, made possible in large part by the age-old devaluation of women's labor. The assumption that women will provide certain services to society — feeding, clothing, sexually satisfying, housing, educating, and giving birth to reproduce the labor force — because these roles are "natural" to women applies even when those services are provided outside the home. Thus, female service workers like waitresses, who do for strangers what wives also do, are paid not as though they are workers but as though they are wives. Such devaluation has deep implications for a nation's economy; on the average a country's gross national product rises 45 percent when women's unpaid labor is counted.[17] Privatization is easiest with services that support children, the elderly, and families, because these are the social arenas in which women will pick up tasks abdicated by the state. Additional burdens on women go unrecognized when policy makers consider costs and benefits of privatization.

The contradiction between women's contribution and the low value of women's work glares at us when we examine child care. Institutions run by men do not consider child care in the wage formula of the free market — less than 2 percent of private sector companies and 9 percent of government agencies offer employer-sponsored day care.[18] Grace Brown, the African American former cochair of the Day Care Justice Committee in Providence, Rhode Island, is contracted by the state to provide child care for families whose incomes approach the poverty level. This child care enables low-income parents to gain and keep their jobs, some to get themselves off the AFDC rolls to achieve the self-sufficiency so important to the New Right. The state pays workers poverty wages, sometimes as little as $2 per hour. The Day Care Justice Committee did its own evaluation of child care to expose the state's assumptions:

> We looked at how much we get per child, per hour, for full-time or part-time care. I have one child now, who I care for fifty hours a week, but get paid only for twenty. Her parents are down to one car and simply can't get back to pick her up. The state does not pay anybody for that free care. We decided that we should be making at least $60,000 a year, more than plumbers and, as a compromise, less than garbage collectors. Men don't have the tenacity to deal with a little child. Men think there are things that keep body and soul together that they don't have to participate in — cooking, cleaning, raising kids with respect so they don't turn psycho on you later.[19]

By adjusting their own lives to care for children, workers, mothers, and other female relatives and friends subsidize the state's inadequate child care programs. Brown started the Day Care Justice Committee as a section of a mixed-gender community organization in Providence called Direct Action for Rights and Equality (DARE).

Another arena in which women's labor is discounted from public policy decisions, by the Left as well as the Right, is in the pending privatization of public education through the voucher system. The issue of school vouchers is the most important one conceived by the New Right to gain control of education. The Left has critiqued the school voucher plan for racial and economic discrimination. In "A Battle for the Soul of Public Education," Los Angeles Board of Education member Warren Furutani writes,

> [it] is no coincidence that funding for public education is receding as our school districts become more populated by children of color.... It is clear that vouchers and choice will be a vehicle for those who have the mobility and the additional dollars to go to the private sector — while at the same time guaranteeing that those who can't augment that voucher will then be relegated to an underfunded, overburdened system. [20]

Yet Furutani's critique misses other hidden costs of this system: the disproportionate effect vouchers will have on women. Women constitute the majority of public school teachers, who will compensate for poorer schools by teaching more students; for lack of materials by purchasing them on their own; for the lack of staff by playing janitor as well as teacher. Mothers constitute the majority of parents involved in their children's education, and they also will subsidize public education, by spending more time going to the school to negotiate with teachers and administrators for their kids, more time tutoring children themselves, more time searching for books in secondhand stores, and more time dealing with the self-esteem problems caused by discriminatory education.

Culture Culture Everywhere, and Nary a Drop that Liberates

Far more than legislation, culture determines what people think. These are confusing times for regular folks who get their ideas, as most of us do, from television and newspapers. On the Christian Broadcasting Network we see women in one role, while on MTV, we see women in a seemingly different role. Neither role is controlled by women, and both institutions represent us as subservient to men.

In the New Right's worldview, the proper position of a woman in the home is defined as one under the authority of her husband, who, in turn, is under the authority of God.[21] Women find dignity and security in this "proper and natural place," and poverty is defined as the punishment for transgression. These assumptions divide women

> into those who are worthy (living by Godly practices) and unworthy (engaging in an ungodly lifestyle), [implying that] many poor women who receive AFDC assistance, or are single mothers, or are otherwise independent of men but dependent on the state, are to be condemned.... It is far less virtuous to pursue a wrong headed notion of equality than to behave appropriately and be assured of respect.[22]

Privatizing the state functions that allow women some measure of independence from a man — AFDC, Legal Services (which the Right calls "state sponsored divorce"), subsidized food or child care, sex education — pushes women back into their rightful place.

By contrast, it may seem that the corporate media, the purveyors of mass culture, stand ready to liberate American women. In contrast to the New Right's sexual repressiveness, the mass culture, shaped by music, theater, television, movies, books, magazines, newspapers, and radio, fetishizes female sexuality. Unfortunately, submitting our sex to men is about all women get to do in the corporate media, where male ownership and control of female sexuality is reinforced constantly; one out of eight Hollywood movies conveys a rape theme, and by age eighteen, the average youth has watched 250,000 acts of violence in the media.[23] The shaping of female desire for a monogamous man who can guarantee financial security, and male desire for pliable women, feeds the global free market; capitalists create a demand for unnecessary, even harmful, products like vaginal douches, push up bras and four kinds of mascara. Cosmetics alone is a $20 billion industry worldwide.[24] Newspapers do their part to render women's other experiences invisible; in February 1991, references to women on front pages of twenty newspapers averaged thirteen percent in proportion to stories about men.[25]

Both cultural trends propagate a profoundly painful epidemic of violence against women and girls. While conservatives of all colors expound the virtues of the nuclear family, the family itself is a well-documented source of violence and sexual exploitation. The leading cause of injury to women aged fifteen to forty-four is still domestic violence, a heavily gendered crime. Ninety percent of murdered women are murdered by men, half of those by male partners or husbands.[26] The family is especially dangerous for girls and teenage women, who can be habitually abused by male family members and friends. The National Center for Health Statistics reports that 67 percent of teenage mothers are impregnated by adult men over twenty; researchers Debra Boyer and David Fine report that the majority of these young women have been sexually abused or raped, usually by men in their own families.[27]

The cultural acceptance of violence against women strikes organizer Sandra Davis as the reason that "90 percent of the girls in Sisters in Portland Impacting Real Issues Together (SPIRIT) have experienced physical and sexual abuse by boys or men they know."[28] Davis is the founding organizer of a one-year-old multiracial organization in Oregon for low-income girls and women of color. SPIRIT has started Project RAGEe (Race and Gender Equity in Education) with a gender analysis of violence in public schools and the school district's violence prevention protocol. Their initial constituency research revealed that "a majority of high school girls report being sexually harassed and violated by male teachers, staff and students at school." Worse yet, the influences of popular culture lead girls to place the blame on each other by insisting that "most girls bring [violence] on themselves by being too loose, too loud, too fast." The consumerism generated by the mass media permeates popular culture, even in communities of color. Davis says that

> Many of the girls I work with clearly identify with a Black youth culture with their own language, music, art and social ways. These girls have all bought into the notion that to be "bomb, you got to wear the latest fashion, and kick it with the boys who got the fast car, money and clout." Many of the girls say they don't mind being seen and treated as a sex object and commodity as long as they are "respected" in that role. One popular R&B artist sings about how his girlfriend is as appealing as his Jeep. When I asked the girls how they felt about the song, one girl's response was "I don't mind if he treats me like his car as long as it's a bomb car like a Lexus or Mercedes, 'cause that means I'll be treated real good."

National studies of teenager attitudes confirm Davis' suspicion that young people contribute to misogyny. The National Victim Center surveys reveal that "42 percent of females and 51 percent of males aged 13–18 feel that it is okay to force sex if 'she gets him excited.'"[29]

What the World Needs Now

For all its strength, the New Right is not invulnerable to our power. Its strategy relies so heavily on the prescribed roles of poor and working women that any disruption of those roles has the potential to throw the Right off track. We can also counteract their divide-and-conquer tactics with a popular analysis and alliance-building strategy that integrates the goals of racial, gender, and economic justice. The elements of such power exist in community organizations, gender analysis, new and creative forms of direct action, and women's leadership. The challenge will be to build on our successes by maximizing the potential of women's leadership, attacking the New Right's vulnerabilities, and eradicating the barriers that limit our effectiveness.

This historic moment requires community organizations to challenge patriarchy and misogyny by integrating the goal of gender equity into all aspects of our work. Community organizations should contribute to a global gender equity movement because it is in our interest that such a movement succeed. To contribute our particular strengths and skills to that project, organizations will have to commit themselves to (1) integrating gender analysis into our research and community education programs; (2) developing direct action campaigns that challenge institutional patriarchy and implement new social structures; and (3) eradicating the barriers to the first two posed by nationalism, an anti-ideological view of the role of the organizer, and the sexual division of labor within our own organizations.

The Role of Community Organizing and the Center for Third World Organizing

Community organizing is a particular social change methodology for collectivizing power among individuals and changing the institutional relations of power between communities. It is distinct from other methods of social change work, for example, legal advocacy or service provision, because it includes a core emphasis on nonviolent direct action, values leadership most as a function of recruitment and community building, and strives for the individual development of members as political agents who own their community and organization, as well as victories on specific and tangible issues.[30] The modern origins of the community organizing universe are usually attributed to Saul Alinsky's founding of Chicago's Back of the Yards Organization and the Industrial Areas Foundation in the 1940s, which utilized an organizing model of joining existing networks like churches and unions to fight on working people's issues.

Gary Delgado, a former ACORN and National Welfare Rights Organization organizer, started CTWO out of frustration with white-dominated organizing net-works.[31] CTWO's early strategy was to train organizers of color and provide technical support to small, struggling community organizations. When I came on the staff in 1988, CTWO was running the country's only field program designed exclusively for new organizers of color, publishing a national magazine to track political trends and organizing news in communities of color, and lending expertise to local education, labor, housing, antipoverty, and environmental campaigns. Through these activities, CTWO began to grow a new generation of organizers, who have founded organiza-tions, staffed and directed some of the most progressive union organizing drives since the mid-1980s, and developed new organizing models. Much of this work has been done by women, who constitute the majority of CTWO's staff, organizing recruits, and members and leaders of local organizing projects.

CTWO's vision of racial and economic equity eschews nationalism (a strategy that demands *primary* communal loyalty along ethnic or racial lines) and challenges market capitalism. More recently, that vision has incorporated the rights of biracial people, women, and gay people to engage and take leadership in community organizing without sacrificing identities or their full range of political interests. By the mid-1980s, all trainings were incorporating racial, class, and gender analysis to nurture a multiracial movement that could fight for fundamental economic and social changes designed by the most affected communities.

By 1989, CTWO had started to test theories for multiracial organizing among people of color by initiating new multiracial community organizations. People United for a Better Oakland set the standard with victories in fair employment practices at the Alameda army base, new patients' rights practices (including ade-quate translation) at the county hospital, and lead poisoning prevention and treat-ment. CTWO continues to start local organizing projects to test new combinations of constituencies and issues; People United members were joined by Action for a Better Community (ABC, 1992) in Denver and Sisters in Portland Impacting Real Issues Together (SPIRIT, 1995) in Oregon.

Also in 1989, we deepened our programmatic commitment to explicit women's organizing and gender issues. Our three national conferences for women organizers and leaders produced gender analysis on racial and economic issues, and on the issue of community and labor organizing itself. Concluding that the strategies community organizations apply to issues have rarely been used to deal with gender systems, and that a number of political arenas are vulnerable to gender analysis, we have shaped a new program area, Winning Action for Gender Equity (WAGE). Our program strategy maximizes the capacity of local or regional constituency-based organizations to integrate gender analysis and action into their work. Such organiza-tions already have a consistent and growing base of members, a solid core of experienced women leaders, some progressive male leaders, and a track record of winning on other issues important to communities of color.

Our goal is to test models for gender analysis and gender equity organizing by supporting, tracking, and evaluating the campaigns such community organizations of color conduct over the next two years. These campaigns should:

- change the relations of power in clearly sexist, probably racist institutions;
- engage people to analyze the construction and institutionalization of masculinity and femininity, and imagine new ways to think about gender roles;
- design clear demands for incremental structural and programmatic changes that will make a real difference in people's lives;
- engage legal, moral, or economic handles that support our analysis and visions;
- shape new organizing goals and tactics.

By supporting and tracking these and other campaigns for gender equity in communities of color for the next two years, we hope to learn several lessons about gender equity organizing:

- What are the most effective gender education and analysis processes?
- Which gender issues resonate most with poor women of color?
- How do men of color react when presented with ideological and action options?
- How does a direct action campaign affect the development of consciousness?
- Which campaigns can be replicated in other cities and towns?

CTWO's ability to facilitate replication, collectivize evaluations of what works and what doesn't, and generate new options for collaborative political action with regional and national impact will determine whether the WAGE project has an impact beyond a small number of local campaigns.

Integrating Gender Analysis and Gender Equity Campaigns

If our goal is to generate winning action for racial, economic, and gender justice, we have to move toward political engagement that is collective, confrontational, and constructive. Collective implies that the members of the organization act as a group because they feel not just connected, but loyal to each other. For collectivity we should not have to sacrifice the willingness to deal with difference and conflict; on the other side of conflict we usually find greater consciousness and more honest cohesion. Our confrontational tactics should surprise and draw out decision makers of targeted institutions and challenge their accountability to poor communities of color. Confrontation, if it relies on *collective* power, can be achieved through many tactics, some loud, some whispery. If we enter the fight, we have to be prepared to construct our solutions, often from foundation to roof; accepting that charge gives us the freedom to use power in new ways, to transform institutions and build new ones. With those goals in mind — collectivity, confrontation, and construction — we utilize a formal gender analysis that engages our constituencies, critiques institutions, and includes men.

All community organizations need a thoughtfully developed political education program that makes the entire organization a consciousness-raising group. Davis says that most organizations know they need a program that fosters political exchange and debate, but don't know how to put one together: "We have to put as much attention to figuring out times where the discussions and exercises are going to happen that surface the issues we want to get at." SPIRIT runs self-defense classes as a recruitment and constituency research tool to define what self-defense means to women and girls of color, combining physical training with a workshop that gets participants to think about racism and sexism and how it affects them. Davis develops those workshops with youth leaders of the organization. SPIRIT also shows movies before the self-defense discussions, then links the movies to the discussions. "Different environments create different moods, different kinds of opportunities for people to get into the discussion. Some girls feel isolated from formal learning situations because of their experiences at schools." Although political education work competes with immediate campaign work for an organizer's time, Davis says the long-term payoff is worth the shift because "the folks we bring in are also involved in developing the political consciousness and plans, goals of the organization."

Lisa Durán, the Chicana coordinator of a breast and cervical cancer screening program in a volunteer clinic run out of a Latino liberation theology church in Denver, Colorado, insists that gender analysis has to be institutional, not just relegated to inter-organizational dynamics "because they feel very personal, don't feel public."

> It's a rare place where I feel [legitimate] raising the issues. In my work with environmental justice and bus rider organizing, issues of gender came out always as oppressive restrictions men would put on women's participation (and I do have a lot of those stories), never as gendered demands on the external institutions the organization was trying to influence. I'd like to find ways to make our gender politics more systemic.[32]

Durán has no problem generating gendered questions about mass transit or the medical industry. Since 50 percent of bus riders are women, what are the dangers posed by the lack of mass transit? How do fare hikes affect women's and men's family responsibilities differently? In the health industry, what are the contradictions between who has the power (male doctors and administrators) and who does the work (female nurse practitioners)? How does that division of labor affect our care? What role does Catholic martyrdom ideology play in women's attitudes toward the industry? The answers to these and other questions deepen, if not change, organizing methods, constituencies, leadership, and the location of proposed changes.

Lastly, gender analysis needs to be done with men as well as women, if mixed-gender community organizations are to contribute to the fight for gender equity. Gwen Hardy, an African American founding leader of People United for a Better Oakland, feels that men could effectively educate other men about gender systems. She suggests educational and training sessions that "would have to be done systematically and repetitively, especially with new men coming into the organization, to get people to decide consciously if they want to be part of such an organization." She makes the flip side of Durán's point, that gender education would require that "an integral part of the organization's plan was to work on male/female dynamics within the organization."[33]

Gender equity projects that explicitly organize women in the context of a mixed-gender organization go a long way toward educating men and other women members about the effects of patriarchy and misogyny. Shannah Kurland, the white executive director of DARE, says that the Day Care Justice Campaign has "led people in the organization to see that women's issues aren't issues defined by women outside of our communities, by women who don't share our race and class analysis. We hope to take that further to build our collective consciousness that women's issues are everyone's issues, and that all issues have a gender dimension."[34] Davis agrees that the active support of male members and staff enables women and girls to take on gender issues without fear:

> the consciousness that already exists at CTWO about why we need to deal with gender allows me freedom to experiment with new organizing models. Communities of color do isolate people who put forth progressive gender politics. I see that's what the fear is for the girls, that they won't have a place anymore in their communities because hardly anybody else thinks like them. Being part of a larger organization that supports raising consciousness allows our women to feel like they are part of the bigger struggle, and that working on these issues does not have to isolate them from their culture and from men.

Gender analysis can redefine our terrain of struggle, revealing new possibilities for demands, targets, handles, and community education. In CTWO's national and collaborative Campaign for Community Safety and Police Accountability, a gender analysis of police brutality forced us to examine our assumption that cops protect property over people. A survey of women's experiences with police misconduct showed that while cops will beat men, they will often intimidate women by attacking our homes, cars, and personal belongings. That understanding gave us the impetus to make important changes in our practice of documenting police misconduct, and in our platform of reforms. The urge to do further research, to understand the gendered nature and experiences of the criminal justice system, was perhaps the most dramatic result of those discussions.

Gender analysis, like any political investigation, cannot be done in the abstract if it is also going to generate activists for the movement. The most effective analytic program, especially with new members, is concretely tied to a project to change our situation. Davis hopes that gender analysis will also shift and broaden our political goals to take on fights that "challenge us to build new communities, rather than simply trying to fix endless flaws of an old, worn-out system, which, in the end, never really changes." SPIRIT is developing a series of programmatic ideas and demands to attack violence at its root, including the multicultural self-defense education model for public schools, and a design for schoolwide conflict resolution centers to be run by students. Davis points out that models of conflict resolution have focused very much on boys and violence between men. Sue Ray Dawson, the sixteen-year-old chair of SPIRIT's Young Women's Committee, attests to the importance of analysis to the committee's goals: "the school just suspends or expels people for fighting, and wants to hire more police and get more metal detectors.

That doesn't stop anybody from fighting, including us [the girls]." Davis adds, "We are moving toward programs that can change the culture of violence at schools, to meet the needs of girls as well as boys."

Adding gender equity to our broad political goals can help us attack New Right policies that affect low-income men/men of color as well as women. Isaiah Bennett, CAFE's African American lead organizer of the Citadel campaign, has high hopes for the potential of the food service workers to challenge South Carolina's subcontracting system, which perpetuates the state's deep anti-union culture. "The whole state is privatizing the majority of the public workforce. Right now the medical university is talking about entering contract agreements with alumnae. This is happening behind closed doors; if we win the Citadel fight, that would open the door for us to fight on all other private contracts." Bennet asserts that gender analysis of the key institutions, the Citadel itself, Aramark, the National Labor Relations Board, and potential unions, will "open up ideas for strategies and demands we can use."[35]

Gender analysis can also challenge organizations to take on bigger issues and be creative with our tactics. The Day Care Justice Campaign has led DARE into a labor relationship with the Rhode Island state legislature, a new dimension to the relations of power between legislators and DARE members. Kurland recalls how this relationship with a male-dominated institution forced the committee to diversify its style:

> Trying to make change in the legislative system drives home the fact that we are not boys. The legislature is male in climate, in its modes of operation; they do their planning sessions at strip joints, we do ours in kitchens. We had to adjust our approaches to be taken seriously, find a means of communication that wasn't based solely on "we're bigger than you." For one thing, we're not bigger, and, for another, they're used to poor women screaming at them by now. We had to find other ways to establish a tone of respect so that we could have a constructive, issue-based discussion.

After three years of fighting for small, procedural changes like getting paychecks on time, then building to their first substantial victory on health insurance, the committee is now ready to fight for collective bargaining. Such an arrangement between a public employer and an independent cooperative would be rare in the United States, and would give the committee real potential for transforming the child care/welfare system entirely. Kurland feels that winning on other core issues like pay scales and lifelong education for workers will require a "tight organization with a very high level of consciousness. We need that as our fight heats up and we want to use more confrontational, controversial, and difficult tactics, for example, shifting child care to the state house for a week or two, or doing other kinds of work stoppage."

A clear gender analysis of constituencies and allies will also lead to nontraditional movement formations that maximize women's strengths. The relationship of women of color to AFL-CIO labor organizations offers important examples of the need for new formations. After several negative experiences with unions that began to organize the Citadel's food service workers, only to drop those efforts in the face of confusion about employer accountability to workers, CAFE is taking a different approach to unionization. Bennett says, "We've had unions looking for a quick fix, and there ain't no quick fix here. Now we're negotiating with unions with the demand that they'll go all the way until the NLRB ruling comes out in our favor. If a union leaves one more time, I don't know what we'll do, so we have to control the partnership from the beginning."

The Day Care Justice Committee has decided to form a cooperative of home day care workers rather than a union. Brown says that "the image of unions leaves a bad taste in almost everyone's mouth. We are turned off by unions because they are male-oriented; unions themselves have given off that aura for too many years. A co-op makes us sound warmer, more homey, and doesn't bring out images of men carrying pitchforks." Brown feels that forming an independent cooperative gives the committee more programmatic freedom: "we're thinking about setting up mutual support systems, like a toy lending library and training programs for providers. We also want to organize the parents into a co-op, so they can get support for their parenting issues, especially as they relate to changes in the welfare system." Brown hopes that these initiatives will give the committee the solidarity it needs to challenge the state.

Eradicating Barriers

Gender systems, as they collude with race and economics, cannot be dismantled without the leadership and participation of women of color. Claire Yoo, former codirector of Action for Community Empowerment in Harlem, New York, insists that nurturing the leadership of women makes sense and is not just political altruism. "We don't pick out women to work with, but that is who emerges as leaders in the organization. Developing women leaders tells us about how women are the central life force of a community. They know everybody, they have a lot of information, they're always figuring out ways for people to get what they need."

Because women dominate community organizations in numbers, participation, staffing, and leadership, we might think that attention to gender is unimportant in these organizations; DARE organizer Conteh Davis asserts that it is actually men who need gendered attention to bring them into the organization.[36] The perception that women completely control community organizing hides the real relations of power between men and women in the progressive movement. Organizers and leaders affirm that taking on gender issues will require organizations to fight three specific barriers within their organization: masculinized nationalism, a narrow view of the organizer's role as purely facilitative, rather than ideological; and the organization's sexual division of labor and leadership.

The Limits of Nationalism

Proponents of a nationalist worldview assert that one's racial/ethnic identity is the *primary* determinant of one's access to power and material resources in the world. Consequently, nationalists from all communities mandate racial and cultural loyalty as the building blocks of a supreme political goal to transform racial systems, which will solve all problems related to that community. Narrow nationalism has severely limited the growth of feminism in communities of color. Proponents of racial nationalism, for example, Nation of Islam leader Louis Farrakhan, link nationalism to the preservation of male supremacy as a cultural entitlement of men of color; women are assigned the role of reproducing rather than creating the politics and culture of their racial community. Women of color raising gender issues are often subject to accusations of "betraying the race," and exhorted to prioritize racial equity.[37] Cynthia Enloe writes in *Bananas, Beaches and Bases* that "every time women succumb to the pressures to hold their tongues about the problems they are having with men in a nationalist organization, nationalism becomes that much more masculinized."[38]

Gender is an unnamed dynamic in most community struggles for power. The influence of nationalist thought creates a political culture in which race and class are far more likely to be addressed by community organizations even when gender is also, even primarily, at work. Depending on the racial demographics of a particular geography, race will be the dominant political category through which people analyze their experiences. Lisa Durán, who recently moved to Denver after organizing with the Los Angeles Bus Riders Union (project of the Labor/Community Strategy Center), compares organizing poor people of color in two cities: "In Denver, because Chicanos are a clear minority and politically and economically marginalized, race is much more important to people than in L.A. Our most successful campaign in L.A. was the mass transit issue, which we defined as a class *and* race issue. In Denver, people still say, if we could only get a Chicano in office, things would be better. People haven't had as much experience here yet of officials of color reneging on commitments to our communities, as people in L.A. have. In both communities, gender came last."

Durán acknowledges that the way constituents look at issues has everything to do with the organizer's own consciousness: "as an organizer, the fact that gender consciousness has come last in my life affected how I engaged people. I'm a latecomer to gender. I would always acknowledge it in the list of issues, but I'm only more recently feeling like it is totally fundamental." The commitment of organizers to deal with gender issues has to be developed as systematically as their ability to do other work in the organization. The notion that organizers can and should influence memberships has radical implications for our view of the role of the organizer and how organizers should be trained.

The Role of the Organizer

Many organizers of color trace community organizing's most prohibitive aspects to Alinksy's tenet that the role of the organizer is nonideological. CTWO founder Gary Delgado writes in *Beyond the Politics of Place* that "Alinsky meant that the organization would originate out of the needs, interests, and issues of the local people. While it is clear from the groups he chose to work with that he had an interest in empowering the 'have-nots', his approach was grounded less in a set ideology than in the application of proven techniques to specific problems."[39] The organizer catalyzed, the community defined and decided on issues, and the organizer served the interests of the community. Alinksy's organizers tended to be white and male, and the extreme behind-the-scenes nature of their presence had a practical as well as political logic. In this way, community organizations neutralized the accusation that they were puppets of "outside agitators."

The nonideological organizer would help an organization choose issues that had clear parameters, that were deeply and widely felt by constituents, that had clear institutional targets and clear demands, and that were winnable and nondivisive. This process often had the result that only the lowest common denominator issues received organizational attention. The policy of nonideology also did not address members' vulnerability to the racist, capitalist, and sexist assumptions of the larger culture. Francis Calpotura, CTWO's codirector and lead organizer of the Campaign for Community Safety and Police Accountability, points to attitudes about crime and punishment in many community organizations as an example:

> Most local community organizations, even those in poor communities of color, are pushing for punitive solutions to crime and violence, more police, more prisons, tougher sentencing laws. Those organizations go with the immediate interests of the community, which, in this case, are driven by fear and congressional agitation on crime. We challenge people to look at all aspects of the issue: the corruption of racist police departments, discrimination in the criminal justice system, and the kinds of economic and social programs that would unify communities, rather than hammer in the wedge.[40]

Sandra Davis of SPIRIT asserts that organizers do not have to submerge their own politics for fear of losing less progressive members, and that building a movement for radical change requires greater skills from organizers than the ability to listen and make the organization accessible. "Our role is not just getting the action done, but also politically developing our people. Organizers have to take any opportunity to engage our members. Hanging out in the office, in the car going home, talking about their day-to-day lives, I'm not just listening, but getting people to connect their experiences to the long-term work of the organization." SPIRIT member Sue Ray Dawson comments on Davis's role in getting the Young Women's Committee to consider the effects of violence between girls: "Sandra kept making us talk about what it means when we fight with each other, how the boys and other people see that."

Because she has been involved in community organizing locally and nationally, Gwen Hardy has also encountered these conflicting definitions of the organizer's role. She acknowledges that past experiences women of color have had with white and male organizers raise issues about the organizer's use of control and power. She acknowledges that organizers wield tremendous power through their relationships with members and their position in the organization, but believes in the ability of regular people to avoid brainwashing. She notes that young feminists of color have enriched, rather than limited, her own experience:

> From them, I learned a great deal about politics and procedures. They were giving me more material to work with to make my own decisions. I know that sometimes in

organizing, you have to use a little bit of manipulation to get people thinking, help that person open up their mind, use different kind of conversational tactics. But I don't believe anyone can be persuaded to do or believe something that did not sit right with them.

The Sexual Division of Labor

In the past ten years, a flood of young women of color have entered organizing from a political framework that embraces gender equity as a principle of community life. All the women organizers and leaders I interviewed agreed that most organizations operate on a sexual and unequal division of labor.

In 1994 I did a campaign management training for advanced organizers who were participating in our year-long Community Partnership Program for advanced organizers. Conducting the exercise in gendered groups revealed dramatic differences between the two women's groups and the one men's group. The exercise provided a campaign and organizational scenario, and asked small groups to (1) list all tasks that needed to be dealt with, (2) assign roles and responsibilities to staff and to leaders, (3) outline a six-week campaign schedule, and (4) create an accountability structure and reporting form. The gendered groups differed in both form and content. The men's group finished thirty minutes earlier than the two women's groups, but forgot an entire portion of the exercise. Ironically, the women spent the most time on the portion the men forgot. The women spent so long assigning roles and responsibilities and plotting the flow of the campaign that I had to cut them off before they could design their form. The men cited their driving goals in fulfilling the exercise as efficiency and clear lines of accountability; the women also cited accountability, but added their concern that each person in the team had a job that s/he could both accomplish and learn something from. The men's list of things to do numbered three: research, turn out, and press. The women's list was much longer: detailed lists for the above three, and also transportation, child care, food, and translation.

I don't use this example to defend an essentialist notion that men and women organize differently. Good organizers organize with attention to development and detail; the lesson is that women are socialized to take care of people's collective needs, which equips us to work with our memberships in a way that is not often required of men. Hardy reflects that "what I see is that the male has the directorship, the strategy work, but females are organizers and members, out front doing the recruitment, actions and managing the group." Durán elaborates on Hardy's observation from her own experience in a mixed-gender organization:

> The organization is directed by a strong male presence; with such a dominant central figure, it's hard to tell how much is personality and how much is a gender dynamic. But I was always told that I was an important force in the organization, the number 2 leader, but in reality I was there to refine and implement the director's ideas. I didn't want to change the strategy, I believed in the strategy, but there are many, many ways to implement a strategy, and all kinds of people contribute different things to that strategy.

Hardy and Durán point to a dangerously gendered division of labor, whose value is reflected in pay scales and power. That division has deep implications for the development of lead organizers and the ability of women to occupy those positions over the long term. The notion that women's base-building work in organizing is less important than men's strategic work also raises serious concerns about the development of male organizers and the effectiveness of organizations. Strategies and memberships symbiotically feed and drive each other. Limited memberships can carry out only limited strategies, which in turn produce narrow, and less powerful, memberships.

The prospect of changing the sexual relations of power within organizations generates both excitement and fear of gender equity work. Again, women organizers agreed that organizations will have to prepare themselves for a stormy transitional period while changing internal gender dynamics. Kurland asserts that leaders from the Day Care Justice Committee act on their gender analysis more than other women in the organization when they "refuse to defer to male leaders because of their gender." Durán predicts that gender equity campaigns will lead to "a social dislocation in the organization. The responsibilities and power of the strong male central figure would be dispersed, and I think men in the organization would have a hard time accepting leadership from someone else." Hardy puts it more bluntly: "Any man that would be part of an organization like this would have to be pretty strong knowing he's not going to control all the agenda. Men think they have to be in power, decide what to do, how to do it; that becomes ingrained programming in their heads." Kurland also wonders whether gender analysis will drive the support of male parents away from the home day care cooperative.

CTWO has been well aware of these challenges as we make the case for our base of community organizations to tackle the gender question. Calpotura reflects that men in the CTWO network, led by male staff and board members, have become willing to tie their own racial and economic interests to those of women because "the whole enterprise of building a movement, the movement we need to gain justice for ourselves, is dead if we can't engage women as our partners and ensure their full liberation."

In community organizing trainings across the country, the 1963 film *Salt of the Earth* is as standard a tool as any easel pad and nontoxic marker. *Salt of the Earth* tells the story of the 1956 New Mexico miners' strike, a classic struggle for power and respect between Chicano and Mexicano miners, their union, and the white company boss. Students of organizing history will immediately see the quintessential race and class struggle. The demands revolve around pay raises, safety standards, and the right to bargain collectively with the company. The white union organizer represents racial solidarity in the working class; the company, a bastion of white male capitalists, stands ready with troops of Chicano scabs and white sheriffs.

A closer look, however, reveals a complicating layer. The film's protagonist is not a miner, but the wife of one. She begins the movie resigned and pregnant, frustrated with her husband's, and his union's, refusal to add running water to the list of strike demands. Over time, when the male miners become too vulnerable to their employer's threats, the women take over the union, the picket line, the county jail, and the strike demands. The men take over the housework and the kids. While the men do not fundamentally change the nature of housework and child rearing, the women totally transform the nature of this particular race and class conflict. Through their leadership, they expand the scope of "labor" issues, redefine the terms of participation in public and private life, and reverse the outcome of the fight.

This essay has suggested that the racial and economic justice movement should be genderized. Genderizing the politics of community organizations of color — giving explicit attention to the different experiences of men and women in the world and in the organization, deepening their gender analysis, and equipping them to take action — can help ensure that community organizing survives the attack of the resurgent Right Wing. As in *Salt of the Earth*, women of color have to lead that project, exercising our collective power and propelling men to acknowledge our legitimate political role. That leadership is the key to a liberating unity for communities of color, which opens the door to victory.

NOTES

1. Chip Berlet, *Eyes Right: Challenging the Right Wing Backlash* (Boston: South End, 1995), 20.

2. Jean Hardisty, "The Resurgent Right: Why Now?," *Public Eye* (Political Research Associates, Boston), fall–winter 1995, 1.

3. Ibid., 12.

4. Teresa Amott and Julie Matthaei, *Race, Gender and Work: A Multicultural History of Women in the United States* (Boston: South End, 1991), 367.

5. Hardisty, 7.

6. Amott and Matthaei, 360.

7. Florence Gardner and Jean McAllister, "Temporary Workers: Flexible or Disposable?" *Poverty and Race Research Action Council Newsletter* (Washington, DC), November–December 1995, 9.

8. Myrna Major, interview by author, 1996.

9. Council on International and Public Affairs, "The Most Unequal Nation in the World Is the United States," *Too Much* (New York), fall 1995, 1.

10. Ibid., 3.

11. Women's Action Coalition, *WAC Stats: The Facts about Women* (New York: New Press, 1993), 58.

12. Ibid., 59.

13. Hardisty, 9.

14. Ibid., 31.

15. Ibid., 40–41.

16. Women's Action Coalition, 7.

17. Kathleen Cloud and Nancy Garrett, "Counting Women's Work," *Dollars and Sense Magazine* (Economic Affairs Bureau, Boston), November–December 1995, 34–35.

18. Women's Action Coalition, 40.

19. Grace Brown, interview by author, 1996.

20. Warren Furutani, "A Battle for the Soul of Public Education," in *False Choices: Why*

School Vouchers Threaten Our Children's Future, ed. Robert Lowe and Barbara Miner (Milwaukee: Rethinking Schools, 1992), 20.

21. Hardisty, 6.

22. Ibid.

23. Women's Action Coalition, 50.

24. Ibid., 35.

25. Ibid., 18.

26. U.S. Department of Justice, *National Report on Violent and Sexual Crimes* (Washington, DC, 1994).

27. Linda Villarosa, "Who's Really Makin' Babies," *Third Force Magazine* (Center for Third World Organizing, Oakland, CA), March–April 1996, 33.

28. Sandra Davis, interview by author, 1995.

29. Women's Action Coalition, 50.

30. Gary Delgado, *Beyond the Politics of Place: New Directions in Community Organizing* (Oakland, CA: Applied Research Center, 1995), 26.

31. These are Citizen Action, National Peoples' Action, ACORN, and the Industrial Areas Foundation.

32. Lisa Durán, interview by author, 1995.

33. Gwen Hardy, interview by author, 1995.

34. Shannah Kurland, interview by author, 1995.

35. Isaiah Bennett, interview by author, 1996.

36. Bill Mesler, "My Brothers Are Saying. . . ," *Third Force Magazine,* March–April 1996, 20.

37. Rinku Sen, *We Are the Ones We Are Waiting For* (Durham, NC: United States Urban Rural Mission, 1995).

38. Cynthia Enloe, *Bananas, Beaches and Bases: Making Feminist Sense of International Politics* (Berkeley: University of California Press, 1989).

39. Delgado, 21.

40. Francis Calpotura, interview by author, 1994.

NINETEEN

Transforming Democracy: Rural Women and Labor Resistance

EVE S. WEINBAUM

Women in low-income rural and urban areas have long served as a low-wage workforce in manufacturing industries. Especially in such labor-intensive industries as textiles and apparel, electronics, and automobile parts, assembly lines are staffed almost exclusively by women. With the advent of the "global economy," these jobs are changing rapidly, and working women are most affected by the restructuring. These industries are especially likely to move jobs overseas, where women in less developed countries will work at much lower cost. In addition, throughout the manufacturing sector in the United States, there has been a dramatic increase in part-time, seasonal, subcontracted, and other forms of contingent work. Within the past five or ten years, the contingent workforce has expanded exponentially, in the service sector as well as in manufacturing. The Bureau of Labor Statistics estimates that by 2000 the number of contingent jobs will surpass full-time jobs in this country. Women and older workers are most affected by this change, which has brought jobs with very low pay, no benefits, and no security.

This essay investigates grassroots organizing efforts among working and unemployed women in East Tennessee who are protesting these trends. Their collective response to economic dislocation has had various aims: to prevent a plant closing, to unionize workers, to mitigate the effects of corporate decisions on the workers and the community, to educate the community about economic changes, and to change local economic development policies and practices to benefit the most vulnerable residents. The fact that political resistance and mobilization took place and was focused on economic issues was itself extraordinary. That it was led by rural women with little or no previous political experience was even more interesting, and completely unforeseen by most political science literature.[1]

These stories of resistance show that the barriers to mobilizing for economic justice are formidable. When small, rural, economically and politically marginalized groups of women confront national and international institutions about the direction of the global economy, change will be difficult and slow, if it comes at all. The women's experiences also show, however, that mobilization and political action lead to important and lasting changes in both the individual participants and their communities. My research among women involved in these struggles illustrates the striking changes in participants' interpretations of their experiences, their place in the economy, and politics more generally. Through political mobilization, individuals come to understand many things in an entirely different way. These transformations, as much as the concrete gains won, demonstrate the power and potential of grassroots organizing to change women's lives.

Changes in the Economic Landscape

For the past decade, economists and policy makers have been documenting a dramatic shift in patterns of employment across the United States. In some ways, recent changes reflect an older, continuing pattern of "deindustrialization" and the economic upheavals resulting from the decline of manufacturing and related industries. But there are signs of new patterns. First is the shift from permanent or full-time to contingent or part-time employment. Second is the globalization of the economy, in the form of both the increasing mobility of capital and the industrialization of developing countries, encouraged by international institutions like the IMF and the World Bank, and treaties like NAFTA and GATT. These changes have especially serious consequences for the lives of working, unemployed, and poor women.

The Rise of Contingent Work

Beginning in the early 1980s, part-time employment began to account for an increasing proportion of employment in all sectors of the economy. The most visible segment of the contingent workforce, the temporary services industry, grew explosively throughout the 1980s, expanding ten times as fast as overall employment. The number of temporary workers grew by almost 400 percent between 1983 and 1993, and the total payroll of temporary help companies increased by almost 3,000 percent between 1970 and 1992 (Parker 1994; Nine to Five 1995; Appelbaum 1992). New methods of hiring nonpermanent employees grew in equal proportion. Some firms created their own, in-house temporary agencies or day-labor pools. Others subcontracted their hiring, paying agencies to supply them with the number of employees needed each day or week. And "temps" began to do much more than only office work. For the first time, temporary work took hold in manufacturing industries. Most industrial firms began to rely on part-time workers to do some piece of the work, and some employers replaced entire assembly lines with subcontracted casual labor forces.[2] For firms, this trend means greater profit margins. For workers, it often means a permanent place among the working poor.

This shift, especially prevalent in low-income areas of the country and in low-wage industries, has been independent of the health of the economy as a whole.

Until the 1990s, employment continued its path of expansion begun in the 1950s. Although many observers remarked on the uneven nature of the recovery since the early 1980s, official unemployment rates remained remarkably low and total employment consistently increased. But closer examination of the facts contradicted this pattern of growth. Although more jobs were available and more workers were working longer hours, expansions in employment were increasingly found in temporary jobs that provided lower wages, no benefits, no advancement opportunities, and no security. This pattern was especially pronounced in "sunbelt" states. In Tennessee, deindustrialization in the 1980s has led to the loss of hundreds of thousands of the best manufacturing jobs in the state. During the same period, contingent work opportunities increased over 420 percent (Gaventa and Wiley 1987; Phillips 1991).

Bureau of Labor Statistics figures predict that within another five years, half of all workers in this country will be employed on a contingent basis; part-time will outnumber full-time workers by the end of this decade (Metzenbaum 1993). For most of these workers, part-time work is not a choice but an involuntary condition of employment; part-time work was the only work available. Voluntary part-time employment has actually declined since 1990, and involuntary part-time employment has accounted for the entire increase in the contingent economy (Appelbaum 1992).

Working and unemployed women suffer most from these trends. Women make up about two-thirds of the "temporary help supply" industry, as calculated by the Bureau of Labor Statistics, and more than twice as many women as men work part-time. Women and people of color are disproportionately represented within the temporary workforce — nearly double their percentages in the total workforce (Belous 1989). This correlation is most often cited by policy makers as evidence that reducing work hours has personal benefits for women and their children, as well as social benefits ranging from energy conservation from fewer trips to work, to more leisure for education, recreation, community service, and family responsibilities (Negrey 1993). But appearances are deceiving. While adult men in every age group have increased their share of part-time employment, women in the primary childbearing years of twenty-two to forty-four — the group most often assumed to be part-time workers — have decreased their rate of part-time work. In fact, studies of women with family responsibilities have shown that they are no more likely to choose temporary employment than other employees.

Economists examining these data have concluded that since 1980 companies have been creating part-time jobs even though workers do not want them (Tilly 1992; Carré 1992). Part-time work is not women's choice. Indeed, in an economy that already undervalues women's work and segregates most forms of labor according to gender, a shift to contingent work only serves to reinforce unequal gender relations (Negrey 1993, 2).

As one economist concludes, "Women are taking the growing number of temp agency jobs because employers are creating more temporary positions in the fields where women typically work, and not because temporary employment better meets their flexibility needs. Rather it is the lack of bargaining power and limited employment alternatives of these workers that make this managerial strategy possible" (Appelbaum 1992, 5).

As the income gap has widened, women, people of color, and workers labeled "unskilled" find it increasingly difficult to support themselves and their families. Faced with increasingly dire and unacceptable choices, they must "choose" the part-time jobs the economy has to offer. Too often, this means surviving without health or retirement benefits and living at a below-poverty wage. The only alternative, as suggested by Appelbaum's quote above, is for women to increase their "bargaining power" through collective action, and to resist the apparently inexorable progression toward poverty. The case study below depicts women involved in exactly this struggle.

The Global Economy

Another important factor in the downward spiral of wages and working conditions has been the pressure of increased international competition. "Competitiveness" in the new "global economy" is probably the most often-cited reason for companies undergoing "downsizing," "restructuring," or other processes of internal reorganization, mass firings, casualization, and concession bargaining. Corporate executives involved in cutting the workforce and reassigning production work most often argue that these changes are necessary to remain competitive in the current economic climate. If their competitors are cutting wages and benefits, subcontracting work to the lowest bidder, and basing corporate decisions on the availability of government subsidies and tax credits, it would be commercial suicide not to do the same.

This has always been standard business practice. What has changed in this decade is the international dimension to this competition. Since "free trade" policies and advancing technologies have made international production and capital mobility easier and less costly, U.S.-based firms now must consider the actions of international corporations. They must remain competitive not only with other U.S.-based manufacturers who pay minimum wage — currently $4.25 an hour — but with transnational firms paying less than this amount in an entire day or sometimes in a week, to workers in Mexico, Guatemala, Indonesia, the Philippines, or other developing countries.

Accordingly, the pressure of international competition and the mobility of capital bring the threat of relocation. While large, transnational corporations have long been able to expand to subsidiaries all over the world, the 1980s and 1990s have seen a surge in companies moving to developing countries. Unskilled production jobs are the easiest to move, as executives seek low wages, weak environmental and labor regulations, and little or no unionization. The pressures toward global reorganization, along with the development of technologies conducive to capital mobility, cause communities whose economies have depended on labor-intensive manufacturing industries to suffer the most serious consequences of deindustrialization (Bluestone and Harrison 1982).

As with the shift to contingent work, women workers in the United States — as well as in developing countries — suffer the most from unchecked transnational corporate capital flight. Since companies move overseas in the first place specifically to procure a low-wage, docile workforce, it is logical that they choose to hire women. In all countries, women have fewer wage-earning opportunities than men, earn less, and are often considered only supplementary income earners in their families. Managers can take advantage of this secondary status by paying women less and hiring and firing at will. For light-assembly or even service work, women are as qualified as men, and are accustomed to working for lower wages in tedious, repetitive occupations. In South Korea, for example, female earnings in manufacturing in the late 1980s were 50 percent of males' earnings in exactly the same jobs and industries (Standing 1989). In free trade zones throughout the developing world, where international companies have "outsourced" production work, light-assembly lines are staffed 80 to 90 percent by women.[3]

Aside from the low cost and availability of women workers, observers have identified two other reasons for women's prominence in these factories. First, governments around the world feel less pressure to protect women workers than men, who are more likely to vote and to make trouble. Accordingly, in the 1980s, with the blessing of the U.S. government, many countries repealed regulations on workplace conditions, in the hope of expanding their export sectors. All of this was more possible with a workforce made up of desperate and powerless women workers (Standing 1989; Barnet and Cavanagh 1994). Second, just as in the United States, women are fit more easily into the "flexible" production schemes that are increasingly important to global corporations. In developing countries, women work uneven hours, sometimes all night long in buildings locked from the inside, and take work home if asked.

Managers of subsidiaries in developing countries have justified their treatment of women workers with claims no longer tenable in the United States, since women here have mobilized for equal rights. Frequent firings, for example, are justified by pointing out that women will quit soon anyway, to get married or have children. They justify hiring an all-woman assembly force by arguing that women have a "natural patience" and superior "manual dexterity" (Fuentes and Ehrenreich 1989). A Malaysian investment brochure declares, "Her hands are small and she works fast with extreme care. Who therefore could be better qualified by nature and inheritance to contribute to the efficiency of a bench-assembly production line than an oriental girl?" (Barnet and Cavanagh 1994; *Global Assembly Line* 1991).[4]

Of course, these workers' exploitation as women is inseparable from both racial and class subjugation. When U.S. corporate executives, paying poor women a tenth of U.S. minimum wages to work and live in dangerously unhealthy circumstances, claim that the workers are thrilled with their new opportunities, it is hard to miss the echoes of apologies for slavery. One American soliciting new business for the Mexican *maquiladoras* (free trade zones) says, "You should watch these kids going to work. You don't have any sullenness here. They smile" (Fuentes and Ehrenreich 1989, 15). Advertisements attracting American companies to move to Mexico tout the easy availability of willing workers and the "excellent labor relations." A primer for businesses interested in opening subsidiaries states that "from their earliest conditioning women show respect and obedience to authority, especially men. The women follow orders willingly, accept change and adjustments easily, and are considerably less demanding" (Fuentes and Ehrenreich 1989, 29–30).

The ability of corporations to move freely in search of available, inexpensive labor has serious ramifications for American workers.[5] In many industries, especially light manufacturing, entire workforces labor under a constant threat that the company will leave if its demands are not met. Vulnerable workers, obviously, do not have the same freedom of choice. Under these conditions, workers are accepting concessions, cuts in their pay and benefits, layoffs, and transitions to segmented, part-time employment. For the individual worker and for the entire community, anything is preferable to losing all those jobs. Thus the same global conditions that lead to exploitation and intolerable working conditions in developing countries have the same effect in the United States. Workers are caught in the global spiral toward lower wages and less power on the job and in the community.

Women Mobilize

Against this forbidding backdrop of both economic and political trends, we may tend to see women with assembly line jobs in poor, rural areas of the United States as powerless victims of an irrefutable global system. But this would be presumptuous. In cities, towns, and rural areas all across the country, women are refusing to accept the dire choices presented them.

My research begins with workers and unemployed people in their communities in East Tennessee. In order to investigate women's political responses to global restructuring, I interviewed women who had been victims of a devastating, yet increasingly common, repercussion of the international mobility of capital: plant closings. In this setting, workers are experiencing one of the most extreme forms of economic dislocation and powerlessness. I studied plant closings in three Tennessee communities, attended meetings and protests, worked with people in their campaigns, and interviewed women in depth, in order to explore several questions: Do women mobilize to resist the threat to their livelihoods? What forms does this resistance take? What difference does political activity make if it happens, and how do different types of activity produce different results? In all cases, some form of resistance occurred. But the goals of the activity, the understandings of participants, the forms of activity, and the outcomes varied dramatically. I will discuss here only one instance of mobilization, which occurred in Morristown, Tennessee. It allows a close look at the potential for collective action to lead to education, politicization, and transformation.

In Morristown, General Electric (GE) was considered one of the best and most prestigious places to work. Wages were higher than at many smaller companies, and employees were well treated. But in 1988, new management took over and instituted changes that upset the workers. After a union organizing drive was begun, the company counterattacked with parties, picnics, and prizes for workers, but also with threats, captive-audience meetings, scary anti-union films, and other propaganda. At the last minute, the company made a movie about "the GE family," complete with footage of the workers with their families. The film touted GE's commitment to Morristown — as opposed to the "outsiders" from the union — and included an original country music song the company had commissioned for the occasion. The workers were scared and convinced, and voted against the union, by a margin of three to one. The next week, GE suddenly closed its warehouse and laid off about two hundred workers.

The GE workers had had no prior warning that their jobs would disappear. They expected for a while to be called back to work. Within a few weeks, by listening to the radio, they learned that the business was not reopening. It had moved thirty miles down the road, to the next county, and reopened under a new name. More than the name had changed; the warehouse jobs were now all subcontracted through a company called USCO, which did all the hiring. Furthermore, all employees were part-time and temporary, earning half of what the Morristown workers had earned, with no benefits, job security, vacations, or regular schedule. The laid-off workers in Morristown attempted to contact their old supervisors, willing to negotiate concessions in order to keep their jobs, but to no avail. Finally some drove the thirty miles to Mascot to seek work even in its new form, but all were rejected.

The worst news came when the fired workers went to apply for unemployment insurance and asked at the state employment offices where to look for new job opportunities. They were told that all the openings were at temporary agencies; even manufacturing jobs now hired through these labor contractors. To these workers, who had considered themselves among the most privileged, skilled, and loyal employees in the county, this was a great shock. A group of women got together and decided to form an organization called Citizens against Temporary Services, or CATS. They would protest the transition to temporary work and fight for fair labor laws in the state of Tennessee.

Over the next few years, CATS members took on several ambitious campaigns. They first attempted to sue GE for sex discrimination, age discrimination, and government fraud (since it had received tax incentives and economic development grants from the next county). The suit was lost when their attorney withdrew and the workers could not afford a new one. They then attempted to lobby the state economic development agency to prevent GE from moving. This was also unsuccessful, although they did get the state to revoke GE's job training grant, since it is illegal to use state monies to train workers for jobs from which other workers are laid off. Finally, CATS undertook a legislative campaign, introducing a bill that would define temporary work and regulate the abuse of long-term temporary workers. With major opposition from Tennessee's largest corporations as well as the National Association of Temporary Services, this campaign also lost.

Despite the failures, the organizing campaign in which CATS members participated alerted public opinion to the dangers of temporary work and transformed previously apolitical women into engaged citizens. The group organized events that had never happened in Morristown before, including a march through the city on a Saturday to raise publicly the issue of contingent work; town meetings with up to seven hundred people attending and testifying to the damage of temporary employment; public hearings on fair labor laws in Tennessee; and trips to Nashville to lobby state representatives. The women met with their local officials and chamber of commerce leaders to discuss local economic development policies. And they appeared all over town in their red CATS T-shirts, becoming readily identifiable as "those uppity CATS women." An entire group of women emerged out of the campaign as educated and articulate opponents of the new economic order.

The Process of Grassroots Organizing

CATS's formation and struggle is unusual; most plant closings happen quietly or with brief protest. Even the naming of the organization was unusual; they did not call themselves "Citizens against GE" or "The GE Workers' Committee," as most plant-closing groups do, but took on the much larger issues of contingent work and economic justice. With the help of others, CATS was encouraged to foster an understanding of its members' experiences within a wider context. Primarily because of CATS's close alliance with other organizations in East Tennessee — and because of the region's rich history of community organizing struggles — the GE workers were able to form a lasting organization and agitate for real political change.

Many factors went into the ongoing politicization of CATS members. Perhaps most important was the contribution of organizing expertise and an organizing structure. Bill Troy of the Tennessee Industrial Renewal Network (TIRN), Susan Williams of the Highlander Research and Education Center, and staff and members of Save Our Cumberland Mountains (SOCM) worked closely with the CATS group, helping them strategize, build a local coalition, plan events, and carry out an entire campaign. The CATS activists credit Troy and Williams with inspiring them, helping them think things through, planning next steps after disappointments, and keeping them going when they felt like giving up. The president of CATS calls them a "lifeline" and says she would not have survived without their aid: "I would go through it fifty more times just for their friendship. What's most important is you have to have a lifeline, someone who you can call up, who's always there on the other end, and will be strong. People who don't have a lifeline will drown. People *do* end up committing suicide, or letting their lives fall apart, if they don't have that lifeline" (Reinhardt 1993). This is more than individual friendship. In plant closings where this support is not available, resistance turns to bitterness, demoralization, and quiescence. A structure and institutional grounding are essential to a group's ability to analyze its situation, decide on goals, remain focused, and persevere over time.

The Highlander Center and the examples of organizers from other groups also provided essential training in leadership skills. CATS members participated in workshops at Highlander with community activists and organizers from all over the South and Appalachia, and learned about how similar struggles were handled in similar communities. They were encouraged to speak publicly, to persuade others to get involved, and to confront decision makers — all of which were entirely new experiences for the women involved.

Connections with other organizations also provided CATS with the opportunity to connect their immediate crisis with ongoing struggles. CATS members spoke to a national audience at the TIRN founding conference in Chattanooga about the effects of deindustrialization on local communities, and to statewide audiences at rallies and forums in Knoxville and Memphis. They went with TIRN leaders to speak with other displaced workers about the practical issues surrounding plant closings, but also about the larger changes that are needed to better serve the needs of working people. Some went to a conference in Washington, D.C., sponsored by the Women's Bureau of the U.S. Department of Labor, about women in the changing workplace. These events challenged the workers to speak out in public and advocate for their cause. This in itself was an important step in their personal and political growth. Once they did it, they found that they were not as alone and isolated as they had felt after GE closed. They began to see themselves as fighting for a cause that went beyond their particular situation. They were representatives of a national problem, inspiring others first to name the problem and then to resist.

Through the connections they made, CATS members were exposed to communities very different from their own. By traveling around Tennessee and meeting with other groups in the context of their fight for fair labor laws, CATS members were educated about changes in the economy and their effects on all kinds of groups. But the most dramatic example of this process was a trip to the *maquiladora* zone in Mexico, sponsored by TIRN. Two CATS leaders participated in the trip, along with eight other women workers from East Tennessee. They visited a GE plant in Mexico, among others, and were horrified by the impoverished living and working conditions provided by American corporations. They learned to make the connections between their own experiences and the experiences of Mexican women working in the *maquiladoras* for very low wages and with no job security or organizing rights. Beyond the personal, they learned how the "global economy" — and specifically, international trade with Mexico and NAFTA, celebrated by government and corporate leaders in Tennessee — was impacting their own community and similar communities in Mexico. When they returned, they prepared a presentation and slide show, which they took to other labor, community, and church groups. They were able to discuss the situation in Mexico and compare it to their own. The poverty among workers at American-owned plants was shocking. As one participant said,

> The whole thing shocked me to death. I had seen pictures; I had seen it on TV; but I never ever dreamed what I saw with my own eyes. . . . I think my heart sunk to my stomach. I thought, "This is not for real. They don't treat human beings like this. People don't do this." But they do. . . . It's something you'll never forget. . . . It changed something inside me.

She continues, "We got to talk to some of the workers, and it made me realize too that we've got some of the same problems here, that they have there" (Clark 1994). Mexican workers were not that different from them. They were struggling with similar problems, fighting the same enemies, and trying to make the best possible life for themselves and their families, given a very limited set of options.

The women returned to Tennessee and taught others in their community to resist the racist message of companies like GE, who told workers that Mexican women were stealing the jobs of Americans. One of the participants on the exchange explained that she "wanted to see if it was really true what they said about the Mexican people. . . . A lot of us went down there with the understanding the same as a lot of people here today: they're taking our jobs." Now, she says, "I don't blame them; I blame our government. . . . I don't believe in slavery. And that's what Mexico is — that's what the American government and manufacturers are making out of the Mexican people" (Hargis 1994). Another echoes this view: "I blamed the corporations — that was my first instinct. And then after I had sense enough to figure it out, [I thought] the government's letting these corporations do it. And to think that they thought that those people weren't human beings and could live in those deplorable conditions — it was beyond me" (Clark 1994). The Tennessee women learned the importance of solidarity across racial and national boundaries. This is remarkable, especially considering the racist rhetoric of companies, politicians, and radio talk show hosts during this time. Many have documented the prevalence of racism within the U.S. working class, especially in predominantly white workforces like East Tennessee's. And yet this group of women, provided the structure, leadership, and guidance of local organizations, overcame some very deep prejudices. They began to see connections between themselves and others, and were able to find fault with structural economic and political forces, rather than with other workers. This laid the groundwork for all of these women to participate in later campaigns, around international issues such as NAFTA and GATT, and around local economic issues as well. It was possible only because of the intensive efforts of grassroots organizers to educate and mobilize ordinary people to do extraordinary things.

The Potential of Collective Action

Through all these experiences, the CATS participants underwent a dramatic political education and transformation. Until 1988, they had been very lucky. They had held some of the best, most secure, and highest-paying jobs in Hamblen County. With a sudden decision by management, they became not only laid-off factory workers but, even worse, workers who were qualified only for the most unstable, poorest-paying positions with temporary services. This changed how they saw not just themselves but others as well. Shirley Reinhardt, a CATS leader, described the changes she saw in herself. She used to consider people on welfare to be lazy cheats, different from herself. "I got up every day, and I went to work, and I made good money, and a lot of times when I went to the grocery store and I saw somebody that had food stamps, I always thought, you know, 'Oh, that *little* kind of people, they ought to get a job and go to work.' " She describes how her attitude has changed.

> I must have been a shallow person. Because, see, I was in my own world. . . . I think I was a snob. . . . Now I'm grateful that I'm able to look and see and have compassion for people, because they're having a hard time. I wrote Al Gore a letter and told him that I fully believe that 98 percent of our society would work, if they could make a decent wage to where they can survive. . . . I really think if you give people the incentive that they'll work. (Reinhardt 1993)

Another CATS leader expressed the same change in her thinking:

> I used to think *I* wouldn't work for a temporary service. . . . That is so easy to say. Words are so easy to form and let them trip off your tongue, but they are so hard to take back. And when I think now how foolish that was, to even think such a thing. Because people who work for these services *are just like me*, they're just trying to make a living, they're just trying to get by, and that's all you got. (Adams 1993)

Besides attitudes, their political behavior changed as they organized CATS. Not one member had ever been to the state capitol in Nashville, and very few had ever so much as written a letter to a public official. As Reinhardt says, "When I worked at GE I would've never asked my government a question. I would've never challenged them on anything. Now I challenge them on *everything*. I mean, I wouldn't take their word for nothing. . . . I can see beyond what they say." This was a major change for Reinhardt. "I had all these ideas that there was justice in the Labor Department. Even when I lost my job, I thought well, not to worry, I'll go out and find another job, and then when reality started setting in I thought, well, our government won't let GE do this. And when you realize, they *will* let 'em do it, they're doing it every day, then I began to ask questions" (Reinhardt 1993). Eventually CATS participants learned that not only the plant managers at GE deserved blame. The government itself, including their own elected representatives, was enabling or even encouraging the very changes that had destroyed lives and livelihoods in Morristown. Deindustrialization in their town, as in so many others, was facilitated by the state (see Harrison and Bluestone 1988, 102 ff; LeRoy 1994).

This conclusion may seem straightforward, but when CATS members are contrasted with survivors of other plant closings, the differences are remarkable. Where there is no organization or structure in place to help workers understand and act together, the results are the opposite. Workers blame themselves or each other, usually scapegoating those more marginal than themselves: the young, the old, other ethnic groups, or welfare recipients. With no leadership other than local elites to interpret their experience, many workers accept the explanation that it was workers' own fault that the companies did not succeed, and that workers elsewhere would try harder and do better. Knowing they themselves did their best, people blame other groups. They become bitter, resentful, divided, and demoralized. They often decide never to trust authority or participate in politics again (Weinbaum 1994).

The process of beginning to ask questions and doubt long-held beliefs and trust in authority was extremely difficult for many of the GE workers. Among other things, it required giving up their idea of themselves as a privileged elite and facing their own powerlessness. They had to reconsider the idea that they were better — because of their skills, work ethic, social connections — than others in their community who had less. They had to question the rules by which they had been taught to play the game all their lives. They had to face the possibility that their relatively superior position had been a matter of sheer luck. Shirley Reinhardt points out that none of the CATS members had ever fought anything like this before.

> I was the type of person, I guess that if they [GE] had told me to go out in a lake and jump in, I would've went on, because I thought they knew what was best for me. . . . I

had been brought up to think that if you got a job you did the very best you could, you worked as hard as you could, you did what they said, because they were boss — and you'd be OK! When I realized that didn't work, it was hard, it was really hard. (Reinhardt 1993)

Others explained how they learned to identify with other oppressed people, rather than with the better-off. Lodis Adams thought a lot about Native Americans: "I can imagine how they feel, when they moved out and thought, 'This was mine and you took it.' You know, when you think about it, that's exactly how we are. This was ours, and they took it, and they gave it to somebody else" (Adams 1993).

These hard-learned lessons stuck. More than most participants involved in typical plant-closing struggles, the members of CATS continue to participate in political activities. As the Morristown chapter of Save Our Cumberland Mountains (SOCM), a regional grassroots organization, CATS has now become involved in local and statewide issues of environmental justice. Reinhardt has become a leader in a new campaign to get city drinking water for people living in a neighborhood near a polluted landfill. Other members have led and worked in union campaigns — including several who were previously virulently anti-union. Several have been activists in international trade issues, leading the protests against NAFTA in 1993. All the members interviewed were extremely knowledgeable about NAFTA, welfare reform, labor law reform, and other national economic issues. They continue to write letters and meet with legislators at every opportunity. Most important, they have learned to stand up for themselves, both individually and collectively. Each one tells stories of confronting authorities, at work and elsewhere, when injustice was being done. These small demonstrations of resistance, taken together, have had an impact on many lives.

These transformations have created democratic citizens and political actors out of individuals. The change in participants' understanding of their identity, but also in their behavior, is remarkable. CATS became a classroom of democracy. Some of the lessons learned were very difficult ones — including the fact of workers' own relative powerlessness and their betrayal by political representatives and elites. Nevertheless, when combined with the skills and experience of participation in strong collective action, it was an essential education. Previously quiescent, atomized individuals became political actors and true democratic citizens.

CATS also transformed Morristown. Anyone in Morristown who has a problem in the workplace knows to contact a CATS leader. A small group of them serve as job counselors for nearly the entire city's population. Moreover, although CATS has become a SOCM chapter and has quieted down during the past four years, public officials in Morristown remember CATS. The county executive and chamber of commerce officials refer to CATS as the strongest protest about jobs and the economy Hamblen County has ever seen. Although CATS may have lost the immediate battle, its legacy can be detected in the ongoing decisions made by local officials who have known their organized power and will always, even unconsciously, anticipate their reactions. In this sense, CATS has had a positive effect on the Morristown economy and polity.

Finally, CATS has transformed the institutional landscape of East Tennessee. Their struggle inspired the newly forming TIRN to decide to focus on contingent work as one of its major organizing programs. TIRN has continued to bring together workers and activists from all over the state to discuss the problem and to strategize. The Highlander Center has also taken on the issue, incorporating exercises and materials on the problems of temporary work into its workshops on the global economy and on community organizing in Appalachia and the South. This in turn has inspired other organizations to take on the issue. One of these, the Carolina Alliance for Fair Employment, for example, recently held a "temp school," inviting long-term temporary workers to come from all over South Carolina for a paid week of discussion and education. The contingent workers participated in workshops, teaching the organizers about their situation and prospects. By the end, they had come up with exciting plans to continue talking and perhaps planning campaigns around temporary work in their state. The Southeastern Regional Economic Justice Network (REJN) has also determined to address the problem of contingent work as one of the centerpieces of its campaign on economic justice. And with grant support from Oxfam America and other organizations, TIRN recently hired a full-time organizer in Nashville to work exclusively on contingent work issues. With the example of the early activists from CATS, other groups and networks have taken up the effort and will continue fighting for greater economic justice for displaced workers.

CATS demonstrates that rural women not only are capable of involvement in political affairs on the most global scale, but are also leading organized efforts at resisting political trends. They are acting not only on their own behalf, or to protect their families and relationships; they are protesting changes that imperil an entire class of people, across borders, genders, and races. And in so doing, they are liberating themselves and discovering the power they can achieve by joining with others.

Their example provides two important lessons to groups organizing around these issues in other areas. First, the economic and political arrangements now labeled the "global economy" present an unparalleled challenge for workers all over the world. Working conditions are deteriorating at a rapid pace, and the gap between rich and poor is widening. The barriers to organizing for economic rights have never been higher. Collective action against economic injustices must now take place on a national or even international level, for very few important decisions are made locally. Making a difference in the international arena requires a measure of re-sources usually beyond the capacities of working-class people. It will require a concerted effort, with the eventual support of more privileged and powerful groups, to resist current trends. In addition, however, CATS shows how this collective action can begin. Through small local efforts, organizers can generate the necessary political discussion, education, and transformation. Workers can transcend their particular circumstances and prejudices, and join with allies elsewhere to make change. CATS, especially in the context of other deindustrialization stories, shows the possibility of bringing out solidarity, politicization, and empathy rather than hatred, isolation, and violence. In the 1990s, this is exactly what must happen if a democratic system is to survive. Only the process of intensive local organizing, in workplaces and communities across America, can form the bedrock on which a new democratic political movement can be built.

This research on rural women's political resistance challenges basic paradigms of political science. Women are clearly capable of acting politically, and not only in their roles as mothers, church leaders, and community builders. Women are taking on the most important and overwhelming political and economic issues facing the nation — issues of global justice — and resisting traditional categories, fighting powerful elites, educating their communities, and leading a movement. Further analysis of women's relationship to their work and communities, their political participation and leadership, and their efforts at mobilization and change will force us to reconceive assumptions about political behavior and may lead to new ways of understanding the practice of politics itself.

NOTES

1. The gaps are striking in several bodies of literature. The literature on women in politics, for the most part, has focused on electoral behavior and used survey research to assess voting and representation patterns. It concludes, therefore, that women are more likely to participate in political activity if they have higher levels of education and income, higher employment status, children, and a greater sense of civic obligation (e.g., Jaquette 1974; Almond and Verba 1965; Gelb and Palley 1987; Sapiro 1983; Beckwith 1986; Kelly and Boutilier 1978). This ignores grassroots workplace- or community-based women activists. Similarly, the vast body of theoretical literature on collective action concentrates mostly on large, organized social movements and neglects local resistance efforts, especially by women. Neither would predict the activity described here.

2. Even as these practices become more prevalent, however, management experts contest their desirability. Shifting from stable to contingent labor does produce immediate, short-term savings for firms. It cuts labor costs, fragments tasks, permits subcontracting, and makes work hours less rigid and predictable. On the other hand, it inhibits a more genuine long-term flexibility that relies on cooperation among a group of well-trained, experienced workers, in an environment conducive to continuous learning, opportunity, and productivity (Piore 1989).

3. This presents a striking contrast to the fact that a full 98 percent of those currently involved in capital and financial transactions on the global level are men (Falk 1993, 43).

4. As Fuentes and Ehrenreich (1989) point out, the idea that women of color are not only happy to work but biologically predisposed to do this work is often fostered by the governments of developing countries. Under pressure from the IMF and World Bank to pursue aggressive industrialization and "structural adjustment," these governments often advertise the availability of a low-wage, hardworking, pliant workforce in order to attract business investment.

5. On the other hand, some are benefiting extraordinarily from globalization. One study of seventy-eight top executives of U.S. transnational corporations showed that their annual compensation averaged $2,651,825 in 1994. Executives at Ford and General Motors received raises of over 130 percent. The CEO of Allied Signal Corporation, Lawrence Bossidy, earned

$12.4 million, an amount that exceeds the combined *total* annual wages of all of Allied's four thousand employees in Mexico (Anderson et al. 1995).

BIBLIOGRAPHY

Adams, Lodis. 1993. Interview by author. Morristown, TN, December 9.

Almond, Gabriel, and Sidney Verba. 1965. *The Civic Culture: Political Attitudes and Democracy in Five Nations*. Boston: Little, Brown.

Anderson, Sarah, John Cavanagh, and Jonathan Williams. 1995. "Workers Lose, CEOs Win (II)." Washington, DC: Institute for Policy Studies.

Appelbaum, Eileen. 1992. "Structural Change and the Growth of Part-Time and Temporary Employment." In *New Policies for the Part-Time and Contingent Workforce*, ed. Virginia L. duRivage. Armonk, NY: M. E. Sharpe.

Barnet, Richard J., and John Cavanagh. 1994. *Global Dreams: Imperial Corporations and the New World Order*. New York: Simon and Schuster.

Beckwith, Karen. 1986. *American Women and Political Participation*. New York: Greenwood.

Belous, Richard. 1989. *The Contingent Economy: The Growth of the Temporary, Part-Time and Subcontracted Workforce*. Washington, DC: National Planning Association.

Bishop, Bobbie. 1993. Interview by author. Clinton, TN, December 6.

Bluestone, Barry, and Bennett Harrison. 1982. *The Deindustrialization of America*. New York: Basic Books.

Bluestone, Barry, Bennett Harrison, and Lawrence Baker. 1981. *Corporate Flight: The Causes and Consequences of Economic Dislocation*. Washington, DC: Progressive Alliance.

Boyte, Harry C. 1980. *The Backyard Revolution: Understanding the New Citizen Movement*. Philadelphia: Temple University Press.

Bray, Brenda. 1993. Interview by author. Lake City, TN, December 7.

Brecher, Jeremy, John Brown Childs, and Jill Cutler. 1993. *Global Visions: Beyond the New World Order*. Boston: South End.

Carré, Françoise J. 1992. "Temporary Employment in the Eighties." In *New Policies for the Part-Time and Contingent Workforce*, ed. Virginia L. duRivage. Armonk, NY: M. E. Sharpe.

Clark, Luvernel. 1994. Interview by author. Knoxville, TN, February 2.

Cobb, James C. 1993. *The Selling of the South: The Southern Crusade for Industrial Development, 1936–1990*. Urbana: University of Illinois Press.

duRivage, Virginia L., ed. 1992. *New Policies for the Part-Time and Contingent Workforce*. Armonk, NY: M. E. Sharpe.

Falk, Richard. 1993. "The Making of Global Citizenship." In *Global Visions: Beyond the New World Order*, ed. Jeremy Brecher et al. Boston: South End.

Fuentes, Annette, and Barbara Ehrenreich. 1989. *Women in the Global Factory*. Boston: South End.

Gaventa, John, and Peter Wiley. 1987. "The Deindustrialization of the Tennessee Economy." New Market, TN: Highlander Research and Education Center.

Gelb, Joyce, and Marian Lief Palley. 1987. *Women and Public Policies*. Princeton: Princeton University Press.

Global Assembly Line. 1991. PBS Video.

Hargis, June. 1994. Interview by author. Knoxville, TN, January 24.

Harrison, Bennett, and Barry Bluestone. 1988. *The Great U-Turn: Corporate Restructuring and the Polarizing of America*. New York: Basic Books.

Jaquette, Jane S., ed. 1974. *Women in Politics.* New York: John Wiley and Sons.

Jenkins, J. Craig. 1987. "Nonprofit Organizations and Policy Advocacy." In *The Nonprofit Sector: A Research Handbook,* ed. Walter W. Powell. New Haven: Yale University Press.

Kelly, Rita Mae, and Mary Boutilier. 1978. *The Making of Political Women.* Chicago: Nelson-Hall.

LeRoy, Greg. 1994. *No More Candy Store: States and Cities Making Job Subsidies Accountable.* Chicago and Washington, DC: Federation for Industrial Retention and Renewal and the Grassroots Policy Project.

Metzenbaum, Senator Howard. 1993. "Toward a Disposable Work Force: The Increasing Use of 'Contingent' Labor." Hearing before the Subcommittee on Labor, Committee on Labor and Human Resources, U.S. Senate, June 15.

Milofsky, Carl. 1988. *Community Organizations: Studies in Resource Mobilization and Exchange.* New York: Oxford University Press.

Negrey, Cynthia. 1993. *Gender, Time, and Reduced Work.* Albany: State University of New York Press.

Nine to Five. 1995. "National Profile of Working Women." Washington, DC: Nine to Five.

Parker, Robert E. 1994. *Flesh Peddlers and Warm Bodies: The Temporary Help Industry and Its Workers.* New Brunswick: Rutgers University Press.

Phillips, Lyda. 1991. "Full-Time Benefits Sought for State's 'Temporaries.' " *Nashville Banner,* February 21, D1.

Piore, Michael J. 1989. "Fissure and Discontinuity in U.S. Labor Management Relations." In *The State and the Labor Market,* ed. Samuel Rosenberg. New York: Plenum.

Putz, Susan, and Nina Gregg. 1995. "Organizing Contingent Workers in a Right-to-Work State: Steps toward an Agenda for Action." Unpublished report.

Reinhardt, Shirley. 1993. Interview by author. Morristown, TN, December 10.

Rosenberg, Samuel, ed. 1989. *The State and the Labor Market.* New York: Plenum.

Sapiro, Virginia. 1983. *The Political Integration of Women: Roles, Socialization and Politics.* Urbana: University of Illinois Press.

Scriver, Chris. 1993. Interview by author. Clinton, TN, December 10.

Standing, Guy. 1989. "Global Feminization through Flexible Labor." *World Development* 17, no. 7: 1077–86.

Tilly, Chris. 1992. "Short Hours, Short Shrift: The Causes and Consequences of Part-Time Employment." In *New Policies for the Part-Time and Contingent Workforce,* ed. Virginia L. duRivage. Armonk, NY: M. E. Sharpe.

Weinbaum, Eve. 1994. "Local Economic Development, Democracy, and the State: Mobilizing against Poverty in East Tennessee." Paper presented at Midwest Political Science Association.

Williamson, Robert. 1993. Interview by author. Morristown, TN, December 8.

Yount, Linda, and Susan Williams. 1990. "Temporary in Tennessee: CATS for Stable Jobs." *Labor Research Review* 15: 74–80.

PART THREE

Participation, Electoral Politics, and Movement Building

Negotiating and Transforming the Public Sphere: African American Political Life in the Transition from Slavery to Freedom

ELSA BARKLEY BROWN

On April 15, 1880, Margaret Osborne, Jane Green, Susan Washington, Molly Branch, Susan Gray, Mary A. Soach, and "over two hundred other prominent sisters of the church" petitioned the Richmond, Virginia, First African Baptist Church's business meeting to allow women to vote on the pastor:

> We the sisters of the church feeling that we are interested in the welfare of the same and also working hard to finish the house and have been working by night and day. . . . We know you have adopted a law in the church that the business must be done by the male members. We don't desire to alter that law, nor do we desire to have anything to do with the business of the church, we only ask to have a vote in electing or dismissing him. We whose names are attached to this petition ask you to grant us this privilege.[1]

The circumstances surrounding these women's petition suggest the kinds of changes taking place internally in late nineteenth- and early twentieth-century black Richmond and other southern black communities. In the immediate post–Civil War era, women had voted in mass meetings and Republican Party conventions held at First African, thus contradicting gender-based assumptions within the larger society about politics, political engagement, and appropriate forms of political behavior. Now, women sitting in the same church were petitioning for the right to vote in an internal community institution, couching the petition in terms designed to minimize the request and avoid a challenge to men's authority and position.

Scholars' assumptions of an unbroken line of exclusion of African American women from formal political associations in the late nineteenth century has obscured fundamental changes in the political understandings within African American communities in the transition from slavery to freedom. Women in First African and in other arenas were seeking in the late nineteenth century not a new authority but rather a lost authority, one they now often sought to justify on a distinctively female basis. As these women petitioned for their rights within the church and as other women formed voluntary associations in turn-of-the-century Richmond, they were not, as often depicted in the scholarly literature, emerging into the political arena through such actions. Rather, these women were attempting to retain space they traditionally had held in the immediate post-emancipation period. This essay explores the processes of public discourse within Richmond and other southern black communities and the factors that led to increasingly more clearly gendered and class spaces within those communities to understand why women by the 1880s and 1890s needed to create their own pulpits from which to speak — to restore their voices to the community. This exploration suggests how the ideas, process, meanings, and practice of freedom changed within late nineteenth-century southern African American communities and what the implications of those changes may be for our visions of freedom and for the possibilities of African American community in the late twentieth century.

After emancipation, African American men, women, and children, as part of black communities throughout the South, struggled to define on their own terms the meaning of freedom and in the process to construct communities of struggle. Much of the literature on Reconstruction portrays freed African Americans as rapidly and readily adopting a gendered private-public dichotomy.[2] Much of the literature on the nineteenth-century public sphere constructs a masculine liberal bourgeois public with a female counterpublic.[3] This essay, focusing on the civic geography of post–Civil War black Richmond, suggests the problematic of applying such generalizations to African American life in the late nineteenth-century South. In the immediate post-emancipation era, black Richmonders enacted their understandings of democratic political discourse through mass meetings attended and participated in (including voting) by men, women, and children and through mass participation in Republican Party conventions. They carried these notions of political participation into the state capitol, engaging from the gallery in the debates on the constitutional convention floor.

Central to African Americans' construction of a fully democratic notion of political discourse was the church as a foundation of the black public sphere.[4] In the post-slavery era, church buildings also served as meeting halls and auditoriums as well as educational and recreational facilities, employment and social service bureaus, and bulletin boards. First African, especially, with a seating capacity of nearly four thousand, was the site of large political gatherings. Schools such as Richmond Theological Seminary and Richmond Colored High and Normal School held their annual commencement exercises at First African Baptist, allowing these events to become community celebrations. Other groups, such as the Temperance Union, were regularly granted the church for their meetings or rallies. As a political space occupied by men, women, and children, literate and nonliterate, ex-slave and formerly free, church members and nonmembers, First African enabled the construction of political concerns in democratic space. This is not to suggest that official versions and spokespersons were not produced, but these official versions were the product of a fairly egalitarian discourse and therefore represented the conditions of black Richmonders of differing classes, ages, and genders. Within black Richmonders' construction of the public sphere, the forms of discourse varied from the prayer to the stump speech to the testimonies regarding outrages against freedpeople to shouted interventions from the galleries into the debates on the legislative floor. By the very nature of their participation — the inclusion of women and children, the engagement through prayer, the disregard of formal rules for speakers and audience, the engagement from the galleries in the formal legislative sessions — Afro-Richmonders challenged liberal bourgeois notions of rational discourse. Many white observers considered their unorthodox political engagements to be signs of their unfamiliarity and perhaps unreadiness for politics.[5]

In the decades following emancipation, as black Richmonders struggled to achieve even a measured amount of freedom, the black public sphere emerged as more fractured and perhaps less democratic at the end of the nineteenth century, yet even then it retained strong elements of a democratic agenda. This essay examines the changing constructions of political space and community discourse in the post-emancipation era.

Envisioning Freedom

In April 1865, when Union troops marched into Richmond, jubilant African American men, women, and children poured into the streets and crowded into their churches to dance, kiss, hug, pray, sing, and shout. They assembled in First African, Third Street African Methodist, Ebenezer, and Second African not merely because of the need to thank God for their deliverance but also because the churches were the only institutional spaces, and in the case of First African certainly the largest space, owned by African Americans themselves.[6] As the process of Reconstruction unfolded, black Richmonders continued to meet regularly in their churches, now not merely to rejoice. If Afro-Richmonders had thought freedom would accompany emancipation, the events of the first few weeks and months of Union occupation quickly disabused them of such ideas. Throughout the summer and fall of 1865 black Richmonders reported numerous violations of their rights. Among them were pass and curfew regulations designed to curtail black mobility and force African American men and women out of the city to labor in the rural areas. Pass and curfew violators (eight hundred in the first week of June) were detained in bullpens — one for women and children, a separate one for men — away from and often unknown to family members. Black Richmonders also detailed numerous incidents of disrespectful treatment, verbal abuse, physical assault, and torture. "Many poor women" told "tales of their frights and robberies"; vendors told of goods destroyed by military police. Private homes were not immune to the intrusions of civilian and military white men. One couple were confronted by soldiers, one of whom stood over them in bed "threatening to blow out their brains if they moved" while others "pillage[d] the house of money, watches, underclothing, etc."[7] Many spoke of the sexual abuse of black women: "gobbling up of the most likely looking negro women, thrown into the cells, robbed and ravished at the will of the guard." Men and women in the vicinity of the jail testified "to hearing women scream frightfully almost every night."[8]

The regular meetings in the African churches, originally ones of jubilation, quickly became the basis for constructing a discourse about freedom and organizing large-scale mass protest. On June 10, 1865, over three thousand assembled at First African to hear the report of the investigating committee, which had conducted hearings and gathered the evidence and depositions necessary to present black Richmonders' case directly to Governor Francis H. Pierpoint and to the "chief head of all authority," the president of the United States. The protest memorial drawn up during the meeting was ratified at meetings in each of the other churches, and money was raised through church collections to send six representatives (one from each church in Richmond and one from First Baptist, Manchester) to Washington. On Friday, June 16, these delegates delivered the mass meeting's protest directly to President Andrew Johnson:[9] "Mr. President: We have been appointed a committee by a public meeting of the colored people of Richmond, Va., to make known . . . the wrongs, as we conceive them to be, by which we are sorely oppressed." In their memorial, as in their meetings, black Richmonders not only recounted the abuses, they also used their individual stories to construct a collective history and to combat the idea of being "idle negroes" unprepared for freedom.[10]

> We represent a population of more than 20,000 colored people, including Richmond and Manchester, . . . more than 6,000 of our people are members in good standing of Christian churches, and nearly our whole population constantly attend divine services. Among us there are at least 2,000 men who are worth $200 to $500; 200 who have property valued at from $1,000 to $5,000, and a number who are worth from $5,000 to $20,000. . . .
>
> The law of Slavery severely punished those who taught us to read and write, but, not withstanding this, 3,000 of us can read, and at least 2,000 can read and write, and a large number of us are engaged in useful and profitable employment on our own account.

The community they described was one based in a collective ethos; it was not merely their industry but also their responsibility that was the basis on which they claimed their rights.

> None of our people are in the alms-house, and when we were slaves the aged and infirm who were turned away from the homes of hard masters, who had been enriched by their toil, our benevolent societies supported while they lived, and buried when they died, and comparatively few of us have found it necessary to ask for Government rations, which have been so bountifully bestowed upon the unrepentant Rebels of Richmond.

They reminded Johnson of the efforts black men and women in Richmond had taken to support the Union forces against the Confederacy.

> During the whole of the Slaveholders' Rebellion we have been true and loyal to the United States Government; . . . We have given aid and comfort to the soldiers of Freedom (for which several of our people, of both sexes, have been severely punished

by stripes and imprisonment). We have been their pilots and their scouts, and have safely conducted them through many perilous adventures.

They declared themselves the loyal citizens of the United States, those the federal government should be supporting. Finally, they invoked the religious destiny that emancipation had reaffirmed, reminding the president of a "motto once inscribed over the portals of an Egyptian temple, '*Know all ye who exercise power, that God hates injustice!*' "[11]

Mindful of others' versions of their history, standing, and entitlements, black Richmonders also moved to have their own story widely circulated. When local white newspapers refused to publish their account, they had it published in the *New York Tribune.*[12] Throughout 1865 and 1866 black Richmonders continued to meet regularly in mass meetings where men, women, and children collectively participated in constructing and announcing their own story of community and freedom.[13] The story told in those mass meetings, published in northern white newspapers, and carried in protest to Union officials was also carried into the streets as black Richmonders inserted themselves in the preexisting national political traditions and at the same time widened those traditions. John O'Brien has noted that in the immediate aftermath of emancipation, black Richmonders developed their own political calendar, celebrating four civic holidays: January 1, George Washington's birthday, April 3 (emancipation day), and July 4.[14] White Richmonders were horrified as they watched former slaves claim civic holidays and traditions they believed to be the historical possession of white Americans and occupy spaces, like Capitol Square, that had formerly been reserved for white residents.[15]

The underlying values and assumptions that would pervade much of black people's political struggles in the city were forged in slavery and war and in the weeks following emancipation. Military regulations that limited black mobility and made finding and reunifying family members even more difficult placed the economic interests of white men and women above the material and social interests of African Americans. The bullpens, which detained many away from their families, and the raids on black homes, which made all space public and subject to the interests of the state, obliterated any possible distinctions between public and private spheres. Demanding passes and evidence of employment denied black Richmonders the right to act and to be treated not as economic units and/or property but as social beings and family members. The difficulty of finding decent housing at affordable prices further impeded freedpeople's efforts to bring their families together. All these obstacles to and expectations of family life were part of what Eric Foner speaks of as the " 'politicization' of every day life."[16]

These political issues underpinned Afro-Richmonders' petition to Johnson and would continue to underpin their political struggles in late nineteenth-century Richmond. Even as they fashioned individual stories into a collective history, black Richmonders could and did differ on the means by which they might secure freedom — vigorously debating issues such as the necessity of confiscation.[17] But they also understood freedom as a collective struggle. When they entered the formal political arena through Republican Party politics in 1867, this understanding was the foundation for their initial engagement with issues of suffrage and democracy. As Julie Saville has observed for South Carolina, freedpeople in Richmond "were not so much converted to the Republican party as they were prepared to convert the Republican party to themselves."[18] The post–Civil War southern black public sphere was forged in jubilation and struggle as African American men, women, and children claimed their own history and set forth their own political ideals.

All the resources of black Richmonders became elements in their political struggles. The *Richmond Whig*, intending to ridicule the inappropriateness of freedpeople's behaviors and assumptions, highlighted the politicized nature of all aspects of black life during Reconstruction; the freedpeople's "mass meetings, committee meetings, and meetings of the different societies all have political significance. The superstitions of the colored people are availed on, and religion and Radicalism are all jumbled together. Every night they have meetings and musterings, harangues and sermons, singing and praying — all looking to political results."[19] Similarly the *Richmond Dispatch* reported an 1867 Republican meeting that began with "Harris, colored" offering "the most remarkable" prayer "we have ever heard. It was frequently interrupted by laughter and manifestations of applause":

> Oh, Lord God, bless our enemies — bless President Johnson. We would not even have him sent to hell. Come, oh come, good Lord, and touch his heart even while I am talking with you here to-night. [Amen.] Show him the error of his ways. Have mercy upon our "Moses," [Sarcastic. Great laughter and amens.] who, like Esau, has sold his birthright for a morsel of pottage — took us in the wilderness and left us there. Come down upon him, oh Lord, with thy blessing. God bless us in our meeting to-night, and help us in what we do. God forbid that we should choose any Conservative that has the spirit of the devil in his heart, and whose feet take hold on hell. God bless our friend — true and tried — Mr. Hunnicut, who has stood a great many sorrows and I think he can stand a great many more. [Laughter.] Bless our judge, Mr. Underwood, who is down here among us, and don't let anything harm a hair of his head.[20]

What the *Whig* and the *Dispatch* captured was a political culture in which the wide range of institutional and noninstitutional resources of individuals and the community as a whole became the basis for defining, claiming, and securing freedom in post-emancipation Richmond. The church provided more than physical space, financial resources, and a communication network; it also provided a cultural base that validated emotion and experience as ways of knowing, and drew on a collective call and response, encouraging the active participation of all.[21]

Virginia's rejection of the Fourteenth Amendment brought the state under the Reconstruction Act of 1867; a constitutional convention became prerequisite for full restoration to the Union. Black men, enfranchised for the delegate selection and ratification ballots, were to have their first opportunity to engage in the political parties and legislative chambers of the state. The struggles in which they had engaged in the two years since emancipation influenced the manner of black Richmonders' initial participation in the formal political arena of conventions and voting. On August 1, 1867, the day the Republican state convention opened in Richmond to adopt a platform for the upcoming state constitutional convention, thousands of African American men, women, and children absented themselves from their employment and joined the delegates at the convention site, First African Baptist Church.[22] Tobacco factories, lacking a major portion of their workers, were forced to close for the day.

This pattern persisted whenever a major issue came before the state and city Republican conventions held during the summer and fall of 1867, or the state constitutional convention, which convened in Richmond from December 1867 to March 1868. A *New York Times* reporter estimated that "the entire colored population of Richmond" attended the October 1867 local Republican convention where delegates to the state constitutional convention were nominated. Noting that female domestic servants were a large portion of those in attendance, the correspondent reported, "as is usual on such occasions, families which employ servants were forced to cook their own dinners, or content themselves with a cold lunch. Not only had Sambo gone to the Convention, but Dinah was there also."[23]

These men and women did not absent themselves from work just to be onlookers at the proceedings, but to be active participants. They assumed as equal a right to be present and participate as the delegates themselves, a fact they made abundantly clear at the August 1867 Republican state convention. Having begun to arrive four hours before the opening session, African American men and women had filled the meeting place long before the delegates arrived. Having showed up to speak for themselves, they did not assume delegates had priority — in discussion or in seating. Disgusted at the scene, as well as unable to find a seat, the conservative white Republican delegates removed to the Capitol Square to convene an outdoor session. That was quite acceptable to the several thousand additional African American men and women who, unable to squeeze into the church, were now still able to participate in the important discussions and to vote down the proposals of the conservative faction.[24]

Black men, women, and children were also active participants throughout the state constitutional convention. A *New York Times* reporter commented on the tendency for the galleries to be crowded "with the 'unprivileged,' and altogether black." At issue was not just these men and women's presence but also their behavior. White women, for example, certainly on occasion sat in the convention's gallery as visitors silently observing the proceedings; these African Americans, however, participated from the gallery, loudly engaging in the debates. At points of heated controversy, black delegates turned to the crowds as they made their addresses on the convention floor, obviously soliciting and relying on mass participation. Outside the convention hours, mass meetings were held to discuss and vote on the major issues. At these gatherings vote was either by voice or rising, and men, women, and children voted. These meetings were not mock assemblies; they were important gatherings at which the community made plans for freedom. The most radical black Republican faction argued that the major convention issues should actually be settled at these mass meetings, and that delegates should merely cast the community's vote on the convention floor. Though this did not occur, black delegates were no doubt influenced by both the mass meetings and the African American presence in the galleries, both of which included women.[25]

Black Richmonders were operating in two separate political arenas: an internal one and an external one. While these arenas were related, they each proceeded from different assumptions, had different purposes, and therefore operated according to different rules. Within the internal political process women were enfranchised and participated in all public forums — the parades, rallies, mass meetings, and the conventions themselves.[26] Richmond was not atypical in this regard.[27]

It was the state constitutional convention, however, that would decide African American women's and men's status in the political process external to the African American community. When the Virginia convention began its deliberation regarding the franchise, Thomas Bayne, a black delegate from Norfolk, argued the inherent link between freedom and suffrage, and contended that those who opposed universal suffrage were actually opposing the freedom of African American people. In rejoinder, E. L. Gibson, a conservative white delegate, enunciated several principles of republican representative government. Contending that "a man might be free and still not have the right to vote," Gibson explained the fallacy of assuming that this civil right was an inherent corollary to freedom: if the right were inherent then it would belong to both sexes and to all from "the first moment of existence" and to foreigners immediately. This was "an absurdity too egregious to be contemplated."[28] And yet this "absurd" notion of political rights was what was in practice in the Richmond black community — males and females voted without regard to age; the thousands of rural migrants who came into Richmond suffered no waiting period but immediately possessed the full rights of the community. What was absurd to Gibson and most white men — Republican or Democrat — was obviously quite rational to many black Richmonders. Two very different conceptions of freedom and public participation in the political process were in place.

In the end only men obtained the legal franchise. The impact of this decision is neither inconsequential nor fully definitive. African American women were by law excluded from the formal political arena external to their community. Yet this does not mean that they were not active in that arena; witness Richmond women's participation in the Republican and constitutional conventions. Southern black men and women debated the issue of women's suffrage in both the external and internal political arenas. In Nansemond County, Virginia, for example, the mass meetings resolved that women should be granted the legal franchise; in Richmond, while a number of participants in a mass meeting supported female suffrage, the majority opinion swung against it.[29] But the meaning of that decision was not as straightforward as it may seem. The debate as to whether women should be given the vote in the external political arena occurred in internal political arena mass meetings where women participated and voted not just before and during, *but also after* the negative decision regarding legal enfranchisement. This maintained the status quo in the external community; ironically enough, the status quo in the internal community was maintained as well — women continued to have the vote. African American men and women clearly operated within two distinct political systems.

Focusing on formal disfranchisement obscures women's continued participation in the external political arena. In Richmond and throughout the South, exclusion from legal enfranchisement did not prevent African American women from shaping the vote and the political decisions. Throughout the late 1860s and 1870s women continued to participate in political meetings in large numbers and to organize political societies. Some, like the Rising Daughters of Liberty and the Daughters of the Union Victory in Richmond or the United Daughters of Liberty organized by coal miners' wives living outside Manchester, had all-female memberships. Others, like the two thousand-member National Political Aid Society, the Union League of Richmond, and the Union Equal Rights League of Manchester, had male and female members. Even though white Republicans made efforts to exclude them from further participation in political meetings by the late 1860s, African American women in Virginia, South Carolina, Louisiana, and elsewhere were still attending these meetings in the 1870s.

Women's presence at these meetings was anything but passive. In the violent political atmosphere of the last years of Reconstruction, they had an especially important and dangerous role. In South Carolina, for example, while the men participated in the meeting, the women guarded the guns — thus serving in part as the protectors of the meeting. For those women and men who lived in outlying areas of Richmond and attended outdoor meetings, political participation was a particularly dangerous matter, a fact they clearly recognized. Meetings were guarded by posted sentinels with guns who questioned the intent of any suspicious people, usually white men, coming to the meeting. A reporter for the *Richmond Daily Dispatch* described one such encounter when he attempted to cover a political meeting of fifty women and twenty-five men.[30]

Women as well as men took election day off from work and went to the polls. Fraud, intimidation, and violence became the order of election days. White newspapers and politicians threatened loss of jobs, homes, and lives. Afro-Richmonders countered with a group presence. Often even those living within the city and short distances from the polling places went early, even the night before, and camped out at the polls, hoping that their early presence would require the acceptance of their vote and that the group presence would provide protection from violence and intimidation. In the highly charged political atmosphere of late nineteenth-century Richmond, it was no small matter for these women and men to participate in political meetings and show up at the election sites. The reasons for the group presence at the polls were varied. African American women in Virginia, Mississippi, South Carolina, and elsewhere understood themselves to have a vital stake in African American men's franchise. The fact that only men had been granted the vote did not at all mean that only men should exercise the vote. Women throughout the South initiated sanctions against men who voted Democratic; some went along to the polls to insure a properly cast ballot. As increasing white fraud made black men's voting more difficult, early arrival at the polls was partly intended to counter such efforts.

Although election days in Richmond were not as violent as they were elsewhere throughout Virginia and other parts of the South, guns were used to intimidate and defraud. It is also probable that in Richmond, as elsewhere throughout the South, when black men went to camp out overnight at the polls, households feared leaving women and children unprotected at home. Thus the women's presence, just as the group presence of the men, may have been a sign of the need for collective protection. If Richmond women were at all like their sisters in South Carolina and Danville, they may have carried weapons with them — to protect themselves and/or help protect the male voters.[31] Women and children's presence reflects their excitement about the franchise but also their understanding of the dangers involved in voting. The necessity for a group presence at the polls reinforced the sense of collective enfranchisement. Women's presence at the polls was both a negative sanction and a positive expression of the degree to which they understood the men's franchise to be a new political opportunity for themselves as well as their children.

In the dangerous political atmosphere of the late nineteenth century, the vote took on a sacred and collective character. Black men and women in Richmond, as throughout the South, initiated sanctions against those black men perceived as violating the collective good by supporting the conservative forces. Black Democrats were subject to the severest exclusion: disciplined within or quite often expelled from their churches and mutual benefit societies, and denied board and lodging with black families. Additionally, mobs jeered, jostled, and sometimes beat black Democrats or rescued those who were arrested for such acts. Women were often reported to be in the forefront of this activity. Similarly, black women were said to have "exercised a positive influence upon some men who were inclined to hesitate or be indifferent" during the early 1880s Readjuster campaigns.[32]

All of this suggests that African American women and men understood the vote as a collective, not an individual, possession; and furthermore, that African American women, unable to cast a separate vote, viewed African American men's vote as equally theirs. They believed that franchise should be cast in the best interest of both. This is not the nineteenth-century patriarchal notion that men voted on behalf of their wives and children. By that assumption women had no individual wills; rather, men operated in women's best interest because women were assumed to have no right of input. African American women assumed the political rights that came with being a member of the community even though they were denied the political rights they thought should come with being citizens of the state.

To justify their political participation, Richmond and other southern black women in the immediate post–Civil War period did not need to rely on arguments of superior female morality or public motherhood. Their own cultural, economic, and political traditions provided rationale enough. An understanding of collective autonomy was the basis on which African Americans reconstructed families, developed communal institutions, constructed schools, and engaged in formal politics after emancipation. The participation of women and children in the external and internal political arenas was part of a larger political worldview of exslaves and free men and women, a worldview fundamentally shaped by an understanding that freedom, in reality, would accrue to each of them individually only when it was acquired by all of them collectively. Such a worldview contrasted sharply with the "possessive individualism" of liberal democracy.[33] This sense of suffrage as a collective, not an individual, possession was the foundation for much of African American women's political activities in the post–Civil War era.[34] Within these understandings, the boundary lines between men's and women's political behavior were less clearly drawn, and active participation in the political arenas — internal or external — seldom required a retreat into womanhood or manhood as its justification.

Even in the organization of militia units, post-emancipation black Richmonders, at least for a time, rejected the liberal bourgeois ideal of a solely male civic domain. By 1886 black men had organized three militia companies. By the late 1870s black women had also organized a militia company, although apparently only for ceremonial purposes; it reportedly was active only before and during emancipation celebrations. Its members conducted preparatory drills on Broad Street, one of Richmond's main thoroughfares. Frank Anthony, the man who prepared and drilled the women's company, demanded military precision and observance of regular military commands.[35] Unlike the men participating in the militias, who came from working-class, artisan, business, and professional backgrounds, the women were probably working-class. Although they served no self-defense role, their drilling in Richmond streets and marching in parades challenged ideas and assumptions about appropriate public behavior held by both white southerners and white Unionists. The women's unit not only challenged, as did the men's, the idea of black subservience, but also suggested wholly new forms and meanings of respectable female behavior. There is no evidence concerning how long this women's unit survived or the causes of its demise. We can speculate that, besides horrifying whites, such a unit may have also become unacceptable to a number of black Richmonders. Increasingly, concerns about respectable behavior were connected to the public behavior of the working class and of women. This black women's militia, however, suggests the fluidity of gender notions in the early years of emancipation. The brevity of its appearance suggests how questions of public behavior became integral within black Richmond, just as they had been within the larger society. Yet for a time the actions of these women declared that perhaps no area of political participation or public ceremony was strictly a male domain.

Renegotiating Public Life

The 1880 First African women's petition followed three contentious church meetings, some lasting until two or three o'clock in the morning, at which the congregants considered dismissing and/or excluding the pastor, the Reverend James H. Holmes. This discussion was initiated at an April 5 meeting where two women were charged with fighting about the pastor. The April 6 meeting considered charges of "unchristian conduct" on the part of Holmes; those men present voted to exclude Holmes. A meeting on April 11 endorsed a protest signed by all but two of the deacons against the earlier proceedings. The protest charged the anti-Holmes faction with trying to "dispose of the deacons, take charge of prayer meetings, the Sunday school and revolutionize things generally." The discussions that ensued over the next two months split the congregation; the May and June church business meetings were "disorderly" and "boisterous." Holmes and the deacons called in the mayor, city court judge, and chief of police to support the pastor and the police to remove or arrest those members of the congregation designated as "rebellious." After the anti-Holmes faction was removed from the church, the June meeting expelled forty-six men for "rebelliously attempting to overthrow and seize upon the church government." It also excluded the two women initially charged, one for fighting and the other for tattling; exonerated Holmes "from all false" accusations; and thanked the civil officers who attended the meeting and restored order. Only after these actions did the church consider the women's petition, which had been presented in the midst of the controversy more than two months earlier.[36]

First African's records do not adequately reveal the nature of gender relations within the church in the late 1860s and 1870s. We do know that the pre–Civil War sex-segregated seating patterns were abandoned by Richmond black Baptist churches immediately after the Civil War and that by the late 1860s women "not only had a voice, but voted in the business meetings" of Ebenezer Baptist Church.[37] Women who voted in political meetings held in First African in the 1860s and 1870s may have carried this participation over to church business meetings. Often in the immediate post–Civil War period, business and political meetings were not clearly distinguishable.

The petition of the women of First African makes clear, however, that by the early 1880s, while women attended and apparently participated in church meetings, the men had "adopted a law in the church that the business must be done by the male members." Whether Margaret Osborne, Jane Green, and others thought that their voices and interests were being inadequately represented, even ignored by the deacons, or wanted to add their voices to those, including the deacons, who were struggling to retain Holmes and control of First African, these women understood that they would have to defend their own rights. The women argued their right to decide on the pastor, justifying their petition by both their work on behalf of the church and the importance of their economic support to the church's ongoing activities and to the pastor's salary. Not until after the matter of Holmes's exclusion was settled were the petitioners granted their request. Since they apparently remained within First African, the petitioners' organization probably indicates that they were not among those dissatisfied with Holmes. It does suggest, however, their dissatisfaction with church procedure and the place of women in church polity. Still, the petition was conservative, and the women denied any intention to demand full voting rights in church matters. The petition was not taken as a challenge to church authority, as were the actions of the anti-Holmes faction. When brought up for a vote in the June meeting, the women's petition was adopted by a vote of 413 to 16.[38]

The women's petition and the vote in favor of it suggest the tenuous and ambiguous position that women had come to occupy both within First African and within the internal political arena more generally. They participated actively in church meetings, but the authority for that participation and the question of limiting women's role resurfaced throughout the late nineteenth century. In the 1890s the women of First African would again have to demand their rights, this time against challenges to their very presence at church meetings, when a deacon sought to prohibit women from even attending First African business meetings. The women protested and the church responded quickly by requiring the deacon to apologize to the women and assure them that they were welcome at the meetings. The degree of women's participation and decision-making powers, however, remained ambiguous.

In 1901–2, during another crisis period in First African, a number of men sought to blame the problems on women. John Mitchell, Jr., a member of First African and editor of the *Richmond Planet,* cited the active participation of women ("ladies who knew nothing of the machinery at work or the deep laid plans on foot") and children ("Sunday School scholars from 8 years of age upward") in church affairs, suggesting that they did not comprehend the proceedings and had been easily misled or manipulated by male factions. Deacon J. C. Farley cited women's active participation in church meetings as the problem, reminding the congregation that "it was the rule of the church" that women were allowed only to vote on the pastor but had extended their participation far past that. And the new minister, the Reverend W. T. Johnson, admonished the women, saying that "the brethren could almost fight in the church meeting and when they went out they would shake hands and laugh and talk. But the sisters would talk about it going up Broad St. and everybody would know what they had done." First African women rejected these assessments of their church's problems. A significant number walked out rather than have their participation censured; those who remained reportedly refused to be silent but continually "talked out in the meeting." Sister Margaret Hewlett later sought out the editor of the *Richmond Planet* to voice her opposition to the men's denunciation of women's roles and to make clear that the women thought the church's problems lay in the male leadership, saying specifically "the deacons were the cause of all the trouble anyway." [39]

In the early 1890s the *Virginia Baptist* publicized its belief that women, in exceeding their proper places in the church by attempting to preach, and in the community by their "deplorable" efforts to "exercise the right of suffrage," would lose their "womanliness." [40] The complexity of gender relations within the African American community was such that at the same time First African was debating women's attendance at church meetings and the *Virginia Baptist* was advocating a severely restricted women's role, other women such as Alice Kemp were known throughout the community as the authors of prominent male ministers' sermons and women such as the Reverend Mrs. Carter were establishing their reputations as "soul-stirring" preachers. The *Richmond Planet* reported these women's activities without fanfare, as if they were commonplace. The debate over women's roles also had become commonplace. The Reverend Anthony Binga, pastor of First Baptist (Manchester), noted the debate in his sermon on church polity; Binga supported women teaching Sunday school, participating in prayer meetings, and voting "on any subject pertaining to the interest of the church," including the pastor; but he interpreted the Bible as forbidding women "throwing off that modesty that should adorn her sex, and taking man's place in the pulpit." The subject received community-wide attention in June 1895 when Ebenezer Baptist Church staged a debate between the ministers of Second Baptist (Manchester) and Mount Carmel, judged by other ministers from Fourth Baptist, First African, First Baptist (Manchester), and others on the subject "Resolved that a woman has every right and privilege that a man has in the christian church." [41]

The debates within First African and other churches over women's roles were part of a series of political struggles within black Richmond in the late nineteenth and early twentieth centuries. As formal political gains, initially secured, began to recede and economic promise became less certain and less surely tied to political advancement, the political struggles over relationships between the working class and the newly emergent middle class, between men and women, between literate and nonliterate, increasingly became issues among Afro-Richmonders. Briefly examining how the sites of public discourse changed and how discussions regarding qualifications for and the nature of individual participation developed suggests the degree to which debates over space and relationships represented important changes in many black Richmonders' assumptions about freedom itself.

The authority of the church in personal and civil matters decreased over the late nineteenth and early twentieth centuries. The church quietly acknowledged these changes without directly confronting the issue of its changed authority. The use of civil authorities to resolve the church dispute, especially since individual members continued to face censure if they relied on civil rather than church sanctions in a dispute with another member, suggests the degree to which First African tried to maintain its traditional authority over its members while acknowledging the limitations of its powers. First African turned outside not only itself but also the black community by inviting the intervention of the mayor, police chief, and judge.[42] The decreasing authority of the church, however, accompanied a shrinking sphere of influence and activity for the church and the development of secular institutions and structures to take over, compete for, or share functions traditionally connected to the church as institution and structure. The changing church axis suggests important developments in the structures, nature, and understandings of community in black Richmond.

After the Reverend James Holmes and the deacons of First African survived the 1880 challenge to their leadership, one of their first actions was to establish a regulation that church business meetings be closed to all but members. They had argued that it was outside agitators who had instigated and sustained the disorder and opposition. While this reflects concerns about internal church business, the closing off of the church was reflected in other central ways that potentially had more far-reaching consequences, and suggests the particularization of interests, concerns, and functions of internal community institutions, and the changed nature of internal community politics. Having completed, at considerable expense, their new edifice, First African worried about avoiding damage and excess wear and tear. In November 1882 the church adopted regulations designed to eliminate the crowds of people attending weddings in the church by requiring guest lists and tickets, and to deny entirely the use of the main auditorium with the largest capacity for "programmes, closing of public schools, political meetings or feasts." In February 1883, when the Acme Lyceum requested use of the main auditorium for a lecture by Frederick Douglass, the church, following its new regulations, refused to grant the request, although it did offer as substitute the use of its smaller lecture room. That same year it denied the use of the church for the Colored High and Normal closing. The paucity of facilities available to black Richmonders meant that these activities now had to be held in much smaller facilities, and the possibilities for the large mass meetings that First African had previously hosted were now reduced. Political meetings and other activities moved to other, smaller church sites or to some of the new halls being erected by some of the societies and businessmen. The latter, however, were more expensive to obtain since their rental was a major source of revenue for the group or individual owner; it also often particularized the meeting or occasion to a specific segment of the community. Without the large facility of First African, graduations and school closings could no longer be the traditional community-wide mass celebrations. Denied the use of First African and barred from the Richmond Theatre where the white high school students had their graduation, the 1883 Colored High and Normal graduation class held their exercises in a small classroom where very few could attend.[43]

First African did not initiate and was not singly responsible for the changing nature of Republican Party participation, but its actions reinforced the narrower sense of party politics that white Republicans had tried to enforce. Disturbed at black influence over Republican meetings, beginning in 1870 white Republicans took steps to limit popular participation and influence in party deliberations. First they moved the conventions from First African to the U.S. courtroom, a facility that held fewer people and was removed from the black community; then they closed the gallery, thus allowing only official delegates to attend and participate. In such a setting they were able to adopt a more conservative platform. Black Republicans had continued, however, to hold mass meetings, often when dissatisfied with the official Republican deliberations. When they were dissatisfied with Republican nominees for municipal office that came from the 1870 closed party convention, for example, black Republicans agreed to convene their own sessions and make their own nominations.[44]

In increasingly delimiting the church's use, distinguishing more clearly between sacred and secular activities as when it began to disallow certain kinds of entertainments in its facilities or on its behalf, and attempting to reserve the church for what was now designated as the "sacred," First African contributed to the increasing segmentation of black Richmond.[45] With the loss of the largest-capacity structure, some black Richmonders recognized the need to reestablish a community space. Edward A. Randolph, founder and first editor of the *Richmond Planet*, used Acme Literary Association meetings to argue regularly throughout 1883 and 1884 for the construction of a hall, a public meeting place within the community. His call was reinforced when the Choral Association was denied use of the Richmond Theatre and had to have its production in a small mutual benefit society hall, an inadequate facility for such a production. The construction of a large auditorium on the top floor of the Grand Fountain, United Order of True Reformers' bank and office building when it opened in 1890 was an effort to provide that space. It could hold larger gatherings than the other halls and most churches, but still had only a small percentage of the seating capacity of First African.[46] A mass meeting on the scale common in the 1860s and 1870s could be held only outside the community, and the facilities for such were often closed to African Americans.

As political meetings moved to private halls rather than church buildings, they became less mass meetings not only in the numerical sense; they also became more gatherings of an exclusive group of party regulars. This signaled not only a change in the role of the church but also a change in the nature of politics in black Richmond. The emerging format gave business and professional men, especially, greater control over the formal political process. First African's prohibitions against mass meetings, school closings, and other programs did not last long; the need and desire of members and other Afro-Richmonders for a space that could truly contain a community-wide activity eventually led members to ignore their prohibition. But instituting the prohibition had not only significantly affected community activities in the early 1880s; it also meant that, even after strict enforcement was curtailed, decisions about using the church for graduation exercises, political meetings, and other activities were now subjects of debate. Afro-Richmonders could no longer assume the church as a community meeting place; instead they had to argue such. The church remained an important community institution, but it increasingly shared power with both civil authorities and other community institutions such as mutual benefit and fraternal societies.

The efforts by white Republican officials to limit popular decision making and the decreased accessibility of First African as a community-wide meeting place affected a politics that had been based in mass participation. Mass meetings were still held throughout the late nineteenth century, but they were now less regular. These changes were exacerbated by the struggle to retain the vote and officeholding and the necessity, therefore, to counter various tactics of both white Republicans and Democrats. The fraudulent tactics employed in the 1890s to eliminate black voters, for example, led some black Republicans like John Mitchell, who continued to argue against literacy qualifications for voting, to encourage nonliterate black men to abstain from voting. Not only could difficulty with many of the election officials' questions and with the ballots delay the line, but also the nonliterate voter's rights and/or ballot would more likely be challenged. Mitchell thought it important to get those least likely to be challenged or disqualified, and most capable of correctly marking the ballots, through the lines first before polls closed on them. While Mitchell argued for a temporary change in practice — not perspective — regarding the right of all to vote, his and other prominent black Republicans' prioritizing of the literate voter significantly changed the makeup of the presumed electorate.

As the divisions between black and white Republicans became deeper in the 1890s, Mitchell and other black Republicans began to hold small Republican caucuses in selected homes, in essence attempting to control ward conventions by predetermining nominees and issues. The ward conventions themselves were often held in halls rather than the larger churches. The organization in 1898 of a Central Republican League, which would oversee black Republican activities through sub-leagues in all the city's wards, reinforced the narrowing party politics framework. Republican Party decision making was now more clearly limited to party regulars; the mass of black voters and other election activists were expected to support these channels of decision making.[47] These changes, consistent with democratic politics and republican representative government as practiced in the late nineteenth-century United States, served to limit the power and influence of most black Richmonders in the electoral arena. If many black men abandoned electoral politics even before formal disfranchisement, it was in large measure due to the effectiveness of the extralegal disfranchisement efforts of white men. The exclusion from real decision-making power within the Republican Party and, in this respect, within the community, was also decisive.

The increasingly limited notion of political decision makers that these changes encouraged is also evident in other ways. In 1896 during a factional dispute among black Republicans, John Mitchell challenged the decisions made in one meeting by noting that a substantial portion of those attending and participating were not even "legal voters," that is, they were women. Although he espoused feminine dress and comportment, Mitchell supported women's rights and championed Dr. Sarah G. Jones's success as a physician as evidence of women's equality. He also endorsed women's suffrage while advising black women to understand the racism of the white women's suffrage movement and not to align themselves with it. Despite these personal convictions, Mitchell could dismiss or minimize opposing factions by a reference to the participation of women, suggesting the ways the meanings and understandings of politics, of appropriate political actors, and even of the ownership of the franchise had changed in the late nineteenth century.[48]

Questions of qualifications for participation in the external political arena and internal community institutions were now frequent. During the conflictual 1901 business meeting at First African, for example, John Mitchell, Jr., questioned his opponents' right to participate even though they were all church members by pointing out their unfamiliarity with parliamentary procedure or their inelegant ways of speaking. The women, who were the targets of much of Mitchell's challenge, refused to accept these as criteria for their participation and even denigrated what he put forth as his formal qualifications by talking out when he got up to speak, saying derisively, "Don't he look pretty."[49] Questions of formal education had already affected the congregation in fundamental ways, most obviously in the late nineteenth-century debate over song, a debate that represented a significant change in the basis of collective consciousness.

The antiphonal nature of the traditional church service at First African and many black churches reinforced a sense of community. The services included spontaneous verbal and nonverbal interaction between minister and prayer, speaker and congregation, thus allowing for the active participation of everyone in the worship service. It was this cultural discourse that was carried over into the political meetings. One important element that bound the congregation together was song; as Lawrence Levine has noted, through their collective song churchgoers "meld[ed] individual consciousness into the group consciousness."[50] However, the practice of lining hymns, which was basic to collective song, was one that white visitors often referred to when they described what they perceived as the unrefined black church services. Some black churchgoers saw the elimination of this practice as part of the work of uplifting the religious style and uplifting the race. But with the elimination of this practice, those unable to read and follow the lyrics in a songbook were now unable to participate, to be fully a part of the community, the collective. It was the equivalent of being deprived of a voice, all the more significant in an oral culture. Daniel Webster Davis, a member of First African and pastor of Second Baptist

(Manchester) as well as a public school teacher, suggested such in his poem, "De Linin' Ub De Hymns":

> Dar's a mighty row in Zion, an' de debbil's gittin' high,
> . . . .
> 'Twuz 'bout a berry leetle thing — de linin' ub a hymn.
> De young folks say 'tain't stylish to lin' um out no mo';
> Dat dey's got edikashun, an' dey wants us all to know
> Dey likes to hab dar singin'-books a-holin' fore dar eyes,
> An' sing de hymns right straight along 'to manshuns in de skies.'
> . . . .
> An' ef de ol' folks will kumplain 'cause dey is ol' an' blin',
> An 'slabry's chain don' kep' dem back frum larnin' how to read —
> Dat dey mus' take a corner seat, an' let de young folks lead.
> . . . .
> We don' edikate our boys an' gals, an' would do de same again;
> . . . .
> De sarmon's highfalutin', an' de church am mighty fin';
> . . . .
> De ol'-time groans an' shouts an' moans am passin' out ub sight —
> Edikashun changed all dat, an' we belebe it right,
> We should serb God wid 'telligence; fur dis one thing I plead:
> Jes' lebe a leetle place in church fur dem ez kin not read.[51]

The debates about women's roles in the church and in the more formal political arenas, like the debate over lining the hymns, were part of widespread discussions about the nature of community, of participation, and of freedom.

The proliferation of scholarly works centered on the flowering of black women's political activity in the late nineteenth and early twentieth centuries[52] has perhaps left the impression that this was the inaugural moment or even height of black women's participation in politics. Overt or not, the suggestion seems to be that black women came to political prominence as (because) black men lost political power.[53] In much of this scholarship the reasons for black women's "emergence" are usually tied to external factors. For example, the development of black women's clubs in the late nineteenth century and their important roles in the political struggles of the twentieth century most often have been seen by historians as the result of the increasing development of such entities in the larger society and as reaction to vitriolic attacks on the morality of black women. Such a perspective explains this important political force solely in terms of external dynamics, but external factors alone cannot account for this development.[54] The internal political arena, which in the immediate post–Civil War era was grounded in the notion of a collective voice that gave men, women, and children a platform and allowed them all participation, came increasingly in the late nineteenth century to be shaped by a narrowing notion of politics and appropriate political behavior.

While mass meetings continued to be held, the more regular forums for political discussions were literary societies, ward meetings, mutual benefit society and fraternal society meetings, women's clubs, labor organizations, newspapers, streetcorners, kitchens, washtubs, and saloons. In the development of literary societies as a primary venue for public discussion, one can see the class and gender assumptions that by the turn of the century came to be central to the political organization of black Richmond. While some, like the Langston Literary Association, had male members only, most of the literary societies founded in the 1880s and 1890s had middle-class and working-class men and women members. Despite the inclusive nature of the membership and often of the officers, the form of discussion that developed privileged middle-class males. Unlike mass meetings where many people might take the floor in planned and unplanned expositions and attendees might freely interrupt or talk back to speakers, thus allowing and building mass participation, literary forums announced discussion topics in advance; charged individual members, apparently almost always male, to prepare a paper on the subject; and designated specific, also male, members to reply.

The discussions that then ensued were open to all present, but the structure privileged those familiar with the conventions of formal debate. Women, who served as officers and attended in large numbers, may have joined in the discussion but their official roles were designated as the cultural arm of the forum — reading poetry, singing songs, often with political content appropriate to the occasion. The questions under consideration at the meetings often betrayed the class bias of the forum. Even when the discussions centered on some aspect of working-class life and behavior, the conversation was conducted by middle-class men. The purpose of the forums, as articulated by the Acme Literary Society, suggested the passive observer/learner position that most were expected to take: to hold "discussions, lectures, and to consider questions of vital importance to our people, so that the masses of them may be drawn out to be entertained, enlightened, and instructed thereby."[55] Given the exclusionary nature of the discussion in these literary forums, it is understandable that far more working-class black men and women saw the Knights of Labor as their principal political vehicle in the late 1880s.[56]

In the late nineteenth century, working-class men and women and middle-class women were increasingly disenfranchised in the black community, just as middle-class black men were increasingly disenfranchised in the larger society. Men and women, working-class and middle-class, at the turn of the century were struggling to move back to a political authority they once had — internally and externally. As they did so they each often justified such authority along distinctively gendered and class-based lines.

African American men countered the image of themselves as uncivilized, beastly rapists — an image white southerners used to justify disfranchisement, segregation, and violence — with efforts to demonstrate their own manhood and to define white males as uncivilized and savage.[57] While white Richmonders told stories of black barbarity, John Mitchell, Jr., inverted the tale. The *Richmond Planet*, for example, repeatedly focused on the sexual perversions of white men with cases of rape and incest and spoke of white men in terms designed to suggest their barbarism: "Southern white folks have gone to roasting Negroes, we presume the next step will be to eat them."[58] In the process of unmanning white males, however, Mitchell and others developed a narrative of endangered black women. Urban areas, once sites of opportunity for women, became sexually dangerous places for the unprotected female, easy prey to deceitful and barbarous white males.[59] Black men's political rights were essential so that they could do as men should — protect their communities, homes, families, women. The focus on manhood could, initially, be the venue for discussing domestic violence as well. For example, the Reverend Anthony Binga, sermonizing against physical abuse of one's wife, drew on the discourse of manhood: "I have never seen a man whip his wife. I mean a *man*. Everyone who wears a hat or a coat is not a *man*. I mean a *man*." And the members of First African took as a serious issue of concern the case of a husband who had infected his wife with syphilis.[60] Concurrent with the narrative of sexual danger in the city and the larger society was an implied corollary narrative of protection within one's own community. Thus the discourse on manhood could keep the concern with violence against women in the public discussion while at the same time setting the stage for issues of domestic abuse and other forms of intraracial violence, which could be evidence of the uncivility of black men, to be silenced as politically dangerous.

In drawing on the new narrative of endangered women, middle-class black women, increasingly disfranchised by the connections between manhood and citizenship in the new political discourse, turned the focus from themselves and on to the working class, enabling middle-class women to project themselves as the protectors of their less fortunate sisters. In this manner they reinserted themselves into a public political role.[61] Autonomous women's organizations, such as the Richmond Women's League (later the Richmond Mothers' Club) or women's divisions within other organizations such as the Standing Committee on Domestic Economy of the Hampton Negro Conference, developed to serve these functions. These associations promulgated class-specific ideas of respectability, in part justifying their public role through the need to impart such protective measures to working-class women. Specific constructions of womanhood, like those of manhood, thus became central to the arguments for political rights. Through discussions of manhood and womanhood, middle-class men and women constructed themselves as respectable and entitled, and sought to use such constructions to throw a mantle of protection over their working-class brothers and sisters. By increasingly claiming sexual violence as a women's issue, middle-class black women claimed a political/public space for themselves, but they also contributed to an emerging tendency to divert issues of sexual violence to a lesser plane and to see them as the specific interest of women, not bound up in the general concerns and struggle for freedom. This set the stage for the masculine conception of liberation struggle that would emerge in the twentieth century.[62]

Collective History/Collective Memory

In July 1895 three black women — Mary Abernathy, Pokey Barnes, and her mother, Mary Barnes — were convicted in Lunenberg County, Virginia, of murdering a white woman. When the women were moved to the state penitentiary in Richmond their case became a cause célèbre in the black community there. For over a year black men and women in Richmond struggled to keep the Lunenberg women from being hanged or returned to Lunenberg County for a retrial, fearing that a return to Lunenberg would mean death, the women lynched at the hands of an angry white mob. The community succeeded, and the three women were eventually released.

The organization of black Richmonders in defense of these women partly illustrates the increasingly gendered nature of internal community politics. Men and women were portrayed as having decidedly different roles in the defense; one avenue of defense was to draw on ideas of motherhood in defending these three women; and the Lunenberg women's release called forth very particular discussions of respectability and womanhood. John Mitchell, Jr., portrayed himself as the militant defender of the women. Women, led by schoolteacher Rosa Dixon Bowser, organized the Richmond Women's League for the purposes of raising funds for the women's defense, visiting them in jail and supporting their husbands and families. Through her column in the *Woman's Era* and her participation in the National Federation of Afro-American Women, Bowser, as did Mitchell, brought the case to national attention. The front-page stories in Mitchell's *Planet* emphasized the Lunenberg women as mothers, especially reporting on Mary Abernathy's pregnancy and the birth of her child in her jail cell. While the pictures and stories during the fourteen-month struggle for their release portrayed the women as simply clad, barefoot farm women, the announcement of Pokey Barnes's final victory was accompanied by a photograph of her now transformed into a true Victorian woman with elegant balloon-sleeved dress, a symbol of respectable womanhood. Later descriptions of Barnes, on speaking engagements, emphasized her dress: "a neat fitting, changeable silk gown and . . . a black felt hat, trimmed with black velvet and ostrich plumes." Mitchell emphasized the importance of this transformation: "The picture showing what Pokey Barnes looked like when brought to Richmond the first time and what she appears to-day will be a startling revelation to the public and will fill with amazement the conservative people everywhere when they realize what a terrible blunder the execution of this young woman would have been." He thus suggested that it was her ability to be a respectable woman (signified superficially by a class-based standard of dress) that was the justification for his and others' protection of her.[63]

But the yearlong discussion of these women's fates (the front page of nearly every issue of the *Richmond Planet* from July 1895 through the early fall of 1896 was devoted to these cases and included pictures of the women and sketches of their cabins) occurred alongside stories about lynchings or near lynchings of black men. Importantly, therefore, when black Richmonders spoke of lynching in the late nineteenth century, they had no reason to assume the victim to be male. When a freed Pokey Barnes rode as "mascot" in the 1896 Jackson Ward election rally parade, the idea of Mitchell and other black men as defenders was reinforced. But also affirmed was the underlying understanding that violence, including state repression, was a real threat to African American women as much as men. This meant that the reconstruction of clearly delineated notions of womanhood and manhood as the basis for political activism remained relatively ambiguous in late nineteenth-century black Richmond. But issues of class and gender were increasingly evident, as when Pokey Barnes and Mitchell accepted public speaking engagements — ones in which she was clearly expected to be the silent symbol of oppression and he the vocal proponent of resistance. Barnes, countering that assumption, set forth her own understandings of her role and qualifications, contradicting the class and gender assumptions of Mitchell and of those who invited them: "she said that she was not an educated lecturer and did not have any D.D.'s or M.D.'s to her name, but she was simply Pokey Barnes, c.s. (common sense)." Her two-hour lecture on her ordeal, while giving credit to Mitchell, established herself as not only victim but also heroine.[64]

The rescue of the Lunenberg women by black Richmonders brought women's struggles to the fore of black rights and reaffirmed violence against women as part of their collective history and struggle. At the same time, black Richmonders struggled to create a new category of womanhood that would be respected and protected, and of middle-class womanhood and manhood that could protect.[65] The plight of the Lunenberg women reaffirmed the collective history of black men and women at the same time as it invigorated increasingly distinct political vehicles for middle-class black men and women.

Just as disfranchisement, segregation, lynching, and other violence denied the privileges of masculinity to African American men, segregation, lynching, sexual violence, and accusations of immorality denied the protections of womanhood to African American women. Increasingly black women relied on constructing not only a respectable womanhood but, in large measure, an invisible womanhood. Hoping that a desexualized persona might provide the protection to themselves and their communities that seemed otherwise unobtainable, many black women carefully covered up all public suggestions of sexuality, even of sexual abuse. In the process issues specific to black women were increasingly eliminated from public discussion and collective memory.[66] In the late twentieth century, therefore, many African Americans have come to link a history of repression and racial violence exclusively to challenges to black masculinity and thus to establish a notion of freedom and black liberation that bifurcates public discussion and privileges men's history and experiences. In 1991, when Supreme Court justice nominee Clarence Thomas challenged his questioners by calling the Senate Judiciary Committee hearings a "high-tech lynching," black Americans were divided in their response. Some men and women supported his analysis; others opposed either Thomas's analogy or his right to, in using such, assume the mantle of black manhood that he had so often rejected. Few people, however, questioned the assumption basic to Thomas's analogy that lynching and other forms of violence had historically been a masculine experience. Similarly, when black people across the country responded to the video of Los Angeles policemen's brutal beating of Rodney King, a narrative of state repression against black men followed.[67] The masculine focus is most evident in the widespread public discussion of "endangered" black men. While appropriately focusing attention on the physical, economic, and social violence that surrounds and engulfs many black men in the late twentieth-century United States, much of this discussion trivializes or ignores the violence of many black women's lives — as victims of rape and other forms of sexual abuse, murder, drugs and alcohol, poverty, and the devastation of AIDS. Seldom are discussions of rape and domestic violence included in summits on black-on-black crime. The masculinization of race progress that this implies often has some black leaders, looking to ways to improve the lot of men, not only omitting women from the picture but often even accepting the violence against women. What else can explain how Mike Tyson, even before he was charged with the rape of an eighteen-year-old black woman, would have been projected by ministers of the National Baptist Convention as a role model for young black men? By what standards would a man who had already publically acknowledged that he enjoyed brutalizing women have been put forward as a role model — unless rescuing black men from poverty and inner-city death at any price, including violence against women, was the standard by which the good of the race was being defined?

Such is the long-term consequence of political strategies developed in the late nineteenth century to empower black men and black women. Understandable and necessary in their day, they served to maintain a democratic agenda even as black political life became more divided. Eventually, however, the experiences of men were remembered as central to African Americans' struggles, but the experiences of women, including the physical violence — lynchings, rapes, sexual and other forms of physical abuse as employees in white homes, domestic abuse — as well as the economic and social violence that has so permeated the history of black women in the United States, were not as vividly and importantly retained in our memory. We give life and validity to our constructions of race, community, and politics by giving those constructions a history. Those who construct masculine notions of blackness and race progress and who claim only some forms of violence as central to African American liberation struggles are claiming/remembering a particular history. African American collective memory in the late twentieth century often appears partial, distorted, and dismembered. The definitions and issues of political struggle that can come from that partial memory are limited. Before we can construct truly participatory discussions around a fully democratic agenda where the history and struggles of women and men are raised as issues of general interest necessary to the liberation of all, we have some powerful lot of reremembering to do.[68]

NOTES

1. Petition of Mrs. Margaret Osborne et al. to the deacons and members of the First Baptist Church, April 15, 1880, recorded in First African Baptist Church, Richmond City, Minutes, Book 2, June 27, 1880 (microfilm), Archives, Virginia State Library and Archives, Richmond, Virginia (hereafter cited as FABC).

2. The idea of the immediate adoption of a gendered public-private dichotomy pervades much of the historical literature on post–Civil War black communities. It is most directly argued by Jacqueline Jones: "the vitality of the political process, tainted though it was by virulent racial prejudice and violence, provided black men with a public forum distinct from the private sphere inhabited by their womenfolk. Black men predominated in this arena because, like other groups in nineteenth-century America, they believed that males alone were responsible for — and capable of — the serious business of politicking." *Labor of Love, Labor of Sorrow: Black Women, Work, and the Family from Slavery to the Present* (New York:

Basic Books, 1985), 66. But it is also an accepted tenet of otherwise rigorous analyses such as Eric Foner, *Reconstruction: America's Unfinished Revolution, 1863–1877* (New York: Harper and Row, 1988), esp. 87.

3. Many recent discussions of the public sphere among U.S. scholars have orbited around the work of Jürgen Habermas, whose 1962 *Strukturwandel der Öffentlichkeit* was published in 1989 in English as *The Structural Transformation of the Public Sphere: An Inquiry into a Category of Bourgeois Society*, trans. Thomas Burger with assistance of Frederick Lawrence (Cambridge: MIT Press). See also Jürgen Habermas, "The Public Sphere: An Encyclopedia Article (1964)," *New German Critique* 1 (fall 1974): 49–55. Critics who have emphasized the masculine bias in the liberal bourgeois public sphere and posited a female counterpublic include Nancy Fraser, "Rethinking the Public Sphere: A Contribution to the Critique of Actually Existing Democracy" and Mary Ryan, "Gender and Public Access: Women's Politics in Nineteenth-Century America," both in *Habermas and the Public Sphere*, ed. Craig Calhoun (Cambridge: MIT Press, 1992), 109–42 and 259–89, respectively. See also Nancy Fraser, "What's Critical about Critical Theory? The Case of Habermas and Gender," in *Unruly Practices: Power, Discourse, and Gender in Contemporary Social Theory* (Minneapolis: University of Minnesota Press, 1989); Mary Ryan, *Women in Public: Between Banners and Ballots, 1825–1880* (Baltimore: Johns Hopkins University Press, 1990); Joan B. Landes, *Women and the Public Sphere in the Age of the French Revolution* (Ithaca: Cornell University Press, 1988); Rita Felski, *Beyond Feminist Aesthetics: Feminist Literature and Social Change* (Cambridge: Harvard University Press, 1989), 154–82. Focusing on contemporary politics, Iris Marion Young offers a critique of an ideal public sphere in which the universal citizen is not only masculine but also white and bourgeois. *Justice and the Politics of Difference* (Princeton: Princeton University Press, 1990).

4. For a study that conceptualizes the history of the black church in relation to Habermas's theory of the public sphere, see Evelyn Brooks Higginbotham, *Righteous Discontent: The Women's Movement in the Black Baptist Church, 1880–1920* (Cambridge: Harvard University Press, 1993), esp. 7–13. Higginbotham describes "the black church not as the embodiment of ministerial authority or of any individual's private interests and pronouncements, but as a social space for discussion of public concerns" (10).

5. Similar negotiations and pronouncements occurred in other post-emancipation societies. For a discussion of the ways British colonial officers sought to impose ideas of a liberal democratic moral and political order, with its attendant gender relations, on former slaves in the West Indies and then pronounced these ex-slaves incapable of responsible citizenship when they failed to wholly adopt such, see Thomas C. Holt, " 'The Essence of the Contract': The Articulation of Race, Gender, and Political Economy in British Emancipation Policy, 1838–1866" (paper presented at "The Black Public Sphere in the Reagan-Bush Era Conference," Chicago Humanities Institute, University of Chicago, October 1993), cited with permission of Holt.

6. The question of ownership was one of the first issues Afro-Richmonders addressed, as antebellum law had required the titles to be in the names of white male supervising committees although the black congregants had themselves bought and paid for the buildings. Through a series of struggles, black churchgoers had by the end of 1866 obtained titles to all of their church buildings. See *New York Tribune*, June 17, 1865; Peter Randolph, *From Slave Cabin to Pulpit* (Boston: Earle, 1893), 94–95; John Thomas O'Brien, Jr., "From Bondage to Citizenship: The Richmond Black Community, 1865–1867" (Ph.D. diss., University of Rochester, 1974), 273–75.

7. Statement of Jenny Scott, wife of Ned Scott, colored, June 8, 1865; Statement of

Richard Adams, colored, June 8, 1865; Statement of Nelson E. Hamilton, June 9, 1865; Statement of Lewis Harris, June 9, 1865; Statement of Wm. Ferguson, June 9, 1865; Statement of Albert Brooks, colored, June 10, 1865; Statement of Thomas Lucas, colored, June 12, 1865; Statement of Washington Hutchinson, Summer 1865; Statement of Edward Davenport, n.d.; Statement of Bernard H. Roberts, n.d.; Statement of Albert Williams, n.d.; Statement of Thos. J. Wayer, n.d.; Statement of Harry R. Jones, n.d.; Statement of Wellington Booker, n.d.; Statement of Stephen Jones, n.d.; Statement of John Oliver of Mass., n.d.; Wm. M. Davis to Col. O. Brown, June 9, 1865, all in Records of the Assistant Commissioner for the State of Virginia, Bureau of Refugees, Freedmen and Abandoned Lands, 1865–1869, Record Group 105, M1048, reel 59, National Archives, Washington, D.C.; *New York Tribune*, June 12, 17, August 1, 8, 1865; *Richmond Times*, July 26, 1865; S.E.C. (Sarah Chase) to Mrs. May, May 25, 1865, in *Dear Ones at Home: Letters from Contraband Camps*, ed. Henry L. Swint (Nashville: Vanderbilt University Press, 1966), 159–60; Julia A. Wilbur in *The Pennsylvania Freedman's Bulletin* 1 (August 1865): 52, quoted in John T. O'Brien, "Reconstruction in Richmond: White Restoration and Black Protest, April–June 1865," *Virginia Magazine of History and Biography* 89, 3 (July 1981): 273, 275.

8. *New York Tribune*, August, 1, 8, 1865. One of the most neglected areas of Reconstruction history and African American history in general is that of violence against women. This has led to the still prevalent assumption that black women were less likely to be victims of racial violence and the generalization that this reflects the fact that black women were less threatening than black men. Historian W. Fitzhugh Brundage, for example, concludes that black women had "greater leeway" to "voice their opinions and anger without suffering extralegal violence themselves." *Lynching in the New South: Georgia and Virginia, 1880–1930* (Urbana: University of Illinois Press, 1993), 80–81, 322–23n. This reflects both the emphasis on lynching as the major form of racial violence and the limited historical attention to the black women who were lynched (at least fifteen between 1889 and 1898; at least seventy-six between 1882 and 1927). Even those ostensibly attuned to issues of gender and sexuality still assume that "the greatest violence was reserved for black men"; see, for example, Martha Hodes, "The Sexualization of Reconstruction Politics: White Women and Black Men in the South after the Civil War," *Journal of the History of Sexuality* 3 (January 1993): 404. Yet the evidence from Richmond and elsewhere suggests that the extent of violence against black women is greater than previously recognized, even greater than reported at the time. One North Carolina man, Essic Harris, giving testimony to the Senate committee investigating Ku Klux Klan terror, reported that the rape of black women was so frequent as to be "an old saying by now." Essic Harris testimony, July 1, 1871, in U.S. Congress, *Testimony Taken by the Joint Select Committee to Inquire into the Condition of Affairs in the Late Insurrectionary States*, vol.: *North Carolina* (Washington, DC: GPO, 1872), 100. Only recently have historians begun to uncover and analyze sexual violence against black women as an integral part of Reconstruction history. See, for example, the dissertation-in-progress by Hannah Rosen, University of Chicago, which examines the rapes connected with the 1866 Memphis race riot. See also Catherine Clinton, "Reconstructing Freedwomen," in *Divided Houses: Gender and the Civil War*, ed. Catherine Clinton and Nina Silber (New York: Oxford University Press, 1992), chap. 17.

9. *New York Tribune*, June 12, 17, 1865.

10. The *Richmond Times* (May 24, 1865), in refusing to publish black Richmonders' statements of protest, reasoned that they were mistaken in believing that they were all oppressed by the military and civilian officials; only the "idle negroes" were targets of military restrictions and inspections. Throughout the early months of emancipation both white

southerners and white Unionists defined freedpeople's mobility in search of family or better jobs and in expression of their newfound freedom as evidence of an unwillingness to work. Similarly, those who chose to vend goods on city streets rather than signing work contracts with white employers were seen as lazy or idle. See O'Brien, "From Bondage to Citizenship," 117–31; see also various communications among the military command reprinted in U.S. War Department, *The War of the Rebellion: A Compilation of the Official Records of the Union and Confederate Armies*, series 1, vol. 45, pt. 3, *Correspondence, Etc.* (Washington, DC: GPO, 1894), 835, 932–33, 1005–6, 1091, 1094–95, 1107–8, 1131–32.

11. *New York Tribune*, June 17, 1865.

12. Black Richmonders were countering the very different image of their community put forth not only by white southerners but also by Union officers. Major-General H. W. Halleck, for example, emphasized the goodwill between Rebel and Union soldiers, both "brave and honest men, although differing in opinion and action"; justified the military restrictions on African Americans; and reported a lack of marriage relationships among African Americans "and the consequent irresponsibility of the parents for the care and support of their offspring." He argued that "colored females," especially, needed legal restrictions, supervision, and suitable punishments, because "being released from the restraints imposed by their former masters and mistresses, . . . naturally fall into dissolute habits." H. W. Halleck, Major-General, Commanding, Headquarters Military Division of the James, Richmond, Va. to Hon. E. M. Stanton, Secretary of War, June 26, 1865, in U.S. War Department, *The War of the Rebellion*, 1295–97. Halleck was one of the Union officers who was reassigned to a different command as a result of the June protest.

13. O'Brien details these meetings in "From Bondage to Citizenship," chaps. 6–9.

14. O'Brien, "From Bondage to Citizenship," 326.

15. See, for example, *Richmond Enquirer*, February 23, 1866; *Richmond Dispatch*, July 6, 1866; *Richmond Times*, July 6, 1866.

16. Foner, *Reconstruction*, 122.

17. *Richmond Dispatch*, April 19, 1867; *New York Times*, April 19, 1867.

18. Julie Saville, "A Measure of Freedom: From Slave to Wage Laborer in South Carolina, 1860–1868" (Ph.D. diss., Yale University, 1986), 273.

19. *Richmond Whig*, April 1, 1867.

20. *Richmond Dispatch*, October 5, 1867.

21. Aldon Morris makes a similar argument regarding the church and the modern civil rights movement, emphasizing the ways the church served as a physical, financial, and cultural resource, with its sermons, songs, testimonies, and prayers becoming political resources in the mobilization of participants and in the construction and communication of political ideology. *The Origins of the Civil Rights Movement: Black Communities Organizing for Change* (New York: Free Press, 1984). See also Robin D. G. Kelley, " 'Comrades, Praise Gawd for Lenin and Them!': Ideology and Culture among Black Communists in Alabama, 1930–1935," *Science and Society* 52, 1 (spring 1988): 59–82; Brenda McCallum, "Songs of Work and Songs of Worship: Sanctifying Black Unionism in the Southern City of Steel," *New York Folklore* 14, 1–2 (1988): 9–33. For an argument that eliminating emotions and aesthetics from acceptable forms of public discourse becomes a means to eliminate particular groups of people from active participation in public life, see Irish Marion Young, "Impartiality and the Civic Public: Some Implications of Feminist Critiques of Moral and Political Theory," in *Feminism as Critique: On the Politics of Gender*, ed. Seyla Benhabib and Drucilla Cornell (Minneapolis: University of Minnesota, 1987), 56–76.

22. The following discussion of collective enfranchisement as the basis for black women's

political activism in the post–Civil War era is drawn from Elsa Barkley Brown, "To Catch the Vision of Freedom: Reconstructing Southern Black Women's Political History, 1865–1880," in *To Be a Citizen*, ed. Arlene Avakian, Joyce Berkman, John Bracey, Bettye Collier-Thomas, and Ann Gordon (Amherst: University of Massachusetts Press, forthcoming).

23. *Richmond Dispatch*, August 1, 2, September 30, October 9, 1867; *New York Times*, August 1, 2, 6, October 18, 1867. My discussion of these events follows closely Peter J. Rachleff, *Black Labor in the South: Richmond, Virginia, 1865–1890* (Philadelphia: Temple University Press, 1984), 45–46. See also Richard L. Morton, *The Negro in Virginia Politics, 1865–1902*, Publications of the University of Virginia Phelps-Stokes Fellowship Papers, (Charlottesville: University of Virginia Press, 1919), 40–43. Similar reports issued from other areas throughout the South, causing one chronicler to report that "the Southern ballot-box" was as much "the vexation of housekeepers" as it was of farmers, businessmen, statesmen, or others: "Elections were preceded by political meetings, often incendiary in character, which all one's servants must attend." Election day itself could also be a problem. As one Tennessean reported in 1867, "Negro women went [to the polls], too; my wife was her own cook and chambermaid." Myrta Lockett Avary, *Dixie after the War: An Exposition of Social Conditions Existing in the South, During the Twelve Years Succeeding the Fall of Richmond* (New York: Doubleday, Page and Co., 1906; reprint, New York: Negro Universities Press, 1969), 282–84. See also Susan Bradford Eppes for similar occurrences in Florida, *Through Some Eventful Years* (1926; reprint, Gainesville: University of Florida Press, 1968).

24. *Richmond Dispatch*, August 1, 2, 1867; *New York Times*, August 2, 6, 1867; see also Rachleff, *Black Labor in the South*, 45; Morton, *Negro in Virginia Politics*, 40–43.

25. The October 1867 city Republican ward meetings and nominating convention adopted the practice common in the black community's mass meetings: a voice or standing vote that enfranchised men, women, and children. See, for example, the October 8 Second Ward meeting for delegate selection: "All who favored Mr. Washburne were first requested to rise, and forty were found on the floor, including women." *Richmond Dispatch*, September 20, October 9, 1867; January 2, 4, 14, 23, 24, February 15, 25, April 3, 8, 25, 1868; *New York Times*, August 6, October 15, 18, 1867; January 11, 1868; Rachleff, *Black Labor in the South*, 45–49; Avary, *Dixie after the War*, 229–31, 254.

The issue of children's participation is an interesting one, suggestive of the means by which personal experience rather than societal norms shaped ex-slaves' vision of politics. A similarly telling example was in the initial proposal of the African National Congress that the new South African constitution set the voting age at fourteen, a testament to those young people, as those in Soweto, who experienced the ravages of apartheid and whose fight against it helped bring about the political negotiations to secure African political rights and self-determination.

26. Compare black women's active participation in Richmond's formal politics — internal and external — in the first decades after the Civil War to Michael McGerr's assessment that nineteenth-century "women were allowed into the male political realm only to play typical feminine roles — to cook, sew, and cheer for men and to symbolize virtue and beauty. Men denied women the central experiences of the popular style: not only the ballot but also the experience of mass mobilization." McGerr's analysis fails to acknowledge the racial basis of his study, that is, it is an assessment of white women's political participation. Michael McGerr, "Political Style and Women's Power, 1830–1930," *Journal of American History* 77 (December 1990): 864–85, esp. 867. My analysis also differs substantially from Mary P. Ryan, *Women in Public*. Ryan gives only cursory attention to African Americans but finds black women's political expression in the Civil War and Reconstruction eras restricted "with

particular severity" and "buried beneath the surface of the public sphere" (146–47, 156, *passim*).

27. For women's participation in political parades in Louisville, Kentucky, Mobile, Alabama, and Charleston, South Carolina, see Herbert G. Gutman, *The Black Family in Slavery and Freedom* (NY: Pantheon 1976), 380; *Liberator*, July 21, 1865 and *New York Daily Tribune*, April 4, 1865, both reprinted in *The Trouble They Seen: Black People Tell the Story of Reconstruction*, ed. Dorothy Sterling (Garden City, NY: Doubleday, 1976), 2–4. In other areas of Virginia besides Richmond and in South Carolina and Louisiana, men and women participated in the political meetings. See, for example, Vincent Harding, *There Is a River: The Black Struggle for Freedom in America* (New York: Harcourt Brace Jovanovich, 1981), 294–97; Rupert Sargent Holland, ed., *Letters and Diary of Laura M. Towne Written from the Sea Islands of South Carolina, 1862–1884* (Cambridge: Riverside Press, 1912; reprint, New York: Negro Universities Press, 1969), 183; testimony of John H. Burch given before a Senate committee appointed to investigate the exodus of black men and women from Louisiana, Senate Report 693, 46th Cong., 2d sess., pt. 2, 232–33, reprinted in *A Documentary History of the Negro People in the United States*, 2 vols., ed. Herbert Aptheker (New York: Citadel Press, 1951), 2: 721–22; Thomas Holt, *Black over White: Negro Political Leadership in South Carolina during Reconstruction* (Urbana: University of Illinois Press, 1977), 34–35. Graphic artists recognized the participation of women as a regular feature of parades, mass meetings, and conventions, as evidenced by their illustrations. See "The Celebration of Emancipation Day in Charleston" from *Leslie's Illustrated Newspaper*, reprinted in Francis Butler Simkins and Robert Hilliard Woody, *South Carolina during Reconstruction* (Chapel Hill: University of North Carolina Press, 1932; reprint, Gloucester, MA: Peter Smith, 1966), facing 364; "Electioneering at the South," *Harper's Weekly*, July 25, 1868, reprinted in Foner, *Reconstruction*, vol. 386; "Colored People's Convention in Session," reprinted in Sterling, *The Trouble They Seen*, 65.

28. *New York Times*, January 11, 22, 1868; *The Debates and Proceedings of the Constitutional Convention of the State of Virginia, Assembled at the City of Richmond* (Richmond, 1868), 505–7, 524–27.

29. *Richmond Dispatch*, June 18, 1867; Rachleff, *Black Labor in the South*, 48.

30. Rachleff, *Black Labor in the South*, 31–32; *Richmond Daily Dispatch*, May 10, 1867; *New Nation*, November 22, 29, December 6, 1866; Holt, *Black over White*, 35; Avary, *Dixie after the War*.

31. Barkley Brown, "To Catch the Vision of Freedom"; *Richmond Enquirer*, October 22, 1867; *Richmond Whig*, October 19, 1867; Robert E. Martin, "Negro Disfranchisement in Virginia," *Howard University Studies in the Social Sciences* 1 (1938): 65–79; *Richmond Afro-American*, December 2, 1962; Mrs. Violet Keeling's testimony before Senate investigating committee, February 18, 1884, Senate Report No. 579, 48th Cong., 1st sess., reprinted in Aptheker, *Documentary History*, 2: 739–41.

32. Barkley Brown, "To Catch the Vision of Freedom"; Howard N. Rabinowitz, *Race Relations in the Urban South, 1865–1880* (New York: Oxford University Press, 1978), 222; Alrutheus Ambush Taylor, *The Negro in the Reconstruction of Virginia* (Washington, DC: Association for the Study of Negro Life and History, 1926), 181, 269; Michael B. Chesson, "Richmond's Black Councilmen, 1871–96," in *Southern Black Leaders of the Reconstruction Era*, ed. Howard N. Rabinowitz (Urbana: University of Illinois Press, 1982), 219n; Peter J. Rachleff, "Black, White and Gray: Working-Class Activism in Richmond, Virginia, 1865–1890" (Ph.D. diss., University of Pittsburgh, 1981), 473, 488n; *Richmond Dispatch*, October 25, 26, 1872; September 14, 1874; Avary, *Dixie after the War*, 285–86, 347; Thomas J. Evans,

Alexander Sands, N. A. Sturdivant, et al., Richmond, to Major-General Schofield, October 31, 1867, reprinted in *Documents of the Constitutional Convention of the State of Virginia* (Richmond: Office of the *New Nation*, 1867), 22–23; John H. Gilmer to Gen. Schofield, reprinted in *New York Times*, October 30, 1867; *New York Times*, November 3, 1867; Wendell P. Dabney, "Rough Autobiographical Sketch of His Boyhood Years" (typescript, n.d.), 98–99, microfilm copy in Wendell P. Dabney Papers, Cincinnati Historical Society, Cincinnati, Ohio; Proceedings before Military Commissioner, City of Richmond, October 26, 1867, in the case of Winston Jackson filed as G-423 1867 Letters Received, ser. 5068, 1st Reconstruction Military District, Records of the U.S. Army Continental Commands, Record Group 393, Pt. 1, National Archives [SS-1049] (bracketed numbers refer to files in the Freedmen and Southern Society Project, University of Maryland; I thank Leslie S. Rowland, project director, for facilitating my access to these files); George F. Bragg, Jr., Baltimore, Maryland, to Dr. Woodson, August 26, 1926, reprinted in "Communications," *Journal of Negro History* 11 (1926): 677.

33. See Thomas C. Holt, " 'An Empire over the Mind'": Emancipation, Race, and Ideology in the British West Indies and the American South," in *Region, Race, and Reconstruction: Essays in Honor of C. Vann Woodward*, ed. J. Morgan Kousser and James M. McPherson (New York: Oxford University Press, 1982), 283–314; also David Montgomery, *The American Civil War and the Meanings of Freedom: An Inaugural Lecture Delivered before the University of Oxford on 24 February 1987* (Oxford: Clarendon Press, 1987), 11–13.

34. This is not to suggest that African American women did not desire the vote nor that they did not often disagree with the actions taken by some black men. One should, however, be careful about imposing presentist notions of gender equality on these women. Clearly for them the question was not an abstract notion of individual gender equality but rather one of community. That such a vision might become over time a lead into a patriarchal conception of gender roles is not a reason to dismiss the equity of its inception.

35. Dabney, "Rough Autobiographical Sketch," 17–18.

36. FABC 2, April 5, 6, 11, May 3, June 27, 1880.

37. First African minutes for 1841–59 and 1875–1930 are available at First African and on microfilm in Archives, Virginia State Library. The Civil War and immediate post-emancipation minutes apparently have not survived. Peter Randolph, who came to Richmond from Massachusetts within weeks of emancipation and became the first black man elected pastor of Ebenezer Baptist, attributed both the change in seating patterns and the formal inclusion of women as voters in church business meetings to his own progressivism. Whether or not he initiated such measures, it is unlikely either change would have been effected without wide acceptance within the congregation. Randolph, *From Slave Cabin to Pulpit*, 89.

38. FABC 2, June 27, 1880.

39. FABC 3, November 7, 20, 1899; *Richmond Planet*, July 6, 20, August 10, 31, 1901, March 8, 15, 1902. Similar debates must have occurred in Ebenezer Baptist Church as well. In approving the conduct of business at Ebenezer, Mitchell noted that "only the male members were permitted to vote" on the appointment of a new pastor. *Richmond Planet*, September 14, 1901. These debates over gender roles within black churches occurred on congregational and denominational levels. For studies that examine these debates at the state and/or national level, see, for example, Higginbotham, *Righteous Discontent*; Glenda Gilmore, "Gender and Jim Crow: Women and the Politics of White Supremacy in North Carolina, 1896–1920" (Ph.D. diss., University of North Carolina, Chapel Hill, 1992); Cheryl Townsend Gilkes, " 'Together and in Harness': Women's Traditions in the Sanctified Church," *Signs: Journal of Women in Culture and Society* 10 (summer 1985): 678–99.

40. *Virginia Baptist*, cited in *Woman's Era* 1 (September 1894): 8.

41. *Richmond Planet*, July 26, 1890; June 8, 1895; September 17, 24, November 19, 1898; September 9, 1899; Anthony Binga, Jr., *Sermons on Several Occasions* (Richmond, 1889), 1: 97–99. Both Kemp and Carter were Baptist. A few women also conducted services in the Methodist church. Evangelist Annie E. Brown, for example, conducted two weeks of revival services at Leigh Street Methodist Episcopal Church in 1900. *Richmond Planet*, April 28, 1900. Even when one "female preacher ... took up station" outside a Manchester barbershop and preached against the male members, claiming they were "leading the young down to perdition," the *Planet's* Manchester correspondent did not denounce her right to preach but rather suggested that if she "is called to preach the gospel, and is sanctified, as some say, why not organize a church of sanctification," rather than stand on street corners issuing "broad and uncalled for" attacks on other ministers. *Richmond Planet*, December 12, 1896.

42. In July 1880 a council representing nine Richmond black Baptist churches censured First African for having called the police. "The First African Baptist Church, Richmond, Virginia, to the Messengers & Churches in General Ecclesiastical Council Assembled," in FABC 2, following April 3, 1881, minutes. For late nineteenth-century disciplinary procedures with regard to members who got civil warrants against other members, see, for example, FABC 2, January 7, October 6, 1884; February 3, 1890.

43. FABC 2, June 27, November 6, 1882; February 5, April 2, 1883. Wendell P. Dabney, a member of that 1883 graduating class, remembered the students as having met in early June and "determined not to go to any church. That we would go to the Richmond Theatre or no where." He calls this "the first school strike by Negro pupils on record in the United States." First African had, however, already denied the use of its facilities because of its new regulation. There is some evidence that, subsequent to the students' action, other black churches may have supported the young people by denying their facilities as well. Dabney, "Rough Autobiographical Sketch," 107–9; Wendell P. Dabney, *Maggie L. Walker and the I. O. of Saint Luke: The Woman and Her Work* (Cincinnati: Dabney Publishing Co., 1927), 32–33. *New York Globe*, June 23, 1883.

44. Rachleff, "Black, White, and Gray," 307–9.

45. See, for example, the discussion of the reconfiguration of leisure space, including the barring of cakewalks and other dancing from the church, in Elsa Barkley Brown and Gregg D. Kimball, "Mapping the Terrain of Black Richmond," *Journal of Urban History* 21 (1995): 296–346.

46. *New York Globe*, October 1883–January 1884. Estimates of the True Reformers' auditorium's seating capacity range from 900 to 1,500 to 2,000. Nearly 4,000 people had been able to attend the March 1867 mass meeting held in First African in support of the Federal Sherman Bill. With their new edifices erected in 1890, Sixth Mount Zion and Sharon Baptist Churches had seating capacity of 1,400 and 1,200 respectively; most churches seated far fewer. Rachleff, *Black Labor in the South*, 40; *Richmond Planet*, March 14, May 31, 1890.

47. For information on the Central Republican League, see *Richmond Planet*, August–September 1898; *Richmond Evening Leader*, August 6, 16, 24, 27, 30, September 1, 28, October 12, 1898; *Richmond Times*, August 3, September 3, 11, 1898; *Richmond Dispatch*, September 14, 1898.

48. *Richmond Planet*, January 26, 1895; October 17, 1896. Similarly, when black Republican men formed the Negro Protective Association in 1898 to organize to retain their vote and political influence, one of the most controversial discussions concerned whether to allow a women's auxiliary, the main purpose of which would be to raise monies for electoral

activities. Because of heated opposition the proposal was abandoned. *Proceedings of the Negro Protective Association of Virginia, Held Tuesday, May 18th, 1897, in the True Reformers' Hall, Richmond, Va.*

49. *Richmond Planet,* July 6, 1901.

50. Lawrence Levine, *Black Culture and Black Consciousness: Afro-American Folk Thought from Slavery to Freedom* (New York: Oxford University Press, 1977).

51. Daniel Webster Davis, " 'De Linin' Ub De Hymns," in *'Weh Down Souf and Other Poems* (Cleveland: Helman-Taylor, 1897), 54–56.

52. The scholarly emphasis on this latter period is not merely a reflection of available sources. It also reflects the conceptual paradigms that have guided the investigation of black women's politics: a focus on the national level, often with minimal attention to different patterns within the North and the South; the acceptance of what Suzanne Lebsock has called the "consensus . . . that for women the standard form of political participation" in the nineteenth century "was the voluntary association"; an emphasis on autonomous women's organizations; and a focus on excavating political (and feminist) texts. This scholarly emphasis has produced a number of insightful works about the period; among them are Higginbotham, *Righteous Discontent*; Gilmore, "Gender and Jim Crow"; Hazel V. Carby, *Reconstructing Womanhood: The Emergence of the Afro-American Woman Novelist* (New York: Oxford University Press, 1987); Claudia Tate, *Domestic Allegories of Political Desire: The Black Heroine's Text at the Turn of the Century* (New York: Oxford University Press, 1992). Quote is from Suzanne Lebsock, "Women and American Politics, 1880–1920," in *Women, Politics, and Change,* ed. Louise A. Tilly and Patricia Gurin (New York: Russell Sage Foundation, 1990), 36.

53. Seeing the 1880–1920 period as "the greatest political age for women (including black women)," Suzanne Lebsock raises the question, "what does it signify" that such occurred at "the worst" age for black people; "an age of disfranchisement and increasing legal discrimination." "Women and American Politics," 59, 37. Glenda Gilmore, in an otherwise thoughtful and nuanced study, contends that black women in North Carolina gained political prominence at the turn of the century as (because) black men vanished from politics — either leaving the state altogether or sequestering themselves in a nonpolitical world. "Gender and Jim Crow," chap. 5. It is an idea, however, that is often unstated but implicit in much literature that imagines black women's turn-of-the-century club movement as their initial emergence into politics. Such a narrative contributes to the fiction that black women were safer in the Jim Crow South than were black men.

54. I am indebted to Stephanie J. Shaw for making the point that it was internal community dynamics more so than external factors that gave rise to the black women's clubs in the late nineteenth century. See Stephanie J. Shaw, "Black Club Women and the Creation of the National Association of Colored Women," *Journal of Women's History* 3 (1991): 10–25. In the end, my analysis of what those internal factors were differs somewhat from Shaw's; she attributes their rise to migration and the resultant presence of a newly migrated group within the community in the 1890s, who sought to recreate in these communities the associational life they had left in their home communities.

55. *New York Globe,* 1883 and 1884, passim; Acme quote is June 23, 1883; *Richmond Planet,* July 26, 1890; January 12, 1895; 1890–1895, passim.

56. For a discussion of black Richmonders' participation in the Knights of Labor, see Rachleff, *Black Labor in the South,* chaps. 7–12.

57. Efforts to demonstrate manhood increasingly took on class and status dimensions. For an example of this, see the discussion of black militias and the military ritual taken on by

black fraternal orders such as the Knights of Pythias, in Barkley Brown and Kimball, "Mapping the Terrain."

58. See for example, *Richmond Planet*, June 11, 1891; February 24, September 22, 1900; February 16, 1901; October 25, November 1, December 20, 1902. Ida Wells-Barnett, in her struggle against the violence aimed at black women and black men, also challenged the links between white supremacy and manliness. For a discussion of Wells-Barnett's writings in this regard, see Gail Bederman, " 'Civilization,' the Decline of Middle-Class Manliness, and Ida B. Wells' Antilynching Campaign (1892–94)," *Radical History Review* 52 (winter 1992): 5–30. Similarly, Frances Ellen Watkins Harper and Anna Julia Cooper associated Anglo-Saxon "imperialism with unrestrained patriarchal power," depicting white males as bestial devourers "of lands and peoples." Hazel V. Carby, " 'On the Threshold of Woman's Era': Lynching, Empire, and Sexuality in Black Feminist Theory," *Critical Inquiry* 12 (autumn 1985): 265.

59. The idea of sexual danger had been a part of the Reconstruction-era discourse, as evidenced in the mass indignation meetings and testimonies. Then, however, it was constructed as a matter of general interest, part of the general discussion of repression of African Americans. Now a more clearly gendered discourse developed where violence against men was linked to state repression and the struggle against it to freedom, and violence against women became a matter of specific interest, increasingly eliminated from the general discussions.

60. First African also excluded men found to have physically abused their wives. Binga, "Duty of Husband to Wife," in Binga, *Sermons on Several Occasions*, 1: 304–5 (emphasis in original); FABC 2, August 6, September 3, November 5, 1883; April 7, 1884. Ultimately the members of First African were at a loss as to how to deal with the sexually transmitted disease, but the persistence of the church's efforts to take it up suggests the degree to which some members considered this a serious issue.

61. It is important to note the constructed nature of this narrative. Suzanne Lebsock has taken the development of women's clubs with these concerns as possible evidence of the increased instances of exploitation of women. "Women and American Politics," 45. I suggest that the exploitation is not increased or even of greater concern, but that the venues for expressing and acting on that concern and the ideology through which this happens — both the narrative of endangerment and the narrative of protection — are the new, changed phenomenon. While the emphasis on motherhood and womanly virtues that undergirded the ideology of middle-class women as protectors may resonate with much of the work on middle-class white women's political activism in this period, it is important to bear in mind two distinctions: African American women's prior history of inclusion, not exclusion, shaped their discourse of womanhood and their construction of gender roles; they did so not in concert with ideas in the larger society but in opposition as white Americans continued to deny African Americans the privileges of manhood or the protections of womanhood, reinforcing the commonality rather than the separateness of men's and women's roles.

62. James Oliver Horton and Lois E. Horton suggest that a masculine conception of liberation, based on violence as an emancipatory tool available principally to men, developed within African American political rhetoric in the North in the antebellum period. "Violence, Protest, and Identity: Black Manhood in Antebellum America," in James Oliver Horton, *Free People of Color: Inside the African American Community* (Washington, DC: Smithsonian Institution Press, 1993), chap. 4.

63. Abernathy's and the Barnes' trials, incarceration, retrials, and eventual releases can be followed in the *Richmond Planet*, July 1895–October 1896; *Richmond Times*, July 23, 1895; *Richmond Dispatch*, September 13–19, October 2, 23, November 8, 9, 12, 14, 16, 21, 23, 24, 27,

28, 1895; July 5, 1896. For Bowser's discussion of the formation of the Women's League to protect the Lunenberg women, see *Woman's Era*, October and November 1895; Charles Wesley, *History of the National Association of Colored Women* (Washington, D.C.: The Association, 1984). The first photographs of the women in the *Planet* appear on August 3, 1895. The first picture of "Mary Abernathy and Her Babe" was published on February 15, 1896. The post-release photograph of Pokey Barnes and Mitchell's comment regarding it appeared on June 27, 1896. For a description of Barnes's attire, see March 6, 1897. Discussions of the case can be found in Brundage, *Lynching in the New South*; and Samuel N. Pincus, *The Virginia Supreme Court, Blacks and the Law, 1870–1902* (New York: Garland, 1990), chap. 11. Brundage emphasizes the role of Governor O'Ferrall, and Samuel Pincus emphasizes the legal maneuverings that prevented the women's certain lynching. While emphasizing the importance of Mitchell's stands against lynching, Ann Alexander dismisses the prolonged front-page coverage of the Lunenberg case in the *Richmond Planet* as mere sensationalism. "Black Protest in the New South: John Mitchell, Jr., (1863–1929) and the *Richmond Planet*" (Ph.D. diss., Duke University, 1973), 152–53. Yet it is certain that it was the continuous efforts of black men and women in Richmond that created the climate of protection for Pokey Barnes, Mary Abernathy, and Mary Barnes, keeping their cases in the public eye, encouraging government and judicial officials to intervene, and providing the financial resources necessary to acquire a team of prominent white men as defense attorneys and advocates for the Lunenberg women. Pamela Henry has pointed to the focus on motherhood as a central point of the *Planet*'s defensive strategy and suggested the futility of such a strategy in an era when black women were denied the protections of Victorian womanhood. Pamela J. Henry, "Crime, Punishment and African American Women in the South, 1880–1940" (paper for Research Seminar in African American Women's History, University of Michigan, fall 1992), cited by permission of Henry. I am uncomfortably cognizant of the fact that my narrative also, for the most part, silences Mary Abernathy and Pokey and Mary Barnes. This reflects my primary interest in understanding what this case illuminates about black Richmond. Abernathy and the Barneses, their lives and their cases, are certainly worthy of investigation in their own right; Suzanne Lebsock is currently undertaking such a study.

64. *Richmond Planet*, March 6, 1897.

65. The narrative of class and gender, protectors and protected, was not uncontested. For example, the women of the Independent Order of Saint Luke offered a counternarrative that emphasized the possibilities of urban life not only for the middle class but importantly the possibilities of urban life for single, working-class black women who, through their collective efforts, could be their own protectors. Still further, they suggested that women — working-class and middle-class — through their political and economic resources, could become men's protectors. Reinterpreting the standards for "race men" to require support for women's rights, they thus reinserted women's condition and rights as a barometer of freedom and progress. Some aspects of the Saint Lukes' ideas regarding the relationship between the well-being of women and the well-being of men and of the community as a whole are traced in Elsa Barkley Brown, "Womanist Consciousness: Maggie Lena Walker and the Independent Order of Saint Luke," *Signs: Journal of Women in Culture and Society* 14, 3 (spring 1989): 610–33.

66. It is important to understand this desexualization of black women as not merely a middle-class phenomenon imposed on working-class women. Many working-class women resisted and forged their own notions of sexuality and respectability. But many working-class women also, independently of the middle-class and from their own experiences, embraced a

desexualized image. Who better than a domestic worker faced with the sexual exploitation of her employer might hope that invisibility would provide protection? Histories that deal with respectability, sexuality, and politics in all their complexity in black women's lives have yet to be written. For beginning discussions, see Darlene Clark Hine, "Rape and the Culture of Dissemblance: Preliminary Thoughts on the Inner Lives of Black Midwestern Women," *Signs: Journal of Women in Culture and Society* 14 (summer 1989): 919–20; Elsa Barkley Brown, " 'What Has Happened Here': The Politics of Difference in Women's History and Feminist Politics," *Feminist Studies* 18 (summer 1992): 295–312; Paula Giddings, "The Last Taboo," in *Race-ing Justice, En-gendering Power: Essays on Anita Hill, Clarence Thomas, and the Construction of Social Reality*, ed. Toni Morrison (New York: Pantheon, 1992), 441–63.

67. Bytches With Problems, "Wanted," is one effort by young black women to democratize the discussion of repressive violence; focusing on the often sexualized nature of police brutality against black women, they remind us that such is often less likely to be included in statistics or acknowledged in the public discussion. *The Bytches* (Noface Records, 1991).

68. Elsa Barkley Brown, "Imaging Lynching: African American Women, Communities of Struggle, and Collective Memory," in *African American Women Speak Out: Responses to Anita Hill-Clarence Thomas*, ed. Geneva Smitherman (Detroit: Wayne State University, 1995).

TWENTY-ONE

From Three-Fifths to Zero
Implications of the Constitution for
African American Women, 1787–1870

MAMIE E. LOCKE

During the summer months of 1787, in Philadelphia, Pennsylvania, fifty-five men argued, debated, suggested, compromised, and eventually hammered out a document that would form the basis of the government of the United States of America. In 1788, the requisite number of states had ratified this document — the Constitution. The Constitution has been called a living, flexible piece of work that is the cornerstone of American democracy. It has been argued that the Constitution established the privileges and rights of citizenship, raised to new heights the rights of individuals, and acknowledged the fundamental principles of life, liberty, and the pursuit of happiness. In the bicentennial year of the ratification of the U.S. Constitution, a simple question can be posed: Was the primacy of individual rights and equality truly reflected in the Constitution as it was written in 1787? The response to this question is equally simple: no, given the omission, for various reasons, of more than half the population. At the bottom of the heap of omissions was to be found the African American woman.

In his controversial remarks on the bicentennial of the Constitution, U.S. Supreme Court justice Thurgood Marshall argued that the meaning of the Constitution was not "fixed" in 1787; furthermore, the wisdom, sense of justice, and foresight of the framers who are being hailed in celebration was not all that profound, particularly since they created a defective government from the beginning. Marshall further stated that there were intentional omissions, namely, blacks and women (Marshall 1987, 2). It is the purpose of this essay to discuss a group of people encompassing both characteristics of exclusion — African American women. It is also the purpose of this essay to elaborate on Justice Marshall's interpretation of the meaning of the Constitution, specifically as it relates to the document's exclusion of

African American women in 1787 and again in 1870. Also to be discussed are African American women's struggles against peripheral status and the consequences of exclusion.

The framers of the Constitution were careful to avoid using terms designating sex or color. The words "slave," "slavery," and "female" are not to be found in the original document. What one does find are phrases such as "persons held to service or labor" (Article 4, section 2) or "three fifths of all other persons" (Article 1, section 2). Those persons held to service or labor and designated as three-fifths were African Americans, females and males. Thus the African American woman started her life in this new government created by men of "wisdom, foresight and a sense of justice" as three-fifths of a person. The struggle for wholeness was begun almost immediately, yet the African American woman usually found herself on the periphery of such struggles. She participated, but she watched as her status moved from three-fifths, in the 1787 document, to zero — total exclusion — with the passage of the Fifteenth Amendment in 1870.

Once, when a speaker at an antislavery meeting praised the Constitution, Sojourner Truth, that prolific sage of the nineteenth century, responded in this way:

> Children, I talks to God and God talks to me. I go out and talks to God in de fields and de woods. Dis morning I was walking out and I got over de fence. I saw de wheat a holding up its head, looking very big. I goes up and talks holt of it. You b'lieve it, dere was no wheat dere. I says, "God, what is de matter wid dis wheat?" and he says to me, "Sojourner, dere is a little weasel in it." Now I hears talkin' bout de Constitution and de rights of man. I come up and talks holt of dis Constitution. It looks mighty big, and I feels for my rights, but dere ain't any dere. Den I say, "God, what ails dis Constitution?" He says to me, "Sojourner, dere is a little weasel in it." (Bennett 1964, 146)

Thus, when the Constitution was written, it advocated equality, opportunity, and the rights of all, yet it condoned the institution of slavery, where men and women alike were reduced to property. Or were they persons? In the "Federalist 54," James Madison argued that slaves were considered not only property but also persons under the federal Constitution. According to Madison, "the true state of the case is that they partake of both these qualities; being considered by our laws, in some respects, as persons, and in other respects, as property . . . the Federal Constitution . . . views them [slaves] in the mixt character" (Madison 1961, 337). In this essay, Madison sought to explain the use of such "weasel" phraseology as "three fifths of all other persons" and "the migration or importation of such persons" (Article 1, section 9).

When antislavery advocates compromised their principles and allowed the institution of slavery to be sanctioned by the very foundation of the new government, the Constitution, they relegated the African American to a status of insignificance. The three-fifths compromise, by counting African Americans for the purpose of taxation and representation, created an interesting paradox. It gave to African Americans the dual status of person and property — however, more property than person.

What did all this mean for the African American woman? Involuntary servitude had a tremendous impact on African Americans, as it was both an economic and a political institution designed to manipulate and exploit men and women. As active participants in the labor market during the slavery era, African American women worked not only in the plantation fields and in the masters' homes but in their own homes as well. They took on many roles and virtually had to be everything to everybody. They were, inter alia, mothers, lovers (willing and unwilling), laborers, and producers of labor. After 1808, the supply of slaves abated somewhat due to congressional legislation prohibiting the importation of Africans into the country. Consequently, additional slave labor was to be created through natural increase. Once again the onus was on the shoulders of the African American woman, who fell prey to further victimization and exploitation. Her fertility was viewed as an asset, yet she had no control over the children born to her; they, too, were the property of the slaveowner, to be bought and sold at the owner's demand.

Interpretation of the Constitution and state laws and statutes merely reinforced the notion of the property rights of slaveholders. For example, the defeminization of African American women made it easy for them to be exploited: they "were never too pregnant, too young, too frail, to be subject to the harsh demands of an insensitive owner" (Horton 1986, 53). African American women were not allowed the protections that were accorded to white women. They were expected to work hard for the slaveowner and to maintain their own homes as well. Their status can be summed up in the folk wisdom given to Janie Sparks by her grandmother in Zora Neale Hurston's novel *Their Eyes Were Watching God*: "De white man throw down the load and tell de nigger man to pick it up. He pick it up because he have to, but he don't tote it. He hand it to his womenfolks. De nigger woman is de mule of the world so far as Ah can see" (Hurston 1969, 29).

The seeds of this reality for the African American woman were planted in slavery. Hence, African American women had few illusions that they held the favored position accorded white women.

African American women did not complacently accept their lot in life. They engaged in resistance in many ways (see Davis 1971; Hine and Wittenstein 1981). They also initiated their own groups such as literary societies and temperance, charitable, and education groups, and of course antislavery groups. Although some white feminists of the nineteenth century, such as Lucy Stone and Susan B. Anthony, invited African American women to participate in the women's struggle, the reform groups actively discriminated against African American women. Their dislike of slavery did not extend to an acceptance of African Americans as equals. For example, attempts by African American women to participate in a meeting of an antislavery society in Massachusetts nearly caused the collapse of that group. According to historical documents, African American men were more readily accepted into the inner sanctums of abolitionist societies than were African American women. It is no surprise, then, that the most well-known advocates of women's rights among African Americans were males, for example, Frederick Douglass, James Forten (Sr. and Jr.), and Robert Purvis. The most prominent female was Sojourner Truth (Terborg-Penn 1981, 303). African American women did, however, participate through their own initiative in both the antislavery and women's movements.

Armed with beliefs such as "It is not the color of the skin that makes the man or woman, but the principle formed in the soul" (Stewart 1973, 565), women such as the Forten sisters, Maria Stewart, and Milla Granson, to name a few, spoke out against racial and sexual injustices. For example, Maria Stewart often attacked racial injustice in the United States. Her outspokenness was accepted and applauded by African American men until her criticisms were aimed at them for not doing as much as they could for the race. Stewart realized then the limitations placed on her as an African American woman. She could speak out on behalf of civil rights and abolition but could not address sexism among African American men. This dilemma, or duality of oppression, is a burden that African American women still bear.

In the period preceding the Civil War, African American and white men and women worked together as abolitionists. All saw a future where slaves and women would be liberated and elevated to equal status under the Constitution of the United States. But would this Constitution incorporate women and slaves? Political abolitionists and Garrisonian abolitionists (followers of William Lloyd Garrison) debated the role and the significance of the Constitution. Many felt that the American political system was corrupt and that this corruption stemmed from the Constitution. As a Garrisonian, Frederick Douglass felt that supporting the Constitution was also supporting slavery. He argued that endorsement of the Constitution meant that one served two masters, liberty and slavery. This argument was articulated also by abolitionist Wendell Phillips. Phillips felt that one should not hold an office in which an oath of allegiance to the Constitution was required. He argued that, since the Constitution was a document upholding slavery, anyone who supported it was a participant in the moral guilt of the institution of slavery (Hofstadter 1948, 148; Lobel 1987, 20).

Douglass later moved away from the Garrisonian view and came to support the political abolitionists' natural-law theory. This view of the Constitution justified participation in the political process (Garrisonians argued for nonparticipation in government), which would allow radical lawyers and judges to argue against and eventually end slavery. It is the natural-law interpretation of the Constitution that led Douglass to assert that the three-fifths compromise "leans to freedom" (Lobel 1987, 20). But did it in fact? According to chief justice Roger Taney in the case of *Dred Scott v. Sandford* (1857), persons of African descent were not citizens under the Constitution. Taney reemphasized the Declaration of Independence's and Constitution's denial of African American citizenship, for the Constitution, he argued, clearly showed that Africans were not to be regarded as people or citizens under the government formed in 1787; they were, and would continue to be, property.

Even before the *Dred Scott* decision, a future president was voicing his opposition to suffrage and equality for African Americans: in a letter to the *New Salem Journal* in 1836, Abraham Lincoln wrote that he supported suffrage for all whites, male and female, if they paid taxes or served in the military. In 1858, a year after the infamous *Dred Scott* decision, Lincoln confirmed this view by stating that he in no way advocated social and political equality between whites and blacks and that he was as much in favor as anyone of whites having a superior position over blacks (Catt and Shuler 1969, 70; Hofstadter 1948, 116).

Armed with political agitation, men and women, whites and African Americans, toiled long and hard toward the quest for equality and liberation. This agitation culminated in a bloody Civil War that ended with the South in ruins and another struggle in store. Who would secure political rights in the postwar period — white women, African Americans, or both? Where would the African American woman be, once the smoke cleared?

The democratization of America, it has been said, has not been the result of the Constitution, the equalitarian ideals of voters, or even the demands of nonvoters; however, these things have played a role, albeit a secondary one. What, then, has brought about democratic change in American society? To some observers, the motivating force behind the major democratic reforms has been partisan advantage. Those reforms thought to be advantageous to a political party have passed; others have been shelved (Elliott 1974, 34).

An all-important question during the period following the Civil War was, "What is to be done with the freedman?" Senator Charles Summer of Massachusetts felt that African Americans should be given the ballot and should be treated like men. Thaddeus Stevens of Pennsylvania said they should be given forty acres of land and should be regarded as human beings. Abraham Lincoln suggested deportation but was told that that idea was virtually impossible (Bennett 1964, 186–87). So what was to be done?

Two groups saw advantages to using the freedmen for their own purposes. First, leaders of the women's rights movement saw an opportunity to channel constitutional discussions around universal suffrage. They supported passage of the Thirteenth Amendment (which ended slavery) and continually pointed out that universal suffrage was a direct outgrowth of the principle of unconditional emancipation. The doors that had formerly been closed to African Americans were slowly opening. As both federal and state constitutions were amended to accommodate the African American, women pushed forward, hoping that they could pass through the same doors as the freedmen (DuBois 1987, 845; Papachristou 1976, 48). Women were not to be as lucky as the freedmen, however. With the doors closing to them, conflict was brewing that would lead to an irreparable schism between women and African Americans, a schism that would carry over to the twentieth-century struggles of blacks and women.

The second group looking for personal gain on the backs of the freedmen was the Republican Party. Republican leaders saw an opportunity to consolidate their power base by enfranchising the freedmen. It was felt that African Americans, out of gratitude, would support the party with their votes. So the wheels were put into motion to enfranchise the freedmen. Were women to be included? Would suffrage be universal?

In 1863, Angelina Grimké stated that the civil and political rights of women and of African Americans were closely connected. She declared that she wanted to be identified with African Americans, because women would not get their rights until

African Americans received theirs (Weld 1970, 80). Did this include African American women, or just men and white women?

President Andrew Johnson opposed granting suffrage to any African American, male or female. In a meeting with George Downing and Frederick Douglass in 1866, Johnson made his position clear:

> While I say that I am a friend of the colored man, I do not want to adopt a policy that I believe will end in a contest between the races, which if persisted in will result in the extermination of one or the other. . . . Yes, I would be willing to pass with him through the Red sea to the Land of Promise, to the land of liberty; but I am not willing . . . to adopt a policy which I believe will only result in the sacrifice of his life and the shedding of his blood. (Fishel and Quarles 1970, 276)

Despite Johnson's position, the radical Republicans circumvented many of his actions, to the point of impeaching him and nearly convicting him and ousting him from office.

There were national and state fights brewing over the issue of universal suffrage. At the state level, several states, including Kansas and New York, proposed changes to their constitutions advocating suffrage for African Americans and women. In Kansas both proposals were rejected, whereas in New York the proposal for women was rejected. At the national level, after the Thirteenth Amendment ended slavery, the Fourteenth Amendment was proposed. This amendment created a serious controversy between women suffragists and men. The major area of contention was the wording of the Fourteenth Amendment, which granted suffrage specifically to males. For the first time, the Constitution explicitly defined voters as men. Section 2 reads,

> Representatives shall be apportioned among the several states according to their respective numbers, counting the whole number of persons in each state. . . . But when the right to vote at any election . . . is denied to any of the male inhabitants of such state, being twenty-one years of age, and citizens of the United States . . . the basis of representation therein shall be reduced in the proportion which the number of such male citizens shall bear to the whole number of male citizens twenty-one years of age in such state.

Speaking before the annual meeting of the Equal Rights Association in 1866, Frederick Douglass argued that acquisition of the franchise was vital for African American men, whereas it was merely desirable for women (Terborg-Penn 1981, 305). Although Douglass attempted to keep the support of white women behind the movement for African American suffrage, the rift between the two groups was widening.

The greatest controversy arose over the proposal and passage of the Fifteenth Amendment. White women continued to press for universal suffrage but were being told to wait until the suffrage amendment for African American males had been passed. This period was deemed the "Negro's hour" (Stanton 1970). The controversy over the Fifteenth Amendment polarized the Equal Rights Association. The Fifteenth Amendment aided the freedmen and rejected women. Where did this leave African American women? They remained on the periphery as discussion centered on African American men and white women.

The Equal Rights Association drifted into two factions, the old abolitionists (headed by William Lloyd Garrison, Wendell Phillips, and Frederick Douglass) and the ardent suffragists (headed by Susan B. Anthony and Elizabeth Cady Stanton). The former group argued for support of the Fifteenth Amendment and urged women not to jeopardize the freedmen's opportunity to obtain suffrage. The latter group opposed the Fifteenth Amendment and started its own newspaper, the *Revolution*. This suffragist faction also joined forces with George Train, a racist Democrat (Papachristou 1976, 56); the association with Train exacerbated the already growing rift between the two groups.

The suffragists used the *Revolution* and other forums to voice their opposition to passage of the Fifteenth Amendment. This excerpt from the *Revolution* summarizes their point of view and also includes their views on the position of African American women:

> Manhood suffrage? Oh! no, my friend, you mistake us, we have enough of that already. We say not another man, black or white, until woman is inside the citadel. What reason have we to suppose the African would be more just and generous than the Saxon has been? Wendell Phillips pleads for black men; we for black women, who have known a degradation and sorrow of slavery such as man has never experienced. (Papachristou 1976, 57)

The issue of African American women was discussed further in an exchange between Douglass, Anthony, Stanton, and others at a meeting of the Equal Rights Association where the subject of debate was the Fifteenth Amendment. Douglass argued that there was not the same sense of urgency for women as for the freedmen. He indicated that women were not treated like animals, were not insulted or hanged from lampposts, and did not have their children taken from them simply because they were women. When asked whether the same things did not happen to African American women, Douglass replied that they did — but because they were black, not because they were women. Thus Douglass underscored the primacy of race over sex. Elizabeth Stanton argued that if African American women in the South were not given their rights then their emancipation could be regarded simply as another form of slavery (Papachristou 1976, 64; Stanton 1970, 81). Even though African American women were victims of both racism and sexism, they were being put in a position of having to choose which oppression was the more debilitating.

Responding to Douglass's remarks, Phoebe Couzins stated,

> While feeling extremely willing that the black man shall have all the rights to which he is justly entitled, I consider the claims of the black woman of paramount importance . . . the black women are, and always have been, in a far worse condition than the men. As a class, they are better, and more intelligent than the men, yet they have been subjected to greater brutalities, while compelled to perform exactly the same labor as men toiling by their side in the fields, just as hard burdens imposed upon them, just as severe punishments decreed to them, with the added cares of maternity and household work, with their children taken from them and sold into bondage; suffering a thousandfold more than any man could suffer. (Papachristou 1976, 64)

Couzins was one of the few white women who identified with the plight of African American women and spoke on their behalf. Along with other suffragists, she advocated universal suffrage and felt that the Fifteenth Amendment should not be passed unless women were included. She felt that men were not any more intelligent nor any more deserving than women: "The Fifteenth Amendment virtually says that every intelligent, virtuous woman is the inferior of every ignorant man, no matter how low he may be sunk into the scale of morality, and every instinct of my being rises to refute such doctrine" (Papachristou 1976, 64).

African American women were themselves divided over the issue of suffrage. Sojourner Truth spoke for those doubly oppressed by race and sex:

> There is a great stir about colored men getting their rights, but not a word about the colored women; and if colored men get their rights, and not colored women theirs, you see the colored men will be masters over the women, and it will be just as bad as it was before. So I am for keeping the thing going while things are stirring; because if we wait till it is still, it will take a great while to get it going again. (Truth 1973, 569)

Truth supported the Fifteenth Amendment but voiced her concern about men being granted suffrage over women.

The suffragist Frances Harper posed the question whether white women were willing to encompass African American women in their struggle, to which Anthony and others replied that they were. Harper supported passage of the Fifteenth Amendment; she declared that, if the country could only address one issue at a time, she would rather see African American men obtain the vote (Papachristou 1976, 64). The debate raged, but when the smoke cleared African American men had obtained the vote and all women were disenfranchised and remained effectively outside the foundation of the American political system.

It has been argued that the Reconstruction Era focused more attention on the rights of African Americans and women than ever before (see DuBois 1987, 846). However, it is apparent that the focus was more on the rights of African American men and white women. African American women were pushed to the periphery of any discussions, or were acknowledged only nominally, despite the fact that they existed as persons who were both female and black. According to bell hooks (1981), the support of African American male suffrage revealed the depth of sexism, particularly among white males, in American society. To counter this sexism, white women began to urge racial solidarity in opposition to black male suffrage. This placed African American women in the predicament of choosing between discriminatory precepts — white female racism or African American patriarchy (hooks 1981, 3). As Sojourner Truth knew, sexism was as real a threat as racism. This issue remains unresolved.

Because they were excluded from the constitutional furor of the Reconstruction period, especially the controversy surrounding the Fourteenth and Fifteenth Amendments, white female suffragists amplified racist themes in their struggles. They claimed that enfranchising black men created "an aristocracy of sex" because it elevated all men over all women. Women suffragists criticized the Fifteenth Amendment because "a man's government is worse than a white man's government" and because the amendment elevated the "lowest orders of manhood" over "the higher classes of women" (DuBois 1987, 850). They, of course, meant white women.

Passage of the Fifteenth Amendment did not grant universal suffrage, just as the framers were not the proclaimed visionaries who created "a more perfect union." Passage of the Fifteenth Amendment elevated African American men to a political status that thrust them into the patriarchal world. White women remained on their pedestals, cherished positions to be revered and envied. African American women had once again been omitted from the cornerstone of American democracy, the Constitution of the United States. There was a difference made in 1870, however: she was no longer to be counted as three-fifths of a person; she was zero.

REFERENCES

Bennett, Lerone. 1964. *Before the Mayflower: A History of the Negro in America, 1619–1964.* Baltimore: Penguin Books.

Catt, Carrie Chapman, and Nettie Rogers Shuler. 1969. *Woman Suffrage and Politics.* Seattle: University of Washington Press.

Davis, Angela. 1971. "The Black Woman's Role in the Community of Slaves." *Black Scholar* 2:3–14.

Dred Scott v. Sandford. 1857. 60 U.S. 19 Howard 393.

DuBois, Ellen Carol. 1987. "Outgrowing the Compact of the Fathers: Equal Rights, Woman Suffrage, and the United States Constitution, 1820–1878." *Journal of American History* 74:836–62.

Elliott, Ward E. Y. 1974. *The Rise of Guardian Democracy: The Supreme Court's Role in Voting Rights Disputes, 1845–1869.* Cambridge: Harvard University Press.

Fishel, Leslie, Jr., and Benjamin Quarles. 1970. *The Black American: A Documentary History.* Glenview, IL: Scott, Foresman.

Hine, Darlene, and Kate Wittenstein. 1981. "Female Slave Resistance: The Economics of Sex." In *The Black Woman Cross-Culturally,* ed. Filomina Chioma Steady. Cambridge, MA: Schenkman.

Hofstadter, Richard. 1948. *The American Political Tradition.* New York: Vintage Books.

hooks, bell. 1981. *Ain't I a Woman: Black Women and Feminism.* Boston: South End.

Horton, James Oliver. 1986. "Freedom's Yoke: Gender Conventions among Antebellum Free Blacks." *Feminist Studies* 12:51–76.

Hurston, Zora Neale. 1969. *Their Eyes Were Watching God.* New York: Negro Universities Press.

Lobel, Jules. 1987. "The Constitution and American Radicalism." *Social Policy* 18:20–23.

Madison, James. 1961. "Federalist 54." In Alexander Hamilton, James Madison, and John Jay, *The Federalist Papers,* ed. Clinton Rossiter. New York: New American Library. (Original work published in 1788.)

Marshall, Thurgood. 1987. "Justice Thurgood Marshall's Remarks on the Bicentennial of the U.S. Constitution." *Signs* 13:2–6.

Papachristou, Judith. 1976. *Women Together: A History in Documents of the Women's Movement in the United States.* New York: Knopf.

Stanton, Elizabeth Cady. 1970. "This Is the Negro's Hour." In *Voices from Women's Liberation,* ed. Leslie B. Tanner. New York: Signet Books.

Stewart, Maria. 1973. "What if I Am a Woman?" In *Black Women in White America,* ed. Gerda Lerner. New York: Vintage Books.

Terborg-Penn, Rosalyn. 1981. "Discrimination against Afro-American Women in the Women's

Movement, 1830–1920." In *The Black Woman Cross-Culturally*, ed. Filomina Chioma Steady. Cambridge, MA: Schenkman.

Truth, Sojourner. 1973. "I Suppose I Am About the Only Colored Woman That Goes About to Speak for the Rights of Colored Women." In *Black Women in White America*, ed. Gerda Lerner. New York: Vintage Books.

Weld, Angelina Grimkée. 1970. "The Rights of Women and Negroes." In *Voices from Women's Liberation*, ed. Leslie B. Tanner. New York: Signet Books.

TWENTY-TWO

Assimilating or Coloring Participation? Gender, Race, and Democratic Political Participation

JANE JUNN

To the extent that political participation constitutes the universal and free expression of voice through democratic deliberation, most observers of American representative democracy agree that more political participation among individual citizens is good. More political activity in the mass public is considered desirable for two reasons. The first reason — consistent with Western liberal or Enlightenment political theory — is that more citizens participating means more individual opinions and preferences are being taken into account. The democratic process, so the argument goes, is a neutral mechanism that aggregates revealed individual preferences and produces an outcome approximating the common good for the polity. Equal levels of participation among groups in society is desirable so that everyone gets a chance to express their preferences in order to have an impact on the outcome. The more voices that are taken into account, the more just or fair that outcome is. Differences in rates or patterns of participation among groups — between men and women, or between racial and ethnic groups — are problematic, because differences in participatory input imply inequality in political outcomes.

A second reason for wanting more citizen participation in democracy has its origin in another set of democratic theories, in particular, those with a participatory-republican perspective. Here, political participation by individuals benefits citizens not by virtue of the political outcomes of preference aggregation; rather, it aids the individual herself in her development as a citizen of the political community. Becoming a democratic citizen is something citizens learn through interaction and participation in politics. Thus, more participation is good because taking part in politics helps citizens develop both their own individual political opinions and the skills and confidence to voice those preferences.

Both of these reasons provide compelling justification for the desirability of more political participation among citizens in democracy, especially for feminists. Under either of the two frameworks, increasing levels of political activity among women in America can help accomplish the twin goals of creating public policies that take women's interests into account and empowering women to take political stands to develop and forward their interests. Many Western feminist theorists have either explicitly or implicitly adopted the normative goal of more political participation and democratic deliberation.[1] In fact, recent feminist theory has found some common ground with critical theory on this very point.[2] The political ideal of the practice of political discourse in a "public sphere" described by Habermas[3] appears to be consistent with one of the main struggles of feminism to eradicate the ideology of domination.

However, the justification of more participation works if and only if two critical assumptions are met. First, more participation can help eradicate the ideology of domination only if the structures and institutions of democracy are indeed *neutral*. That is, for democracy to be better with more participation, the process itself must not favor some group or ideology. Second, more participation can help eradicate the ideology of domination only if the common understanding of agency and citizenship is *fluid*; the conception of democracy cannot uphold some a priori static definition of the model citizen. Competing visions of citizenship must be recognized and embraced,[4] and the construction of the meaning of political being must reflect the composition of all within the political community, including those who differ systematically from the already existing cultural norm. As such, democracy cannot require assimilation to the current model; rather, the conception of the democratic citizen must itself be colored by the diversity of the population.

Why are these two assumptions necessary in order for more participation to be good? If either assumption is not met, more participation works in exactly the opposite direction from which it is intended. Instead of eradicating domination, more participation amid structures and institutions of democracy that replicate the already existing domination in society and economy will only reinforce and legitimate it. Likewise, more participation in a polity where norms are constructed from a static conception of the political being forces groups who are different to choose between assimilation or exit. Instead of participation *coloring* democracy with a range of shades of diversity, the static understanding of agency and citizenship requires *assimilating* to the already existing norm.[5] Thus, if either assumption of neutrality or fluidity is violated, more participation will reinforce and legitimate, rather than eradicate, domination as it already exists.

One way to evaluate the extent to which these assumptions are realistic in the United States is to examine data about the "actually existing democracy."[6] Women, especially women of color, need look no further than our own experiences in political, social, and economic life to illustrate the fallacy of both of the assumptions. As Audre Lorde observed, "the master's tools will never dismantle the master's house."[7] Insofar as it is true that neither neutrality nor fluidity is present in American democracy, more participation by women — and in particular, more political activity among women of color — will not necessarily have its intended consequences.

In this essay I present data from a recent survey of Americans on the political activity of women of color and white women in the United States. How much and what kinds of political and social activities do women engage in? What differences are there between men and women, and between women of color and white women? The data show that there are big differences in the rate at which white women, African American women, Latina women, and Asian women take part in political activity. The most common interpretation of this finding — one that is consistent with the notion that more participation is good — is that these differences should be eliminated, and groups equalized. What often follows from this interpretation is that minority women who participate less than white women in politics should participate more, "raising themselves up" to this standard. However, arguing for more participation by women of color both assumes the neutrality of the democratic system and upholds some static (white) conception of the democratic citizen. When the democratic system is not neutral, but biased culturally, racially, and by gender, this interpretation of the relative inactivity of women of color becomes problematic. Moreover, when the conception of the democratic citizen is not fluid, but some static notion based on liberal methodological individualism, women of color are required to assimilate to the already existing standard. Group-based notions are negated. Thus, the benefits of more voice in democracy can accrue only under certain circumstances, in particular, if and only if both the structures and institutions of the democratic process and the conception of the political citizen are constructed within the context of differences inherent among groups of citizens.

Political Participation by Women in America

For more than half of the history of the American republic, female voices were legally and systematically excluded from the public process of democratic deliberation. The political domain was virtually entirely male. Since the time women gained the right to vote, political scientists and journalists have documented the fact that women vote less frequently, talk about politics less, make fewer campaign contributions, and are far less likely to run for political office.[8] These conclusions about the political behavior of women were based on data gathered on citizen activity between the mid-1950s and the early 1970s, and drawn from measures of political activity that were limited to the traditionally male-dominated arenas of electoral and legislative politics. Feminists took issue with this narrow conceptualization of both activity and the political,[9] arguing that the circumscribed definition of political activity underestimated the rate at which women were active in political life.

Since the mid-1970s, the gap in political participation between men and women has begun to narrow and disappear. Now better-educated, more likely to be employed outside the home, and with more access to economic resources, women are almost as likely as men to take part in politics. The intervening two decades witnessed an explosion in the numbers of women in official and elected positions at all levels of government,[10] along with increased mass participation by women in electoral politics. In addition, more recent studies of mass political behavior have incorporated a broader definition of political participation, extending the world of the political beyond elections, and in so doing, capturing more adequately the range of activities Americans engage in. Examining data from the 1990 Citizen Participation Study, Schlozman, Burns, and Verba find that few if any differences exist between men and women in their political activity, once the resources that facilitate political activity are accounted for.[11] The 1990 Citizen Participation Study extended measures of political participation beyond traditional electoral activities such as voting and campaign activity, and included a much wider range of political activities, including group-based and communal activity, contacting elected officials, protesting, and working with others in religious and charity groups.[12]

In addition to the range of political and social activities, a second unique feature of the 1990 Citizen Participation Study is the large number of African Americans, Latinos, and Asians included in the sample. Typical national surveys draw a sample of people to interview of between one thousand and two thousand adults who are representative of the U.S. population. Because minority Americans are outnumbered by whites by a more than four-to-one margin, only small numbers of minority Americans are interviewed in most national surveys. For example, in a typical survey of 1,500 adult Americans, between 90 and 120 Latinos will be interviewed, with roughly half being Latina women. The Citizen Participation Study gathered data from interviews with more than fifteen thousand Americans — ten times the size of the typical national sample; therefore, much larger samples of minority Americans are available for analysis.

Thus, the 1990 Citizen Participation Study presents a unique opportunity to view the differences between women and men, and between white women and women of color, in terms of political and social activity. The first two columns in table 22.1 show the proportion of women and men who are active in each of thirteen types of political activities, including electoral activity, contacting, local community activity, organizational activity, protesting, and church and charity activity. The third column shows the difference between women and men in each of these activities. The data show that there are small differences between men and women in the rate of participation in most forms of political and social activity. Women are as active as men in most electoral activities, but less likely to give money to a political campaign (15 percent as opposed to 22 percent). Women contact government officials at the local or national level less frequently than do men (31 percent versus 38 percent). Fewer women are members of political and social organizations; 41 percent of women say they belong to an organization, while more than half of men belong (52 percent). However, women are more active than men in working with others in church (43 percent of women and 37 percent of men), and more active doing charity work (38 percent versus 35 percent). Women and men protest and participate in local community activity at about the same rates.

Table 22.1 provides support for the notion that women's voices are being heard more frequently and with more volume in American politics today than in the past. But which women's voices are being heard? Which women participate? Which remain silent? Most of what we know about women's participation in the mass public is about white women. The political behavior, characteristics, and beliefs of

TABLE 22.1.
Political Activity of Women and Men in the United States

	% Women active (N = 8,574)	% Men active (N = 6,479)	Difference
Electoral Activity			
Registered to vote	79	80	−1
Voted in 1988 presidential election	71	71	0
Voted in most or all local elections	54	55	−1
Worked on a political campaign in last 5 years	10	11	−1
Gave money to a political campaign in last year	15	22	−7
Contacting Activity			
Contacted a government official (local or national) in last 5 years	31	38	−7
Local Community Activity			
Served on a local board or council in last 5 years	8	9	−1
Worked with others in the local community in last year	28	32	−4
Organizational Activity			
Member of any social or political organization	41	52	−11
Protesting Activity			
Participated in a protest (non-strike-related) in last 5 years	5	6	−1
Church and Charity Activity			
Worked with others in church	43	37	+6
Did charity work	38	35	+3
Gave money to charity	67	67	0

SOURCE: 1990 Citizen Participation Study.

women of color in the United States have been marginalized and frequently subsumed under studies of race or gender.[13] There are studies of differences between ethnic and racial groups and mass political behavior,[14] but there are no national studies of the political and social participation of women of color. Despite important contributions about the political activity of women of color,[15] our invisibility in data collections and in scholarship contributes to the "continuing marginality" of women of color.

How active are African American women, Latina women, and Asian women? The data in table 22.2 provide some insight into the extent to which women of color take part in a range of political and social activities. Columns 1 through 4 display the percentage of women in each of these categories who reported taking part in the thirteen political activities listed.[16] For women of color, the difference between their participation rate and the participation rate of white women is shown in parentheses. For example, while 57 percent of white women say they voted in most or all local elections, only 23 percent of Asian women said they voted — a difference of 34 percent. Column 5 shows the largest percentage difference between groups of women of color and white women.

The differences are dramatic. White women are more likely than women of color to take part in the thirteen political activities. For only one type of political activity —

TABLE 22.2.
Political Activity of Women in the United States, by Ethnic Background

	(1) % White (N = 6,837)	(2) % African American (N = 881)	(3) % Latina (N = 552)	(4) % Asian (N = 80)	(5) Largest % difference
Electoral Activity					
Registered to vote	81	82 (+1)	58 (−23)	49 (−32)	−40
Voted in 1988 presidential election	74	68 (−6)	46 (−28)	40 (−34)	−46
Voted in most or all local elections	57	52 (−5)	32 (−25)	23 (−34)	−59
Worked on a political campaign in last 5 years	10	12 (+2)	8 (−2)	5 (−5)	−50
Gave money to a political campaign in last year	15	14 (−1)	9 (−6)	11 (−4)	−40
Contacting Activity					
Contacted government official (local or national) in last 5 years	35	22 (−13)	15 (−20)	14 (−21)	−60
Local Community Activity					
Served on a local board or council in last 5 years	8	11 (+3)	8 (0)	4 (−4)	−50
Worked with others in local community in last year	29	31 (+2)	20 (−9)	21 (−8)	−31
Organizational Activity					
Member of social or political organization	44	33 (−11)	21 (−23)	30 (−14)	−52
Protesting Activity					
Participated in a protest (non- strike-related) in last 5 years	5	8 (+3)	4 (−1)	10 (+5)	+100
Church and Charity Activity					
Worked with others in church	45	46 (+1)	29 (−16)	27 (−18)	−40
Did charity work	39	34 (−5)	25 (−14)	28 (−11)	−36
Gave money to charity	71	54 (−17)	43 (−28)	50 (−21)	−39
Percent of population	80	10	6	1	

SOURCE: 1990 Citizen Participation Study.

NOTE: In columns 2–4, figures in parentheses are percentage point differences from white women.

protesting—do white women participate less than African American women and Asian women (and about the same rate as Latina women). This makes perfect sense, especially given the nature of political protest, a form of political activity that does not include working with and within current structures and institutions of existing democracy. However, the data also clearly show that generalizing about all women of color hides many of the interesting differences between African American women, Latina women, and Asian women. African American women are considerably more active than either Latina women or Asian women. In fact, African American women are more likely to be registered to vote, work on political campaigns, serve on a community board, work with others in the local community, march in a protest, and work with others in church than are white women. For almost half of the political activities, African American women are more active than white women. Alternatively, Latina women are less active than white women in each of the thirteen political activities, and Asian women participate at the lowest rate across the three groups of women of color, with the exception of protesting.

Interpreting the Differences

What are we to make of the differences in activity among women? One response might disregard the survey data entirely, and argue that the conceptualization of the political and the scope of the questions asked in the survey are far too circumscribed. Clearly, the survey data do not address all forms of politics and activity, but they do provide information on the more conventional forms of democratic participation. Another popular interpretation of the differences among white women and women of color attributes the variation to the fact that white Americans on average have more social and economic resources. Being educated and having money are among the two strongest and most robust explanations of how and why people become active in politics.[17] The differences in the rates of political participation among the groups might thus be explained away if the fact that whites are both economically and educationally advantaged is accounted for.

Table 22.3 displays a profile of political, educational, and economic resources of women in the United States from the 1990 Citizen Participation Study. The data show several interesting patterns. First, almost all white and African American women are citizens by birth, while only a little more than half of Latina women and one-quarter of Asian women were born in the United States.[18] In addition, two-thirds of Latina women spoke Spanish as the first home language.[19] Citizenship and language are clearly two areas in which Latina women and Asian women are disadvantaged. The next set of characteristics on educational and employment status shows that while white women are advantaged in terms of educational resources—22 percent of white women have a college degree or higher, while 14 percent and 9 percent of African American and Latina women have the same educational standing—they are less advantaged than Asian women, of whom 37 percent have a college degree. Nevertheless, white women are on average far more active than Asian women, despite an educational disadvantage. The third set of characteristics of income and homeownership show a similar incongruity with the conventional

TABLE 22.3.
Resource Profile of Women in the United States, by Ethnic Background

	(1) % White (N = 6,837)	(2) % African American (N = 881)	(3) % Latina (N = 552)	(4) % Asian (N = 80)
U.S. Citizenship and Language				
Born in the United States	97	96	58	23
First home language is Spanish	—	—	67	—
Education and Employment Status				
College degree or higher	22	14	9	37
Employed full-time outside the				
home	44	50	42	45
Keeping house full-time	20	17	31	16
Income and Homeownership				
Total family income less than				
$15,000	20	30	31	18
Total family income more than				
$50,000	23	17	14	31
Owns home	70	45	50	50
Percent of population	80	10	6	1

SOURCE: 1990 Citizen Participation Study

wisdom that economic resources drive political activity. The row displaying the proportion of women in each category whose total family income is more than $50,000 shows that Asian women are the most advantaged, followed by white women, African American women, and Latina women. Despite the disparity in income resources, white women and African American women participate at a much higher rate than do Asian women. Interpreting the differences in participation as a function of the systematic variation in political, educational, and social differences can take us only so far.

What are we to make, then, of the vast differences in levels of political participation among white women and women of color? In other words, why are we uncomfortable with the fact that there are differences between women and men, and between women of color and white women? A third and the most common interpretation is that differences in rates of political activity are undesirable — especially differences favoring whites — because if women of color participate less than white women, the opinions and preferences of women of color are not adequately being expressed publicly and communicated to representatives. In order to remedy such a situation, feminists have frequently argued for increasing political participation among women of color — up to the level set by white women — by breaking down barriers and mobilizing women of color. But advocating more participation by women of color can result in forcing assimilation to the system as it already exists. In many cases changes in language, styles of interpersonal communication, and dress, for example, are required of new entrants into the system. Change is demanded of those who enter the structures of participation, rather than of the system itself.

So what would it take to make more participation good? As an ideal, more participation is desirable; it expands the voice of groups and interests traditionally excluded from American politics. However, advocating more participation by women is justifiable only under circumstances where the structures and institutions of the process of decision making incorporate difference, and when the conceptualization of the citizen is contested and fluid. When the structures are biased, and when concepts of political beings are fixed, advocating more participation does not empower or emancipate those who have been previously dominated. Rather, more participation legitimates those biased structures, and forces assimilation into that which already exists. In shattering barriers and gaining access to politics for women, we cannot neglect to reconstruct the politics we seek to influence.[20]

What it would take to make more participation good is to grapple seriously with the problems of incorporating difference — that is, of coloring participation. Feminists must recognize that incorporating difference may require a restructuring of modern representative democracy in the United States. While some feminists have addressed these issues,[21] others have called for the strengthening of liberal democracy, and in so doing, are relying on the current democratic process as the mechanism by which difference can be incorporated. But it is not at all clear how Western notions of liberty and equality and the universalization of women's experiences[22] can be liberating and incorporating of difference.[23] As bell hooks observed, "The rhetoric of feminism with its emphasis on resistance, rebellion, and revolution created an illusion of militancy and radicalism that masked the fact that feminism was in no way a challenge or a threat to capitalist patriarchy."[24] Perhaps it is the very nature of liberal notions of equality — based squarely on the preeminence of individual right — that makes the incorporation of difference in democracy so difficult.

NOTES

1. While the theorists differ dramatically, and the norms they advocate range from participatory democracy to socialist feminist democracy to radical pluralism, all appear to agree that more participation in democracy is good. See, e.g., Carole Pateman, *Participation and Democratic Theory* (New York: Cambridge University Press, 1970); Jane Mansbridge, *Beyond Adversary Democracy* (New York: Basic Books, 1980); Anne Phillips, *Democracy and Difference* (University Park: Pennsylvania State University Press, 1994); Zillah Eisenstein, *The Color of Gender: Reimaging Democracy* (Los Angeles: University of California Press, 1994).

2. See Nancy Fraser, "Rethinking the Public Sphere: A Contribution to the Critique of Actually Existing Democracy," in *Habermas and the Public Sphere*, ed. Craig Calhoun (Cambridge: MIT Press, 1992), 109–42.

3. Jurgen Habermas, *The Structural Transformation of the Public Sphere: An Inquiry into a Category of Bourgeois Society*, trans. Thomas Burger with Frederick Lawrence (Cambridge: MIT Press, 1989).

4. Michael Dawson, "Desperation and Hope: Competing Visions of Race and American Citizenship" (unpublished manuscript, 1995); Michael G. Hanchard, "Identity, Meaning and the African-American," *Social Text* 8 (1990): 31–42.

5. The definition of "assimilate" is to incorporate. I use "assimilate" here to mean engulf or take in. Such an understanding implies that which is taken in does the changing, while that which does the incorporating remains the same.

6. See Fraser.

7. Audre Lorde, "The Master's Tools Will Never Dismantle the Master's House," in *This Bridge Called My Back: Writings by Radical Women of Color*, ed. Cherríe Moraga and Gloria Anzaldúa (New York: Kitchen Table: Women of Color Press, 1983), 99. In a similar vein, and in arguing against the freedom of all types of speech, feminist legal theorist Catharine MacKinnon argues, "One genius of the system we live under is that the strategies it requires to survive it from day to day are exactly the opposite of what is required to change it." Catharine MacKinnon, *Feminism Unmodified* (Cambridge: Harvard University Press, 1987). 16. Black feminist bell hooks has observed, "Largely because feminists themselves, as they attempted to take feminism beyond the realm of radical rhetoric into the sphere of American life, revealed that they remained imprisoned in the very structures they hoped to change." bell hooks, *Ain't I a Woman: Black Women and Feminism* (Boston: South End, 1981), 190.

8. Angus Campbell, Philip E. Converse, Warren E. Miller, and Donald E. Stokes, *The American Voter* (New York: Free Press, 1960), 483–94; Robert E. Lane, *Political Life: Why People Get Involved in Politics* (New York: Free Press, 1959), 208–13, 354–55; Bernard Berelson, Paul F. Lazarsfeld, and William McPhee, *Voting: A Study of Opinion Formation in a Presidential Campaign* (Chicago: University of Chicago Press, 1954).

9. See, e.g., Susan C. Bourque and Jean Grossholtz, "Politics as Unnatural Practice: Political Science Looks at Female Participation," *Politics and Society* 4 (1974): 225–66.

10. See, e.g., Debra L. Dodson, ed., *Gender and Policymaking: Studies of Women in Office* (New Brunswick, NJ: Center for the American Woman and Politics, 1991); Janet Flamang, ed., *Political Women: Current Roles in State and Local Government* (Beverly Hills: Sage, 1984); Debra L. Dodson and Susan J. Carroll, *Reshaping the Agenda: Women in State Legislatures* (New Brunswick, NJ: Center for the American Woman and Politics, 1991); Timothy Bledsoe and Mary Herring Munro, "Victims of Circumstances: Women in Pursuit of Political Office in America," *American Political Science Review* 84 (March 1990): 213–24.

11. See Kay Lehman Schlozman, Nancy Burns, and Sidney Verba, "Gender and the Pathways to Participation: The Role of Resources," *Journal of Politics* 56, no. 4 (November 1994): 963–90; see also Kay Lehman Schlozman, Nancy Burns, Sidney Verba, and Jesse Donahue, "Gender and Citizen Participation: Is There a Different Voice?" *American Journal of Political Science* 39, no. 2 (May 1995): 267–93.

12. For a full description of the study, see Sidney Verba, Kay Lehman Schlozman, and Henry E. Brady, *Voice and Equality: Civic Voluntarism in American Politics* (Cambridge: Harvard University Press, 1995).

13. See Cathy J. Cohen, "A Portrait of Continuing Marginality: Studying Women of Color in American Politics" (paper presented at the Center for the American Woman and Politics conference on Research on Women and American Politics, April 1994); Marianne Githens and Jewel L. Prestage, eds., *A Portrait of Marginality: The Political Behavior of the American Woman* (New York: David McKay, 1977).

14. In a recent article, Verba et al. find that there are differences among racial/ethnic groups in political participation, with African American respondents being slightly less active and Latinos significantly less active than whites. After controlling for differences in economic and political resources, however, Verba et al. show that these differences recede. See Sidney Verba, Kay Lehman Schlozman, Henry E. Brady, and Norman H. Nie, "Race, Ethnicity, and Political Resources: Participation in the United States," *British Journal of Political Science* 23 (1993): 453–97; see also Katherine Tate, *From Protest to Politics: The New Black Voters in American Elections* (New York: Russell Sage Foundation, 1993) for an analysis of African American voters.

15. See Jo Ann Gibson, *The Montgomery Bus Boycott and the Women Who Started It*

(Knoxville: University of Tennessee Press, 1987); Carol Hardy-Fanta, *Latina Politics, Latino Politics: Gender, Culture, and Political Participation in Boston* (Philadelphia: Temple University Press, 1993); Karin Aguilar-San Juan, ed., *The State of Asian America: Activism and Resistance in the 1990s* (Boston: South End, 1994).

16. The categories of white, African American, Latina, and Asian are convenient but highly problematic. In particular, women of various national identities and immigrant generations are all lumped together. For example, all East Asian women in America — Chinese women, Korean women, Philippine women, Japanese women — are a single category; first-generation Mexican women are combined with fourth-generation Cuban women. Unfortunately, separating the categories further is impossible because no data on national origin were gathered, and would further reduce the size of the subsamples of women.

17. See, for example, Sidney Verba and Norman H. Nie, *Participation in America: Political Democracy and Social Equality* (New York: Little Brown, 1972).

18. A much greater proportion of Latina and Asian women may be citizens by naturalization. Unfortunately, this information was not asked on the 1990 Citizen Participation Study.

19. While there was no comparable question for first home language other than Spanish, it is very likely that Asian women not born in the United States spoke a language other than English at home. In addition, while the questionnaire was conducted in Spanish as well as English, no other additional languages were accounted for.

20. Jones makes a similar point in her discussion of authority: she argues that feminists have spent more energy figuring out how to make women and women's lives authoritative, and less examining the nature of authority itself. "Our efforts have been directed more at investigating how to remove the remaining obstacles to women's being in authority, or how to integrate women into politics, than inquiring about whether women's entering the field of authority as gendered subjects would challenge the terms of authority itself" (ix). Kathleen Jones, *Compassionate Authority: Democracy and the Representation of Women* (New York: Routledge, 1993).

21. See Phillips.

22. See, for example, Okin's recent attempt to universalize the experiences of all women, in particular the experiences of third world women as "the same but worse" as Western women's. Susan Moller Okin, "Gender Inequality and Cultural Differences," *Political Theory* 22, no. 1 (February 1994): 5–24.

23. See Maivan Clech Lam, "Feeling Foreign in Feminism," *Signs* 19, no. 4 (summer 1994): 865–93.

24. hooks, 191.

TWENTY-THREE

Gender, Participation, and the Black Urban Underclass

YVETTE ALEX-ASSENSOH
AND KARIN STANFORD

Current empirical research has underscored unequivocally that the structure of American families and neighborhoods has changed dramatically over the last two decades (Jargowsky and Bane 1991; Green 1990, 1991; Wilson 1980, 1987; Wilson and Wacquant 1989). The growth of households headed by never-married, separated, widowed, or divorced women with young children, and the emergence of so-called concentrated poverty or ghetto poor neighborhoods in predominantly white and black areas are indicative of these changes. Research has also indicated that these two trends — which appear to have converged in central city communities — have political consequences (Cohen and Dawson 1993; Alex 1993; Alex-Assensoh 1995).

Residents of concentrated poverty or ghetto neighborhoods are, however, often treated as a homogeneous group (Wilson 1987; Lemann 1991; Murray 1984; Mead 1992). Yet women and men, entrapped in the mire of debilitating neighborhood and family contexts, are known to have faced different kinds of social and economic constraints, which in turn may have differentiating influences on political participation (Abzug 1984; Gelpi et al. 1986; McLanahan and Garfinkel 1989; Hochschild 1989). For example, women continue to face more downward mobility than men as a result of divorce, welfare dependency, and raising children single-handedly. Given the inequities of women's positions in the labor force and local economy, it is likely that women have life experiences that affect their overall participation differently than that of men.

Indeed, while a few studies have examined the political consequences of living in concentrated poverty communities, only scant attention has been devoted to gender differences. Instead, scholars have devoted more efforts to understanding how differences in family structure and neighborhood contexts influence political participation. Although the emphases on family structure and neighborhood context are important, the differences between men and women in those contexts are also significant. This study, therefore, seeks to address the foregoing apparent shortcomings in two ways: First, it examines the extent to which gender differences in political participation exist among residents in urban underclass communities. Second, it examines the direction of those differences by using a wide range of political attitudes and activities.

Research Context

Unfortunately, research on the political participation of the black underclass is virtually silent on the issue of gender.[1] However, a small body of available literature on gender differences in black political behavior and beliefs illuminates several interesting findings. First, it is shown that black women do not fit the typical pattern of female participation in politics, whereby women lag significantly behind men in political activity. In fact, studies have shown that the rate of increase in voting by black women since 1952 has been greater than the rates for white males, white females, and black males (Lansing 1977; Baxter and Lansing 1983). Second, although men are generally known to be more successful than women in bids for elective offices, black women are typically more successful than their white counterparts (Darcy and Hadley 1988). Third, black women are also typically known to be more partisan, more politically engaged, and more likely to report that they are registered voters than their black male counterparts (Williams 1987). Fourth, black women participate in voluntary associations of all kinds at a higher rate than black men (Williams 1987; Carson 1987; Giddings 1984).

Several theories have been advanced to explain the enigma of black female political participation. One camp of theorists has argued that higher levels of education and occupational status among black women account for higher levels of participation (Williams 1987). However, subsequent studies have shown that black women outpace black men even when they occupy similar educational and occupational strata (Baxter and Lansing 1983). The "dual oppression" or "double whammy" thesis has also been utilized to explain the higher levels of participation among black women when compared to black men.[2] This theory suggests that their dual oppression as women and blacks accounts for higher levels of participation among black women above and beyond what socioeconomic status and race would predict (Lansing 1977; Pierce, Avery, and Carey 1973; Almquist 1979; Baxter and Lansing 1983). Various studies that examine the relationship between feminist ideas and political participation have also suggested that feminism explains the increased level of participation among black women (Lansing 1977; Baxter and Lansing 1983). The increased awareness of gender discrimination heightens political interest, awareness, and political participation (Welch and Secret 1981).

Perhaps the most applicable explanation for the gap between black women and men is the theory of matrifocality, especially as it relates to the urban underclass phenomenon of female-headed households. More generally, it dictates that black women, as a result of racism and economic necessity, have been forced to adopt many of the roles, responsibilities, and duties assigned to men. This role-reversal relationship, wherein women have assumed primary responsibility for maintaining the household, presumably makes voting more appropriate behavior for the independent and aggressive female (Pierce, Avery, and Carey 1973).[3] In large measure, the literature on gender differences in political participation celebrates the so-called independence of women, which very often manifests itself in female-headed households. In contrast, research on the urban underclass suggests that female-headed families in inner-city communities are indicative of a failing economic system that leads to unemployment, low-paying jobs, family dissolution, nonmarriage, and dependence on government assistance (McLanahan and Garfinkel 1989).

Unlike the mother-only families of the 1970s that were made up of working mothers who lived in stable neighborhood environments, many present-day female-headed households are increasingly isolated from mainstream society by virtue of the fact that they are not in the labor force (McLanahan and Garfinkel 1989). While black men and women alike face similar daunting economic circumstances in inner-city communities, women are more imperiled by a series of devastating circumstances. In a recent study of urban poverty in Chicago's urban underclass communities, black women were more than twice as likely as black men to be currently receiving welfare aid and to have household incomes below $7,500 (Wilson and Wacquant 1989). They were two to three times less likely than black men to have checking or savings accounts, a home, or a car. Moreover, men were more likely to report that they had a best friend who worked steadily, while black women were more likely to report that their best friend was on public aid. These data indicate that women face a much more severe opportunity structure than black men. The data also suggest that black women in inner-city communities are more socially isolated. Above all is the fact that women have lower volumes of social capital — including the networks of friends, family, and partners that can assist in the time of need — than do men. The implication of the urban underclass literature is that women should participate less than men in political activity as a result of the lack of resources, social isolation, limited opportunity structures, and the added responsibilities of heading a household.

While considering the previous research literature on the urban underclass and gender differences in black political participation, this study empirically examines the extent to which gender differences emerge. Moreover, in light of the role reversal in the responsibilities of women and men in urban environments (Wilson 1987; Wilson and Wacquant 1989), the study empirically assesses the direction of those differences. An interesting question is whether the increased responsibility of parenthood, the lack of work, and the debilitating neighborhood and family environments that women face in today's urban underclass communities facilitate or impede participation.

Data, Study Area, and Methodology

To a large extent, the lack of adequate data has prevented scholars with research interests in political participation from examining gender differences in the political activities of residents in concentrated poverty communities. However, the data being utilized in this study consist of both individual-level and contextual data, all of which were specifically collected to assess the political behavior and attitudes of residents in urban underclass communities of Columbus, Ohio.[4]

The city of Columbus is an ideal choice for a study of concentrated poverty. First, it is a frostbelt city that has experienced massive job loss in the manufacturing sector and that once served as the economic backbone of the state, providing jobs for poorly skilled and undereducated workers. Second, in part as a consequence of deindustrialization, Columbus was one of the ten cities that witnessed the largest increases in the number of ghetto poor between 1970 and 1980 (Jargowsky and Bane 1991).

Table 23.1 illustrates the gross disparities between residents of Columbus as a whole and the residents of the South Linden neighborhood, which is the site of this study. While less than 15 percent of the residents in Columbus live below the poverty line, almost 50 percent of the residents in South Linden live on incomes that are below the national poverty standard.

In terms of education, over 80 percent of Columbus residents hold a high school degree. In South Linden, only 50 percent of the residents hold a high school diploma. This statistic is extremely troubling, when one considers the fact that a high school diploma is a basic requirement for minimum wage employment. If residents do not acquire such credentials, poverty and social isolation will have intergenerational consequences. The margin of difference is even greater in the area of college education. Almost 30 percent of Columbus residents hold a bachelor's degree or higher, compared to less than 5 percent of South Linden residents.

Finally, while neighborhood poverty and urban underclass behaviors are known to prevail among whites (Alex-Assensoh 1995), the South Linden neighborhood is overwhelmingly black as compared with the city of Columbus as a whole, where blacks make up less than one-third of the population. The social consequences of

TABLE 23.1.
Neighborhood and Citywide Statistics

Indicators (Citywide)	Columbus, Ohio (%)	South Linden neighborhood (%)
Poverty		
People living below the poverty line	12	49
Families below the poverty line	9	49
Education		
High school degree or above	81	50
Bachelor's degree or above	27	3
Race		
White	74	7
African American	23	91
Other	3	2

SOURCE: 1990 Census and 1991 Columbus, Ohio, Neighborhood Study.

TABLE 23.2.
Concepts and Operationalizations

Concepts	Operationalizations
Political Attitudes	Do you feel left out of things going on around you?
	Do you feel that most people in power try to take advantage of people like yourself?
	Do you think the public has control over what politicians do in office?
	Do you think people running this city care about what you think?
	Do you think people running this country care about what you think?
	How much of the time do you trust the government in Washington to do what is right?
Political Participation	How often do you attend religious services?
	Are you currently registered to vote?
	Since you were old enough to vote, have you voted most of the time, some of the time, or hardly ever in presidential elections? (The same question was asked for local elections.)
	Please name the organizations that you currently belong to.
	In the last four years, has anyone encouraged you to participate in political activities?
Civil Disobedience Tactics	Would you approve of the tactic of refusing to obey a law you think is unfair?
	Supposing that other forms of participation like voting, petitioning, and campaigning have failed, would you approve of trying to stop government from going about its usual activities with sit-ins and demonstrations?
	Do you think people are justified in (1) rioting, (2) staging sit-ins and demonstrations, or (3) refusing to obey an unjust law, when other methods have failed?

concentrated poverty neighborhoods and isolation are definitely evident in South Linden. At this juncture, it is important to assess gender differences in political participation among black men and women in this beleaguered neighborhood environment.

Building on previous research dealing with the black urban "underclass," this analysis examined six political attitudes and nine types of political behavior. Table 23.2 provides a list of these concepts and their operationalizations. The reliability of the measures were validated by factor analysis and cronbach's alpha. Examined is the extent to which men and women who live in predominantly black underclass communities harbor similar political beliefs and have similar rates of participation. If differences do exist, the study also assesses the direction of those differences. Chi-square tests were used to assess the extent to which the political attitudes and behaviors were statistically different among black men and women. The results of the chi-square tests are presented on tables 23.3–23.17.

Findings

The literature on gender differences in the political attitudes of blacks reveals that women have less positive attitudes about the political system than their male counterparts (Pierce, Avery, and Carey 1973; Tate 1993). In an effort to assess the extent to which this assertion is true for blacks who live in concentrated poverty neighborhoods like South Linden and comprise the so-called underclass, we examine several different political attitudes. They include political efficacy, political alienation, trust in government, and the extent to which respondents believed that people running the city and country care about what they think.

Tables 23.3 and 23.4 present the findings for political alienation and political exploitation, respectively. Contrary to expectations, there are no differences between black women and black men. In fact, the findings show that all blacks, regardless of gender, often feel alienated and taken advantage of by government. While various studies have shown a general increase in the level of political alienation among all Americans, the lack of variance among blacks is extremely sobering (Aberbach 1969; Abramson 1983).

Table 23.5 presents the findings for political efficacy. Approximately 40 percent of women, compared to 29 percent of men, stated that the public has control over politicians. The overwhelming majority of black men were very pessimistic about their political efficacy, especially so as 71 percent expressed that the public has no control over politicians. Black women were somewhat less pessimistic; 60 percent stated that they had no control over politicians. This may be due to the greater role black women, as representatives of their households, play in dealing with agents of the system. Additionally, the statistically significant difference in the political efficacy of black men and women perhaps foreshadows differences in political participation.

The findings on table 23.6 reveal that 45 percent of women compared with 33 percent of men expressed the belief that people running the city did care about them. This is a statistically significant difference, which might also suggest that local officials

TABLE 23.3.
Do You Feel Left Out of Things Going On Around You?

	Males (N=129)	Females (N=250)
Yes	100%	100%
No	0	0

NOTE: Statistical evaluations are unavailable because of the lack of variance of the dependent variables.

TABLE 23.4.
Do People in Power Take Advantage of You?

	Males (N=135)	Females (N=255)
Yes	100%	100%
No	0	0

NOTE: Statistical evaluations are unavailable because of the lack of variance of the dependent variables.

TABLE 23.5.
Does the Public Have Control over Politicians?

	Males (N = 130)	Females (N = 243)
Yes	29%	40%
No	71	60

NOTE: Chi-Square = .02; significant at the .05 level.

TABLE 23.6.
Do People Running the City Care about What You Think?

	Males (N = 131)	Females (N = 230)
Yes	33%	45%
No	67	55

NOTE: Chi-Square = .03; significant at the .05 level.

are more responsive to black women's issues than issues that either influence or affect black men. Interestingly, however, table 23.7 shows that men and women are almost on par in expressing a belief that people running the country do not care about them. Almost 90 percent of black men and women alike feel uncared for by officials at the national level. These findings, indeed, reveal an interesting relationship between the level of government and political beliefs about the responsiveness of government officials. Events at the national level, including the rightward shift of the Democratic Party and the conservative political climate, may account for these findings.

Presented on table 23.8 are the results of the contingency table analysis for trust in government. In large measure, the findings have revealed that black men and women have similar levels of trust in government. Overwhelmingly, blacks — regardless of gender — expressed lower levels of trust in government. Almost 66 percent of black men and 69 percent of black women stated that they trusted government only some of the time. These findings are consistent with the Pierce et al. study, which found minimal gender differences in black political beliefs.

As political attitudes are only one aspect of the political participation study, we now turn to analyses of differences in political activities. Toward that end, we examine voting, voting registration, organizational membership, mobilization, church attendance, and propensity to participate in civil disobedience tactics.

While church attendance is not seen as a political activity, religious involvement has always served as a catalyzing force for black political participation (Dawson 1993; Harris 1994; Brown and Wolford 1994). The findings shown on table 23.9 reveal that blacks are frequent church attenders, as a majority report going to church more than several times a month. However, women are much more likely than their male counterparts to attend church services on a consistent basis. Almost 50 percent of black women reported attending church every week or more, compared to about 28 percent of black men. Indeed, this statistically significant difference is very critical because church involvement often provides the experience and the skills necessary for participation in politics (Verba and Nie 1972; Verba et al. 1993; Tate 1993).

Indeed, some churches provide parishioners with the opportunity for voter registration as well as information about the candidates seeking political office.

Table 23.10 presents the findings from the contingency table analysis for registering to vote. The findings reveal that more blacks reported being registered than not registered. However, statistically significant gender differences are evident. Black women (92 percent) are more likely than black men (81 percent) to report being registered to vote.[5] Since it is impossible to vote without being registered, these differences are likely to lead to differences in voting participation as well.

Consistent with expectations, statistically significant differences emerge when the voting activities of black men and women are examined (table 23.11). Approximately 62 percent of all black women, compared with only 45 percent of black men, reported that they had voted most of the time in presidential and local elections.

The literature on gender differences in political participation has also chronicled the fact that women are more likely to belong to various organizations and associa-

TABLE 23.7.
Do People Running the Country Care about What You Think?

	Males (N = 180)	Females (N = 357)
Yes	14%	14%
No	86	86

NOTE: Chi-Square = .90

TABLE 23.8.
Do You Trust the Government in Washington to Do What Is Right?

	Males (N = 139)	Females (N = 251)
Never	21%	22%
Some of the time	66	69
Most of the time	11	8
Just about always	2	1

NOTE: Chi-Square = .69

TABLE 23.9.
How Often Do You Attend Religious Services?

	Males (N = 126)	Females (N = 249)
Never	8%	3%
Less than once a year	2	2
About once or twice a year	11	4
Several times a year	12	7
Once a month	14	6
Two to three times a month	12	16
Nearly every week	13	14
Every week or more than once a week	28	48

NOTE: Chi-Square = .00; significant at the .001 level

TABLE 23.10.
Are You Registered to Vote?

	Males (N = 140)	Females (N = 261)
Yes	81%	92%
No	19	8

NOTE: Chi-Square = .00; significant at the .001 level.

TABLE 23.11.
Voting in Presidential and Local Elections

	Males (N = 140)	Females (N = 263)
Rarely vote	20%	16%
Vote sometimes	35	22
Vote most of the time	45	62

NOTE: Chi-Square = .00; significant at the .001 level.

tions than their male counterparts (Carson 1987, 1989). In large measure, therefore, the statistically significant findings shown on table 23.12 are consistent with prior research. Twenty-seven percent of black men, as compared with 18 percent of black women, reported that they do not belong to any organizations. In contrast, 14 percent of black men, compared with 23 percent of black women, reported that they belong to three to five organizations. Like church membership and attendance, organizational affiliation frequently serves as a catalyst for participation in voting and nonelectoral activities aimed at political actors and officials.

Mobilization has consistently been shown to be an important aspect of political participation. Political parties have often played the role of mobilizers (Erie 1988; McNickle 1993; Grimshaw 1992). During election campaigns, elected officials and/ or other concerned citizens mobilize or encourage others to participate in politics (Nelson and Meranto 1979). Table 23.13 shows important and statistically significant gender differences in the mobilization rates of black men and women. Black men more frequently report less mobilization, or encouragement to participate, than black women. Since mobilization is very highly correlated with political participation, these statistically significant differences are important in understanding why women may out-participate men in various political activities. Additionally, it is important to remember that black women in this study have reported a higher level of involvement in church activities than black men and, therefore, have benefited more from the mobilization activities of the church.

While voting involves the most traditional and typical form of political participation, nonelectoral participation involves activities that are grassroots and community-oriented in nature. Table 23.14 presents the findings for the contingency table analysis of nonelectoral activities. The findings reveal very little difference between the nonelectoral activities of black men and women. Approximately 53 percent of black men and 55 percent of black women reported participating in one to three nonelectoral activities.

While table 23.14 examined differences in the nonelectoral activities of black men and women, tables 23.15–23.17 examine the propensity to participate in civil disobedience tactics similar to those employed by blacks during the late 1960s and early 1970s. As revealed in table 23.15, when asked whether they approved of stopping government with sit-ins and demonstrations, black women (45 percent) were more likely than black men (32 percent) to disapprove. This statistically significant finding is similar to the statistically significant findings revealed in table 23.16, which asks black men and women whether they approve of stopping government by rioting. This finding is consistent with the investigations of the riots/rebellions of the 1960s. For instance, studies showed that black men under thirty were among the most active participants (Feagan and Hahn 1973; Sears and McConahay 1973). While

TABLE 23.12.
Organizational Membership

	Males (N=140)	Females (N=263)
None	27%	18%
One to two organizations	56	56
Three to five organizations	14	23
More than five organizations	3	3

NOTE: Chi-Square = .06; significant at the .10 level.

TABLE 23.13.
Summary of Mobilization

	Males (N=140)	Females (N=263)
One to four mobilizers	54%	59%
Five to eight mobilizers	33	22
Nine to twelve mobilizers	7	8
Over twelve mobilizers	6	10

NOTE: Chi-Square = .09; significant at the .10 level.

TABLE 23.14.
Summary of Nonelectoral Activities

	Males (N=140)	Females (N=263)
One to three activities	53%	55%
Four to six activities	36	32
Over six activities	11	12

NOTE: Chi-Square = .67.

TABLE 23.15.
Do You Approve of Stopping Government with Sit-Ins and Demonstrations?

	Males (N=173)	Females (N=348)
Disapprove	32%	45%
Approve	68	55

NOTE: Chi-Square = .02; significant at the .05 level.

TABLE 23.16.
Do You Approve of Stopping Government by Rioting?

	Males (N = 123)	Females (N = 229)
Disapprove	68%	78%
Approve	32	22

NOTE: Chi-Square = .03; significant at the .05 level.

TABLE 23.17.
Do You Approve of Refusing to Obey a Law?

	Males (N = 121)	Females (N = 220)
Disapprove	47%	60%
Approve	53	40

NOTE: Chi-Square = .02; significant at the .05 level.

blacks overwhelmingly disapprove of rioting, black men (68 percent) are less likely than black women (78 percent) to disapprove of rioting, a difference that is also statistically significant. Table 23.17 shows the differences in the responses of black men and women who either approved or disapproved of stopping government by refusing to obey a law. Again, statistically significant differences emerge: black women (60 percent) are more likely than black men (47 percent) to disapprove of refusing to obey a law.

To recapitulate, this study assessed gender differences in the political participation of the black urban underclass. The findings can be summarized in four major points.

First, in large measure, black men and women harbor similar impressions of and attitudes about the political system. In fact, black women and black men differed on only two of the six sampled political attitudes. Compared to black men, black women were more efficacious about their control over politicians (table 23.5) and more positive about governmental responsiveness at the local level (table 23.6). Generally, however, blacks — regardless of gender — harbor negative attitudes about politics and the American political system.

Second, the similarities in political attitudes and outlook do not translate into similar levels of political participation. Overwhelmingly, black women participate in more types of activities and participate more frequently than their black male counterparts. A key to understanding these differences is the greater involvement of black women in organizations and church activities. Additionally, black women are more likely than black men to be encouraged to participate, a factor that is very important to political participation.

Third, the only area in which black men express more interest in participation than black women is in civil disobedience. Unlike the traditional forms of participation like voting and registering, this type of political activity involves challenging unjust laws by refusing to obey them, rioting, or staging sit-ins and demonstrations. Black men were more likely to approve of these tactics than black women. This suggests that black men in urban underclass environments are more likely than women to use radical approaches to political participation.

Fourth, the findings reveal that although the black urban underclass may participate at lower rates than their counterparts who live in working-class, middle-class, and affluent communities, the patterns of participation confirm many of the contentions advanced by earlier studies. Although this study did not explicitly include an examination of the matrifocality or dual oppression theories, we have no reason to believe that both cannot apply to this population. Women of the black urban underclass certainly take on characteristics that are traditionally associated with men, and are oriented toward feminism (Wilcox 1990). Therefore, despite the implications of the urban underclass literature that female-headed households are socially isolated and lack the strength, fortitude, time, and energy to participate, black women are more active participants in political activities than their male counterparts. Our conclusion implies that women of the urban underclass may not be as alienated from society as it is often stated. The evidence shows that they attempt to empower themselves despite the lack of resources and attention given to their communities.

NOTES

1. Cohen and Dawson (1993) included gender as a variable in their study of the black urban underclass in Detroit, Michigan.

2. This research is very much related to the literature on racial group identification, which suggests that group identification is a political resource that raises participation rates in the black community (Verba and Nie 1972; Tate 1990). If race identification promotes black political participation in general, then a gender consciousness combined with a race consciousness is expected to promote greater participation among black women.

3. Examples of the role-reversal phenomenon are described in Wilson and Wacquant 1989.

4. The telephone interviewing was conducted by the professional staff of Polimetrics Laboratory at the Ohio State University, under the direction of Drs. Aage Clausen and Kathleen Carr. The data collection phase commenced on September 27, 1992, and concluded on November 2, 1992. The survey produced 1,165 completed interviews with 432 respondents from the predominantly black, concentrated poverty neighborhoods, 327 from the predominantly white, concentrated poverty neighborhood, 205 from the predominantly black, low-poverty neighborhood, and 201 from the predominantly white, low-poverty neighborhood.

Originally, it was collected for the purpose of conducting dissertation research that focused on the political consequences of living in concentrated poverty neighborhoods. However, the data set includes a wide variety of family, neighborhood, and individual-level characteristics that will be useful in this research project. Respondents were asked about the participation habits of household members and the extent to which they were encouraged to participate in political activity by someone at home, at work, in the neighborhood, and at church. Respondents were also queried about their involvement in social organizations and their religious affiliation. The survey also explored the economic situations of respondents to determine whether they were able to purchase all the things they needed, whether they had to seek additional employment to make ends meet, and whether last year's economic policies had an adverse impact on their personal economic situation. In addition to the usual demographic questions that are posed at the end of surveys, respondents were asked detailed questions about their families, including the extent to which household members received benefits and the extent to which they owned basic resources like a home and an automobile.

The funds to conduct the study came from a variety of sources; the lion's share of the money came from the National Science Foundation and the Social Science Research Council.

5. The registration responses were not verified.

REFERENCES

Aberbach, Joel D. 1969. "Alienation and Political Behavior." *American Political Science Review* 63:76–89.

Abramson, Paul R. 1983. *Political Attitudes in America*. San Francisco: W. H. Freeman.

Abzug, Bella. 1984. *Gender Gap*. Boston: Houghton Mifflin.

Alex, Yvette. 1993. "Assessing the Effects of Family and Neighborhood Contexts on Political Orientations and Behavior." Ph.D. diss., Ohio State University.

Alex-Assensoh, Yvette. 1995. "Myths about Race and the Urban Underclass." *Urban Affairs Review* (formerly known as the *Urban Affairs Quarterly*), September.

Almquist, Elizabeth. 1979. "Black Women and the Pursuit of Equality." In *Women: A Feminist Perspective*, ed. Joe Freeman. Palo Alto, CA: Mayfield.

Baxter, Sandra, and Marjorie Lansing. 1983. *Women and Politics: The Visible Majority*. Ann Arbor: University of Michigan Press.

Brown, Ronald, and Monica L. Wolford. 1994. "Religious Resources and African American Political Activity." *National Political Science Review* 4:30–48.

Carson, Emmett D. 1987. "The Contemporary Charitable Giving and Volunteerism of Black Women." Presented at Women and Philanthropy Past, Present and Future Conference, City University of New York, Center for the Study of Philanthropy, June 17–18.

———. 1989. *Charitable Appeal Fact Book: How Black and White Americans Respond to Different Types of Fund-Raising Efforts*. Washington, DC: Joint Center for Political Studies.

Cohen, Cathy J., and Michael Dawson. 1993. "Neighborhood Poverty and African American Politics." *American Political Science Review* 87 (2): 286–302.

Darcy, R., and Charles D. Hadley. 1988. "Black Women in Politics: The Puzzle of Success." *Social Science Quarterly* 69 (3): 629–45.

Dawson, Michael C. 1993. *Behind the Mule*. Princeton: Princeton University Press.

Erie, Steven. 1988. *Rainbow's End*. Berkeley: University of California Press.

Feagan, Joe R., and Harlan Hahn. 1973. *Ghetto Revolts*. New York: Macmillan.

Gelpi, Barbara, Nancy Hartsock, Clare Novak, and Myra H. Strober, eds. 1986. *Women and Poverty*. Chicago: University of Chicago Press.

Giddings, Paula. 1984. *When and Where I Enter: The Impact of Black Women on Race and Sex in America*. New York: Morrow.

Green, Richard R. 1990. "Poverty Concentration Measures and the Urban Underclass." *Economic Geography* 67 (3): 240–52.

———. 1991. "Poverty Area Diffusion: The Depopulation Hypothesis Examined." *Urban Geography* 12: 526–41.

Grimshaw, William J. 1992. *Bitter Fruit.* Chicago: University of Chicago Press.

Harris, Frederick C. 1994. "Something Within: Religion as a Mobilizer of African-American Political Activism." *Journal of Politics* 56 (1): 42–68.

Hochschild, Jennifer. 1989. "Equal Opportunity and the Estranged Poor." *Annals of the American Academy* 501 (22): 143–55.

Jargowsky, Paul A., and Mary Jo Bane. 1991. "Ghetto Poverty in the United States." In *The Urban Underclass,* ed. Christopher Jencks and Paul E. Peterson, 235–73. Washington, DC: Brookings Institution.

Lansing, Marjorie. 1977. "The Voting Patterns of American Black Women." In *A Portrait of Marginality: The Political Behavior of the American Woman,* ed. Marianne Githens and Jewel Prestage. New York: David McKay.

Lemann, Nicholas. 1991. *The Great Migration and How It Changed America.* New York: Knopf.

McLanahan, Sara, and Irwin Garfinkel. 1989. "Single Mothers, the Underclass and Social Policy." *Annals of the American Academy* 501 (22): 92–104.

McNickle, Chris. 1993. *To Be Mayor of New York.* New York: Columbia University Press.

Mead, Lawrence. 1992. *The New Politics of Poverty.* New York: Basic Books.

Murray, Charles. 1984. *Losing Ground.* New York: Basic Books.

Nelson, William E., and Phillip J. Meranto. 1979. *Electing Black Mayors: Political Action in the Black Community.* Columbus: Ohio State University Press.

Pierce, John C., William Avery, and Addison Carey, Jr. 1973. "Sex Differences in Black Political Beliefs and Behavior." *American Journal of Political Science* 17:422–30.

Prestage, Jewel. 1991. "In Quest of African American Political Woman." *Annals of the American Academy* 515:88–103.

Sears, David O., and John B. McConahay. 1973. *The Politics of Violence: The New Urban Blacks and the Watts Riot.* Boston: Houghton Mifflin.

Tate, Katherine. 1990. "Bloc Voters, Black Voters and the Jackson Candidacies, 1984–1988." Paper presented at the annual meeting of the American Political Science Association, San Francisco, August 30–September 2.

———. 1993. *From Protest to Politics.* Cambridge: Harvard University Press.

Verba, Sidney, and Norman H. Nie. 1972. *Participation in America.* Evanston: University of Chicago Press.

Verba, Sidney, Kay Schlozman, Henry Brady, and Norman Nie. 1993. "Citizen Activity: Who Participates? What Do They Say?" *American Political Science Review* 87 (2): 303–18.

Welch, Susan, and Philip Secret. 1981. "Sex, Race and Political Participation." *Western Political Quarterly* 34 (1): 5–16.

Wilcox, Clyde. 1990. "Black Women and Feminism." *Women and Politics* 9:65–84.

Williams, Linda. 1987. "Black Political Progress in the 1980s: The Electoral Arena." In *The New Black Politics.* New York: Longman.

Wilson, William J. 1980. *The Declining Significance of Race.* Chicago: University of Chicago Press.

———. 1987. *The Truly Disadvantaged.* Chicago: University of Chicago Press.

Wilson, William J., and Loic J. D. Wacquant. 1989. "The Cost of Racial and Class Exclusion in the Inner City." *Annals of the American Academy of Political and Social Science* 501 (22): 8–25.

TWENTY-FOUR

Breaking Barriers to Representation Chicana/Latina Elected Officials in California

PAULE CRUZ TAKASH

Feminist theorists are credited with significantly broadening our understanding of what constitutes politics and who may be deemed political actors. Mainstream definitions of politics in the United States have focused primarily on institutions and practices falling within the electoral political realm. Despite an earlier scholarship whose focus on the political activities of the working class also challenged elite notions of political participation (Thompson 1963; Zinn 1980; Wolf 1982), politics as practiced by women generally escaped academic attention until the development of women's studies. Focusing on the activities of working-class women, feminist scholars have recovered from virtual obscurity the rich history of the political participation of persons often depicted as passive and politically apathetic. Contributors to Bookman and Morgen's edited volume, *Women and the Politics of Empowerment* (1988), exemplify the contribution of gender analysis to the reconstruction of what is political. According to these scholars, politics is reconstituted by the "activities that are carried on in the daily lives of ordinary people and are enmeshed in the social institutions and political-economic processes of their society. When there is an attempt to change the social and economic institutions that embody the basic power relations in our society — that is politics" (Morgen and Bookman 1988, 3–4).

Latina feminists also underscore that politics is much more than electoral participation. Patricia Zavella's (1987) study of Chicana cannery workers' union organizing in San Jose, California; Magdalena Mora and Adelaida Del Castillo's (1980) edited volume on Latina activists; Vicki Ruiz's (1987) historical treatment of Mexicana unionization struggles in the food processing industry; Cordova et al.'s (1986) research on Chicana women, among other work, are by now standard reading for serious students of gender, race, and class politics. Mary Pardo (1990, 1) observes, "political activism is conceptualized by social scientists, who often use a narrow definition confined to electoral politics." In her research on working-class Latina mobilization against environmental racism in poor Los Angeles neighborhoods, Pardo emphasizes the transformation these women embody in their development of a political consciousness and their response to issues broader than those affecting hearth and home. Yet despite the wealth of mainstream academic study on electoral politics, scholarly inquiry about Latina activity in traditional electoral arenas is remarkable not by its redundancy but rather by its near absence. Although Latinas have only recently penetrated federal and state elective office, they have a much longer history of participation in representational politics and officeholding at the local and county levels, positions often gained after years spent in community-based struggles. Latinas are rendered invisible, and stereotypes of Latina and Latino quiescence in formal political institutions and processes are perpetrated. Latinas' broad political repertoire, which has included electoral as well as community activism, is thus diminished.

Sierra and Sosa-Riddell (1994) find that Chicano scholars have reinforced rather than rectified the scholarly neglect or misrepresentation of Latina political experience. Santillan (1988), for example, characterizes Latinas as less interested in politics than Latino men, and women and men of other ethnoracial heritage. Feminist research on women officeholders has also failed to remedy the situation, as it is generally focused on federal and state legislators and/or drawn from large national surveys, which are unable to adequately sample for the experiences of nonwhite women (Carroll and Strimling 1983; Carroll 1991). Hardy-Fanta (1993, 20) remarks, "[r]esearch is conducted on women as a minority group, but *minority women* in politics are less likely to receive attention" (emphasis in original).

Inattention to Latina electoral activism also reinforces a prevailing and false dichotomy between politics as representational politics and grassroots politics. If politics and women's political participation are to be understood in their broadest application, neither electoral nor grassroots politics can be excluded from the equation. While some individuals and/or groups may in fact operate only in electoral realms, and others may entirely eschew representational politics, many groups excluded from formal institutions of political power mount grassroots campaigns to elect representatives who will promote not only their group interests, but also a more participatory model of politics.[1] Commenting on the tendency of scholars to dichotomize between electoral and grassroots activities, and their failure to distinguish between electoral activism for access to political institutions and efforts for more fundamental social change, James Jennings (1992, 32) remarks,

> It is no longer accurate to describe Black leadership and activism along a divided continuum of activism and electoral activity. . . . activists are using and exploring the potential of the electoral arena for social change in America. . . . Presuming that electoral activism is a totally different category from protest activity obscures the vision of how the former has become part of the latter.

This essay presents ongoing research into Latina political empowerment and the links between the various political arenas in which Latinas engage. Emerging from my political ethnography of a California town where Latinas were major political actors in grassroots and representational politics (Takash 1990), the research presented here focuses on the political trajectories of Chicana/Latina elected and appointed officials in California. Providing the first profile ever of Latina officeholders in the United States and their experiences of penetrating formal political office, it allows us to begin constructing a more comprehensive picture of Latina political activity.

Recent scholarship suggests that Latinas perceive politics and power differently than Latinos and also select different kinds of political strategies based on these perceptions (Hardy-Fanta 1993). Whereas Latinos generally define the political as what happens in electoral realms and concentrate their energies within those contexts, Latinas focus on a broader, more participatory politics, which does not, however, exclude mainstream political participation. It is their construction of politics as "connectedness, collectivity, community, and consciousness" that, according to Hardy-Fanta, may provide a more general paradigm of participatory democracy with the potential to challenge institutionalized forms of politics and power. A major question for future research regarding Latinas active in electoral politics is whether they go beyond a traditional political activism that emphasizes access, to embrace a politics of difference that seeks more fundamental changes in existing social and economic relationships. A brief discussion of Latina activists in Watsonville that explores this last issue precedes the presentation of the survey results. The survey findings suggest that in regard to gender issues, the majority of Latina elected officials are indeed part of the vanguard demanding equity between the sexes and between white and nonwhite women.

The profile of Chicana/Latina elected officials provided here is based on a survey conducted from September 1992 to June 1993. Results of this study are limited, as it encompasses only those women serving in California. Nonetheless, the study helps counter stereotypes of Latina and Latino nonparticipation in formal political institutions and processes and Latina disinterest in politics. It also challenges weak but pervasive cultural explanations for the lack of representational parity experienced by Latinos in the United States.[2] Finally, while we have recently come to know much about a few Latina elected officials profiled frequently in the media (Gloria Molina, Los Angeles Board of Supervisors; Miriam Santos, Chicago city treasurer; Lena Guerrero, former Texas state railroad commissioner), we know little about the "average" Latina officeholder.

This research begins to provide answers about Latinas who are in formal positions to effect public policy decisions of consequence to Latino communities and to the broader society. What are Latina elected officials' positions on child care, immigration, noncitizen suffrage, the Equal Rights Amendment, feminism, and the women's movement, among other issues? Are gender, race, culture, and class barriers to their winning office? What influenced these women to seek political office; what political experience did they have, if any, prior to winning office? Can we speak of a distinct Latina politics that differs from that of their non-Latina female and Latino counterparts? Future research should also reveal whether Latina elected representatives indeed have stronger social networks than Latino officeholders; whether they maintain community-based relationships once in office; and, more important, whether they practice a more inclusionary politics that challenges existing arrangements of wealth and power. Findings from the survey follow a short review of the literature on the relationship between traditional electoral and community politics.

The Relationship between Community-Based Activism and Electoral Politics

Although Latino and other nonwhite scholars have long documented their ethnic groups' political histories and advanced theories about their sociopolitical positions in this country (Acuña 1981; Barrera 1979; *Daedalus* 1981; Ruiz 1987), a serious examination of nonwhite electoral politics by mainstream academia is only now emerging; recent work emphasizes coalition politics between nonwhite groups and white liberals (Browning, Marshall, and Tabb 1984, 1990; Uhlaner, Cain, and Kiewiet 1989; Jackson and Preston 1991; Erie and Brackman 1993; Sonenshein 1990). When discussed, community activism and electoral participation are generally depicted as entirely different arenas of political activity (see citations in Jennings 1992, 30). In addition, minority demands for representation are generally equated with their desire for access to the status quo; rarely are they interpreted as movements to change existing relations of power (Jennings 1992, 30).

Browning, Marshall, and Tabb (1984) exemplify the latter proclivity in their comparative study of African American and Latino protest and demand politics and electoral activities in ten northern California cities. While underscoring the importance of protest and demand to minority electoral gains, the authors nonetheless depict these struggles as efforts for access; protest precedes political incorporation, which in turn better ensures greater minority political efficacy: "We know that protest is not enough. Protest alone is not sufficient for representation and the *stronger forms of access and responsiveness.* Something more is needed, and electoral effort is the key. Protest must be translated into electoral organizing" (emphasis added, 1984, 263). Browning et al. document the variability of electoral outcomes in the cities they studied. In regard to Latinos, they underscore the importance of protest and demand activities to the development of Latino leadership and their eventual gains in local government. Dispelled are simplistic theories that Latino political potential depends on the absolute size of their populations. Nonetheless, some of their conclusions about the trajectory of Latino political mobilization remain unsatisfactory, as when they conclude that local Black protest and demand contributed to local Latino protest and finally, to Latino electoral officeholding. Whereas this may be the case in the cities examined by Browning et al., it does not explain successful Latino protest and demand activities followed by significant electoral gains in those cities where the African American population is practically nonexistent.

The authors note that local Black electoral gains did not necessarily follow protest and demand but rather were stimulated by the 1960s national African American civil rights mobilization. Our research in California (Takash and Avila 1989) suggests that not unlike the African American case, a score of local-level political "takeovers" were stimulated by the national Chicano movement, most directly by the United Farm Workers Union (UFW), California Rural Legal Assistance (CRLA), and Chicano student activism. In agricultural towns such as Parlier, Huron, and Orange Cove in the Central Valley, and Colton and Coachella in San Bernadino and Riverside Counties, Latinos wrested power from dominant white city councilmembers from the mid-1960s through mid-1970s. Forming majorities on the city councils at the time, Chicanos have maintained control of these local governments to date. Although Rose (1988) provides an excellent analysis of three types of Latina leadership in the United Farm Workers Union, Latinas' roles as community organizers in these impacted towns are as yet undocumented. We do know that Latinas had also penetrated city council offices in Coachella, Mendota, Colton, and Soledad before 1980. In none of the cities studied by Browning et al. was there more than one Latino council member (1984, 258). It appears that despite the comparative value of their research, the variability of the routes to electoral office for Latinos and Latinas is not entirely captured by the urban cities they examined.[3]

Also absent from Browning, Marshall, and Tabb's study is a gender analysis of the Black and Latino activists whose political careers they followed. Feminist theory posits that where one finds grassroots political activity one finds women activists. Given the authors' focus on protest and demand politics, one might expect women to have emerged in force in their investigation; instead, women are barely mentioned. They do note, however, that a large number of Latino activists developed their leadership positions in federally funded community-based organizations created in the late 1960s and early 1970s. Hardy-Fanta (1993) observes in her Boston research on Latina politics that despite a preponderance of Latinas working in community agencies, Latinos generally became the directors of these organizations, leadership positions from which electoral political careers were launched.

Jennings's (1992) research on the transformation of African American activism more specifically examines how progressive activists try to effect political and economic change through their participation in representational politics. Unlike most scholars, he clearly differentiates between a traditional African American activism for access to established American institutions and that of Black empowerment. To Jennings, Black empowerment is an emerging social movement with the potential to challenge existing relations of power. For examples, he draws on the campaigns of Harold Washington, the late mayor of Chicago, Gus Newport, former mayor of Berkeley, and activists Al Vann in Brooklyn and Mel King in Boston. Although he does not explicitly analyze the participation of Black and other minority women in these empowerment struggles, he did interview a number of African American women and Latinas. Among the latter, Hartford, Connecticut, activist Maria Borrero discussed her initial disregard of representational politics until she realized how government bodies influence housing decisions. Chicago activist Maria Cerda underscored the importance of Harold Washington's vision for an economic and social agenda that eschewed politics as business as usual in order to mobilize minority voters new to, and those long disaffected with, electoral and party politics. Jennings (1992, 18) contends that "[t]he development of a populist economics may be more significant than any change in the racial style of new Black politicians and activists."

While not claiming that minority empowerment now represents a considerable threat to entrenched power and wealth, he does posit an emerging challenge by activists across the country utilizing electoral means to achieve a greater redistribution of wealth and a more participatory politics.

Hardy-Fanta's (1993) recent book on Latino politics in Boston also addresses issues of participatory democracy focusing on the relationship of gender, Latino culture, and Latina political activity. Intending to examine broad nongender-specific questions regarding Latino political participation, Hardy-Fanta (1993, ix) immediately noted that Latino men and women defined the political differently; these differences in perception manifest themselves in Latinas' and Latinos' political strategies and choice of political arenas. Unlike most work, which focuses either on grassroots or electoral politics, Hardy-Fanta's study examines Latinas' participation across both political arenas. Included in the latter are Latinas who are active in party politics, electoral campaigns, voter registration, and get-out-the-vote drives, those who work as legislative aides, and Latinas elected to local office. Still, the bulk of her analysis is based on the political activities and strategies of Latina grassroots activists who are part of *la gente del pueblo* (the "common folk"). These nonelected community representatives, *las alcadesas* (recognized leaders), are able to mobilize large numbers of people around issues confronting the Latino community, an organizing capacity based on interpersonal relationships that connect them to local residents. Telling is her conclusion that "the ability to generate Latino political participation is linked to gender" (1993, 25). When she asked her informants who can best mobilize Latino community members, over 60 percent of those named were women; when she asked who are Boston's Latino reputational leaders, those featured in the media or with official statuses, 60 percent of those mentioned were men. According to Hardy-Fanta (40, 187), it is these women and their politics of connectedness ("connecting people to each other, developing and building on personal relationships, and blending personal ties with political purposes") who offer a prescription for an American politics, today characterized by exclusion rather than participation of the greatest number of people.

Latina Political Mobilization in Watsonville, California

My original research on Watsonville conducted during 1986–89 was not guided by a gender analysis; at the time, I was more interested in how white Americans were responding socioculturally and politically to the fact that they were becoming a numerical minority in that agricultural community (Takash 1990). Watsonville was founded in the mid-1800s by Yankees from the East Coast and European immigrant settlers. Structural changes in agribusiness in the second half of the twentieth century resulted in local growers needing a near year-round agricultural labor force; larger numbers of Mexican families thus settled in and around the city. By 1980, Watsonville was Latinized, Mexican-origin people having come to constitute the majority of the city's population.

Prior to 1988, no Latino had ever been elected to the Watsonville city council despite repeated efforts to do so. From 1971 through 1988, ten Latinos ran for office in the citywide, at-large election system and lost; four of the candidates were women. The entrenched white majority city council was finally ousted from power in December 1989 with the dismantling of at-large elections and implementation of federal court-ordered district elections. The five-year struggle for district elections was spearheaded by a Chicana activist, Cruz Gomez. While firmly rooted in grass-roots politics, she also advocated representational politics and twice ran unsuccessfully for city council. The defeat of a Chicana candidate in 1985 prompted Gomez and other advocates for the Latino community to inquire into legal remedies to an at-large electoral system, which, they contended, structurally discriminated against Latinos. The Mexican American Legal Defense and Education Fund (MALDEF), a national Chicano/Latino civil rights organization, agreed to pursue the case and won it at the federal court level in July 1988 (*Gomez et al. vs. City of Watsonville* 1988). The conservative, majority white city council was displaced in Watsonville's first district elections by a progressive to moderate slate supported by the majority of the Latino community and their liberal to progressive allies. One member of this slate was of Latino origins and is today the mayor of Watsonville.

Latina women were major actors in this election as they had been in earlier Latino and Latina electoral campaigns. Many were politicized in struggles for union representation and wage parity; housing and immigrant rights advocacy; bilingual education and other issues regarding education equity; and voter registration and get-out-the-vote campaigns. During the two-year period I resided in Watsonville, Latinas supplanted male leadership in the local chapter of the League of United Latin American Citizens (LULAC), the only viable Latino organization in the city at the time. Designated a "friend of the court," LULAC formally supported the MALDEF lawsuit and was instrumental in demonstrating community support for the case at critical moments. Outside their participation as LULAC officers, the Latina leadership founded or participated in groups that selected and/or legitimated who they would support as city council candidates, determined what issues would be included in a Latino agenda, and otherwise strategized how best to confront a conservative political order that was unresponsive to the needs of the poor and the Latino community. Two of these women recently won elective office, Rebecca Garcia to the Cabrillo Community College Board and Lucha Ortega to the Hollister Board of Education. A third woman, Celia Organista, has been approached to run for county supervisor but has thus far declined. Arriving in Watsonville over twenty-five years ago to work in the strawberry fields, Organista has since become a recognized community activist whose political influence extends beyond the city.

Watsonville Latinas also predominated in rank-and-file union and strike activities. One thousand one hundred frozen-food workers staged an eighteen-month-long strike (September 1985 to February 1987) against the country's leading frozen-food plants; the majority were Mexicana single heads of households. Gloria Bettancourt, a twenty-three-year veteran frozen-food worker at the time of the Watsonville cannery strike, emerged as a major strike leader; serving on the strike support committee, she was frequently profiled in local and national media. Bettancourt also challenged the majority white, all-male union representatives, running unsuccessfully for president of the Teamsters Local 912 in 1986. Given her high profile during the strike and the mobilization efforts of the strikers and their supporters, Bettancourt was elected to serve as a Jesse Jackson delegate to the 1988 Democratic convention.

Although the MALDEF district elections struggle was viewed by some as the political efforts of professional and middle-class Chicanos, former Mexicana frozen-food strikers were major participants in subsequent district elections. The relationship between popular struggle and elected officialdom was articulated by Bettancourt ("Forward" 1987, 13) during the *huelga* (strike) and prior to the implementation of district elections in Watsonville: "In the upcoming elections we have to unite and vote to give Latinos more representation, because all the people that form the executive board are white, the City Council members. The times we [strikers] have gone there, it has been very noticeable that they see us with great indifference. They don't care about Raza workers."

Cuca Lomeli, another *huelgista* (striker), drew a connection between the power wielded by capitalists and the support they receive from local and extra-local government. She remarked,

> [President] Reagan's support for business can be seen in the strike. . . . Mort Console [former owner of Watsonville Canning Co.] has so much political support. . . . [A]mong the working class . . . another one of the injustices here in the U.S. is that Chicanos and Latinos have always been discriminated against. And the same thing is happening here with the City Council and the politicians. They don't support us . . . if we organized ourselves well . . . perhaps we can change the future in Watsonville. ("Forward" 1987, 13)

During the first district election campaigns in 1989, former strikers mobilized behind strike organizer Oscar Rios to represent working-class Latino interests in a newly created Latino district. Formerly a member of a left-wing, multinational organization, Rios presently serves as mayor of Watsonville; there is some anticipation he will soon run for county or state office.

Clearly not all Latinas and Latinos participating in Watsonville representational politics are interested only in access to local government positions and resources. Just as some LULAC members and other community members pursue a politics to make fundamental changes in the economic and social relationships in their city, frozen-food workers sought representation that potentially could change power relations between those who govern and workers. Latinas have been prominent in all these efforts.

What can we say about California Chicana/Latina officeholders in terms of their participation in both community and representational politics? Interestingly, Latina participation in all manner of political activities as documented in Hardy-Fanta's study and my own ethnography is supported by the survey research. Over 61 percent of the respondents include community activism in their descriptions of their political experiences prior to their first elective or appointed office. Community activism included organizing and/or participating in neighborhood watch programs, anti-graffiti campaigns; serving as board members for nonprofit organizations and on a variety of public school committees; and taking part in actions for housing, environmental, and educational equity. An even greater percentage (68 percent) claim to have participated in political campaign activity prior to their winning office, while only 4 percent state that they had been professional community organizers.

Latina Elected Officials in California: Data and Methodology

The implications of the political experiences of California Latina officeholders and of a host of findings drawn from the survey will be considered in the pages that follow; a profile of California Chicana/Latina elected officials also emerges. My ethnographic field research in Watsonville and in Latino-dominated towns in the California Central Valley informed the development of the questionnaire. The data are based on a survey of 117 forced-response and open-ended questions subsumed under thirteen categories, including background on the most current political office held by the respondents and their past political experiences; individuals and other factors influencing their decisions to run; organizational, occupational network, and political party support of their campaigns; campaign and constituency profiles; potential obstacles to winning office; personal and family characteristics; their position on current issues; and whether they were the first Latina and/or woman to hold their current position. The questionnaire was constructed by myself in consultation with Dr. Adaljiza Sosa-Riddell, coordinator of the Chicana/Latina Research Center at the University of California, Davis, and three women, two Chicanas and a Filipina, active in San Diego city and county politics. It was also adapted to a nationwide survey of women's political routes to office conducted by the Center for the American Woman and Politics, Eagleton Institute of Politics, Rutgers University (Carroll and Strimling 1983).

While findings from the California Chicana/Latina Elected Officials Survey would be more meaningful in the context of all California officeholders, of office-holders in general, and of female elected officials in particular, comparisons are difficult or impossible given the lack of comparative data currently available. The Center for the American Woman and Politics (CAWP) at Rutgers University is perhaps the best research center providing firsthand survey data about women in politics and government. Its nationwide comparison between women and men in elective office (Carroll and Strimling 1983), widely cited and useful in its own right, is not directly applicable to the California Chicana/Latina survey for three reasons. The CAWP survey included men and women serving as state representatives, members of county and local governing boards, and mayors; it does not include elected members of school boards, which account for the bulk of all California Chicana/Latina elected officials and all Latino elected officials in the United States. The CAWP survey results are also over ten years old, based on data from 1980 and 1981. Although it provides a useful baseline regarding women's routes to elective office, the experiences of women and Latinas winning office a decade later may differ given recent breakthroughs in national gender politics.[4] While the CAWP survey sampled all women officeholders in the categories aforementioned, including women of color in proportion to their numbers of female elected representatives, the fact that fewer Latinas held elective office ten years ago also dilutes the comparative value of the former survey. More important, the CAWP survey did not ask questions to determine the role of race and culture in the women of color candidates' political experiences, their decisions to run, and their campaigns, among other issues.[5] Data comparable to that generated by the California Latina survey regarding Latino males' routes to elective office at the state or national levels do not yet exist; gender differences within the Latino elected officials population are thus impossible or difficult to ascertain. In those instances where data are available or suggestive, comparisons are drawn.

The questionnaire was mailed in September 1992 to all Chicanas/Latinas elected or appointed to office in California listed in the 1991 National Roster of Hispanic Elected Officials and to an additional eight Latinas who won office in April 1992, for a total of 150 persons. Follow-up telephone calls were made at two- and four-month intervals, and a second mailing was sent to all nonrespondents to encourage them to return the survey. The resulting response rate was 50.6 percent, or seventy-six responses.[6]

This is the first study of its kind about Latina officeholders. We believe our focus on California is warranted given the scrutiny women running for office in this state received in 1992, which had been proclaimed the "Year of the Woman." The Boxer and Feinstein U.S. senatorial races and victories captured the attention of the nation. Lucille Roybal-Allard became the first Chicana elected to the U.S. House of Representatives, and four Chicanas won California State Assembly seats. The latter have created a greater female presence in the California Latino Legislative Caucus (a ratio of four women to eleven men); prior to their election only two women were members of this body, but never at the same time. A score of Latinas at the municipal level also joined the ranks of Latinos serving at other levels of government. Again, while we believe the findings to be significant, they may not be generalizable to Latina officials in other states or to Latinas in regions where non–Mexican-origin Latinos predominate.

California Chicana/Latina Elected Officials Profile

Despite the substantial gains made by Latino officeholders in the past decade, they hold less than 1 percent (4,994) of all elected offices in the United States (504,404); women constitute 17.5 percent of the national total of elected officials (NALEO 1992, vii, ix). Proportionally, more Latinas serve as elected officials than women in general, accounting for 30 percent of all Latino officeholders (NALEO 1992, ix). Nonetheless, Latinas remain underrepresented in all levels of government, especially at the federal and statewide levels. Ileana Ros-Lehtinen (R-FL), the first Latina elected to Congress in 1989, was recently joined by two others in November 1992, Nydia Velazquez (D-NY) and Lucille Roybal-Allard (D-CA). Constituting less than 1 percent (.05 percent) of the fifty-four women in the 103rd U.S. Congress, Latinas together with other women of color (African American and Asian American) number fourteen, or 26 percent of all Congresswomen currently in office (CAWP 1993). Women of color make up 13 percent (202) of the 1,517 woman state legislators, with Latinas accounting for twenty-seven, or .01 percent, of this body. Only one Latina holds a statewide elective executive office (New Mexico secretary of state Stephanie

Gonzales) out of seventy-two women in these positions (CAWP 1993). Nationally, Latinas serve mainly as county and school board representatives, while in California, the overwhelming majority (140 of 197) are school board trustees (NALEO 1992). In the past year, California Latinas have made gains in municipal offices, rising from thirty-three in 1992 to forty-two in 1993 (NALEO 1992).

What are the general demographic characteristics of the "average" Latina office-holder in California? The majority of our seventy-six respondents were born in California (64 percent), are of Mexican origins (68 percent), are second-generation, which we defined as U.S.-born, daughter of immigrants (51 percent), and Catholic (71 percent). Most stated that they had spoken English and Spanish (36 percent) or only Spanish (35 percent) in their childhood homes but identified English (53 percent) as their major language today. Thirty-six percent of the Latina officeholders surveyed are between the ages of forty and forty-nine; 76 percent are forty or over. The majority are married (78 percent) and mothers of children over eighteen (52 percent).

Almost 100 percent of the California Latina elected officials are of working-class origins. The majority identified their fathers' occupations as laborers, construction workers, gardeners, and agricultural workers; and their mothers' occupations as housewives or service sector workers. While 72 percent of the women surveyed have experienced greater occupational mobility than their parents, most (41 percent) are in nonexecutive professions such as teaching (K-12), real estate, and social work. A full 45 percent work in educational settings. In terms of formal education, 39 percent are credentialed at the bachelor of arts and sciences level or above. More respondents (33 percent) reported an annual family income of $50,000–$75,000, although almost as many (28 percent) have incomes falling between $25,001 and $50,000. Given their working-class origins, these elected officials may introduce policy perspectives more responsive to the needs of poor and working-class people; an analysis of policy enacted by Latina officeholders is needed, however, before this correlation can be substantiated.

Only 15 percent of the respondents were born in a country other than the United States, 16 percent of Latin American origins other than Mexican. Another 16 percent identified themselves as Latinas of mixed heritage, the majority being white and Latina. Foreignborn, naturalized Latina officeholders (first-generation) accounted for 18 percent of the total. Thirty percent are third-generation (or more) Americans of Latino origins. Few respondents are Protestant (10.6 percent); just as many (10.6 percent) identified themselves as having faiths other than Catholicism or Protestantism, while 8 percent claimed to have no religion. Interestingly, fewer Latinas who were monolingual English speakers as children (27 percent) have become elected officials. Forty-four percent remain bilingual Spanish and English speakers.

In regard to education, more Latina representatives (22.3 percent) identified themselves as having "some college" (less than an associate arts degree); those with master's degrees (21 percent) made up the next largest category of the highest level of education achieved by these women. Most fell into the higher-income brackets, 61.6 percent having family incomes from $50,000 to $100,001 and above. As 56.5

percent are not compensated above $500 for their public office service, 14 percent receiving no compensation, the ability of low-income Latinas to hold elective office is likely to be impaired. It may be instructive to investigate how those Latina officials whose family incomes fall between $10,000 and $25,000 (9.5 percent) afford serving in these positions.

Gloria Molina's election to the Los Angeles County Board of Supervisors in 1991 captured the attention of the country, not only because she became the first woman ever to win a seat on that body, but also because she is the first person of Mexican heritage in this century to hold this powerful office. Like Molina, the majority (68.6 percent) of the women surveyed are the first Latinas to serve in the positions they now hold; 15 percent report being the first woman in their office as well. One respondent quipped that while she was neither the first Latina nor woman on the city council, she was the first pregnant mayor the city had ever had!

Ninety-four percent of the representatives were elected, not appointed, to their current positions; 50 percent of them served in these positions for two or more terms. While the majority ran in nonpartisan elections, California Latina officeholders overwhelmingly identify themselves as Democrats (82.4 percent), as do their male counterparts and 92 percent of Hispanic elected officials nationwide (NALEO 1992, x). Latinas' strong Democratic Party affiliation also corresponds with that of women of color serving in federal or state legislative elected positions; numbering 202, or 13.3 percent of 1,517 women state legislators in the country, only six, or 2.9 percent, are non-Democrats. Put another way, 97 percent of the women of color holding federal and statewide offices are members of the Democratic Party (CAWP 1993).

Single-member district elections enhance minority candidates' chances for success at the polls (Grofman and Davidson 1992; Fraga 1993a), yet the majority of California cities have at-large electoral systems. Racially polarized voting practices, where the electorate votes for candidates of their own race, are also well documented in this state (*Gomez et al.* vs. *City of Watsonville* 1988). Nonetheless, over 67 percent of the Latinas surveyed ran and won in at-large elections. Importantly, although 60.3 percent reported having majority Latino constituencies, 74.2 percent are dependent on white voting electorates.

This circumstance may have implications for the ability of Latina officeholders to adequately respond to the needs of their nonwhite constituents and for Latina candidates to be seen as willing and/or able to represent the needs of non-Latino voters. Responding to a question about ethnic barriers faced by the candidates, several women cited the latter problem. One said, "I was the first elected Mexican woman to the —— city council. They were concerned that I would be only for Latinos and [I] had to reinforce that I would work for all constituents." A second remarked, "My many years of being involved in local Chicano organizations was used against me as being a one issue candidate, only concerned about Hispanics."

In terms of political experience prior to winning their current position, 64 percent had never before held elective or appointive office; 84.5 percent never served on the staff of an elected public official.[7] Sixty-eight percent had, however, participated in political campaign work, and 61 percent claimed community activism. Seventy percent had served as board members of local organizations, 33.7 percent as local and extralocal commissioners, and 55.8 percent had received awards in recognition of their community service. California Latina officeholders also gained political experience in non-Latina women's organizations (43 percent) and in Latino organizations (40 percent); fewer claimed having gained political experience in Latina organizations (26.3 percent).

Of the women's organizations to which these Latinas belong, the National Women's Political Caucus was mentioned most frequently, followed by the National Organization for Women, and third, the Comisíon Femeníl Méxicana. Nonetheless, the majority of Latinas (53.9 percent) claimed that women's groups had not supported their first bids for office. This may be interpreted as a greater neglect by non-Latina women's organizations than by Latina groups, as the women participate in the former to a greater extent. At least one respondent, however, did mention Latina nonsupport in her written comments: "[M]y only regret is that I *can't* say that Latina Groups helped me" (emphasis in original). The majority (61 percent) also claim that their major role model was not a woman.

Carroll (1991, 64) states, "Without the strategy of women helping women, there undoubtedly would be fewer women holding office at the state and other levels of government." The general lack of support for California Latina candidates may also be explained by the fact that the majority ran in local-level elections, while national women's organizations, which do provide financial and other means of support, tend to focus on state and federal campaigns. At these levels, Carroll (1991) finds that women candidates have received considerable support from women's and feminist organizations and political action committees. For women of color candidates, some change appears to be imminent; several women's groups such as the National Women's Political Caucus have recently committed themselves to supporting women of color candidates both in terms of preparing them to run (candidate workshops) and in extending campaign funds to local-level contests. In California, a statewide political action committee, Latina PAC, was founded recently specifically to support Latina candidates. One community college trustee states, "I was helped by Latina PAC — the moral support that they gave me was more profound than the money; I mean, the money really mattered, but the fact that these women wanted to see me in that position and were willing to give me some of their resources . . ."

Few (14.4 percent) California Latina officeholders report being raised in a political family. In response to a question about the one most important event, factor, or influence leading them to run the first time for office, more (22.2 percent) claimed a dissatisfaction with politics or incumbent politicians; almost as many (20.3 percent) claimed a "general concern with social change." Ideologically, 44.5 percent call themselves politically middle-of-the-road (moderate), while 37.7 percent describe themselves as liberal or very liberal.

Barriers to Elective Office: Ethnicity, Class, Sexuality, Ideology, Gender, and Money

Zavella (1988, 202) reminds feminist theorists that the totality of women's experience must be taken into account, as nonwhite women "experience gender, class and racial statuses concurrently." The Latina officeholders surveyed, while successfully surmounting these and other systemic barriers to traditional politics, nonetheless provide evidence of obstacles faced by women candidates and barriers unique to Latinas and other women of color seeking political office. We asked the women if a Latina's ethnicity, class, and gender may present obstacles to her winning elective office. Although many answered "no" to ethnicity (40 percent), class (42.4 percent), and gender (39.4 percent), the majority answered "yes" or "somewhat" (ethnicity, 60 percent; class, 56 percent; gender, 60.5 percent). In regard to racial discrimination, women wrote, "I am the first and only person in the entire community who is Latino and who has ever been elected to office at any level — Race is an issue"; "Many whites don't know how to treat a Mexican in a high power position, [u]sually attitudes were condescending or inappropriate"; and "I was opposed by the old white political machine." Still others commented that their competency was questioned because of their race and gender, charges they met by having to be more prepared than other candidates. They remarked, "The same way a woman doing 'a man's job' has to prove herself and show she is better than the average, a minority person has to do the same"; "I needed to be more dynamic, well-educated on all issues, . . . understand the perception of the Anglo culture — Be above all candidates"; and "I had to be better informed and work harder than male candidates."

We also asked whether they themselves had to overcome any of these barriers in their own campaigns, and here included the dimensions of sexual orientation and political ideology. While many claimed to have encountered ethnic (46 percent) and gender (41 percent) barriers during their campaigns, the majority did not (ethnicity, 53.9 percent; gender, 58.9 percent). Eighty-one percent said that their class presented no obstacle to getting elected, nor had their sexual orientation (88 percent) or political ideology (72.3 percent). The women who answered affirmatively in regard to the latter dimension most often describe themselves as liberal or very liberal. One woman who describes herself as "middle-of-the-road" remarked that because she is Latina she was "associated with being too liberal/radical."

The lack of financial resources for campaign costs may discourage women from seeking elective office especially at the state and federal levels; women state legislators claimed that knowing that sufficient campaign funds were forthcoming significantly affected their decision to run (Carroll and Strimling 1983, 8–9). While most (49 percent) of the Latina representatives' campaigns cost a maximum of $5,000, reflecting local political races, 46 percent of the women stated that the assurance of having sufficient financial resources was very or somewhat important to their decision to seek office. Interestingly, 42 percent won their bids for elective office despite their opponents' outspending them. The candidates' working-class origins and/or the class status of their constituents may affect their ability to raise sufficient campaign funds. One woman stated, "Trying to raise money was a difficult experience. Also, I have only a high school diploma. No university experience." Another Latina officeholder noted, "the working poor have a difficult time being able to make contributions [for] a person running for office. If you come from a working poor background you must seek support outside your community. Not every candidate can do that."

Impact of Child-Rearing Responsibilities on Latina Elected Officials

Cultural and societal expectations are such that Latinas and women in general still bear the largest responsibility for the welfare of the family and children. Many Latina elected officials express feelings of guilt, of neglecting their parental and familial duties, even when their children are grown but remain at home. At a recent session on Latinas and policy making sponsored by the Congressional Hispanic Caucus Institute in Washington, D.C., San Diego Community College district president Maria Nieto Senour confessed having put off her political career until her children were grown. She continued, "I think we need to address that emotional bind that we as women are all in . . . all of us want to do the right thing all the time, and the right thing is to serve our community and to live up to our talents and our abilities, but the right thing is also to nurture our children and to make sure they're o.k., . . . or is it? So we have to keep weighing these things for ourselves and those are very real for us as women."

Most Latina officeholders are forty to fifty-nine years old; the majority of all respondents stated that they have children over eighteen. Not surprisingly then, 22.3 percent responded that a question about child care arrangements was not applicable to them, while 38 percent stated that their children are old enough to take care of themselves. Carroll (1991, 61) reports that for elected officials in general, "women were less likely than men to be under forty or over sixty," suggesting that women wait until their children are older or grown before making their first bids for political office. Telling is the finding that male elected officials are more likely to have younger children than are women officeholders (Carroll and Strimling 1983, 27–28).

A significant number of California Latina elected officials (42 percent), nonetheless, have children under eighteen; the majority (64.5 percent) have children between the ages of six and eleven. For these women, child care is an immediate issue. Twenty-six percent reported that having satisfactory child care arrangements was "very important" to their decision to run for the office they now hold; 11 percent noted that it was "somewhat important." Of the ten options for child care arrangements listed in the survey, most use a battery of arrangements, reporting more frequently that parents or other relatives (older children) care for young children, that they have a cooperative arrangement with a spouse, and/or that they use day care facilities. Only five women claim that their spouses take care of the children most of the time. When we asked the Latina officeholders whether we had failed to ask any questions they thought important, one councilwoman suggested, "[s]ome questions regarding the sacrifices in running or being in public office need to be studied. *Latinas' commitment to familia is really tested*" (emphasis added). Of potential importance for public policy related to child care, 55 percent of the Latina officeholders describe themselves as advocating more governmental responsibility for providing child care services and tax incentives; another 1.1 percent advocate more governmental and private sector responsibility for child care.

Views on Issues: Feminism, the Women's Movement, and Abortion

Latina officeholders obviously must contend with issues that are not gender-specific. Lucille Roybal-Allard's (D-CA) appointment to the Committee on Small Business and Subcommittee on Consumer Credit and Insurance, and Congresswoman Nydia Velazquez's (D-NY) appointment to the Banking Committee are evidence of Latina legislators' interest in and capacity to develop policy about nongender-specific problems. While the women surveyed were asked questions regarding nongender-specific issues faced by their communities and American society at large, space constraints prevent a full disclosure of these responses at this time. As gender and participatory democracy are the underlying themes in this article, California Latina officeholders' views on abortion, feminism, the women's movement, immigration, and noncitizen suffrage are considered in the remaining pages.

Women of color often evaluate American feminism and the women's movement as white and middle-class, and as having failed to consider the dimensions of class and race faced by the majority of nonwhite women (Pesquera and Segura 1993; Cordova et al. 1986; DuBois and Ruiz 1990; Moraga and Anzaldúa 1981). Seventy-five percent of the Latina representatives surveyed stated that many issues faced by women of color are different from those faced by white women. Sixty-seven percent strongly agreed or agreed with the statement, "In general, the women's movement has failed to respond adequately to issues affecting women of color." Nonetheless, to assume that all Latinas are neither feminists nor supportive of agendas that address gender discrimination is to misread this population (Pesquera and Segura 1993). Fifty-eight percent of the Latina officeholders strongly agreed that the Equal Rights Amendment should be ratified; another 19.4 percent agreed with that statement. While most of the Latina respondents state that they do not call themselves feminists (51.3 percent), the overwhelming majority (84.2 percent) still claim to support feminist goals. Here, how the question was asked bears some mention. Knowing from the ethnographic evidence that many women of color are, in their actions, supportive of feminist goals despite their rejection of the label feminist, we presented the question to reflect that reality along with several other possible responses. We asked, "In regard to feminism, how do you describe yourself?" Forced-response categories included (a) I call myself a feminist; (b) I am somewhat ambivalent about feminism, do not call myself a feminist but support many of the issues feminists advocate; (c) I do not call myself a feminist and do not support most of the issues feminists advocate; and, (d) other circumstance. Again, the majority (51.3 percent) chose (b), while another 32.8 percent unequivocally describe themselves as feminists. Less than 12 percent of the women state they do not support feminist agendas.

Latinas are also often portrayed as opposed to abortion rights because of the large number who identify their religion as Catholic. In posing this question to the California Latina representatives, we again provided more possible responses than merely affirming or negating legalized abortion. We asked, "In regard to abortion rights, how do you describe yourself?" Possible answers included (a) I support a woman's right to make her own choice; (b) I support a woman's right to make her own choice, although personally I may not consider abortion a viable alternative for myself; (c) I do not support a woman's decision to have an abortion, except in the cases of rape, incest and/or when the life of the mother is clearly endangered; (d) there should be a constitutional amendment to prohibit abortion under all circumstances; and (e), other position. Interestingly, more women (42 percent) selected (a); less surprising, 39 percent chose (b). Despite Latina elected officials' personal beliefs about abortion, 81 percent support a woman's right to make her own decision in regard to an unplanned pregnancy.

Views on Issues: Immigration and Noncitizen Suffrage

Mexico accounts for the largest proportion of all immigration to the United States; augmented by immigrants and migrants from other Latin American countries, immigration is a concern to Latino policy makers. Given the current tendency to blame immigrants for many of the social and economic ills faced by the country, we attempted to discern Latina officeholders' support or nonsupport for recent immigrants by asking whether immigrants use more public funds and resources than they contribute to their local communities. While a significant number (28 percent) agree with that statement, more (34.3 percent) disagree. An even greater number (37.3 percent), however, remain neutral on this subject or state that they do not know.

Numerous economic studies of the 1980s established that immigrants and undocumented workers contribute more in taxes than they extract in services (McCarthy and Valdez 1986; Borjas and Tienda 1985; Bean et al. 1987; Tienda 1988; Hinojosa-Ojeda et al. 1992). Recent studies, however, suggest that local governments bear a disproportionate share of the social costs for this population, as the greater proportion of immigrant wages ends up in federal coffers (ISD Report 1992; Parker and Rea 1993). In light of this information, officials agreeing that immigrants use more public funds than they contribute may or may not be reflecting an anti-immigrant position. Liberals and conservatives are presently calling on the federal government to return monies collected from immigrants to those communities rich in immigrant settlers and poor in revenues. Perhaps more revealing of their position about legal and/or undocumented immigrants would be a question asking whether recent immigrants and/or undocumented persons should be denied access to health, education, and other social amenities.

Enfranchisement of noncitizens, especially in school board and city elections, is here interpreted as support for a more democratic participatory politics. Proponents of noncitizen suffrage argue persuasively that the "hard currency" of political efficacy is the vote; without it, the needs of noncitizen communities are frequently ignored (Raskin 1993; Raskin n.d.; Aviva Shimmelman 1992, 1). Raskin (1993, 452) remarks, "The federal Civil Rights Commission recently documented the District of Columbia's dreadful neglect of the social needs of its heavily alien Latino population. . . . It is widely believed that this official malign neglect is only possible because of the alien community's political marginality."[8]

We asked the California Latina elected officials whether, in regard to extending voting rights to resident noncitizens, they would support noncitizens voting in school board elections if they had children in school; in all local elections in the community in which they live; in all local, state, and national elections; or whether they do not support noncitizen suffrage. The majority (51.3 percent) state that they do not support noncitizen suffrage; 24 percent support noncitizens voting in school board elections only. A mere 5 percent are willing to extend voting rights to noncitizens in all local elections; another 5 percent opine that resident noncitizens should be allowed to vote in elections at all levels of government. It appears that on this measure of a more inclusionary polity, Latina officeholders more closely resemble those who define formal democratic political participation as a right limited to citizens.

While the literature reinforces the notion that electoral politics and community politics are entirely different arenas of activity, Latinas in California and elsewhere demonstrate the relationship between the two. The majority of this generation of California Latina elected officials gain political experience through their participation in community activism and by working in electoral campaigns. Hardy-Fanta (1993, 192) observes, "[a] more participatory vision of politics does not in any way preclude support for the electoral side of politics."

The survey findings also suggest that in regard to gender, the majority of Latina elected officials will challenge existing gender relationships as well as racial inequality between nonwhite and white women. Less clear is whether a Latina politics of "connectedness, collectivity, community, and consciousness" is entirely transferred to electoral realms, if California Latina officeholders' position on noncitizen suffrage is any kind of indicator. While at the grassroots level a Latina model of participatory democracy transcends legal and social norms of who can participate politically (Hardy-Fanta 1993, 100–102), few Latina (or Latino) elected officials in California have yet to imagine an electorate expanded to facilitate the participation of noncitizens in local-level representational politics beyond accepted naturalization and voter registration efforts.

Obviously, other issues of import compete for attention, the response to which must also be included in any assessment of whether Latina representatives practice a politics of difference. While the majority of Latina officeholders support feminist agendas and may be expected to promote legislation on women's rights, they express more concern with issues facing the Latino community as a whole, such as employment, access to education and retention, and safe neighborhoods, issues largely stemming from institutionalized racism and classicism. Fraga (1993b, 18) remarks, "[a]cross the nation the experience of Latinos much more closely approximates the experience of African Americans than it does that of women."

A comprehensive examination of nonwhite elected officials requires a race, class, and cultural analysis in addition to a gender analysis. In-depth interviews and research on actual policy decisions taken by Latina officeholders are needed, as are comparative studies of politics practiced by Latinos and non-Latina women and men, if we are to further substantiate claims of a distinctive Latina electoral politics.

NOTES

I would like to thank all the California Latina officeholders who took the time from their very busy schedules to participate in this study. Thanks also to the staff at the Center for the American Woman and Politics, particularly Lucy Baruch, who have at all times been generous with their data. My colleagues Ada Sosa-Riddell and Patricia Zavella provided cogent advice regarding the Latina elected officials project and valuable comments on this essay. To all my student research assistants, especially Maria Soto and Ivonne Avila, who readily assisted me with mailings, phone calls, and data entry — *mil gracias*. Funding for this research was made available by a University of California San Diego Academic Senate Research Grant.

1. Several ethnographies examine Latino social movements in the United States in which activists are engaged in both grassroots mobilization and electoral activities. Foley et al. (1988) examine the Mexicano community's "takeover" of local government in a Texas Winter Garden town. An agricultural region known for its fertility, it proved fertile ground for the formation of a third party, La Raza Unida Party, which challenged entrenched Texas Democratic party politics in the 1960s and early 1970s. Trujillo (1993a) recounts La Raza Unida mobilization in Crystal City, the party's birthplace, its foray there into school board politics, and bilingual/bicultural education struggles from 1969 to 1989. While neither he nor Foley et al. focus on Latina political mobilization, Trujillo claims women were active participants in La Raza Unida, having refused at the outset an inferior role as a women's auxiliary (personal communication, September 1993). For a more comprehensive review of the anthropological study of U.S. Latino politics, see Menchaca (1993).

2. See Erie and Brackman's (1993, 16) discussion of the "cultural importation" theory.

3. Takash and Avila (1989) also identified six California urban/suburban cities in which Latinos dominated the city councils. San Fernando (pop. 17,731) was 69 percent Latino. La Raza Unida was very active in this town during the 1970s and 1980s, one of its members eventually becoming mayor of the town. The largest one, Pico Rivera (pop. 53,459), was 71 percent Latino.

4. Here I am thinking of the discernable change in the national political climate in regard to gender politics and women running for office. A national survey of all women officeholders conducted today would come after a vice presidential bid by Geraldine Ferraro (1984), a presidential bid by Patricia Schroeder (1988), and the Anita Hill-Clarence Thomas Senate Judiciary Committee confirmation hearings (1991). The latter event is credited with catapulting the issue of gender representational inequity before a national audience and galvanizing an unprecedented number of women across the country, not only to run for elective office, but also to contribute financially to women's campaigns. Witt, Paget, and Matthews (1993) state in their recent book, *Running as a Woman*, "[b]ut we were sensing something new in 1990. Not numbers, but a new level of confidence among women candidates. A new sense of legitimacy and entitlement. Gone was the old defensive posture."

5. CWAP did conduct a study of African American women officeholders in 1981, which provided comparative data for black and white women representatives. While some race-specific features are explored, the researchers noted that they did not ask certain questions that would have been included in a study focused on Black political participation (Carroll and Strimling 1983, 142).

6. The 1991 NALEO roster lists 163 Latina elected officials in California. Eight women identified themselves to us as white American married to Latino men; three women were

listed twice. We thus subtracted 11 from the NALEO count for a total of 152. Another 10 women could not be located; we thus also subtracted them from the total number of Latinas to be surveyed. With the eight women winning office in April 1992, the total number of Latinas surveyed is 150.

7. Generalizing from a California study of minority officeholders in the state congressional delegation and Los Angeles City Council (Guerra 1991), Witt et al. (1993, 111) conclude that two-thirds of California male and female minority elected officials served as aides to politicians prior to running for local or state office. Our findings demonstrate that this is not the case for the average Latina officeholder, underscoring the need to broaden our research inquiries from a focus on megalopolis (Los Angeles) and state-level politics.

8. In 1991, voting rights were extended to noncitizen residents of Takoma Park, Maryland, home to a large number of Central Americans. Any parent, regardless of their voter registration or citizenship statuses, may vote in New York City community school board elections as long as they have children in the school system. In 1993, the New York State Assembly Task Force on New Immigrants introduced a bill to the State Assembly to allow municipalities to grant the vote to noncitizen legal residents.

REFERENCES CITED

Acuña, Rodolfo. 1981. *Occupied America: A History of Chicanos.* 2d ed. New York: Harper and Row.

Aviva Shimmelman, Wendy. 1992. "Local Voting Rights for Non-U.S. Citizen Immigrants in New York City: A Report Prepared for the Center for Immigrant Rights."

Barrera, Mario. 1979. *Race and Class in the Southwest: A Theory of Racial Inequality.* Notre Dame: University of Notre Dame Press.

Bean, Frank D., B. Linsay Lowell, and Lowell J. Taylor. 1987. "Undocumented Mexican Immigrants and the Earnings of Other Workers in the United States." *Demography* 25 (1): 35–52.

Bookman, Ann and Sandra Morgen, eds. 1988. *Women and the Politics of Empowerment.* Philadelphia: Temple University Press.

Borjas, George J., and Marta Tienda, eds. 1985. *Hispanics in the U.S. Economy.* Orlando, FL: Academic Press.

Browning, Rufus P., Dale Rogers Marshall, and David H. Tabb. 1984. *Protest Is Not Enough: The Struggle of Blacks and Hispanics for Equality in Urban Politics.* Berkeley: University of California Press.

———. 1990. *Racial Politics in American Cities.* White Plains, NY: Longman.

Carroll, Susan J. 1991. "Women in State Elective Office: Problems, Strategies, and Impact." In *Women, Black, and Hispanic State Elected Leaders,* ed. Susan J. Carroll, 55–74. New Brunswick, NJ: Eagleton Institute of Politics, Rutgers University.

Carroll, Susan, and Wendy Strimling. 1983. *Women's Routes to Elective Office.* New Brunswick, NJ: Center for the American Woman and Politics.

Center for the American Woman and Politics (CAWP). 1993. "Women of Color in Elective Office 1993: Congress, Statewide, State Legislature, Fact Sheet." Rutgers University, New Brunswick, NJ.

Cordova, Teresa, et al. 1986. *Chicana Voices: Intersections of Class, Race, and Gender.* Austin: Center for Mexican American Studies Publications.

Daedalus, Journal of the American Academy of Arts and Sciences. 1981. Issue on American Indians, Blacks, Chicanos, and Puerto Ricans. 110 (2).

DuBois, Ellen Carol, and Vicki L. Ruiz, eds. 1990. *Unequal Sisters: A Multicultural Reader in U.S. Women's History.* New York: Routledge.

Erie, Stephen P., and Harold Brackman. 1993. "Paths to Political Incorporation for Latinos and Asian Pacifics in California." California Poilcy Seminar, University of California.

Foley, Douglas E., with C. Mota, D. Post, and I. Lozano. 1988. *From Peones to Politicos: Class and Ethnicity in a South Texas Town, 1900–1987.* Austin: University of Texas Press.

"Forward. Round-Table Discussion with the Watsonville Workers." 1987. *Journal of Socialist Thought* 7 (11): 3–25.

Fraga, Louis. 1993a. "Latinos in State Elective Office: Progressive Inclusion in Critical Perspective." In *Women, Black, and Hispanic State Elected Leaders,* ed. Susan J. Carroll, 99–104. New Brunswick, NJ: Eagleton Institute of Politics, Rutgers University.

————. 1993b. "Panel on Women, Black, and Hispanics in State Elective Office." In *Women, Black, and Hispanic State Elected Leaders,* ed. Susan J. Carroll, 15–31. New Brunswick, NJ: Eagleton Institute of Politics, Rutgers University.

Gomez et al. vs. City of Watsonville. 1988. Opinion No. 87 1751 DC No. CV-85-20319 WAI: Appeal from the United States District Court for the Northern District of California, William A. Ingram, Presiding. Argued and submitted 15 January 1988, San Francisco, CA before Alfred T. Goodwin and Dorothy W. Nelson, Circuit Judges, and Earl B. Gilliam, District Judge (27 July).

Grofman, Bernard, and Chandler Davidson. 1992. *Controversies in Minority Voting: The Voting Rights Act in Perspective.* Washington, DC: Brookings Institute.

Guerra, Fernando. 1991. "The Emergence of Ethnic Officeholders in California." In *Racial and Ethnic Politics in California,* ed. Byran O. Jackson and Michael B. Preston, 117–31. Berkeley: IGS Press.

Hardy-Fanta, Carol. 1993. *Latina Politics, Latino Politics: Gender, Culture, and Political Participation in Boston.* Philadelphia: Temple University Press.

Hinojosa-Ojeda, Raul, Sherman Robinson, and Goetz Wolff. 1992. "The Impact of a North American Free Trade Agreement on California: A Summary of Key Research Findings." Lewis Center for Regional Policy Studies. UCLA Working Paper no. 3.

Internal Service Department (ISD) Report. 1992. "Impact of Undocumented and Other Immigrants on Costs, Revenues and Services in Los Angeles County." Los Angeles County Board of Supervisors, 6 November.

Jackson, Byran O., and Michael B. Preston. 1991. *Racial and Ethnic Politics in California.* Berkeley: IGS Press.

Jennings, James. 1992. *The Politics of Black Empowerment: The Transformation of Black Activism in Urban America.* Detroit: Wayne State University Press.

McCarthy, Kevin, and R. Burciaga Valdez. 1986. *Current and Future Effects of Mexican Immigration in California.* Santa Monica, CA: Rand Corporation.

Menchaca, Martha. 1993. Latino Political Attitudes and Behavior in Five Neighborhoods. In *Barrio Ballots: Latino Politics in the 1990 Elections,* ed. Rudolfo de la Garza and Louis DeSipio. Boulder: Westview.

Mora, Magdalena, and Adelaida Del Castillo, eds. 1980. *Mexican Women in the United States: Struggles Past and Present.* Los Angeles: Chicano Studies Research Center, UCLA.

Moraga, Cherríe, and Gloria Anzaldúa. 1981. *This Bridge Called My Back: Writings by Radical Women of Color.* New York: Kitchen Table Press.

Morgen, Sandra, and Ann Bookman. 1988. "Rethinking Women and Politics: An Introductory Essay." In *Women and the Politics of Empowerment*, ed. Ann Bookman and Sandra Morgen, 3–29. Philadelphia: Temple University Press.

NALEO. 1991. *National Roster of Hispanic Elected Officials*. Washington, DC: NALEO Educational Fund.

———. 1992. *National Roster of Hispanic Elected Officials*. Washington, DC: NALEO Educational Fund.

Pardo, Mary. 1990. "Mexican American Women Grassroots Community Activists: 'Mothers of East Los Angeles.' " *Frontiers* 11 (1): 1–7.

Parker, Richard, and Louis Rea. 1993. "Illegal Immigration in San Diego County: An Analysis of Costs and Revenues." Report to the California State Senate Special Committee on Border Issues. September.

Pesquera, Beatriz M., and Denise A. Segura. 1993. "There Is No Going Back: Chicanas and Feminism." In *Chicana Critical Issues*, ed. Norma Alarcon et al., 95–115. Berkeley: Third Woman Press.

Raskin, Jamin B. 1993. "Time to Give Aliens the Vote (Again)." *Nation*, April 5.

———. n.d. "Legal Aliens, Local Citizens: The Historical, Constitutional and Theoretical Meanings of Alien Suffrage." Unpublished manuscript.

Rose, Margaret E. 1988. "Women in the United Farm Workers: A Study of Chicana and Mexicana Participation in a Labor Union, 1950–1980." Unpublished dissertation, University of California, Santa Barbara.

Ruiz, Vicki L. 1987. *Cannery Women/Cannery Lives: Mexican Women, Unionization, and the California Food Processing Industry, 1930–1950*. Albuquerque: University of New Mexico Press.

Santillan, Richard. 1988. "The Latino Community in State and Congressional Redistricting: 1961–1985." In *Latinos and the Political System*, ed. F. Chris Garcia, 467–79. Notre Dame: University of Notre Dame Press.

Sierra, Christine Mane, and Adaljiza Sosa-Riddell. 1994. "Chicanas as Political Actors: Rare Literature, Complex Practice." *National Political Science Review* 4:297–317.

Sonenshein, Raphael J. 1990. "Biracial Coalitions in Big Cities: Why They Succeed, Why They Fail." In *Racial Politics in American Cities*, ed. Rufus P. Browning, Dale Rogers Marshall, and David H. Tabb, 193–211. White Plains, NY: Longman.

Takash, Paule Cruz. 1990. "A Crisis of Democracy: Community Responses to the Latinization of a California Town Dependent on Immigrant Labor." Unpublished dissertation, Department of Anthropology, University of California, Berkeley.

Takash, Paule Cruz, and Joaquin Avila. 1989. "Latino Political Participation in Rural California." Working Paper no. 8. Davis: California Institute for Rural Studies.

Tienda, Marta. 1988. "Looking to 1990: Immigration, Inequality, and the Mexican Origin People in the United States." *Ethnic Affairs* (2): 1–22.

Thompson, E. P. 1963. *The Making of the English Working Class*. London: V. Gollanez.

Trujillo, Armando L. 1993a. "Community Empowerment and Bilingual/Bicultural Education: A Study of the Movimiento in a South Texas Community." Unpublished dissertation, Department of Anthropology, University of Texas, Austin.

——— (1993b). Personal telephone communication. September 15.

Uhlaner, Carole, Bruce Cain, and D. Roderick Kiewiet. 1989. "Political Participation of Ethnic Minorities in the 1980s." *Political Behavior II* (September): 195–231.

Witt, Linda, Karen M. Paget, and Glenna Matthews. 1993. *Running as a Woman: Gender and Power in American Politics*. New York: Free Press.

Wolf, Eric R. 1982. *Europe and the People without a History.* Berkeley: University of California Press.

Zavella, Patricia. 1987. *Women's Work and Chicano Families: Cannery Workers of the Santa Clara Valley.* Ithaca: Cornell University Press.

———. 1988. "The Politics of Race and Gender: Organizing Cannery Workers in Northern California." In *Women and the Politics of Empowerment,* ed. Ann Bookman and Sandra Morgen, 202–24. Philadelphia: Temple University Press.

Zinn, Howard. 1980. *A People's History of the United States.* New York: Harper and Row.

TWENTY-FIVE

Relative Privilege? Reconsidering White Women's Participation in Municipal Politics

BARBARA A. CROW

More women now hold office at the municipal level than ever before; thus municipal politics is an increasingly important site of political participation for women.[1] However, little research has been done on this phenomenon. Lack of attention to any aspect of the municipal level in the study of political participation has meant that significant increases in women's political representation have not been analyzed. This lack of attention reveals biases, such as the privileging of elite politics, in the work on political participation.[2] It is this gap in the literature that this essay attempts to fill.

Vickers (1978), Stewart (1980), and Kopinak (1985) explore elected women's participation in municipal politics, arguing that women's increased representation at this level can best be explained by the character of municipal politics in relation to higher levels of office. The municipal level is (1) a less competitive realm, decreasing both campaign costs and time commitments; (2) a level of office that does not require relocation; and (3) a stepping stone for other levels. The relative unimportance of women's increased representation at this level is assumed in all these studies. Few researchers have empirically verified such assertions, nor have they considered that individuals might have different reasons for being attracted to municipal rather than provincial or federal politics. Clearly, if we want to better understand the individuals who run at this level and their effects, we must ask them why they ran for office.

Why do such characteristics as low campaign cost, infrequent travel, less competition, and nonpartisanship cause municipal elections to be perceived as less powerful and unimportant? What do municipal politicians have to say about provincial and federal politics? What do women say about the municipal offices that continue to attract them? What do women like about the municipal level of government? Who are the women who hold this level of office? Does feminism inform their work?

Studies of political participation have been premised on the liberal democratic assumption that the public and the private are separable. This dichotomy associates men with rationality, objectivity, culture, aggressiveness, politics, and agency (the public sphere). It associates women with emotionalism, subjectivity, nature, passivity, sexuality, and the family (the private sphere). If women are associated with the private sphere, it is difficult to even acknowledge their political participation. The association of men with the public and political and women with the private and social sphere has made it difficult for women to be full partners in the political process; it has also diminished the political contributions women have made. Moreover, conflating women with the familial removes accountability and responsibility from the concept of the political and continues to make women's alleged nonparticipation a purely "female" problem.

Municipal politics has been neglected by the disciplines of sociology and political science not only because it is marginal to the traditional definition of political participation, but also because the separation between the public and private spheres is not easily demarcated. Also, acknowledging the interrelationship between the public and private spheres fundamentally challenges the traditional definition of politics. Female municipal politicians are one population who can assist us with the challenge of expanding the traditional definition of politics.

The lack of research on women in municipal politics, in spite of the large number of elected representatives at this level, the relationship of this level to higher officeholding (Barrie and Gibbins 1989), and the significant increase of female officeholders in the last two decades suggests that research on municipal politics may have been ignored because the concerns of the "private" sphere are more immediate than at any other level of office.

In Western democracies, a liberalism premised on a public/private dichotomy that gets reproduced in the separate disciplines of political science and sociology has dominated the discourse of political participation. The discipline of political science focuses on men's participation in politics qua politics (the public sphere), while sociology focuses on women's participation in the social qua family (the private sphere). The identification of women with the family operates in such a manner that the category "woman" is discussed almost exclusively as though women *are* the family.[3] Additionally, little attention is given to how the institution of the family is integral to politics. Consequently the association of women with politics is inherently problematic. Notwithstanding the importance of examining the role that the family plays in political socialization, the disciplines of sociology and political science have difficulty discussing women as political actors without the appropriate nod to their family activities. Furthermore, this alignment of men with politics and the public sphere and women with the family and the private sphere shapes the kinds of assumptions and inquiries made regarding the possibilities and character of women's political participation. As a result, the literature on participation discusses women only as "familial" political actors — unlike the discourse concerning men as political agents.

More troubling, this discussion is reproduced in the feminist academic community.[4] In terms of empirical analyses, much of this feminist research has dealt with how issues of gender were neglected in the study of political participation; how traditional assumptions and untested hypotheses were utilized to perpetuate women's lack of political participation; and how male political behavior was the norm used to measure political participation. In summary, it has showed how much of the study of political participation has defined women outside the political, using androcentric models of "the political" (Bourque and Grossholtz 1974; Goot and Reid 1975; Siltanen and Stanworth 1984). While this work illustrates and identifies inadequate methodologies and androcentric evaluations of women's political participation, it focuses mainly on "bad" science. Little feminist work has been done linking theoretical critiques of liberalism with its empirical progeny. Some feminist scholars like Owen and Zerilli (1991) and Pateman (1988) have spoken to this omission and discuss how empirical work has reproduced the public/private dichotomies inherent in liberalism. These scholars suggest that we need to explore more critically the important link between liberal theory and practice. However, they do not specifically discuss how feminist empiricists have yet to respond to or incorporate feminist critiques of liberalism;[5] their discussions focus more on generalizations than detailed analyses of the relationship between liberal theory and feminist empiricism.

A series of feminist articles have summarized and categorized the "development" or "trends" of feminist critiques of sociology and political science (Carroll 1979, 1980; Siltanen and Stanworth 1984; Elshtain 1990; Ferguson 1987; Smith 1987; Sydie 1987; Kandal 1988; Owen and Zerilli 1991; Vickers 1989; Silverberg 1990; Randall 1991; Pateman 1992; Tronto 1992; Carroll and Zerilli 1993). Interestingly, these developments have been bifurcated such that we have one feminist community summarizing the feminist challenge to classic sociological and political theory and another informing empirical studies. While the feminist critiques of both sociological and political theory and empirical studies are in some ways very similar, there have been few attempts to link them. Feminist critiques of liberalism could be utilized more fruitfully in critiquing feminist empirical work. The intersection of these two streams of feminist criticism could affect the kinds of questions we ask about women's political participation. For example, how has the public/private dichotomy shaped assumptions about women's and men's political participation?

Moreover, the dismantling of the historical construction of the public/private dichotomy in liberalism is critical to our effort to broaden our understanding of what constitutes the "political." Kimberlè Crenshaw (1989), Patricia Hill Collins (1990), and Chandra Talpade Mohanty et al. (1991) have discussed how the public/private dichotomy is not useful for understanding the intersecting relations between racial and gender oppression. They argue that this dichotomy is based on a view of reality in which differences are obscured. Relying on a model that takes white, male, heterosexual, middle-class experience as the norm and adds difference to it does not allow for difference to challenge the norm itself. Addressing the activities of women, people of color, First Nations people, and gays and lesbians requires a radical reassessment of politics that acknowledges that the political is gendered and racialized.

Liberal political theory is founded on a separation of public from private, mind from body, rational from irrational, knower from known. These dichotomies have been translated into ideas and practices of representation that have contributed to the barriers women, people of color, First Nations people, and gays and lesbians face when entering the public world of the state and its institutions. Feminist theory has made clear that these distinctions are themselves political and serve particular interests. Whose interests does the public/private dichotomy serve? Sexism, racism, heterosexism, and classism require dichotomous thinking, and they are perpetuated as much in the private as the public sphere. But we do not look at the private sphere as political in this way, nor see the link between the public and private arenas. Thus we continue to view the world as though family and work can be understood separately, for instance. However, what happens when we ask men, as women have been asked, questions regarding their families and the role that family work plays in their political careers? Such questions highlight the fact that both men's and women's participation in politics is shaped by their relationship to their families and to their socially constructed genders.

Recent shifts in feminist empirical work have begun to focus on female candidates and the impact of female officeholders (Dodson and Carroll 1991). In part, this shift has occurred because there is now a relatively large aggregate pool of female elected officeholders. Once feminist empiricist scholars were able to identify the barriers women face in attaining elected office, barriers that are not intrinsically linked to being female, they began to investigate what female elected officials were like once elected.

Feminist empirical work has yet to meet the conceptual challenges posed by feminist critics of liberal theory, that is, what are the consequences for feminism if we choose to focus on "getting what men have"? Focusing only on what women have to do in order to be "successful" perpetuates the male as the standard measure. We have to be asking men about their relations to the private sphere. We have to talk about how legislators' actions impact on the private sphere. Ultimately, feminist empirical work does not address the problem of gender and race. The focus of this work is how to get women to elected office, not on how the construction of gender and race continues to situate women's political participation in relation to men.

Sociological theories, focused on the family/private/woman/social construction, and political theories, focused on the individual/public/man/political construction, need to find common ground. The study of municipal politics may be one site where theorists and methodologists can find a meeting place.

The task for feminist empiricists is to begin from the premise that the two spheres are interrelated, move beyond the barriers that women face in running for elected office, begin to acknowledge women's agency by looking at the places where they are politically active, and see men's political choices, like women's, as framed by their family relations.

Pateman (1988), in her critique of feminist empirical work, has argued that

> Despite the claims of empirical theorists, they have not produced a convincing account
> of the relationship between the pattern of attitudes and activity revealed in their

findings and the political structures of the liberal democracies (142). . . . empirical theory all too often obscures or denies the existence of problems, and presents evidence of socially structured inequalities as "natural facts" about the world that constitute insurmountable barriers to increased participation. (174)

These criticisms can be leveled at feminist empiricists who continue to study women's electoral participation at the provincial, state, and national levels of office. An investigation of municipal officeholders provides us with a locale in which to begin an examination of the interrelationship of the public and private spheres. In fact, it is precisely because of the sense that municipal politics verges on the private that female officeholders have been for the most part bypassed.

The public/private dichotomy still informs the study of women's participation in electoral politics. The adherence to this separation of spheres suggests that women can become political actors only by emulating men and dissociating themselves from domestic activities. Feminist empirical studies of women's political participation accept the political system as it is currently structured and thus ask only, "What does women's participation look like?" (Amundsen 1971; Baxter and Lansing 1983; Darcy et al. 1987). Rarely do these studies explore the premises that shape their inquiry or assumptions.[6] Most of this feminist empirical work on women's electoral participation adds women to the current studies of electoral participation without questioning the traditional model and measures of participation,[7] and the gendered and racialized assumptions that undergird their constitution. Even with these limitations, feminist empiricist analyses can have a radical component, and their findings have forced liberals to see the kinds of barriers women face in running for and winning elected office. Yet the work operates from the premise that white women must act like white men to be more successful in politics.[8]

Studies that move beyond the issue of barriers have begun to ask what "new" perspectives women bring to office and whether women officeholders make a difference while in office (Young 1993; Dodson and Carroll 1991; Dodson 1991). It remains the case, however, that few studies address these issues in the context of municipal politics, even though it is an area where women's participation has tripled in the last two decades. Women's participation in municipal politics has not received the same critical attention as women's participation in provincial, state, and national politics because the traditional critique, which focuses on barriers to participation and associates politics with the public sphere, does not hold at the municipal level.

In summary, the little work on women's participation in municipal politics is located in feminist scholarship and in a related subdiscipline of political science called "women and politics." Although the literature is still quite small, it can be characterized in two ways. One set of works argues that women's participation in municipal politics is impeded by the assumption that women run at the municipal level because it is less competitive, does not require one to relocate, and is a stepping stone to higher levels of office. Such assumptions make the study of women's participation at this level of politics seem relatively unimportant. A second and more recent set of works has shifted the analysis from documentation to an exploration of the different priorities and political practices of female municipal politicians

(CRIAW 1986; Flammang 1984; Boles 1986). This literature is based on the premise that public and private spheres are interrelated and that local and municipal politics best serves these women's political interests.

In combination, these two literatures suggest that women's increased success at the municipal level of politics may be the result of women's longer history of involvement in municipal politics. It appears that changes in provincial and federal politics will follow the trend of municipal politics. However, it may also be the case that women are attracted to municipal politics for other substantive reasons, which need to be investigated — not for what they lack, but for what they promise. A study of municipal politics has much to offer in terms of understanding the complex reasons women choose to go into electoral politics, and how they fare once they have made that decision.

The study of municipal politicians can enhance our understanding of political participation. The fact that there has been so little research on this group in spite of the large number of elected representatives at this level; the relationship of this level to higher officeholding (Barrie and Gibbins 1989); and the significant increase of female officeholders in the last two decades (CAWP 1991) suggest that municipal politics has been ignored quite possibly because it challenges traditional liberal analyses of political participation. At this level of office more than any other, the concerns of the "private" sphere seem more immediate and compelling.

What is revealed to us when an empirical study of female mayors in Ontario acknowledges the interrelationship between the public and the private spheres?[9] Unfortunately, there were not sufficient data to allow me to make the kinds of claims I wanted to make about the interrelationship between the public and the private spheres. These mayors locate their political agency at the municipal level of office where they can best serve their communities and support a democratic model that allows for a variety of representation, provides easy access to services, and addresses their immediate local concerns.

Given what we know about elected women at the provincial, state, and national levels, in what ways were female mayors similar or different? The female mayors in Ontario differed significantly from female provincial and federal officeholders in their age, educational backgrounds, marital status, and parental status. Generally, the mayors are likely to support issues that have been associated with the women's movement, particularly in relation to child care and abortion. Finally, a finding that emerged requiring further investigation is the role that organized religion plays for women at the local level. This may provide us with further insights into settings where women may be developing leadership skills and ideological values. It may also provide a way to address the conventional wisdom regarding women's conservatism at the municipal level. However, the female mayors and federally and provincially elected officeholders seem to differ in terms of where they feel they can provide the best service to their communities.

In the discussion of why they chose to serve at the municipal level rather than the provincial or federal levels, many mayors argued that the municipal level of office most directly affected their private lives, making clear once again that these women do not consider the "public" and the "private" to be in opposition.

Well, first of all I have no desire to leave my community. My family and my roots are too deep. (Mayor 31)

I really felt that I could do more at the municipal level. (Mayor 26)

The municipal level of government is closer to affecting the family. (Mayor 17)

The issues that were paramount to me were those day to day issues, the community infrastructure, the way that we talk to our people, respect for the individual. These were things that I could make a difference at, I felt, and they were at the municipal level. (Mayor 11)

These women argued that the best way to serve the community was to be there. They did not envision this role as passive "mothering," but as strong and independent action, requiring autonomy as well as responsibility to the community.

Another factor that suggests that female mayors in Canada are different from provincially and federally elected women is that municipally elected female officials have not organized any caucuses, auxiliaries, or committees addressing women's representation in municipal politics. This lack of organization to promote women's interests contrasts markedly with the United States, where the National League of Cities[10] has had an active women's caucus.[11] The analogous body in Canada, the Canadian Federation of Municipalities, has no such caucus or mechanism to address issues of gender in either representation or municipalities.

Perhaps there has been insufficient time for such organizations to emerge. We have seen a dramatic increase in women's elite representation at the municipal level only since 1978. In addition, many of the female mayors hesitated to acknowledge sexism, racial privilege, or classism as barriers to attaining office at the municipal level. Therefore, until there are both consciousness and articulation of gendered and racialized interests, women's organizations at the municipal level will not likely evolve.

One final explanation for the lack of municipally elected women's organizations is that the situation reflects the kind of women currently holding office. If, as I have suggested, these women choose the municipal arena because it allows for the integration of the public and private spheres, then these municipally elected women do not require organizations to service their gendered interests. This level of office directly addresses them.

Another factor that can assist us in understanding the interrelatedness of the public and the private spheres is the policy issues that the female mayors chose to focus on while in office. Quite clearly the female mayors were concerned with both public and private issues. These ranged from economic policy, land use, the provision of social services, and quality of life. These mayors viewed these policy issues as interrelated and important to their own quality of life as well as that of their communities. They did not focus specifically on "public" or "private" issues, nor understand them as contradictory sets of interests.

The results from this study only scratch the surface of a rich field of investigation into women and politics. Feminist geographers and planners have discussed the links between individual women, women's groups, and consumption services at the local level (MacKenzie and Rose 1983; MacKenzie 1987; Andrew and Milroy 1988;

Little et al. 1988; Fielding and Halford 1993; Preston et al. 1993). However, little work has been done on the relationship among women as local consumers of services, activists, and municipally elected officials. An investigation of the interaction between these various actors could reveal more about the relationship between gender, race, class, and sexual orientation at the local level of politics. Also, further study of municipal politicians from various provinces and states may also reveal idiosyncratic practices of various localities that require us to rethink municipal politics.

The current political climate in Canada and the United States has been fueled and shaped by renewed federalism and neoconservativism. Solutions for the nation's fiscal problems have been increasingly "dumped" on municipalities. As municipalities struggle with fiscal strategies to deal with the nation's debt load, the public has become more attuned to the responsibilities of municipalities. Voters demand a "new" kind of politician to solve these problems. This climate can partially explain women's increased rate of participation at the municipal level. The public's dissatisfaction with current officeholders has caused voters to agitate for elected officials who will "clean up" politics. Furthermore, some see these "new" municipal politicians as bearing characteristics traditionally associated with the feminine and private sphere.

A "different" profile of municipally elected women has emerged from this research. It seems clear that the public and private spheres are interrelated, and not dichotomous, for these women. They do see themselves as political, but their definition of politics is reflected in the level of office they hold. The municipal level is important to them because they value a politics that both provides their community with easy access to its elected representatives and offers elected officials like themselves easy access to their communities. In addition, they appreciate that it does not cost an enormous amount of money to run for municipal office and that they can remain independent of the party system. These characteristics of political office provide these women with agency, knowing that they support a level of office that is more democratic. Finally, they value the fact that their positions have given them the power to shape the issues affecting their communities.

NOTES

1. In Canada, the Canadian Advisory Council on the Status of Women (1988) found that the percentage of female officeholders in municipal politics increased from 7 percent in 1981 to 19 percent in 1988. In the United States, women's officeholding at the municipal level has tripled since 1970. Currently, women constitute approximately 15 percent of municipally elected representatives (*CAWP Fact Sheet* 1991).

2. Political participation, as it has been traditionally defined, refers to voting, attitudes, candidacies, parties, and officeholding. Politics is equated with elite activity, generally in formal democratic structures. This definition operates to marginalize both nonelite activity and activity outside these structures.

3. Riley (1988) makes a similar kind of argument in *"Am I That Name?" Feminism and the Category of "Women" in History.*

4. Several classical sociological and political theorists have played an important role in shaping our understanding of women's and men's participation in politics. Over the past decades, there have been a number of feminist anthologies and full-length books that have been dedicated to the treatment of women in these classical sociological and political theory texts (Clarke and Lange 1979; Elshtain 1981; Okin 1979, 1989; Lloyd 1984; Pitkin 1984; Saxonhouse 1985; Benhabib and Cornell 1987; Coole 1988; Kandal 1988; Nye 1988; Brown 1988; Gatens 1991).

5. Harding (1986) characterizes feminist empiricism as an attempt to deal with sexist and androcentric biases in scientific inquiry. Its claims rest on the assumption that there exists a world independent of the knower; thus it accepts the basic tenets of philosophical realism (Hawkesworth 1990).

Code (1991) argues that feminist empiricism does not adequately acknowledge that facts are not found or discovered, but are produced. Like its predecessor — empiricism — it assumes a vantage point that is on the outside looking in. It is premised on an objective discoverable world that, via proper scientific investigation, will be uncovered.

6. The current exception is Sue Tolleson Rinehart in her most recent publication, *Gender Consciousness and Politics* (1992).

7. I want to make a distinction between the study of women's "political" participation in mainstream politics and the study of their participation in nontraditional places that are not defined as political. This second group of studies assumes that women are political actors and goes to the places where women organize. For example, the women's movement would be one such site.

8. In the past two decades, there have emerged a number of studies on women's participation in electoral politics in North America, and several scholars, such as Sylvia Bashevkin and Susan Welch, now have considerable reputations for their expertise in this area (Bashevkin 1983a, 1983b, 1985, 1989; Welch 1975, 1977, 1978; Welch and Hibbing 1992). The research in Canada and the United States on women's participation in electoral politics tends to focus on the national, provincial, or state level and continues the separation of the private and public spheres. The central concerns for most of these studies are the barriers to women's participation.

9. In order to investigate women's participation in municipal politics, I focused on female mayors holding office in Ontario, 1990–93. A questionnaire was developed and administered to the total population of female mayors (N = 38). The survey was administered in an interview format; there were thirty-seven responses.

The mayors were interviewed between January 8 and October 20, 1991. Before arranging these interviews, I sent an initial letter explaining the project. I then followed up this letter with a telephone call to arrange an interview. The mayoral interviews lasted from twenty to ninety minutes.

In 1991, 17 percent of the total population of mayors in Ontario were female, the largest number of female mayors to serve to date. Women's rates of participation in elite positions (reeves, mayors, chairs, and wardens) in municipal politics had been consistently low (from .06 percent to 1.6 percent) between 1948 and 1970. The most dramatic increase occurred in 1978, when female elites in municipal politics doubled in one year, from 1.9 percent to 4.5 percent. Since 1978, the numbers have increased at an incremental rate of 1 percent per year. In 1991, women held 14.2 percent of these elite positions. For more information about this study, see Crow 1994.

10. This is the national organization that represents municipalities in the United States.

11. This caucus is called Women in Municipal Government. It was established in 1974.

BIBLIOGRAPHY

Amundsen, K. 1971. *The Silenced Majority: Women and American Democracy*. Englewood Cliffs: Prentice-Hall.

Andrew, C., and B. Moore Milroy, eds. 1988. *Life Spaces: Gender, Household, Employment*. Vancouver: University of British Columbia Press.

Barrie, D., and R. Gibbins. 1989. "Parliamentary Careers in the Canadian Federal State." *Canadian Journal of Political Science* 22 (1): 137–46.

Bashevkin, S. 1983a. "Social Change and Political Partisanship: The Development of Women's Attitudes in Quebec." *Comparative Political Studies* 16 (2): 147–72.

———. 1983b. "Social Background and Political Experience: Gender Differences among Provincial Elites." *Atlantis* 9 (1): 1–12.

———. 1985. *Toeing the Lines: Women and Party Politics in English Canada*. Toronto: University of Toronto Press.

———. 1989. "Political Parties and the Representation of Women." In *Canadian Parties in Transition*, ed. A. Gagnon and B. Tanguay, 446–60. Toronto: Nelson.

Baxter, S., and M. Lansing, eds. 1983. *Women and Politics: The Invisible Majority*. Ann Arbor: University of Michigan Press.

Benhabib, S., and D. Cornell, eds. 1987. *Feminism as Critique*. Minneapolis: University of Minnesota Press.

Boles, J., ed. 1986. *The Egalitarian City: Issues of Rights, Distribution, Access and Power*. New York: Praeger.

Bourque, S. C., and J. Grossholtz. 1974. "Politics an Unnatural Practice: Political Science Looks at Female Participation." *Politics and Society* 4:225–66.

Brown, W. 1988. *Manhood and Politics: A Feminist Reading in Political Theory*. Totowa, NJ: Rowman and Littlefield.

Canadian Advisory Council on the Status of Women. 1988. *Women in Politics: Becoming Full Partners in the Political Process*. Ottawa: Canadian Advisory Council on the Status of Women.

Carroll, B. A. 1979. "Political Science, Part I: American Politics and Political Behavior." *Signs* 5:289–306.

———. 1980. "Political Science, Part II: International Politics, Comparative Politics, and Feminist Radicals." *Signs* 5:449–58.

Carroll, S. J., and L. M. G. Zerilli. 1993. "Feminist Challenges to Political Science." In *The State of the Discipline II*, ed. A. Finifter. Washington, DC: American Political Science Association.

CAWP Fact Sheet. 1991. New Brunswick, NJ: Center for the American Woman and Politics.

Clarke, L., and L. Lange. 1979. *The Sexism of Social and Political Theory: Women and Reproduction from Plato to Nietzsche*. Toronto: University of Toronto Press.

Code, L. 1991. *What Can She Know? Feminist Theory and the Construction of Knowledge*. Ithaca: Cornell University Press.

Collins, P. Hill. 1990. *Black Feminist Thought: Knowledge, Consciousness, and the Politics of Empowerment*. New York: Routledge, Chapman and Hall.

Coole, D. H. 1988. *Women in Political Theory: From Ancient Misogyny to Contemporary Feminism*. Boulder: Lynne Rienner.

Crenshaw, K. 1989. "Demarginalizing the Intersection of Race and Gender in Antidiscrimination Law: Feminist Theory and Antiracist Politics." *University of Chicago Legal Forum*, 139–67.

CRIAW. 1986. "Women's Involvement in Political Life: A Pilot Study." Ottawa: Canadian Research Institute for the Advancement of Women.

Crow, B. A. 1994. "Female Mayors in Ontario." Diss., York University, North York, Ontario.

Darcy, R., S. Welch, and J. Clark. 1987. *Women, Elections, and Representation.* New York: Longman.

Di Stefano, C. 1991. *Configurations of Masculinity: A Feminist Reading in Modern Political Theory.* Ithaca: Cornell University Press.

Dodson, D. L., ed. 1991. *Gender and Policymaking: Studies of Women in Office.* New Brunswick, NJ: Center for the American Woman and Politics.

Dodson, D. L., and S. J. Carroll. 1991. *Reshaping the Agenda: Women in State Legislatures.* New Brunswick, NJ: Center for the American Woman and Politics.

Eisenstein, Z. 1981. *The Radical Future of Liberal Feminism.* New York: Longman.

Elshtain, J. B. 1981. *Public Man, Private Woman: Women in Social and Political Thought.* Princeton: Princeton University Press.

———. 1990. "Feminism and Politics." *Partisan Review* 57 (spring): 181–92.

Ferguson, K. 1987. "Male-Ordered Politics: Feminism and Political Science." In *Idioms of Inquiry: Critique and Renewal in Political Science,* ed. T. Ball, 209–29. Albany: State University of New York Press.

Fielding, A., and S. Halford. 1993. "Geographies of Opportunity: A Regional Analysis of Gender-Specific Social and Spatial Mobilities in England and Wales, 1971–81." *Environment and Planning A* 25 (October): 1421–40.

Flammang, J. A., ed. 1984. *Political Women: Current Roles in State and Local Government.* Beverly Hills: Sage.

Gatens, M. 1991. *Feminism and Philosophy: Perspectives on Difference and Equality.* Bloomington: Indiana University Press.

Goot, M., and E. Reid. 1975. *Women and Voting Studies: Mindless Matrons or Sexist Scientism?* Sage Professional Papers in Contemporary Political Sociology, no. 8. London: Sage.

Harding, S. 1986. *The Science Question in Feminism.* Ithaca: Cornell University Press.

Hawkesworth, M. 1990. *Beyond Oppression: Feminist Theory and Political Strategy.* New York: Continuum.

Kandal, T. R. 1988. *The Woman Question in Classical Sociological Theory.* Miami: Florida International University Press.

Kopinak, K. 1985. "Women in Canadian Municipal Politics: Two Steps Forward, One Step Back." *Canadian Review of Sociology and Anthropology* 22 (3): 394–410.

Little, J., L. Peake, and P. Richardson. 1988. *Women in Cities: Gender and the Urban Environment.* New York: New York University Press.

Lloyd, G. 1984. *The Man of Reason: "Male" and "Female" in Western Philosophy.* Minneapolis: University of Minnesota Press.

MacKenzie, S. 1987. "Women's Responses to Economic Restructuring: Changing Gender, Changing Space." In *The Politics of Diversity,* ed. R. Hamilton and M. Barrett, 81–100. Montreal: Book Centre.

MacKenzie, S., and D. Rose. 1983. "Industrial Change, the Domestic Economy and Home Life." In *Redundant Spaces in Cities and Regions? Studies in Industrial Decline and Social Change,* ed. J. Anderson et al., 155–300. London: Academic Press.

Mohanty, C. T., A. Russo, and L. Torres, eds. 1991. *Third World Women and the Politics of Feminism.* Bloomington: Indiana University Press.

Nye, A. 1988. *Feminist Theory and the Philosophies of Man.* New York: Routledge.

Okin, S. Moller. 1979. *Women in Western Political Thought*. Princeton: Princeton University Press.

———. 1989. *Justice, Gender, and the Family*. New York: Basic Books.

Owen, D., and L. Zerilli. 1991. "Gender and Citizenship." *Society* 28 (July/August): 27–34.

Pateman, C. 1988. *The Sexual Contract*. Stanford: Stanford University Press.

———. 1992. "Political Obligation, Freedom and Feminism." *American Political Science Review* 86 (1): 179–82.

Pitkin, H. 1984. *Fortune Is a Woman: Gender and Politics in the Thought of Niccolo Machiavelli*. Berkeley: University of California Press.

Preston, V., S. McLafferty, and E. Hamilton. 1993. "The Impact of Family Status on Black, White, and Hispanic Women's Commuting." *Urban Geography* 14 (3): 228–50.

Randall, V. 1991. "Feminism and Political Analysis." *Political Studies* 39:513–32.

Riley, D. 1988. *"Am I That Name?" Feminism and the Category of "Women" in History*. Minneapolis: University of Minnesota Press.

Rinehart, S. Tolleson. 1992. *Feminist Consciousness and Politics*. New York: Routledge, Chapman and Hall.

Saxonhouse, A. 1985. *Women in the History of Political Thought: Ancient Greece to Machiavelli*. New York: Praeger Special Studies.

Siltanen, J., and M. Stanworth. 1984. *Women and the Public Sphere: A Critique of Sociology and Politics*. London: Hutchinson.

Silverberg, H. 1990. "What Happened to the Feminist Revolution in Political Science?" *Western Political Quarterly* 43 (4): 886–903.

Smith, D. 1987. *The Everyday World as Problematic: A Feminist Sociology*. Toronto: University of Toronto Press.

Stewart, D., ed. 1980. *Women in Local Politics*. London: Scarecrow Press.

Sydie, R. 1987. *Natural Women, Cultured Men: A Feminist Perspective in Sociological Theory*. Vancouver: University of British Columbia Press.

Tronto, J. 1992. "Politics and Revision: The Feminist Project to Change the Boundaries of American Political Science." In *Revolutions in Knowledge: Feminism in the Social Sciences*, ed. S. Rosenberg Zalk and J. Gordon-Kelter, 91–110. Boulder: Westview.

Vickers, J. 1978. "Where Are the Women in Canadian Politics?" *Atlantis* 3:2, pt. 2.

———. 1989. "Feminist Approaches to Women in Politics." In *Beyond the Vote: Canadian Women and Politics*, ed. L. Kealey and J. Sangster, 16–36. Toronto: University of Toronto Press.

Welch, S. 1975. "Dimensions of Political Participation in a Canadian Sample." *Canadian Journal of Political Science* 8 (September): 553–59.

———. 1977. "Women as Political Animals: A Test of Some Explanations for Male-Female Political Participation Differences." *American Journal of Political Science* 21:711–30.

———. 1978. "Recruitment of Women to Public Office: A Discriminant Analysis." *Western Political Quarterly* 31:372–80.

Welch, S., and J. Hibbing. 1992. "Financial Conditions, Gender, and Voting in American Elections." *Journal of Politics* 54: 197–213.

Young, L. 1993. "Fulfilling the Mandate of Difference: Cross-Party Cooperation among Women in the Canadian House of Commons." Paper presented at Canadian Political Science Association Annual Meeting, Carleton University, June 6–8.

TWENTY-SIX

Election Systems and the Representation of Black Women in American State Legislatures

R. DARCY, CHARLES D. HADLEY, AND JASON F. KIRKSEY

Blacks and women are two overlapping groups that remain radically underrepresented in American state legislatures. While each first gained representation in the nineteenth century, their progress toward increased representation has been very slow. Blacks first were elected during Reconstruction and briefly were a majority in the South Carolina lower house. Clara Cressingham, Francis S. Klock, and Carrie C. Holly, the first women legislators, were elected by Colorado voters in 1894 (Anthony and Harper 1902, 521). Today (1991) blacks hold 5.7 percent of the lower house seats in the several state legislatures, a number about half that expected given their numbers in the population. Women, on the other hand, hold 19.4 percent of the seats, or about 36 percent of the number expected from their population proportions.

Solutions to the underrepresentation of blacks and women take different directions. Gerrymandering single-member districts can guarantee black representation simply by redrawing boundaries to create districts with black majorities. Multimember districts, on the other hand, can be organized to deny black representation if districts are drawn large enough to swamp black votes with those of whites (e.g., Davidson and Korbel 1981; Engstrom and McDonald 1981, 1986; MacManus 1978; MacManus and Bullock 1988). The result, especially in jurisdictions covered by the Voting Rights Act, is a shift from multimember to single-member districts in places with significant black populations.

Women, in contrast, gain greater representation in multimember district systems because of ticket balancing and a campaign style that focuses on the candidate's own program rather than an attack on an opponent ("give me *one* of your votes" versus "give me your vote") (see, for example, Bullock and MacManus 1991; Darcy, Welch, and Clark 1987, 1985; MacManus and Bullock 1988; Rule 1990b, 445; Welch 1990; Welch and Studlar 1990).

Black women did not enter state legislatures until 1928, when Minnie Harper was appointed to fill the remainder of her husband's term in the West Virginia Senate (Breckinridge 1933). Crystal Bird Fauset became the first elected black woman state legislator (Pennsylvania House of Representatives) in 1938 (Githens and Prestage 1977). In 1989–90 black women held only 1.5 percent of the lower house seats, or about 28 percent of what would be merited by their population proportions. Black women, then, are less well represented than women generally or blacks generally. This appears to confirm the double disadvantage hypothesis: black women suffer politically from being women and from being black (Baxter and Lansing 1981; Carroll and Strimling 1983; Epstein 1973; Githens and Prestage 1977; King 1975, 1977).

More recent research documents the fact that black women actually made greater gains than white women within their respective electoral environments (Darcy and Hadley 1988; Moncrief, Thompson, and Schuhmann 1991). The explanation is that black women benefited from the overall gains made by black Americans, especially in the South. The source of electoral gains for black women is to some extent structural. Black Americans gained new congressional, state legislative, and local districts when black women were there to take advantage. Nevertheless, black women remain greatly underrepresented; therefore, we need to understand the structural factors that inhibit or encourage the election of black women.

Wilma Rule (1990a, 15), in an exploratory study of lower houses in American state legislatures in 1985, concluded that states with multimember districts with greater than 5 percent black population provide both white and black women with the best opportunity for legislative election. A more guarded conclusion was reached by Herrick and Welch (1989, 7) in their study of city council elections (based on 1988 data). They found that

> Black women are substantially under-represented in all three of the major district systems [single-member, at-large, and mixed] (though their representation approaches parity in the four multi-member district cities not examined here). Interestingly, they [black women] are slightly better represented in at-large rather than mixed, and mixed rather than single member district cities, but they are severely under-represented in all three.

Both Rule and Herrick and Welch are sensitive to the problem of balancing the advantage of being women against possible disadvantages of being black (see also Darcy, Welch, and Clark 1987, 126). Herrick and Welch (1989, 12), moreover, go on to point out that for city councils, at least, "The combination of low representation of black women in all electoral systems combined with much better black male representation in district elections leads to the overall conclusion that district elections provide a considerably more equitable representation for blacks as a group than do at-large elections." Concern with black representation, then, leads toward electoral arrangements favorable to black representation over those more favorable to women.

True, blacks are greatly underrepresented in elected bodies given their numbers in the U.S. population, but most, if not all, of this underrepresentation is due to the underrepresentation of black women. Black men either achieved parity or are even overrepresented in proportion to their presence in the population. Welch and Herrick (1992) report that black men have about 142 percent of the representation on city councils expected from their population proportions, while black women have only 33 percent. The situation is the same in state legislatures. Rule (1990a) found black men overrepresented in eighteen states and at a level of between 80 and 99 percent of their expected representation in eleven other states.[1]

In fact, if we use Rule's population proportions for each state as a base multiplied by the number of legislators in each state and totaled across the fifty states, we find that black men merit election to 259 lower house seats, and black women to 286 (table 26.1). Since black men in 1989 actually held 235 seats, they held 91 percent of their expected representation given their population proportions ([235/259] $\times$ 100 = 91). By the same calculation, black women held only 28 percent of their expected seats merited by their populations ([80/286] $\times$ 100 = 28).[2] By 1991, electoral gains resulted in 240 black men and 103 black women state legislators. Black men had risen to 93 percent of the expected legislative representation merited by their population proportions and black women increased to 36 percent. Men, moreover, held 72 percent of the seats among all black state legislators and 82 percent among all white state legislators.

The underrepresentation of blacks and women in elected bodies, then, is largely one and the same problem — the underrepresentation of women, both black and white. The problem of black underrepresentation cannot ignore the underrepresentation of black women; strategies for increasing black representation, then, must be directed at bringing more black women into public office. If black women achieve gains in representation at the expense of black men, then black representation overall remains unaffected at the same time the women gain. On the other hand, gains by black women at the expense of white men would result in gains for both blacks and women. Two other possibilities appear remote at this point given population distributions: (1) gains by white women at the expense of black men (which would increase the representation of women at the expense of blacks); or, (2) gains by black women at the expense of white women (which would increase black representation without changing that of women). A shift to political structures that promote the election of more black women in predominantly black constituencies will increase the proportion of women without hurting black representation. Alternatively, a shift to political structures that promote the election of more black women in predominantly white constituencies will increase the proportions of both blacks and women.

The work of Rule (1990a) and Herrick and Welch (1989) suggests that an increase in the representation of black women could be achieved if electoral arrangements were altered. On the other hand, there is a reason for caution. Both papers use the entire elected body as the unit of analysis rather than the actual election district. Consider Georgia. Rule shows it to be a state using multimember legislative districts with a proportion of black women above the national median. The implication is

TABLE 26.1.
State Lower House Delegations, by Region, Sex, and Race, 1989–90

State	Total members	Men	Women	Blacks	Black men	Black women	District type
Northeast							
Connecticut	151	117	34	5	5 (5)	0 (6)	SMD
Maine	151	104	47	0	0 (0)	0 (0)	SMD
Massachusetts	160	130	30	5	3 (3)	2 (4)	SMD
New Hampshire	400	270	130	3	1 (0)	2 (1)	S&MMD/T
New Jersey	80	72	8	6	4 (5)	2 (6)	MMD/T
New York	150	132	18	16	9 (11)	7 (12)	SMD
Pennsylvania	203	188	15	15	13 (9)	2 (9)	SMD
Rhode Island	100	86	14	5	5 (2)	0 (2)	SMD
Vermont	150	101	49	2	1 (0)	1 (0)	SMD/T
Midwest							
Iowa	100	81	19	0	0 (1)	0 (1)	SMD
Illinois	118	97	21	14	9 (9)	5 (10)	SMD
Indiana	100	89	11	6	5 (4)	1 (4)	S&MMD/T
Kansas	125	92	33	3	3 (3)	0 (4)	SMD
Michigan	110	90	20	14	9 (7)	5 (8)	SMD
Minnesota	134	107	27	1	1 (1)	0 (1)	SMD
Missouri	163	136	27	13	10 (8)	3 (9)	SMD
Nebraska	49	41	8	0	0 (1)	0 (1)	SMD
North Dakota	106	87	19	0	0 (0)	0 (0)	MMD/T
Ohio	99	85	14	11	8 (5)	3 (6)	MMD/T
South Dakota	70	57	13	0	0 (0)	0 (0)	MMD/T
Wisconsin	99	68	31	4	1 (2)	3 (2)	SMD
South							
Alabama	105	98	7	18	14 (13)	4 (14)	SMD
Arkansas	100	92	8	5	4 (8)	1 (9)	SMD
Florida	120	104	16	9	8 (8)	1 (9)	SMD
Georgia	180	158	22	23	16 (23)	7 (25)	S&MMD/P
Louisiana	105	102	3	15	12 (15)	3 (17)	SMD
Mississippi	122	115	7	20	19 (21)	1 (23)	SMD
North Carolina	120	99	21	12	11 (13)	1 (14)	S&MMD/T
South Carolina	124	112	12	16	13 (18)	3 (20)	SMD
Tennessee	99	89	10	10	8 (8)	2 (8)	SMD
Texas	150	134	16	13	10 (8)	3 (9)	SMD
Virginia	100	88	12	7	5 (9)	2 (10)	SMD
Border South							
Delaware	41	35	6	2	2 (3)	0 (4)	SMD
Kentucky	100	94	6	1	1 (3)	0 (4)	SMD
Maryland	141	106	35	22	14 (16)	8 (18)	MMD/T
Oklahoma	101	94	7	3	2 (3)	1 (4)	SMD
West Virginia	100	82	18	1	1 (2)	0 (2)	S&MMD/T
West							
Alaska	40	31	9	1	1 (1)	0 (1)	SMD
Arizona	60	38	22	2	1 (1)	1 (1)	MMD/T
California	80	66	14	5	2 (3)	3 (3)	SMD
Colorado	65	43	22	3	1 (1)	2 (1)	SMD
Hawaii	51	40	11	0	0 (0)	0 (1)	SMD
Idaho	84	62	22	0	0 (0)	0 (0)	MMD/P
Montana	100	79	21	0	0 (0)	0 (0)	SMD
Nevada	42	32	10	2	2 (1)	0 (1)	SMD
New Mexico	70	59	11	0	0 (0)	0 (1)	SMD
Oregon	60	49	11	1	0 (0)	1 (0)	SMD
Utah	75	64	11	0	0 (0)	0 (0)	SMD
Washington	98	66	32	1	1 (1)	0 (1)	MMD/P
Wyoming	64	46	18	0	0 (0)	0 (0)	S&MMD/T
TOTAL N	5,515	4,507	1,008	315	235 (259)	80 (286)	
PERCENT	100.0	81.7	18.3	5.7	4.3 (4.7)	1.4 (5.2)	

SOURCES: Authors' calculations from *Black Elected Officials: A National Roster* (Washington, DC: Joint Center for Political Studies, 1989); *National Directory of Women Elected Officials* (Washington, DC: National Women's Political Caucus, 1989); *Redistricting Provisions: 50 State Profiles* (Denver: National Conference of State Legislatures, 1989); and *State Elective Officials and the Legislatures, 1989–90* (Lexington, KY: Council of State Governments, 1989).

T = Top vote getters win the available seats.   P = Post, candidates must run for a specific seat, e.g., A, B, C.
SMD = Single-member district.   MMD = Multimember district.
S&MMD = Single and multimember district.
Figures in parentheses are authors' calculation of expected seats, from data in Rule 1990a and sources cited in table 26.2.

that multimember districts lead to increased proportions of elected women. On closer examination, however, some Georgia state legislative districts are multimember while others are single-member (see table 26.2).

All the black Georgia representatives, both women and men, come from the single-member districts.[3] Certainly the presence of some multimember districts in the state is not evidence of the causal effect of district system on the representation of black women (or men). The Georgia case, moreover, is not likely to be unique. Because multimember or at-large election district systems historically were used to deny blacks representation, as in Georgia, courts have had a tendency to remedy the situation by requiring single-member district systems in areas with substantial black constituencies. Evidence presented by Herrick and Welch (1989), for example, shows that areas with predominantly black voting populations, hence areas from which black officials are elected, tend to have single-member district or mixed election systems, while at-large city council elections are more likely to be present where there are small black voting populations. In this context, it is likely to mean the use of single-member districts where black voters predominate and another system for areas dominated by white voters. Consequently, few, if any, black men or women will be elected from multimember districts.

The fact that blacks are not elected in multimember election systems, however, is an artifact of the tendency toward single-member districts where there are significant black voting populations rather than an outcome of the election system itself. While it is difficult to estimate the number of multimember districts that can be created in areas with predominantly black constituencies, there are some with black populations substantial enough to allow us to expect multiple legislative representation, areas of Chicago, New York, Atlanta, Philadelphia, and Los Angeles, for example. Voting in multimember districts that cover areas with predominantly black constituencies is likely to produce black officials just as contemporary single-member districts do now.

The total distribution of state legislative seats for black men and women by election district type is shown in table 26.3, highlighting the advantages and disadvantages of district systems.[4] In absolute terms, black men are much better served by single-member district election systems than are black women. About 10 percent more black women are elected from multimember than from single-member district systems, but the difference fails significance (p <.07). Either the type of district

TABLE 26.2.
Members of the Georgia House of Representatives, by Race, Sex, and District Type, 1989

Race	Sex	Single-member	Multimember	Total
White	Men	107	35	142
	Women	13	2	15
Black	Men	16	0	16
	Women	7	0	7
Total		143	37	180

SOURCES: See table 26.1.

TABLE 26.3.
Black State Representatives, by Sex and District Type, 1989

Holder of seat	Single-member (%)	Multimember (%)
Man	76.0	66.0
Woman	24.0	34.0
Total	100.0	100.0
(n)	(271)	(44)

$z = 1.428$ $p < .0764$

SOURCES: See table 26.1.

system does not make a difference, or single-member district systems are more advantageous to black men and multimember districts better serve the representation of black women. Given the large number of findings associating the election of more women with multimember districts in a number of contexts (see Darcy, Welch, and Clark 1987) in the United States and elsewhere, the lack of significance here is likely attributable to the small number of cases rather than the absence of an effect. Thus, areas with majority black constituencies that have multimember districts (but still kept predominantly black) either would not change the black gender balance or, more likely, would improve the ratio of women to men elected officials without the loss of black representation.

If multimember districts help improve the representation of black women in areas with majority black constituencies without hindering the representation of blacks generally, can it also work in areas with predominantly white constituencies? We can answer this question by examining the demographics of and types of election districts represented by black women. As table 26.4 shows, fewer than 4 percent (3.75) of all the districts represented by a black woman have populations less than 5 percent black.[5] Few black women are elected from overwhelmingly white constituencies; but all those represented by black women have multimember districts. Therefore, we can conclude that, while single-member districts do not increase black female representation in areas with overwhelmingly white constituencies, multimember districts might, an expectation from previous work on the effect of single- and multimember districts on the election of women.

Six of the eight states (75 percent) with legislative delegations of women at or higher than the 18 percent national average have multimember districts; in contrast, the thirty-eight single-member district states divide evenly. The multimember districted Arizona lower house stands out, in that 36 percent of its members are women. The state with the largest number of black women in its legislature is Maryland, with eight. This is 10 percent of the total number of black women legislators nationally, and all of them were elected in multimember districts (table 26.1). Looking at the districts from which women state legislators come (lower house, 1991), we see that 18 percent of all the state legislators elected in the country from single-member districts are women. In contrast, 24 percent of those elected from multimember districts are women. Regardless of race, women fare better in multimember district systems.

TABLE 26.4.
Black Women State Representatives, by Black Population Size and
District Type, 1989

% Black population	Single-member	Multimember	Total
Less than 5%	0	3	3
More than 5%	65	12	77
Total	65	15	80

SOURCES: *County and City Data Book, 1988*, U.S. Department of Commerce, Bureau of the Census (Washington, DC: GPO, 1988); *Black Elected Officials: A National Roster* (Washington, DC: Joint Center for Political Studies, 1989); *National Directory of Women Elected Officials* (Washington, DC: National Women's Political Caucus, 1989); *Redistricting Provisions: 50 State Profiles* (Denver: National Conference of State Legislatures, 1989); and *State Elective Officials and the Legislatures, 1989–90* (Lexington, KY: Council of State Governments, 1989).

The problems of the underrepresentation of blacks and women are one and the same. Black men have achieved rates of representation in local and state legislative bodies that come close to or exceed expectations based on their population proportions. Black women, like white women, have not. It is reasonable to turn attention to the election of more of the disproportionately underrepresented black women.

In regard to single-member versus multimember district systems, multimember districts are not harmful to black representation in and of themselves, as areas with predominantly black constituencies can have multimember districts with no loss of black representation. In areas with predominantly white constituencies, too, there is some suggestion that multimember district systems might be advantageous to the election of black women. If multimember districts can be used to facilitate the election of black women without the loss of black representation overall, they should be favored over single-member districts. Multimember districts, moreover, appear to facilitate the election of women regardless of race.

NOTES

1. Lower houses of the state legislatures vary in size from forty (Alaska) to four hundred (New Hampshire). The black population varies greatly from state to state, as well. Estimates of how many seats blacks merit in state legislatures based on their population proportions, then, should be calculated within states and totaled across all states, as is done here. The number should not be calculated from national totals, as might be appropriate for women, whose population proportions do not vary significantly from state to state.

2. The expected number of seats in table 26.1, by carrying numbers to three decimal places, is 256 for black men and 286 for black women; however, the total number for black men in the table is a slightly larger 259 due to rounding to whole numbers for the cell entries.

3. The black women in the lower house and the district from which they were elected in 1989–90 were Betty Clark (55), Grace Davis (29), Diane Johnson (123), Georgianna Sinkfield (37), LaNett Stanley (33), Juanita Williams (54), and Mary Young-Cummings (134).

4. We determined the numbers of men and women who are members of the lower houses of the state legislatures by subtracting the number of women holding seats from the total

number of seats. Then the numbers of black men and women who hold such seats are subtracted from the numbers of men and women, yielding the numbers of white men and white women who hold seats. See the note at table 26.2 for the data sources.

5. While 5 percent is an arbitrary cutoff, it is the common standard used in previous research, some of the more recent being Herrick and Welch 1989; Welch and Studlar 1990; Welch 1990, 1056–61, 1071; and Rule 1990a.

REFERENCES

Anthony, Susan B., and Ida Husted Harper, eds. 1902. *The History of Woman Suffrage*. Vol. 4: Rochester, NY: Susan B. Anthony.

Baxter, Sandra, and Marjorie Lansing. 1981. *Women and Politics: The Invisible Majority*. Ann Arbor: University of Michigan Press.

Breckinridge, Sophonisba P. 1933. *Women in the Twentieth Century*. New York: McGraw-Hill.

Bullock, Charles S., and Susan A. MacManus. 1991. "Municipal Election Structure and the Election of Councilwomen." *Journal of Politics* 53: 75–89.

Carroll, Susan, and Wendy Strimling. 1983. *Women's Routes to Elective Office: A Comparison with Men's*. New Brunswick, NJ: Center for the American Woman and Politics.

Darcy, R., and Charles D. Hadley. 1988. "Black Women in Politics: The Puzzle of Success." *Social Science Quarterly* 69: 629–45.

Darcy, R., Susan Welch, and Janet Clark. 1985. "Women Candidates in Single and Multi-Member Districts." *Social Science Quarterly* 66: 945–53.

———. 1987. *Women, Elections, and Representation*. New York: Longman.

Davidson, Chandler, and George Korbel. 1981. "At-Large Elections and Minority Group Representation: A Re-Examination of Historical and Contemporary Evidence." *Journal of Politics* 43: 982–1005.

Engstrom, Richard L., and Michael D. McDonald. 1981. "The Election of Blacks to City Councils: Clarifying the Impact of Electoral Arrangements on the Seats/Population Relationship." *American Political Science Review* 75: 344–54.

———. 1986. "The Effect of At-Large Versus District Elections on Racial Representation in U.S. Municipalities." In Bernard Grofman and Arend Lijphart, eds., *Electoral Laws and Their Political Consequences*, 203–25. New York: Agathon Press.

Epstein, Cynthia Fuchs. 1973. "Black and Female: The Double Whammy." *Psychology Today* 7: 57–99.

Githens, Marianne, and Jewel L. Prestage, eds. 1977. *A Portrait of Marginality: The Political Behavior of American Women*. New York: McKay.

Herrick, Rebekah, and Susan Welch. 1989. "The Impact of At-Large Elections on the Representation of Black and White Women." Paper presented at the annual meeting of the Midwest Political Science Association, Chicago.

King, Mae C. 1975. "Opposition and Power: The Unique Status of the Black Woman in the American Political System." *Social Science Quarterly* 56: 116–28.

———. 1977. "The Politics of Sexual Stereotypes." In Githens and Prestage, eds., *A Portrait of Marginality*, 346–65.

MacManus, Susan A. 1978. "City Council Election Procedures and Minority Representation: Are They Related?" *Social Science Quarterly* 59: 153–61.

MacManus, Susan A., and Charles S. Bullock III. 1988. "Minorities and Women *Do* Win at Large." *National Civic Review* 77: 231–44.

Moncrief, Gary F., Joel A. Thompson, and Robert Schuhmann. 1991. "Gender, Race, and the State Legislature: A Research Note on the Double Disadvantage Hypothesis." *Social Science Journal* 28: 481–87.

Rule, Wilma. 1990a. "Multimember Districts, Contextual Factors, and Black and Anglo Women's Recruitment to State Legislatures." Paper presented at the annual meeting of the American Political Science Association, San Francisco.

———. 1990b. "Why More Women Are State Legislators: A Research Note." *Western Political Quarterly* re: 437–48.

Welch, Susan. 1990. "The Impact of At-Large Elections on the Representation of Blacks and Hispanics." *Journal of Politics* 52: 1050–76.

Welch, Susan, and Rebekah Herrick. 1992. "The Impact of At-Large Elections on the Representation of Minority Women." In Wilma Rule and Joseph F. Zimmerman, eds., *United States Electoral Systems: Their Impact on Women and Minorities*, 153–66. New York: Greenwood.

Welch, Susan, and Donley Studlar. 1990. "Multi-Member Districts and the Representation of Women: Evidence from Britain and the United States." *Journal of Politics* 52: 391–412.

TWENTY-SEVEN

Nothing Distant about It: Women's Liberation and Sixties Radicalism

ALICE ECHOLS

On 7 September 1968 the sixties came to the Miss America Pageant when one hundred women's liberationists descended on Atlantic City to protest the pageant's promotion of physical attractiveness and charm as the primary measures of women's worth. Carrying signs that declared, "Miss America Is a Big Falsie," "Miss America Sells It," and "Up against the Wall, Miss America," they formed a picket line on the boardwalk, sang anti–Miss America songs in three-part harmony, and performed guerrilla theater. The activists crowned a live sheep Miss America and paraded it on the boardwalk to parody the way the contestants, and, by extension, all women, "are appraised and judged like animals at a county fair." They tried to convince women in the crowd that the tyranny of beauty was but one of the many ways that women's bodies were colonized. By announcing beforehand that they would not speak to male reporters (or to any man for that matter), they challenged the sexual division of labor that consigned women reporters to the "soft" stories and male reporters to the "hard" news stories. Newspaper editors who wanted to cover the protest were thus forced to pull their female reporters from the society pages to do so.[1]

The protesters set up a "Freedom Trash Can" and filled it with various "instruments of torture" — high-heeled shoes, bras, girdles, hair curlers, false eyelashes, typing books, and representative copies of *Cosmopolitan*, *Playboy*, and *Ladies' Home Journal*. They had wanted to burn the contents of the Freedom Trash Can but were prevented from doing so by a city ordinance that prohibited bonfires on the boardwalk. However, word had been leaked to the press that the protest would include a symbolic bra-burning, and, as a consequence, reporters were everywhere.[2] Although they burned no bras that day on the boardwalk, the image of the bra-burning, militant feminist remains part of our popular mythology about the women's liberation movement.

The activists also managed to make their presence felt inside the auditorium during that night's live broadcast of the pageant. Pageant officials must have known that they were in for a long night when early in the evening one protester sprayed Toni Home Permanent Spray (one of the pageant's sponsors) at the mayor's booth. She was charged with disorderly conduct and "emanating a noxious odor," an irony that women's liberationists understandably savored. The more spectacular action occurred later that night. As the outgoing Miss America read her farewell speech, four women unfurled a banner that read, "Women's Liberation," and all sixteen protesters shouted "Freedom for Women," and "No More Miss America" before security guards could eject them. The television audience heard the commotion and could see it register on Miss America's face as she stumbled through the remainder of her speech. But the program's producer prevented the cameramen from covering the cause of Miss America's consternation.[3] The television audience did not remain in the dark for long, because Monday's newspapers described the protest in some detail. As the first major demonstration of the fledgling women's liberation movement, it had been designed to make a big splash, and after Monday morning no one could doubt that it had.

In its wit, passion, and irreverence, not to mention its expansive formulation of politics (to include the politics of beauty, no less!), the Miss America protest resembled other sixties demonstrations. Just as women's liberationists used a sheep to make a statement about conventional femininity, so had the Yippies a week earlier lampooned the political process by nominating a pig, Pegasus, for the presidency at the Democratic National Convention.[4] Although Atlantic City witnessed none of the violence that had occurred in Chicago, the protest generated plenty of hostility among the six hundred or so onlookers who gathered on the boardwalk. Judging from their response, this new thing, "women's liberation," was about as popular as the antiwar movement. The protesters were jeered, harassed, and called "commies" and "man-haters." One man suggested that it "would be a lot more useful" if the protesters threw themselves, and not their bras, girdles, and makeup, into the trash can.[5]

Nothing — not even the verbal abuse they encountered on the boardwalk — could diminish the euphoria women's liberationists felt as they started to mobilize around their own, rather than other people's, oppression. Ann Snitow speaks for many when she recalls that in contrast to her involvement in the larger, male-dominated protest Movement,[6] where she had felt sort of "blank and peripheral," women's liberation was like "an ecstasy of discussion." Precisely because it was about one's own life, "there was," she claims, "nothing distant about it."[7] Robin Morgan has contended that the Miss America protest "announced our existence to the world."[8] That is only a slight exaggeration, for as a consequence of the protest, women's liberation achieved the status of a movement both to its participants and to the media; as such, the Miss America demonstration represents an important moment in the history of the sixties.[9]

Although the women's liberation movement began to take shape only toward the end of the decade, it was a paradigmatically sixties movement. It is not just that many early women's liberation activists had prior involvements in other sixties movements, although that was certainly true, as has been ably documented by Sara Evans.[10] And it is not just that, of all the sixties movements, the women's liberation movement alone carried on and extended into the 1970s that decade's political radicalism and rethinking of fundamental social organization, although that is true as well. Rather, it is also that the larger, male-dominated protest Movement, despite its considerable sexism, provided much of the intellectual foundation and cultural orientation for the women's liberation movement. Indeed, many of the broad themes of the women's liberation movement — especially its concern with revitalizing the democratic process and reformulating "politics" to include the personal — were refined and recast versions of ideas and approaches already present in the New Left and the black freedom movement.

Moreover, like other sixties radicals, women's liberationists were responding at least in part to particular features of the postwar landscape. For instance, both the New Left and the women's liberation movement can be understood as part of a gendered generational revolt against the ultradomesticity of that aberrant decade, the 1950s. The white radicals who participated in these movements were in flight from the nuclear family and the domesticated versions of masculinity and femininity that prevailed in postwar America. Sixties radicals, white and black, were also responding to the hegemonic position of liberalism and its promotion of government expansion both at home and abroad — the welfare/warfare state. Although sixties radicals came to define themselves in opposition to liberalism, their relation to liberalism was nonetheless complicated and ambivalent. They saw in big government not only a way of achieving greater economic and social justice, but also the possibility of an increasingly well managed society and an ever more remote government.

In this chapter I will attempt to evaluate some of the more important features of sixties radicalism by focusing on the specific example of the women's liberation movement. I am motivated by the problematic ways "the sixties" has come to be scripted in our culture. If conservative "slash and burn" accounts of the period indict sixties radicals for everything from crime and drug use to single motherhood, they at least heap guilt fairly equally on antiwar, black civil rights, and feminist activists alike. By contrast, progressive reconstructions, while considerably more positive in their assessments of the period, tend to present the sixties as if women were almost completely outside the world of radical politics. Although my accounting of the sixties is in some respects critical, I nonetheless believe that there was much in sixties radicalism that was original and hopeful, including its challenge to established authority and expertise, its commitment to refashioning democracy and "politics," and its interrogation of such naturalized categories as gender and race.

Women's discontent with their place in America in the sixties was, of course, produced by a broad range of causes. Crucial in reigniting feminist consciousness in the sixties was the unprecedented number of women (especially married white women) being drawn into the paid labor force, as the service sector of the economy expanded and rising consumer aspirations fueled the desire of many families for a second income.[11] As Alice Kessler-Harris has pointed out, "homes and cars, refrigerators and washing machines, telephones and multiple televisions required higher incomes." So did providing a college education for one's children. These new patterns of consumption were made possible in large part through the emergence of the two-income family as wives increasingly "sought to aid their husbands in the quest for the good life." By 1960, 30.5 percent of all wives worked for wages.[12] Women's growing participation in the labor force also reflected larger structural shifts in the U.S. economy. Sara Evans has argued that the "reestablishment of labor force segregation following World War II ironically reserved for women a large proportion of the new jobs created in the fifties due to the fact that the fastest growing sector of the economy was no longer industry but services."[13] Women's increasing labor force participation was facilitated as well by the growing number of women graduating from college and by the introduction of the birth control pill in 1960.

Despite the fact that women's "place" was increasingly in the paid workforce (or perhaps because of it), ideas about women's proper role in American society were quite conventional throughout the 1950s and the early 1960s, held there by a resurgent ideology of domesticity — what Betty Friedan called the "feminine mystique." But, as Jane De Hart-Mathews has observed, "the bad fit was there: the unfairness of unequal pay for the same work, the low value placed on jobs women performed, the double burden of housework and wage work."[14] By the mid-1960s at least some American women felt that the contradiction between the realities of paid work and higher education on the one hand and the still pervasive ideology of domesticity on the other had become irreconcilable.

Without the presence of other oppositional movements, however, the women's liberation movement may not have developed at all as an organized force for social change. It certainly would have developed along vastly different lines. The climate of protest encouraged women, even those not directly involved in the black movement and the New Left, to question conventional gender arrangements. Moreover, many of the women who helped form the women's liberation movement had been involved as well in the male-dominated Movement. If the larger Movement was typically indifferent, or worse, hostile to women's liberation, it was nonetheless through their experiences in that Movement that the young and predominantly white and middle-class women who initially formed the women's liberation movement became politicized. The relationship between women's liberation and the larger Movement was at its core paradoxical. If the Movement was a site of sexism, it also provided white women a space in which they could develop political skills and self-confidence, a space in which they could violate the injunction against female self-assertion.[15] Most important, it gave them no small part of the intellectual ammunition — the language and the ideas — with which to fight their own oppression.

Sixties radicals struggled to reformulate politics and power. Their struggle confounded many who lived through the sixties as well as those trying to make sense of the period some thirty years later. One of the most striking characteristics of sixties radicals was their ever-expanding opposition to liberalism. Radicals' theoretical disavowal of liberalism developed gradually and in large part in response to liberals'

specific defaults — their failure to repudiate the segregationists at the 1964 Democratic National Convention, their lack of vigor in pressing for greater federal intervention in support of civil rights workers, and their readiness (with few exceptions)
to support President Lyndon B. Johnson's escalation of the Vietnam War. But
initially some radicals had argued that the Movement should acknowledge that
liberalism was not monolithic but contained two discernible strands — "corporate"
and "humanist" liberalism. For instance, in 1965 Carl Oglesby, an early leader of
the Students for a Democratic Society (SDS), contrasted *corporate liberals*, whose
identification with the system made them "illiberal liberals," with *humanist liberals*,
who he hoped might yet see that "it is this movement with which their own best
hopes are most in tune." [16]

By 1967 radicals were no longer making the distinction between humanist and
corporate liberals that they once had. This represented an important political shift
for early new leftists in particular who once had felt an affinity of sorts with
liberalism. [17] Black radicals were the first to decisively reject liberalism, and their
move had an enormous impact on white radicals. With the ascendancy of black
power many black militants maintained that liberalism was intrinsically paternalistic, and that black liberation required that the struggle be free of white involvement.
This was elaborated by white radicals, who soon developed the argument that
authentic radicalism involved organizing around one's own oppression rather than
becoming involved, as a "liberal" would, in someone else's struggle for freedom. For
instance, in 1967 Gregory Calvert, another SDS leader, argued that the "student
movement has to develop an image of its own revolution . . . instead of believing
that you're a revolutionary because you're related to Fidel's struggle, Stokely's struggle, always someone else's struggle." [18] Black radicals were also the first to conclude
that nothing short of revolution — certainly not Johnson's Great Society programs
and a few pieces of civil rights legislation — could undo racism. As leftist journalist
Andrew Kopkind remembered it, the rhetoric of revolution proved impossible for
white new leftists to resist. "With black revolution raging in America and world
revolution directed against America, it was hardly possible for white radicals to think
themselves anything less than revolutionaries." [19]

Radicals' repudiation of liberalism also grew out of their fear that liberalism
could "co-opt" and thereby contain dissent. Thus, in 1965 when President Johnson
concluded a nationally televised speech on civil rights by proclaiming, "And we
shall overcome," radicals saw in this nothing more than a calculated move to
appropriate Movement rhetoric in order to blunt protest. By contrast, more established civil rights leaders reportedly cheered the president on, believing that his
declaration constituted a significant "affirmation of the movement." [20] Liberalism,
then, was seen as both compromised and compromising. In this, young radicals were
influenced by Herbert Marcuse, who emphasized the system's ability to reproduce
itself through its recuperation of dissent. [21]

Just as radicals' critique of materialism developed in the context of relative
economic abundance, so did their critique of liberalism develop at a time of
liberalism's greatest political strength. The idea that conservativism might supplant
liberalism at some point in the near future was simply unimaginable to them. (To

be fair, this view was not entirely unreasonable given Johnson's trouncing of Barry Goldwater in the 1964 presidential election.)

This was just one of many things that distinguished new leftists from old leftists, who, having lived through McCarthyism, were far more concerned about the possibility of a conservative resurgence. For if sixties radicals grew worlds apart from liberals, they often found themselves in conflict with old leftists as well. In general, new leftists rejected the economism and virulent anticommunism of the non-communist Old Left. In contrast to old leftists, whose target was "class-based economic oppression," new leftists (at least before 1969, when some new leftists did embrace dogmatic versions of Marxism) focused on "how late capitalist society creates mechanisms of psychological and cultural domination over *everyone*."[22] For young radicals the problem went beyond capitalism and included not only the alienation engendered by mass society, but also other systems of hierarchy based on race, gender, and age. Indeed, they were often more influenced by existentialists like Camus or social critics like C. Wright Mills and Herbert Marcuse, both of whom doubted the working class's potential for radical action, than by Marx or Lenin. For instance, SDS president Paul Potter contended that it would be "through the experience of the middle class and the anesthetic of bureaucracy and mass society that the vision and program of participatory democracy will come."[23] This rejection of what Mills dubbed the "labor metaphysic" had everything to do with the different circumstances radicals confronted in the sixties. As Arthur Miller observed, "The radical of the thirties came out of a system that had stopped and the important job was to organize new production relations which would start it up again. The sixties radical opened his eyes to a system pouring its junk over everybody, or nearly everybody, and the problem was to stop just that, to escape being overwhelmed by a mindless, goalless flood which marooned each individual on his little island of commodities."[24]

If sixties radicals initially rejected orthodox and economistic versions of Marxism, many did (especially over time) appropriate, expand, and recast Marxist categories in an effort to understand the experiences of oppressed and marginalized groups. Thus exponents of what was termed "new working-class theory" claimed that people with technical, clerical, and professional jobs should be seen as constituting a new sector of the working class, better educated than the traditional working class, but working class nonetheless. According to this view, students were not members of the privileged middle class, but rather "trainees" for the new working class. And many women's liberationists (even radical feminists who rejected Marxist theorizing about women's condition) often tried to use Marxist methodology to understand women's oppression. For example, Shulamith Firestone argued that just as the elimination of "economic classes" would require the revolt of the proletariat and their seizure of the means of production, so would the elimination of "sexual classes" require women's revolt and their "seizure of control of reproduction."[25]

If young radicals often assumed an arrogant stance toward those remnants of the Old Left that survived the 1950s, they were by the late 1960s unambiguously contemptuous of liberals. Women's liberationists shared new leftists' and black radicals' rejection of liberalism, and, as a consequence, they often went to great

lengths to distinguish themselves from the liberal feminists of the National Organization for Women (NOW). (In fact, their disillusionment with liberalism was more
thorough during the early stages of their movement building than had been the case
for either new leftists or civil rights activists because they had lived through the
earlier betrayals around the Vietnam War and civil rights. Moreover, male radicals'
frequent denunciations of women's liberation as "bourgeois" encouraged women's
liberationists to distance themselves from NOW.) NOW had been formed in 1966 to
push the federal government to enforce the provisions of the 1964 Civil Rights Act
outlawing sex discrimination — a paradigmatic liberal agenda focused on public
access and the prohibition of employment discrimination. To women's liberation
activists, NOW's integrationist, access-oriented approach ignored the racial and class
inequities that were the very foundation of the "mainstream" that NOW was dedicated to integrating. In the introduction to the 1970 bestseller *Sisterhood Is Powerful*,
Robin Morgan declared that "NOW is essentially an organization that wants reforms
[in the] second-class citizenship of women — and this is where it differs drastically
from the rest of the Women's Liberation Movement."[26] In *The Dialectic of Sex*,
Shulamith Firestone described NOW's political stance as "untenable even in terms
of immediate political gains" and deemed it "more a leftover of the old feminism
rather than a model of the new."[27] Radical feminist Ti-Grace Atkinson went even
further, characterizing many in NOW as only wanting "women to have the same
opportunity to be oppressors, too."[28]

Women's liberationists also took issue with liberal feminists' formulation of wom-
en's problem as their exclusion from the public sphere. Younger activists argued
instead that women's exclusion from public life was inextricable from their subordination in the family and would persist until this larger issue was addressed. For
instance, Firestone claimed that the solution to women's oppression was not inclusion in the mainstream, but rather the eradication of the biological family, which
was the "tapeworm of exploitation."[29]

Of course, younger activists' alienation from NOW was often more than matched
by NOW members' disaffection from them. Many liberal feminists were appalled (at
least initially) by women's liberationists' politicization of personal life. NOW founder
Betty Friedan frequently railed against women's liberationists for waging a "bedroom
war" that diverted women from the real struggle of integrating the public sphere.[30]

Women's liberationists believed that they had embarked on a much more ambitious project — the virtual remaking of the world — and that theirs was the real
struggle.[31] Nothing short of radically transforming society was sufficient to deal with
what they were discovering: that gender inequality was embedded in everyday life.
In 1970 Shulamith Firestone observed that "sex-class is so deep as to be invisible."[32]
The pervasiveness of gender inequality and gender's status as a naturalized category
demonstrated to women's liberationists the inadequacy of NOW's legislative and
judicial remedies and the necessity of thoroughgoing social transformation. Thus,
whereas liberal feminists talked of ending sex discrimination, women's liberationists
called for nothing less than the destruction of capitalism and patriarchy. As defined
by feminists, patriarchy, in contrast to sex discrimination, defied reform. For example, Adrienne Rich contended, "Patriarchy is the power of the fathers: a familial-

social, ideological, political system in which men — by force, direct pressure, or through ritual, tradition, law and language, customs, etiquette, education, and the division of labor, determine what part women shall or shall not play, and in which the female is subsumed under the male." [33]

Women's liberationists typically indicted capitalism as well. Ellen Willis, for instance, maintained that "the American system consists of two interdependent but distinct parts — the capitalist state, and the patriarchal family." Willis argued that capitalism succeeded in exploiting women as cheap labor and consumers "primarily by taking advantage of women's subordinate position in the family and our historical domination by man." [34]

Central to the revisionary project of the women's liberation movement was the desire to render gender meaningless, to explode it as a significant category. In the movement's view, both masculinity and femininity represented not timeless essences, but rather "patriarchal" constructs. (Of course, even as the movement sought to deconstruct gender, it was, paradoxically, as many have noted, trying to mobilize women precisely on the basis of their gender.) [35] This explains in part the significance abortion rights held for women's liberationists, who believed that until abortion was decriminalized, biology would remain women's destiny, thus foreclosing the possibility of women's self-determination." [36]

Indeed, the women's liberation movement made women's bodies the site of political contestation. The "colonized" status of women's bodies became the focus of much movement activism. The discourse of colonization originated in Third World national liberation movements but, in an act of First World appropriation, was taken up by black radicals who claimed that African Americans constituted an "internal colony" in the United States. Radical women trying to persuade the larger Movement of the legitimacy of their cause soon followed suit by deploying the discourse to expose women's subordinate position in relation to men. This appropriation represented an important move and one characteristic of radicalism in the *late* 1960s, that is, the borrowing of conceptual frameworks and discourses from other movements to comprehend the situation of oppressed groups in the United States — with mixed results at best. In fact, women's liberationists challenged not only tyrannical beauty standards, but also violence against women, women's sexual alienation, the compulsory character of heterosexuality and its organization around male pleasure (inscribed in the privileging of the vaginal over clitoral orgasm), the health hazards associated with the birth control pill, the definition of contraception as women's responsibility, and, of course, women's lack of reproductive control. They also challenged the sexual division of labor in the home, employment discrimination, and the absence of quality child care facilities. Finally, women's liberationists recognized the power of language to shape culture.

The totalism of their vision would have been difficult to translate into a concrete reform package, even had they been interested in doing so. But electoral politics and the legislative and judicial reforms that engaged the energies of liberal feminists did little to animate most women's liberationists. Like other sixties radicals, they were instead taken with the idea of developing forms that would prefigure the utopian community of the imagined future. [37] Anxious to avoid the "manipulated consent" that they believed characterized American politics, sixties radicals struggled to develop alternatives to hierarchy and centralized decision making.[38] They spoke often of creating "participatory democracy" in an effort to maximize individual participation and equalize power. Their attempts to build a "democracy of individual participation" often confounded outsiders, who found Movement meetings exhausting and tedious affairs.[39] But to those radicals who craved political engagement, "freedom" was, as one radical group enthused, "an endless meeting."[40] According to Gregory Calvert, participatory democracy appealed to the "deep anti-authoritarianism of the new generation in addition to offering them the immediate concretization of the values of openness, honesty, and community in human relationships."[41] Women's liberationists, still smarting from their firsthand discovery that the larger Movement's much-stated commitment to egalitarianism did not apply equally to all, often took extraordinary measures to try to ensure egalitarianism. They employed a variety of measures in an effort to equalize power, including consensus decision making, rotating chairs, and the sharing of both creative and routine movement work.

Fundamental to this "prefigurative politics," as sociologist Wini Breines terms it, was the commitment to develop counterinstitutions that would anticipate the desired society of the future.[42] Staughton Lynd, director of the Mississippi Freedom Schools and a prominent new leftist, likened sixties radicals to the Wobblies (labor radicals of the early twentieth century) in their commitment to building "the new society within the shell of the old."[43] According to two early SDSers, "What we are working for is far more than changes in the structure of society and its institutions or the people who are now making the decisions. . . . The stress should rather be on wrenching people out of the system both physically and spiritually."[44]

Radicals believed that alternative institutions would not only satisfy needs unmet by the present system, but also, perhaps, by dramatizing the failures of the system, radicalize those not served by it but currently outside the Movement. Tom Hayden proposed that radicals "build our own free institutions — community organizations, newspapers, coffeehouses — at points of strain within the system where human needs are denied. These institutions become centers of identity, points of contact, building blocks of a new society from which we confront the system more intensely."[45]

Among the earliest and best known of such efforts were the Mississippi Freedom Democratic Party and the accompanying Freedom Schools formed during Freedom Summer of 1964. In the aftermath of that summer's Democratic National Convention, Bob Moses [Parris] of the Student Nonviolent Coordinating Committee (SNCC) even suggested that the Movement abandon its efforts to integrate the Democratic Party and try instead to establish its own state government in Mississippi. And as early as 1966 SNCC's Atlanta Project called on blacks to "form our own institutions, credit unions, co-ops, political parties."[46] This came to be the preferred strategy as the sixties progressed and disillusionment with traditional politics grew. Rather than working from within the system, new leftists and black radicals instead formed alternative political parties, media, schools, universities, and assemblies of oppressed and unrepresented people.

Women's liberationists elaborated on this idea, creating an amazing panoply of counterinstitutions. In the years before the 1973 Supreme Court decision decriminalizing abortion, feminists established abortion referral services in most cities of any size. Women's liberationists in Chicago even operated an underground abortion clinic, "Jane," where they performed about one hundred abortions each week.[47] By the mid-1970s most big cities had a low-cost feminist health clinic, a rape crisis center, and a feminist bookstore. In Detroit, after "a long struggle to translate feminism into federalese," two women succeeded in convincing the National Credit Union Administration that feminism was a legitimate "field" from which to draw credit union members. Within three years of its founding in 1973, the Detroit credit union could claim assets of almost one million dollars. Feminists in other cities soon followed suit. Women's liberation activists in Washington, D.C., formed Olivia Records, the first women's record company, which by 1978 was supporting a paid staff of fourteen and producing four records a year.[48] By the mid-1970s there existed in most cities of any size a politicized feminist counterculture, or a "women's community."

The popularity of alternative institutions was that at least in part they seemed to hold out the promise of political effectiveness without co-optation. Writing in 1969, Amiri Baraka (formerly LeRoi Jones), a black nationalist and accomplished poet, maintained, "But you must have the cultural revolution. . . . We cannot fight a war, an actual physical war with the forces of evil just because we are angry. We can begin to build. We must build black institutions . . . all based on a value system that is beneficial to black people."[49]

Jennifer Woodul, one of the founders of Olivia Records, argued that ventures like Olivia represented a move toward gaining "economic power" for women. "We feel it's useless to advocate more and more 'political action' if some of it doesn't result in the permanent material improvement of the lives of women."[50] Robin Morgan termed feminist counterinstitutions "concrete moves toward self-determination and power."[51] The situation, it turned out, was much more complicated. Women involved in nonprofit feminist institutions such as rape crisis centers and shelters for battered women found that their need for state or private funding sometimes militated against adherence to feminist principles.

Feminist businesses, by contrast, discovered that while they were rarely the objects of co-optation, the problem of recuperation remained. In many cases the founders of these institutions became the victims of their own success, as mainstream presses, recording companies, credit unions, and banks encroached on a market they had originally discovered and tapped.[52] For instance, by the end of the 1970s Olivia was forced to reduce its staff almost by half and to scuttle its collective structure.[53] Today k. d. lang, Tracy Chapman, Michelle Shocked, and Sinead O'Connor are among those androgynous women singers enjoying great commercial success, but on major labels. Although Olivia helped lay the groundwork for their achievements, it finds its records, as Arlene Stein has observed, "languishing in the 'women's music' section in the rear [of the record store] if they're there at all."[54]

The move toward building counterinstitutions was part of a larger strategy to develop new societies "within the shell of the old," but this shift sometimes had unintended consequences. While feminist counterinstitutions were originally conceived as part of a culture of resistance, over time they often became more absorbed in sustaining themselves than in confronting male supremacy, especially as their services were duplicated by mainstream businesses. In the early years of the women's liberation movement this alternative feminist culture did provide the sort of "free space" women needed to confront sexism. But as it was further elaborated in the mid-1970s, it ironically often came to promote insularity instead — becoming, as Adrienne Rich has observed, "a place of emigration, an end in itself," where patriarchy was evaded rather than confronted.[55] In practice, feminist communities were small, self-contained subcultures that proved hard to penetrate, especially to newcomers unaccustomed to their norms and conventions. The shift in favor of alternative communities may have sometimes impeded efforts at outreach for the women's liberationists, new leftists, and black radicals who attempted it.

On a related issue, the larger protest Movement's great pessimism about reform — the tendency to interpret every success a defeat resulting in the Movement's further recuperation (what Robin Morgan called "futilitarianism") — may have encouraged a too-global rejection of reform among sixties radicals. For instance, some women's liberation groups actually opposed the Equal Rights Amendment (ERA) when NOW revived it. In September 1970 a New York–based group, The Feminists, denounced the ERA and advised feminists against "squandering invaluable time and energy on it."[56] A delegation of Washington, D.C., women's liberationists invited to appear before the senate subcommittee considering the ERA testified, "We are aware that the system will try to appease us with their [sic] paper offerings. We will not be appeased. Our demands can only be met by a total transformation of society which you cannot legislate, you cannot co-opt, you cannot *control*."[57] In *The Dialectic of Sex*, Firestone went so far as to dismiss child care centers as attempts to "buy women off" because they "ease the immediate pressure without asking why the pressure is on *women*."[58]

Similarly, many SDS leaders opposed the National Conference for New Politics (NCNP), an abortive attempt to form a national progressive organization oriented around electoral politics and to launch an antiwar presidential ticket headed by Martin Luther King, Jr., and Benjamin Spock. Immediately following NCNP's first and only convention, in 1967, the SDS paper *New Left Notes* published two front-page articles criticizing NCNP organizers. One writer contended that "people who recognize the political process as perverted will not seek change through the institutions that process has created."[59] The failure of sixties radicals to distinguish between reform and reformism meant that while they defined the issues, they often did little to develop policy initiatives around those issues.[60] Moreover, the preoccupation of women's liberationists with questions of internal democracy (fueled in part by their desire to succeed where the men had failed) sometimes had the effect of focusing attention away from the larger struggle in an effort to create the perfect movement. As feminist activist Frances Chapman points out, women's liberation was "like a generator that got things going, cut out and left it to the larger reform engine which made a lot of mistakes."[61] In eschewing traditional politics rather than entering them skeptically, women's liberationists, like other sixties radicals, may have lost an opportunity to foster critical debate in the larger arena.

If young radicals eschewed the world of conventional politics, they nonetheless had a profound impact on it, especially by redefining what is understood as "political." Although the women's liberation movement popularized the slogan "the personal is political," the idea that there is a political dimension to personal life was first embraced by early SDSers who had encountered it in the writings of C. Wright Mills.[62] Rebelling against a social order whose public and private spheres were highly differentiated, new leftists called for a reintegration of the personal with the political. They reconceptualized apparently personal problems — specifically their alienation from a campus cultural milieu characterized by sororities and fraternities, husband and wife hunting, sports, and careerism, and the powerlessness they felt as college students without a voice in campus governance or curriculum — as political problems. Thus SDS's founding Port Huron Statement of 1962 suggested that for an American New Left to succeed, it would have to "give form to . . . feelings of helplessness and indifference, so that people may see the political, social, and economic sources of their private troubles and organize to change society."[63] Theirs was a far more expansive formulation of politics than what prevailed in the Old Left, even among the more renegade remnants that had survived into the early sixties.[64] Power was conceptualized as relational and by no means reducible to electoral politics.

By expanding political discourse to include personal relations, new leftists unintentionally paved the way for women's liberationists to develop critiques of the family, marriage, and the construction of sexuality. (Of course, nonfeminist critiques of the family and sexual repressiveness were hardly in short supply in the 1950s and 1960s, as evidenced by *Rebel without a Cause, Catcher in the Rye,* and Paul Goodman's *Growing Up Absurd,* to mention but a few.) Women's liberationists developed an understanding of power's capillarylike nature, which in some respects anticipated those being formulated by Michel Foucault and other poststructuralists.[65] Power was conceptualized as occupying multiple sites and as lodging everywhere, even in those private places assumed to be the most removed from or impervious to politics — the home and, more particularly, the bedroom.

The belief of sixties radicals that the personal is political also suggested to them its converse — that the political is personal. Young radicals typically felt it was not enough to sign leaflets or participate in a march if one returned to the safety and comfort of a middle-class existence. Politics was supposed to unsettle life and its routines, even more, to transform life. For radicals the challenge was to discover, underneath all the layers of social conditioning, the "real" self unburdened by social expectations and conventions. Thus, SNCC leader Stokely Carmichael advanced the slogan, "Every Negro is a potential black man."[66] Shulamith Firestone and Anne Koedt argued that among the "most exciting things to come out of the women's movement so far is a new daring . . . to tear down old structures and assumptions and let real thought and feeling flow."[67] Life would not be comfortable, but who wanted comfort in the midst of so much deadening complacency? For a great many radicals, the individual became a site of political activism in the sixties. In the black freedom movement the task was very much to discover the black inside the Negro, and in the women's liberation movement it was to unlearn niceness, to challenge the taboo against female self-assertion.[68]

Sixties radicalism proved compelling to many precisely because it promised to transform life. Politics was not about the subordination of self to some larger political cause; instead, it was the path to self-fulfillment. This ultimately was the power of sixties radicalism. As Stanley Aronowitz notes, sixties radicalism was in large measure about "infus[ing] life with a secular spiritual and moral content" and "fill[ing] the quotidian with personal meaning and purpose."[69] But "the personal is political" was one of those ideas whose rhetorical power seemed to sometimes work against or undermine its explication. It could encourage a solipsistic preoccupation with self-transformation. As new leftist Richard Flacks presciently observed in 1965, this kind of politics could lead to "a search for personally satisfying modes of life while abandoning the possibility of helping others to change theirs."[70] Thus the idea that "politics is how you live your life, not who you vote for," as Yippie leader Jerry Rubin put it, could and did lead to a subordination of politics to lifestyle.[71] If the idea led some to confuse personal liberation with political struggle, it led others to embrace an asceticism that sacrificed personal needs and desires to political imperatives. Some women's liberation activists followed this course, interpreting the idea that the personal is political to mean that one's personal life should conform to some abstract standard of political correctness. At first this tendency was mitigated by the founders' insistence that there were no personal solutions, only collective solutions, to women's oppression. Over time, however, one's self-presentation, marital status, and sexual preference frequently came to determine one's standing or ranking in the movement. The most notorious example of this involved the New York radical group The Feminists, who established a quota to limit the number of married women in the group.[72] Policies such as these prompted Barbara Ehrenreich to question "a feminism which talks about universal sisterhood, but is horrified by women who wear spiked heels or call their friends 'girls.' "[73] At the same time, what was personally satisfying was sometimes upheld as politically correct. In the end, both the women's liberation movement and the larger protest Movement suffered, as the idea that the personal is political was often interpreted in such a way as to make questions of lifestyle absolutely central.

The social movements of the sixties signaled the beginning of what has come to be known as "identity politics," the idea that politics is rooted in identity.[74] Although some New Left groups by the late 1960s did come to endorse an orthodox Marxism whereby class was privileged, class was not the pivotal category for these new social movements.[75] (Even those New Left groups that reverted to the "labor metaphysic" lacked meaningful working-class participation.) Rather, race, ethnicity, gender, sexual preference, and youth were the salient categories for most sixties activists. In the women's liberation movement, what was termed "consciousness-raising" was the tool used to develop women's group identity.

As women's liberationists started to organize a movement, they confronted American women who identified unambiguously as women, but who typically had little of what Nancy Cott would call "we-ness," or "some level of identification with 'the group called women.' "[76] Moreover, both the pervasiveness of gender inequality and the cultural understanding of gender as a natural rather than a social construct made it difficult to cultivate a critical consciousness about gender even among women. To engender this sense of sisterhood or "we-ness," women's liberationists developed consciousness-raising, a practice involving "the political reinterpretation of personal life."[77] According to its principal architects, its purpose was to "awaken the latent consciousness that . . . all women have about our oppression." In talking about their personal experiences, it was argued, women would come to understand that what they had believed were personal problems were, in fact, "social problems that must become social issues and fought together rather than with personal solutions."[78]

Reportedly, New York women's liberationist Kathie Sarachild was the person who coined the term *consciousness-raising*. However, the technique originated in other social movements. As Sarachild wrote in 1973, those who promoted consciousness-raising "were applying to women and to ourselves as women's liberation organizers the practice a number of us had learned in the civil rights movement in the South in the early 1960's."[79] There they had seen that the sharing of personal problems, grievances, and aspirations — "telling it like it is" — could be a radicalizing experience. Moreover, for some women's liberationists consciousness-raising was a way to avoid the tendency of some members of the movement to try to fit women within existing (and often Marxist) theoretical paradigms. By circumventing the "experts" on women and going to women themselves, they would be able to not only construct a theory of women's oppression but formulate strategy as well. Thus women's liberationists struggled to find the commonalities in women's experiences in order to formulate generalizations about women's oppression.

Consciousness-raising was enormously successful in exposing the insidiousness of sexism and in engendering a sense of identity and solidarity among the largely white, middle-class women who participated in "c-r" groups. By the early 1970s even NOW, whose founder Betty Friedan had initially derided consciousness-raising as so much "navel-gazing," began sponsoring c-r groups.[80] But the effort to transcend the particular was both the strength and the weakness of consciousness-raising. If it encouraged women to locate the common denominators in their lives, it inhibited discussion of women's considerable differences. Despite the particularities of white, middle-class women's experiences, theirs became the basis for feminist theorizing about women's oppression. In a more general sense the identity politics informing consciousness-raising tended to privilege experience in certain problematic ways. It was too often assumed that there existed a kind of core experience, initially articulated as "women's experience." Black and white radicals (the latter in relation to youth) made a similar move as well. When Stokely Carmichael called on blacks to develop an "ideology which speaks to our blackness," he, like other black nationalists, suggested that there was somehow an essential and authentic "blackness."

With the assertion of difference within the women's movement in the 1980s, the notion that women constitute a unitary category has been problematized. As a consequence, women's experiences have become ever more discretely defined, as in "the black female experience," "the Jewish female experience," or "the Chicana lesbian experience." But, as Audre Lorde has argued, there remains a way in which, even with greater and greater specificity, the particular is never fully captured.[81] Instead, despite the pluralization of the subject within feminism, identities are often still imagined as monolithic. Finally, the very premise of identity politics — that identity is the basis of politics — has sometimes shut down possibilities for communication, as identities are seen as necessarily either conferring or foreclosing critical consciousness. Kobena Mercer, a British film critic, has criticized the rhetorical strategies of "authenticity and authentication" that tend to characterize identity politics. He has observed, "if I preface a point by saying something like, 'as a black gay man, I feel marginalized by your discourse,' it makes a valid point but in such a way that preempts critical dialogue because such a response could be inferred as a criticism not of what I say but of what or who I am. The problem is replicated in the familiar cop-out clause, 'as a middle-class, white, heterosexual male, what can I say?' "[82]

The problem is that the mere assertion of identity becomes in a very real sense irrefutable. Identity is presented as not only stable and fixed, but also insurmountable. While identity politics gives the oppressed the moral authority to speak (perhaps a dubious ground from which to speak), it can, ironically, absolve those belonging to dominant groups from having to engage in a critical dialogue. In some sense, then, identity politics can unintentionally reinforce Other-ness. Finally, as the antifeminist backlash and the emergence of the New Right should demonstrate, there is nothing inherently progressive about identity. It can be, and has been, mobilized for reactionary as well as for radical purposes.[83] For example, the participation of so many women in the antiabortion movement reveals just how problematic the reduction of politics to identity can be.

Accounts of sixties radicalism usually cite its role in bringing about the dismantling of Jim Crow and disfranchisement, the withdrawal of U.S. troops from Vietnam, and greater gender equality. However, equally important, if less frequently noted, was its challenge to politics as usual. Sixties radicals succeeded both in reformulating politics, even mainstream politics, to include personal life, and in challenging the notion that elites alone have the wisdom and expertise to control the political process. For a moment, people who by virtue of their color, age, and gender were far from the sites of formal power became politically engaged, became agents of change.

Given the internal contradictions and shortcomings of sixties radicalism, the repressiveness of the federal government in the late 1960s and early 1970s, and changing economic conditions in the United States, it is not surprising that the movements built by radicals in the sixties either no longer exist or do so only in attenuated form. Activists in the women's liberation movement, however, helped bring about a fundamental realignment of gender roles in this country through outrageous protests, tough-minded polemics, and an "ecstasy of discussion." Indeed, those of us who came of age in the days before the resurgence of feminism know that the world today, while hardly a feminist utopia, is nonetheless a far different, and in many respects a far fairer, world than what we confronted in 1967.

NOTES

1. See Carol Hanisch, "A Critique of the Miss America Protest," in *Notes from the Second Year: Women's Liberation,* ed. Shulamith Firestone and Anne Koedt (New York: Radical

Feminism, 1970), 87; and Judith Duffet, "Atlantic City Is a Town with Class — They Raise Your Morals While They Judge Your Ass," *Voice of the Women's Liberation Movement* 1, no. 3 (October 1968). The protesters also criticized the pageant's narrow formulation of beauty, especially its racist equation of beauty with whiteness. They emphasized that in its forty-seven-year history, the pageant had never crowned a black woman Miss America. That weekend the first Black Miss America Pageant was held in Atlantic City.

2. See Lindsy Van Gelder, "Bra Burners Plan Protest," *New York Post*, 4 September 1968, which appeared three days before the protest. The *New York Times* article by Charlotte Curtis quoted Robin Morgan as having said about the mayor of Atlantic City, "He was worried about our burning things. He said the boardwalk had already been burned out once this year. We told him we wouldn't do anything dangerous — just a symbolic bra-burning." Curtis, "Miss America Pageant Is Picketed by 100 Women," *New York Times*, 8 September 1968.

3. See Jack Gould's column in the *New York Times*, 9 September 1968.

4. The Yippies were a small group of leftists who, in contrast to most of the Left, had enthusiastically embraced the growing counterculture. For a fascinating account of the 1968 convention, see David Farber, *Chicago '68* (Chicago: University of Chicago Press, 1988).

5. Curtis, "Miss America Pageant."

6. For the sake of convenience, I will use the term *Movement* to describe the overlapping protest movements of the sixties — the black freedom movement, the student movement, the antiwar movement, and the more selfconsciously political New Left. I will refer to the women's liberation movement as the *movement*; here I use the lower case simply to avoid confusion.

7. Snitow, interview by author, New York, 14 June 1984. Here one can get a sense of the disjuncture in experiences between white and black women; presumably, black women had not felt the same sense of distance about their civil rights activism.

8. Robin Morgan, *Going Too Far: The Personal Chronicle of a Feminist* (New York: Random House, 1978), 62.

9. Yet virtually all the recently published books on the sixties either slight or ignore the protest. This omission is emblematic of a larger problem, the failure of authors to integrate women's liberation into their reconstruction of that period. Indeed, most of these books have replicated the position of women in the larger, male-dominated protest Movement — that is, the women's liberation movement is relegated to the margins of the narrative. Such marginalization has been exacerbated as well by the many feminist recollections of the sixties that demonize the Movement and present women's liberation as its antithesis. Sixties books that textually subordinate the women's liberation movement include James Miller, *Democracy Is in the Streets: From Port Huron to the Siege of Chicago* (New York: Simon and Schuster, 1987); Tom Hayden, *Reunion: A Memoir* (New York: Random House, 1988); Todd Gitlin, *The Sixties: Years of Hope, Days of Rage* (New York: Bantam, 1987); and Nancy Zaroulis and Gerald Sullivan, *Who Spoke Up? American Protest against the War in Vietnam* (Garden City, NY: Doubleday, 1984). A notable exception is Stewart Burns, *Social Movements of the 1960's: Searching for Democracy* (Boston: Twayne, 1990).

10. Sara Evans, *Personal Politics: The Roots of Women's Liberation in the Civil Rights Movement and the New Left* (New York: Vintage Books, 1979).

11. Sara Evans has argued that in their attempt to combine work inside and outside the family, educated, middle-class, married white women of the 1950s were following the path pioneered by black women. See Evans, *Born for Liberty: A History of Women in America* (New York: Free Press, 1989), 253–54. As Jacqueline Jones and others have demonstrated, black women have a "long history of combining paid labor with domestic obligations."

According to Jones, in 1950 one-third of all married black women were in the labor force, compared to one-quarter of all married women in the general population. One study cited by Jones "concluded that black mothers of school-aged children were more likely to work than their white counterparts, though part-time positions in the declining field of domestic service inhibited growth in their rates of labor force participation." Jones, *Labor of Love, Labor of Sorrow: Black Women, Work, and the Family, from Slavery to the Present* (New York: Vintage Books, 1986), 269.

12. Alice Kessler-Harris, *Out to Work: A History of Wage-Earning Women in the United States* (New York: Oxford University Press, 1982), 302.

13. Evans, *Born for Liberty*, 252.

14. Jane De Hart-Mathews, "The New Feminism and the Dynamics of Social Change," in *Women's America: Refocusing the Past*, 2d ed., ed. Linda Kerber and Jane De Hart-Mathews (New York: Oxford University Press, 1987), 445.

15. I think that this was an experience specific to white women. The problem of diffidence seems to have been, if not unique to white women, then especially acute for them. This is not to say that issues of gender were unimportant to black women activists in the sixties, but that gender seemed less primary and pressing an issue than race. However, much more research is needed in this area. It could be that the black women's noninvolvement in women's liberation had as much, if not more, to do with the movement's racism than any prioritizing of race.

16. Carl Oglesby, "Trapped in a System," reprinted as "Liberalism and the Corporate State," in *The New Radicals: A Report with Documents*, ed. Paul Jacobs and Saul Landau (New York: Vintage Books, 1966), 266. For a useful discussion of the New Left's relationship to liberalism, see Gitlin, *The Sixties*, 127–92.

17. See Howard Brick, "Inventing Post-Industrial Society: Liberal and Radical Social Theory in the 1960's" (paper delivered at the 1990 American Studies Association Conference). In September 1963 the electoral politics faction of SDS had even succeeded in getting the group to adopt the slogan "Part of the Way with LBJ." Johnson's official campaign slogan was "All the Way with LBJ." See Gitlin, *The Sixties*, 180.

18. Gregory Calvert, interview, *Movement* 3, no. 2 (1967): 6.

19. Andrew Kopkind, "Looking Backward: The Sixties and the Movement," *Ramparts* 11, no. 8 (February 1973): 32.

20. That evening seven million people watched Johnson's speech to Congress announcing voting rights legislation. According to C. T. Vivian, "a tear ran down" Martin Luther King's cheek as Johnson finished his speech. Juan Williams, *Eyes on the Prize: America's Civil Rights Years, 1954–65* (New York: Penguin, 1988), 278.

21. Elinor Langer discusses the ways Marcuse's notion of repressive tolerance was used by the Movement. See her wonderful essay, "Notes for Next Time," *Working Papers for a New Society* 1, no. 3 (fall 1973): 48–83.

22. Ellen Kay Trimberger, "Women in the Old and New Left: The Evolution of a Politics of Personal Life," *Feminist Studies* 5, no. 3 (fall 1979): 442.

23. Potter quoted from Miller, *Democracy Is in the Streets*, 196.

24. Miller quoted from Gitlin, *The Sixties*, 9. Although the broad outlines of Miller's argument are correct, some recent scholarship on 1930s radicalism suggests that it was considerably more varied and less narrowly economistic than has been previously acknowledged. For example, recent books by Paula Rabinowitz and Robin Kelley demonstrate that some radicals in this period understood the salience of such categories as gender and race. See Paula Rabinowitz, *Labor and Desire: Women's Revolutionary Fiction in Depression*

America (Chapel Hill: University of North Carolina Press, 1991); Robin Kelley, *Hammer and Hoe: Alabama Communists during the Great Depression* (Chapel Hill: University of North Carolina Press, 1990).

25. Shulamith Firestone, *The Dialectic of Sex: The Case for Feminist Revolution*, rev. ed. (New York: Bantam Books, 1971), 10–11.

26. Robin Morgan, in *Sisterhood Is Powerful*, ed. Morgan (New York: Vintage Books, 1970), xxii.

27. Firestone, *The Dialectic of Sex*, 33. For a very useful history of women's rights activism (as opposed to women's liberation) in the postwar years, see Cynthia Harrison, *On Account of Sex: The Politics of Women's Issues, 1945–68* (Berkeley: University of California Press, 1988).

28. Ti-Grace Atkinson, *Amazon Odyssey* (New York: Link Books, 1974), 10. In contrast to other founders of early radical feminist groups, Atkinson came to radicalism through her involvement in the New York City chapter of NOW, admittedly the most radical of all NOW chapters. Atkinson made this remark in October 1968 after having failed badly in her attempt to radically democratize the New York chapter of NOW. Upon losing the vote she immediately resigned her position as the chapter's president and went on to establish The Feminists, a radical feminist group.

29. Firestone, *The Dialectic of Sex*, 12.

30. Betty Friedan, *It Changed My Life: Writings on the Women's Movement* (New York: Random House, 1976), 153. Friedan was antagonistic to radical feminism from the beginning and rarely missed an opportunity to denounce the man-hating and sex warfare that she claimed it advocated. Her declamations against "sexual politics" began at least as early as January 1969.

31. Due to limitations of space and the focus of this chapter, I do not discuss the many differences among women's liberationists, most crucially, the conflicts between "radical feminists" and "politicos" over the relationship between the women's liberation movement and the larger Movement and the role of capitalism in maintaining women's oppression. This is taken up at length in Alice Echols, *Daring to Be Bad: Radical Feminism in America, 1967–75* (Minneapolis: University of Minnesota Press, 1989).

32. Firestone, *The Dialectic of Sex*, 1. It is the opening line of her book.

33. Adrienne Rich quoted from Hester Eisenstein, *Contemporary Feminist Thought* (Boston: G. K. Hall, 1983), 5.

34. Ellen Willis, "Sequel: Letter to a Critic," in *Notes from the Second Year*, ed. Firestone and Koedt, 57.

35. See Ann Snitow, "Gender Diary," *Dissent*, spring 1989, 205–24; Carole Vance, "Social Construction Theory: Problems in the History of Sexuality," in *Homosexuality, Which Homosexuality?* ed. Anja van Kooten Niekark and Theo van der Maer (Amsterdam: An Dekken/Schorer, 1989).

36. Ellen Willis discusses the centrality of abortion to the women's liberation movement in the foreword to *Daring to Be Bad*. For the young, mostly white middle-class women who were attracted to women's liberation, the issue was forced reproduction. But for women of color, the issue was as often forced sterilization, and women's liberationists would tackle that issue as well.

37. Stanley Aronowitz, "When the New Left Was New," in *The Sixties without Apology*, ed. Sohnya Sayres, Anders Stephanson, Stanley Aronowitz, and Fredric Jameson (Minneapolis: University of Minnesota Press, 1984), 32.

38. C. Wright Mills quoted from Miller, *Democracy Is in the Streets*, 86.

39. The phrase is from SDS's founding statement, "The Port Huron Statement," which is

reprinted in full as an appendix to Miller's book, *Democracy Is in the Streets*, 333. For instance, Irving Howe, an influential member of the Old Left who attended a couple of SDS meetings, called them "interminable and structureless sessions." Howe, "The Decade That Failed," *New York Times Magazine*, 19 September 1982, 78.

40. The statement appeared in a pamphlet produced by the Economic Research and Action Project of SDS. Miller quotes it in *Democracy Is in the Streets*, 215.

41. Gregory Calvert, "Participatory Democracy, Collective Leadership, and Political Responsibility," *New Left Notes*, 2, no. 45 (18 December 1967): 1.

42. See Breines's summary of prefigurative politics in *Community and Organization in the New Left, 1962–68* (New York: Praeger, 1982), 1–8.

43. Staughton Lynd, "The Movement: A New Beginning," *Liberation* 14, no. 2 (May 1969).

44. Pat Hansen and Ken McEldowney, "A Statement of Values," *New Left Notes*, 1, no. 42 (November 1966): 5.

45. Tom Hayden, "Democracy Is . . . in the Streets," *Rat* 1, no. 15 (23 August–5 September 1968): 5.

46. The Atlanta Project's position paper has been reprinted as "SNCC Speaks for Itself," in *The Sixties Papers: Documents of a Rebellious Decade*, ed. Judith Clavir Albert and Stewart Albert (New York: Praeger, 1984), 122. However, the title assigned it by the Alberts is misleading because at the time it was written in the spring of 1966, it did not reflect majority opinion in SNCC.

47. Rosalind Petchesky, *Abortion and Woman's Choice: The State, Sexuality, and Reproductive Freedom* (New York: Longman Press, 1984), 128.

48. Michelle Kort, "Sisterhood Is Profitable," *Mother Jones*, July 1983, 44.

49. Amiri Imanu Baraka, "A Black Value System," *Black Scholar*, November 1969.

50. Jennifer Woodul, "What's This about Feminist Businesses?" *off our backs* 6, no. 4 (June 1976): 24–26.

51. Robin Morgan, "Rights of Passage," *Ms.*, September 1975, 99.

52. For a fascinating case study of this as it relates to women's music, see Arlene Stein, "Androgyny Goes Pop," *Out/Look* 3, no. 3 (spring 1991): 26–33.

53. Kort, "Sisterhood Is Profitable," 44.

54. Stein, "Androgyny Goes Pop," 30.

55. Adrienne Rich, "Living the Revolution," *Women's Review of Books* 3, no. 12 (September 1986): 1, 3–4.

56. Quoted from Jane Mansbridge, *Why We Lost the ERA* (Chicago: University of Chicago Press, 1986), 266.

57. "Women's Liberation Testimony," *off our backs* 1, no. 5 (May 1970): 7.

58. Firestone, *The Dialectic of Sex*, 206.

59. Steve Halliwell, "Personal Liberation and Social Change," *New Left Notes*, 2, no. 30 (4 September 1967): 1; see also Rennie Davis and Staughton Lynd, "On NCNP," *New Left Notes* 2, no. 30. (4 September 1967): 1.

60. See Charlotte Bunch, "The Reform Tool Kit," *Quest* 1, no. 1 (summer 1974).

61. Frances Chapman, interview by author, New York, 30 May 1984. Here Chapman was speaking of the radical feminist wing of the women's liberation movement, but it applies as well to women's liberation activists.

62. For more on the prefigurative, personal politics of the sixties, see Breines, *Community and Organization in the New Left*; Miller, *Democracy Is in the Streets*; and Aronowitz, "When the New Left Was New."

63. Quoted from Miller, *Democracy Is in the Streets,* 374.

64. Although individual social critics such as C. Wright Mills influenced the thinking of new leftists, the noncommunist Left of the 1950s and early 1960s remained economistic and anticommunist. Indeed, the fact that the board of the League for Industrial Democracy — the parent organization of SDS in SDS's early years — ignored the values section of the Port Huron Statement suggests the disjuncture between old and new leftists. For another view stressing the continuities between the Old and the New Left, see Maurice Isserman, *If I Had a Hammer . . . The Death of the Old Left and the Birth of the New Left* (New York: Basic Books, 1987).

65. See Judith Newton, "Historicisms New and Old: 'Charles Dickens' Meets Marxism, Feminism, and West Coast Foucault," *Feminist Studies* 16, no. 3 (fall 1990): 464. In their assumption that power has a source and that it emanates from patriarchy, women's liberationists part company with Foucauldian approaches that reject large-scale paradigms of domination.

66. Carmichael quoted from Clayborne Carson, *In Struggle: SNCC and the Black Awakening of the 1960's* (Cambridge: Harvard University Press, 1981), 282.

67. Firestone and Koedt, "Editorial," in *Notes from the Second Year,* ed. Firestone and Koedt.

68. However, the reclamation of blackness was often articulated in a sexist fashion, as in Stokely Carmichael's 1968 declaration, "Every Negro is a potential black man." See Carmichael, "A Declaration of War," in *The New Left: A Documentary History,* ed. Teodori Massimo (Indianapolis: Bobbs-Merrill, 1969), 277.

69. Aronowitz, "When the New Left Was New," 18.

70. Richard Flacks, "Some Problems, Issues, Proposals," in *The New Radicals,* ed. Jacobs and Landau, 168. This was a working paper intended for the June 1965 convention of SDS.

71. Excerpts from Jerry Rubin's book, *Do It,* appeared in *Rat* 2, no. 26 (26 January–9 February 1970).

72. "The Feminists: A Political Organization to Annihilate Sex Roles," in *Notes from the Second Year,* ed. Firestone and Koedt, 117.

73. Ehrenreich quoted from Carol Ann Douglas, "Second Sex 30 Years Later," *off our backs* 9, no. 11 (December 1979): 26.

74. The term *identity politics* was, I think, first used by black and Chicana feminists. See Diana Fuss, *Essentially Speaking: Feminism, Nature, and Difference* (New York: Routledge, 1989), 99.

75. Jeffrey Weeks locates the origins of identity politics in the post-1968 political flux. He argues that "identity politics can be seen as part of the unfinished business of the 1960's, challenging traditionalist hierarchies of power and the old, all-encompassing social and political identities associated, for example, with class and occupation." Perhaps Weeks situates this in the post-1968 period, because class held greater significance for many British new leftists than it did for their American counterparts. Weeks, "Sexuality and (Post) Modernity" (unpublished paper).

76. Nancy Cott, *The Grounding of Modern Feminism* (New Haven: Yale University Press, 1987), 5.

77. Amy Kesselman, interview by author, New York, 2 May 1984.

78. "The New York Consciousness Awakening Women's Liberation Group" (handout from the Lake Villa Conference, November 1968).

79. Kathie Sarachild, "Consciousness-Raising: A Radical Weapon," in *Feminist Revolution,* ed. Redstockings (New Paltz, NY: Redstockings, 1975), 132.

80. Betty Friedan, *It Changed My Life* (New York: Norton, 1985), 101.

81. Audre Lorde, *Zami: A New Spelling of My Name* (Freedom, CA: Crossing Press, 1982), 226.

82. Lorraine Kenney, "Traveling Theory: The Cultural Politics of Race and Representation: An Interview with Kobena Mercer," *Afterimage*, September 1990, 9.

83. Mercer makes this point as well in Kenney, "Traveling Theory," 9.

TWENTY-EIGHT

Organizational Mobilizations, Institutional Access, and Institutional Change

DEBRA C. MINKOFF

Women's political and social gains in recent decades owe much to their organizational mobilizations — both within and outside the electoral arena. The mainstream women's movement, building on established histories of social action among privileged white women, brought pressure to bear on political, economic, and social life. During the 1970s in particular, women's organizations expanded at a rapid pace, at the same time that key movement organizations became more professionalized and women's interests were presumably institutionalized in the political arena. In tandem with this trend, the more radical and less formalized wing of the feminist movement faced an increasingly restrictive environment for political action and tended to move into less visible and more local arenas (Ferree and Hess 1985; Ferree and Martin 1995; Costain 1992; Taylor and Whittier 1993).

This trend toward the professionalization of national social movement organizations, combined with the prevalence of white middle-class women in leadership positions, has also represented a significant limitation on the work of the mainstream feminist movement. Lack of attention to the concerns of women of color, working-class women, lesbians, and other marginalized constituencies has meant that the movement has pursued a limited equal opportunity agenda (Davis 1983; Garcia 1990; King 1988; Higginbotham 1993). This exclusion and narrowness has been an important factor in the proliferation of national women of color organizations since the 1970s, such as the National Black Feminist Organization, the National Conference of Puerto Rican Women, and the Mexican American Women's Association. The National Congress of Neighborhood Women was created in support of working-class women in 1974, which was the same year that the Coalition of Labor Union Women was founded (Balser 1987; Ferree and Hess 1985).

As often as the limitations of the mainstream women's movement are elaborated, very little is documented about the actual differences in national organizing styles between predominantly white women's groups and those organizations established by women of color and working-class women, as well as among such groups themselves (on the latter point see Hernandez 1991; Barnett 1995). Nor do we really understand the implications of such different organizational choices for women's political action. The main purposes of this chapter are to describe the variety of ways that white women and women of color have organized nationally since the mid-1950s, and to suggest how the diversity in women's interests, organizations, and traditions of voluntary action has shaped their current access to, and ability to change, conventional interest group and social movement politics.

My argument is that to the extent that women of color organizations choose less traditional combinations of goals, strategy, and structure, this acts as one more mechanism isolating these constituencies from centers of power and decision making, since such institutions favor established forms of organization.[1] At the same time, by actualizing alternative organizational profiles, such groups increase the potential for institutional inclusiveness and change — if they are able to survive, grow, and gain a credible voice without being co-opted. Successful organizational mobilizations expand the boundaries of what are defined as legitimate constituencies and forms of action, even if change in progressive directions is incremental.

National Organizations and Activism in the United States

Sociological research on social movements shows that to understand the development of activism by marginalized constituencies, we must examine the traditions of social action and community infrastructures on which they build (Morris 1984; Taylor 1989); the political and resource environment in which activism develops (McCarthy and Zald 1977; McAdam 1982); and the range and diversity of organizational goals, structures, and strategies that make up various movements for social change and the social movement sector more generally (Garner and Zald 1987; Zald and McCarthy 1980; Minkoff 1995). In the U.S. context, it is especially important to consider the organizational dimension of activism, since interest groups, voluntary associations, and nonprofit community service providers are relied on to supplement a weak welfare state (Ferree and Martin 1995). The dominance of organizations also reflects the greater responsiveness of authorities to the mobilization of organizations over protest mobilizations — which are more likely to meet with state repression (McAdam 1982; Jenkins and Ekert 1986). At the same time, protest is unlikely to emerge without the support of an organizational infrastructure that provides resources and networks for its diffusion (McAdam 1982; Morris 1984). It is therefore essential to understand how the organizational bias of U.S. politics delimits the amount and type of organizations established by women of color.

Importantly, national organization building has not been the only (or even the primary) mode of collective action by women of color. The resources and community support necessary for national mobilization are not readily available to socially and economically marginalized groups (Piven and Cloward 1978). Focusing on national organizations thereby understates the total collective action of women of color who do not have equal access to this method of institutional challenge. Also, the simultaneity of race, class, and gender oppression has meant both alignment with and exclusion from national social movements such as the civil rights movement, the women's movement, and the labor movement. Engagement has usually meant subsuming one set of interests for another — in many cases with nationalist concerns taking precedence (Garcia 1990; Davis 1983; hooks 1981, 1984; King 1988).

Classifying women of color organizations in terms of their emphasis on feminist concerns is problematic to the extent that it simplifies a multifaceted commitment to interlocking strategies to challenge gender, racial, and class inequalities (Davis 1983; Crenshaw 1989; hooks 1984; Garcia 1990; Pardo 1995). My interest in this chapter, however, is specifically the contours of those national organizations that explicitly identify themselves with struggles against sexism. Although I hesitate to call such organizations feminist — especially since many women of color reject this term as specific to white middle-class liberal feminism (Garcia 1990; King 1988) — Patricia Martin's (1990) definition is useful in clarifying the organizations that I include in my conceptualization of the white women's and women of color organizational sectors. She suggests that a feminist politics "favors changes to improve women's collective status, living conditions, opportunities, power, and self-esteem" (Martin 1990, 184). How the organizations formed and maintained to these ends by women of color differ from those established and run mainly by white women is the empirical question that motivates this study.

White Women's Mobilization

Nationally visible activism by women has been associated mostly with organizations dominated by white middle-class women — in terms of leadership, staff, membership, and reform agendas that privilege traditional bourgeois liberalism. Mainstream feminism has tended to emphasize equal opportunities for women, especially with respect to access to the paid labor force and escape from the domestic sphere (Dill 1983; King 1988). These objectives are of less consequence to women of color, who have had historically higher rates of labor force participation. In addition, women of color have viewed white women's access to a private family sphere as a privilege rather than a constraint. Such divergent interests have thus limited the movement's relevance for women of color (Dill 1983; Collins 1991).

Liberal feminist organizations are associated with the more reform-oriented wing of the contemporary women's movement (Ferree and Hess 1985). This branch of the movement has utilized more established methods of interest group and social movement politics, such as lobbying, litigation, research, and information dissemination, along with demonstrations and disruptions. This approach entailed the creation of national social movement organizations and interest groups in the late 1960s, for example, the National Organization for Women, the Women's Equity Action League, and the National Women's Political Caucus. These national associations tended to be constructed around predominantly hierarchical and centralized models of organization and were moderate with respect to national-level movement goals and tactics.[2] During the emergent phase of the contemporary feminist movement, which was between 1963 and 1970 according to Ferree and Hess (1985), white middle-class feminists drew on a tradition of associational activity and owed a great deal in the way of resources and access to traditional women's organizations such as the League of Women Voters and the YWCA, where many of them gained leadership skills (Gelb and Paley 1982; Klein 1984; Taylor 1989). Many of these established voluntary associations also began to address gender inequality in the 1970s, adding to the number and diversity of national organizations (Gelb and Paley 1982).

The younger branch of the women's movement has historically been more local and decentralized. As a result, it has constituted a smaller segment of the national women's group structure (Ferree and Martin 1995; Whittier 1995). As Evans (1979) describes it, many of the women in this younger branch were motivated by their deep frustration with the contradictions between progressive politics and practice in the civil rights and student movements of the 1960s to organize independently against male-dominated institutions. They formed a variety of smaller, less formal groups that engaged in more disruptive collective action and direct resource provision to women (shelters, health clinics, abortion referral information, etc.), as well as consciousness-raising activities (Evans 1979; Freeman 1973; Whittier 1995). For the most part, liberation groups sought more radical structural change and were committed to collectivist, participatory models of decision making and organization.

By 1980, the women's movement had become an institutionalized actor in the political arena, forming a dense and diverse field of organizational activity (Costain 1992). There is a great deal of heterogeneity in this national organizational system, which includes mass-based membership associations such as NOW; specialized litigation and research groups such as the Center for Women Policy Studies; single-issue groups like the National Abortion Rights Action League; coalitions of direct service providers, for example, the Displaced Homemakers Network; traditional voluntary associations such as the YWCA; and an electoral campaign sector that includes political action committees and campaign-oriented groups such as Women's Campaign Fund (Gelb and Paley 1982; Spalter-Roth and Schreiber 1995). Ferree and Martin (1995) suggest that three decades of antifeminism have curtailed national organizations in the 1990s, but that local feminist organizations remain vibrant if not visible (see also Katzenstein 1990; Taylor and Whittier 1993; Whittier 1995).

Women of Color Activism

As Angela Davis noted more than a decade ago, there have been (and still are) "two distinct continuums of the women's movement, one visible and another invisible, one publicly acknowledged and another ignored except by the conscious progeny of the working-class women — Black, Latina, Native American, Asian, and white — who forged that hidden continuum" (1983, 7). The greater visibility of white women's organizations, combined with the greater access of middle-class white women to the means of intellectual production and communication, means that much more is known about such organizations than about the set of organizations representing the interests of women of color at the national level.

Recent scholarship on women of color activism has concentrated on making visible the historical contributions of women of color to a diverse set of collective efforts at social change (Davis 1983; Gilkes 1994; Higginbotham 1993; Barnett 1995; Crawford, Rouse, and Woods 1990). There are also important efforts to document their exclusion from more recent collective challenges such as the contemporary feminist movement and debates about the desirability of coalition with middle-class white women given significant divergences in social location and political interests, commitments, and resources (Giddings 1984; King 1988; Dill 1983; hooks 1981; Garcia 1990; Chow 1987). These combined projects illustrate the limits placed on Black women activists by racism and sexism and the resolution of the women who have challenged such constraints. There are also an increasing number of parallel projects that clarify the nature and extent of Latina and Asian American feminist consciousness and activism (Garcia 1990; Hardy-Fanta 1993; Chow 1987; Pardo 1995).

Activism by women of color has multiple dimensions. At the community level, African American women have engaged in what Cheryl Townsend Gilkes (1994) calls community work and Patricia Hill Collins (1991) refers to as the struggle for group survival. At its core, "community work is focused on internal development and external challenge, and creates ideas enabling people to think about change" (Gilkes 1994, 230). Latinas and Asian American women also have long traditions of broad-based community activism that have centered on empowering and improving the quality of life for group members through the provision of resources, services, and education (Naples 1992). Although not limited to challenging gender oppression, community-based activism is at once gendered and feminist with respect to such qualities as a rejection of hierarchy, collective sharing of leadership and power, and an emphasis on collective rather than individual empowerment (Pardo 1995; Hardy-Fanta 1993; Chow 1987; Gilkes 1994; Higginbotham 1993).

Along with these forms of community work, women of color have pursued a "politics of institutional transformation" (Collins 1991) both locally and nationally. Political action has centered on grassroots social movement activism, institutional politics, and pressure group activity to challenge racial, class, and gender inequalities. Collective institutional challenges have taken place both within and outside Black, Asian, and Latino nationalist movements and mainstream white women's organizations (Collins 1991; King 1988; Garcia 1990; Chow 1987). Explicit institutional challenges against gender oppression by women of color became more visible and organized in the early 1970s, marked by the 1973 formation of the National Black Feminist Organization and the founding of the Combahee River Collective in 1974 (Giddings 1984). During this period, Black women became more willing to organize primarily around feminist issues (King 1988; Chow 1987; Garcia 1990). The result was varied — political organizations, cultural enterprises, Black feminist scholarship, as well as participation in the mainstream women's movement (King 1988; Giddings 1984).[3]

Latina and Asian American feminists followed a similar trajectory, initially dismissing the mainstream women's movement as limited by racism and classism and then establishing autonomous feminist organizations that sought a more comprehensive attack on inequality and oppression in the United States. In much the same way that Black women were mobilized by sexism in the civil rights and Black Power movements, the Chicano movement in the late 1960s was a spur to activism for Chicana feminists (Garcia 1990). Somewhat later in the 1970s, Asian American women followed Black and Hispanic women in organizing against gender inequality. Their efforts took the form of establishing women's caucuses in traditional Asian American organizations, creating new pan-ethnic coalitions such as the National Network of Asian and Pacific Women, and engaging in community-based activism around domestic abuse, health projects, and cultural activities. As Chow (1987, 288) points out, however, "many of these groups were short-lived because of lack of funding, grass-roots support, membership, credible leadership, or strong networking."

These new organizations and challenges have represented innovations in the established "repertoire of collective action" (Tilly 1978). Case studies suggest that women of color have a more established, historical commitment to a collectivist perspective (Barnett 1995; Dill 1983; Pardo 1995; Hardy-Fanta 1993). This translates into organizing and leadership styles that reject traditional models of organization based on centralization of power and decision making (Collins 1991). In this respect, women of color activism contrasts with the dominant trend in national white women's organizations, although there are parallels to the commitment to participatory democracy found in the more radical branch of the feminist movement (Whittier 1995). Carol Hardy-Fanta (1993) also demonstrates that Latina women reject hierarchy in organizational settings in favor of collective structures; in her words, "connectedness, attention to the interplay between private and public life, development of political consciousness, and collective, nonhierarchical organizational structures are all ways Latina women expand both the meaning of politics and the methods of achieving increased political participation in the community" (Hardy-Fanta 1993, 154).

Trends in National Activity

The combined information presented in figure 28.1 and table 28.1 offers a clear depiction of the development of national women's organizations since 1955.[4] There was a visible increase in organizational activity over the 1960s, as white women took advantage of an improved climate for group formation and collective action. The civil rights movement and the more general climate of insurgency in the 1960s opened up the political arena to a variety of new constituencies, and white women in particular benefited from lower costs of mobilization during this period (Tarrow 1994). This growth in women's organizations also reflects a growing feminist consciousness among both white women and women of color that correlates with activism and organizational activity (Ferree and Hess 1985; Giddings 1984; Klein 1984). Still, there was only a handful of national Black women's organizations by 1970, and virtually no national organizational activity by Asian American and Latina women before then.

The most dramatic rise in the number of white women's and women of color organizations took place over the 1970s, which coincides with the most active years

FIG. 28.1.
National White Women and Women of Color Organizations

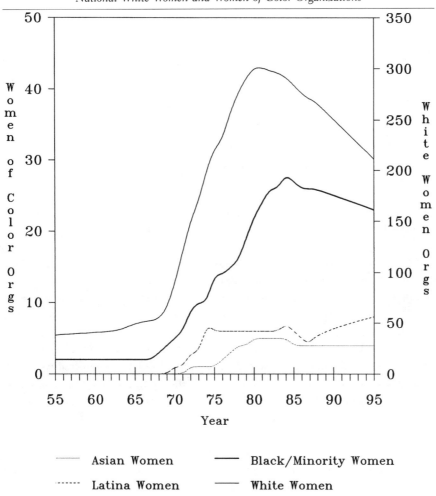

SOURCE: *Encyclopedia of Associations*, vols. 1–23, 29 (Detroit, Gall Research Company, 1985).

of feminist collective action (Ferree and Hess 1985). The number of white women's organizations rose from almost ninety in 1970 to roughly three hundred in 1980. The rate of increase was highest in the first half of the decade, when the number of groups expanded by 148 percent. Women of color did not begin to increase their organizational presence until after 1970 (slightly later for Asian American and Latina women). Between 1970 and 1975 alone, the number of women of color organizations increased by 250 percent.

By 1975, the mainstream women's movement had peaked with respect to feminist protest and institutional confrontation, but organizational expansion continued through 1980 at a slower rate (Costain 1992). This corresponds with the transition of the women's movement from a social movement to a more established interest group actor (Costain 1992; Gelb and Paley 1982). After 1980 there was a gradual decline in predominantly white women's organizations, attributable to, among other

TABLE 28.1.
Number and Percentage Change in National White Women's and Women of Color Organizations, 1960–95

	1960	1965	1970	1975	1980	1985	1995
White women's organizations	41	49	89	221	301	284	211
		(19)	(81)	(148)	(36)	(−6)	(−26)
Women of color organizations	2	2	6	21	33	37	35
		(0)	(200)	(250)	(57)	(12)	(−5)
Total national organizations	43	51	95	242	334	321	246
		(19)	(86)	(155)	(38)	(−4)	(−23)

SOURCE: *Encyclopedia of Associations*, vol. 1, *National Organizations* (Detroit: Gale Research Company, 1985, 1995).
NOTE: Figures in parentheses are percentage change.

things, the failure to get the ERA ratified at the state level, the explicit antifeminism of the Reagan-Bush presidencies, and a widespread turn to conservatism by much of the American public (Costain 1992; Spalter-Roth and Schreiber 1995). Between 1985 and 1995 there was a fairly substantial (35 percent) decline in the number of predominantly white women's social and political organizations.

In an important contrast, women of color managed to increase their presence nationally through 1985 and to resist a more dramatic contraction over the next ten years. The rate of organizational growth continued to increase 57 percent from 1975 to 1980, and 12 percent again between 1980 and 1985; by 1985 there were upwards of thirty-seven national women of color organizations. In fact, at the point when white women's organizations were beginning to decline, women of color organizations continued to expand. It was not until later that the women of color sector began to contract. Between 1985 and 1995, the number of women of color organizations diminished by 5 percent, much lower than the comparable decrease of 35 percent in white women's groups; Latina women's organizations even show some increase. These trends are striking, since they suggest that during a decade of intensified official racism and antifeminism associated with the Reagan and Bush presidencies, women of color organizations were able to maintain a national presence.

Organizing and Surviving in the 1990s

What accounts for the different vulnerabilities of white women's and women of color organizations over the past decade? How do white women's and women of color organizing styles differ in ways that might explain their distinct development at the national level? In establishing an autonomous sphere of national organizations, women of color were responding to their exclusion from the mainstream feminist movement, building on strong feminist, race, and class-conscious analyses. They were also facing more significant limits on resources and institutional access compared with the white middle-class women who dominated women's organizations. National organizations constructed by Black, Latina, and Asian American women in recent decades should reflect such differences in political and organizational choices and constraints.

Tables 28.2, 28.3, and 28.4 summarize percentage distributions and average differences along key organizational attributes that influence organizational survival (see Minkoff 1993). The ability to maintain organizations over time has fundamental implications for future activism by women of color. Organizational innovation and, ultimately, institutional access depend on the extent to which women of color organizations diverge from the dominant model of white women's organizations and are still able to maintain a national presence. In this way they will be able to gain greater voice for themselves and greater legitimacy for more progressive organizational models.

Strategy, Goals, and Targets of Action

Organizational strategies or practices reflect group choices about how to get the work of the organization done. Unlike ideology and goals, which reflect the ideal objectives of the organization's members, the actual means chosen are more likely to be determined by resource constraints and instrumental concerns (Martin 1990). White women's and women of color organizations have tended to combine four sets of practices: protest, advocacy, service or resource provision, and cultural production or sponsorship. Protest refers to a range of institutional disruptions, including demonstrations, marches, sit-ins, boycotts, and the like. Advocacy represents more established forms of pressure group activity such as lobbying, class-action litigation, information dissemination, networking, and coalition formation. A third type of strategy is service or resource provision. This category includes traditional forms such as educational support and career training, as well as progressive forms such as women's health centers, consciousness-raising, political education, and related grassroots efforts. At the national level, coalitions of service providers also play an active role (Spalter-Roth and Schreiber 1995). Cultural activities, such as producing women's theater, sponsoring music festivals, putting on art exhibits, or maintaining libraries, museums, and so forth, represent a final form of women's organizational action.[5]

The information provided in table 28.2 shows that national white women's organizations pursue a diverse combination of practices and that women of color organizations tend to cluster around advocacy and service activities. White women appear more likely to pursue direct institutional challenge through advocacy and limited protest, but there is still a substantial amount of institutional action by women of color. For both groups, however, advocacy tends to be combined with a service component, implying that this dual-pronged approach is the most viable tactic for addressing gender discrimination. The majority of women of color organizations — 43 percent — indicate that they pursue a combination of advocacy and service/resource provision; only 17 percent indicate that advocacy is their primary purpose. This compares with 29 percent of white women's organizations that express an exclusive commitment to advocacy and 36 percent of these organizations that combine advocacy with service provision. A handful of white women's organizations also engage in protest, which is typically combined with a resource agenda. There are also a small number of organizations that include cultural activities as part of

TABLE 28.2.
National White Women's and Women of Color Organizations:
Strategies, Goals, Targets
(Percentage Distributions)

	National white women organizations		National women of color organizations	
	N	%	N	%
Strategy				
advocacy/protest	1	1	0	0
advocacy	60	29	6	17
service/protest	3	2	0	0
service/advocacy	74	36	15	43
service	61	30	14	40
culture/advocacy	3	2	0	0
culture/service	2	1	0	0
Total	204	100	35	100
Goals				
External				
structural change	4	2	0	0
equality/opportunity	47	23	6	17
participation	21	10	14	39
interests	60	29	4	11
public awareness	15	7	3	8
Internal				
empowerment	14	7	5	14
coalition/cooperation	12	6	1	3
group awareness	1	1	1	3
group capacity	30	15	2	6
Total	204	100	36	100
Targets				
electoral/political	7	3	5	14
legal	11	5	1	3
media	2	1	1	3
general social system	9	4	11	31
multiple targets	64	31	0	0
economic	46	22	7	20
educational	28	14	4	11
cultural	13	6	1	3
religious	15	7	3	9
social welfare	10	5	2	6
Total	205	100	35	100

SOURCE: Data collected from *Encyclopedia of Associations*, vol. 1, *National Organizations* (Detroit: Gale Research Company, 1995). See text for description of data collection and measurement.

their overall agenda, but these do not constitute a significant dimension of the national white women's group structure.

The goals that motivate women's activism can be classified according to a continuum of external — directed toward society and societal transformation — and internal — directed toward the constituency and personal transformation (Martin 1990). Goals can be further distinguished by how comprehensive or radical their vision of change is. For example, external goals can include radical structural transformation of established hierarchies or reform of prevailing institutions to increase women's participation or opportunities within them. In either case, they imply direct challenge to institutional elites. Similarly, internal goals can have the intent of empowering women to challenge oppression or increase the group's ability to participate more equally in social, political, and economic life.

Both white women and women of color emphasize external social transformation, although in the case of white women there are more organizations that combine this goal with a comprehensive, or radical, vision of structural change. The majority of women of color organizations — 39 percent — seek greater participation and visibility in social institutions; 17 percent work toward equality and increased opportunities for women of color; and 11 percent represent the interests of women of color in policy debates, public affairs, and general social institutions. Only three organizations are coded as having an interest in promoting public awareness of discrimination and improving images of women of color. Taken together, 75 percent of women of color organizations pursue external goals that are oriented toward change in power relations and established institutions, compared with a slightly lower 71 percent of white women's groups. One important difference is that a handful of predominantly white women's organizations espouse radical structural change as their objective, but these organizations represent only 2 percent of the white women's group structure.

Internal goals include promoting cooperation and coalition among women, providing resources and services to improve the ability of women to participate in society, and promoting awareness of discrimination among women. Twelve percent of women of color organizations pursue one of these three more moderate internal goals. Fifteen percent of white women's organizations seek to improve women's capacity to participate in society, 6 percent advocate cooperation, and 1 percent pursue awareness of discrimination among women. Fourteen percent of all women of color organizations seek a fourth internal goal — community empowerment to increase the collective capacity for activism and social change. Although its immediate reference is the community, the ultimate goal is more extensive institutional change. In contrast, only 7 percent of white women's groups advocate more comprehensive change through collective empowerment.

If we examine the differences in goals and activities, we see that white women's organizations seem more likely to use service or resource provision to improve the capacity of women to participate in society, while women of color organizations use similar strategies for collective empowerment. Even though women of color are less likely to use protest and advocacy, which are more direct methods of institutional influence, they are no less likely to advocate direct societal transformation. Despite their ideological commitments and political visions, women of color may not have the resources and legitimacy to mobilize direct pressure tactics — at least without combining them with more indirect forms of service, education, and resource provision. Marginalization from centers of power and decision making limits the available forms of leverage and increases the risks of repression (Piven and Cloward 1978).

A final element in the organizing profiles of these groups is the target of their activities. Women's organizations mobilize for change within a variety of institutional settings, such as the political-electoral sphere, legal institutions, the media, economic organizations, and even religious institutions. Similarly, resource provision may be geared to economic, political, educational, or cultural empowerment. Collectively, it appears that women of color organizations are slightly more likely than white women to target general social relations, along with what can be considered the core sites of oppression: political/electoral institutions, legal structures, and the media. These institutions have inordinate power to shape the laws, policies, and dominant understandings and political treatment of marginalized groups. Altogether, close to 52 percent of women of color organizations challenge these central political institutions (denoted as electoral/political, legal, media, and general in table 28.2). This compares with 14 percent of white women's organizations that operate in political, legal, media, and general institutional arenas. Thirty-one percent of white women's organizations also target multiple institutions. Similar proportions of women of color and white women's organizations challenge the economic system, which is an equally significant locus of inequality (20 and 22 percent, respectively). Although the greater number of white women's organizations might allow them to challenge, and be represented more extensively in, a variety of institutions, women of color are more focused in seeking change in core sites of oppression.

Age, Size, and Structure

Organizational age, size, and structure also influence the survival of organizations over time (see tables 28.3 and 28.4). White women's organizations are, on average, older than women of color organizations. In 1995, the mean age of white women's organizations was 26 years of activity (ranging from 3 to 137 years), compared with a mean of 20 years of activity for women of color organizations (ranging from 10 to 60). Among national organizations it appears that between 1985 and 1995 any new women of color organizations that were established also failed within the decade. This is consistent with other research I have conducted, which found that, in the aggregate, racial-ethnic and women's organizations face what is called a "liability of newness" (Stinchcombe 1965) until they survive past the ten-year mark, when survival rates improve significantly (Minkoff 1993).[6] Older organizations have a considerable advantage with respect to garnering external resources and obtaining the sort of legitimacy that buffers them from contractions in the political opportunity structure (Minkoff 1993).

Most research finds that in addition to liabilities of newness there are also "liabilities of smallness" that put smaller groups in a more tenuous position with respect to organizational survival. Not surprisingly, white women's organizations appear to have an edge with respect to membership size: the average size of white women's organizations is 21,749 members, compared with 3,457 members for women of color groups. Two of the largest white women's organizations are the National Federation of Democratic Women (300,000 members) and NOW (280,000 members). The National Council of Negro Women claims membership upwards of 40,000; it is followed in size by the National Association of Negro Business and Professional Women's Clubs and the National Network of Hispanic Women, each of which lists 10,000 members.

TABLE 28.3.
National White Women and Women of Color Organizations: Age, Size, and Budget
(Means and Standard Deviations)

	Mean	Standard deviation	Minimum	Maximum	N
White women's organizations					
Age	26	21	3	137	198
Number of members	21,749	95,475	5	750,000	156
Number of paid staff	10	19	1	150	96
Budget	$636,546	$899,355	$1,500	$4.5 million	66
Women of color organizations					
Age	20	11	10	60	36
Number of members	3,457	7,575	80	40,000	29
Number of paid staff	8	14	1	53	13
Budget	$397,272	$587,730	$5,000	$1.6 million	13

SOURCE: Data collected from *Encyclopedia of Associations*, vol. 1, *National Organizations* (Detroit: Gale Research Company, 1995). See text for description of data collection and measurement.

TABLE 28.4.
National White Women and Women of Color Organizations:
Membership Structure

	White women organizations		Women of color organizations	
	N	%	N	%
Individuals as members	164	79	33	92
Organizations as members	44	21	3	8

SOURCE: Data collected from *Encyclopedia of Associations*, vol. 1, *National Organizations* (Detroit: Gale Research Company, 1995).

Differences in budgets are also consistent with this pattern: the average budget for the sixty-six white women's groups that reported annual information is close to $636,500. The highest budget listed was $4.5 million and was reported by Women in Community Service, a service coalition that pursues community welfare with an emphasis on the needs of younger women. The corresponding figure for the thirteen women of color groups responding was approximately $397,000; the largest budget, $1.6 million, was reported by the National Black Women's Health Project.

Despite apparently large differences in age and size among these organizations, there is not much difference in the average size of paid staff, which is an indicator of the degree of organizational formalization (McCarthy and Zald 1973, 1977; Minkoff 1993). In 1995, the mean staff size for white women's groups was ten, compared to eight for women of color organizations. Here the key difference is in the range: white women's organizations may have up to 150 staff, compared with a maximum of 53 staff persons in women of color organizations.

A related indicator of organizational structure is the type of membership composition, for example, whether a group has a mass-based membership or is an organizational coalition or umbrella group that counts autonomous associations as its members. Organizations made up of other organizations, such as Women in Community Service, tend to be more formal and professionalized. Twenty-one percent of white women's organizations comprise other organizations as opposed to individuals, compared with only 8 percent of women of color organizations (see table 28.4). This suggests that white women's organizations are more formally structured at the national level, which is thought to allow less room for constituency involvement and creates a hierarchy that is antithetical to progressive social change (Staggenborg 1989).

Organizational Innovation and Institutional Change, or Politics by Any Means

What can we learn from this type of organizational census, which is aggregated over time and across a variety of organizational forms? The available information on white women's and women of color organizations confirms the general impression that mainstream women's organizations are more formal and institutionalized. This is consistent with Steady's (1993, 98) suggestion that "what we are witnessing . . . is the emergence of an articulated female model which, within a female context, is itself a dominant model. For the most part it is being articulated and actualized primarily by women who have access to the instruments of communication, to information and, directly or indirectly, to the means of production, control and domination." She concludes that as long as women of color, working-class women, lesbians, and other marginalized women "continue to remain outside the structures of articulation [domination], the objectives of the women's movement to promote gender equity and to end gender-based discrimination, etc., will be only partially achieved" (Steady 1993, 99).

This outsider position can also be considered from a more proactive vantage point. The organizational profiles I have described in this chapter provide some additional evidence that women of color organizations are more grassroots and collectivist than national white women's organizations (Barnett 1995; Collins 1991; Steady 1993). The smaller size of women of color organizations — with respect to members, staff, and budgets — suggests that these organizations may be able to effectively resist the dominant model of professionalized, staff-run organizations that substitute donations for real involvement and centralized decision making for grassroots, nonhierarchical forms of participation. They thus provide some compelling illustration of what kinds of innovations in organizational structure and activities might be viable over the long run, thus modifying the dominance of traditional organizational models at the national level.

The choice of less traditional combinations of strategies and structures can thus be seen as a source of both constraint and innovation. Established, professionalized, and bureaucratic forms of organization tend to have greater external legitimacy, which is correlated with organizational survival and success for obvious resource-related reasons (Gamson 1990; Minkoff 1993). Therefore, the fact that women of color organizations do not or cannot necessarily construct themselves according to this dominant organizational model is one more mechanism that isolates their constituencies from institutional centers of power and decision making. However, by successfully implementing and maintaining divergent organizing styles, those groups that are able to survive may ultimately increase the potential for institutional inclusiveness and change. Successful organizational mobilizations expand the boundaries of what are defined as legitimate constituencies and forms of action, even if change in progressive directions happens slowly (Clemens 1993; Minkoff 1995). Increasingly, women of color organizations are surviving past the "danger zone" of ten years of activity. This suggests that women of color organizers and activists are finding ways to secure the infusion of resources, energy, and commitment into their organizations, ensuring that their organizational models are available to serve as templates for future efforts. This is no small contribution.

The point I would like to end on returns us to the dynamism of social movement development. The combination of three consecutive Republican presidential administrations, a more general backlash against feminist advances, and more visible resurgences in racism and racist rhetoric has shaped efforts by white women and women of color separately. By 1995 there was a dramatic decline in the number of white women's national advocacy groups, and this constituency became less likely to target political institutions. Contractions in the political climate have reinforced the tendency of women of color to establish and maintain service or resource organizations at the national level. However, this has not been at the expense of targeting core social and political institutions. The central point is that there is a high probability that women of color will mount comprehensive, systemic challenges, whether through advocacy, service, or a combination of the two.

The notion that women of color use a variety of means to pursue comprehensive social change and challenge entrenched power relations strikes me as particularly important, given the tendency of scholars and activists alike to dismiss the significance of less direct or less publicly radical forms of organization and action. Ferree and Martin's (1995, 11) discussion of noninstitutionalized, primarily white feminist organizations makes this point as well: "social movement researchers who deplore the ideological and procedural imperfections of feminist organizations may be underappreciating these groups' practical situations and their role in producing fundamental political and social change." What I have tried to show in this chapter is that by combining established traditions of "community work" with a politics of institutional transformation, women of color are exploring new organizing styles with potentially innovative implications. By linking political work to a variety of organizational forms, such initiatives by women of color challenge the parameters of activity established by elites — not only those in traditional positions of power but also the women who currently hold leadership positions in the national feminist social movement community.

APPENDIX: NATIONAL WOMEN OF COLOR ORGANIZATIONS

African American Women's Clergy Association (1962)

Alliance of Minority Women for Business and Political Development (1982)

American Association of African American Women Business Owners (1982)

Asian-Indian Women in America (1980)

Association of Black Women in Higher Education (1979)

Black, Indian, Hispanic, Asian Women in Action (1983)

Black Women in Church and Society (1982)

Black Women in Publishing (1979)

Black Women Organized for Educational Development (1984)

Black Women's Educational Alliance (1976)

Chicana Research and Learning Center (1974)

Comisión Feminil Mexicana Nacional (1970)

Commission on South Asian Women (1982)

Committee on Women in Asian Studies (1972)

Global Women of African Heritage (1982)

International Black Women's Congress (1983)

Las Hermanas — USA (1971)

National Association of Black Women Attorneys (1972)

National Association of Black Women Entrepreneurs (1979)

National Association of Cuban-American Women (1972)

National Association of Minority Women in Business (1972)

National Association of Negro Business and Professional Women's Clubs (1935)

National Black Women's Consciousness Raising Project (1975)

National Black Women's Health Project (1981)

National Coalition of 100 Black Women (1981)

National Conference of Puerto Rican Women (1972)

National Council of Hispanic Women (1981)

National Council of Negro Women (1935)

National Federation of Cuban-American Women (1982)

National Hook-Up of Black Women (1975)

National Identification Program/Advancement of Women in Higher Education (1977)

National Latinas Caucus (1985)

National Network of Hispanic Women (1981)

National Network of Minority Women in Science (1978)

Organization of Chinese American Women (1977)

Organization of Pan Asian American Women (1976)

Trade Union Women of African Heritage (1961)

Women for Racial and Economic Equality (1975)

SOURCE: *Encyclopedia of Associations*, vol. 1, *National Organizations* (Detroit: Gale Research Company, 1995).

NOTES

1. Organizational structure is the "intentional or emergent plan of organization, strategy, and goals that may or may not be reproduced in official tables of organization, constitutions, and job descriptions" (Martin 1990, 185). Organizational plan refers to the administrative arrangements and other structural attributes that characterize an organization, for example, whether decision making is participatory-democratic or hierarchical, extent of reliance on staff and voluntary members, size, and age. Goals are the objectives that orient internal and external action. Strategies represent the primary activities members engage in to reach these objectives.

2. This is an ideal-type representation of mainstream feminist groups; in practice many organizations adopt a mix of hierarchical and participatory modes of organization (Ferree and Martin 1995; Staggenborg 1989). This may especially be the case with local chapters of national organizations that diverge from the national blueprint with regard to the structure of decision making and strategies.

3. Buechler (1990, 154) suggests that "by the early 1970s, the tendency for working-class women and women of color to selectively appropriate and refashion feminist insights and ideology to fit their particular situation was taking organizational form." More accurately, the ability of women of color to assert and implement the traditions of participation and leadership that made possible both white women's feminism and the civil rights struggles of the 1960s was becoming organized in innovative and public ways.

4. This information was compiled from each of the first twenty-three editions of the *Encyclopedia of Associations*, vol. 1, *National Organizations* (Detroit: Gale Research Company); see Minkoff 1995. I updated the database for the current chapter from the 1995 edition. This directory provides descriptive information on the structure, objectives, and activities of *national* membership associations. It does not include staff-run and/or nonprofit organizations that are nonmembership. This excludes organizations such as the National Institute for Women of Color, the Women of Color Partnership Program, and the National Congress of Neighborhood Women. It also excludes women's businesses, such as Olivia Records and Kitchen Table Press. The appendix provides the names and founding dates of the Black, Latina, and Asian American women's organizations listed in the 1995 edition.

Listed organizations are initially contacted by research staff or through referrals; entries are based on questionnaires filled out by organizational representatives. My goal was to collect information on all forms of voluntary organizations, both activist and more traditional membership associations (see also Ferree and Martin 1995). Limitations to this database include underrepresentation of small, short-lived, and more radically oriented groups. Thus the most innovative and least institutionalized forms of action are not likely to be visible. Women of color organizations are therefore more likely to be underrepresented in the database than are white women's organizations. As a final point, the information provided in each entry represents the views of respondents and is not necessarily an objective assessment of the organization.

5. Examples of organizations that do protest are Women's Health Action and Mobilization (WHAM!) and the National Black Feminist Organization. Advocacy is the mainstay of such organizations as NOW and the Organization of Pan Asian American Women. Traditional resource provision is carried out by the YWCA and the National Council of Negro Women, while progressive direct services/resources are the focus of such groups as the national Black Women's Consciousness Raising Project and the Chicana Research and Learning Center. Two examples of cultural organizations are Women Make Movies and Women in the Arts Foundation.

6. Striking confirmation of this is that of twenty-one national women of color organizations once listed in the *Encyclopedia of Associations* and currently defunct, inactive, or address unknown, only four had been active for ten or more years. The oldest was the Sisterhood of Black Single Mothers, established in 1973 and listed as address unknown since 1991, followed by the Black Women's Association (1970–85); Chicana Rights Project (1974–87); and the National Black Feminist Organization (1973–83).

REFERENCES

Balser, Diane. 1987. *Sisterhood and Solidarity.* Boston: South End.

Barnett, Bernice McNair. 1995. "Black Women's Collectivist Movement Organizations: Their Survival in the Doldrums." In *Feminist Organizations: Harvest of the New Women's Movement*, ed. Myra Marx Ferree and Patricia Yancey Martin, 199–219. Philadelphia: Temple University Press.

Buechler, Steven. 1990. *Women's Movements in the U.S.* New Brunswick: Rutgers University Press.

Chow, Esther Ngan-Ling. 1987. "The Development of Feminist Consciousness among Asian American Women." *Gender and Society* 1:284–99.

Clemens, Elisabeth. 1993. "Women's Groups and the Transformation of U.S. Politics, 1892–1920." *American Journal of Sociology* 98:755–98.

Collins, Patricia Hill. 1991. *Black Feminist Thought: Knowledge, Consciousness, and the Politics of Empowerment.* New York: Routledge.

Costain, Anne. 1992. *Inviting Women's Rebellion.* Baltimore: Johns Hopkins University Press.

Crawford, Vicki, Jacqueline Rouse, and Barbara Woods, eds. 1990. *Women in the Civil Rights Movement.* Bloomington: Indiana University Press.

Crenshaw, Kimberlè. 1989. "Demarginalizing the Intersection of Race and Sex: A Black Feminist Critique of Antidiscrimination Doctrine, Feminist Theory and Antiracist Politics." *University of Chicago Legal Forum*, 139–67.

Davis, Angela. 1983. *Women, Race, and Class.* New York: Vintage Books.

Dill, Bonnie Thornton. 1983. "Race, Class, and Gender: Prospects for an All-Inclusive Sisterhood." *Feminist Studies* 9 (spring): 131–50.

Evans, Sara. 1979. *Personal Politics.* New York: Vintage Books.

Ferree, Myra, and Beth Hess. 1985. *Controversy and Coalition.* Boston: Twayne.

Ferree, Myra Marx, and Patricia Yancey Martin. 1995. "Doing the Work of the Movement: Feminist Organizations." In *Feminist Organizations: Harvest of the New Women's Movement*, ed. Myra Marx Ferree and Patricia Yancey Martin, 3–23. Philadelphia: Temple University Press.

Freeman, Jo. 1973. "The Origins of the Women's Liberation Movement." *American Journal of Sociology* 78:792–811.

Gale Research Company. 1955–95. *Encyclopedia of Associations.* Vol. 1, *National Organizations.* Editions 1–23, 29.

Gamson, William. 1990. *The Strategy of Social Protest.* 2d ed. Belmont, CA: Wadsworth.

Garcia, Alma M. 1990. "The Development of Chicana Feminist Discourse, 1970–1980." In *Unequal Sisters: A Multicultural Reader in U.S. Women's History*, ed. Ellen Carol DuBois and Vicki L. Ruiz, 418–31. New York: Routledge.

Garner, Roberta Ash, and Mayer N. Zald. 1987. "The Political Economy of Social Movement Sectors." In *Social Movements in an Organizational Society*, ed. Mayer N. Zald and John D. McCarthy, 293–317. New Brunswick, NJ: Transaction Publishers.

Gelb, Joyce, and Marian Paley. 1982. *Women and Public Policy*. Princeton: Princeton University Press.

Giddings, Paula. 1984. *When and Where I Enter*. New York: Bantam Books.

Gilkes, Cheryl Townsend. 1994. " 'If It Wasn't for the Women . . .': African American Women, Community Work, and Social Change." In *Women of Color in U.S. Society*, ed. Maxine Baca Zinn and Bonnie Thornton Dill, 229–46. Philadelphia: Temple University Press.

Hardy-Fanta, Carol. 1993. *Latina Politics, Latino Politics*. Philadelphia: Temple University Press.

Hernandez, Aileen. 1991. *National Women of Color Organizations: A Report to the Ford Foundation*. New York: Ford Foundation.

Higginbotham, Evelyn Brooks. 1993. *Righteous Discontent: The Women's Movement in the Black Baptist Church, 1880–1920*. Cambridge: Harvard University Press.

hooks, bell. 1981. *Ain't I a Woman: Black Women and Feminism*. Boston: South End.

———. 1984. *Feminist Theory: From Margin to Center*. Boston: South End.

Jenkins, J. Craig, and Craig M. Ekert. 1986. "Channeling Black Insurgency." *American Sociological Review* 51:812–29.

Katzenstein, Mary. 1990. "Feminism within Institutions: Unobtrusive Mobilization in the 1980s." *Signs* 16:27–54.

King, Deborah. 1988. "Multiple Jeopardy, Multiple Consciousness: The Context of Black Feminist Ideology." *Signs* 14:42–72.

Klein, Ethel. 1984. *Gender Politics*. Cambridge: Harvard University Press.

Martin, Patricia Yancey. 1990. "Rethinking Feminist Organization." *Gender and Society* 4:182–206.

McAdam, Doug. 1982. *Political Process and the Development of Black Insurgency*. Chicago: University of Chicago Press.

McCarthy, John D., and Mayer N. Zald. 1973. *The Trend of Social Movements in America: Professionalization and Resource Mobilization*. New Brunswick, NJ: Transaction Publishers.

———. 1977. "Resource Mobilization and Social Movements." *American Journal of Sociology* 82:1212–41.

Minkoff, Debra C. 1993. "The Organization of Survival." *Social Forces* 71:887–908.

———. 1995. *Organizing for Equality: The Evolution of Women's and Racial-Ethnic Organizations in America, 1955–1985*. New Brunswick: Rutgers University Press.

Morris, Aldon. 1984. *The Origins of the Civil Rights Movement*. New York: Free Press.

Naples, Nancy A. 1992. "Activist Mothering: Cross-Generational Continuity in the Community Work of Women from Low-Income Urban Neighborhoods." *Gender and Society* 6:441–63.

Pardo, Mary. 1995. "Community Activists, Border Feminists?" In *Feminist Organizations: Harvest of the New Women's Movement*, ed. Myra Marx Ferree and Patricia Yancey Martin, 356–71. Philadelphia: Temple University Press.

Piven, Frances Fox, and Richard Cloward. 1978. *Poor People's Movements*. New York: Pantheon.

Spalter-Roth, Roberta, and Ronnie Schreiber. 1995. "Outsider Issues and Insider Tactics: Strategic Tensions in the Women's Policy Network during the 1980s." In *Feminist Organizations*, ed. Myra Marx Ferree and Patricia Yancey Martin, 105–27. Philadelphia: Temple University Press.

Staggenborg, Suzanne. 1989. "Stability and Innovation in the Women's Movement: A Comparison of Two Movement Organizations." *Social Problems* 36 (February): 75–92.

Steady, Filomina Chioma. 1993. "Women and Collective Action: Female Models in Transition." In *Theorizing Black Feminisms*, ed. Stanlie M. James and Abena P. A. Busia, 90–101. New York: Routledge.

Stinchcombe, Arthur. 1965. "Social Structure and Organizations." In *Handbook of Organizations*, ed. James March, 142–93. New York: Rand McNally.

Tarrow, Sidney. 1994. *Power in Movement: Social Movements, Collective Action and Politics.* New York: Cambridge University Press.

Taylor, Verta. 1989. "Social Movement Continuity: The Women's Movement in Abeyance." *American Sociological Review* 54 (October): 761–75.

Taylor, Verta, and Nancy Whittier. 1993. "The New Feminist Movement." In *Feminist Frontiers III*, ed. Laurel Richardson and Verta Taylor, 533–48. New York: McGraw-Hill.

Tilly, Charles. 1978. *From Mobilization to Revolution.* New York: Random House.

Whittier, Nancy. 1995. *Feminist Generations.* Philadelphia: Temple University Press.

Zald, Mayer N., and John D. McCarthy. 1980. "Social Movement Industries: Competition and Cooperation among Movement Organizations." *Research in Social Movements, Conflict and Change* 3:1–20.

PART FOUR

Pitfalls, Paradoxes, and Futures
of Feminist Politics

TWENTY-NINE

Crime and Justice: Paradoxes for Theory and Action

KATHLEEN DALY

Paradox: a statement that is seemingly contradictory or opposed to common sense and yet is perhaps true . . . an argument that apparently derives self-contradictory conclusions by valid deduction from acceptable premises.

Policies on crime and justice are riddled with paradoxes for theory and action. To develop sound policy, feminists and allied groups must address them.

Paradox 1: Power-based theories of crime and justice are more applicable to race-ethnicity than to gender relations.

Paradox 2: Feminist efforts to reduce men's violence against women, while important, can contribute to a conservative policy stance.

Paradox 3: Equal treatment policies may improve and worsen female lawbreakers' treatment in the justice system.

Paradox 4: Media and feminist attention to celebrated crime cases, though important, may also be harmful.

Before explicating these paradoxes, I will review the sources of statistical data on crime and justice, along with problems in using them.[1]

Sources of Data

Crime

"Crime" is not easy to count and classify: it is a socially and historically constructed category, not a natural phenomenon. The same behavior may be a "crime" in one context but not another or in one time period but not another. Increases in the crime rate over time may reflect changes in citizens' inclinations to report crime and police professionalism in recording crime, but no change in "actual" levels of crime. The crimes counted in official statistics are individual acts of theft, violence, and breaches of public order; we have no national counts of organizational or occupational crimes, although these forms of "white-collar" crime involve higher losses of property and injury to citizens than does common crime (Coleman 1989).

In the United States the two national sources of crime data are the Uniform Crime Report (UCR) and the National Crime Victimization Survey (NCVS).[2] The UCR, begun in 1930, contains information gathered by police departments on the number of crimes reported to the police for seven "index" offenses: four violent crimes (criminal homicide, rape, aggravated assault, and robbery) and three property crimes (larceny/theft, burglary, and motor vehicle theft).[3] Thus, the crime rate is calculated from a selected set of offenses that citizens report to the police (or less often, that police officers witness themselves) and that the police record as crimes.[4]

The UCR also tallies the number of arrests for the index and over twenty other offenses. Scholars use these arrest data to describe and explain race-, age-, and gender-based differences in rates of involvement in crime; but there are problems in using them. First, most crimes reported to the police do not result in arrest.[5] Second, arrest data are subject to shifts in the organizational management of crime; that is, they reflect policing activity and record-keeping practices as much as criminal activity (Steffensmeier 1993, 422–23). Third, arrest data are presented by "race"[6] or by gender; published data do not give arrest rates for black women, white women, black men, and so on. Moreover, there is no measure of the economic status (or class standing) of those arrested.

The NCVS began in 1973 with the aim of gathering more complete information on crime. The data are gathered by a sample survey of about fifty thousand U.S. households.[7] The crimes surveyed are assault (both aggravated and simple), rape, robbery, larceny/theft, burglary, and motor vehicle theft. Respondents are asked about their victimization experiences, whether they reported an incident to the police, whether they were injured, the value of property taken, among many other items. NCVS data can be used to estimate annual rates of victimization for individuals (e.g., age-specific rates of violent victimization experienced by black men and black women) and households (e.g., rates of household burglaries and thefts experienced by low-, moderate-, and high-income households).

Until recently, the NCVS has underestimated the incidence of rape and family violence (Bachman and Taylor 1994; Eigenberg 1991). The screen questions did not directly ask those interviewed whether they had been sexually assaulted in some way.[8] For family violence, the NCVS has recently introduced a more sensitive interview protocol, and it has reduced its practice of interviewing couples together.

From the NCVS, we learn that victims are more likely to report incidents to the police when they are "serious," that is, when they involve high dollar losses and serious injury (Bureau of Justice Statistics 1988). We also learn that more people report crime to the police today (39 percent) than when the NCVS first began (32 percent) (Maguire and Pastore 1994, 254).

Criminal Courts

Compared to crime statistics, national data on state criminal courts are recent,[9] the National Judicial Reporting Program (NJRP) having begun in 1986. The NJRP contains information on sentences for convicted defendants only. Like the UCR arrest data, published NJRP data do not show sentences for black women, white women, black men, and so on, but rather for women, men, whites, and so on.[10] Nor can the NJRP data be used to determine whether some crimes and defendants are more likely to be prosecuted, to plead guilty, or to be found guilty at trial.[11]

Prisons and Jails

National data on state and federal prisoners have been gathered since 1925.[12] Unlike crime and court data, published prisoner data are disaggregated by race and gender; thus we can calculate the rate of imprisonment for black women, white women, black men, and so on. Data on jail populations are more recent.[13] In addition to inmate counts, the Bureau of Justice Statistics (BJS) surveys prisoners and jail inmates to learn more about their circumstances at the time of arrest.

How the Statistics Add Up

As we shall see, across all statistical indicators, female lawbreakers are more favorably positioned than their male counterparts: they are less likely to be involved in crime and to be arrested or prosecuted for violent offenses, their prior criminal history is less serious than men's, and their care for children and efforts to help themselves may render them more conventional and reformable (see Daly 1994a). This gender structure offers fundamental challenges to theories of crime and justice. It informs our first paradox.

Four Paradoxes

Paradox 1: Power-based theories of crime and justice are more applicable to race-ethnicity than to gender relations.

The story of crime and justice is typically about the disproportionate presence of racial and ethnic minority group members among those arrested, prosecuted, and incarcerated. However, the gender disproportionalities are as great or greater. In 1990–91, women were 51 percent of the U.S. population, but they were 18 percent of all UCR arrests, 11 percent of arrests for the index violent crimes, 14 percent of those convicted in felony court, 9 percent of new court commitments to prison, 5 percent of those in prison, and 1 percent of those under penalty of death. In 1990–91, blacks were 12 percent of the U.S. population, but they were 29 percent of all UCR arrests, 45 percent of arrests for the index violent crimes, 47 percent of those convicted in felony court, 54 percent of new court commitments to prison, 46 percent of those in prison, and 40 percent of those under penalty of death (see table 29.1). If we move

TABLE 29.1.

Female and Black Share of Arrests, Felony Court Convictions, New Court Commitments to Prisons, and Those in Prison, by Selected Offenses, 1990–91

Offense	(1) Share of arrests	(2) Share of felony convictions	(3) Share of new court commitments to prison	(4) Share of those in prison
			Women	
Murder and non-negligent manslaughter	10	10	7	6
Rape	1	1	1	—
Robbery	8	6	5	3
Aggravated assault	13	9	6	4
Burglary	9	5	3	2
Larceny and m/v theft	29	18	13	12
Drug sale/possession	14	16	12	8
All offenses[a]	18	14	9	5.4
			Blacks[b]	
Murder and non-negligent manslaughter	55	56	57	44
Rape	43	33	40	40
Robbery	61	63	71	59
Aggravated assault	38	44	57	47
Burglary	30	42	44	39
Larceny and m/v theft	32	42	50	44
Drug sale/possession	41	55	66	53
All offenses[a]	29	47	54	46

SOURCES: Column 1: UCR data for 1990: Flanagan and Maguire 1992, 442 for female share; 444 for black share. The female share is drawn from Flanagan and Maguire rather than Steffensmeier 1993, 416–17 for comparability with the black share. Column 2: NJRP data for 1990: BJS 1993, 16. Column 3: Corrections data for 1991: Maguire and Pastore 1994, 625. Column 4: Corrections data for 1991: for female share, BJS 1994c, 4; for black share, calculated from data in Maguire and Pastore 1994, 612.

[a] Includes offenses not listed.

[b] The black share of those in prison (column 4) is black, non-Hispanic; in the preceding three columns, black includes Hispanic and non-Hispanic.

from column 1 to column 3 in table 29.1, we see that in general, the female share *decreases* from arrest to court commitments to prison, whereas the black share *increases*. This suggests a funnelling process whereby a higher proportion of female cases are *dropped* from the felony process whereas a higher proportion of black cases are *retained*.

Feminist theorists have yet to explain why, if men have more power than women, men are at greater risk of being under criminal justice control. Nonfeminist theorists often avoid the question of why women are more law-abiding than men, even when living in similar conditions of economic marginality, poverty, and powerlessness.

Arrest data, experiences with victimization, and profiles of those in prison and jail will be examined in more detail. We shall see that the expectations of power-based theories hold for men and women arrested and imprisoned; yet power-based theories cannot explain the disproportionate presence of men under formal criminal justice control.

Arrests for Crime

According to UCR arrest data for 1990 (as analyzed by Steffensmeier 1993),[14] the female share of arrests is highest for larceny/theft (30 percent), forgery (34 percent), embezzlement (37 percent), and fraud (43 percent).[15] The female share is lower for violent offenses such as homicide (12 percent) and aggravated assault (13 percent), and lowest for robbery and burglary (8 percent each).[16]

To analyze race and gender together, scholars draw from selected portions of UCR data, NCVS data, and adolescents' self-reported involvement in crime and delinquency. Studies show that women are less likely than men to be involved in crime, but that black women's involvement is higher than white women's (Chilton and Datesman 1987; Hill and Crawford 1990; Laub and McDermott 1985; Lewis 1981; Simpson 1991; Young 1980). The typical ordering from most to least likely to be arrested for common crimes is black men, white men, black women, and white women. Racial differences are especially evident for violent crime, but less so for property crime.[17]

An obvious question one may pose is this: what part of race differences in arrests reflects police actions in responding to crime (including racism and increased surveillance of racial-ethnic minority group communities) and what part reflects "actual" race differences in crime involvement?[18] Most scholars would argue that relations of class and race-ethnicity are embedded in the history and organizational practices of policing (see, e.g., Hawkins 1994, 1995; Mann 1993) and that certain groups and neighborhoods are subjected to heightened police patrols and surveillance (Miller 1994). Moreover, several studies find that the police are more quick to arrest black than white women (Smith, Visher, and Davidson 1984; Visher 1983). At the same time, varied data sources suggest that there are race differences in crime involvement, especially street forms of violent crime (for which blacks have higher rates) and elite or white-collar forms of property crime (for which whites have higher rates) (see Harris and Meidling 1994).

Victimization

NCVS data for 1987–91 show that women's victimization rate for violent crime (25 per 1,000) is about 60 percent of men's (41 per 1,000); black women's rate of violent crime victimization (32 per 1,000) is greater than white women's (24 per 1,000) (table 29.2). The male-female ratio in violent crime victimization is identical for blacks and whites (60 percent). Compared to white women, black women's higher violent crime victimization is evident for robbery, but not for rape or simple assault (table 29.3).

Victim-offender relations in violent crime victimizations suggest that black and white women experience similar rates of violence committed by intimates and other relatives; however, black women's rate of violent victimization by acquaintances and strangers is higher than white women's (table 29.4). Class-related indicators of education and income show differences in women's victimization by intimates: college graduates are three times *less* likely to be victimized than are high school

TABLE 29.2.
Annual Rate of Victimization per Thousand, by Gender, 1987–91

	Males violence	Theft	Females violence	Theft
All	41	72	25	64
Race				
White	39	71	24	65
Black	56	77	32	59
Other	39	72	23	58
Ethnicity				
Hispanic	50	68	29	60
Non-Hispanic	40	72	24	64
Education				
Some high school or less	54	66	32	59
High school graduate	33	59	20	48
Some college	49	93	28	83
College graduate or more	23	76	18	87
Family income				
Less than $10 K	69	80	43	60
$10 to $20 K	45	65	27	60
$20 to $30 K	38	69	24	64
$30 to $50 K	33	71	17	65
$50 K or higher	29	77	15	78

SOURCE: BJS 1994a, 2.
NOTE: Rates are rounded up or down from the more precise published numbers that report tenths. Violence includes rape, robbery, and all assaults; theft is personal larceny, with and without contact.

TABLE 29.3.
Annual Rate of Victimization per Thousand Females, 1987–91

	Total	Rape	Robbery	Aggravated assault	Simple assault
All women	25	1	4	5	14
Race					
White	24	1	3	5	14
Black	32	2	9	8	14
Other	23	1	4	5	13
Ethnicity					
Hispanic	29	1	7	7	15
Non-Hispanic	24	1	4	5	14
Education					
Some high school or less	32	2	5	7	19
High school graduate	20	1	4	4	11
Some college	28	2	5	6	16
College graduate or more	18	1	4	3	11
Family income					
Less than $10 K	43	2	7	10	23
$10 to $20 K	27	1	5	6	16
$20 to $30 K	24	1	3	5	11
$30 to $50 K	17	1	2	3	11
$50 K or higher	15	<1	2	3	10

SOURCE: BJS 1994a, 3.
NOTE: Rates are rounded up or down from the more precise published numbers that report tenths.

graduates or those with some college; women with less than $10,000 in family income are about five times *more* likely to be victimized than women with family incomes of $30,000 or more.

Both UCR arrest data and NCVS data on victims' perceptions of offenders show that young men are the most likely demographic group to be common crime

TABLE 29.4.
Annual Rate of Single-Offender Violent Victimization per Thousand Females,
by Victim-Offender Relationship.

	Intimate	Other relative	Acquaintance	Stranger
All women	5	1	8	5
Race				
White	5	1	7	5
Black	6	1	11	7
Other	4	<1	6	5
Ethnicity				
Hispanic	5	1	6	7
Non-Hispanic	5	1	8	5
Education				
Some high school or less	5	2	12	5
High school graduate	6	1	5	4
Some college	6	1	7	8
College graduate or more	3	1	6	6
Family income				
Less than $10 K	11	2	13	8
$10 to $20 K	7	1	8	6
$20 to $30 K	6	1	8	5
$30 to $50 K	3	1	6	4
$50 K or higher	2	1	5	4

SOURCE: BJS 1994a, 7.
NOTE: Rates are rounded up or down from the more precise published numbers that report tenths. Violence includes rape, robbery, and all assaults.

offenders and victims, that black men are more likely than white men to be violent crime offenders and victims, and that black women are more likely than white women to be violent crime offenders and victims (Harris and Meidling 1994; Hindelang 1978; Simpson 1991; Steffensmeier 1993). How class relates to these race differences has not been assessed adequately because we lack indicators of class standing in UCR arrest data and victims' perceptions of offenders in NCVS data.

Incarceration

In 1980 there were about 330,000 prisoners in state and federal institutions; by mid-1994, the population exceeded one million (BJS 1995, 1). In 1980, black men's prison incarceration rates were six times those of white men's; by 1992, they were seven times greater (table 29.5). Black women's incarceration rates were seven times those of white women's in 1980 and 1992. Gender differences in rates of incarceration are even more pronounced. Black men's incarceration rates were nineteen times those of black women's in 1992 (they were twenty-five times greater in 1980). White men's incarceration rates were also nineteen times those of white women's in 1992 (they were twenty-eight times greater in 1980).

A 1991 BJS survey of prison inmates shows that the majority of men and women (64–65 percent) were members of minority groups (black, Hispanic, and Native American/Asian) and most had not graduated from high school (see table 29.6). Over half the women and 31 percent of the men were unemployed at the time of arrest. More imprisoned men (close to half) were in prison for violent offenses than

TABLE 29.5.
Sentenced Prisoners per 100,000 Residents, 1980–92

Year	All[a]	Male White	Black	Female White	Black
1980	139	168	1,111	6	45
1982	170	206	1,345	8	57
1984	187	228	1,459	9	63
1986	216	261	1,695	12	77
1988	244	290	1,951	15	91
1990	292	339	2,376	19	135
1992	344	372	2,678	20	143

SOURCE: Adapted from BJS 1994b, 9.
[a]All includes prisoners of other races.

TABLE 29.6.
Demographic, Offense, and Criminal History Profiles of Men and Women in State Prisons in 1991 and in Jails in 1989.

	In prison Males (%)	Females (%)	In jail Males (%)	Females (%)
Race-ethnicity				
White, Non-Hispanic	35	36	39	38
Black, Non-Hispanic	46	46	42	43
Hispanic	17	14	17	16
Other	2	4	2	3
Education				
8th grade or less	20	16	16	12
Some high school	46	46	38	38
High school graduate or more	34	38	46	50
Pre-arrest employment				
Employed	69	47	68	38
Unemployed, looking	16	19	20	28
Unemployed, not looking	15	34	12	34
Offense				
Violent	47	32	24	13
Property	25	29	30	32
Drugs				
Possession	7	12	9	15
Sale	13	20	12	17
Public order	7	6	23	19
Other	1	1	2	4
Criminal history				
No prior record	20	29	22	33
One conviction	19	22	21	20
Two or more convictions	61	49	57	47

SOURCES: Data on prisons are adapted from BJS 1994c, 2–4. Data on jails are from BJS 1992, 3–6.
NOTE: The Ns upon which these percentages are based may vary depending on whether there is complete information. For prison data, the N of women and men is about 38,700 and 670,000, respectively. For jail, the N is for all inmates, convicted and awaiting trial. In 1989, there were about 36,500 women and 344,500 men.
Median age for men in prison is thirty years, for women, thirty-one. Median age in jail is twenty-eight for both men and women.

were women (one-third). Higher proportions of imprisoned men (61 percent) had two or more convictions compared to women (49 percent).

Added to prisoners are 440,000 adults in jails (Maguire and Pastore 1994, 591, 1992 data). Just under half (about 218,000) were convicted and serving sentences; the rest were awaiting trial (594). The number of adults in local jails has nearly doubled from 1984 to 1992. A 1989 BJS survey of jail inmates shows that women were 9 percent of jail inmates; most men and women (61–62 percent) were members of minority groups (black, Hispanic, and Native American/Asian), and slightly more women (50 percent) than men (46 percent) had completed high school. More jailed women had never been convicted of a crime (33 percent) compared to jailed men (22 percent).

These crime and justice numbers caution against making glib claims about how relations of power operate in the wider society and in the criminal justice system. Race-ethnicity (and other relations such as class and age) operate as we might expect: members of racial-ethnic minority groups (blacks and, to a lesser degree, Latinos) are disproportionately more likely to be represented in arrest, court, and prison populations. But members of the socially subordinate gender group (women) are disproportionately less likely to be represented in arrest, court, and prison populations.

Even the most enlightened policy discussion on crime ignores the gender dimension. Class and race relations are the focus of such policies, which ask questions such as, How can we create more jobs? How can we revitalize neighborhoods? How can we provide a more equitable distribution of opportunities and resources such as good schools and recreational facilities? These questions are important, but incomplete. Missing in the policy discussion are the criminalizing consequences of masculinity and trying to be "a man." Also missing is a recognition that current justice system responses can *escalate* a crime-promoting masculinist identity. These include the military regimes used in "shock incarceration" (or boot camps) (MacKenzie and Shaw 1990; Morash and Rucker 1990), "get tough" police surveillance and tactical approaches toward gangs (Hagedorn 1988; Huff 1990; Sanchez Jankowski 1991), court procedures that demonize male defendants (Braithwaite and Daly 1994), and prisons that "intensify the most negative aspects of masculinity" (Sim 1994, 103; also see Messerschmidt 1993; Newburn and Stanko 1994).

Paradox 2: Feminist efforts to reduce men's violence against women, while important, can contribute to a conservative policy stance.

During the 1970s and 1980s major legal changes occurred in the police and prosecutorial responses to rape (Bienen 1983; Spohn and Horney 1992), spouse assault (Dobash and Dobash 1992), and child abuse and neglect (Myers 1992). Movement activists viewed men's violence against women as one expression of male domination and power in intimate relations.

It is useful to distinguish this form of victim advocacy from victim-*centered* advocacy. The latter refers to a single-minded focus on individual victims' rights of redress without a broader understanding of the societal conditions conducive to violence. Victim-centered advocacy is amenable to punitive responses to crime that center on more punishment and offer little hope of reforming and reintegrating offenders.

Victim-centered advocacy is part of a general conservative turn in criminal justice policy that was consolidated in the early 1980s. This conservative shift occurred just as feminist advocates were pushing for changes in police and prosecutorial procedures to make the criminal justice system more responsive to men's violence against women. Some academic and grassroots feminists participated in a conservative, law-and-order response to crime. It is easy to understand why this occurred: the victim advocacy movement of the 1970s, largely voluntary and autonomous, increasingly began to rely on state resources and the machinery of criminal justice (Dobash and Dobash 1992; Schechter 1982). But there is another source of feminist conservatism that may be more intractable. The criminal justice system leaves few options for those working on behalf of victimized women: one can take a victim-centered stance or a defendant-centered stance. The sharp-edged win-lose criminal court adversarial process is transacted in a discourse of stigma: each side attempts to win by destroying or demonizing the other. Working in this context, feminist activists and attorneys must paint victimized women as "truly innocent" and male victimizers as "truly evil" (defense attorneys will do just the opposite).

For the development of sound policy, two points should be considered. First, we will not reduce crime — including men's violence against women — by creating more criminal laws, arresting more people for crime, punishing people more harshly, or putting more resources into the machinery of criminal justice (more police, courts, or prisons) (Nettler 1989; Walker 1989). Even well-known conservatives argue that putting more resources into criminal justice may reduce crime only marginally (Wilson 1983). Second, a just response to crime should include both victims and victimizers. We may need to shift from a largely stigmatizing and warehousing model of criminal justice to a more humane system that envisions welfare, restoration, and reintegration as its principles (see Daly 1989a; Braithwaite and Daly 1994).

Paradox 3: Equal treatment policies may improve and worsen female lawbreakers' treatment in the justice system.

National court data show substantial gender gaps in the likelihood of receiving an incarceration sentence (men's likelihood is higher by seventeen to twenty percentage points) and in the length of an incarceration sentence (men's are eighteen months longer). By comparison, there is no race difference in likelihood of receiving an incarceration sentence, though there is for length of sentence (three to thirteen months) (see tables 29.7 and 29.8). These bivariate-level data seem to suggest that the court treats women more leniently than men but that race differences are more variable.[19] Research on gender and race disparities in noncapital sentencing shows a higher fraction of studies with "sex effects" favoring women (45 percent) than "race effects" favoring whites (9 percent) (Daly and Bordt 1995). These studies, which include controls for the offense charged, the defendant's prior record, and other variables, suggest little evidence of racial disparity against blacks but a good deal more evidence of gender disparity favoring women. What do we make of these results?

Statistical studies may give the misleading impression that women are treated more leniently than men in the courts (see Daly 1994a; Daly and Bordt 1995). When the details of the cases are examined at closer range, it can be seen that gender differences are small but not entirely absent. A major problem is that we cannot know from the statistical evidence alone whether gender gaps in sentencing result

TABLE 29.7.
Percentage of Defendants Sentenced to Prison or Jail, 1986 and 1990

	Male 1986	1990	Female 1986	1990	Black 1986	1990	White 1986	1990
All (includes other offenses not listed)	70	74	50	57	69	75	66	73
Murder and non-negligent manslaughter	95	96	95	88	95	95	94	96
Rape	88	86	75	84	91	89	89	87
Robbery	89	91	69	79	88	92	89	91
Aggravated assault	74	75	44	58	66	75	73	76
Burglary	74	78	70	65	74	82	72	78
Larceny and m/v theft	67	70	49	49	69	70	61	69
Drug sale	65	79	53	69	67	78	56	77

SOURCES: 1986 data from BJS 1990, 5; 1990 data from BJS 1993, 19–20.

TABLE 29.8.
Average (Mean) Length of Sentence Imposed on Defendants Sentenced to Prison and Jail,
1986 and 1990
(in Months)

	Male 1986	1990	Female 1986	1990	Black 1986	1990	White 1986	1990
All (includes other offenses not listed)	60	54	42	36	59	58	62	45
Murder and non-negligent manslaugther	217	234	168	173	220	233	228	206
Rape	129	128	124	75	170	157	123	98
Robbery	128	98	85	48	111	99	162	85
Aggravated assault	66	52	71	42	72	57	59	44
Burglary	57	62	54	45	57	63	62	55
Larceny and m/v theft	32	35	29	23	36	40	31	29
Drug sale	42	52	43	44	38	56	46	41

SOURCES: 1986 data from BJS 1990, 6; 1990 data from BJS 1993, 21–22.
NOTES: Sentence lengths for women in 1990 are corrected from those given in BJS 1993, 21.
Sentences combine defendants who pleaded guilty and those who were found guilty at trial. Sentence lengths for those convicted at trial are typically longer than those pleading guilty.
Each offense category contains a wide range of offense seriousness.
Published NJRP reports do not report sentences for black men, black women, and so forth.

from warranted sources of disparity (e.g., differences in crime contexts) or those we may deem unwarranted.

To appreciate contemporary sentencing policy, we need some historical perspective. In the last part of the nineteenth century, an optimistic rehabilitation-oriented approach emerged, which was based on individualized treatment. This stance provided both therapy and restraint: some individuals were deemed reformable; others, dangerous. Indeterminate sentences allowed for wide-ranging discretion by probation officers and parole boards to decide when individuals were reformed or were not a threat to community safety.

Sentencing policy and practices became politicized in the late 1960s. Sentencing reform advocates were concerned with abuses of state power and with racial disparities in time served in prison. Radical and liberal commentators called for limits on officials' discretionary power, and a shift away from the individualized treatment model to equal treatment in sentencing. Their focus was on disparities of treatment among men. What happened when they considered women and gender differences? They had three options: to punish women more like men, to punish men more like women, or to shift both groups to achieve an average of past sentencing practices (split-the-difference) (Blumstein et al. 1983, 114). Reformers reasoned that if strong versions of equality were to be applied to men to reduce racial disparities, then they should also be used to redress potential gender disparities.

Such a stance illustrates how equal treatment can make things worse for women. The problem is not equal treatment in the abstract, but the male-centered terms in which it is conceptualized and implemented. The logic is that we need to bring women's sentences in line with (that is, "raised to") a male standard. There are other ways to implement equal treatment: we could, for example, use women as the standard by which to set average penalties and to imagine the varied circumstances and contexts leading to crimes (see Daly 1994a).[20]

Just as important is the need to recognize conflicts in joining feminist and antiracist understandings of equality. In general, all women may fare better under weaker versions of "equality" with some attention to gender differences, whereas male members of racial and ethnic minority groups may fare better under stronger versions of "equality" and a muting of racial differences (see Daly 1994c). Several types of equality standards, not just one, may be required.

For justice system institutions such as jails, prisons, halfway houses, and treatment programs, legal arguments that draw from the Eighth and Fourteenth Amendments to the U.S. Constitution have been used. Litigation on behalf of female prisoners, although less developed than that for male prisoners, has centered on educational and training programs, medical and mental health services, and access to the courts (Daly, Geballe, and Wheeler 1988; Leonard 1983; Rafter 1990). Such litigation, if successful and if followed through with state resources, can help women. But when male prisoners are used as the norm, the services or programs that female prisoners currently require (e.g., maintaining relations with children, medical care in pregnancy) are outside the legal frame (Resnik 1987; Wheeler et al. 1989).[21]

Equal treatment can lead to spin-off paradoxes that haunt feminist activists. If a state has no prison for women (as was the case in Hawaii in the 1970s), do you push for building a women's prison? (see Chesney-Lind 1991). More generally, do you call for more resources for women in the criminal justice system because, in principle, such resources should be more equitably distributed? Or do you call for shifting resources away from institutions of criminal justice to job training and education, welfare supports, and care for dependents?

The failure of equality doctrine has been documented by numerous feminist scholars in family, employment, and antidiscrimination law (e.g., Crenshaw 1989; Fineman 1991; MacKinnon 1987; Vogel 1993). Similar problems are evident in crime and justice, but with a twist: strong versions of equality may continue to resonate with a politics of racial redress (among men), whereas weaker versions of equality with an emphasis on gender specificity may continue to resonate with a politics of gender redress. Feminist and antiracist coalitions will need to acknowledge and work with these tensions (see Daly 1994b, 1994c).

Paradox 4: Media and feminist attention to celebrated crime cases, though important, may also be harmful.

There are major differences between crimes "in the news" and crimes in criminological studies and statistics (Barak 1994; Chermak 1994; Daly 1995; Ericson, Baranek, and Chan 1991; Fishman 1978; Graber 1980; Surette 1992; Warr 1994). Crime news focuses disproportionately on violent offenses and atypical cases. Why does this occur? News organizations select "newsworthy" crimes and cases. These are *not* representative but are instances of the exceptional, unusual, and dramatic (Katz 1987; Roshier 1973).

Media interest in newsworthy crime is recapitulated, not challenged, in feminist analyses. Two stories are commonly featured: women who are raped and those who fight back against abusive mates. Rape features in Benedict's (1992) analysis of media reporting of "sex crimes," in which she analyzes four celebrated cases. Benedict argues that media organizations and journalists need to cover cases like these with greater sensitivity. She may be right, but we should press the more radical questions. Why do media institutions and feminist commentators spend so much time on these stories when they are a small fraction of women's experiences as crime victims or offenders? Might attention to these cases contribute to an impoverished, sensationalized analysis of crime rather a critical understanding of it? How do these celebrated cases relate to the more routine, hidden, and unanalyzed cases? Feminist research and commentary should seek to displace media attention on the unusual by focusing on the routine and apparently unremarkable circumstances that bring men and women before the law.

In the last decade, we have witnessed a shrinkage in state supports for health, education, and welfare, and a concomitant increase in supports for police, prisons, and the management of justice systems. U.S. culture extols the acquisition of material goods and wealth beyond all else, and it proclaims that all can succeed (Merton 1938). That materialism and idealism are set against the reality of several generations of kids now growing up who have little to look forward to but short-term material gain and excitement; they (predominantly boys) learn to live by their wits and street smarts in earning money and respect in the informal and illegal economy. Initial conditions of disadvantage spawn disabling and adaptive responses such as escape via illegal drugs and alcohol abuse, disinterest in school, running away from abusive families, a desire to form associations with others who are more "like family," among other reasons (see, e.g., Anderson 1990; Arnold 1990; Campbell 1991; Carlen 1988; Currie 1991; Gilfus 1992; Hagedorn 1988; Miller 1986; Moore 1991; Sanchez Jankowski 1991; Sullivan 1989). These responses continue to move marginal segments of the population toward even greater marginality. And it is these marginal group members who are the primary targets of U.S. criminal law.: the young, brown-black-yellow-red racialized, gendered Other of middle-class fear and loathing.[22] We should ask why this group is targeted, why young men are especially affected by the nexus of criminal action and state reaction, and why gender and young women feature so strongly yet invisibly as axes of differential power and social control.

All citizens, feminist and otherwise, need to confront core paradoxes in crime and justice. Crime should be understood as an integral feature of all societies, constitutive of social organization and culture, not the result of individual pathology (Durkheim 1964; Merton 1938). For significant change to occur in patterns of crime, fundamental changes need to occur in a society, but most U.S. citizens are not prepared to accept these changes. We will therefore continue to muddle through, trying to find politically acceptable ways to redistribute wealth, ameliorate misery, and create stronger nets of informal social control.

Contemporary debates on crime and justice are informed by dramatic crime stories and cases rather than by a sociohistorical or comparative understanding of broad patterns and trends. Such an understanding may give little solace to those who have been victimized by crime or to those who feel unsafe. But it may offer a way to think more clearly about crime in setting a different policy course.

I have identified four paradoxes that could be a focus of policy reflection and discussion. We can decide to face these paradoxes, work with them, and deal with their complexity. Or we can decide to avoid them, but feel a fleeting sense of empowerment in marching to "take back the night." I propose that we begin to confront these paradoxes and take back the day.

NOTES

I appreciate Valerie Blum's careful reading and comments on an earlier draft.

1. I do not include interview, observational, and archival studies of gender, crime, and justice. For examples of this work, see Carlen and Worrall 1987; Gelsthorpe and Morris 1990; Maher and Curtis 1992; and Newburn and Stanko 1994. My focus is on the relative presence of men and women by minority and majority group status in the criminal justice system. How gender, race-ethnicity, class, age, and so forth structure the conditions of lawbreaking (e.g., drug dealing, prostitution, and violence) invites a different analytic focus than I take here.

2. These sources give different pictures of crime trends: the UCR data show that the violent crime rate has increased from 1973 to 1992, whereas the NCVS data show that the violent crime rate has remained the same (see Reiss and Roth 1993, appendix B for a discussion of these trends). The sources are similar in showing that violent crime is about 12 to 17 percent of crimes reported to the police or experienced by victims.

3. An eighth index offense, arson, was added in 1978; but it is often dropped from studies of crime trends.

4. The UCR crime rate is driven largely by larcenies, which constitute 55 percent of *all* index crimes reported to the police. The UCR violent crime rate is driven largely by aggravated assaults, which account for 57 percent of violent crimes reported to the police.

5. Of the UCR violent and property crimes reported to the police, 45 and 18 percent, respectively, are cleared by arrest (Maguire and Pastore 1994, 462).

6. "Race" is a social construction, no less so in crime data. UCR arrest data from the 1950s through the 1970s used these race-ethnic categories: White, Negro, Indian, Chinese, Japanese, and "all others." In 1980, the categories were White, Black, American Indian or

Alaskan Native, and Asian or Pacific Islander. NCVS, on the other hand, uses the census categories of "black/white" and "Hispanic/non-Hispanic." I shall use black and white (without quotes) in describing patterns of arrest, court, and imprisonment, even though they capture neither ethnic nor class variation.

7. Those twelve years of age and older are asked about their experiences of victimization in the previous six months; and respondents are interviewed twice a year for three years.

8. The NCVS introduced the new survey methodology to a portion of households in 1991 and to all households in 1993. Estimates for rape victimization using the redesigned survey have just been released ("With New Questions" 1995, A10); they show a doubling of the number of rapes, which BJS officials attribute to how the rape victimization questions were asked. For another estimate of rape victimization, see Denno 1994, who utilizes a report by the National Victim Center 1992.

9. By comparison, data on criminal cases in federal courts have been available for several decades. There is a large literature on state criminal courts that describes patterns of case disposition and actions of court officials, but it typically focuses on just one or several jurisdictions (see Myers 1994 for a review).

10. While published NJRP reports do not disaggregate sentences by race and gender groups, one could request the datafile and compute them.

11. Such detail can be found in other publications; see Bureau of Justice Statistics 1988.

12. See Shover and Inverarity 1994 for an overview of prisons and jails, and Maguire and Pastore 1994 (598–600) for prisoner data from 1925 to the present. National counts of federal and state prisoners are gathered by the National Corrections Reporting Program.

13. Prisons hold those sentenced to more than a year, and jails hold those awaiting trial and sentenced to less than a year. See Bureau of Justice Statistics 1988 for an overview.

14. The data reported in Steffensmeier 1993 on the female share of arrests differ slightly (by 1 percent or so) from that presented in Flanagan and Maguire 1992 (442) because Steffensmeier calculated the female share from arrests rates for those aged ten to sixty-four.

15. The categories of forgery, embezzlement, and fraud can be misleading. In an analysis of federal court defendants convicted of white-collar offenses, I found that men's white-collar crimes were both petty and major, but almost all the women's were petty (Daly 1989b). Most women convicted of bank embezzlement were tellers, and 30 to 45 percent of women convicted of credit fraud and postal fraud were not employed. No one has analyzed the content of the UCR offense categories of fraud, forgery, and embezzlement to determine their range of seriousness.

16. The female share of UCR rape arrests is small, less than 1 percent; Steffensmeier dropped this offense from his analysis. In the UCR, rapes are counted only when women are victimized, whereas the NCVS estimates rape victimization of men and women.

17. Several arrest categories contain a disproportionate white share: driving under the influence, violation of liquor laws, and drunkenness. In comparing arrest rates for larceny, some scholars find that they are similar for white men and black women (Chilton and Datesman 1987).

18. The same question is posed for gender differences in arrest rates. Scholars who have conducted cross-national analyses of gender and arrest rates suggest that one reason women's arrest rates are higher in more economically developed countries is that police recording practices are more formal and bureaucratic (see Steffensmeier, Allan, and Streifel 1989).

19. While my focus is on gender- and race-based disparities in sentencing, it should be stressed that the severity of the offense and the defendant's prior record are stronger predictors of sentencing than are defendant attributes such as race and gender (see Blumstein et al. 1983).

20. I see the progressive possibilities of using women as the "norm" in sentencing policy in much the same way that male union activists in the late nineteenth century in the United States decided to "fight the battle behind women's petticoats" (Kessler-Harris 1982, 184, quoting Elizabeth Brandeis). Specifically, men recognized that they could benefit from women's claims for shorter hours and better factory sanitation and safety.

21. Services or programs "for women" could also be provided to men. The problem is that current prison services and programs are male-centered, not inclusive.

22. This group has been the target of criminal law and social control policy in the United States since the early nineteenth century. Although a cyclical sense of "crisis" pervades the popular imagination, there is nothing new about the crime problem in the United States.

REFERENCES

Anderson, Elijah. 1990. *Streetwise*. Chicago: University of Chicago Press.

Arnold, Regina. 1990. "Processes of victimization and criminalization of black women." *Social Justice* 17 (3): 153–66.

Bachman, Ronet, and Bruce M. Taylor. 1994. "The measurement of family violence and rape by the redesigned National Crime Victimization Survey." *Justice Quarterly* 11 (3): 499–512.

Barak, Gregg, ed. 1994. *Media, Process, and the Social Construction of Crime*. New York: Garland.

Benedict, Helen. 1992. *Virgin or Vamp*. New York: Oxford University Press.

Bienen, Leigh. 1983. "Rape reform legislation in the United States: A look at some practical effects." *Victimology: An International Journal* 8: 139–51.

Blumstein, Alfred, Jacqueline Cohen, Susan E. Martin, and Michael H. Tonry, eds. 1983. *Research on Sentencing: The Search for Reform*. Vol. 1. Washington, DC: National Academy Press.

Braithwaite, John, and Kathleen Daly. 1994. "Masculinities, violence, and communitarian control." In *Just Boys Doing Business?* ed. Tim Newburn and Betsy Stanko, 189–213. New York: Routledge.

Braithwaite, John, and Philip Pettit. 1990. *Not Just Deserts: A Republican Theory of Criminal Justice*. Oxford: Oxford University Press.

Bureau of Justice Statistics (BJS). 1988. *Report to the Nation on Crime and Justice*. 2d ed. Washington, DC: U.S. Department of Justice, Office of Justice Programs.

———. 1990. "Profile of felons convicted in state courts, 1986," by Patrick A. Langan and John M. Dawson. Washington, DC: U.S. Department of Justice, Office of Justice Programs.

———. 1992. "Women in jail, 1989," by Tracy L. Snell. Washington, DC: U.S. Department of Justice, Office of Justice Programs.

———. 1993. "National judicial reporting program, 1990," by Patrick A. Langan and Richard Solari. Washington, DC: U.S. Department of Justice, Office of Justice Programs.

———. 1994a. "Violence against women," by Ronet Bachman. Washington, DC: U.S. Department of Justice, Office of Justice Programs.

———. 1994b. "Prisoners in 1993," by Darrell K. Gilliard and Allen J. Beck. Washington, DC: U.S. Department of Justice, Office of Justice Programs.

———. 1994c. "Women in prison, 1991," by Tracy L. Snell and Danielle C. Morton. Washington, DC: U.S. Department of Justice, Office of Justice Programs.

————. 1995. "Press release on prisoners at midyear 1994." Washington, DC: U.S. Department of Justice, Office of Justice Programs.

Campbell, Anne. 1991. *The Girls in the Gang*. 2d ed. Cambridge, MA: Basil Blackwell.

Carlen, Pat. 1988. *Women, Crime and Poverty*. Philadelphia: Open University Press.

Carlen, Pat, and Anne Worrall, eds. 1987. *Gender, Crime, and Justice*. Philadelphia: Open University Press.

Chermak, Steven M. 1994. "Body count news: How crime is presented in the news media." *Justice Quarterly* 11 (4): 561–82.

Chesney-Lind, Meda. 1991. "Patriarchy, prisons, and jails: A critical look at trends in women's incarceration." *Prison Journal* 71 (1): 51–67.

Chilton, Roland, and Susan K. Datesman. 1987. "Gender, race, and crime: An analysis of urban arrest trends, 1960–1980." *Gender and Society* 1: 152–71.

Coleman, James W. 1989. *The Criminal Elite*. 2d ed. New York: St. Martin's.

Crenshaw, Kimberlè. 1989. "Demarginalizing the intersection of race and sex: A black feminist critique of antidiscrimination doctrine, feminist theory, and antiracist politics." *University of Chicago Legal Forum*, 139–67.

Currie, Elliott. 1991. Dope and Trouble. New York: Pantheon.

Daly, Kathleen. 1989a. "Criminal justice ideologies and practices in different voices: Some feminist questions about justice." *International Journal of the Sociology of Law* 17: 1–18.

————. 1989b. "Gender and varieties of white-collar crime." *Criminology* 27 (4): 769–94.

————. 1994a. *Gender, Crime, and Punishment*. New Haven: Yale University Press.

————. 1994b. "Criminal law and justice system practices as racist, white, and racialized." *Washington and Lee Law Review* 51 (2): 431–64.

————. 1994c. "Race and gender politics in punishment policy." Paper presented at the annual meeting of the Law and Society Association, Phoenix, June.

————. 1995. "Celebrated crime cases and the public's imagination: From bad press to bad policy?" *Australian and New Zealand Journal of Criminology*, Special Issue: 6–30.

Daly, Kathleen, and Rebecca L. Bordt. 1995. "Sex effects and sentencing: An analysis of the statistical literature." *Justice Quarterly* 12 (1): 143–77.

Daly, Kathleen, Shelley Geballe, and Stanton Wheeler. 1988. "Litigation-driven research: A case study of lawyer/social scientist collaboration." *Women's Rights Law Reporter* 10 (4): 221–40.

Denno, Deborah. 1994. "Why rape is different." Introduction to panel discussion, "Men, Women and Rape." *Fordham Law Review* 63: 125–38.

Dobash, R. Emerson, and Russell P. Dobash. 1992. *Women, Violence, and Social Change*. New York: Routledge.

Durkheim, Emile. 1964. *The Rules of Sociological Method*. 1895. Reprint, New York: Free Press.

Eigenberg, Helen. 1991. "The National Crime Survey and rape: The case of the missing question." *Justice Quarterly* 7 (4): 655–71.

Ericson, Richard V., Patricia M. Baranek, and Janet B. L. Chan. 1991. *Representing Order: Crime, Law, and Justice in the News Media*. Toronto: University of Toronto Press.

Fineman, Martha. 1991. *The Illusion of Equality*. Chicago: University of Chicago Press.

Fishman, Mark. 1978. "Crime waves as ideology." *Social Problems* 25 (5): 530–43.

Flanagan, Timothy J., and Kathleen Maguire, eds. 1992. *Sourcebook of Criminal Justice Statistics — 1991*. Washington, DC: U.S. Department of Justice, Bureau of Justice Statistics.

Gelsthorpe, Loraine, and Allison Morris, eds. 1990. *Feminist Perspectives in Criminology.* Philadelphia: Open University Press.

Gilfus, Mary E. 1992. "From victims to survivors to offenders: Women's routes of entry and immersion into street crime." *Women and Criminal Justice* 4 (1): 63–89.

Graber, Doris. 1980. *Crime News and the Public.* New York: Praeger.

Hagedorn, John. 1988. *People and Folks.* Chicago: Lake View Press.

Harris, Anthony R., and Lisa R. Meidling. 1994. "Criminal behavior: Race and class." In *Criminology,* 2d ed., ed. Joseph F. Sheley, 115–412. Belmont, CA: Wadsworth.

Hawkins, Darnell F. 1994. "Ethnicity: The forgotten dimension of American social control." In *Inequality, Crime, and Social Control,* ed. George S. Bridges and Martha A. Myers, 99–116. Boulder: Westview.

———. 1995. "Ethnicity, race, and crime: A review of selected studies." In *Ethnicity, Race, and Crime,* ed. Darnell Hawkins, 11–45. Albany: State University of New York Press.

Hill, Gary D., and Elizabeth M. Crawford. 1990. "Women, race and crime." *Criminology* 28: 601–26.

Hindelang, Michael. 1978. "Race and involvement in common law personal crimes." *American Sociological Review* 46: 461–74.

Huff, C. Ronald. 1990. "Denial, overreaction, and misidentification: A postscript on public policy." In *Gangs in America,* ed. C. Ronald Huff, 310–17. Newbury Park, CA: Sage.

Katz, Jack. 1987. "What makes crime 'news'?" *Media, Culture and Society* 9: 47–75.

Kessler-Harris, Alice. 1982. *Out to Work.* New York: Oxford University Press.

Laub, John H., and M. Joan McDermott. 1985. "An analysis of serious crime by young black women." *Criminology* 23: 81–98.

Leonard, Eileen. 1983. "Judicial decisions and prison reform: The impact of litigation on women prisoners." *Social Problems* 31 (1): 45–58.

Lewis, Diane. 1981. "Black women offenders and criminal justice: Some theoretical considerations." In *Comparing Female and Male Offenders,* ed. Marguerite Warren, 89–105. Beverly Hills: Sage.

MacKenzie, Doris Layton, and James W. Shaw. 1990. "Inmate adjustment and change during shock incarceration: The impact of correctional boot camp programs." *Justice Quarterly* 7 (1): 125–50.

MacKinnon, Catharine. 1987. *Feminism Unmodified.* Cambridge: Harvard University Press.

Maguire, Kathleen, and Anne L. Pastore. 1994. *Sourcebook of Criminal Justice Statistics — 1993.* Washington, DC: U.S. Department of Justice, Bureau of Justice Statistics.

Maher, Lisa, and Richard Curtis. 1992. "Women on the edge of crime: Crack cocaine and the changing contexts of street-level sex work in New York City." *Crime, Law and Social Change* 18: 221–58.

Mann, Coramae Richey. 1993. *Unequal Justice: A Question of Color.* Bloomington: Indiana University Press.

Merton, Robert. 1938. "Social structure and anomie." *American Sociological Review* 3: 672–82.

Messerschmidt, James W. 1993. *Masculinities and Crime.* Lanham, MD: Rowman and Littlefield.

Miller, Eleanor. 1986. *Street Woman.* Philadelphia: Temple University Press.

Miller, Jerome G. 1994. "From social safety net to dragnet: African American males in the criminal justice system." *Washington and Lee Law Review* 51 (2): 479–90.

Moore, Joan W. 1991. *Going Down to the Barrio: Homeboys and Homegirls in Change*. Philadelphia: Temple University Press.

Morash, Merry, and Lila Rucker. 1990. "A critical look at the idea of boot camp as a correctional reform." *Crime and Delinquency* 36 (2): 204–22.

Myers, John E. B. 1992. *Legal Issues in Child Abuse and Neglect*. Newbury Park, CA: Sage.

Myers, Martha. 1994. "The courts: Prosecution and sentencing." In *Criminology*, 2d ed., ed. Joseph Sheley, 407–26. Belmont, CA: Wadsworth.

National Victim Center. 1992. *Rape in America: A Report to the Nation*. Arlington, VA: National Victim Center.

Nettler, Gwynn. 1989. *Criminology Lessons*. Cincinnati: Anderson.

Newburn, Tim, and Betsy Stanko, eds. 1994. *Just Boys Doing Business?* New York: Routledge.

Rafter, Nicole Hahn. 1990. *Partial Justice*, 2d ed. New Brunswick, NJ: Transaction.

Reiss, Albert J., Jr., and Jeffrey A. Roth, eds. 1993. *Understanding and Preventing Violence*. Washington, DC: National Academy Press.

Resnik, Judith. 1987. "The limits of parity in prison." *National Prison Project Journal* 13: 26–28.

Roshier, Bob. 1973. "The selection of crime news by the press." In *The Manufacture of News*, ed. Stan Cohen and Jock Young, 28–39. Beverly Hills: Sage.

Sanchez Jankowski, Martin. 1991. *Islands in the Street*. Berkeley: University of California Press.

Schechter, Susan. 1982. *Women and Male Violence: The Vision and Struggle of the Battered Women's Movement*. Boston: South End.

Shover, Neal, and James Inverarity. 1994. "Adult segregative confinement." In *Criminology*, 2d ed., ed. Joseph Sheley, 429–51. Belmont, CA: Wadsworth.

Sim, Joe. 1994. "Tougher than the rest? Men in prison." In *Just Boys Doing Business?* ed. Tim Newburn and Betsy Stanko, 100–117. New York: Routledge.

Simpson, Sally. 1991. "Caste, class, and violent crime: Explaining difference in female offending." *Criminology* 29: 115–35.

Smith, Douglas A., Christy Visher, and Laura Davidson. 1984. "Equity and discretionary justice: The influence of race on police arrest decisions." *Journal of Criminal Law and Criminology* 75: 234–49.

Spohn, Cassia, and Julie Horney. 1992. *Rape Law Reform*. New York: Plenum.

Steffensmeier, Darrell. 1993. "National trends in female arrests, 1960–1990: Assessment and recommendations for research." *Journal of Quantitative Criminology* 9 (4): 411–41.

Steffensmeier, Darrell, Emilie Allan, and Cathy Streifel. 1989. "Modernization and female crime: A cross-national test of alternative explanations." *Social Forces* 68: 262–83.

Sullivan, Mercer L. 1989. *"Getting Paid": Youth Crime and Work in the Inner City*. Ithaca: Cornell University Press.

Surette, Ray. 1992. *Media, Crime, and Criminal Justice*. Pacific Grove, CA: Brooks/Cole.

Tonry, Michael. 1994. *Malign Neglect: Race, Crime, and Punishment in America*. New York: Oxford University Press.

Visher, Christy. 1983. "Gender, police arrest decisions, and notions of chivalry." *Criminology* 21: 5–28.

Vogel, Lise. 1993. *Mothers at Work: Maternity Policy in the U.S. Workplace*. New Brunswick: Rutgers University Press.

Walker, Samuel. 1989. *Sense and Nonsense about Crime*, 2d ed. Pacific Grove, CA: Brooks/Cole.

Warr, Mark. 1994. "America's perceptions of crime and punishment." In *Criminology*, 2d ed., ed. Joseph F. Sheley, 15–30. Belmont, CA: Wadsworth.

Wheeler, Patricia A., Rebecca Fuller, Jim Thomas, and Jennifer Findlay. 1989. "Persephone chained: Equality or parity in women's prisons?" *Prison Journal* 69: 88–102.

Wilson, James Q. 1983. *Thinking about Crime*, 2d ed. New York: Basic Books.

"With new questions used, F.B.I. doubles its estimate of rapes." 1995. *New York Times*, August 17, A10.

Young, Vernetta. 1980. "Women, race and crime." *Criminology* 18: 26–34.

THIRTY

Smashing Icons: Disabled Women and the Disability and Women's Movements

MARIAN BLACKWELL-STRATTON,
MARY LOU BRESLIN,
ARLENE BYRNNE MAYERSON,
AND SUSAN BAILEY

When Miss America, a vibrant, glowing image on the television screen, first walks down the stage runway, crying, laughing, nervously clutching a bouquet of roses, millions of women sigh in envy. This woman embodies a collective faith — that beauty, determined by youth and specific physical proportions, guarantees fun, happiness, money, success, and sexual desirability. To be Miss America, says the emcee, is every girl's dream.

But when the five-year-old child in the Jerry Lewis Telethon walks slowly across the stage in her braces and crutches, no one envies her, although she too embodies another collective faith. She represents our belief in both technology and beauty. She too can have the rewards of beauty — but only when she is cured. The emcee reminds us that the child is a victim, the victim of a terrible tragedy that we can offset only by giving money.

These two images, the beauty queen and the poster child, could not be further apart. They represent the extremes, the outside limits of physical attributes. A woman viewer can perhaps take pleasure in imagining that she is close to the beauty queen and remote from the crippled child. To the viewer who is both a woman and disabled, however, it is impossible to escape the reproach of either image. How can she fight against the admonishment, seen not only on television but in every advertising medium, that a perfect body is essential for happiness?

More important, how can she assert herself against the belief that a disabled person is like an eternal poster child: cute, but not sexy; always the cared for, never the caring? Unlike the nondisabled woman, who has societally sanctioned roles as mother and wife (restrictive though they be), the disabled woman has no adult roles. Neither mother nor wife nor worker shall she be. This sense of rolelessness is reinforced by a public assumption that disabled women are inappropriate as mothers or sexual beings (*International Rehabilitation Review* 1977). Statistics reveal that disabled women are less likely to be married, more likely to marry later, and more likely to be divorced than are nondisabled women (Franklin 1977). In comparison to disabled men, disabled women are more likely to have a marriage in which the partner is absent, either through separation, divorce, or widowhood. Few disabled women are wage earners. Fewer than one-fourth of all disabled women are even in the labor force (Bowe 1984).

The effect of this rolelessness is that the disabled woman lives as a kind of social nomad. There is no place in society she can call her own. Her dual status as woman and disabled person endows her with a perspective that at times differs from those of both nondisabled women and disabled men. Quite naturally, this different perspective influences her formulation of political concerns and priorities. For the disabled feminist, neither the disability nor the women's movement fully addresses her concerns. In the disability movement the disabled feminist has to contend with sexism. In the feminist movement she must contend with colleagues who do not understand her disability-based political concerns. In response to this predicament, she far too often opts out of the political process altogether. As both disabled women and feminists, the authors believe that we must educate both movements in the issues specifically affecting disabled women, especially since the women's movement has shown a previous willingness to learn about the issues affecting other women of dual identities such as women of color, working-class women, lesbians, and survivors of incest.

This chapter shows how the following issues — parenting a disabled child, abortion/Baby Doe, education, voting rights, and employment — specifically affect disabled women, and how the women's movement can work with the disability rights movement. While the specific aim is to show how disabled women's issues can be integrated within the women's movement, the larger purpose is to describe the bonds that exist between the two movements. Topics are framed in the context of society's perceptions of women and disabled people. By tracing common history and images throughout a discussion of differing approaches to political issues, activists in both movements may gain a deeper understanding of how and why the other has selected its political priorities.

Cracked Mirrors: Beauty Pageant and Telethon

When the feminist and the disability rights activist view their political agendas in the context of society's past and present attitudes of prejudice, they may discover that the most dissimilar of society's icons — the tall, elegant beauty queen and the cute, awkward, crippled child — have in fact much to say to each other. These television images appear in the context of a programming format that invariably clues the viewer to society's perceptions of women and disabled people. The beauty pageant, for instance, is a contest: the women compete against each other for the favor of the judges. The competition separates women, encouraging them to compare themselves against all others. Rarely do the contestants perform together in the talent section of the pageant. Subtly but surely, society discourages women's friendship. In advertising, for example, women are usually pictured with a man, a child, or simply with the product to be sold. Only occasionally are they seen with other women; when they are, their attention is almost always directed to a man or the product. The women's movement, quite rightly, has recognized that it must challenge society's contention that women should be competitive with each other, for trust in other women is the key element of concerted political action.

But what about the poster child? While television bombards women with images of themselves as sex objects, disabled children are seldom seen on series, specials, or commercials. Once a year, the telethon saturates the screen with images of disabled children for twenty-four to forty-eight hours. After that, the disabled child, like the disabled adult, is "out of sight, out of mind." This programming format contributes to the popularly held notion that disabled and nondisabled children should be separate, an idea that translates easily into segregated schools for disabled kids, resulting in an absence of disabled children from every aspect of community life. Thus, while the beauty pageant format tries to separate women from each other, the telethon format separates disabled children from everybody.

More insidiously still, the message of the telethon is also that of separation. The telethon portrays disabled people as victims who need only to be cured, reinforcing the belief that disabled people can never fit into society unless they are cured. Quite wrongly, the telethon suggests that cures are the only acceptable solution to the exclusion of disabled people — and that society has no current obligation to accommodate those disabled people labeled "incurable." To a telethon supporter, a disabled person's inability to go to the second floor of a building is not due to the lack of an elevator or a wheelchair ramp; it is the result of the individual's sad "condition." By portraying disabled children as victims of a tragic fate, telethon organizers depend on the sympathy a crippled child engenders in the telethon viewer, knowing that pity will encourage the viewer to give money. But money alone, without efforts to eliminate the existing physical and attitudinal barriers that keep disabled people separate, is merely a salve for society's conscience.

Both disabled people and the parents of disabled children have strongly criticized the false images telethons generate and perpetuate. Disability rights advocates who themselves were poster children now view that experience in the context of a disability civil rights perspective, speaking out against telethons because they contribute so significantly to the public's negative perception of disabled people. Disability rights advocates have thus paralleled the efforts of feminists who have attacked beauty pageants for their commercial exploitation of women's bodies. To view pageants and telethons in terms of their exploitation of women and disabled children binds the women's and disability movements in a fundamental way. We are both exploited for grossly commercial purposes and for deeply rooted motives that reach far back into history. When we as disabled women and feminists can see a part of the other in the "mirror" of the telethon/beauty pageant, we will have come a long way in understanding the overlapping goals of our respective movements. But we must also remember that beauty pageants and telethons are liked cracked mirrors. Everything we see in them is distorted. The closer we get, the more we can see how the images and programming format skew our perceptions. Yet a step backwards also can be instructive. If the feminist steps back and views the telethon, for instance, from a historical and political perspective, she will see that the program accurately reflects a centuries-old tradition of prejudice toward and exclusion of disabled people.

The nature and history of prejudice toward disabled people was recently documented in an amicus brief for the U.S. Supreme Court case *Consolidated Rail Corp. v. Darrone:*[1]

> Disabled people throughout history have been regarded as incomplete human beings — "defectives." In early societies this view of disabled people resulted in persecution, neglect, and death. These practices gradually gave way to the more humanitarian belief that disabled people should be given care and protection. Persecution was largely replaced by pity, but the exclusion and segregation of disabled people remained unchallenged. Over the years, the false belief that disabled people were incompetent and dependent upon charity, custodial care, and protection became firmly imbedded in the public consciousness. The invisibility of disabled Americans was simply taken for granted and the innate biological and physical "inferiority" of disabled people was considered self-evident. (1248).

For a woman staring into the telethon mirror, the assumptions about a disabled person's "self-evident" physical inferiority closely parallel those arguments once used to deny women an education and the right to vote. The particular argument contended that a woman's small stature and lesser muscle strength obviously proved that women were physically and mentally inferior to men.[2] This "innate inferiority" theory served to justify the exclusion of women from all aspects of society. Looking deeper into the telethon mirror, the feminist will see that "disability" implies much more than mere physical limitation:

> For the individual who does have a physical or mental limitation the social consequences of this limitation bear no relationship to the disabling condition. For example, being paralyzed means far more than being unable to walk — it has meant being excluded from public school, being denied employment opportunities, and being deemed an "unfit" parent. These injustices co-exist in an atmosphere of charity and concern for disabled people. (*Con. Rail v. Darrone*, 13)

The dominant attitude of "charitable concern," which guided disability policy for decades, underwent a profound and historic shift in the 1970s. On the federal level, two landmark laws were enacted that set the stage for disabled children and adults to lead more meaningful, integrated, and independent lives: the Education for All Handicapped Children Act, also known as PL 94-142, enacted in 1976, and Section 504 of the 1973 Rehabilitation Act.[3] PL 94-142 requires that all disabled children, regardless of the nature or severity of their disability, receive a free, appropriate public education with nondisabled children to the maximum extent possible. Section 504 bars discrimination on the basis of disability in federally funded programs; a 1974 amendment to the rehabilitation act provided a comprehensive definition of disability, which takes into account society's stigmatizing views of certain types of disabilities.[4] For example, a burned person may have facial scars but be lacking in any impairment that limits a life activity. If a federally funded employer refuses to hire such a person out of fears that clients will be uncomfortable with the scars, the scarred individual is protected under the law and can file a discrimination complaint.

These laws were passed in a climate of changing legal mandates affecting not only disabled people but also women and racial minorities, who paved the way in the 1960s with the passage of the Civil Rights Act. Title VI of the act prohibits racial discrimination in all programs receiving federal funds; Title VII prohibits employment discrimination against women and minorities, extending provisions to all employers engaging in interstate commerce, not merely those who receive federal funds. Women further benefited from the changing times by scoring two more significant victories in the seventies. The Supreme Court decision *Roe v. Wade* upheld a woman's right to abortion, and the passage of Title IX of the Education Amendments of 1972 prohibited sex discrimination in educational institutions receiving federal funds.[5]

Title VI of the Civil Rights Act and Title IX of the Education Amendments are the legal antecedents of Section 504. Section 504 is patterned after and has antidiscrimination language almost identical to both statutes.[6] This similarity in language attests to the federal government's recognition that disabled people as a group have been subject to discrimination and deserve the same basic civil rights protections that have been given to minorities and women. Yet despite the passage of laws guaranteeing the rights of disabled people, society persists in its view that disabled people are inferior beings.

The feminist before the mirror — who now has a firm grasp of the historical roots of prejudice toward disabled people and a specific understanding of the rolelessness of disabled women in society — must see fully one more aspect of a disabled woman's life if she is to integrate disabled women's issues into her political work. She must understand how the dual status of being both disabled and female affects the disabled woman's political concerns and priorities. A disabled woman formulates her political priorities from a unique identity, one that forces her to evaluate her political goals and choices differently from her nondisabled sisters. For instance, a disabled woman may be drawn to issues that affect her primarily because of her identity as a disabled individual, and secondarily because of her gender. Disabled people have been denied, and in some cases are still denied, equal voting access due to physical barriers and restrictive laws.

Second, a disabled woman's dual status as both disabled and female influences her approach to political issues. Often, nondisabled and disabled women will agree on the larger issue but differ on either the solution to or the formulation of the specific problem. Say, for example, that both groups are protesting violence against women. The nondisabled women will organize a march to persuade the city council to allocate more money for street lighting. The disabled women, in contrast, will organize a different protest to persuade the para-transit bus company to operate wheelchair-accessible buses at night. The disabled woman has limited access to evening activities. What access she does have will be increased and made safer if she spends less time on the street. While the solution of better street lighting certainly benefits the disabled woman, unless her higher priority of night transportation is addressed, it is unlikely that the march organizers will get any disabled women to participate.

In another example, a meeting may be called to protest police harassment of prostitutes. The disabled woman agrees that police harassment is an issue, but her concern may be directed toward police behavior that assumes any woman with slurred speech is drunk, ignoring the possibility that she may have a speech impairment. Or the disabled woman's concern may be with an officer's patronizing attitude that a disabled woman out alone should be escorted home "for her own good." While disabled and nondisabled women agree on the theme, the specifics of the issue differ.

Finally, the disabled woman determines her political priorities on the basis of "double" discrimination. This doubling of the discrimination factor can be seen in education, where sex discrimination combined with the segregation of disabled children has had a devastating effect on the education of disabled girls. The attempts of educators to remedy sexist curriculum materials never reach the disabled girl, because those nonsexist materials never get to the special classes in the segregated school. In employment, the double discrimination effect can be seen in the relative wage amounts of disabled women. Disabled women make less, on the average, than either nondisabled women or disabled men (Bowe 1984).

It should be clear by now that cracked mirrors, though occasionally useful, are more often dangerous, for they perpetuate stereotypes and divide women whose stronger political image is a united one. To both the politically minded disabled woman and the activist feminist, the benefits of coalition work between the women's movement and the disability rights movement must be obvious. Disabled women represent 8.5 percent of all working-age women in the United States (Bowe 1984). The women's movement, by incorporating disability issues in its political agenda, moves a step closer to its goal of including all women in its movement. The disability rights movement, in turn, by aligning itself with the women's movement, gains a valuable ally in its struggle for the full participation of disabled people within all aspects of society.

What may be less obvious, however, is that the political ties between the two movements can be effected best by yet a third group of women: the mothers of disabled children. Like disabled women, they must cope with issues that link them to both movements. In all the following areas — abortion/Baby Doe, education, voting, and employment — the mother of a disabled child has a stake because of her disabled child. Early in her child's life the mother of a disabled child will begin battling for her child's educational rights. Later, when the child is grown, the mother will be looking for needed services and civil rights laws that will enable her son or daughter to achieve an independent adulthood. The women's movement can give the parent of a disabled child support as a mother; it can also remedy her child care needs by linking them with the child care needs of all mothers. The disability rights movement can give her support as an advocate for her child.

For feminists, the inclusion of mothers of disabled children into the women's movement can serve as a bridge to the issues of the disability rights movement. Both feminists and mothers of disabled children have the same relationship to the disability rights movement: they have vital interests in seeing movement goals realized, but they will always be a little apart from it simply because they themselves are not disabled. This is not to say that feminists and mothers of disabled children have secondary roles in the disability rights movement; it merely means that their relationship to the movement is different from that of a disabled person.

New Visions: Movement Issues, Coalition Efforts

Parenting a Disabled Child: A Feminist Issue

In recent years the women's movement, recognizing that mothers, too, are working women, has given priority to such issues as child care in setting working agendas. However, the child care needs of mothers of disabled children are virtually invisible in the development of consciousness and policy. It is estimated that 10 percent of children under the age of twenty-one are disabled (Gliedman and Roth 1980). Almost one-fourth of all disabled children are raised by single parents. Among disabled children under age seventeen, 23 percent are living with only one parent, compared to only 16 percent of nondisabled children (Czajka 1984).

The reality of the lives of mothers of disabled children radically extends the traditionally perceived boundaries of motherhood. Mothers of disabled children must not only become experts in education and medicine; they must also become advocates and organizers in order to ensure the most basic rights and services for their children. The need to become an advocate and organizer is especially true for the mother who tries to secure an appropriate education for her disabled child. This process is inherently politicizing. It forces women to deal with the system. It is assertiveness-training boot camp.

The experience of these women is of critical importance to the women's movement, for mothers of disabled children have all the issues of other mothers and more. The women's movement cannot ignore these women. As with all disabled people, families with disabled children too often become isolated — out of sight and out of mind. Not only do these women need the support of the women's movement, they also have much to contribute to it.

Before these mothers can be integrated into the women's movement, however, their needs must be addressed. One important need is child care/caretaking. While all mothers expect their infants and small children to be dependent, they also know that the dependence will lessen as the child grows up; changing diapers, feeding, and dressing last only so long.[7] Some parents of disabled children can, of course, look forward to the same progression. For others, however, primary daily caretaking does not end with early childhood. Parents of severely disabled children often must dress, feed, bathe, lift, transport, and groom their children until the parents die or the child leaves home. This is not only incredibly time-consuming but also emotionally and physically draining. Changing diapers for two or three years is different from changing diapers for twenty-one.

If the parent cannot find adequate child care services, her child must be institutionalized. Not only is institutionalization damaging to the child, it is many times more expensive than providing decent in-home services, which could enable the family to stay intact. In-home care for a severely disabled child costs approximately seven thousand dollars per year, compared to thirty-eight thousand dollars annually to institutionalize that child (U.S. Congress 1985). Nevertheless, public policy penalizes parents who choose to keep their severely disabled children at home. There are virtually no support services available. As bad as the child care situation is for all mothers and children, it is worse for severely handicapped children. Generic services in the community for preschool children either lack access or simply refuse to admit severely disabled children. Mothers of young, school-age children often rely on neighborhood teenagers to baby-sit after school hours, but this option is generally unavailable for mothers of severely disabled children. Moreover, the need for care and supervision of severely disabled children extends beyond the age for nondisabled children. Even a highly assertive, self-directing sixteen-year-old quadriplegic may still need some assistance in using a bathroom.

Child care services have been given top priority by the women's movement. In promoting this cause, the women's movement has exposed the nation to the needs of nontraditional families — single mothers, working mothers, poor mothers, and minority mothers. More attention needs to be given to mothers of disabled children — mothers who might often also be single, working, minority, and poor.

The lack of child care/caretaking services is only the first problem facing mothers of disabled children. The second most pressing issue is securing an appropriate education for her disabled child. It is here that the mother's advocacy skills are tested to the extreme. As important as an education is for any child, it is only within the past ten years that disabled children have had a legal right to receive a public education. In 1975, Congress passed the Education for All Handicapped Children Act (referred to as the EHA, or PL 94-142). As mentioned earlier, this law was enacted in response to a long history of segregation and outright exclusion of disabled children from school.

The EHA is landmark legislation not only because it recognizes the right of every disabled child to a free, appropriate education in the least restrictive environment, but also because it gives parents a key role in educational planning and the ability to challenge school district decisions through a comprehensive system of due-process protections. However, as with all laws, the EHA is not self-executing, and theory and reality are often quite different. School administrators, trained to see themselves as professional experts with ultimate knowledge of what is best for the child, have not always welcomed the new role of parents. Special-education systems have been established around this "professional expertise" and its authority; parents who have been taught that the school knows best and who have relied on the advice of professionals since their child's birth also may have trouble assuming authority.

Mothers have the additional burden of being women within a largely male-dominated hierarchical system.

In order for a mother to assure an appropriate education for her child, she must learn the skills to interact in this realm of professionalism and bureaucracy. Not only must she develop the knowledge to evaluate educational and medical advice, but she must also learn to advocate, negotiate, and organize.

As with any entrenched system, there is a vested interest in the status quo, and there is too much work and too little time. The child of an inactive mother will get what is available, which is not always what the child needs. In order to assure that the needs of the child will be addressed, mothers must learn to confront and manipulate the system. Thousands of "ordinary housewives" have become activists through the experience of having a disabled child, and the supermom syndrome has been imposed through necessity: in addition to providing daily care, rearing other children, running a home, and often having a job, mothers of disabled children also must constantly fight for services and for an appropriate education for their children.

Through the years, mothers of disabled children have learned (as have women in the women's movement) that individual efforts alone are not enough to effect systemic change. In addition to becoming experts in education, medicine, transportation, recreation, equipment, and so on, mothers of disabled children also have become potent community organizers. All across the country mothers have organized into parent groups, which press for positions before school boards and community councils and lobby for legislation in state capitols.

These women are part of the women's movement, yet neither they nor the women's movement may know it. These women have developed skills and strategies that could help reform all education. This is a resource that should be tapped. Here are women who have developed leadership in the context of working as part of a community. These women should be seen as role models — not idealized as valiant heroes in the face of tragedy, but hailed as women who have learned to take charge and make change.

Unfortunately, the vast majority of mothers of disabled children still do not know their rights and have not been given the support they need to confront the system. These women, too, must be a concern to the women's movement. These women are isolated; the women's movement should reach out to bring them in.

The Abortion/Baby Doe Controversy: A Disability Perspective

Just as the mothers of disabled children have a different perspective on parenting issues, so too do disabled women have a different perspective on abortion rights and the Baby Doe controversy. The disabled woman is concerned not only with abortion rights but also with the right to be free from involuntary sterilization. Further, the Baby Doe controversy involves the disabled woman both as a parent or potential parent and as a disability rights advocate.

The disabled woman's concern with the right to be free from involuntary sterilization stems from an important difference in the social roles of disabled and nondisabled women. In the past, feminists have struggled with being cast only in the limited role of mothers. As a U.S. Supreme Court case justifying the enactment of protective work legislation for women stated, "And as healthy mothers are essential to vigorous offspring, the physical well being of women becomes an object of public interest and care in order to preserve the strength and vigor of the race." [8]

Thus, the perception that women are weaker than men and are to be seen primarily as mothers has sometimes resulted in protective legislation. Disabled women, however, have never been considered fit as mothers. One psychologist comments, "Historically, child custody suits almost always have ended with custody being awarded to the nondisabled parent, regardless of whether affection or socio-economic advantages could have been offered by the disabled parent" (Vash 1981, 115). The presumed inferiority of the disabled person has been translated frequently into social policy that condones the involuntary sterilization of mentally retarded boys and girls. In 1930, for example, twenty-eight states had sterilization statutes on the books (Burgdorf and Burgdorf 1977). In light of this history, it is imperative that reproductive rights activists advocate social policy that accounts for the right of all women to decide whether or not to have a child.

The second issue, the Baby Doe controversy, is a hotly contested debate involving the right of a parent to withhold life-sustaining medical treatment from a severely disabled infant. In "Baby Doe" situations, the infant is born with a severe disability and needs medical attention to survive. If given, the medical treatment will prolong the life of the child, but it will not lessen the child's disability. An example is that of an infant with Down's syndrome. She or he has a permanent mental impairment that may range from mild to severe. Let us say that shortly after birth the infant develops a blood infection and needs medical treatment to save its life. But the treatment, which may be very expensive, will not lessen the infant's mental impairment. These parents decide they would rather withhold treatment, thus pitting their right to privacy in making decisions regarding the welfare of their child against the right of the disabled child to live. Part of the parents' rationale for withholding medical treatment relies on the telethon "disability as tragedy" theory. Applied in this context, that argument says that a disabled infant imposes such an emotional and financial burden on the family that the state has no right to prohibit the parents from relieving themselves of the burden. Viewed from the parents' perspective, the argument appears compelling; take away the blinders imposed by the "disability as tragedy" theory, however, and the Baby Doe issue becomes a clear-cut case of civil rights. Viewed from a civil rights context, a disabled infant should not receive a different standard of medical care solely because of her or his disability. If a nondisabled infant developed a blood infection, there would be no question of a right to life-sustaining medical treatment.

In a recent case involving the validity of regulations prohibiting discriminatory treatment of disabled newborns, two public-interest law firms representing disability rights and women's rights (the Disability Rights, Education and Defense Fund and the Women's Defense Fund) filed a joint friend-of-the-court brief. It argued that the civil rights protections that apply to disabled adults also should apply to disabled infants, noting that the outdated stereotypes once used to exclude women and minorities from medical care (society's perception that women and minorities are "subhuman," "sick," or "inferior") are now used to limit a disabled infant's right to medical care.[9]

The cooperation between the women's movement and the disability rights movement in the Baby Doe controversy illustrates how effectively coalition work can function when viewed in the context of civil rights.

Flexing Muscles: The Struggle for Civil Rights

In the past hundred years, the women's movement has been fairly successful in gaining for women many of the civil rights that many male Americans took for granted. These rights, including the right of equal opportunity for education, equal access to the ballot box, and equal opportunity for employment, form the basis for political power in this country. No movement for self-determination of its people can succeed unless it has achieved three goals: an educated leadership that provides role models for an educated and politically informed citizenry; equal access to the voting booth so that politicians perceive the group as a voting bloc whose needs must be addressed; and economic power, based on the jobs of the constituency, allowing movement strategies such as boycotts, class-action lawsuits, and campaign contributions to sympathetic politicians to be implemented. More basically, everyone needs jobs to survive. When movement goals include employment rights, the movement directly benefits constituents.

The women's movements have produced the unrestricted right to vote since 1920, strong federal employment protections since 1964, and protection from discrimination in education since 1972.[10] For the disability rights movement, successes have been much more recent. The first disability civil rights statute, Section 504 of the Rehabilitation Act, wasn't passed until 1973. Implementing regulations were not signed until 1977.[11] The Equal Access to Voting Rights Act was passed in 1984.[12]

Disabled women's struggles for education, voting rights, and employment force them to fight the sexism and disability discrimination inherent in all of society's institutions. In all three issues, the work done by the disability movement and women's movement provides fertile ground for coalition work.

The Right to an Education

The disabled woman's struggle for an education is plagued by double stereotyping and a lack of role models. One disabled woman in six has had fewer than eight years of formal education, as compared to only one out of every twenty-eight nondisabled women. Only 16 percent of all disabled women are likely to report some college education, compared with 31 percent of all nondisabled women (Bowe 1984). One way to show the devastating effect of the lack of role models for disabled women is to contrast the disabled woman's plight with the successful efforts of nondisabled women to obtain higher education and to show the positive effects of role models on nineteenth-century feminists.

A hundred years ago, society believed that the sole purpose of educating women was to serve men better. Rousseau (1908) stated,

> The whole education of women ought to be relative to men. To please them, to be useful to them, to make themselves loved and honored by them, to educate them when young, to care for them when grown, to counsel them, to console them and to make life sweet and agreeable to them — these are the duties of women at all times and what should be taught them from their infancy. (263)

Early education for women in the United States consisted of embroidery, French, singing, and playing the harpsichord (Flexner 1972).

Feminists believed that education was the first step toward solving the problems of women's inequality. But women who wanted to learn something more than domestic skills had to start their own schools. The first school for women, Troy Female Seminary, opened its doors in New York State in 1821. The school endeavored to teach the natural, as well as the domestic, sciences. Mount Holyoke, the first college for women, opened in 1837. Gradually, women were allowed into state-supported colleges, although their curriculum differed from that of the men (Clinton 1984).

In the 1870s there were still many obstacles. Women were thought to be biologically unable to compete with men because a study showed that the average man's brain weighed forty-nine grams and the average woman's brain weighed forty-four grams (Clinton 1984). Even more damaging was the notion that a woman who pursued a college education would become disabled. A best-selling book in 1873, *Sex in Education*, stated that "identical education of the two sexes is a crime before God and humanity, that physiology protests against, and experience weeps over" (Clarke 1873, 127). The author maintained that "amenorrhoea, menorrhagia, dysmenorrhea, hysteria, anemia, chorea and the like" resulted from college education for women (48).

Despite male opposition, some women did obtain an education — but the only way they could put it to use was by teaching small children. This was seen as an extension of motherhood and was therefore acceptable. It was not acceptable for women to teach high school or to become school administrators. And a woman certainly was not allowed to teach at a university. A woman who was intelligent and wanted to teach at a college could teach only at one of the women's colleges, and she often had to go to a European university to obtain a Ph.D.

The visible presence of women professors in female universities — for example, two-thirds of the faculty at Smith were women (Clinton 1984) — first created role models for the young women of the generation after the Civil War. The educated middle-class women who emerged from these women's colleges provided the constituency and leadership for the feminist movement. A woman who was reminded of Rousseau's dictum on the education of women could point to M. Carey Thomas, the dean of Bryn Mawr; or to Belva Lockwood, the first woman admitted to practice law before the U.S. Supreme Court; or to Alice Freeman Palmer, who combined marriage and academics (Clinton 1984). She could respond to a comment on her small brain by mentioning Martha Mitchell, who discovered a comet; Margaret

Maltby, the first American woman to do original work in physics; or Elizabeth Blackwell, the first woman doctor. As for the notion that education would make her sick, she could note that all the college professors she had seen appeared to be in fine health.

But for disabled women, the situation was far different. Nondisabled women could justify some amount of learning as a necessity in order to educate their children and to be pleasing to men. Disabled women were not seen as being able to take care of men, nor were they seen as competent to have or to care for children. They could not fit the Rousseauistic ideal of a nurturer. Also, the biological arguments that impeded women also applied to disabled women.

On the other hand, a disabled woman's education was vital to achieving any kind of independence. As one woman put it, "We can't do manual labor, so we have to cultivate our minds. The more disabled you are, the more you need a good education" (Matthews 1983, 46). However, disabled children, when they were educated, were educated in special, segregated schools. Blind and deaf children, for example, were educated in large state residential facilities where they were taught braille and lipreading (Burgdorf and Burgdorf 1977). The education disabled children received in these segregated schools was vastly inferior to that in public elementary schools. After all, the belief went, if a disabled girl would never have to carry the burdens of motherhood or wifehood, why should education provide anything more than the survival skills necessary to prevent the child from becoming a beggar or a criminal?

The disabled woman who aspired to a higher education (assuming she received some education at a special school and had learned to read and write, or was educated at home) had no role models save one: Helen Keller. *Her* achievement was so singular as to be the exception that proves the rule. Twenty female college professors together show that a woman can be a professor; one educated disabled woman alone seems only to show how difficult it is. The typical disabled woman had no role models, no one to support her ambitions, and no school that would modify a physically inaccessible campus to admit her. The impetus for higher education that derived from female role models and a supportive community of educated women did not extend to the woman with a disability.

The difference is clear. Nondisabled women in the nineteenth century were struggling for the right to go to college. Disabled women barely were able to achieve an elementary education. In the 1970s the situation appeared to change when Congress passed amendments to the education act. Title IX prohibited discrimination on the basis of sex in all activities that received federal funding. This law affected all levels of education but has had most effect on the inclusion of women in higher education. In 1973, Section 504 of the Rehabilitation Act, using language similar to that in Title IX, prohibited all federally funded programs from discriminating against disabled people. The 504 regulations, enacted to specify an institution's obligation under the law, stated that disabled people had the right to an equal opportunity to participate in all school programs and activities, even if that meant making a building accessible to wheelchairs, or providing readers and equipment for blind students. It seemed that disabled girls and women, by the end of the seventies, had laws in place protecting them from both sex and disability discrimination in their attempts to secure an education.

In 1983, however, the Supreme Court ruled on a case that severely restricted the discrimination protections of women and disabled people. In *Grove City v. Bell*, the court narrowed the definition of recipient to include only the department that received federal financial assistance.[13] Previous to this decision any federal money a university received obligated every department of the university to comply with the requirements of Title IX. This case referred specifically to Title IX, but because the court interpreted language common to both statutes, the implications for disabled people are just as restrictive. Thus, it is now conceivable that within a university, an anthropology department that directly receives a federal grant cannot discriminate against women or disabled people in its policies or practices, whereas the chemistry department, if it receives no direct federal assistance, is under no such obligation.

The *Grove City* decision sparked a coalition effort between disability and women's groups. Recognizing that the similar language of Title IX and Section 504 meant that an attack on one was an attack on all, both groups have actively supported legislation designed to overturn the Supreme Court decision. Called the Civil Rights Restoration Act of 1985, this legislative effort marks the first time disability and women's groups have worked together in passing legislation. Though the bill did not survive the legislative session, it has been reintroduced in subsequent sessions, and the continuing coalition effort to get this bill passed will no doubt pave the way for more joint efforts.

The successful strategies to achieve educational equity for disabled and nondisabled women have much in common. As we have seen, role models are as important to disabled girls as to nondisabled girls. Authors of sex-equity materials need to include positive images of disabled women. And yet those images will not help disabled girls if they remain in segregated classrooms, isolated from other students. This is where women's groups, parent groups, and disability organizations need to work together to ensure the mainstreaming of disabled children into regular classrooms whenever possible.

The battle to learn for disabled and nondisabled children begins at the kindergarten door. Only when the disability and women's movements work together at all levels of education — primary, secondary, and postsecondary — can there be a chance for educational equity for every child.

The Right to Vote

The nineteenth-century feminists who strove to educate themselves soon looked to the ballot box as a way of acquiring political selfdetermination.

It took women seventy-two years to get the vote. From 1848, the year women resolved to "secure themselves their sacred right to the elective franchise,"[14] to 1920, the year ratification of the Nineteenth Amendment affirmed their right to vote, women battled stereotypes that they were biologically inferior to men, eternally childlike, and mentally unfit.[15]

Today, women's right to vote is unquestioned, yet a woman who is disabled still may be denied this basic right. If she has a mental disability she may be subject to state laws that prohibit her from voting.[16] If she is physically disabled she may face architectural and communication barriers that limit her right.

Laws denying mentally disabled people the right to vote are based on the premise that it is in the state's interest to exclude from voting those individuals unable to make a rational decision. Each state has the power to determine its voter qualifications. All but ten states have some statute restricting the voting rights of mentally disabled people. The problem with many of these statutes is that they unfairly generalize about the ability of certain classes of people labeled "mentally disabled" to make rational decisions. The assumption of these laws is that an individual judged to be mentally disabled within the meaning of the statute is totally incapacitated for all purposes, including voting. For example, take guardianship. Twenty-four states disqualify from voting those individuals placed under guardianship. However, the criterion for placing someone under guardianship is merely that the individual is incapable of handling his or her financial affairs. It is possible that an individual may not be able to save money or balance a checkbook, but may be able to decide rationally which candidate to support. The inability to handle money does not imply that the individual is incompetent in every area of life ("Mental Disability" 1979).

A similar argument may be made against the laws that prohibit voting by anyone adjudged "insane" ("Mental Disability" 1979). While there may be certain individuals within that classification who should not vote, the law risks excluding those who are capable of voting. One psychiatric study of "insane" individuals in institutions concluded that most had the ability to comprehend the act of voting (Klein and Grossman 1968).

The stereotypes underlying these laws — that *all* individuals under guardianship are incompetent to vote, and *all* individuals labeled insane are similarly unfit to vote — must be examined. If the decision to deny an individual the right to vote is to be based on an inability to make rational decisions, that judgment should be made on a case-by-case basis and not as the result of an individual's mental disability classification.

Another problem with laws denying mentally disabled people the right to vote is the often vague definition of mental capacity in the statutes. Several states deny the right to vote to persons considered idiots. Idiocy has been interpreted broadly to mean "mental feebleness."[17]

In the beginning of the twentieth century, an attempt to define and identify "feeblemindedness" was developed in the form of an IQ test. In 1912 Henry Goddard administered his intelligence test to immigrants. The results showed that 83 percent of the Jews, 80 percent of the Hungarians, 79 percent of the Italians, and 87 percent of the Russians tested were "feeble-minded" (Goddard 1913). Because the test was given in English to largely non-English speaking people, it is easy to see why so many people failed it.

While individuals labeled mentally disabled have had to contend with laws that unfairly stereotype their abilities, physically disabled people have had their right to vote restricted by physical and communications barriers. These barriers affect those who are blind, deaf, and orthopedically disabled. They include architecturally inaccessible sites, voting machines that are impossible to use without assistance, ballots that are not in braille or in language that a learning-disabled person can understand. The right to privacy is denied when a disabled person is barred from choosing her own assistant to help operate an inaccessible voting machine or to read the ballot. In some states, disabled people may vote by absentee ballot. However, this method prevents disabled people from considering and reacting to last-minute political developments because absentee ballots must be mailed several days in advance of an election.

Advocates tried for years to pass legislation mandating accessible voting sites. In 1984, the Equal Access to Voting Rights Act (PL 98-435) was passed, mandating either accessible precinct polling places or accessible alternative polling places. Paper ballots must be provided for those unable to operate a voting machine, and blind people are able to have a person of their choice assist them. The law, however, applies only to federal elections. Each state will have to pass similar legislation to secure the rights of disabled individuals in state and municipal elections.

Unlike their nondisabled counterparts, who secured the right to vote in every election without restriction, disabled women still must look to each state to determine their status as voting citizens. Legal and physical barriers that make it difficult for disabled women to vote discourage involvement in the political process. The women's movement can do much to encourage the political involvement of disabled women by working on voter access issues. This is yet another area where the women's and disability rights movements can effectively combine forces. For example, women's groups can do voter outreach to disabled women. That means having fact sheets and issue papers in braille and on tape. Voter outreach extends to registration: women's groups need to visit nursing homes, state hospitals, and mental hospitals to register women to vote. Later, they must be ready to defend their newly registered voters from challenges of unfitness by state officials. Also, women's groups that support candidates for office should know their candidate's position on removing restrictions on the voting rights of disabled people. Finally, political clubs should lobby state voting officials to identify accessible polling places within the materials the state mails to voters. The clubs also can survey accessible voting places in precincts and encourage officials to provide as many accessible places as possible.

Employment Rights

In the analysis of employment discrimination, those flickering images of the beauty queen and the poster child return to haunt us. The intelligent, professional, career-seeking woman still is plagued by the constraints of the beauty queen image. She faces career stagnation and frustration caused by the closed male mentor, or "old boy," network. To those men who still wield power, the career woman too often is merely an elegant, dispensable ornament, not to be taken seriously. Viewed this way, she is almost never considered an integral part of a management team.

Ornament though she be, the beauty queen fares better than the poster child. Disabled people, and disabled women especially, are not considered able to work. Their inability to work is seen as a natural result of their disabling condition. Only

23.5 percent of disabled women are in the labor force. Of this percentage, 15.5 percent are unemployed. Compare those figures to the employment percentages of nondisabled women. Sixty-four percent of nondisabled women are in the labor force; their unemployment rate is 7.5 percent (Bowe 1984). That the high unemployment rate among disabled women can be attributed partially to disability discrimination can be seen from surveys reflecting employers' attitudes toward disabled people. In one study, employers were asked to rank various groups in terms of which ones they would be most likely to hire. The list included physically and mentally disabled groups, minority groups, student militants, prison parolees, senior citizens, and "neutral" groups such as whites and Canadians. The study showed that physically disabled groups ranked lower than all minority groups, senior citizens, student militants, and prison parolees, but higher than all mentally disabled groups (Colbert, Kalish, and Chang 1973). In another study, employers were found more likely to hire a prison parolee or a formal mental patient than a person with epilepsy (Triandis and Patterson 1963). In a third study, 50 percent of the employers queried said they would never consider hiring a blind or mentally retarded person for any type of job (Williams 1972).

Disabled women, unlike disabled men, must contend with yet another aspect of societal stereotyping. This is the effect of a disabled woman's rolelessness. Nondisabled women, by virtue of their roles as mothers and nurturers, traditionally have been limited to job categories such as teaching and nursing. The disabled woman has been denied even these opportunities. While feminists struggle to enter nontraditional jobs, to a disabled woman every job is a nontraditional job.

Take teaching as an example. In the late sixties in New York City, a woman in a wheelchair was denied a license to teach in the city's schools on the ground that "being confined to a wheelchair as a result of poliomyelitis, she was physically and mentally unsuited for teaching." As a result of a lawsuit by the woman, the board of education reversed itself and granted the plaintiff a license and a teaching position. In another example, a blind English teacher was denied a job with the Philadelphia School District because she was certified as having a "chronic or acute physical defect." The court found this stereotyping unconstitutional.[18]

Thus, a disabled woman seeking employment risks discrimination twice: once by virtue of her gender, again by virtue of her disability. This double dose of discrimination is reflected strikingly in the economic disparity between disabled women and disabled men or nondisabled women. Almost 30 percent of all disabled women have incomes that fall below the poverty line. Compare this figure to 20 percent of all disabled men and 10 percent of all nondisabled women who have incomes below the poverty line. Nondisabled women earn 58 percent of what nondisabled males earn; disabled women earn only 51 percent (Bowe 1984).

These statistics are in part the result of employer policies that operate to systemically exclude women or disabled people from jobs. Two of these practices are the bona fide occupational qualification (or BFOQ) and the use of blanket medical standards. A BFOQ often presumes that a job position can be performed only by a member of a specified sex. Often the assumption is based on the belief that women cannot lift heavy weights, cannot supervise men, or should not work late at night. In one case the Maryland Racing Commission denied a jockey's license to a woman, arguing that only men could be jockeys. This was ruled illegal. In another case the court ruled against prohibiting a woman from transferring to another position simply because company officials believed the job too "strenuous" for one of her sex.[19]

The assumption that only men can perform certain kinds of jobs finds a disability parallel in blanket medical standards. These medical standards merely reveal the presence of a disability rather than indicate any job-related limitation. Some employers, for example, exclude all applicants with a history of cancer. Others refuse to hire anyone who has lost a leg (DREDF 1982). One employer fired a truck assembler when it was discovered he had only one kidney.[20] Others exclude from all job positions those with a history of epilepsy (DREDF 1982). Most of these blanket medical standards have been found illegal unless it can be shown that the medical standard is related to the essential requirements of the job.[21]

Existing statutes prohibit employment discrimination against both women and disabled people. However, women have broader employment protections. Title VII of the Civil Rights Act prohibits employment discrimination based on sex by all employers with fifteen or more employees. Disabled people's protections, for the most part covered under the 1973 Rehabilitation Act, are limited to employers who are federal contractors or recipients of federal funds.

The laws that prohibit discrimination based on sex and disability have as their larger purpose the inclusion and participation of women and disabled people in society. That means eliminating discriminatory practices and in some cases instituting affirmative action programs to remedy past discrimination. However, the disabled job-seeker faces an additional barrier besides the attitudinal ones: she or he faces physical barriers. A disabled person who is qualified to perform a job still faces discrimination when the employer says, "Yes, you are qualified for the job, but your wheelchair cannot get into the office because of the two steps, so I won't hire you." Or the employer might say, "Sure, you can fill out the forms, but you cannot reach the shelf where the forms are stored, so I will not hire you." The disabled job-seeker, first victimized by prejudice, now is hindered by an inaccessible environment. The solution for this dilemma — to require employers to make "reasonable accommodations to the known physical or mental limitation of an otherwise qualified handicapped applicant or employee" — is the heart of Section 504.[22] The reasonable accommodation requirement means, in essence, that employers should try to adjust the job to the individual. That can entail such simple remedies as removing a physical barrier, providing a piece of equipment that will enable the person to do the job, or adjusting a work schedule. The qualified disabled person who could not get into the office because of two steps could be accommodated through a ramp. The woman who could not reach the forms could be accommodated if the forms were moved or the shelf were lowered.

The law requires employers only to make "reasonable" accommodations. Recent court decisions have been defining the parameters of what is reasonable. In *Nelson v. Thornburgh*, the court ruled that an employer had to provide readers for blind employees. In *Coleman v. Casey Board of Education*, a school district was ordered to allow a bus driver with only one leg to drive a bus modified with a hand clutch. Accommodations also are required for applicants. In *Stutt v. Freeman*, the court ruled that a dyslexic person who could not read a written examination for a heavy-equipment operator had to be accommodated by means of an oral test.[23]

The concept of reasonable accommodation to remedy employment discrimination is not unique to disability. In one case of sex discrimination, the court said that the refusal to hire a woman welder because there were no women's bathrooms was illegal. The judge then ordered the company to install a women's bathroom. In another sex discrimination case, one involving height requirements, the court ruled that if a woman worker's inability to reach the machinery was due to her height, a platform should be built to accommodate her.[24]

The reasonable accommodation argument also has sprung up in another women's rights issue, that of pregnancy leave. There are two schools of thought on this. One group says that a woman who becomes pregnant should be treated exactly the same as anyone else who has a temporarily disabling condition, and she should be subject to the standard leave policy of her company. In other words, if she has to be off work for six weeks following birth, but the company provides only a four-week leave policy, then the company can legally terminate her. The theory is that equal treatment in the workplace means equal opportunity to compete for the high-paying jobs that men have.

Women have been striving for equal treatment in the workplace from the time protection laws were enacted in the early twentieth century. The equal treatment argument flows from the nonaccepted notion that "protective" legislation undermines and restricts women's job opportunities. Some of this legislation has included weight-lifting limits; restrictions on the hours a woman could work; and mandatory, additional rest periods that were denied to men (Kanowitz 1969). Women have fought for many years to eliminate the paternalistic notion that as a class they cannot do certain kinds of labor. Having realized that protective legislation often prevents their access to skilled labor jobs, their rallying cry is equal treatment to compete for jobs (Williams 1982).

The second school of thought opposes this logic as it relates to the issue of pregnancy leave. Feminists of this school say that in the area of pregnancy leave, equal treatment of the sexes results in inequality for women. A company that applies a four-week leave policy to all workers has a disproportionate impact on women. Many pregnant women require more than four weeks leave and therefore face almost certain termination — a hardship that no man has to bear. They argue that an adequate leave policy — one that allows a pregnant woman time to deal with pregnancy, delivery, and recovery from childbearing — should not be viewed as an additional benefit that borders on protective legislation. In fact, they argue, an adequate leave time merely equalizes the outcomes for women in the job market. It removes a barrier to continued employment that exists only for women. They further draw the analogy that just as a disabled person is entitled to reasonable accommodation to remove a unique barrier presented by her or his disability, so too should a woman be allowed adequate leave time to remove the barrier presented by her pregnancy (Krieger and Cooney 1983).

It is too early to tell which argument will win favor with the divided feminist community. The use of a primarily disability-based solution to a women's rights issue merely illustrates again the crossover of issues and answers between the women's movement and the disability rights movement.

The disability rights movement and the women's movement share common goals for their members: equality of opportunity and full participation in all aspects of society. This includes parenting, reproductive choice, education, voting, and employment. However, equal opportunity and full participation can exist only in a society that values the individual as part of the social collective. This new society will allow all women, disabled or nondisabled, to make life choices based on their needs. It will fit jobs to people instead of discarding people who don't fit jobs. It will recognize our right to control our bodies, to educate ourselves, and to value both work and motherhood. No longer will the images of beauty queen and poster child reflect a woman's or a disabled person's lesser status in society. In our new society, each individual will be able to live in a community that mirrors her true self, undistorted by the icons of a past age.

NOTES

1. *Consolidated Rail Corp. v Darrone*, 104 S.Ct. 1248 (1984). A brief submitted in support of the argument that Section 504 of the Rehabilitation Act covers employment discrimination. Amici's argument attempted to prove the existence of widespread discrimination against disabled people. The court agreed and held that Section 504 does cover employment.

2. One nineteenth-century judge remarked, "Man is or should be woman's protector and defender. The natural and proper timidity and delicacy which belongs to the female sex evidently unfits it for many of the occupations of civil life." *Bradwell v. Illinois*, 83 U.S. (15 Wallace) 130 (1873). This opinion upheld the right of a state to deny a woman an application for a license to practice as an attorney.

3. Education for All Handicapped Children Act, PL 94-142, 89 Stat. 773 (codified as amended at 20 USC 1400–1420 (1976 & supp. V 1981); Rehabilitation Act of 1973, PL 93-112, 504, 87 Stat. 355 (codified as amended at 29 USC 794) (supp. V 1981).

4. Rehabilitation Act Amendments of 1974, PL 93-516, 88 Stat. 1617.

5. Civil Rights Act of 1964, 601, PL 88-352, 78 Stat. 252 (codified at 42 USC 2000d (1976); Title VII, 42 USC 2000e; *Roe v. Wade*, 93 S.Ct. 705 (1972); Education Amendments of 1972, 901(a), PL 93-318, 86 Stat. 373 (codified at 20 USC 168(a) (1982).

6. Title VI reads, "No person in the United States shall, on the ground of race, color, or national origin, be excluded from participation in, be denied the benefits of, or be subjected to discrimination under any program or activity receiving Federal financial assistance."

Title IX reads, "No person in the United States shall, on the basis of sex, be excluded from participation in, be denied the benefits of, or be subjected to discrimination under any education program or activity receiving Federal financial assistance."

Section 504 reads, "No otherwise qualified handicapped individual in the United States shall, solely by reason of his handicap, be excluded from participation in, be denied the benefits of, or be subjected to discrimination under any program or activity receiving Federal financial assistance."

7. Reference throughout to mothers is not intended to dismiss the involvement of fathers. It simply recognizes that mothers are most often primary caretakers.

8. *Muller v. Oregon*, 208 U.S. 412 (1908).

9. Brief of Amici Curie for Petitioners, *Margaret M. Heckler v. American Hospital Association*, no. 84-1529 (2 Cir. 1985), cert. granted.

10. Voting rights: "The right of citizens of the United States to vote shall not be denied or abridged by the United States, or any state on account of sex" (U.S. const. amend. XIX); employment protection: Title VII of the 1964 Civil Rights Act. 42 USC 2000e; education rights: Title IX of the Education Amendments of 1972, 20 USC 1681.

11. 42 Fed. Reg. 22,676 (1977), found at 34 CFR 104 and 45 CFR 84.

12. Equal Access to Voting Rights Act, PL 98-435.

13. *Grove City v. Bell*, 103 S.Ct. 1181 (1983).

14. Declaration of Sentiments and Resolutions Adopted by the Seneca Falls Convention, July 19–20, 1848.

15. One example from a nineteenth-century religious figure: "We do not believe women . . . are fit to have their own head. . . . Without masculine direction or control, she is out of her element, and a social anomaly, sometimes a hideous monster" (see Gurko 1974).

16. The term "mental disability" used here is meant to be a generic reference to anyone suffering or presumed to be suffering from a mental health problem. It includes people who are labeled "mentally retarded" as well as those labeled "mentally ill."

17. *In Re South Charleston Beal Law Election*, 3 Ohio NP, NS 373 (1905), the court noted that definitions such as "insanity," "idiocy," "lunacy," "imbecility," and "feeblemindedness" are general terms and refer to manifestation in language or conduct of a disease or a defect of the brain.

18. *Heumann v. Board of Education of the City of New York*, 320 F. Supp. 623, 624 (S.D. N.Y. 1970); *Gurmankin v. Constanzo*, 411 F. Supp. 982 (E.D. Pa. 1976), aff'd 556 F.2d 184 (3 Cir. 1977).

19. *In Re Kusner v. Maryland Racing Commission*, no. 37,044 Circuit Court, Prince George's County, Md. (1968); *Weeks v. Southern Bell Telegraph and Telephone Co.*, 408 F.2d 228 (5 Cir. 1969).

20. *Dairy Equipment Co. v. Wis. DILHR*, 95 Wis. 2d 319, 290 NW 2d 330 (1980).

21. "Once a Plaintiff shows an employer denied him employment because of physical condition, the burden of persuasion shifts to the Federal employer to show that the criteria used are job related and the Plaintiff could not safely and effectively perform the essentials of the job." *Treadwell v. Alexander*, 707 F. 2d 473 474 (11 Cir. 1983).

22. 34 CFR 104.12(a), 45 CFR 84.12(a) (1982).

23. *Nelson v. Thornburgh*, 567 S. Supp. 369 (ED Pa. 1983), aff'd 732 F.2d 146 (3 Cir. 1984); *Coleman v. Casey Board of Education*, 510 F. Supp. 310 (WD Ky. 1980); *Stutt v. Freeman*, 694 F. 2d 666 (11 Cir. 1983).

24. EEOC Dec. No. 70-558, Feb. 19, 1970; EEOC Dec. No. 71-1418.

REFERENCES

Bowe, F. 1984. *Disabled women in America*. Washington, DC: President's Committee on Employment of the Handicapped.

Burgdorf, R., and M. Burgdorf. 1977. The wicked witch is almost dead: Buck v. Bell. *Temple Law Quarterly* 50:995.

Clarke, E. 1873. *Sex in education; or, A fair chance for the girls.* New York: Arno Press. Reprinted 1972.

Clinton, C. 1984. *The other civil war.* New York: Hill and Wang.

Colbert, J., R. Kalish, and P. Chang. 1973. Two psychological portals of entry for disadvantaged groups. *Rehabilitation Literature* 32 (7): 194.

Czajka, J. 1984. *Digest of data on persons with disabilities.* Washington, DC: Congressional Research Service, Library of Congress.

DREDF. 1982. *Medical standards project: Final report.* Disability Rights Education and Defense Fund and Employment Law Center, Berkeley, CA.

Flexner. E. 1972. *Century of struggle: The women's rights movement in the United States.* New York: Atheneum.

Franklin, P. 1977. Impact of disability on the family structure. *Social Security Bulletin* 40 (5): 3–18.

Gliedman, J., and W. Roth. 1980. *The unexpected minority: Handicapped children in America.* New York: Harcourt Brace Jovanovich.

Goddard, H. H. 1913. The Binet tests in relation to immigration. *Journal of Psycho-Asthetics* 18:105.

Gurko, M. 1974. *The ladies of Seneca Falls: The birth of the women's rights movements.* New York: Schocken Books.

International Rehabilitation Review. 1977. February. Entire issue.

Kanowitz, L. 1969. *Women and the law: The unfinished revolution.* Albuquerque: University of New Mexico Press.

Klein, M., and S. A. Grossman. 1968. Voting competence and mental illness. *Proceedings of the 76th Annual Convention, American Psychological Association* 3:701.

Kreiger, L. J., and P. N. Cooney. 1983. The Miller-Wohl controversy: Equal treatment, positive action and the meaning of women's equality. *Golden Gate Law Review* 3 (summer).

Matthews, G. F. 1983. *Voices from the shadows.* Toronto: Women's Educational Press.

"Mental Disability and the Right to Vote." 1979. *Yale Law Review* 88.

Rousseau, J. 1908. *L'Emile; or, A treatise on education,* ed. W. H. Payne. New York: D. Appleton.

Safilios-Rothschild, C. 1977. Discrimination against disabled women. *International Rehabilitation Review,* February, 4.

Triandis, H. C., and C. H. Patterson. 1963. Indices of employer prejudice toward disabled applicants. *Journal of Applied Psychology* 47:52.

U.S. Congress. 1985. *Families with disabled children: Issue for the 80s. Hearings before the Select Committee on Children, Youth and Families,* 99th Cong., 1st sess.

Vash, C. 1981. *The psychology of disability.* New York: Springer.

Williams, C. A. 1972. Is hiring the handicapped good business? *Journal of Rehabilitation* 38 (2): 30.

Williams, W. 1982. The equality crisis: Some reflections on culture, courts, and feminism. *Women's Rights Law Reporter* 7:175.

THIRTY-ONE

Presenting the Blue Goddess: Toward a National Pan-Asian Feminist Agenda

SONIA SHAH

We all laughed sheepishly about how we used to dismiss the South Asian women in our lives as doormats irrelevant to our feminist lives. For most of us in that fledgling South Asian American women's group in Boston, either white feminists or black feminists had inspired us to find our Asian feminist heritage. Yet neither movement had really prepared us for actually finding any. The way either group defined feminism did not, could not, define our South Asian feminist heritages. That, for most of us, consisted of feisty immigrant mothers, ball-breaking grandmothers, Kali-worship (Kali is the blue goddess who sprang whole from another woman and who symbolizes "shakti" — Hindi for womanpower), social activist aunts, freedom-fighting/Gandhian great-aunts. In many ways, white feminism, with its "personal is political" maxim and its emphasis on building sisterhood and consciousness raising, had brought us together. Black feminism, on the other hand, had taught us that we could expect more — that feminism can incorporate a race analysis. Yet, while both movements spurred us to organize, neither included our South Asian American agendas — battery of immigrant women, the ghettoization of the Indian community, cultural discrimination, and bicultural history and identity.

I felt we were starting anew, starting to define a South Asian American feminism that no one had articulated yet. As I began to reach out to other Asian American women's groups over the years and for this chapter, however, that sense faded a bit. Asian American women have been organizing themselves for decades, with much to show for it.

Our shakti hasn't yet expressed itself on a national stage accessible to all our sisters. But we are entering a moment in our organizing when we will soon be able to create a distinctly Asian American feminism, one that will be able to cross the class and culture lines that currently divide us.

The first wave of Asian women's organizing, born of the women's liberation and civil rights movements of the 1960s, established groups like Asian Women United in San Francisco, Asian Sisters in Action in Boston, and other more informal networks of primarily professional, East Asian American women. They focused on empowering Asian women economically and socially and accessing political power. Asian Women United, for example, has produced videos like *Silk Wings*, which describes Asian women in nontraditional jobs, and books like *Making Waves*, an anthology of Asian American women's writing.

In contrast, the second wave of organizing, politicized by the 1980s multicultural movements, includes the many ethnically specific women's groups that tend to start out as support networks, some later becoming active in the battered women's movement (like Manavi in New Jersey, Sneha in Hartford, and the New York Asian Women's Center, which offer battery hotlines and shelter for Asian women) and others working in the women-of-color and lesbian/gay liberation movements. Culturally, these groups are Korean, Indian, Cambodian, Filipina, and from other more recently arrived immigrant groups who may not have felt part of the more established, primarily East Asian women's networks. These different groups are divided by generation, by culture, and by geographic location. Anna Rhee, a cofounder of the Washington Alliance of Korean American Women (WAKAW), a group of mostly 1.5 generation (those who emigrated to the United States in early adulthood) and second-generation Korean American women, with an average age of twenty-seven to twenty-eight, says she felt "we were starting anew, because of the focus on English speaking Korean women, which was different from any other group we had seen." WAKAW, like many similar groups, started as a support group, but has since evolved into activism, with voter registration and other projects.

Talking to various Asian American women activists, I was inspired by the many projects they have undertaken, and impressed with the overwhelming sense women had that the Asian American women's community today stands at a crossroads and has great potential. The New York Asian Women's Center, which runs several programs fighting violence against Asian women, just celebrated its tenth birthday. The Pacific Asian American Women's Bay Area Coalition honors Asian American women with Woman Warrior (á la Maxine Hong Kingston's novel) leadership awards, catapulting their honorees on to other accolades. Indian Subcontinent Women's Alliance for Action (ISWAA) in Boston just assembled a grassroots arts exhibit of works by and for South Asian women. Asian Women United, in addition to several other videos, is working on a video of Asian American visual artists. The Washington Alliance for Korean American Women is taking oral histories of Korean mothers and daughters. Everyone has a story of another group starting up, another exciting Asian American woman activist.

So far, Asian American women activists have used two general organizing models. The first is based on the fact that Asian women need each other to overcome the violence, isolation, and powerlessness of their lives; no one else can or will be able to help us but each other. The groups that come together on this basis focus on the immediate needs of the community: housing battered women, finding homes for abandoned women and children, providing legal advocacy for refugee women, and so forth.

The second model is based on shared identity and the realization that both Asian and U.S. mainstream cultures make Asian American women invisible. The groups that come together on this basis work on articulating anger about racism and sexism, like other women of color groups, but also on fighting the omnipresent and seductive pressure to assimilate, within ourselves and for our sisters.

Today, our numbers are exploding, in our immigrant communities and their children, and subsequently, in our activist communities. Our writers, poets, artists, and filmmakers are coming of age. Our activist voices against anti-Asian violence, battery, and racism are gaining legal, political, and social notice. We still have much ground to cover in influencing mainstream culture: we must throw those exoticizing books about Asian women off the shelf and replace them with a slew of works on pan-Asian feminism; women of color putting together collections of radical essays must be able to "find" Asian American feminists; *Ms.* magazine must offer more than a colorful photo of an Indian mother and daughter with less than three lines about them in a related cover article; critics must stop touting Asian American women's fiction as "exotic treasures"; Fifth Avenue advertising executives must stop producing ads that exploit tired stereotypes of Asian female "exotic beauty" and "humble modesty" with images of silky black hair and Asian women demurely tucking tampons into their pockets.

Our movement faces crucial internal challenges as well. Longtime Asian American feminist activists, such as Helen Zia, a contributing editor to *Ms.*, wonder, "What makes us different from white feminists or black feminists? What can we bring to the table?" and complain that "these questions haven't really been developed yet." Others, such as Jackie Church, a Japanese American activist, state that "there just aren't enough Asian American feminists who aren't doing five different things at once."

On the one hand, our national Asian women's groups, while inclusive across Asian ethnicities, haven't yet developed an Asian feminism *different* from black or white feminism. On the other, our ethnically specific groups, while emotionally resonant and culturally specific, are still remote and inaccessible to many of our sisters.

The movements of the 1960s colluded with the mainstream in defining racism in black and white terms; racism is still defined as discrimination based on skin color, that is, race. They also, to some extent, elevated racism, defined in this way, to the top of layers of oppression. This narrow definition has distorted mainstream perception of anti-Asian racism and even our perception of ourselves — as either nonvictims of racism or victims of racism based on skin color. By these assumptions, an Indian assaulted because she "dresses weird" is not a victim of racism; a Chinese shopkeeper harassed because she has a "funny accent" is not a victim of racism. Mainstream culture finds neither of these incidents as disturbing, unacceptable, or even downright "evil" as racism. By this definition, one must be in either the black or white camp to even speak about racism, and we are expected to forget ourselves. Whites try to convince us we are really *more like them*; depending on our degree of sensitivity toward racist injustice, we try to persuade blacks that we are more like them.

For example, many Asian American women have described Asian women's experience of racism as a result of stereotypes about "exotica" and "china dolls," two stereotypes based on our looking different from white people. But our experiences of racism go far beyond that. Rather than subvert the definition of racism itself, or uncover new layers of oppression just as unacceptable and pernicious as racism but based on what I call cultural discrimination, we have attempted to fit our experience of discrimination into the given definition. We too assume that racism is the worst kind of oppression, by emphasizing that racism against us is based on skin color and racial differences. Indeed, when we forged our first wave of women's movement, solidarity with other people of color whose activism revolved around black/white paradigms of oppression was a matter of survival. And organizing around racially based oppressions served as common ground for all ethnic Asians.

Yet our experiences of oppression are, in many qualitative ways, different from those of black and white people. For me, the experience of "otherness," the formative discrimination in my life, has resulted from culturally different (not necessarily racially different) people thinking they were culturally central: thinking that *my* house smelled funny, that *my* mother talked weird, that *my* habits were strange. They were normal; I wasn't.

Today, a more sophisticated understanding of oppression is emanating from all people of color groups. The Los Angeles riots, among other ethnic conflicts, unmasked to belated national attention the reality of an ethnic conflict (between blacks and browns, as well as between the white power structure and oppressed people of color) impossible to explain away simply as white-against-black racism. Multicultural movements and growing internationalism have raised questions about our hierarchy of oppressions. Asian American men and women activists are beginning to create legal and social definitions of cultural discrimination. Our movement can march beyond black/white paradigms that were once useful, and start to highlight cultural discrimination — our peculiar blend of cultural and sexist oppression based on our accents, our clothes, our foods, our values, and our commitments. When we do this successfully, we will have not just laid a common ground for all ethnic Asian women for the practical goal of gaining power, we will have taken an important political step toward understanding and, from there, struggling against the many layers of oppression.

The search for identity that has compelled Asian American women to separate into cultural-, age-, generation-, class-, and geographic-specific groups will ensure that the emerging pan–Asian American feminism retains emotional resonance. Although the very specificity that makes them so useful limits these groups, as their numbers grow, coalition building and networking become not only viable options, but necessary for advancing difficult agendas requiring extensive resources and support. These coalitions and networks must struggle to find common ground that retains emotional resonance while being inclusive.

Our common ground must be more than our simply being "Asian," which encompasses so much diversity as to be practically useless as an ethnic category, particularly since our specific cultural heritages are so much more meaningful. The general "feminist" agenda, commonly understood as that of the mainstream white middle-class women's movement, is also problematic. The racism and classism of the traditional white women's movement, as well as the threat of violence from our community's patriarchy, has sometimes held us back from calling ourselves feminists. "The whole attitude" of white feminism, says Sunita Mani of Indian Subcontinent Women's Alliance for Action, "is that my strong-mindedness is my American-ness, not my Asian-ness." The heightened demand for specificity that grows out of groups like ISWAA makes the simple grafting of the feminist label onto our organizing untenable: we need something that recognizes our Asian activist heritage and our cultural specificity. As Carol Ito, a board member of the Pacific Asian American Women's Bay Area Coalition in San Francisco, says, "We didn't want to be called feminist." "Feminism was seen as a white, middle-class concern," says Korean American Elaine Kim, literary critic and a member of Asian Women United. "Race discrimination was much more vivid than sexism."

Our movement owes much to black feminism. But while white feminism seemed to ignore race and culture analyses, black feminism, on the other hand, worked under the black/white paradigms and according to a hierarchy of oppressions, which Asian American women can neither accurately nor powerfully organize under. The black/white paradigms of both feminist and civil rights struggles create false divisions and false choices for Asian American women. Recently, a group of 1.5-generation South Asian women who organize against battery held a conference on South Asian women. This group, demographically, having emigrated later than the parents of second-generation South Asian Americans, tends to hail from greater class privilege. Second-generation South Asian American activists boycotted the conference, charging that the organizers, because of their class privilege and their relative newness to the Asian American community, sidelined issues of U.S.-based racism and discrimination.

This is a false division, especially dangerous in such a relatively small activist community. When first faced with American racism and its black/white constructs, immigrants with class privilege, even activist ones, are apt to dismiss racism as "not their problem." (As the mainstream defines it, strictly speaking, it isn't.) Efforts by second-generation activists and beyond, confined as we have been to black/white paradigms, to convince our sisters at other locations on the culture/class continuum that what we suffer is similar to what the black community suffers will necessarily be difficult if not impossible. Yet we are natural allies, given a broader critique of oppression that includes cultural discrimination and an accurate portrayal of our own experiences of racism on a continuum of oppressions linked to imperialism, immigration policy, and sexism, across real divisions of immigration status and class and certainly across the false divisions of black/white race analysis and black/white feminism.

As Asian Americans, Asians in America, Americans of Asian descent, or however we choose to think of ourselves, we all grapple with conflicting signals and oppressions in our lives because we are all situated, to differing degrees, in both Asian and American cultural milieus. As any of these, we suffer not only cultural discrimination as men also do, but also our own form of cultural schizophrenia, from the mixed and often contradictory signals about priorities, values, duty, and meaning our families and greater communities convey. We encounter sexist Asian tradition, racist and sexist white culture, antiracist nonfeminist women heroes, racist feminist heroes, strong proud Asian women who told us not to make waves, strong proud non-Asian women who told us *to* make waves, and on and on.

Black/white paradigms have informed the conception of cultural or racial differ-ence as well: white people are all white, black people are all black. No room exists for cultural duality in a world where one is automatically relegated to one camp or another based on biology. Yet the problems of cultural duality as well as the concomitant experience of cultural discrimination are exactly what unite the Asian American women's community across our differences. We all reconcile these ten-sions and oppressions in different ways, by acting out a model minority myth, for some; by suffering silently, for others; by being activist, for still others. As we grapple with conflicting signals and oppressions in our lives and struggle against cultural discrimination, we can reimagine and reinvent ourselves and our priorities, with the support of our sisters. We can politicize the process of cultural reconciliation, and tag it for feminism and liberation.

This broader critique that the Asian American women's community is groping toward does and must continue to include this empowering and activist commonal-ity among Asian American women: not just the fact and nature of our oppressions, but the nature of our responses to oppression, which I call bicultural feminism.

The plea for bicultural feminism is not simply that Asian American women activists call themselves bicultural feminists. It is a call for an agenda that subverts the black/white paradigms, articulates cultural discrimination and how it illuminates and connects to other processes of oppression, and politicizes the process of cultural reconciliation for feminism and liberation.

A poor immigrant Asian woman follows an abusive husband to the United States; she doesn't speak English and is cut off from the women who supported her in her home country; she is beaten nearly to death by her one contact to the outside world. This woman needs a bicultural feminism. Within black/white constructs of racism, she cannot name the threats to her with the authority that racism carries. Within narrow white feminist paradigms and essentialist notions of cultural difference, she is presented with false choices for liberation: either become a prototypical "American" woman, with all the alien cultural cues that implies, or go back to Asia. She needs an activism that struggles against the danger she encounters as a non-English speaking Asian woman in America; she needs an activism that empowers her to liberate herself in this country (with money, legal services, shelter, and support) while recognizing and politicizing the cultural reconciliation she must undergo to liberate herself (by reimagining her duty as an Asian wife as a duty to herself, for example).

When my little sister, who is just beginning to see herself as a sexual person, thinks she is a "slut" for wearing tight jeans, she needs this bicultural feminism. Not a mainstream white feminism, which might suggest she throw away her tight jeans because she is objectifying herself, nor one that simply suggests she revert to the dress of her "homeland" and wear a revealing sari — but one that would affirm that she doesn't have to abandon Indian values or filial respect or whatever it is that makes her fear appearing "slutty."

It is possible that first-generation Indians reject the trappings of American sexuality, such as tight jeans, as culturally alien. The subsequent interpretation by their children and their greater American communities, however, that they are anti-sexuality stems from the dominant paradigm of a monoculture: white culture and black culture, which is simply the poor, darker version of the white culture. An Asian American feminism that emphasized cultural duality and reconciliation would subvert this notion. There are many cultures, many sexualities, and many trappings of such. My sister needs to name the cultural conflicts she is involved in for what they are, and reconcile her visions of sexuality and empowerment within the cultural confines of white patriarchy and Indian patriarchy. A bicultural feminism would ensure that she does this in a feminist, liberated way.

As bicultural feminists, we are empowered to enter the broader discussion and struggles around us with something more substantial than identity politics and our slightly different take on racism within the black/white dichotomy. As we approach the concept and practice of the extended family, for example, we can apply our critical reinventions to the struggle for accessible child care, by shifting the turgid debate away from paid care and toward building cooperative care centers and work-sharing. As we approach social and linguistic difference within Asian American families, we can apply our insights to the current debates about gay parents raising potentially straight children, or to white families raising children of color, for example, by advocating for the fitness of the child's cultural community rather than for the "fitness" of the parent. As we remember our histories as Asian women, we can apply our sense of outrage, over the internment, the brain drain, and the treatment of refugees, to the struggle for just immigration policy. We can reinterpret Asian paradigms of filial and familial duty as social responsibility. We can use antimaterialism as a basis for building an ecological society.

I remember that in that South Asian American women's group, we were all looking forward to Mira Nair's film, *Mississippi Masala*. We took Nair as a kind of model — a seemingly progressive Indian woman filmmaker who had gained the kind of financial backing necessary for reaching wide sectors of the South Asian community. *Masala* was the first film we knew of that would portray an Indian American woman in her cultural milieu as the protagonist.

I don't know what Nair's intentions were, but her Indian American protagonist was little more than a standard Western-defined beauty, her biculturalism little more than occasional bare feet and a chureedar thrown over her shoulder. Although a refugee from Uganda living in Mississippi with Indian parents, she was phenomenally unconcerned with issues of race, history, culture, and gender. Given the dearth of accessible activist commentary on biculturalism and feminism beyond the black/white divide, even a sympathetic "opinion maker" like Nair can hurt our movement by portraying us as little more than exotic, browner versions of white women, who by virtue of a little color can bridge the gap between black and white (not through activism, of course, just romantic love). If Asian American women's movements can effectively unite within bicultural feminist agendas, we can snatch that power away from those willing to trivialize us, and *Masala* and our less sympathetic foes beware.

RESOURCES

Washington Alliance of Korean American Women, 1623-J Carriage House Terrace, Silver Spring, MD 20904-5681.

Pacific Asian American Women's Bay Area Coalition, 450 Taraval, Suite 283, San Francisco, CA 94116.

Indian Subcontinent Women's Alliance for Action, call Riti Sachdeva in Boston, MA, (617) 232-5165.

Asian Women United, c/o Lilia Villanueva, 1218 Spruce Street, Berkeley, CA 94704.

Asian Sisters in Action, PO Box 38-0331, Cambridge, MA 02238.

New York Asian Women's Center, 39 Bowery, Box 375, New York, NY 10002.

Manavi, PO Box 614, Bloomfield, NJ 07003.

Sneha, c/o Hansa Shah, 100 Woodpond Rd., Glastonbury, CT 06033.

THIRTY-TWO

Beyond Racism and Misogyny
Black Feminism and 2 Live Crew

KIMBERLÈ WILLIAMS CRENSHAW

Violence against women is a central issue in the feminist move-
ment. As part of an overall strategy to change patterns of individual and institutional
behavior to better women's lives, academics and activists have challenged the ways
violence against women — primarily battering and rape — is perpetuated and condoned within our culture.

Much of this challenge has occurred within legal discourse because it is within
the law that cultural attitudes are legitimized through organized state power. Feminists have struggled with some success to end the representation of battering and
rape as a "private family matter" or as "errant sexuality" and make clear that these
are specific sites of gender subordination. These battles have taken place over issues
such as mandatory arrest for batterers, the admissibility of a victim's sexual history in
sexual assault cases, and the admissibility of psychological evidence, such as the
battered women's syndrome in cases involving women who kill their batterers and
rape trauma syndrome in sexual assault cases.

If recent events are indicative, the process may continue to bear some political
fruit. The governors of Ohio and Maryland have commuted sentences of women
convicted of murdering abusive husbands, and other states are considering similar
actions. Moreover, legislation is pending before Congress that would make violence
"motivated by gender" a civil rights violation.[1]

The emphasis on gender, however, tends to downplay the interaction of gender
subordination with race and class. The attitude is largely consistent with doctrinal
and political practices that construct racism and sexism as mutually exclusive. Given
the assumption that all women stand to benefit from efforts to politicize violence
against women, concerns about race may initially seem unnecessarily divisive. Indeed, it seems that what women have in common — the fact that they are primary
targets of rape and battering — not only outweighs the differences among them but

may render bizarre the argument that race should play a significant role in the analysis of these issues.

Although racial issues are not explicitly a part of the politicization of gender, public controversies show that racial politics is often linked to gender violence in the way that the violence is experienced, how the interventions are shaped, or the manner in which the consequences are politicized and represented. The controversies over the Central Park jogger case, the 2 Live Crew case, the St. John's rape trial, and the perhaps lesser known issue of Shahrazad Ali's book *The Blackman's Guide to the Blackwoman* [2] all present issues of gender violence in which racial politics is deeply implicated, but in ways that seem impossible to capture fully within existing frameworks that separate racial politics from gender politics. These separations are linked to the overall problem of the way racism and sexism are understood and how these understandings inform organizing around antiracism and feminism.

Reformist efforts to politicize these issues exclusively around gender are thus problematic both for women of color and for those engaged in feminist and antiracist politics generally. Discursive and political practices that separate race from gender and gender from race create complex problems of exclusion and distortion for women of color. Because monocausal frameworks are unlikely to provide a ready means for addressing the interplay of gender and race in cultural and political discourse on violence, it is necessary to recenter inquiries relating to violence against women from the vantage point of women of color. On the simplest level, an intersectional framework uncovers how the dual positioning of women of color as women and as members of a subordinated racial group bears upon violence committed against us. This dual positioning, or as some scholars have labeled it, double jeopardy, renders women of color vulnerable to the structural, political, and representational dynamics of both race and gender subordination. A framework attuned to the various ways these dynamics intersect is a necessary prerequisite to exploring how this double vulnerability influences the way that violence against women of color is experienced and best addressed.

Second, an intersectional framework suggests ways in which political and representational practices relating to race and gender interrelate. This is relevant because the separate rhetorical strategies that characterize antiracist and feminist politics frequently intersect in ways that create new dilemmas for women of color. For example, political imperatives are frequently constructed from the perspectives of those who are dominant within either the race or gender categories in which women of color are situated, namely, white women or men of color. These priorities are grounded in efforts to address only racism or sexism — as those issues are understood by the dominant voices within these communities. Political strategies that challenge only certain subordinating practices while maintaining existing hierarchies not only marginalize those who are subject to multiple systems of subordination, but also often result in oppositionalizing race and gender discourses. An intersectional critique is thus important in uncovering the ways the reformist politics of one discourse enforces subordinating aspects of another.

The observations that follow are meant to explore the ways intersections of race and gender bear on depictions of violence against women, particularly women of color. My observations are also meant to explore the bearing of these intersections on the broader efforts to politicize violence against all women. I explicitly adopt a Black feminist stance in my attempt to survey violence against women of color. I do this with cognizance of several tensions that this perspective entails. The most significant one relates to the way feminism has been criticized for speaking *for* women of color through its invocation of the term "woman" even as it fails to examine differences, and for *excluding* women of color by grounding feminism on the experiences and interests of white women. I think it is important to name the perspective from which my own analysis is constructed, and that is as a Black feminist. I also think it is important to acknowledge that the materials on which my analysis are based relate primarily to Black women. At the same time, I see my own work as part of a broader effort among feminist women of color to broaden feminism to include, among other factors, an analysis of race. Thus, I attempt to reach across racial differences to share my thinking and tentatively suggest ways the theory may apply to other women of color.

This chapter focuses on the problem of representational intersectionality. After a brief introduction to the theory of intersectionality, I will consider the ways media representations of women of color reinforce race and gender stereotypes. These stereotyped representations encourage and incite violence against us. But they do much more than that: they create a dominant narrative that forces actual women of color to the margins of the discourse and renders our own accounts of such victimization less credible. These media images define the spaces that women of color may occupy in dominant consciousness and problematize our efforts to construct a political practice and cultural critique that address the physical and material violence we experience.

This project is not oppositional to the overall effort to recode violence against women; rather, it is an attempt to broaden and strengthen the strategies available by exploring sites where race and gender converge to create the cultural and political grounding for gender violence. It is important also to ensure that these reform efforts do not reinforce racist sensibilities within the larger culture or ignore the need to challenge patriarchy within subcultures.

An Examination of Intersectionality

Intersectionality is a core concept both provisional and illustrative. Although the primary intersections that I explore here are between race and gender, we can and should expand the concept by factoring in issues such as class, sexual orientation, age, and color. I conceive of intersectionality as a provisional concept that links contemporary politics with postmodern theory. In examining the intersections of race and gender, I engage the dominant assumptions that these are essentially separate; by tracing the categories to their intersections, I hope to suggest a methodology that will ultimately disrupt the tendencies to see race and gender as exclusive or separable categories. Intersectionality is thus in my view a transitional concept that links current concepts with their political consequences, and real world politics with postmodern insights. It can be replaced as our understanding of each category becomes more multidimensional. The basic function of intersectionality is to frame the following inquiry: How does the fact that women of color are simultaneously situated within at least two groups that are subjected to broad societal subordination bear on problems traditionally viewed as monocausal — that is, gender discrimination or race discrimination? I believe three aspects of subordination are important: the structural dimensions of domination (structural intersectionality), the politics engendered by a particular system of domination (political intersectionality), and the representations of the dominated (representational intersectionality). These intersectionalities serve as metaphors for different ways women of color are situated between categories of race and gender when the two are regarded as mutually exclusive. I hope that a framework of intersection will facilitate a merging of race and gender discourses to uncover what lies hidden between them and to construct a better means of conceptualizing and politicizing violence against women of color. It is important to note that although I use these concepts in fairly specific ways, as metaphors their boundaries are neither finite nor rigid. Indeed, representational intersectionality is not only implicated in the political interactions of race and gender discourses, it can also be inclusive of these intersections. Moreover, political and representational intersectionality can also be included as aspects of structural intersectionality.

Structural Intersectionality

I use the term *structural intersectionality* to refer to the way in which women of color are situated within overlapping structures of subordination. Any particular disadvantage or disability is sometimes compounded by yet another disadvantage emanating from or reflecting the dynamics of a separate system of subordination. An analysis sensitive to structural intersections explores the lives of those at the bottom of multiple hierarchies to determine how the dynamics of each hierarchy exacerbates and compounds the consequences of another. The material consequences of the interaction of these multiple hierarchies in the lives of women of color is what I call structural intersectionality. Illustrations of structural intersectionality suggest that violence against a woman usually occurs within a specific context that may vary considerably depending on the woman's race, class, and other social characteristics. These constraints can be better understood and addressed through a framework that links them to broader structures of subordination that intersect in fairly predictable ways.

One illustration of structural intersectionality is the way in which the burdens of illiteracy, responsibility for child care, poverty, lack of job skills, and pervasive discrimination weigh down many battered women of color who are trying to escape the cycle of abuse. That is, gender subordination — manifested in this case by battering — intersects with race and class disadvantage to shape and limit the opportunities for effective intervention.

Another illustration of structural intersectionality is the way in which battered immigrant women's vulnerabilities were particularly exploited by the Immigration Marriage Fraud Amendments of 1986,[3] which imposed a two-year wait for permanent-resident status on women who moved to this country to marry U.S. citizens or permanent residents, and which required that both spouses file the application for the wife's permanent-resident status. When faced with what they saw as a choice between securing protection from their batterers and securing protection from deportation, many women, not surprisingly, chose the latter. Even now that these provisions have been amended — primarily at the urging of immigration activists, not feminists, which is perhaps another testament to immigrant women's isolation under intersecting structures of subordination — immigrant women are still at risk. The amendment waives the two-year wait only for battered women who produce evidence of battering from authorities (such as police officers, psychologists, and school officials) to which immigrant women may have little access, and immigrant women may still lack the English-language skills, the privacy on the telephone, and the courage to transgress cultural barriers to ask for help. Further, women married to undocumented workers may suffer in silence for fear that the security of their entire family will be jeopardized should they seek help.

A final illustration of structural intersectionality is the way in which rape crisis centers in poor minority or immigrant communities must address rape survivors' homelessness, unemployment, poverty, hunger, distrust of law enforcement officers, and perhaps their lack of English-language skills as well, often hindered by funding agency policies premised on the needs of middle-class white rape survivors.

Political Intersectionality

I use the term *political intersectionality* to refer to the different ways in which political and discursive practices relating to race and gender interrelate, often erasing women of color. On some issues, the frameworks highlighting *race* and those highlighting *gender* are oppositional and potentially contradictory. These discourses are sometimes presented as either/or propositions: the validity of each necessarily precluding the validity of the other. Manifestations of this oppositionality are found in antiracist and feminist rhetorical postures that implicitly or explicitly legitimize the dynamics of either racial or gender subordination. An extreme example is Shahrazad Ali's controversial book, *The Blackman's Guide to the Blackwoman* (1989), which blames the deteriorating conditions within the Black community on the failure of Black men to control their women. Ali recommends, among other practices, that Black men "discipline" disrespectful Black women by slapping them in the mouth — the mouth "because it is from that hole, in the lower part of her face, that all her rebellion culminates into words. Her unbridled tongue is a main reason she cannot get along with the Blackman."[4] More commonly, the need to protect the political or cultural integrity of the community is interpreted as precluding any public discussion of domestic violence. But suppressing information about domestic violence in the name of antiracism leaves unrevealed, and thus unaddressed in public discourse within our communities, the real terror in which many women of color live.

In other instances, women of color are erased when race and gender politics proceed on grounds that exclude or overlook the existence of women of color. Such an erasure took place in the rhetorical appeals made by sponsors of the Violence against Women Act (1991).[5] White male senators eloquently urged passage of the bill because violence against women occurs everywhere, not just in the inner cities. That is, the senators attempted to persuade other whites that domestic violence is a problem because "these are *our* women being victimized." White women thus came into focus, and any authentic, sensitive attention to our images and our experience, which would probably have jeopardized the bill, faded into darkness.

But an erasure need not take place for us to be silenced. Tokenistic, objectifying, voyeuristic inclusion is at least as damaging as exclusion. We are as silenced when we appear in the margins as we are when we fail to appear at all.

Political intersectionality as it relates to violence against women of color reveals the ways in which politics centered around mutually exclusive notions of race and gender leave women of color without a political framework that will adequately contextualize the violence that occurs in our lives.

Representational Intersectionality

A final variant on the intersectional theme is *representational intersectionality*, referring to the way that race and gender images, readily available in our culture, converge to create unique and specific narratives deemed appropriate for women of color. Not surprisingly, the clearest convergences are those involving sexuality, perhaps because it is through sexuality that images of minorities and women are most sharply focused. Representational intersectionality is significant in exploring violence against women of color because it provides cues to the ways our experiences are weighed against counternarratives that cast doubt on the validity and harm of such violence. I will analyze examples of representational intersectionality in images of violence against women — images that wound — in the next section.

Representational Intersectionality and Images That Wound

Representational intersectionality is manifest in the familiar images of women of color within popular culture. Here I examine the cultural images widely disseminated in the mainstream movies *Angel Heart, Colors, Year of the Dragon*, and *Tales from the Darkside: The Movie*. Next, I will discuss a video game called *General Custer's Revenge*. Finally, I will consider in more detail the debate surrounding the obscenity prosecution of 2 Live Crew's album *Nasty As They Wanna Be*.

Media images provide cues to understanding the ways in which women of color are imagined in our society. The images of Latina, African American, Asian American, and Native American women are constructed through combinations of readily available race and gender stereotypes. Because the stereotypes depicted in these presentations are quite familiar, collectively they form images of women of color that are specific and categorically unique.

Consider first the film *Colors*. *Colors* was a controversial film, but unfortunately none of the criticism addressed its portrayal of women. Yet the film was rife with familiar stereotypes. The obligatory sexual relationship in that movie occurred between a hotheaded white cop played by Sean Penn and a young Latina played by Maria Conchita Alonso, whom he encountered working at a fast-food stand. Their relationship and her characterization progressed as follows: In scene 1, he flirts, she blushes. In scene 2, she accompanies him to a family outing at his partner's home. In scene 3, the crucial scene, he drops her off at her home. She almost maintains the "good girl" image that had been carefully constructed from the onset, but when she reaches her door, she reconsiders and turns back to invite him in for a night of sex. In subsequent scenes this nice, hardworking ethnic girl increasingly turns into a promiscuous, schizophrenic Latina. In her final appearance, the transformation is complete. The scene begins with the young cop arriving to investigate a noisy house party. She is seen putting on her clothes in a bedroom from which a black man has departed. She wears a low-cut, loud dress and six-inch heels. She is very loud and brash now, laughingly tormenting the distraught and disappointed Sean Penn, who upon seeing her, attempts to escape. She follows him; with her hands on her hips, demanding now in a very heavy and exaggerated accent — "Look at me. This is part of me too!"

This image of the good ethnic fiery Latina is contrasted with an image of Black sexuality also constructed in *Colors*. In another scene, the police converge on a house to serve a warrant on a suspect named Rock-it. As they approach the house, the viewer hears a rhythmic squeaking and loud screams. The camera takes several seconds to track through the ramshackle house. There is little in the house except a stereo apparently playing the loud, pulsating music accenting the sound track. The camera turns a corner and finds a Black man and a Black woman on a bed, atop a single white sheet, so earnestly and frantically copulating that they are wholly oblivious to the several police officers surrounding them with guns drawn. When they finally become aware of the officers' presence, the man makes a sudden move and is shot several times in the back. As his lover screams hysterically, he gasps that he was simply reaching for his clothes.

In *Angel Heart*, the descent of an African American woman into her own uncontrolled sexuality ends in tragic horror. Epiphany Proudfoot, played by Cosby-kid Lisa Bonet, is introduced washing her hair at a well. She appears at first the model of youth, reticent and exotic. Yet she's slightly fallen: she has a child whose father is unknown. Later we see her as a voodoo priestess dancing a blood-curdling ritual and collapsing in an uncontrolled sexual frenzy. The movie culminates in a vicious pornographic scene between Epiphany and Harry Angel (played by Mickey Rourke) that gives new meaning to the phrase "sex and violence." Sex — initiated by Epiphany — soon becomes gruesome as dripping water turns into blood, intercut with rivers of blood, deep thrusting, and screams of agony and horror. The visual narrative splits after this scene: Epiphany appears normal, singing a lovely lullaby and wistfully twisting her hair as she bathes, but later we discover that Epiphany is in fact dead. Her body sprawls across the bed, her legs spread open. A deep pool of blood surrounds her pelvic area. The movie's final scene plays out across her dead body. We discover the cause of her death when the Southern sheriff questioning Angel drawls, "Is that your gun up her snatch?" The horror is not yet complete, for we have still to discover that not only has Harry Angel killed his lover, but that this lover is actually his daughter. So this Cosby kid hits big time, being multiply victimized by incest, rape, and murder.

Perhaps it is happenstance that Lisa Bonet played Epiphany and that the imagery in this big-budget Hollywood film is so violent. Yet I wonder whether a Michelle Pfeiffer, a Kim Basinger, or even a Madonna would be asked to play such a role? I don't think so. The film, by relying on race-sex exoticism, works differently from the way it would with a white female. In fact, the presence of a woman of color often "makes" the story, as is still more clearly shown in an episode from *Tales from the Dark Side: The Movie.* The life of a young white artist is spared by a sixteen-foot talking gargoyle upon the artist's promise that he will never tell anyone that he has ever seen this gargoyle. Later that night he meets a Black woman, played here by Rae Dawn Chong, whom he later marries and with whom he has two lovely children. With the support of his wife he becomes enormously successful, and they live a happy, fulfilled life. On their tenth anniversary, he decides to tell his wife this secret as a part of his expression of affection to her. Presenting her with a full-sized sculpture of the monster, he tells her how his life was spared upon making a vow never to reveal that the monster exists. After he tells her the story, she becomes hysterical and, as "fate" would have it, begins to turn into the sixteen-foot gargoyle. Their two children emerge from the adjoining room as baby gargoyles. The wife disregards the artist's frantic efforts to profess his love for her, stating that she "loved him too but when the vow was broken their fate was sealed." She monstrously tears out his throat, gathers up the "children," and swoops through the ceiling. Here the drop-of-blood rule really works: the children, although half human, are little monsters, too. Can anyone doubt the message — white male miscegenators, beware! Exotica and danger go hand in hand.

Mickey Rourke, apparently bidding to be everybody's favorite racist/sadomasochist/rapist/murderer, turns up again in *Year of the Dragon.* There he plays Captain Stanley White, a New York cop, who pursues a brash and independent Asian American television newscaster. He encounters her on the street, addresses her as a prostitute, taunts her with racist epithets (apparently learned from his days in Vietnam). After she invites him up to her apartment, he continues to assault her verbally, before physically doing so. He tells her that he hates everything about her, and then taking down his pants, he queries, "So why do I want to fuck you so badly?" The worst is yet to come: as our heroine rallies enough outrage to ask him to leave, he calls her a slanteyed cunt. She slaps him once, pauses, and slaps again. He then grabs her, throws her down, rips off her clothes, and has forcible sex with her.

The next image comes not from a movie but from a video game, *General Custer's Revenge.* A Native American woman is tied to a pole. The player, General Custer, must traverse an obstacle course to get to the woman before getting shot. His saberlike penis leads him forward. The player wins when General Custer reaches the Native American woman and pounces on her. She "kicks up her legs in dubious delight" as he commits "what opponents call a rape and the manufacturer claims is a willing sex act." (A spokesman for the manufacturer commented, "There is a facsimile of intercourse. The woman is smiling.") Every stroke is a point. The motto: "When you score, you score."[6]

These four representations confirm both the feminist claim that women are legitimate targets for violence and the more specific observation that these targets are often represented with distinct racialized images. The Latina is two-sided: she is both a sweet, hardworking ethnic and a loud, unscrupulous, racialized "other." The Black woman is wild and animal-like. In *Tales from the Darkside: The Movie*, she *is* an animal or, worse yet, a monster. The Asian American woman is passive. She can be verbally abused and physically assaulted, yet she still stands ready to please. The Native American woman is a savage. She has no honor and no integrity. She doesn't fight rape; in fact, being tied up and ravished makes her smile. She enjoys it.

In each of these cases the specific image is created within the intersection of race and gender. Although some claim that these images reflect certain attitudes that make women of color targets of sexual violence, the actual effect of images on behavior is still hotly contested. Whatever the relationship between imagery and actions is, it seems clear that these images do function to create counternarratives to the experiences of women of color that discredit our claims and render the violence that we experience unimportant. These images not only represent the devaluation of women of color, they may also reproduce it by providing viewers with both conscious and unconscious cues for interpreting the experiences of "others." Because both the actual experience of violence and the representations of those experiences constitute the "problem" of gender violence, feminists of color must address how race and gender intersect in popular discourse as well as in feminist and antiracist politics.

Addressing the Intersectionalities in the 2 Live Crew Controversy

The different intersectionalities discussed above converge in my thinking on the controversy surrounding the obscenity prosecution of 2 Live Crew. The entire problem spurred by the prosecution of 2 Live Crew — the question of how to construct a Black feminist approach to the virulent misogyny in some rap music — has vexed me for some time, and as I suggested at the outset, prompted my attempt to construct a Black feminist understanding of gender violence.

The prosecution of 2 Live Crew began several months after the release of their *Nasty As They Wanna Be* album. In the midst of the Mapplethorpe controversy and Tipper Gore's campaign to label offensive rock music, the Broward County sheriff, Nick Navarro, began investigating 2 Live Crew's *Nasty* recording at the behest of Jack Thompson, a fundamentalist attorney in Miami, Florida. The sheriff obtained an ex parte order declaring the recording obscene and presented copies of the order to local store owners, threatening them with arrest if they continued to sell the recording. 2 Live Crew filed a civil rights suit, and Sheriff Navarro sought a judicial determination labeling 2 Live Crew's *Nasty* recording obscene.[7] A federal court ruled that *Nasty* was obscene but granted 2 Live Crew permanent injunctive relief because the sheriff's action had subjected the recording to unconstitutional prior restraint. Two days after the judge declared the recording obscene, 2 Live Crew members were charged with giving an obscene performance at a club in Hollywood, Florida. Additionally, deputy sheriffs arrested a merchant who was selling copies of the *Nasty* recording. These events received national attention and the controversy quickly polarized into two camps. Writing in *Newsweek*, political columnist George Will staked out a case for the prosecution. He argued that *Nasty* was misogynistic filth. Will characterized the performance as a profoundly repugnant "combination of extreme infantilism and menace" that objectified Black women and represented them as suitable targets for sexual violence.[8]

The most prominent defense of 2 Live Crew was advanced by Professor Henry Louis Gates, Jr., an expert on African American literature. In a *New York Times* op-ed piece and in testimony at the criminal trial, Gates contended that 2 Live Crew were literary geniuses operating within and inadvertently elaborating distinctively African American forms of cultural expression.[9] Furthermore, the characteristic exaggeration featured in their lyrics served a political end: to explode popular racist stereotypes in a comically extreme form. Where Will saw a misogynistic assault on Black women by social degenerates, Gates found a form of "sexual carnivalesque" with the promise to free us from the pathologies of racism.

As a Black feminist, I felt the pull of each of these poles but not the compelling attractions of either. My immediate response to the criminal charges against 2 Live Crew was a feeling of being torn between standing with the brothers against a racist attack and standing against a frightening explosion of violent imagery directed to women like me. This reaction, I have come to believe, is a consequence of the location of Black women at the intersection of racial and sexual subordination. My experience of sharp internal division — if dissatisfaction with the idea that the "real issue" is race or gender is inertly juxtaposed — is characteristic of that location. Black feminism offers an intellectual and political response to that experience. Bringing together the different aspects of an otherwise divided sensibility, Black feminism argues that racial and sexual subordinations are mutually reinforcing, that Black women are marginalized by a politics of race and of gender, and that a political response to each form of subordination must at the same time be a political response to both. When the controversy over 2 Live Crew is approached in light of such Black feminist sensibilities, an alternative to the dominant poles of the public debate emerges.

At the legal bottom line, I agree with the supporters of 2 Live Crew that the obscenity prosecution was wrongheaded. But the reasons for my conclusion are not the same as the reasons generally offered in support of 2 Live Crew. I will come to those reasons shortly, but first I must emphasize that after listening to 2 Live Crew's lyrics along with those of other rap artists, my defense of 2 Live Crew, however careful, did not come easily.

On first hearing 2 Live Crew I was shocked; unlike Gates I did not "bust out laughing." One trivializes the issue by describing the images of women in *As Nasty As They Wanna Be* as simply "sexually explicit." We hear about cunts being fucked until backbones are cracked, asses being busted, dicks rammed down throats, and semen splattered across faces. Black women are cunts, bitches, and all-purpose "hos." Images of women in some of the other rap acts are even more horrifying: battering, rape, and rape-murder are often graphically detailed. Occasionally, we do hear Black women's voices, and those voices are sometimes oppositional. But the response to opposition typically returns to the central refrain: "Shut up, bitch. Suck my dick."

This is no mere braggadocio. Those of us who are concerned about the high rates of gender violence in our communities must be troubled by the possible connections between such images and violence against women. Children and teenagers are listening to this music, and I am concerned that the range of acceptable behavior is being broadened by the constant propagation of antiwomen imagery. I'm concerned, too, about young Black women who together with men are learning that their value lies between their legs. Unlike that of men, however, women's sexual value is portrayed as a depletable commodity: by expending it, boys become men and girls become whores.

Nasty is misogynist, and a Black feminist response to the case against 2 Live Crew should not depart from a full acknowledgment of that misogyny. But such a response must also consider whether an exclusive focus on issues of gender risks overlooking aspects of the prosecution of 2 Live Crew that raise serious questions of racism. And here is where the roots of my opposition to the obscenity prosecution lie.

An initial problem concerning the prosecution was its apparent selectivity. Even the most superficial comparison between 2 Live Crew and other massmarketed sexual representations suggests the likelihood that race played some role in distinguishing 2 Live Crew as the first group to ever be prosecuted for obscenity in connection with a musical recording, and one of only a handful of recording groups or artists to be prosecuted for a live performance. Recent controversies about sexism, racism, and violence in popular culture point to a vast range of expressions that might have provided targets for censorship but that were left untouched. Madonna has acted out masturbation, portrayed the seduction of a priest, and insinuated group sex on stage. But she has never been prosecuted for obscenity. Whereas 2 Live Crew was performing in an adults-only club in Hollywood, Florida, Andrew Dice Clay was performing nationwide on HBO. Well known for his racist "humor," Clay is also comparable to 2 Live Crew in sexual explicitness and misogyny. In his show, for example, Clay offers: "Eeny, meeny, miney, mo, suck my [expletive] and swallow slow," or "Lose the bra bitch." Moreover, graphic sexual images — many of them violent — were widely available in Broward County, where 2 Live Crew's performance and trial took place. According to the trial testimony of a vice detective named McCloud, "Nude dance shows and adult bookstores are scattered throughout the county where 2 Live Crew performed."[10] But again, no obscenity charges were leveled against the performers or producers of these representations.

In response to this charge of selectivity, it might be argued that the successful prosecution of 2 Live Crew demonstrates that its lyrics were uniquely obscene. In a sense, this argument runs, the proof is in the prosecution — if they were not uniquely obscene, they would have been acquitted. However, the elements of 2 Live Crew's performance that contributed initially to their selective arrest continued to play out as the court applied the obscenity standard to the recording. To clarify this argument, we need to consider the technical use of "obscenity" as a legal term of art. For the purposes of legal argument, the Supreme Court in the 1973 case of *Miller v. California* held that a work is obscene if and only if it meets each of three conditions: (1) "the average person, applying community standards, would find that the work, taken as a whole, appeals to the prurient interest"; (2) "the work depicts or describes, in a patently offensive way, sexual conduct specifically defined by the applicable state law"; and (3) "the work, taken as a whole, lacks serious literary, artistic, political, or scientific value."[11] The Court held that it is consistent with First Amendment guarantees of freedom of expression for states to subject work that meets each of the three prongs of the *Miller* test to very restrictive regulations.

Focusing first on the prurient interest prong of the *Miller* test, we might wonder how 2 Live Crew could have been seen as uniquely obscene by the lights of the "community standards" of Broward County. After all, as Detective McCloud put it, "Patrons [of clubs in Broward] can see women dancing with at least their breasts exposed" and bookstore patrons can "view and purchase films and magazines that depict vaginal, oral and anal sex, homosexual sex and group sex."[12] In arriving at its finding of obscenity, the court placed little weight on the available range of films, magazines, and live shows as evidence of the community's sensibilities. Instead, the court apparently accepted the sheriff's testimony that the decision to single out *Nasty* was based on the number of complaints against 2 Live Crew, "communicated by telephone calls, anonymous messages, or letters to the police."[13]

Evidence of this popular outcry was never substantiated. But even if it were, the case for selectivity would remain. The history of social repression of Black male sexuality is long, often violent, and all too familiar. Negative reactions against the sexual conduct of Black males have traditionally had racist overtones, especially where that conduct threatens to "cross over" into the mainstream community. So even if the decision to prosecute did reflect a widespread community perception of the purely prurient character of 2 Live Crew's music, that perception itself might reflect an established pattern of vigilante attitudes directed toward the sexual expression of Black males. In short, the appeal to community standards does not undercut a concern about racism; rather, it underscores that concern.

A second troubling dimension of the case against 2 Live Crew was the court's apparent disregard for the culturally rooted aspects of 2 Live Crew's music. Such disregard was essential to a finding of obscenity given the third prong of the *Miller* test, requiring that obscene material lack any literary, artistic, or political value. 2 Live Crew argued that this test was not met because the recording exemplified such African American cultural modes as "playing the dozens," "call and response," and "signifying." As a storehouse of such cultural modes, it could not be said that *Nasty* could be described as completely devoid of literary or artistic value. In each case the court denied the group's claim of cultural specificity by recharacterizing those modes claimed to be African American in more generic terms. For example, the court reasoned that playing the dozens is "commonly seen in adolescents, especially boys, of all ages." "Boasting," the court observed, appears to be "part of the universal human condition." And the court noted that the cultural origins of one song featuring call and response — a song about fellatio in which competing groups chanted "less filling" and "tastes great" — were to be found in a Miller beer commercial, not in African American cultural tradition. The possibility that the Miller beer commercial may have itself evolved from an African American cultural tradition was lost on the court.

In disregarding this testimony the court denied the artistic value in the form and style of *Nasty* and, by implication, rap music more generally. This disturbing dismissal of the cultural attributes of rap and the effort to universalize African American modes of expression flattens cultural differences. The court's analysis here manifests in the law a frequently encountered strategy of cultural appropriation. African American contributions accepted by mainstream culture are considered simply "American" or found to be "universal." Other modes associated with African American culture that resist absorption and remain distinctive are neglected or dismissed as "deviant."

An additional concern has as much to do with the obscenity doctrine itself as with the court's application of it in this case. The case illustrates the ways in which obscenity doctrine asks the wrong questions with respect to sexual violence and facilitates the wrong conclusions with respect to racially selective enforcement. As I mentioned earlier, obscenity requires a determination that the material be intended to appeal to the prurient interest. In making this determination, the court rejected the relevance of 2 Live Crew's admitted motives — both their larger motive of making money and their secondary motive of doing so through the marketing of outrageous sexual humor. Although the prurient interest requirement eludes precise definition — recall Potter Stewart's infamous declaration that "I know it when I see it" — it seems clear that it must appeal in some immediate way to sexual desire. It would be difficult to say definitively what does or does not constitute an appeal to this prurient interest, but one can surmise that the twenty-five-cent peep shows that are standard fare in Broward County rank considerably higher on this scale than the sexual tall tales told by 2 Live Crew.

2 Live Crew is thus one of the lesser candidates in the prurient interest sweepstakes mandated by the obscenity standard, and it is also a lesser contender by another measure that lies explicitly outside the obscenity doctrine: violence. Compared to groups such as N.W.A., Too Short, Ice Cube, and the Geto Boys, 2 Live Crew's misogynistic hyperbole sounds minor league. Sometimes called gangsta' rap, the lyrics offered by these other groups celebrate violent assault, rape, rape-murder, and mutilation. Had these other groups been targeted rather than the comparatively less offensive 2 Live Crew, they may have been more successful in defeating the prosecution. The graphic violence in their representations militates against a finding of obscenity by suggesting an intent to appeal not to prurient interests but instead to the fantasy of the social outlaw. Indeed, these appeals might even be read as political. Against the historical backdrop in which the image of the Black male as social outlaw is a prominent theme, gangsta' rap might be read as a rejection of a conciliatory stance aimed at undermining fear through reassurance in favor of a more subversive form of opposition that attempts to challenge the rules precisely by becoming the very social outlaw that society has proscribed. Thus, so long as obscenity remains preoccupied with finding prurient interests and violent imagery is

seen as distinct from sexuality, obscenity doctrine is ineffectual against more violent rappers.

Yet even this somewhat formal dichotomy between sex, which obscenity is concerned about, and violence, which lies beyond its purview, may provide little solace to the entire spectrum of rappers ranging from the Geto Boys to 2 Live Crew. Given the historical linkages between Black male sexuality and violence, the two are likely to be directly linked in the prurient interest inquiry, even if subconsciously. In fact, it may have been the background images of Black male sexual violence that rendered 2 Live Crew an acceptable target for obscenity in a lineup that included many stronger contenders.

My point here is not to suggest that the distinction between sex and violence should be maintained in obscenity, nor more specifically, that the more violent rappers ought to be protected. To the contrary, these groups trouble me much more than 2 Live Crew. My point instead is to suggest that obscenity doctrine does nothing to protect the interests of those who are most directly implicated in such rap — Black women. On a formal level, obscenity separates out sexuality and violence, thus shielding the more violently misogynist groups from prosecution. Yet the historical linkages between images of Black male sexuality and violence simultaneously single out lightweight rappers for prosecution among all other purveyors of explicit sexual imagery. Neither course furthers Black women's simultaneous interests in opposing racism and misogyny.

Although Black women's interests were quite obviously irrelevant in this obscenity judgment, their bodies figured prominently in the public case supporting the prosecution. George Will's *Newsweek* essay provides a striking example of how Black women's bodies were appropriated and deployed in the broader attack against 2 Live Crew. In "America's Slide into the Sewers," Will told us, "America today is capable of terrific intolerance about smoking, or toxic waste that threatens trout. But only a deeply confused society is more concerned about protecting lungs than minds, trout than black women. We legislate against smoking in restaurants; singing 'Me So Horny' is a constitutional right. Secondary smoke is carcinogenic; celebration of torn vaginas is 'mere words.'"[14]

Notwithstanding these expressions of concern about Black women, Will's real worry is suggested by his repeated references to the Central Park jogger. He writes, "Her face was so disfigured a friend took 15 minutes to identify her. 'I recognized her ring.' Do you recognize the relevance of 2 Live Crew?" Although the connection between the threat of 2 Live Crew and the image of the Black male rapist was suggested subtly in the public debate, it is manifest throughout Will's discussion and in fact bids to be its central theme. "Fact: Some members of a particular age and societal cohort — the one making 2 Live Crew rich — stomped and raped the jogger to the razor edge of death, for the fun of it." Will directly indicts 2 Live Crew in the Central Park jogger rape through a fictional dialogue between himself and the defendants. Responding to one defendant's alleged confession that the rape was fun, Will asks, "Where can you get the idea that sexual violence against women is fun? From a music store, through Walkman earphones, from boom boxes blaring forth the rap lyrics of 2 Live Crew"; because the rapists were young Black males and

Nasty presents Black men celebrating sexual violence, surely 2 Live Crew was responsible. Apparently, the vast American industry that markets misogynistic representation in every conceivable way is irrelevant to understanding this particular incident of sexual violence.

Will invokes Black women — twice — as victims of this music. But if he were really concerned with the threat to Black women, why does the Central Park jogger figure so prominently in his argument? Why not the Black woman from Brooklyn who, within weeks of the Central Park assault, was gangraped and then thrown down an air shaft? What about the twenty-eight other women — mostly women of color — who were raped in New York City the same week the Central Park jogger was raped? Rather than being centered in Will's display of concern, Black women appear to function as stand-ins for white women. The focus on sexual violence played out on Black women's bodies seems to reflect concerns about the threat to Black male violence against the strategy of the prosecutor in Richard Wright's novel *Native Son.*[15] Bigger Thomas, the Black male protagonist, is on trial for killing Mary Dalton, a white woman. Because Bigger burned her body, however, it cannot be established whether Mary was raped. So the prosecutor brings in the body of Bessie, a Black woman raped by Bigger and left to die, to establish that Bigger had raped Mary.

Further evidence that Will's concern about sexual imagery and rape is grounded in familiar narratives of Black sexual violence and white victimhood is suggested by his nearly apoplectic reaction to similar attempts to regulate racist speech. In his assault on 2 Live Crew, Will decries liberal tolerance for lyrics that "desensitize" our society and that will certainly have "behavioral consequences." Proponents of campus speech regulations have made arguments that racist speech facilitates racist violence in much the same way that Will links rap to sexual violence. Yet Will has excoriated such proponents.

Despite his anguish that sexual lyrics "coarsen" our society and facilitate a "slide into the sewer," in Will's view,[16] racist speech is situated on a much higher plane. Apparently, the "social cohort" that is most likely to engage in racial violence — young white men — has sense enough to distinguish ideas from action, whereas the "social cohort" that identifies with 2 Live Crew is made up of mindless brutes who will take rap as literal encouragement to rape. Will's position on racist speech not only indicates how readily manipulable the link between expression and action is, but suggests further reasons why his invocation of Black women seems so disingenuous. One can't help but wonder why Will is so outraged about attacks on Black women's vaginal walls and not concerned about attacks on our skin.

These concerns about selectivity in prosecution, about the denial of cultural specificity, and about the manipulation of Black women's bodies convince me that race played a significant if not determining role in the shaping of the case against 2 Live Crew. While using antisexist rhetoric to suggest a concern for women, the attack simultaneously endorsed traditional readings of Black male sexuality. The fact that most sexual violence involves intraracial assault fades to the background as the Black male is represented as the agent of sexual violence and the white community is represented as his victim. The subtext of the 2 Live Crew prosecution thus becomes a rereading of the sexualized racial politics of the past.

Although concerns about racism fuel my opposition to the obscenity prosecution, I am also troubled by the uncritical support for and indeed celebration of 2 Live Crew by other opponents of that prosecution. If the rhetoric of antisexism provided an occasion for racism, so too, the rhetoric of antiracism provided an occasion for defending the misogyny of Black male rappers.

The defense of 2 Live Crew took two forms, one political and one cultural, both of which were advanced most prominently by Henry Louis Gates, Jr. The political argument was that 2 Live Crew represents an attack against Black sexual stereotypes. The strategy of the attack is, in Gates's words, to "exaggerate [the] stereotypes" and thereby "to show how ridiculous the portrayals are." [17] For the strategy to succeed, it must of course highlight the sexism, misogyny, and violence stereotypically associated with Black male sexuality. But far from embracing that popular mythology, the idea is to fight the racism of those who accept it. Thus, the argument goes, 2 Live Crew and other rap groups are simply pushing white society's buttons to ridicule its dominant sexual images.

I agree with Gates that the reactions by Will and others to 2 Live Crew confirm that the stereotypes still exist and still evoke basic fears. But even if I were to agree that 2 Live Crew intended to explode these mythic fears, I still would argue that its strategy was wholly misguided. These fears are too active and African Americans are too closely associated with them not to be burned when the myths are exploded. More fundamentally, however, I am deeply skeptical about the claim that the Crew was engaged — either in intent or effects — in a postmodern guerrilla war against racist stereotypes.

Gates argues that when one listens to 2 Live Crew, the ridiculous stories and the hyperbole make the listener "bust out laughing." Apparently, the fact that Gates and many other people react with laughter confirms and satisfies the Crew's objective of ridiculing the stereotypes. The fact that the Crew is often successful in achieving laughter neither substantiates Gates's reading nor forecloses serious critique of its subordinating dimensions.

In disagreeing with Gates, I do not mean to suggest that 2 Live Crew's lyrics are to be taken literally. But rather than exploding stereotypes as Gates suggests, I believe that the group simply uses readily available sexual images in trying to be funny. Trading in racial stereotypes and sexual hyperbole are well-rehearsed strategies for achieving laughter; the most extreme representations often do more to reinforce and entrench the image than to explode it. 2 Live Crew departs from this tradition only in its attempt to up the ante through more outrageous boasts and more explicit manifestations of misogyny.

The acknowledgment, however, that the Crew was simply trying to be funny should not be interpreted as constituting a defense against its misogyny. Neither the intent to be funny nor Gates's loftier explanations negate the subordinating qualities of such humor. An examination of the parallel arguments in the context of racist humor suggests why neither claim functions as a persuasive defense for 2 Live Crew.

Gates's use of laughter as a defensive maneuver in the attack on 2 Live Crew recalls similar strategies in defense of racist humor. Racist humor has sometimes been defended as antiracist — an effort to poke fun at or to show the ridiculousness of racism. More simply, racist humor has often been excused as just joking; even racially motivated assaults are often defended as simple pranks. Thus, the racism and sexism of Andrew Dice Clay could be defended either as an attempt to explode the stereotypes of white racists or more simply as simple humor not meant to be taken seriously. Implicit in these defenses is the assumption that racist representations are injurious only if they are devoid of any other objective or are meant to be taken literally. Although these arguments are familiar within the Black community, I think it is highly unlikely that they would be viewed as a persuasive defense of Andrew Dice Clay. Indeed, the historical and ongoing criticism of such humor suggests widespread rejection of such disclaimers. Operating instead under a premise that humor can be nonliteral, perhaps even well intended, but racist nonetheless, African Americans have protested such humor. This practice of opposition suggests a general recognition within the Black community that "mere humor" is not inconsistent with subordination. The question of what people find humorous is of course a complicated one that includes considerations of aggression, reinforcement of group boundaries, projection, and other issues. The claim of intending only a joke may be true, but representations function as humor within a specific social context and frequently reinforce patterns of social power. Even though racial humor may sometimes be intended to ridicule racism, the close relationship between the stereotypes and the prevailing images of marginalized people as well as a presumed connection between the humorist and the dominant audience complicates this strategy. Clearly, racial humor does not always undermine the racism of the character speaking nor indict the wider society in which the jokes have meaning. The endearment of Archie Bunker seems to suggest at least this much.

Thus, in the context of racist humor, neither the fact that people actually laughed at racist humor nor the usual disclaimer of intent have functioned to preclude incisive and often quite angry criticism of such humor within the African American community. Although a similar set of arguments could be offered in the context of sexist humor, images marketed by 2 Live Crew were not condemned, but as Gates illustrates, defended, often with great commitment and skill. Clearly, the fact that the Crew is Black, as are the women it objectifies, shaped this response. There is of course an ongoing issue of how one's positioning vis-à-vis a targeted group colors the way the group interprets a potentially derisive stereotype or gesture. Had 2 Live Crew been whites in blackface, for example, all the readings would have been different. Although the question of whether one can defend the broader license given to Black comedians to market stereotypical images is an interesting one, it is not the issue here. 2 Live Crew cannot claim an in-group privilege to perpetuate misogynistic humor against Black women. Its members are not Black women, and more important, they enjoy a power relationship over them.

Sexual humor in which women are objectified as packages of bodily parts to serve whatever male-bonding/male-competition the speakers please subordinates women in much the same way that racist humor subordinates African Americans. That these are "just jokes" and are not taken as literal claims does little to blunt their demeaning quality — nor, for that matter, does it help that the jokes are told within a tradition of intragroup humor.

Gates offered a second, cultural defense of 2 Live Crew: the idea that *Nasty* is in line with distinctively African American traditions of culture. It is true that the dozens and other forms of verbal boasting have been practiced within the Black community for some time. It is true as well that raunchy jokes, insinuations, and boasts of sexual prowess were not meant to be taken literally. Nor, however, were they meant to disrupt conventional myths about Black sexuality. They were meant simply to be laughed at and perhaps to gain respect for the speaker's word wizardry.

Ultimately, however, little turns on whether the "wordplay" performed by 2 Live Crew is a postmodern challenge to racist sexual mythology or simply an internal group practice that has crossed over into mainstream U.S. society. Both versions of the defense are problematic because both call on Black women to accept misogyny and its attendant disrespect in the service of some broader group objective. Whereas one version argues that accepting misogyny is necessary to antiracist politics, the other argues that it is necessary to maintain the cultural integrity of the community. Neither presents sufficient justification for requiring Black women to tolerate such misogyny. The message that these arguments embrace — that patriarchy can be made to serve antiracist ends — is a familiar one, with proponents ranging from Eldridge Cleaver in the 1960s to Shahrazad Ali in the 1990s. In Gates's variant, the position of Black women is determined by the need to wield gargantuan penises in efforts to ridicule racist images of Black male sexuality. Even though Black women may not be the intended targets, they are necessarily called to serve these gargantuan penises and are thus in the position of absorbing the impact. The common message of all such strategies is that Black women are expected to be vehicles for notions of "liberation" that function to preserve Black female subordination.

To be sure, Gates's claims about the cultural aspects of 2 Live Crew's lyrics do address the legal issue about the applicability of the obscenity standard. As I indicated earlier, the group's music does have artistic and potentially political value; I believe the court decided this issue incorrectly and Will was all too glib in his critique. But these criticisms do not settle the issue within the community. Dozens and other wordplays have long been within the Black oral tradition, but acknowledging this fact does not eliminate the need to interrogate either the sexism within that tradition or the objectives to which that tradition has been pressed. To say that playing the dozens, for example, is rooted in a Black cultural tradition or that themes represented by mythic folk heroes such as Stagolee are Black does not settle the question of whether such practices are oppressive to women and others within the community. The same point can be made about the relentless homophobia in the work of Eddie Murphy and many other comedians and rappers. Whether or not the Black community has a pronounced tradition of homophobic humor is beside the point; the question instead is how these subordinating aspects of tradition play out in the lives of people in the community, people who are otherwise called upon to share the benefits and the burdens of a common history, culture, and political agenda. Although it may be true that the Black community is more familiar with the cultural forms that have evolved into rap, that familiarity should not end the discussion of whether the misogyny within rap is acceptable.

Moreover, we need to consider the possible relationships between sexism in our cultural practices and violence against women. Violence against women of color is not centered as a critical issue in either the antiracist or antiviolence discourses. The "different culture" defense may contribute to a disregard for women of color victimized by rape and violence that reinforces the tendency within the broader community not to take intraracial violence seriously. Numerous studies have suggested that Black victims of crime can count on less protection from the criminal justice system than whites receive. This is true for Black rape victims as well — their rapists are less likely to be convicted and on average serve less time when they are convicted. Could it be that perpetuating the belief that Blacks are different with respect to sexuality and violence contributes to the disregard of Black female rape victims like Bessie in *Native Son* or the woman thrown down an air shaft in Brooklyn?

Although there are times when Black feminists should fight for the integrity of Black culture, this does not mean that criticism must end when a practice or form of expression is traced to an aspect of culture. We must also determine whether the practices and forms of expression are consistent with other interests that we must define. The legal question of obscenity may be settled by finding roots in the culture. But traditional obscenity is not our central issue. Performances and representations that do not appeal principally to "prurient interests" or that may reflect expressive patterns that are culturally specific may still encourage self-hatred, disrespect, subordination, and various other manifestations of intragroup pathology. These problems require an internal group dialogue. Although we have no plenary authority to grapple with these issues, we do need to find ways of using group formation mechanisms and other social spaces to reflect on and reformulate our cultural and political practices.

I said earlier that the political goals of Black feminism are to construct and empower a political sensibility that opposes misogyny and racism simultaneously. Merging this double vision in an analysis of the 2 Live Crew controversy makes clear that despite the superficial defense of the prosecution as being in the interests of women, nothing about the anti–2 Live Crew movement is about Black women's lives. The political process involved in the legal prosecution of 2 Live Crew's representational subordination of Black women does not seek to empower Black women; indeed, the racism of that process is injurious to us.

The implication of this conclusion is not that Black feminists should stand in solidarity with the supporters of 2 Live Crew. The spirited defense of 2 Live Crew was no more about defending the Black community than the prosecution was about defending women. After all, Black women — whose assault is the very subject of the representation — are part of that community. Black women can hardly regard the right to be represented as rape-deserving bitches and whores as essential to their interests. Instead the defense primarily functions to protect the cultural and political prerogative of male rappers to be as misogynistic as they want to be.

The debate over 2 Live Crew illustrates how the discursive structures of race and gender politics continue to marginalize Black women, rendering us virtually voiceless. Fitted with a Black feminist sensibility, one uncovers other issues in which the unique situation of Black women renders a different formulation of the problem than the version that dominates in current debate. Ready examples include rape, domestic violence, and welfare dependency. A Black feminist sensibility might also provide a more direct link between the women's movement and traditional civil rights movements, helping them both to shed conceptual blinders that limit the efficacy of their efforts. In the recent controversy over the nomination of Clarence Thomas to the U.S. Supreme Court, for example, organized groups in both camps — in particular women's groups — initially struggled to produce evidence showing Thomas's negative disposition toward their respective constituencies. Thomas's repeated derogatory references to his sister as the quintessential example of welfare dependency might have been profitably viewed from a Black feminist framework as the embodiment of his views on race, gender, and class, permitting an earlier formulation of a more effective coalition.

The development of a Black feminist sensibility is no guarantee that Black women's interests will be taken seriously. For that sensibility to develop into empowerment, Black women will have to make it clear that patriarchy is a critical issue that negatively impacts the lives of not only African American women, but men as well. Within the African American political community, this recognition might reshape traditional practices so that evidence of racism would not constitute sufficient justification for uncritical rallying around misogynistic politics and patriarchal values. Although collective opposition to racist practice has been and continues to be crucially important in protecting Black interests, an empowered Black feminist sensibility would require that the terms of unity no longer reflect priorities premised on the continued marginalization of Black women.

NOTES

1. 137 Cong. Rec. S597, S610 (1991) (S. 15, H.R. 1502).

2. S. Ali, *The Blackman's Guide to the Blackwoman* (1989).

3. Pub. L. 99-639 (Nov. 10, 1986), Pub. L. 100-525, § 7(a)–(c) (Oct. 24, 1988).

4. Ali, *supra* note 2, at 169.

5. H.R. 1502, S. 15 (102d Cong.).

6. Coraham, *Custer May Be Shot Down Again in Battle of Sexes over X-Rated Video Game*, People Magazine, Nov. 15, 1982.

7. Santoro, *How 2B Nasty: Rap Musicians 2 Live Crew Arrested*, Nation, July 2, 1990, at 4.

8. Will, *America's Slide into the Sewer*, Newsweek, July 30, 1990, at 64.

9. Gates, *2 Live Crew Decoded*, New York Times, June 19, 1990, at A23.

10. *2 Live Crew*, UPI (Oct. 19, 1990).

11. 413 U.S. 15, 24 (1973).

12. *2 Live Crew*, UPI (Oct. 19, 1990).

13. 739 F. Supp. 578, 589 (S.D. Fla. 1990).

14. Will, *supra* note 8.

15. R. Wright, *Native Son* (1966).

16. Will, *Supra* note 8.

17. *An Album Is Judged Obscene; Rap: Slick, Violent, Nasty and, Maybe Helpful*, New York Times, June 17, 1990, at 1.

THIRTY-THREE

Spiraling Discourses of Reproductive and Sexual Rights: A Post-Beijing Assessment of International Feminist Politics

ROSALIND P. PETCHESKY

One of the most important things to happen at the recent Fourth World Women's Conference in Beijing was the adoption, in the Platform for Action, of the following paragraph:

> The human rights of women include their right to have control over and decide freely and responsibly on matters related to their sexuality, including sexual and reproductive health, free of coercion, discrimination and violence. Equal relationships between women and men in matters of sexual relations and reproduction, including full respect for the integrity of the person, require mutual respect, consent and shared responsibility for sexual behavior and its consequences.[1]

This text is remarkable for both its utterances and its silences, what it makes explicit in the repertoire of international declarations (which are nonbinding but morally incumbent on their signatories) and what it leaves still hidden.

Notice that for the first time in any international document women are acknowledged as sexual as well as reproductive beings, with human rights to decide freely about their sexuality without any express qualification regarding age, marital status, or sexual orientation. At the same time, the Beijing Platform goes to great lengths to avoid ever using the expression "sexual rights," much less "sexual orientation"; whereas "reproductive rights" — as "the capability to reproduce and the freedom to decide if, when and how often to do so" — is now indelibly defined and codified within both the Program of Action of the International Conference on Population and Development in Cairo and the Beijing Platform. Moreover, the welcome language of "respect for the integrity of the person" is intended to occlude any reference to "bodily integrity" or the body in any form; nowhere in the platform do sexualized female bodies, claiming pleasures rather than fending off abuses, appear.

On one level, we could analyze these outcomes simply in terms of the micropolitics of the official conference, who was chairing which section, what got traded off for what, and so forth. But I believe the language in the text I just quoted represents the distillates of a complex debate involving major global political actors through several years of intense discursive struggle, both in public international fora and behind the scenes. Thus my aim in this chapter is to uncover a genealogy of this text through three intersecting trajectories: tensions within women's movements about the language of "rights" and "reproduction"; conflicts between women's movements and the global power structures that are contending for domination over this discursive field; and, finally, the three-year evolution of one international feminist project, the International Reproductive Rights Research Action Group (IRR-RAG), and how we in this project have come to understand our conceptual framework. Underlying my analysis is a kind of meta-argument that sees language as a critical terrain in which power is continually contested and redefined through an endless process of spirals of domination, resistance, and reconstitution of discourse.[2] I have watched closely over the past five years how such a process has transformed "reproductive rights" from a Westernist code for abortion into an international feminist and United Nations language denoting women's self-determination over their fertility, motherhood, and — to a limited degree — sexuality. We have much to learn, I think, about the production of feminist thought and practice across nations and regions from the shifts and fault lines through which this particular politics of language has moved.

In some ways, the work of the IRRRAG project can be taken in microcosm as a chart of the tentative and uncertain course of reproductive and sexual rights language during this recent period. In 1992 IRRRAG first embarked on a project to understand the meanings of "reproductive and sexual rights" through the voices and experiences of ordinary women, situated in diverse countries, cultures, and social conditions. Although our research poses many interrelated questions, one primary question motivates the project: How do women across diverse countries and cultures arrive at and negotiate a sense of entitlement with regard to their reproductive and sexual health and well-being? Put another (and apparently more subversive) way, in what circumstances, through what terms and codes, and by means of which strategies do women envision and strive for self-determination over their bodies? Given the diversity of the seven countries we represented and our very different experiences of feminism and women's movements, there was little agreement among us when we began our work about the concepts undergirding these questions. Thus, in order to work internationally as a group of feminists, IRRRAG began its inquiry with a political commitment to ambiguity, denoted by the quotation marks in which we framed every relevant term: "reproductive," "sexual," "rights," "decision-making," "resistance," "accommodation," "entitlement." Not only did these terms provoke political misgivings among some of our participants; they also had no linguistic equivalents in some of our national languages. It required three years of periodically revisiting these concepts, including nearly two years of fieldwork and data interpretation, to arrive at a common ground of meaning, one that avoided the individualist connotations such concepts usually evoke in "Westernized feminist" readings while acknowledging the ways women in all our countries engage in acts of self-construction through their reproductive and sexual decisions.[3]

Feminist thinking (including that of IRRRAG) about reproductive and sexual rights has continually rearticulated its terms and broadened its scope during the past five years in response to three centers of discursive power on the international stage: the population and family planning establishment, with its Malthusian emphasis on curbing population growth by controlling women's fertility; the Vatican and its Islamic fundamentalist allies, joined in opposition to hedonism, individualism, and any forms of human coupling that are not strictly patriarchal, marital, and heterosexual; and the human rights organizations, traditionally focused on state responsibility for the treatment of prisoners and noncombatants in warfare and less concerned with sexual matters or social and economic needs. I will concentrate on the first two of these and mention the third only in passing, all in an attempt to show the complex rhetorical negotiations that have feminized U.N. language and radicalized international feminist language in the 1990s.

Deconstructing the Rhetoric of Population Programs

For decades prior to the historic International Conference on Population and Development in Cairo (ICPD) in 1994, but particularly in the six months preceding that conference, population and family planning groups promoted the rhetoric of a "population time bomb" in relentless media campaigns. According to their dire projections, unless current growth rates are curtailed dramatically, today's world population of 5.6 billion may double or even triple in the twenty-first century, and this will inevitably lead to global economic and environmental catastrophe, including mass migrations from poor southern countries to the more affluent north.[4] The "population bomb" ideology of course has deep roots in the ideas of Thomas Malthus, who in 1798 first theorized that unchecked population growth would geometrically exceed the world's food supply. Malthus himself preferred abstinence to artificial birth control methods, assuming that these would corrupt the morals of the poor and working-class. But his neo-Malthusian successors in the twentieth century rallied behind the strategy of curbing population growth through medically controlled methods of contraception, such as sterilization, the pill, and the IUD and, more recently, long-term injectibles like Norplant and antifertility vaccines (Malthus [1817] 1976; Dixon-Mueller 1993, 34–37; Petchesky 1990, 35–37; Shapiro 1985, 13–16, 30–32).

Historically, neo-Malthusian thinking has resulted in population policies and programs that target specific demographic groups — immigrants, racial and ethnic minorities, the disabled, and other so-called unfit, but above all the masses of poor in both the south and the north. Improving women's health and social status, reducing maternal mortality, or fulfilling individual desires was never more than a means rather than an end of such programs, and often not even that. Meanwhile, although many postcolonial southern nations adhered in the 1970s to the idea that "development is the best contraceptive," by the 1980s governments of these same nations — under pressure from northern donors like U.S. AID and the World Bank, but also to divert attention from their own failed development programs — had shifted their positions and adopted full-scale family planning programs into their domestic policies (Correa 1994, chap. 1; Dixon-Mueller 1993, chap. 4; Hartmann 1995).

While late twentieth-century policies to curb population growth are commonly associated with liberal agendas of alleviating poverty, unemployment, and environmental devastation, in practice they too often belie an underlying attitude of racism and ethnic chauvinism. Contemporary population policies emanating from the United States — those directed at home as well as at the so-called third world — are not immune from this taint (see Dixon-Mueller 1993, chap. 3; Hartmann 1995, chaps. 4, 7, 12, 13; Shapiro 1985, chaps. 4, 5). This is particularly evident in policies to restrict immigration, which have traditionally complemented controls over fertility as a means to reduce population levels within a given territory. As they did during the height of the eugenics era early in this century, northern and white fears of being "overrun" by hordes of darker-skinned (and poorer) peoples today play a real, if sometimes covert, role in motivating such policies. We have only to look at recent attacks on the rights of legal as well as undocumented immigrants — fomented by right-wing Republicans but with the acquiescence of the liberal political establishment and press — to see the most blatant manifestations of this dynamic. In the mid-1990s, with legislative initiatives in California and other states to restrict access of not only undocumented but legal immigrants to most social services, and similar anti-immigrant provisions in the Republican welfare "reform" bill in Congress, the xenophobia of the 1920s has come back to haunt us. And not only in the United States but in France, Germany, Austria, Canada, and Australia, and in the reactionary opposition of northern governments (including the United States) at recent U.N. deliberations in Cairo, Copenhagen, and Beijing when it came to issues of immigrant rights.[5]

Yet according to the distinguished economist Amartya Sen, "[the] apocalyptic view [of population pressures as the cause of immigration] is empirically baseless" (A. Sen 1994). First, it ignores the impact of international capital flows and debt crisis, which are far more significant in creating migratory pressures than are sheer numbers. Second, it ignores both history and regional and local variations: Why should the outnumbering of Europeans and North Americans by Asians and Africans suddenly be thought an "imbalance" when it has been true for much of human history? And if population density is the major impediment to prosperity in Cairo or Calcutta, why is it not so in Miami or Singapore? But Sen also suggests that fears among ethnic and economic elites of being outnumbered, for all their visceral racism, are not illusory. According to U.N. estimates, the populations of Asia and Africa have grown since 1970 from 64 percent of the world to 71 percent and will become over 78 percent by the year 2050. Within North America, demographers have been predicting for the last several years that by the year 2000, with the rising Asian and Hispanic in-migration, people of color will outnumber whites in major urban areas by a ratio of as much as two-thirds to one-third. Such projections fan the flames of entrenched ethnic chauvinism and hatred in the United States.

Racial and ethnic divisions intersect in complicated ways with sexual and gender politics to construct U.S. population policies that target poor women — as welfare recipients, immigrants, and clients of family planning programs (Crenshaw 1991; Eisenstein 1994; hooks 1989; Williams 1991). The most usual strategy for curbing population growth is to reduce women's fertility, often through family planning programs that rely on numerical quotas, high-pressure methods, and "medically effective" technologies (particularly irreversible sterilization and injectible long-lasting hormonal contraceptives). IRRRAG's research subjects in the United States — particularly black and white welfare recipients in rural Georgia and Kentucky — told of having been sterilized without their informed consent and of physicians who refused their requests to remove Norplant implants and dismissed their complaints of troublesome side effects. These are abuses more often associated with women in the "third world" and, according to the ICPD Program of Action (to which the United States is a signatory), are violations of women's human rights (ICPD, Principle 8 and paras. 7.3 and 7.16). Further, conservative politicians defend punitive welfare cuts and disentitlements for immigrants and for all young unmarried women in spite of the fears of Catholic Church bishops and some Catholic legislators that such policies will lead to increased abortions. (For the Republican and neoconservative mainstream, racism, ethnic chauvinism, and "traditional morality" apparently trump even fetal rights!) As in the past, programs aimed at excluding or lowering the fertility of some groups — the poorest and darkest — coexist with fiscal and other incentives (e.g., tax credit proposals) that most advantage the wealthy and middle-class and could be seen as pronatalist incentives to encourage these groups to be fruitful and multiply.[6]

Throughout the 1980s and prior to the ICPD, women's health groups in the south as well as the north (especially women of color groups like the National Black Women's Health Project and the National Latina Health Organization) vocally protested the racism, sexism, and class bias inherent in population control programs and their tendency to target poor, marginalized, and indigenous women. Women's groups in India, Indonesia, and Bangladesh, the Women's Global Network for Reproductive Rights based in Amsterdam, and women's health networks in North America and Latin America have campaigned against reproductive technologies that are either permanent, difficult to remove, controlled by medical providers, or potentially hazardous to women's health. They have opposed the promotion of any family planning methods through coercion, manipulative "social marketing" techniques, or material incentives to users and providers (Garcia-Moreno and Claro 1994; Correa 1994, chap. 2; Dixon-Mueller 1993, chap. 5; Fried 1990; Sen, Germain, and Chen 1994; U.S. Women of Color Delegation 1994; Women's Global Network for Reproductive Rights 1985–present).

Moreover, feminists have argued that the emphasis on fertility reduction through sterilization and hormonal methods ignores the critical need for barrier methods to protect women against HIV/AIDS and other STDs. They have pointed out that such programs are all too often provided instead of, and draw resources away from, the primary health care services that poor women in both the south and the north so desperately lack. Like Amartya Sen, they have cited volumes of research showing that programs that empower women by increasing their access to education, literacy, credit, and mobility are far more effective in generating long-run fertility decline than are family planning programs by themselves (Kerala in India, Sri Lanka, and Thailand and the Grameen Bank borrowers in Bangladesh being the most dramatic examples). In documents prepared for the 1994 ICPD — such as "Women, Population and the Environment: Call for a New Approach" and "Women's Declaration on Population Policies/Women's Voices '94" — they have argued that militarism and uneven consumption patterns in the north play a bigger role in wreaking environmental and economic instability in the south than does population growth. Pointing to countries like Brazil, where poverty continues unabated despite successful fertility reduction campaigns, or Russia, where environmental destruction persists despite low fertility and population decline, feminists deride populationist theories (Correa and Petchesky 1994a; Hartmann 1995; Isis International 1993; Pitanguy and Petchesky 1993).

Against the instrumentalism and narrow goals of neo-Malthusians, women's health advocates in the south and the north in the 1980s developed an expansive concept of reproductive health that encompasses not only safe abortion and contraception, but also comprehensive maternal, prenatal, and infant care; infertility treatment; an end to sterilization abuse, hazardous reproductive technologies, and coercion; an end to sexual and domestic violence, female genital mutilation, and other harmful traditional practices, as well as to unethical medical experimentation; prevention of HIV/AIDS, reproductive tract infections, and other STDs; prevention of gynecological cancers, reproductive hazards, and toxins in the workplace and community; primary health care for women and children everywhere; and transformations in the structural and social conditions blocking poor women's access to all of the above. And they envisioned this broad agenda in a context that paid attention to differences among women across culture, region, race-ethnicity, sexual orientation, and place in the life cycle. Thus, the perspective on reproductive and sexual health that feminists put forward implied a much larger political and social terrain than that encompassed in mainstream approaches to family planning or maternal and child health, which treat women as undifferentiated objects or means rather than ends of population and public health strategies (Boston Women's Health Book Collective 1984; Correa and Petchesky 1994b; Dixon-Mueller 1993, chap. 8; Fried 1990; Garcia-Moreno and Claro 1994; Germain, Nowrojee, and Pyne 1994; Germain and Ordway 1989; Asian and Pacific Women's Resource Collection Network 1990; Women's Global Network for Reproductive Rights 1985–present).

Yet this vision still was framed very much within a health paradigm. By the early 1990s, while women's health movements were growing throughout Latin America, Asia, and Africa, the concept of "reproductive rights" (to say nothing of sexual rights) was still associated with abortion struggles in the United States and Europe. I vividly recall the first meeting of IRRRAG's researcher-activists in November 1992 in Malaysia. Of the twenty-odd women sitting around the table — six Malaysians, two Philippinas, two Indonesians, two Egyptians, two Nigerians, one Indian, three Mexicans, two Brazilians, and three from the United States — only those from the United States, Brazil, and Mexico were entirely comfortable with the term "rights"; others preferred to speak of "health." Moreover, the proposal that our project should investigate women's sexual identities, or even use the word "sexuality," caused grave consternation among some of our participants, particularly those from Egypt, Malaysia, and Nigeria. But within the following year, every one of IRRRAG's groups — and the women's movements of which they were part — had confronted the rising forces of fundamentalism, either the Catholic Church or the Islamist variety, in their own countries. The shape of their discomfort — and their discourse — radically changed.

Confronting Fundamentalisms

By the time of the Cairo conference in 1994, fundamentalist-influenced regimes had formed a strategic coalition under the leadership of the Vatican in defense of pronatalism, cultural and religious relativism, and the patriarchal heterosexual family. While not averse to family planning within traditional marriage and if done through "natural" rather than "artificial" means, these groups bitterly oppose not only abortion and many forms of contraception but also — as stated in a pre-Cairo meeting of the college of cardinals led by John O'Connor of New York — "sexual promiscuity and distorted notions of the family."

The Vatican's opposition to women's (and gay men's) self-determination in reproduction and sexuality is grounded in a philosophical and theological tradition that naturalizes "the" family and sexual and reproductive experience, reducing it to a single conjugal heterosexual norm. To the extent that such experience is codified through natural and divine law, it exists outside the realm of history and public debate, oblivious to the real households of many of the world's people (female-headed, extended, free unions, gay and lesbian partnerships, women alone). At the ICPD in Cairo, the fundamentalist coalition sought high visibility in its attempt to counter the growing influence of feminist organizations like Catholics for a Free Choice and Women Living under Muslim Laws, and its effort to delete references to "safe abortion," "individuals," "reproductive rights," "adolescent sexual health," and "diverse family forms" from the Program of Action. Unsuccessful in these efforts, this small but disruptive group of states and nonstates (the Vatican has "observer" status at the United Nations, which oddly gives it all the privileges of a member state at U.N. conferences) proceeded to register its reservations to the final document. Listen to their drift. Holy See: "With reference to the term 'couples and individuals,' the Holy See reserves its position with the understanding that this term is to mean married couples and the individual man and woman who constitute the couple." And Guatemala, a firm Vatican ally: "We enter a reservation on the whole chapter [related to reproductive health and rights], for the General Assembly's mandate to the Conference does not extend to the creation or formulation of rights." Finally, here is Egypt (pandering to its fundamentalist rivals at home): "our delegation called for the deletion of the word 'individuals' since it has always been our understanding that all the questions dealt with by the Programme of Action . . . relate to harmonious relations between couples united by the bond of marriage in the context of . . . the family as the primary cell of society" (United Nations 1994).

In another move calculated to placate Islamic fundamentalist elements at home, the Egyptian government promulgated a new law following the Cairo conference regarding female genital mutilation (FGM)[7] that has outraged and alienated Egyptian feminists. One of the major gains of the ICPD, thanks to determined efforts by Middle Eastern and African women's NGOs, was the exposure given to the issue of FGM and the severe health deficits it imposes on women. Indeed, the Cairo document "urgently" calls on governments, NGOs, and religious institutions "to prohibit female genital mutilation" and other harmful "practices meant to control women's sexuality," making this a matter of basic human right. Yet, though FGM had been prohibited in public health institutions in Egypt for many years, the Egyptian government, as soon as all the foreign delegates and women's groups had gone home, passed a law permitting the practice in public hospitals. Egyptian feminists have organized strenuously against this new law and in so doing have reconstituted a discourse of reproductive and sexual health as human rights, and of women's "bodily integrity," within a particular political context of southern women under Muslim regimes (Toubia 1995). So the spiral of power and resistance widens.

Indeed, when we observe the surprisingly feminist content, on the whole, of the ICPD Program of Action, we have to ask, given the alignment of forces I described earlier, how did this happen? I have no time here to examine the progressive elements of that document in detail, much less its weaknesses (which were substantial).[8] Nonetheless, consider: (1) the program is almost completely divested of the traditional language and conceptual apparatus of Malthusianism, demographic targets, and family planning, replacing these with the language of reproductive and sexual health and reproductive rights; (2) it fully integrates principles of gender equality (including male responsibility for housework and child care) and women's empowerment into the domain of reproductive and sexual health and declares that "the empowerment and autonomy of women and the improvement of their political, social, economic and health status is a highly important end in itself . . . essential for the achievement of sustainable development"; finally, (3) it recognizes reproductive rights, very broadly defined and including sexual health, as fundamental human rights.

This happened as a result of two political negotiations that occurred shortly before and during the conference. First, population and family planning groups, whose agendas and budgets were threatened by the fundamentalist offensive, also found themselves overshadowed by the strong women's coalition. Fearing marginalization, these groups allied themselves with the women's NGOs and accepted the new reproductive rights discourse.[9] (Of course, the extent to which the populationists' conversion to feminism was sincere or merely tactical is very much an open one that must be tested by time and continued vigilance by women's movements.) Second, many women's NGOs concerned with reproductive and sexual issues began shifting their discourse from a health paradigm to a human rights paradigm. In part this was due to the influential work of women's human rights activists; but even more, this shift came out of a felt need to articulate a strong, militant response to the fundamentalist assault. Rights language provides an effective instrument, universally recognized as political, for making group claims on governments and intergovernmental organizations; and women's movements, along with other popular movements seeking democratization, have embraced it (Bunch 1990; Cook 1994; Copelon and Petchesky 1995; Schuler 1995; Williams 1991).

Having basically lost the verbal contest in Cairo, the Vatican-led fundamentalist alliance conducted a concerted campaign, during the Preparatory Committee meetings and in the media before the Women's Conference in Beijing, designed to taint the concepts of "reproductive and sexual rights" with the labels of "individualism," "Western feminism" and, covertly, lesbianism.[10] This campaign not only opposed "reproductive rights" and "diverse family forms" but also, for a period of time, succeeded in bracketing all references to the word "gender." The reason for this puzzling maneuver, as feminists involved in the third Preparatory Committee meeting learned, was that Vatican agents had gotten hold of a women's studies course packet from the United States containing readings that not only explained gender as a social construct (rather than a biological given) but also evoked the possibility of changing genders, multiple genders, and other shocking heresies. Hence the Vatican delegation's insistence that "sex," not "gender," should be the officially sanctioned terminology.

While the fundamentalist campaign against "gender" and "sexual rights" fronted as a crusade on behalf of "parental rights" in Beijing, its real targets were clearly the sexuality of all unmarried adolescents and lesbian sexuality. A flier distributed at the Beijing conference by a group of North American Vatican-aligned women called Coalition for Women and the Family makes perfectly plain the homophobia that Holy See delegates are far too politic to expose in official U.N. sessions. Entitled "Sexual Rights and Sexual Orientation — What Do These Words Really Mean?" the flier associates "these words" with not only homosexuality, lesbianism, and sexual relationships outside marriage and among adolescents, but also "pedophilia," "prostitution," "incest," and "adultery." And it engages in gay-baiting and fear-mongering (e.g., "Homosexuals have claimed protection for behaviors which everyone knows spread HIV/AIDS").

But the fundamentalist position goes deeper even than the issues of sexual and bodily self-determination of women and gays, challenging the ethical and epistemological basis of these claims to rights. In his *Evangelium Vitae* encyclical — released to the media precisely to coincide with the final Preparatory Committee meeting before Beijing — the pope condemns ideas and practices asserting reproductive and sexual autonomy by associating them with "a hedonistic mentality unwilling to accept responsibility in matters of sexuality" and "a self-centered concept of freedom."[11] In a world historical moment of religious patriarchal revivalism, accusations of "selfishness" and admonitions to self-sacrifice directed toward women have a powerful appeal. (Of course, blaming individuals for their problems has always been the counterface of attacks on "individualism." The morality of self-abnegation is heavily steeped in an individualist sociology.)

Such fundamentalist attacks have successfully catalyzed feminist resistance throughout the Middle East, Asia, Africa, and Latin America as well as in the United States. Women's movements in predominantly Catholic countries or countries where the Catholic Church is powerful, such as the Philippines, Nigeria, and all of Latin America, have struggled to legalize abortion, reduce maternal mortality, and educate about safer sex and condom use. In Bangladesh, according to Sajeda Amin and Sara Hossain (1995), women's organizations have countered brutal attacks on women accused by Islamic religious tribunals of transgressing sexual norms, and groups and individuals who advocate women's reproductive rights and self-determination. In Egypt, Sudan, Somalia, Kenya, and Nigeria, the focus has been on FGM and its tacit or open support by supposedly non-Islamist governments.

My main point here, however, is the discursive terms in which these southern feminist campaigns have been waged. Since the period immediately before and during the ICPD in Cairo, the language of sexual and reproductive health has merged with the language of women's human rights; and this synthesis, in turn, has rearticulated a feminist ethics of bodily integrity and personhood that permeates the Cairo document and directly challenges the moral arsenal of the Vatican and Islamic fundamentalists. Basically, this ethics postulates not only that women must be free from abuse and violation in their bodies, including their fertility and sexuality, but also that they must be treated as principal actors and decision makers, as the ends and not the means of population and development programs. Feminist activists, beginning with the U.N. Conference on Human Rights in Vienna in 1993, have shaken the premises of mainstream human rights discourse, not only by demanding universal standards and enforcement mechanisms to uphold respect for women's bodily integrity and personhood, but also by challenging traditional divisions between "public" and "private." From the standpoint of feminist international jurisprudence, potential violators of women's human rights are not only at the level of states and their agents; they must be held accountable at every level where power operates — through husbands, partners, family members, clinicians, and religious leaders. The in-laws who attempt to block a woman from going to the local clinic; the husband or parent who beats or stones her for being sexually active; the doctor who denies her request to remove Norplant; and the religious figure who condemns her abortion as a heinous crime — all are failing to respect her reproductive and sexual personhood and thus her human rights (Center for Women's Global Leadership 1995; Cook 1994; Copelon and Petchesky 1995; Correa and Petchesky 1994b; Freedman and Isaacs 1993).

Yet I find something disturbing in the way this shift to a feminist ethic of self-determination over our bodies, which I have argued has become a shared discourse across north and south, has opened up through negations, denials, and litanies of violence and abuse behind which the claims to pleasure remain ever silent. Of course, human rights language, especially with the so-called second- and third-generation rights, is supposed to embody affirmative entitlements and not just protections from abuse; they are two sides of a coin (I cannot enjoy my sexual body if I am subjected to the constant fear of battering or unwanted pregnancy). Still, the campaigns around "women's human rights" have generally flourished — that is, gained the widest acceptance — when they parade the worst horrors (sexual violence, genital mutilation, forced pregnancy or forced abortion, sexual trafficking, etc.) and therefore capitalize on the image of women as victims. Given this tendency in "global feminist" human rights discourse, it is no accident that in both the health and the human rights sections of the Beijing Platform, the specter of sexualized bodies claiming pleasures lurked *behind* the debates, present only in the absence of "bodies" and "sexual rights" in the final text. Does this victimizing tendency sometimes evade, or even mirror, more than it directly confronts fundamentalist images of women?

The Discursive Spiral Spinning Home: Feminism and Women's Bodies

I want to revisit this starting point for a moment, to recall these absences, these silences, and explore their seamy underside. Between Cairo and Beijing, the language of "full respect for the integrity of the human body" (para. 7.34, ICPD) got changed to that of "full respect for the integrity of the person" (para. 97, FWCW) — for good tactical reasons: some liberal feminists close to the U.S. delegation discovered that "integrity of the human body" rather closely echoes parts of the Catholic Church catechism and might be turned around to defend the fetus's right to life. At the same time, it should be noted, the U.S. delegation entered an interpretive statement on paragraph 97 — the one I quoted at the outset and the place in the Beijing Platform that comes closest (though not quite) to articulating a human right to sexual freedom. In its exclusive emphasis (repeated three times) on "relationships between women and men" and on "freedom from coercion, discrimination and violence," the U.S. statement seems intended to deflect possible interpretations of this crucial paragraph as including women's right to sexual pleasure or lesbian identity. So much for our illusion that the United States, dastardly on the macroeconomic issues, could at least be depended on to hold firm on the reproductive and sexual ones.

Yet these evasions also remind me of a scene from the annals of the IRRRAG project, an encounter during a work meeting in Bellagio we held in the summer before the Beijing conference. During an informal presentation of our research, the sharp query of a Turkish feminist sociologist set everyone's heads spinning: I'm surprised, she remarked, that no one here has mentioned the focus it seems to me your work is all about — women's bodies, their self-determination over their bodies. At that, our research coordinator from the Philippines rejoined with her typical combativeness: Women in the Philippines would not speak of "the body," she said, but rather of "the self." Culturally, the women of the grass roots would feel alien from any "body" talk. And our Egyptian participant, reflecting her cultural context, heartily agreed.[12]

I will not probe further into the intimate undercurrents behind this exchange — the charged personal struggles over female circumcision, sexual orientation, marital fidelity, and identity that many of our own members have lived in the short history of this project and that fuel the tensions between "body" and "self." What we can say is this: The body evokes the fetal body for some and women's sexualized body, including the lesbian body, for others; either way, it remains dangerous and commands silence. Sexual self-determination and sexual rights imply both the negative freedom against unwanted intrusions, violations, abuses, and the positive capacity to seek and experience pleasures in a variety of ways and situations, including without a man. But the latter is still too dangerous to permit affirmative reiteration among many women's movements.

On the other hand, it is crucial to recognize that these silences I find disturbing are as much based on strategic calculation as they are on deep inner conflict. In many countries still, to speak openly of women's right to varied sexual pleasures is to invite the closing down of your organization, ostracism of its members, verbal and physical attacks, or even death. The spiral of resistance is still, as always, constrained by power. From this vantage point, it is remarkable that the IRRRAG project — working in Egypt, Brazil, Mexico, Malaysia, the Philippines, Nigeria, and the United States — has uncovered so many positive, resistant voices of ordinary women negotiating reproductive and sexual matters. Listen to this rural Malaysian woman we interviewed:

> I am the one to make decisions where family planning is concerned. After I decide, then I tell him that we should not have so many children, or that we should not space them so closely. Childbearing is not by him, his responsibility is only to bring the money back. Getting up in the middle of the night to give them milk, taking them to the doctor when they are ill — all this is my responsibility. He does not suffer, the suffering is all done by me. So when I tell him that we need to use the contraceptive, he cooperates.

The Vatican and its fundamentalist allies might call this woman a "Western feminist" or follower of the "Western feminist model," but the fact is she is a poor rural Malaysian Chinese who never heard of feminism. We interviewed hundreds of women like her, around eight hundred in all, and while most of them did place central value on marriage and motherhood and did see motherhood as a primary source of their identity, they were not willing to sacrifice their own decision-making autonomy or their own health and safety for the sake of traditional family and childbearing roles. In fact, many of the women we interviewed used their status as mothers to justify their autonomy over reproduction and sexual relations.

IRRRAG's researchers found that women engage in many different strategies of accommodation and resistance to exercise their authority over reproductive and sexual decisions. They find inventive ways to protect themselves against domestic violence and to secure their bodily integrity. From the work of our Philippines team, we call these strategies "negotiated entitlements," and we interpret them to mean that low-income women in southern or developing societies, and minority and immigrant women in the United States — women who do not identify as feminists, attend international conferences, or speak about rights — acquire through their own life experience an embedded sense of reproductive and gender justice. IRRRAG's research, then, is centrally concerned with issues of moral agency and women's formulation and pursuit of claims to decision-making authority within the so-called private arenas of family and sexual relations. But we are also interested in power relations within the clinic, the church or mosque, and the community — the local gatekeepers of women's reproductive and sexual behavior. Our inquiry is thus directed at two levels of social reality: (1) how women perceive their entitlements in the light of both community norms and their own (and their children's) most urgent physical and emotional needs; and (2) how they negotiate power relations to translate such needs into deliberate claims of right or justice. A shared premise among all our research teams is that, much of the time, women engage in such negotiations as active agents rather than passive victims.

Notwithstanding the broad, flexible, and gender-sensitive approach to rights that many feminist theorists have deployed, the IRRRAG framework accounts for the reality that, in ordinary discourse (and in most languages), "rights" are still associated with formal arenas and mechanisms of the state and law. In our research we found that, for most people — particularly poor women, and especially those not organized into political or community-based groups — "rights" belong to others, not to them. This may be because those charged with enforcing rights in many societies (police, bureaucrats, hospital personnel) are experienced as alienating, oppressive, or corrupt; or because the harshness of daily life makes the very concept of a "right" unthinkable. Thus, to speak of "reproductive and sexual rights" is meaningless except for those who are already politicized and involved in organized struggles that presume the possibility of justice. At the same time, if women are distrustful or unaware of their rights, it does not necessarily mean they have no sense of justice or are not prepared to act or speak out to secure their own or their children's needs, including in the realm of reproduction and sexuality. IRRRAG thus developed the concept of a sense of entitlement, or negotiated entitlement, to express the place in between a felt sense of need and an articulation of right. "Entitlement" in this understanding signifies those gestures of speech, metaphor, or even unspoken behavior that represent both an aspiration to change one's own or one's children's situation and a sense of authority to do so through one's own words and/or actions.

It is important to distinguish the approach to entitlement and rights I am presenting here from the notion of "individualism." Asserting my authority or agency to make decisions over reproduction and sexuality because it is my own body or health at stake, or because I am a mother who has the major responsibility for what happens to my children, is not the same as being "selfish" or acting only for myself. More often than not — as confirmed by IRRRAG's research findings — women act or decide on their own out of a sense of duty to others (usually their living children). This is not a paradox but rather the result of centuries of patriarchal culture and socialization of women as caretakers who ought to think of everyone else's needs first. IRRRAG has debated in our internal discussions whether a feminist ethics implies a kind of hierarchy that makes acting for oneself in some way superior to, or more politically aware than, acting for others (the traditional role of women). Yet the data from our research (and possibly also our own lives) suggest that women in their everyday deliberations over matters of fertility, sexuality, work, and child care do not necessarily experience their own entitlement and that of their families (particularly children) as operating on different or conflicting levels of decision making. Rather, they interweave the self-other relationship in their moral calculations all the time (Collins 1990; Petchesky 1995; Tronto 1993). In rural Nigerian women's eyes, that their bodies should be rested and conserved after pregnancy is necessary for competent mothering. For urban Brazilian women, that their daughters should have more sexual and reproductive freedom than they had as young women enhances their own dignity and self-worth.

The sense of entitlement becomes manifested in everyday life through a wide range and mix of strategies of accommodation as well as resistance that women use to negotiate reproductive and sexual decisions — strategies that differ depending on the particular cultural and material circumstances in which women find themselves. Our research discovered that in such highly sensitive and controversial areas, women often engage in trade-offs, or strategic accommodations. In other words, they choose to go along with traditional expectations they detest, that blatantly violate their own sense of bodily integrity (for example, a public defloration ritual in marriage or unwanted marital sex), in order to gain other benefits (for example, freedom to work or go about outside the home, or concessions from husbands with regard to housework and child care). Such accommodations remind us that the strategies women adopt to express or act on their sense of entitlement almost always exist in a context of domination and limited power or resources. The very concept of "resistance" implies this reality (MacLeod 1991; Scott 1990).

Often women express their sense of reproductive and sexual entitlement more in actions than in words, even contradicting their words with their actions (for example, saying abortion is *haram*, or a sin, but seeking an abortion anyway). This disjunction between speech and behavior indicates that women may have a practical ethics of childbearing that reflects the compelling circumstances of their lives rather than dominant religious doctrine or tradition. It also shows the lack of empowerment most women still suffer because of their lack of material resources, information, and skills, because of macroeconomic policies that mortgage away public health and education services, and because of cultural biases that still see women as reproductive vessels and deny men's responsibilities for caretaking.

These gaps in resources and public supports for women's sense of reproductive entitlement confirm the necessity of reconnecting the body and the social in our theorizing. As Sonia Correa and I have argued, "bodily integrity . . . is not just an individual but a social right, since without it women cannot function as responsible community members" (1994b, 113). Dichotomizing individuals and society, a derivative of Western classical liberalism, denies the social nature of individuals as well as their connection to multiple communities, out of which they construct their identities. Thus, the pope notwithstanding, individual rights and social solidarity are not in conflict but rather complementary. Moreover, there is a necessary interdependence between such rights (of the person, the body) and the more generally recognized social or solidarity rights — for example, reliable transportation, sanitation, income supports, access to education, and above all the highest available standard of health care — since the latter constitute the enabling conditions without which the former are merely, at best, paper promises. It does a woman little good to have a legal "right" to terminate or bring to term a pregnancy if she lacks means of transportation or payment required to access decent services, or the services do not exist or are under continual threat of retrenchment or terrorist attack.

Such enabling conditions involve correlative obligations on the part of governments and international organizations to treat basic human needs not as market commodities, but as human rights. In turn, the realization of these rights will require macroeconomic changes on a global scale: the elimination of poverty, harsh structural adjustment policies, trade inequities, brutal cuts in social programs, and unsustainable consumption patterns; the shifting of public resources toward social welfare and the quality of life rather than corporate profits and militarism; the establishment of effective accountability mechanisms that involve women as key decision makers and subject international financial institutions as well as governments and transnational corporations to scrutiny (DAWN 1994; Braidotti et al. 1994; Correa 1994). In other words, a feminist politics of reproductive and sexual rights for the year 2000 must rearticulate those rights from the perspective of women's position in the global economy and the gendered dimensions of sustainable human development. If working on women's issues across international boundaries has taught us anything, it is that we must relink the ethics of women's bodily self-determination to the materiality of their bodies in the world.

NOTES

1. United Nations, *Beijing Declaration and Platform for Action,* adopted by the Fourth World Conference on Women: Action for Equality, Development and Peace, Beijing, 15 Sept. 1995, para. 97.

2. This argument follows Michel Foucault (1978, 45, 92–101; 1980, 56–57), and is also influenced by Judith Butler (1993, 9, 15–17, 22), who posits both the "materialization" and the "subjectivation" of sexualized bodies as a continual process of articulation and reiteration. Butler's theory suggests that bodies become "materialized" — that is, conceived as part of the material world — through discourse, which both names them and fastens them to particular, concrete needs, deprivations, and abuses.

3. IRRRAG teams exist in Brazil, Egypt, Malaysia, Mexico, Nigeria, the Philippines, and the United States. For a synopsis of the project's history, goals, methods, and preliminary findings, see International Reproductive Rights Research Action Group, "Negotiating Reproductive Rights: A Seven-Country Study of Women's Views and Practices," informational packet available from IRRRAG, Hunter College, 695 Park Avenue, Room 1713 West, New York, NY 10021.

4. Reliable summaries, either critical or sympathetic, of this position and of recent population policies generally may be found in Camp 1993; Correa 1994; Correa and Petchesky 1994a; Dixon-Mueller 1993; Hartmann 1995; Jacobson 1991; A. Sen 1994; G. Sen 1994; Shapiro 1985; Warwick 1982; and World Bank 1994. For the immediate prelude to the Cairo conference, see also Stevens 1994; Schmidt 1994; U.S. Department of State 1994; and U.S. AID 1993.

5. The main bone of contention at the Cairo International Conference on Population and Development (ICPD) in 1994 was the right of "family reunification," which was strongly

opposed by the United States and most of its northern allies. This is the right of family members, mainly spouses and children, to join their loved ones who are working abroad; so much for the "family values" so frequently touted by American politicians!

6. See Petchesky 1990, chaps. 2 and 3, for a review of how these tensions between population policy and gender and family policy have played out over the course of the twentieth century in the United States.

7. Female genital mutilation (FGM), which is referred to as female circumcision in some countries, is the customary practice of excising the clitoris, or the external labia of the vagina along with the clitoris, of female infants or very young girls. In addition to inhibiting a woman's sexual pleasure in later life (which is its main purpose), the practice frequently results in severe, chronic vaginal infection, incontinence, and difficulties in childbirth. While FGM is most common in countries of North, East, and West Africa (especially Egypt, Somalia, Nigeria, and Kenya), its incidence is increasing among immigrants from those countries in North America. The ICPD Program of Action condemns FGM as "a violation of basic rights and a major lifelong risk to women's health" and enjoins governments to "urgently take steps to stop the practice" (Arts. 7.35, 7.40). See Toubia 1995.

8. For a detailed analysis of the Cairo document, see Petchesky 1996.

9. This point was made convincingly by Gita Sen in a workshop to evaluate the ICPD held at the NGO Forum in Beijing.

10. A sampling of the Vatican's pre- and mid-Beijing antifeminist campaign can be found in Bohlen 1995 (this call was combined with a condemnation of the Beijing draft platform as having been "overly influenced by Western feminist thought"); Tagliabue 1995; "Sovereignty Begins at Home/Protect Parental Rights" and "Sexual Rights and Sexual Orientation — What Do These Words Really Mean?" two fliers distributed by NGO Coalition for Women and the Family at the Beijing conference; and Catholics for a Free Choice, *The Vatican and the Fourth World Conference on Women*, available from CFFC, 1436 U Street NW, Suite 301, Washington, DC 20009.

11. For the complete text of the encyclical, see *New York Times*, March 31, 1955.

12. IRRRAG is grateful for the perceptive comments of Dr. Nilufer Akat Gole of Bogazici University in Istanbul during this discussion and to the Rockefeller Foundation's Bellagio Center for sponsoring our meeting.

REFERENCES

Amin, Sajeda, and Sara Hossain. 1995. "Women's Reproductive Rights and the Politics of Fundamentalism: A View from Bangladesh." *American University Law Review* 44, 4 (April): 1319–43.

Asian and Pacific Women's Resource Collection Network. 1990. *Asia and Pacific Women's Resource and Action Series: Health.* Kuala Lumpur: Asia and Pacific Development Centre.

Bohlen, C. 1995. "Pope Calls for an End to Discrimination against Women." *New York Times,* July 11, A11.

Boston Women's Health Book Collective. 1984. *The New Our Bodies, Ourselves.* New York: Simon and Schuster.

Braidotti, Rosi et al. 1994. *Women, the Environment and Sustainable Development: Toward a Theoretical Synthesis.* London: Zed.

Bunch, Charlotte. 1990. "Women's Rights as Human Rights: Toward a Re-Vision of Human Rights." *Human Rights Quarterly* 12, 4: 486–98.

Butler, Judith. 1993. *Bodies That Matter: On the Discursive Limits of "Sex."* New York: Routledge.

Camp, Sharon L. 1993. "Global Population Stabilization: A 'No Regrets' Strategy." *Conscience: A Newsjournal of Prochoice Catholic Opinion* 14, 3: 7–8.

Center for Women's Global Leadership. 1995. *From Vienna to Beijing: The Cairo Hearing on Reproductive Health and Human Rights.* New Brunswick: Rutgers University.

Collins, Patricia Hill. 1990. *Black Feminist Thought.* Boston: Unwin Hyman.

Cook, Rebecca, ed. 1994. *Human Rights of Women: National and International Perspectives.* Philedelphia: University of Pennsylvania Press.

Copelon, Rhonda, and Rosalind Petchesky. 1995. "Toward an Interdependent Approach to Reproductive and Sexual Rights as Human Rights: Reflections on the ICPD and Beyond." In Schuler, 343–67.

Correa, Sonia. 1994. *Population and Reproductive Rights: Feminist Perspectives from the South.* London: Zed.

Correa, Sonia, and R. Petchesky. 1994a. "Exposing the Numbers Game: Feminists Challenge the Population Control Establishment." *Ms.*, September–October, 10–17.

———. 1994b. "Reproductive and Sexual Rights: A Feminist Perspective." In Sen, Germain, and Chen, 107–23.

Crenshaw, Kimberlè. 1991. "Demarginalizing the Intersection of Race and Sex: A Black Feminist Critique of Anti-Discrimination Doctrine, Feminist Theory, and Anti-Racist Politics." In K. T. Bartlett and R. Kennedy, eds., *Feminist Legal Theory*, 57–80. Boulder: Westview.

DAWN (Development Alternatives with Women for a New Era). 1994. "Challenging the Given: DAWN's Perspectives on Social Development." Presentation by Peggy Antrobus at the Second PREPCOM for the World Summit on Social Development. New York, August 22–September 2.

Dixon-Mueller, Ruth. 1993. *Population Policy and Women's Rights: Transforming Reproductive Choice.* Westport, CT: Praeger.

Eisenstein, Zillah. 1994. *The Color of Gender: Reimaging Democracy.* Berkeley: University of California Press.

Foucault, Michel. 1978. *The History of Sexuality.* Vol. 1, *An Introduction.* New York: Pantheon.

———. 1980. *Power/Knowledge: Selected Interviews and Other Writings, 1972–1977.* Ed. C. Gordon. Brighton, Sussex: Harvester Press.

Freedman, Lynn P. 1995. "Reflections on Emerging Frameworks of Health and Human Rights." *Health and Human Rights* 1, 4: 312–46.

Freedman, Lynn P., and Steven L. Isaacs. 1993. "Human Rights and Reproductive Choice." *Studies in Family Planning* 24, 1: 18–30.

Fried, Marlene Gerber, ed. 1990. *From Abortion to Reproductive Freedom: Transforming a Movement.* Boston: South End Press.

Garcia-Moreno, Claudia, and Amparo Claro. 1994. "Challenges from the Women's Health Movement: Women's Rights versus Population Control." In Sen, Germain, and Chen, 47–61.

Germain, Adrienne, Sia Nowrojee, and Hnin Hnin Pyne. 1994. "Setting a New Agenda: Sexual and Reproductive Health and Rights." In Sen, Germain, and Chen, 27–46.

Germain, Adrienne, and Jane Ordway. 1989. *Population Control and Women's Health: Balancing the Scales.* New York: International Women's Health Coalition.

Hartmann, Betsy. 1995. *Reproductive Rights and Wrongs: The Global Politics of Population Control.* Rev. ed. Boston: South End Press.

hooks, bell. 1989. *Talking Back*. Boston: South End Press.

IRRRAG (International Reproductive Rights Research Action Group). 1995. *Negotiating Reproductive Rights: A Seven-Country Study of Women's Views and Practices*. Information packet. New York: IRRRAG, Hunter College.

Isis International. 1993. *Information Kit: Women's Perspectives on Population Issues*. Quezon City, Philippines: Isis International.

Jacobson, Jodi L. 1991. "People vs. the Environment (review of P. Ehrlich and A. Ehrlich, *The Population Explosion*)." *International Family Planning Perspectives* 17, 2: 70–71.

MacLeod, Arlene Elowe. 1991. *Accommodating Protest: Working Women, the New Veiling, and Change in Cairo*. New York: Columbia University Press.

Malthus, Thomas R. [1817] 1976. *An Essay on the Principle of Population*. Ed. Anthony Flew. Harmondsworth, England: Penguin.

Petchesky, Rosalind P. 1990. *Abortion and Woman's Choice: The State, Sexuality and Reproductive Freedom*. Rev. ed. Boston: Northeastern University Press.

———. 1995. "The Body as Property: A Feminist Re-Vision." In Faye D. Ginsburg and Rayna Rapp, eds., *Conceiving the New World Order: The Global Politics of Reproduction*, 387–406. Berkeley: University of California Press.

———. 1996. "From Population Control to Reproductive Rights: Feminist Fault Lines." *Reproductive Health Matters*, no. 6.

Pitanguy, Jacqueline, and R. Petchesky. 1993. "Women and Population: A Feminist Perspective." *Conscience: A Newsjournal of Prochoice Catholic Opinion* 14, 3: 5–7.

Schmidt, William E. 1994. "U.N. Population Report Urges Family-Size Choice for Women." *New York Times*, August 18, A8.

Schuler, Margaret A., ed. 1995. *From Basic Needs to Basic Rights: Women's Claim to Human Rights*. Washington, DC: Women, Law and Development International.

Scott, James C. 1990. *Domination and the Arts of Resistance: Hidden Transcripts*. New Haven: Yale University Press.

Sen, Amartya. 1994. "Population: Delusion and Reality." *New York Review of Books* 41, 15 (September 22): 62–71.

Sen, Gita. 1994. "Development, Population, and the Environment: A Search for Balance." In Sen, Germain, and Chen, 63–73.

Sen, Gita, Adrienne Germain, and Lincoln C. Chen, eds. 1994. *Population Policies Reconsidered: Health, Empowerment, and Rights*. Cambridge: Harvard University Press.

Shapiro, Thomas M. 1985. *Population Control Politics: Women, Sterilization, and Reproductive Choice*. Philedelphia: Temple University Press.

Stevens, William K. 1994. "Poor Lands' Success in Cutting Birth Rate Upsets Old Theories." *New York Times*, January 2, 8.

Tagliabue, J. 1995. "Vatican Attacks U.S.-Backed Draft for Women's Conference." *New York Times*, August 26, A5.

Toubia, Nahid. 1995. *Female Genital Mutilation: A Call for Global Action*. New York: Rainbo/Women, Ink.

Tronto, Joan C. 1993. *Moral Boundaries: A Political Argument for an Ethic of Care*. New York: Routledge.

United Nations. 1994. *Report of the International Conference on Population and Development*. Cairo, Egypt, September 5–13, 1994. U.N. Doc. No. A/CONF. 171/13 (October 18, 1994).

———. 1995. *Beijing Declaration and Platform for Action*. Fourth World Conference on Women: Action for Equality, Development and Peace. Beijing, September 15, 1995. U.N. Doc. No. A/CONF.

U.S. Agency for International Development. 1993. "Stabilizing World Population Growth and Protecting Human Health: U.S. AID's Strategy." Draft. *U.S. AID Strategy Papers:* LPA Revision, October 5.

U.S. Department of State. 1994. *U.S. National Report on Population.* April.

U.S. Women of Color Delegation. 1994. Statement on Poverty, Development and Population Activities prepared by the U.S. Women of Color Delegation to the International Conference on Population and Development. Washington, DC: National Black Women's Health Project.

Warwick, Donald P. 1982. *Bitter Pills: Population Policies and Their Implementation in Eight Developing Countries.* Cambridge: Cambridge University Press.

Williams, Patricia J. 1991. *The Alchemy of Race and Rights.* Cambridge: Harvard University Press.

Women's Global Network for Reproductive Rights. 1985–present. WGNRR *Newsletter.* Amsterdam.

World Bank. 1994. *World Development Report 1994: Infrastructure for Development.* New York: Oxford University Press.

Yvette Alex-Assensoh is an assistant professor of political science at Indiana University, Bloomington. Her research interests include urban, minority, and gender politics.

M. V. Lee Badgett is an assistant professor of economics at the University of Massachusetts at Amherst.

Susan Bailey, M.D., is a third-year resident in psychiatry at Johns Hopkins Hospital in Baltimore. Her areas of interest include schizophrenia research and psychotherapy, and she is currently writing a series of essays about the spectrum of psychiatry.

Sarah Banet-Weiser is a visiting lecturer in the women's studies department at UCLA, and a research fellow at the University of California Humanities Research Institute. Her book, *Crowning Identities: Performing Nationalism, Femininity, and Race in U.S. Beauty Pageants*, is forthcoming.

Rina Benmayor is a Multidisciplinary Professor at California State University at Monterey Bay. She is the chair of the Institute for Human Communication and the director of the Oral History and Community Memory Institute and archive at CSUMB. Previously, she directed cultural research at the Centro de Estudios Puertorriqueños, Hunter College.

Marian Blackwell-Stratton currently teaches English at Diablo Valley College in California.

Mary Lou Breslin is president and chairperson of the Board of Directors of the Disability Rights Education and Defense Fund (DREDF), a national law and policy center dedicated to advancing the civil rights of people with disabilities. At the University of San Francisco, she is adjunct professor in the McLaren School of Management and a senior researcher for the Disability Rights Archival Media Research Project. She is also the recipient of a 1995 Mary E. Switzer Merit Fellowship.

Elsa Barkley Brown is an associate professor of history and women's studies at the University of Maryland, College Park. She is the associate editor of the two-volume work *Black Women in America: An Historical Encyclopedia*.

Hazel V. Carby is a professor of American studies and professor and chair of African and African-American studies at Yale University. She is the author of *Reconstructing Womanhood: The Emergence of the African-American Woman Nov-*

elist, and is currently completing a book entitled *Race Men: Icons of Race, Nation, and Masculinity.*

Cathy J. Cohen is an assistant professor of political science and African and African American studies at Yale University.

Kimberlè Williams Crenshaw is a professor of law at UCLA and Columbia School of Law in New York. Her articles on race and gender have appeared in the *Harvard Law Review,* the *Stanford Law Review,* and the *University of Chicago Law Review.*

Barbara A. Crow is an assistant professor of women's studies at the University of Calgary. She is the editor of *Radical Feminism: An Historical Reader.*

Kathleen Daly is an associate professor of justice administration at Griffith University in Brisbane. Her book *Gender, Crime, and Punishment* received the 1995 Hindelang Award from the American Society of Criminology.

R. Darcy is Regents Professor of Politics and Statistics at Oklahoma State University. He is the coauthor of *Guide to Quantitative History* and *Women, Elections, and Representation.*

Andrea Densham is an activist and researcher who currently lives in Chicago. Her research interests are focused on community political participation and mobilization.

Alice Echols is the author of *Daring to Be Bad: Radical Feminism in America, 1967–75.* She lives in Los Angeles, where she is currently writing *Nobody's Girl: The Life and Times of Janis Joplin.* A collection of her essays is also forthcoming.

Michelle Habell-Pallán is an assistant professor of Chicana and Chicano studies at Arizona State University, Tempe. Her research on Chicano/Latino performance culture was awarded a UC President's Dissertation Year Fellowship and an Honorable Mention from the Ford Fellowship Foundation.

Charles D. Hadley is a research professor at the University of New Orleans. A past president of the Southern Political Science Association, he is the coauthor of *Transformations of the American Party System.*

Carol Hardy-Fanta is the director of research at the Center for Women in Politics and Public Policy and a senior research associate at the Mauricio Gastón Institute for Latino Community Development and Public Policy at the University of Massachusetts, Boston. She is the author of *Latina Politics, Latino Politics: Gender, Culture, and Political Participation in Boston.*

M. A. Jaimes * Guerrero is an activist and a professor in humanities in the women's studies department at San Francisco State University. She is the editor of the award-winning book *The State of Native America.*

Jennie R. Joe is the director of the Native American Research and Training Center at the University of Arizona, Tucson, where she is also an assistant professor of family and community medicine.

Alethia Jones, currently a Ford Foundation predoctoral fellow, is enrolled in the doctoral program in political science at Yale University. Her main research interests include the politics of new immigrant communities.

Kathleen B. Jones is an associate dean of the College of Arts and Letters and a professor of women's studies at San Diego State University, and the author of *Compassionate Authority.*

Tamara Jones is a doctoral student in the political science department at Yale University. She is a Jamaican immigrant whose political work in the United States has included AIDS education in Black communities and organizing Caribbean lesbians and gays.

Jane Junn is an assistant professor of political science at Rutgers University. She is the coauthor of *Education and Democratic Citizenship in America* and the forthcoming *Educating Emerging Citizens.*

Jason F. Kirksey is Hannah D. Atkins Assistant Professor of Political Science at Oklahoma State University. His research and teaching interests include American government and politics, election systems, and ethnic and racial politics.

Peter Kwong is a professor and the director of the Asian American studies program at Hunter College, City University of New York. His latest book is the revised edition of *The New Chinatown.*

Mamie E. Locke is the dean of the School of Liberal Arts and Education and a professor of political science at Hampton University. Her research and teaching interests include race and gender politics as well as urban and ethnic politics. She is also a member of the Hampton City Council.

Doreen J. Mattingly is an assistant professor of geography and women's studies at San Diego State University. Her research and teaching focus on the gender dynamics of migration, employment, and political participation.

Arlene Byrnne Mayerson is Directing Attorney of the Disability Rights Education and Defense Fund (DREDF), and Co-Director of the Disability Rights Legal Education Clinic in Berkeley, California.

Dorothy Lonewolf Miller, D. S. W., is the president of the Scientific Analysis Corporation in San Francisco, a private, not-for-profit research firm engaged in social research.

Debra C. Minkoff is an associate professor of sociology at Yale University. She is the author of *Organizing for Equality,* which details the organizational aspects of the contemporary women's and civil rights movements in the United States.

Rosalind P. Petchesky is the international coordinator of the International Reproductive Rights Research Action Group (IRRRAG) and a professor of political science and women's studies at Hunter College, City University of New York. She is the author of *Abortion and Women's Choice: The State, Sexuality, and Reproductive Freedom.*

Frances K. Pohl is an associate professor of art history at Pomona College. She is the author of *Behn Shahn: New Deal Artist in a Cold War Climate, Ben Shahn,* and the exhibition catalogue *An Art of Conscience: American Social Commentary, 1930–1970.*

Rachel Roth is a Ph.D. candidate in political science at Yale University, where she is completing her dissertation on the politics of fetal rights in the United States, 1973–1992.

Rinku Sen is the codirector of the Center for Third World Organizing and the political editor of the center's magazine, *Third Force.* She has been organizing low-income women, men, and youth of color since 1985.

Sonia Shah is an editor/publisher in the South End Press Collective. She is currently editing an anthology on Asian American feminism.

Suzanne Shende is a lawyer. She is currently living in Honduras, supporting the Gan Funa community in the struggle for rights to land, education, women's equality, and freedom from racial discrimination.

Sandyha Shukla is an assistant professor of ethnic studies at the University of California at San Diego. Her current research pertains to Indian postcolonial/ immigrant cultures in the United States and Britain.

Karin Stanford is an assistant professor of political science and African American studies at the University of Georgia. Her book on Jesse Jackson's involvement in international politics is forthcoming.

Jacqueline Stevens is an assistant professor of political theory at the University of Michigan. She is completing a manuscript entitled *Reproducing the State.*

Paule Cruz Takash is an assistant professor of ethnic studies at the University of California, San Diego, where she teaches and writes about race, gender, and ethnic politics. She is currently completing a manuscript on the latinization of California and changing white and Latino relations entitled *New Minorities, New Majorities: Whites and Latinos in a Changing Multiracial America.*

Rosa M. Torruellas was the director of the Barrio Popular Education Program from 1985 to 1991. She was the associate director of the Language Education Task Force at the Centro de Estudios Puertorriqueños, Hunter College.

Joan C. Tronto is the coordinator of women's studies and a professor of political science at Hunter College, and the author of *Moral Boundaries.*

Eve S. Weinbaum is the political director for the southern region of the Union of Needletrades, Industrial, and Textile Employees (UNITE). She writes and teaches on social movements and labor and politics.

INDEX

Prepared by Jennifer Leigh Disney